D0473701

Gender through the Prism of Difference

Gender through the Prism of Difference
Second Edition

Edited by

MAXINE BACA ZINN
Michigan State University

PIERRETTE HONDAGNEU-SOTELO
University of Southern California

MICHAEL A. MESSNER
University of Southern California

ALLYN AND BACON
Boston   London   Toronto   Sydney   Tokyo   Singapore

Series Editor: Sarah L. Kelbaugh
Editor-in-Chief, Social Sciences: Karen Hanson
Series Editorial Assistant: Jennifer DiDomenico
Marketing Manager: Brooke Stoner
Production Editor: Christopher H. Rawlings
Editorial-Production Service: Omegatype Typography, Inc.
Composition and Prepress Buyer: Linda Cox
Manufacturing Buyer: Julie McNeil
Cover Administrator: Jennifer Hart
Electronic Composition: Omegatype Typography, Inc.

Copyright © 2000, 1997 by Allyn & Bacon
A Pearson Education Company
160 Gould Street
Needham Heights, MA 02494

Internet: www.abacon.com

All rights reserved. No part of the material protected by this copyright notice may be
reproduced or utilized in any form or by any means, electronic or mechanical, including
photocopying, recording, or by any information storage and retrieval system, without
written permission from the copyright owner.

Library of Congress Cataloging-in-Publication Data

Gender through the prism of difference / edited by Maxine Baca Zinn,
    Pierrette Hondagneu-Sotelo, Michael A. Messner. — 2nd ed.
        p.   cm.
    Rev. ed. of: Through the prism of difference, c 1997.
    Includes bibliographical references.
    ISBN 0-205-30225-4 (alk. paper)
    1. Sex role.   I. Zinn, Maxine Baca.   II. Hondagneu-
Sotelo, Pierrette.   III. Messner, Michael A.   IV. Through the prism
of difference.
HQ1075.G4666   2000
305.3—dc21   99-25085
                                                                        CIP

Credits appear on pages 523–526, which constitute an extension of the copyright page.

Printed in the United States of America
10 9 8 7 6 5 4 3 2 1   04 03 02 01 00 99

CONTENTS

Preface   ix

Introduction: Sex and Gender through the Prism of Difference   1

Part One
Perspectives on Sex, Gender, and Difference

1. Judith Lorber, "Believing Is Seeing: Biology as Ideology"   13
2. Maxine Baca Zinn and Bonnie Thornton Dill, "Theorizing Difference from Multiracial Feminism"   23
3. Barrie Thorne, "Children and Gender: Constructions of Difference"   30
4. Carol B. Stack, "Different Voices, Different Visions: Gender, Culture, and Moral Reasoning"   42
5. R. W. Connell, "Masculinities and Globalization"   49
6. Pierrette Hondagneu-Sotelo and Michael A. Messner, "Gender Displays and Men's Power: The 'New Man' and the Mexican Immigrant Man"   63
7. Margaret L. Andersen, "Studying across Difference: Race, Class, and Gender in Qualitative Research"   75

Part Two
Bodies

Embodiments of Control and Resistance

8. Jane Sprague Zones, "Beauty Myths and Realities and Their Impact on Women's Health"   87
9. Nomy Lamm, "It's a Big Fat Revolution"   104
10. Thomas J. Gerschick and Adam Stephen Miller, "Coming to Terms: Masculinity and Physical Disability"   109
11. Debbie Nathan, "Abortion Stories on the Border"   123

Violence

12. Jack C. Straton, "The Myth of the 'Battered Husband Syndrome'"   126
13. Beth E. Richie and Valli Kanuha, "Battered Women of Color in Public Health Care Systems: Racism, Sexism, and Violence"   129
14. Nancy A. Matthews, "Surmounting a Legacy: The Expansion of Racial Diversity in a Local Anti-Rape Movement"   138
15. Michael A. Messner, "When Bodies Are Weapons"   148

Part Three
Sexualities

Sexual Relations, Intimacy, and Power

16. Deborah L. Tolman, "Doing Desire: Adolescent Girls' Struggles for/with Sexuality"   155

17. Susan Bordo, "Pills and Power Tools"   168
18. Matthew C. Gutmann, "Male Discretion and Sexual Indiscretion in Working Class Mexico City"   171
19. Cynthia Enloe, "It Takes More Than Two: The Prostitute, the Soldier, the State, and the Entrepreneur"   188

Sexuality and Identity

20. Marilyn Frye, "Lesbian 'Sex'"   200
21. Michael A. Messner, "Becoming 100% Straight"   205
22. Arlene Stein, "Seventies Questions for Nineties Women"   211
23. Yen Le Espiritu, "'Americans Have a Different Attitude': Family, Sexuality, and Gender in Filipina American Lives"   222

Part Four
Identities

24. Slavenka Drakulic, "A Letter from the United States: The Critical Theory Approach"   235
25. Michael S. Kimmel, "Judaism, Masculinity, and Feminism"   239
26. Anastasia Higginbotham, "Chicks Goin' at It"   242
27. Peggy McIntosh, "White Privilege: Unpacking the Invisible Knapsack"   247
28. Manning Marable, "The Black Male: Searching beyond Stereotypes"   251

Part Five
Families

Constructing Motherhood and Fatherhood

29. Nancy Scheper-Hughes, "(M)Other Love: Culture, Scarcity, and Maternal Thinking"   261
30. Patricia Hill Collins, "The Meaning of Motherhood in Black Culture and Black Mother–Daughter Relationships"   268
31. Pierrette Hondagneu-Sotelo and Ernestine Avila, "'I'm Here, but I'm There': The Meanings of Latina Transnational Motherhood"   279
32. Judith K. Witherow, "Native American Mother"   295
33. Ralph LaRossa, "Fatherhood and Social Change"   298

Work and Families

34. David D. Gilmore, "Men and Women in Southern Spain: 'Domestic Power' Revisited"   310
35. M. Patricia Fernández Kelly, "Delicate Transactions: Gender, Home, and Employment among Hispanic Women   321
36. Nazli Kibria, "Culture, Social Class, and Income Control in the Lives of Women Garment Workers in Bangladesh"   331
37. Elizabeth Higginbotham and Lynn Weber, "Moving Up with Kin and Community: Upward Social Mobility for Black and White Women"   346

Part Six
Constructing Gender in the Workplace

38. Rosemary Pringle, "Male Secretaries"   357
39. Patti A. Giuffre and Christine L. Williams, "Boundary Lines: Labeling Sexual Harassment in Restaurants"   372
40. Karen J. Hossfeld, "'Their Logic against Them': Contradictions in Sex, Race, and Class in Silicon Valley"   388
41. Teresa Amott, "Shortchanged: Restructuring Women's Work"   401
42. Laura L. Miller, "Not Just Weapons of the Weak: Gender Harassment as a Form of Protest for Army Men"   409

Part Seven
Popular Culture

43. Catherine A. Lutz and Jane L. Collins, "The Color of Sex: Postwar Photographic Histories of Race and Gender in *National Geographic Magazine*"   431
44. Shari Lee Dworkin and Faye Linda Wachs, "'Disciplining the Body': HIV-Positive Male Athletes, Media Surveillance, and the Policing of Sexuality"   438
45. Melissa Klein, "Duality and Redefinition: Young Feminism and the Alternative Music Community"   452

Part Eight
Change and Politics

Resistance and Social Movements

46. Mary Pardo, "Mexican American Women, Grassroots Community Activists: 'Mothers of East Los Angeles'"   461
47. Helen Icken Safa, "Women's Social Movements in Latin America"   467
48. Tracy Bachrach Ehlers, "Debunking Marianismo: Economic Vulnerability and Survival Strategies among Guatemalan Wives"   478
49. Mindy Stombler and Irene Padavic, "Sister Acts: Resisting Men's Domination in Black and White Fraternity Little Sister Programs"   490

Visions of the Future

50. Audre Lorde, "Age, Race, Class, and Sex: Women Redefining Difference"   503
51. Walter L. Williams, "Benefits for Nonhomophobic Societies: An Anthropological Perspective"   509
52. bell hooks and Cornel West, "Breaking Bread"   518

PREFACE

Over the past 25 years, texts and readers intended for use in women's studies and gender studies courses have changed and developed in important ways. In the 1970s and into the early 1980s, many courses and texts focused almost exclusively on women as a relatively undifferentiated category. Two developments have broadened the study of women. First, in response to criticisms by women of color and by lesbians that heterosexual, White middle-class feminists had tended to "falsely universalize" their own experiences and issues, courses and texts on gender began in the 1980s to systematically incorporate race and class diversity. And simultaneously, as a result of feminist scholars' insistence that gender be studied as a relational construct, more concrete studies of men and masculinity began to emerge in the 1980s.

This book reflects this belief that race, class, and sexual diversity among women and men should be central to the study of gender. But this collection adds an important new dimension that will broaden the frame of gender studies. By including some articles that are based on research in countries outside the United States, in nonindustrial societies, and among immigrant groups, we hope that *Gender through the Prism of Difference* will contribute to a transcendence of the often myopic, U.S.-based, and Eurocentric focus in the study of sex and gender. The inclusion of these perspectives is not simply useful for illuminating our own cultural blind spots: It also begins to demonstrate how, as the twentieth century comes to a close, gender relations are increasingly centrally implicated in current processes of globalization.

Because the amount of high-quality research on gender has expanded so dramatically in the past decade, the most difficult task in assembling this collection was deciding *what* to include. The second edition, while retaining the structure of the previous edition, is different and improved. In addition to a new section on popular culture, this edition includes material on gender issues relevant to the college-age generation. Many of the new readings tend toward a more personal narrative style that students will find engaging.

We thank faculty and staff colleagues in the Department of Sociology and the Gender Studies program at the University of Southern California and in the Department of Sociology and the Julian Samora Research Institute at Michigan State University for their generous support and assistance. Other people contributed their labor to the development of this book. We are grateful to our research assistants, Dan Heller of the University of Southern California and Heather E. Dillaway of Michigan State University, who contributed invaluable groundwork.

We acknowledge the helpful criticism and suggestions made by the following reviewers: Susan M. Allbee, University of Northern Iowa; Karen Denton, University of Utah; Ramon Guerra, University of Texas–Pan American; and Rachel K. Jones, Tulane University. Our editor at Allyn & Bacon, Sarah Kelbaugh, has been helpful and encouraging.

Finally, we thank our families for their love and support as we worked on this book. Alan Zinn, Prentice Zinn, and Gabrielle Cobbs provide inspiration through their work for progressive social change. Miles Hondagneu-Messner and Sasha Hondagneu-Messner continually challenge the neatness of Mike and Pierrette's image of social life. Life with a nine-year-old and a six-year-old is less a neat rainbow shining through a stable prism than it is a kaleidoscope of constantly shifting moments and meanings. We do hope, though, that the kind of work that is collected in this book will eventually help them and their generation make sense of the world and move that world into more peaceful, humane, and just directions.

Gender through the Prism of Difference

Introduction
Sex and Gender through
the Prism of Difference

"Men can't cry." "Women are victims of patriarchal oppression." "After divorces, single mothers are downwardly mobile, often moving into poverty." "Men don't do their share of housework and childcare." "Professional women face barriers such as sexual harassment and a 'glass ceiling' that prevent them from competing equally with men for high-status positions and high salaries." "Heterosexual intercourse is an expression of men's power over women." Sometimes, the students in our sociology and gender studies courses balk at these kinds of generalizations. And they are right to do so. After all, some men are more emotionally expressive than some women, some women have more power and success than some men, some men do their share—or more of housework and childcare, and some women experience sex with men as both pleasurable and empowering. Indeed, contemporary gender relations are complex, changing in various directions, and, as such, we need to be wary of simplistic, if handy, slogans that seem to sum up the essence of relations between women and men.

On the other hand, we think it is a tremendous mistake to conclude that "all individuals are totally unique and different" and that therefore all generalizations about social groups are impossible or inherently oppressive. In fact, we are convinced that it is this very complexity, this multifaceted nature of contemporary gender relations that fairly begs for a sociological analysis of gender. In the title of this book, we use the image of "the prism of difference" to illustrate our approach to developing this sociological perspective on contemporary gender relations. *The American Heritage Dictionary* defines *prism,* in part, as "a homogeneous transparent solid, usually with triangular bases and rectangular sides, used to produce or analyze a continuous spectrum." Imagine a ray of light—which to the naked eye, appears to be only one color—refracted through a prism onto a white wall. To the eye, the result is not an infinite, disorganized scatter of individual colors. Rather, the refracted light displays an order, a structure of relationships among the different colors—a rainbow. Similarly, we propose to use the "prism of difference" in this book to analyze a continuous spectrum of people, in order to show how gender is organized and experienced differently when refracted through the prism of sexual, racial/ ethnic, social class, physical abilities, age, and national citizenship differences.

EARLY WOMEN'S STUDIES: CATEGORICAL VIEWS OF "WOMEN" AND "MEN"

Taken together, the articles in this book make the case that it is possible to make good generalizations about women and men. But these generalizations should be drawn carefully, by always asking the questions *"which* women?" and *"which* men?" Scholars of sex and gender have not always done this. In the 1960s and 1970s, women's studies focused on the differences *between* women and men rather than *among* women and men. The very concept of gender, women's studies scholars demonstrated, is based on socially defined difference between women and men. From the macro level of social institutions like the economy, politics, and religion, to the micro level of interpersonal relations, distinctions between women and men structure social relations. Making males and females *different* from one another is the essence of gender. It is also the basis of men's power and domination. Understanding this was profoundly illuminating. Knowing that difference produced domination enabled women to name, analyze, and set about changing their victimization.

In the 1970s, riding the wave of a resurgent feminist movement, colleges and universities began to develop women's studies courses that aimed first and foremost to make women's lives visible. The texts that were developed for these courses tended to stress the things that women shared under patriarchy—having the responsibility for housework and childcare, the experience or fear of men's sexual violence, a lack of formal or informal access to education, exclusion from high-status professional and managerial jobs, political office, and religious leadership positions (Brownmiller, 1976; Kanter, 1977).

The study of women in society offered new ways of seeing the world. But the 1970s approach was limited in several ways. Thinking of gender primarily in terms of differences between women and men led scholars to overgeneralize about both. The concept of patriarchy led to a dualistic perspective of male privilege and female subordination. Women and men were cast as opposites. Each was treated as a homogenous category with common characteristics and experiences. This approach *essentialized* women and men. Essentialism, simply put, is the notion that women's and men's attributes are categorically different. From this perspective, male control and coercion of women produced conflict between the sexes. The feminist insight originally introduced by Simone de Beauvoir in 1953—that women, as a group, had been socially defined as the "other" and that men had constructed themselves as the subjects of history, while constructing women as their objects—fueled an energizing sense of togetherness among many women. As college students read books like *Sisterhood is Powerful* (Morgan, 1970), many of them joined organizations that fought, with some success, for equality and justice for women.

THE VOICES OF "OTHER" WOMEN

Although this view of women as an oppressed "other" was empowering for certain groups of women, some women began to claim that the feminist view of universal sisterhood ignored and marginalized their major concerns. It soon became apparent that treating women as a group united in its victimization by patriarchy was biased by too narrow a focus on the experiences and perspectives of women from more privileged social groups. "Gender" was treated as a generic category, uncritically applied to women. Ironically, this analysis, which was meant to unify women, instead produced divisions between and among them. The concerns projected as "universal" were removed from the realities of many women's lives. For example, it became a matter of faith in second-wave feminism that women's liberation would be accomplished by breaking down the "gendered public–domestic split." Indeed, the feminist call for women to move out of the kitchens and into the workplaces resonated in the experiences of many of the college-educated white women who were inspired by Betty Friedan's 1963 book, *The Feminine Mystique.* But the idea that women's movement into workplaces was itself empowering or liberating seemed absurd or irrelevant to many working-class women and women of color. They were already working for wages, as had many of their mothers and grandmothers, and did not consider access to jobs and public life as "liberating." For many of these women, liberation had more to do with organizing in communities and workplaces—often alongside men—for better schools, better pay, decent benefits, and other policies to benefit their neighborhoods, jobs, and families. The feminism of the 1970s did not seem to address these issues.

As more and more women analyzed their own experiences, they began to address the power relations creating differences among women and the part that privileged women played in the oppression of others. For many women of color, working-class women, lesbians, and women in contexts outside the United States (especially women in non-Western societies), the focus on male domination was a distraction from other oppressions. Their lived experiences could support neither a unitary theory of gender nor an ideology of universal sisterhood. As a result, finding common ground in a universal female victimization was never a priority for many groups of women.

Challenges to gender stereotypes soon emerged. Women of varied races, classes, national origins, and sexualities insisted that the concept of gender be broadened to take their differences into account (Baca Zinn et al., 1986; Hartmann, 1976; Rich, 1980; Smith, 1977). Many women began to argue that their lives are affected by their location in a number of different hierarchies: as African Americans, Latinas, Native Americans, or Asian Americans in the race hierarchy; as young or old in the age hierarchy; as heterosexual, gay, lesbian, or bisexual in the sexual orientation hierarchy; and as women outside of the Western, industrialized nations, in subordinated geopolitical contexts. These arguments made it clear that women were not victimized by gender alone but by the historical and systematic denial of rights and privileges based on other differences as well.

MEN AS GENDERED BEINGS

As the voices of "other" women in the mid- to late 1970s began to challenge and expand the parameters of women's studies, a new area of scholarly inquiry was beginning to stir—a critical examination of men and masculinity. To be sure, in those early years of gender studies, the major task was to conduct studies and develop courses about the lives of women in order to begin to correct centuries of scholarship that rendered women's lives, problems, and accomplishments invisible. But the core idea of feminism—that "femininity" and women's subordination is a social construction—logically led to an examination of the social construction of "masculinity" and men's power. Many of the first scholars to take on this task were psychologists, who were concerned with looking at the social construction of "the male sex role" (e.g., Pleck, 1981). By the late 1980s, there was a growing interdisciplinary collection of studies of men and masculinity, much of it by social scientists (Brod, 1987; Kaufman, 1987; Kimmel, 1987; Kimmel & Messner, 1989).

Reflecting developments in women's studies, the scholarship on men's lives tended to develop three themes: First, what we think of as "masculinity" is not a fixed, biological essence of men but, rather, is a social construction that shifts and changes over time, as well as between and among various national and cultural contexts. Second, power is central to understanding gender as a relational construct, and the dominant definition of masculinity is largely about expressing difference from—and superiority over—anything considered "feminine." Third, there is no singular "male sex role." Rather, at any given time there are various masculinities. R. W. Connell (1987, 1995) has been among the most articulate advocates of this perspective. Connell argues that hegemonic masculinity (the dominant form of masculinity at any given moment) is constructed in relation to femininities *as well as* in relation to various subordinated or marginalized masculinities. For example, in the United States, various racialized masculinities (e.g., as represented by African American men, Latino immigrant men, etc.) have been central to the construction of hegemonic (White, middle-class) masculinity. As Hondagneu-Sotelo and Messner (in this book) argue, this "othering" of racialized masculinities helps to shore up the material privileges that have been historically connected to hegemonic masculinity. When viewed this way, we can better understand hegemonic masculinity as part of a system that includes gender, as well as racial, class, sexual, and other relations of power.

The new literature on men and masculinities also begins to move us beyond the simplistic, falsely categorical, and pessimistic view of men simply as a privileged sex class. When race, social class, sexual orientation, physical abilities, and immigrant or national status are taken into account, we can see that in some circumstances, "male privilege" is partly—sometimes substantially—muted (Kimmel & Messner, 1998). Although it is unlikely that we will soon see a "men's movement" that aims to undermine the power and privileges that are connected with hegemonic masculinity, when we begin to look at "masculinities" through the prism of difference, we can begin to see similarities and possible points of coalition between and among certain groups of women and men (Messner, 1998). Certain kinds of changes in gender relations—for instance, a national family leave policy for working parents—might serve as a means of uniting particular groups of women and men.

GENDER IN INTERNATIONAL CONTEXTS

It is an increasingly accepted truism that late twentieth-century increases in transnational trade, international migration, and global systems of production and communication have diminished both the power of nation-states and the significance of national borders. A much more ignored issue is the extent to which gender relations—in the United States and elsewhere in the world—are increasingly linked to patterns of global economic restructuring. Decisions made in corporate headquarters located in Los Angeles, Tokyo, or London may have immediate repercussions in how women and men thousands of miles away organize their work, community, and family lives (Sassen, 1991). It is no longer possible to study gender relations without attention to global processes and inequalities. Scholarship on women in third-world contexts has moved from liberal concerns for the impact of development policies on women (Boserup, 1970), to more critical perspectives that acknowledge how international labor and capital mobility are transforming gender and family relations (Fernández Kelly, this volume; Hondagneu-Sotelo & Avila, this volume), to theoretical debates on third-world feminisms (Mohanty, 1991), and to analyses of women and post–Cold War political alignments (Enloe, 1993).

Around the world, women's paid and unpaid labor is key to global development strategies. Yet it would be a mistake to conclude that gender is molded from the "top down." What happens on a daily basis in families and workplaces simultaneously constitutes and is constrained by structural transnational institutions. For instance, in the second half of the twentieth century young, single women, many of them from poor rural areas, have been recruited for work in export assembly plants along the U.S.–Mexico border, in East and Southeast Asia, in Silicon Valley, in the Caribbean, and in Central America. While the profitability of these multinational factories depends, in part, on management's ability to manipulate the young women's ideologies of gender, the women—as suggested by various shopfloor ethnographies and by Karen Hossfeld's article in this volume—do not respond passively or uniformly, but they actively resist, challenge, and accommodate. At the same time, the global dispersion of the assembly line has concentrated corporate facilities in many U.S. cities, making available myriad managerial, administrative, and clerical jobs for college educated women. Women's paid labor is used at various points along this international system of production. Not only employment, but also consumption, embodies global interdependencies. There is a high probability that the clothes you wear and the computer you use originated in multinational corporate headquarters and in assembly plants scattered around third-world nations. And if these items were actually manufactured in the United States, they were probably assembled by Latin American and Asian-born women.

Worldwide, international labor migration and refugee movements are creating new types of multiracial societies. Although these developments are often discussed and analyzed with respect to racial differences, gender typically remains absent. As several commentators have noted, the White feminist movement in the United States has not addressed issues of immigration and nationality. Gender, however, has been fundamental in shaping immigration policies (Chang, 1994; Hondagneu-Sotelo, 1994). Direct labor recruitment programs generally solicit either male or female labor (e.g., Filipina nurses, Mexican male farm workers); national disenfranchisement has particular repercussions for women and men; and current immigrant laws are based on very gendered notions of what constitutes "family unification." As Chandra Mohanty suggests, "analytically these issues are the contemporary metropolitan counterpart of women's struggles against colonial occupation in the geographical third world" (1991: 23). Moreover, immigrant and refugee women's daily lives often challenge familiar feminist paradigms. The occupations in which immigrant and refugee women concentrate—paid domestic work, informal sector street vending, assembly or industrial piece work performed in the home—often blur the ideological distinction between work and family and between public and private spheres.

FROM PATCHWORK QUILT TO PRISM

All of these developments—the voices of "other" women, the study of men and masculinities, and the examination of gender in transnational contexts—have helped redefine the study of gender. By working to develop knowledge that is inclusive of the experiences of all groups, new insights about gender have begun to emerge. Examining gender in the context of other differences makes it clear that nobody experiences themselves as solely gendered. Instead, gender is configured through cross-cutting forms of difference that carry deep social and economic consequences.

By the mid-1980s, thinking about gender had entered a new stage that was more carefully grounded in the experiences of diverse groups of women and men. This perspective is a general way of looking at women and men and understanding their relationships to the structure of society. Gender is no longer viewed simply as a matter of two opposite categories of people—males and females—but as a range of social relations among differently situated people. Because centering on difference is a radical challenge to the conventional gender framework, it raises several concerns. Does the recognition that gender can only be understood contextually (meaning that there is no singular "gender" per se) make women's studies and gender studies newly vulnerable to critics in the academy? Does the immersion in difference throw us into a whirlwind of "spiraling diversity" (Hewitt, 1992: 316) where multiple identities and locations shatter the categories *women* and *men*?

Throughout the book, we take a position directly opposed to an empty pluralism. Although the categories *woman* and *man* have multiple meanings, this does not reduce gender to a "postmodern kaleidoscope of lifestyles. Rather, it points to the *relational* character of gender" (Connell, 1992: 736). Not only are masculinity and femininity relational, but different masculinities and femininities are interconnected also through other social structures such as race, class, and nation. Groups are created by their relationships with each other. The meaning of *woman* is defined by the existence of women of different races and classes. Being a White woman in the United States is meaningful only insofar as it is set apart from and in contradistinction to women of color.

Just as masculinity and femininity each depend on the definition of the other to produce domination, differences *among* women and *among* men are also created in the context of structured relationships. Some women derive benefits from their race and class position, and from their location in the global economy, while they are simultaneously restricted by gender. In other words, such women are subordinated by patriarchy, yet their relatively privileged positions within hierarchies of race, class, and the global political economy intersect to create for them an expanded range of opportunities, choices, and ways of living. They may even use their race and class advantage to minimize some of the consequences of patriarchy and/or to oppose other women. Similarly, one can become a man in opposition to other men. For example, "the relation between heterosexual and homosexual men is central, carrying heavy symbolic freight. To many people, homosexuality is the *negation* of masculinity.... Given that assumption, antagonism toward homosexual men may be used to define masculinity" (Connell, 1992: 736).

In the past decade, viewing gender through the prism of difference has profoundly reoriented the field (Acker, 1999; Glenn, 1999; Messner, 1996; West & Fenstermaker, 1995). Yet analyzing the multiple constructions of gender does not mean studying just groups of women and groups of men as different. It is clearly time to go beyond what we call the "patchwork quilt" phase in the study of women and men—that is, the phase in which we have acknowledged the importance of examining differences within constructions of gender, but do so largely by collecting a study here on African American women, a study there on gay men, and a study on working-class Chicanas. This patchwork quilt approach too often amounts to no more than "adding difference and stirring." The result may be a lovely mosaic, but like a patchwork quilt it still tends to overemphasize boundaries, rather than highlighting bridges of interdependency. In addition, this approach too often does not explore the ways that social constructions of femininities and masculinities are based on, and reproduce relations of, power. In short, we think that the substantial quantity of research that has now been done on various groups and subgroups needs to be analyzed within a framework that emphasizes differences and inequalities not as discrete areas of separation, but as interrelated bands of color that together make up a spectrum.

A recent spate of sophisticated sociological theorizing along these lines has introduced some useful ways to think about difference in relational terms. Patricia Hill Collins (1990, 1998) has suggested that we think of race, class, and gender as a socially structured "matrix of domination"; R. W. Connell has pressed us to think of multiple differences not in simple additive ways, but rather as they "abrade, inflame amplify, twist, negate, dampen, and complicate each other" (Kessler et al., 1985). Similarly, Maxine Baca Zinn and Bonnie Thornton Dill (in this volume) have suggested that we consider a body of theory and practice they call "multiracial feminism" as a means of coming to grips with the relations between various systems of inequality.

These are the kinds of concerns that we had in mind in putting together this collection. We sought individual articles that explored intersections or axes in the matrix of domination by comparing different groups. We brought together articles that explored the lives of people who experience the daily challenges of multiple marginality (e.g., Black lesbians, immigrant women), or the often paradoxical realities of those who may identify simultaneously with a socially marginalized or subordinated identity (e.g., gay, poor, physically disabled, Latino) along with a socially dominant identity (e.g., man, White, professional class). When we could not find articles that directly compared or juxtaposed categories or groups, we attempted to juxtapose two or three articles that, together, explored difference and similarities between groups. To this end, we added a fifth dimension to the now commonly accepted "race/class/gender/sexuality" matrix: national origin. Reflecting a tendency in U.S. sociology in general, courses on sex and gender have been far too U.S.-focused and Eurocentric. Focusing on the construction of gender in industrializing societies or the shifting relations of gender among transnational immigrant groups challenges and broadens our otherwise narrow assumptions about the constraints and possibilities facing contemporary women and men. But it is not enough to remain within the patchwork quilt framework, to simply focus on women and men in other nations as though they were somehow separate from processes occurring in the United States.

Again, the metaphor of the prism better illustrates the dual challenges we face in integrating analyses of national inequalities. A central challenge facing scholars today is to understand how constructions of masculinities and femininities move across national borders. In this regard, we need to acknowledge two distinct, but interrelated, outcomes. In the process of moving across national boundaries—through media images, immigration, or global systems of production—gender inequalities are reconstructed and take new shape. At the same time, global movements of gender transform the gendered institutions that they come into contact with. While it may seem ironic to focus on nation in this era that some commentators have termed "postnational," we believe that we need to focus more on national difference precisely because of the increasing number and intensity of global connections and interdependencies.

The second edition of this book continues with all of these themes, but adds attention to two arenas of gender previously neglected: differences of generation and the images of gender propagated by mass media and popular culture. In recent years, pundits have employed the term *Generation X* to refer to the vast and diverse group of the "twenty-something" (and now "early thirty-something") population. Although celebrated by some as a new market for products, and condemned by others as spoiled slackers, Generation X is in fact more heterogeneous than the pundits would allow. The articles we have assembled on generational differences are sprinkled throughout the various sections of this volume, and they underline some of the gender issues in these distinct communities located within the amorphous Generation X. The gendered character of these multiple communities are, in many instances, defined by differences of race, class, sexuality, and nation. Yet these constituencies are also deliberately constructed by young people in ways that underline their distinctiveness, and sometimes oppositional stances, to other groups and older generations.

The second edition of this book also includes a new selection of readings on popular culture and ideology. In recent years, the flourishing scholarship in cultural studies has shown us that our experiences of gender are strongly shaped by mass media, advertisements, consumption, and leisure activities. Music, sports, and the marketing of difference through consumer goods, to cite a few examples, convey particular embodiments of gender. These are all activities that catch us with our guard down, and it is precisely for this reason that they exert such a powerful force over our lives.

We hope this book contributes to a new generation of scholarship in the study of sex and gender—one that moves beyond the patchwork quilt approach that lists or catalogs differences to an approach that takes up the challenge to explore the relations of power that structure these differences. Gloria Anzaldúa (1990), a Chicana lesbian and feminist, uses the border as a metaphor to capture the spatial, ethnic, class, and sexual transitions traversed in one's lifetime. She states in a poem that, "To survive the borderlands you must live *sin fronteras*" (without borders). Breaking down, reassessing, and crossing the borders that divide the patches on the quilt—both experientially and analytically—is key to the difficult task of transforming knowledge about gender. Looking at the various prisms that organize gender relations, we think, will contribute to the kind of bridge-building that is needed to construct broad-based coalitions to push for equality and social justice in the twenty-first century.

REFERENCES

Acker, Joan. 1999. "Rewriting Class, Race and Gender: Problems in Feminist Rethinking." Pp. 44–69 in Myra Marx Ferree, Judith Lorber, and Beth B. Hess (eds.), *Revisioning Gender.* Thousand Oaks, CA: Sage Publications.

Anzaldúa, Gloria. 1990. "To Live in the Borderlands Means You." Pp. 194–195 in Gloria Anzaldúa, *Borderlands La Frontera: The New Mestiza.* San Francisco, CA: Spinsters/Aunt Lute.

Baca Zinn, M., Weber Cannon, L., Higginbotham, E., Thornton Dill, B. 1986. "The Costs of Exclusion-

ary Practices in Women's Studies," *Signs: Journal of Women in Culture and Society 11:* 290–303.

Boserup, Ester. 1970. *Woman's Role in Economic Development.* London: George Allen & Unwin.

Brod, Harry (ed.). 1987. *The Making of Masculinities: The New Men's Studies.* Boston: Allen & Unwin.

Brownmiller, Susan. 1975. *Against Our Will: Men, Women, and Rape.* New York: Simon and Schuster.

Chang, Grace. 1994. "Undocumented Latinas: The New 'Employable Mothers.'" Pp. 259–285 in Evelyn Nakano Glenn, Grace Chang, and Linda Rennie

Forcey (eds.), *Mothering, Ideology, Experience, and Agency.* New York and London: Routledge.

Collins, Patricia Hill. 1990. *Black Feminist Thought: Knowledge, Consciousness, and the Politics of Empowerment.* Boston: Unwin Hyman.

Collins, Patricia Hill. 1998. *Fighting Words: Black Women and the Search for Justice.* Minneapolis: University of Minnesota Press.

Connell, R. W. 1987. *Gender and Power.* Stanford, CA: Stanford University Press.

Connell, R. W. 1992. "A Very Straight Gay: Masculinity, Homosexual Experience, and the Dynamics of Gender," *American Sociological Review 57:* 735–751.

Connell, R. W. 1995. *Masculinities.* Berkeley: University of California Press.

De Beauvoir, Simone. 1953. *The Second Sex.* New York: Knopf.

Enloe, Cynthia. 1993. *The Morning After: Sexual Politics at the End of the Cold War.* Berkeley: University of California Press.

Glenn, Evelyn Nakano. 1999. "The Social Construction and Institutionalization of Gender and Race: An Integrative Framework." Pp. 3–43 in Myra Marx Ferree, Judith Lorber, and Beth B. Hess (eds.), *Revisioning Gender.* Thousand Oaks, CA: Sage.

Hartmann, Heidi. 1976. "Capitalism, Patriarchy, and Job Segregation by Sex," *Signs: Journal of Women in Culture and Society 1:* (3), part 2, Spring: 137–167.

Hewitt, Nancy A. 1992. "Compounding Differences," *Feminist Studies 18:* 313–326.

Hondagneu-Sotelo, Pierrette. 1994. *Gendered Transitions: Mexican Experiences of Immigration.* Berkeley: *University of California Press.*

Kanter, Rosabeth Moss. 1977. *Men and Women of the Corporation.* New York: Basic Books.

Kaufman, Michael. 1987. *Beyond Patriarchy: Essays by Men on Pleasure, Power, and Change.* Toronto and New York: Oxford University.

Kessler, Sandra, Dean J. Ashendon, R. W. Connell, & Gary W. Dowsett. 1985. "Gender Relations in Secondary Schooling," *Sociology of Education 58:* 34–48.

Kimmel, Michael S. (ed.). 1987. *Changing Men: New Directions in Research on Men and Masculinity.* Newbury Park, CA: Sage.

Kimmel, Michael S. 1996. *Manhood in America: A Cultural History.* New York: Free Press.

Kimmel, Michael S., & Michael A. Messner (eds.). 1989. *Men's Lives.* New York: Macmillan.

Kimmel, Michael S. & Michael A. Messner (eds.). 1998. *Men's Lives,* 4th edition. Allyn & Bacon.

Lorber, Judith. 1994. *Paradoxes of Gender.* Oxford University Press.

Messner, Michael A. 1996. "Studying Up on Sex," *Sociology of Sport Journal 13:* 221–237.

Messner, Michael A. 1998. *Politics of Masculinties: Men in Movements.* Thousands Oaks, CA: Sage.

Mohanty, Chandra Talpade. 1991. "Cartographies of Struggle: Third World Women and the Politics of Feminism." Pp. 51–80 in Chandra Talpade Mohanty, Ann Russo, and Lourdes Torres (eds.), *Third World Women and the Politics of Feminism.* Bloomington: Indiana University Press.

Morgan, Robin. 1970. *Sisterhood Is Powerful: An Anthology of Writing from the Women's Liberation Movement.* New York: Vintage Books.

Rich, Adrienne. 1980. "Compulsory Heterosexuality and the Lesbian Experience," *Signs: Journal of Women in Culture and Society 5:* 631–660.

Sassen, Saskia. 1991. *The Global City: New York, London, Tokyo.* Princeton, NJ: Princeton University Press.

Smith, Barbara. 1977. *Toward a Black Feminist Criticism.* Freedom, CA: Crossing Press.

West, Candace, & Sarah Fenstermaker. 1995. "Doing Difference," *Gender & Society 9:* 8–37.

PART ONE

Perspectives on Sex, Gender, and Difference

Are women and men or boys and girls really different, or do we just think and act as though they are different? In other words, are gender differences and inequalities rooted in biology, or are they socially constructed? Today, these questions are rarely answered with simplistic, pat answers. And the questions that gender scholars are asking have also grown more complex. Are these differences constant over time, historically invariant? If women and men are different, then are women—as a group—similar to one another? Do White women share experiences similar to those of women of color? The articles in this opening section reflect a sampling of recent gender scholarship in the social sciences. They tackle tricky questions of difference between women and men, as well as issues of difference among groups of women and among groups of men.

In recent years the concept of "difference feminism" has crept into the vocabulary of women's studies. Difference feminism arose in opposition to liberal feminism, which sought women's equality by appealing to the logic of sameness. If women and men are inherently similar, liberal feminists argued, then, according to meritocratic principles, women deserve the same treatment and opportunities that men receive. Difference feminists sought women's equality by appealing to the logic of difference. By acknowledging and sometimes even underscoring biological, emotional, and social differences between women and men, they argued that women cannot rely on men's strategies to achieve equality.

While difference feminism highlights differences between women and men, another line of thinking questions the basis of difference and equality between women and men. In the first reading, Judith Lorber goes right to the heart of both sexist thinking and difference feminism by questioning what is generally taken for granted: physical, bodily differences between women and men. She deconstructs "the making" of gendered bodies and deftly shows that physiological differences remain meaningless without substantial scaffolding composed of social meanings and practices. It takes a complex ongoing social apparatus to transform physiological differences into gender inequality.

In contrast to difference feminism's premise of a unitary, implied sameness in the category *women* or *men*, the second reading in this part, by Maxine Baca Zinn and Bonnie

Thornton Dill, questions this universalism. Here, the authors focus on differences of race and class between women. They analyze the development of this scholarship, noting both the tensions and the benefits, as they explore theories and concepts of multiracial feminism. A key insight here is recognition of the ways in which the differences between women are historically and socially constructed and the ways in which they intersect.

The remaining readings in Part One bring different points of critique to the categorical "difference" lens applied to women and men. The reading by Barrie Thorne raises important theoretical and methodological questions for scholarship that highlight differences between and within the sexes. Ethnographic research of children in elementary schools leads Thorne to question the "dualistic models of sex differences." She persuasively argues the merits of a more fluid and contextually situated view of gender relations. In the subsequent reading on moral reasoning among African American youth, Carol Stack directly challenges the "difference" findings of Carol Gilligan. Her critique points to the importance of considering race, class, and culture in any sweeping generalization that might be made about young women and men.

How is global restructuring affecting gender? In contrast to the common image of a homogenizing process sweeping the globe to make gender more uniform, global forces are, in fact, creating new gender hierarchies. R. W. Connell untangles the key strands in "the world gender order" to expose the invisible connections between globalization and gender. He shows how masculinities are being reconfigured by transnational relations of power and subordination. In the next reading, Pierrette Hondagneu-Sotelo and Michael Messner look at differences between hegemonic masculinities, characterized by class and race privileges and the marginalized masculinities of Mexican, working-class, undocumented immigrant men. The authors note that popular "common sense" views of masculinity and "machismo" typically fail to distinguish between gender display and structural power.

The final reading in this part turns to questions about research, gender, and difference. Where shall research on gender come from? Who should study gender and under what conditions? Can men study women? Can women study men? Can "outsiders" comprehend the subjectivity of women and men who are different from themselves, or are "insiders" better qualified to conduct research on those of the same gender, race, and sexual orientation? How do the experiences of those who have historically been intellectual outsiders shape their view of social reality?

Questions about insiders and outsiders have been the subject of much debate. As more researchers adopt qualitative approaches in order to capture the nuances of everyday life and as they become more sensitive to difference, questions about social location and research are among the most important issues in feminist scholarship. Margaret L. Andersen draws on her field research in an African American community for lessons in studying groups different from one's own. She encourages White scholars to develop research practices that acknowledge the race, class, and gender relations in which all research activities are situated.

1

Believing Is Seeing

Biology as Ideology

JUDITH LORBER

Until the eighteenth century, Western philosophers and scientists thought that there was one sex and that women's internal genitalia were the inverse of men's external genitalia: the womb and vagina were the penis and scrotum turned inside out (Laqueur 1990). Current Western thinking sees women and men as so different physically as to sometimes seem two species. The bodies, which have been mapped inside and out for hundreds of years, have not changed. What has changed are the justifications for gender inequality. When the social position of all human beings was believed to be set by natural law or was considered God-given, biology was irrelevant; women and men of different classes all had their assigned places. When scientists began to question the divine basis of social order and replaced faith with empirical knowledge, what they saw was that women were very different from men in that they had wombs and menstruated. Such anatomical differences destined them for an entirely different social life from men.

In actuality, the basic bodily material *is* the same for females and males, and except for procreative hormones and organs, female and male human beings have similar bodies (Naftolin and Butz 1981). Furthermore, as has been known since the middle of the nineteenth century, male and female genitalia develop from the same fetal tissue, and so infants can be born with ambiguous genitalia (Money and Ehrhardt 1972). When they are, biology is used quite arbitrarily in sex assignment. Suzanne Kessler (1990) interviewed six medical specialists in pediatric intersexuality and found

that whether an infant with XY chromosomes and anomalous genitalia was categorized as a boy or a girl depended on the size of the penis—if a penis was very small, the child was categorized as a girl, and sex-change surgery was used to make an artificial vagina. In the late nineteenth century, the presence or absence of ovaries was the determining criterion of gender assignment for hermaphrodites because a woman who could not procreate was not a complete woman (Kessler 1990, 20).

Yet in Western societies, we see two discrete sexes and two distinguishable genders because our society is built on two classes of people, "women" and "men." Once the gender category is given, the attributes of the person are also gendered: Whatever a "woman" is has to be "female"; whatever a "man" is has to be "male." Analyzing the social processes that construct the categories we call "female and male," "women and men," and "homosexual and heterosexual" uncovers the ideology and power differentials congealed in these categories (Foucault 1978). This article will use two familiar areas of social life—sports and technological competence—to show how myriad physiological differences are transformed into similar-appearing, gendered social bodies. My perspective goes beyond accepted feminist views that gender is a cultural overlay that modifies physiological sex differences. That perspective assumes either that there are two fairly similar sexes distorted by social practices into two genders with purposefully different characteristics or that there are two sexes whose essential differences are rendered unequal by social practices. I am arguing that bodies differ in many ways physiologically, but they are completely transformed by social practices to fit into the salient categories of a society, the most pervasive of which are "female" and "male" and "women" and "men."

Neither sex nor gender are pure categories. Combinations of incongruous genes, genitalia, and hormonal input are ignored in sex categorization, just as combinations of incongruous physiology, identity, sexuality, appearance, and behavior are ignored in the social construction of gender statuses. Menstruation, lactation, and gestation do not demarcate women from men. Only some women are pregnant and then only some of the time; some women do not have a uterus or ovaries. Some women have stopped menstruating temporarily, others have reached menopause, and some have had hysterectomies. Some women breastfeed some of the time, but some men lactate (Jaggar 1983, 165fn). Menstruation, lactation, and gestation are individual experiences of womanhood (Levesque-Lopman 1988), but not determinants of the social category "woman," or even "female." Similarly, "men are not always sperm producers, and in fact, not all sperm producers are men. A male-to-female transsexual, prior to surgery, can be socially a woman, though still potentially (or actually) capable of spermatogenesis" (Kessler and McKenna [1978] 1985, 2).

When gender assignment is contested in sports, where the categories of competitors are rigidly divided into women and men, chromosomes are now used to determine in which category the athlete is to compete. However, an anomaly common enough to be found in several women at every major international sports competition are XY chromosomes that have not produced male anatomy or physiology because of a genetic defect. Because these women are women in every way significant for sports competition, the prestigious International Amateur Athletic Federation has urged that sex be determined by simple genital inspection (Kolata 1992). Transsexuals would pass this test, but it took a lawsuit for Renée Richards, a male-to-female transsexual, to be able to play tournament tennis as a woman, despite his male sex chromosomes (Richards 1983). Oddly, neither basis for gender categorization—chromosomes nor genitalia—has anything to do with sports prowess (Birrell and Cole 1990).

In the Olympics, in cases of chromosomal ambiguity, women must undergo "a battery of gynecological and physical exams to see if she is 'female enough' to compete. Men are not tested" (Carlson 1991, 26). The purpose is not to categorize women and men accurately, but to make sure men don't enter women's competitions, where, it is felt, they will have the advantage of size and strength. This practice sounds fair only because it is assumed that all men are similar in size and strength and different from all women. Yet in Olympics boxing and wrestling matches, men are matched within weight classes. Some women might similarly successfully compete with some men in many sports. Women did not run in marathons until about twenty years ago. In twenty years of marathon competition, women have reduced their finish times by more than one-and-one-half hours; they are expected to run as fast as men in that race by 1998 and might catch up with men's running times in races of other lengths within the next 50 years because they are increasing their fastest speeds more rapidly than are men (Fausto-Sterling 1985, 213–18).

The reliance on only two sex and gender categories in the biological and social sciences is as epistemologically spurious as the reliance on chromosomal or genital tests to group athletes. Most research designs do not investigate whether physical skills or physical abilities are really more or less common in women and men (Epstein 1988). They start out with two social categories ("women," "men"), assume they are biologically different ("female," "male"), look for similarities among them and differences between them, and attribute what they have found for the social categories to sex differences (Gelman, Collman, and

Maccoby 1986). These designs rarely question the categorization of their subjects into two and only two groups, even though they often find more significant within-group differences than between-group differences (Hyde 1990). The social construction perspective on sex and gender suggests that instead of starting with the two presumed dichotomies in each category—female, male; woman, man—it might be more useful in gender studies to group patterns of behavior and only then look for identifying markers of the people likely to enact such behaviors.

WHAT SPORTS ILLUSTRATE

Competitive sports have become, for boys and men, as players and as spectators, a way of constructing a masculine identity, a legitimated outlet for violence and aggression, and an avenue for upward mobility (Dunning 1986; Kemper 1990, 167–206; Messner 1992). For men in Western societies, physical competence is an important marker of masculinity (Fine 1987; Glassner 1992; Majors 1990). In professional and collegiate sports, physiological differences are invoked to justify women's secondary status, despite the clear evidence that gender status overrides physiological capabilities. Assumptions about women's physiology have influenced rules of competition; subsequent sports performances then validate how women and men are treated in sports competitions.

Gymnastic equipment is geared to slim, wiry, prepubescent girls and not to mature women; conversely, men's gymnastic equipment is tailored for muscular, mature men, not slim, wiry prepubescent boys. Boys could compete with girls, but are not allowed to; women gymnasts are left out entirely. Girl gymnasts are just that—little girls who will be disqualified as soon as they grow up (Vecsey 1990). Men gymnasts have men's status. In women's basketball, the size of the ball and rules for handling the ball change the style of play to "a slower, less intense, and less exciting modification of the 'regular' or men's game" (Watson 1987,

441). In the 1992 Winter Olympics, men figure skaters were required to complete three triple jumps in their required program; women figure skaters were forbidden to do more than *one*. These rules penalized artistic men skaters and athletic women skaters (Janofsky 1992). For the most part, Western sports are built on physically trained men's bodies:

> *Speed, size, and strength seem to be the essence of sports. Women* are *naturally inferior at "sports" so conceived.*
>
> *But if women had been the historically dominant sex, our concept of sport would no doubt have evolved differently. Competitions emphasizing flexibility, balance, strength, timing, and small size might dominate Sunday afternoon television and offer salaries in six figures. (English 1982, 266, emphasis in original)*

Organized sports are big businesses and, thus, who has access and at what level is a distributive or equity issue. The overall status of women and men athletes is an economic, political, and ideological issue that has less to do with individual physiological capabilities than with their cultural and social meaning and who defines and profits from them (Messner and Sabo 1990; Slatton and Birrell 1984). Twenty years after the passage of Title IX of the U.S. Civil Rights Act, which forbade gender inequality in any school receiving federal funds, the *goal* for collegiate sports in the next five years is 60 percent men, 40 percent women in sports participation, scholarships, and funding (Moran 1992).

How access and distribution of rewards (prestigious and financial) are justified is an ideological, even moral, issue (Birrell 1988, 473–76; Hargreaves 1982). One way is that men athletes are glorified and women athletes ignored in the mass media. Messner and his colleagues found that in 1989, in TV sports news in the United States, men's sports got 92 percent of the coverage and women's sports 5 percent, with the rest mixed or gender-neutral (Messner, Duncan, and Jensen

1993). In 1990, in four of the top-selling newspapers in the United States, stories on men's sports outnumbered those on women's sports 23 to 1. Messner and his colleagues also found an implicit hierarchy in naming, with women athletes most likely to be called by first names, followed by Black men athletes, and only white men athletes routinely referred to by their last names. Similarly, women's collegiate sports teams are named or marked in ways that symbolically feminize and trivialize them—the men's team is called Tigers, the women's Kittens (Eitzen and Baca Zinn 1989).

Assumptions about men's and women's bodies and their capacities are crafted in ways that make unequal access and distribution of rewards acceptable (Hudson 1978; Messner 1988). Media images of modern men athletes glorify their strength and power, even their violence (Hargreaves 1986). Media images of modern women athletes tend to focus on feminine beauty and grace (so they are not really athletes) or on their thin, small, wiry androgynous bodies (so they are not really women). In coverage of the Olympics,

> *loving and detailed attention is paid to pixie-like gymnasts; special and extended coverage is given to graceful and dazzling figure skaters; the camera painstakingly records the fluid movements of swimmers and divers. And then, in a blinding flash of fragmented images, viewers see a few minutes of volleyball, basketball, speed skating, track and field, and alpine skiing, as television gives its nod to the mere existence of these events. (Boutilier and SanGiovanni 1983, 190)*

Extraordinary feats by women athletes who were presented as mature adults might force sports organizers and audiences to rethink their stereotypes of women's capabilities, the way elves, mermaids, and ice queens do not. Sports, therefore, construct men's bodies to be powerful; women's bodies to be sexual. As Connell says,

> *The meanings in the bodily sense of masculinity concern, above all else, the superiority of men to women, and the exaltation of hegemonic masculinity over other groups of men which is essential for the domination of women. (1987, 85)*

In the late 1970s, as women entered more and more athletic competitions, supposedly good scientific studies showed that women who exercised intensely would cease menstruating because they would not have enough body fat to sustain ovulation (Brozan 1978). When one set of researchers did a yearlong study that compared 66 women—21 who were training for a marathon, 22 who ran more than an hour a week, and 23 who did less than an hour of aerobic exercise a week—they discovered that only 20 percent of the women in any of these groups had "normal" menstrual cycles every month (Prior et al. 1990). The dangers of intensive training for women's fertility therefore were exaggerated as women began to compete successfully in arenas formerly closed to them.

Given the association of sports with masculinity in the United States, women athletes have to manage a contradictory status. One study of women college basketball players found that although they "did athlete" on the court—pushing, shoving, fouling, hard running, fast breaks, defense, obscenities and sweat" (Watson 1987, 441), they "did woman" off the court, using the locker room as their staging area:

> *While it typically took fifteen minutes to prepare for the game, it took approximately fifteen minutes after the game to shower and remove the sweat of an athlete, and it took another thirty minutes to dress, apply make-up and style hair. It did not seem to matter whether the players were going out into the public or getting on a van for a long ride home. Average dressing time and rituals did not change. (Watson 1987, 443)*

Another way women manage these status dilemmas is to redefine the activity or its result as feminine or womanly (Mangan and Park 1987). Thus women bodybuilders claim that "flex appeal is sex appeal" (Duff and Hong 1984, 378).

Such a redefinition of women's physicality affirms the ideological subtext of sports that physical strength is men's prerogative and justifies men's physical and sexual domination of women (Hargreaves 1986; Messner 1992, 164–72; Olson 1990; Theberge 1987; Willis 1982). When women demonstrate physical strength, they are labeled unfeminine:

It's threatening to one's takeability, one's rape-ability, one's femininity, to be strong and physically self-possessed. To be able to resist rape, not to communicate rapeability with one's body, to hold one's body for uses and meanings other than that can transform what being a woman means. (MacKinnon 1987, 122, emphasis in original)

Resistance to that transformation, ironically, was evident in the policies of American women physical education professionals throughout most of the twentieth century. They minimized exertion, maximized a feminine appearance and manner, and left organized sports competition to men (Birrell 1988, 461–62; Mangan and Park 1987).

DIRTY LITTLE SECRETS

As sports construct gendered bodies, technology constructs gendered skills. Meta-analysis of studies of gender differences in spatial and mathematical ability have found that men have a large advantage in ability to mentally rotate an image, a moderate advantage in a visual perception of horizontality and verticality and in mathematical performance, and a small advantage in ability to pick a figure out of a field (Hyde 1990). It could be argued that these advantages explain why, within the short space of time that computers have become ubiquitous in offices, schools, and homes, work on them and with them has become gendered: Men create, program, and market computers, make war and produce science and art with them; women microwire them in computer factories and enter data in computerized offices; boys play games, socialize, and commit crimes with

computers; girls are rarely seen in computer clubs, camps, and classrooms. But women were hired as computer programmers in the 1940s because

the work seemed to resemble simple clerical tasks. In fact, however, programming demanded complex skills in abstract logic, mathematics, electrical circuitry, and machinery, all of which . . . women used to perform in their work. Once programming was recognized as "intellectually demanding," it became attractive to men. (Donato 1990, 170)

A woman mathematician and pioneer in data processing, Grace M. Hopper, was famous for her work on programming language (Perry and Greber 1990, 86). By the 1960s, programming was split into more and less skilled specialties, and the entry of women into the computer field in the 1970s and 1980s was confined to the lower-paid specialties. At each stage, employers invoked women's and men's purportedly natural capabilities for the jobs for which they were hired (Cockburn 1983, 1985; Donato 1990; Hartmann 1987; Hartmann, Kraut, and Tilly 1986; Kramer and Lehman 1990; Wright et al. 1987; Zimmerman 1983).

It is the taken-for-grantedness of such everyday gendered behavior that gives credence to the belief that the widespread differences in what women and men do must come from biology. To take one ordinarily unremarked scenario: In modern societies, if a man and woman who are a couple are in a car together, he is much more likely to take the wheel than she is, even if she is the more competent driver. Molly Haskell calls this taken-for-granted phenomenon "the dirty little secret of marriage: the husband-lousy-driver syndrome" (1989, 26). Men drive cars whether they are good drivers or not because men and machines are a "natural" combination (Scharff 1991). But the ability to drive gives one mobility; it is a form of social power.

In the early days of the automobile, feminists co-opted the symbolism of mobility as emancipation: "Donning goggles and dusters, wielding tire irons and tool kits, taking the wheel, they announced their intention to move beyond the bounds of women's place" (Scharff 1991, 68). Driving enabled them to campaign for women's suffrage in parts of the United States not served by public transportation, and they effectively used motorcades and speaking from cars as campaign tactics (Scharff 1991, 67–88). Sandra Gilbert also notes that during World War I, women's ability to drive was physically, mentally, and even sensually liberating:

> For nurses and ambulance drivers, women doctors and women messengers, the phenomenon of modern battle was very different from that experienced by entrenched combatants. Finally given a chance to take the wheel, these post-Victorian girls raced motorcars along foreign roads like adventurers exploring new lands, while their brothers dug deeper into the mud of France.... Retrieving the wounded and the dead from deadly positions, these once-decorous daughters had at last been allowed to prove their valor, and they swooped over the wastelands of the war with the energetic love of Wagnerian Valkyries, their mobility alone transporting countless immobilized heroes to safe havens. (1983, 438–39)

Not incidentally, women in the United States and England got the vote for their war efforts in World War I.

SOCIAL BODIES AND THE BATHROOM PROBLEM

People of the same racial ethnic group and social class are roughly the same size and shape—but there are many varieties of bodies. People have different genitalia, different secondary sex characteristics, different contributions to procreation, different orgasmic experiences, different patterns of illness and aging. Each of us experiences our bodies differently, and these experiences change as we grow, age, sicken, and die. The bodies of pregnant and nonpregnant women, short and tall people, those with intact and functioning limbs and those whose bodies are physically challenged are all different. But the salient categories of a so-

ciety group these attributes in ways that ride roughshod over individual experiences and more meaningful clusters of people.

I am not saying that physical differences between male and female bodies don't exist, but that these differences are socially meaningless until social practices transform them into social facts. West Point Military Academy's curriculum is designed to produce leaders, and physical competence is used as a significant measure of leadership ability (Yoder 1989). When women were accepted as West Point cadets, it became clear that the tests of physical competence, such as rapidly scaling an eight-foot wall, had been constructed for male physiques—pulling oneself up and over using upper-body strength. Rather than devise tests of physical competence for women, West Point provided boosters that mostly women used—but that lost them test points—in the case of the wall, a platform. Finally, the women themselves figured out how to use their bodies successfully. Janice Yoder describes this situation:

> I was observing this obstacle one day, when a woman approached the wall in the old prescribed way, got her fingertips grip, and did an unusual thing: she walked her dangling legs up the wall until she was in a position where both her hands and feet were atop the wall. She then simply pulled up her sagging bottom and went over. She solved the problem by capitalizing on one of women's physical assets: lower-body strength. (1989, 530)

In short, if West Point is going to measure leadership capability by physical strength, women's pelvises will do just as well as men's shoulders.

The social transformation of female and male physiology into a condition of inequality is well illustrated by the bathroom problem. Most buildings that have gender-segregated bathrooms have an equal number for women and for men. Where there are crowds, there are always long lines in front of women's bathrooms but rarely in front of men's bathrooms. The cultural, physiological, and demographic combinations of clothing, frequency of urination, menstruation, and child care add up to generally greater bathroom use by

—. 1990. *The conceptual practices of
feminist sociology of knowledge.* Tor-
…rsity of Toronto Press.

…beth. 1988. *Inessential woman: Prob-
…clusion in feminist thought.* Boston: Bea-
…s.

…ancy. 1987. Sport and women's em-
…ment. *Women's Studies International Forum*
…7–93.

…eorge. 1990. Cathy Rigby, unlike Peter, did
…v up. *New York Times* Sports Section, 19
…cember.

…, Tracey. 1987. Women athletes and athletic
…omen: The dilemmas and contradictions of man-

aging incongruent identities. *Sociological Inquiry*
57:431–46.

Willis, Paul. 1982. Women in sport in ideology. In
Sport, culture, and ideology, edited by Jennifer A.
Hargreaves. London: Routledge & Kegan Paul.

Wright, Barbara Drygulski et al., eds. 1987. *Women,
work, and technology: Transformations.* Ann Arbor: University of Michigan Press.

Yoder, Janice D. 1989. Women at West Point: Lessons
for token women in male-dominated occupations.
In *Women: A feminist perspective,* edited by Jo
Freeman. 4th ed. Palo Alto, CA: Mayfield.

Zimmerman, Jan, ed. 1983. *The technological woman:
Interfacing with tomorrow.* New York: Praeger.

women than men. Thus, although an equal number of bathrooms seems fair, equity would mean
more women's bathrooms or allowing women to
use men's bathrooms for a certain amount of time
(Molotch 1988).

The bathroom problem is the outcome of the
way gendered bodies are differentially evaluated
in Western cultures: Men's social bodies are the
measure of what is "human." Gray's *Anatomy,* in
use for 100 years, well into the twentieth century,
presented the human body as male. The female
body was shown only where it differed from the
male (Laqueur 1990, 166–67). Denise Riley says
that if we envisage women's bodies, men's bodies,
and human bodies "as a triangle of identifications,
then it is rarely an equilateral triangle in which
both sexes are pitched at matching distances from
the apex of the human" (1988, 197). Catharine
MacKinnon also contends that in Western society,
universal "humanness" is male because

> *virtually every quality that distinguishes men from
> women is already affirmatively compensated in this
> society. Men's physiology defines most sports, their
> needs define auto and health insurance coverage,
> their socially defined biographies define workplace
> expectations and successful career patterns, their
> perspectives and concerns define quality in schol-
> arship, their experiences and obsessions define
> merit, their objectification of life defines art, their
> military service defines citizenship, their presence
> defines family, their inability to get along with each
> other—their wars and rulerships—define history,
> their image defines god, and their genitals define
> sex. For each of their differences from women,
> what amounts to an affirmative action plan is in ef-
> fect, otherwise known as the structure and values
> of American society. (1987, 36)*

THE PARADOX OF HUMAN NATURE

Gendered people do not emerge from physiology
or hormones but from the exigencies of the social
order, mostly, from the need for a reliable division
of the work of food production and the social (not
physical) reproduction of new members. The
moral imperatives of religion and cultural repre-

sentations reinforce the boundary lines among
genders and ensure that what is demanded, what is
permitted, and what is tabooed for the people in
each gender is well-known and followed by most.
Political power, control of scarce resources, and,
if necessary, violence uphold the gendered social
order in the face of resistance and rebellion. Most
people, however, voluntarily go along with their
society's prescriptions for those of their gender
status because the norms and expectations get
built into their sense of worth and identity as a
certain kind of human being and because they believe their society's way is the natural way. These
beliefs emerge from the imagery that pervades the
way we think, the way we see and hear and speak,
the way we fantasize, and the way we feel. There
is no core or bedrock human nature below these
endlessly looping processes of the social production of sex and gender, self and other, identity and
psyche, each of which is a "complex cultural construction" (Butler 1990, 36). The paradox of "human nature" is that it is *always* a manifestation of
cultural meanings, social relationships, and power
politics—"not biology, but culture, becomes destiny" (Butler 1990, 8).

Feminist inquiry has long questioned the conventional categories of social science, but much
of the current work in feminist sociology has
not gone beyond adding the universal category
"women" to the universal category "men." Our
current debates over the global assumptions of
only two categories and the insistence that they
must be nuanced to include race and class are
steps in the direction I would like to see feminist
research go, but race and class are *also* global categories (Collins 1990; Spelman 1988). Deconstructing sex, sexuality, and gender reveals many
possible categories embedded in the social experiences and social practices of what Dorothy Smith
calls the "everyday/everynight world" (1990, 31–
57). These emergent categories group some people together for comparison with other people
without prior assumptions about who is like
whom. Categories can be broken up and people regrouped differently into new categories for com-

parison. This process of discovering categories from similarities and differences in people's behavior or responses can be more meaningful for feminist research than discovering similarities and differences between "females" and "males" or "women" and "men" because the social construction of the conventional sex and gender categories already assumes differences between them and similarities among them. When we rely only on the conventional categories of sex and gender, we end up finding what we looked for—we see what we believe, whether it is that "females" and "males" are essentially different or that "women" and "men" are essentially the same.

REFERENCES

Birrell, Susan J. 1988. Discourses on the gender/sport relationship: From women in sport to gender relations. In *Exercise and sport science reviews.* Vol. 16, edited by Kent Pandolf New York: Macmillan.

Birrell, Susan J., and Sheryl L. Cole. 1990. Double fault: Renée Richards and the construction and naturalization of difference. *Sociology of Sport Journal* 7:1–21.

Boutilier, Mary A., and Lucinda SanGiovanni. 1983. *The sporting woman.* Champaign, IL: Human Kinetics.

Brozan, Nadine. 1978. Training linked to disruption of female reproductive cycle. *New York Times,* 17 April.

Butler, Judith. 1990. *Gender trouble: Feminism and the subversion of identity.* New York and London: Routledge & Kegan Paul.

Carlson, Alison. 1991. When is a woman not a woman? *Women's Sport and Fitness* March:24–29.

Cockburn, Cynthia. 1983. *Brothers: Male dominance and technological change.* London: Pluto.

———. 1985. *Machinery of dominance: Women, men and technical know-how.* London: Pluto.

Collins, Patricia Hill. 1990. *Black feminist thought: Knowledge, consciousness, and the politics of empowerment.* Boston: Unwin Hyman.

Connell, R. W. 1987. *Gender and power.* Stanford, CA: Stanford University Press.

Donato, Katharine M. 1990. Programming for change? The growing demand for women systems analysts. In *Job queues, gender queues: Explaining women's inroads into male occupations,* written and edited by Barbara F. Reskin and Patricia A. Roos. Philadelphia: Temple University Press.

Duff, Robert W., and Lawrence K. Hong, 1984. Self-images of women bodybuilders. *Sociology of Sport Journal* 2:374–80.

Dunning, Eric. 1986. Sport as a male preserve: Notes on the social sources of masculine identity and its transformations. *Theory, Culture and Society* 3: 79–90.

Eitzen, D. Stanley, and Maxine Baca Zinn. 1989. The deathleticization of women: The naming and gender marking of collegiate sport teams. *Sociology of Sport Journal* 6:362–70.

English, Jane. 1982. Sex equality in sports. In *Femininity, masculinity, and androgyny,* edited by Mary Vetterling-Braggin. Boston: Littlefield, Adams.

Epstein, Cynthia Fuchs. 1988. *Deceptive distinctions: Sex, gender and the social order.* New Haven, CT: Yale University Press.

Fausto-Sterling, Anne. 1985. *Myths of gender: Biological theories about women and men.* New York: Basic Books.

Fine, Gary Alan. 1987. *With the boys: Little League baseball and preadolescent culture.* Chicago: University of Chicago Press.

Foucault, Michel. 1978. *The history of sexuality: An introduction.* Translated by Robert Hurley. New York: Pantheon.

Gelman, Susan A., Pamela Collman, and Eleanor E. Maccoby. 1986. Inferring properties from categories versus inferring categories from properties: The case of gender. *Child Development* 57: 396–404.

Gilbert, Sandra M. 1983. Soldier's heart: Literary men, literary women, and the Great War. *Signs: Journal of Women in Culture and Society* 8:422–50.

Glassner, Barry. 1992. Men and muscles. In *Men's lives,* edited by Michael S. Kimmel and Michael A. Messner. New York: Macmillan.

Hargreaves, Jennifer A., ed. 1982. *Sport, culture, and ideology.* London: Routledge & Kegan Paul.

———. 1986. Where's the virtue? Where's the grace? A discussion of the social production of gender relations in and through sport. *Theory, Culture, and Society* 3:109–21.

Hartmann, Heidi I., ed. 1987. *Computer chips and paper clips: Technology and women's employment.* Vol. 2. Washington, DC: National Academy Press.

Hartmann, Heidi I., Robert E. Kraut, and Louise A. Tilly, eds. 1986. *Computer chips and paper clips: Technology and women's employment.* Vol. 1. Washington, DC: National Academy Press.

Haskell, Molly. 1989. Hers: He drives me crazy. *New York Times Magazine,* 24 September, 26, 28.

Hudson, Jackie. 1978. Physical parameters used for female exclusion from law enforcement and athletics. In *Women and sport: From myth to reality,* edited by Carol A. Oglesby. Philadelphia: Lea and Febiger.

Hyde, Janet Shibley. 1990. Meta-analysis and the psychology of gender differences. *Signs: Journal of Women in Culture and Society* 16:55–73.

Jaggar, Alison M. 1983. *Feminist politics and human nature.* Totowa, NJ: Rowman & Allanheld.

Janofsky, Michael. 1992. Yamaguchi has the delicate and golden touch. *New York Times,* 22 February.

Kemper, Theodore D. 1990. *Social structure and testosterone: Explorations of the socio-biosocial chain.* Brunswick, NJ: Rutgers University Press.

Kessler, Suzanne J., 1990. The medical construction of gender: Case management of intersexed infants. *Signs: Journal of Women in Culture and Society* 16:3–26.

Kessler, Suzanne J., and Wendy McKenna. [1978] 1985. *Gender: An ethnomethodological approach.* Chicago: University of Chicago Press.

Kolata, Gina. 1992. Track federation urges end to gene test for femaleness. *New York Times,* 12 February.

Kramer, Patricia E., and Sheila L. Lehman. 1990. Mismeasuring women: A critique of research on computer ability and avoidance. *Signs: Journal of Women in Culture and Society* 16:158–72.

Laqueur, Thomas. 1990. *Making sex: Body and gender from the Greeks to Freud.* Cambridge, MA: Harvard University Press.

Levesque-Lopman, Louise. 1988. *Claiming reality: Phenomenology and women's experience.* Totowa, NJ: Rowman & Littlefield.

MacKinnon, Catharine. 1987. *Feminism unmodified.* Cambridge, MA: Harvard University Press.

Majors, Richard. 1990. Cool pose: Black masculinity in sports. In *Sport, men and the gender order: Criti-*

Theorizing Difference from Multiracial Feminism

MAXINE BACA ZINN
BONNIE THORNTON DILL

Women of color have long challenged the hegemony of feminisms constructed primarily around the lives of white middle-class women. Since the late 1960s, U.S. women of color have taken issue with unitary theories of gender. Our critiques grew out of the widespread concern about the exclusion of women of color from feminist scholarship and the misinterpretation of our experiences,[1] and ultimately "out of the very discourses, denying, permitting, and producing difference."[2] Speaking simultaneously from "within and against" *both* women's liberation and antiracist movements, we have insisted on the need to challenge systems of domination,[3] not merely as gendered subjects but as women whose lives are affected by our location in multiple hierarchies.

Recently, and largely in response to these challenges, work that links gender to other forms of domination is increasing. In this article, we examine this connection further as well as the ways in which difference and diversity infuse contemporary feminist studies. Our analysis draws on a conceptual framework that we refer to as "multiracial feminism."[4] This perspective is an attempt to go beyond a mere recognition of diversity and difference among women to examine structures of domination, specifically the importance of race in understanding the social construction of gender. Despite the varied concerns and multiple intellectual stances which characterize the feminisms of women of color, they share an emphasis on race as a primary force situating genders differently. It is

the centrality of race, of institutionalized racism, and of struggles against racial oppression that link the various feminist perspectives within this framework. Together, they demonstrate that racial meanings offer new theoretical directions for feminist thought.

TENSIONS IN CONTEMPORARY DIFFERENCE FEMINISM

Objections to the false universalism embedded in the concept "woman" emerged within other discourses as well as those of women of color.[5] Lesbian feminists and postmodern feminists put forth their own versions of what Susan Bordo has called "gender skepticism."[6]

Many thinkers within mainstream feminism have responded to these critiques with efforts to contextualize gender. The search for women's "universal" or "essential" characteristics is being abandoned. By examining gender in the context of other social divisions and perspectives, difference has gradually become important—even problematizing the universal categories, "women" and "men." Sandra G. Harding expresses the shift best in her claim that "there are no gender relations *per se,* but only gender relations as constructed by and between classes, races, and cultures."[7]

Many feminists now contend that difference occupies center stage as *the* project of women studies today.[8] According to one scholar, "difference has replaced equality as the central concern of feminist theory."[9] Many have welcomed the change, hailing it as a major revitalizing force in U.S. feminist theory.[10] But if *some* priorities within mainstream feminist thought have been refocused by attention to difference, there remains an "uneasy alliance"[11] between women of color and other feminists.

If difference has helped revitalize academic feminisms, it has also "upset the apple cart," and introduced new conflicts into feminist studies.[12] For example, in a recent and widely discussed essay, Jane Rowland Martin argues that the current preoccupation with difference is leading feminism into dangerous traps. She fears that in giving privileged status to a predetermined set of analytic categories (race, ethnicity, and class), "we affirm the existence of nothing but difference." She asks, "How do we know that for us, difference does not turn on being fat, or religious, or in an abusive relationship?"[13]

We, too, see pitfalls in some strands of the difference project. However, our perspectives take their bearings from social relations. Race and class difference are crucial, we argue, not as individual characteristics (such as being fat) but insofar as they are primary organizing principles of a society which locates and positions groups within that society's opportunity structures.

Despite the much-heralded diversity trend within feminist studies, difference is often reduced to mere pluralism; a "live and let live" approach where principles of relativism generate a long list of diversities which begin with gender, class, and race and continue through a range of social structural as well as personal characteristics.[14] Another disturbing pattern, which bell hooks refers to as "the commodification of difference," is the representation of diversity as a form of exotica, "a spice, seasoning that livens up the dull dish that is mainstream white culture."[15] The major limitation of these approaches is the failure to attend to the power relations that accompany difference. Moreover, these approaches ignore the inequalities that cause some characteristics to be seen as "normal" while others are seen as "different" and thus, deviant.

Maria C. Lugones expresses irritation at those feminists who see only the *problem* of difference without recognizing *difference*.[16] Increasingly, we find that difference *is* recognized. But this in no way means that difference occupies a "privileged" theoretical status. Instead of using difference to rethink the category of women, difference is often a euphemism for women who differ from the traditional norm. Even in purporting to accept difference, feminist pluralism often creates a social reality that reverts to universalizing women:

> So much feminist scholarship assumes that when we cut through all of the diversity among women created by differences of racial classification, ethnicity, social class, and sexual orientation, a "universal truth" concerning women and gender lies buried underneath. But if we can face the scary possibility that no such certainty exists and that persisting in such a search will always distort or omit someone's experiences, with what do we replace this old way of thinking? Gender differences and gender politics begin to look very different if there is no essential woman at the core.[17]

WHAT IS MULTIRACIAL FEMINISM?

A new set of feminist theories have emerged from the challenges put forth by women of color. Multiracial feminism is an evolving body of theory and practice informed by wide-ranging intellectual traditions. This framework does not offer a singular or unified feminism but a body of knowledge situating women and men in multiple systems of domination. U.S. multiracial feminism encompasses several emergent perspectives developed primarily by women of color: African Americans, Latinas, Asian Americans, and Native Americans, women whose analyses are shaped by their unique perspectives as "outsiders within"— marginal intellectuals whose social locations provide them a particular perspective on self and society.[18] Although U.S. women of color represent many races and ethnic backgrounds—with different histories and cultures—our feminisms cohere in their treatment of race as a basic social division, a structure of power, a focus of political struggle and hence a fundamental force in shaping women's and men's lives.

This evolving intellectual and political perspective uses several terms. While we adopt the label "multiracial," other terms have been used to describe this broad framework. For example, Chela Sandoval refers to "U.S. Third World feminisms,"[19] while other scholars refer to "indigenous feminisms." In their theory text-reader, Alison M. Jagger and Paula M. Rothenberg adopt the label "multicultural feminism."[20]

We use "multiracial" rather than "multicultural" as a way of underscoring race as a power system that interacts with other structured inequalities to shape genders. Within the U.S. context, race, and the system of meanings and ideologies which accompany it, is a fundamental organizing principle of social relationships.[21] Race affects all women and men, although in different ways. Even cultural and group differences among women are produced through interaction within a racially stratified social order. Therefore, although we do not discount the importance of culture, we caution that cultural analytic frameworks that ignore race tend to view women's differences as the product of group-specific values and practices that often result in the marginalization of cultural groups which are then perceived as exotic expressions of a normative center. Our focus on race stresses the social construction of differently situated social groups and their varying degrees of advantage and power. Additionally, this emphasis on race takes on increasing political importance in an era where discourse about race is governed by color-evasive language[22] and a preference for individual rather than group remedies for social inequalities. Our analyses insist upon the primary and pervasive nature of race in contemporary U.S. society while at the same time acknowledging how race both shapes and is shaped by a variety of other social relations.

In the social sciences, multiracial feminism grew out of socialist feminist thinking. Theories about how political economic forces shape women's lives were influential as we began to uncover the social causes of racial ethnic women's

subordination. But socialist feminism's concept of capitalist patriarchy, with its focus on women's unpaid (reproductive) labor in the home failed to address racial differences in the organization of reproductive labor. As feminists of color have argued, "reproductive labor has divided along racial as well as gender lines, and the specific characteristics have varied regionally and changed over time as capitalism has reorganized."[23] Despite the limitations of socialist feminism, this body of literature has been especially useful in pursuing questions about the interconnections among systems of domination.[24]

Race and ethnic studies was the other major social scientific source of multiracial feminism. It provided a basis for comparative analyses of groups that are socially and legally subordinated and remain culturally distinct within U.S. society. This includes the systematic discrimination of socially constructed racial groups and their distinctive cultural arrangements. Historically, the categories of African American, Latino, Asian American, and Native American were constructed as both racially and culturally distinct. Each group has a distinctive culture, shares a common heritage, and has developed a common identity within a larger society that subordinates them.[25]

We recognize, of course, certain pitfalls inherent in an uncritical use of the multiracial label. First, the perspective can be hampered by a biracial model in which only African Americans and Whites are seen as racial categories and all other groups are viewed through the prism of cultural differences. Latinos and Asians have always occupied distinctive places within the racial hierarchy, and current shifts in the composition of the U.S. population are racializing these groups anew.[26]

A second problem lies in treating multiracial feminism as a single analytical framework, and its principle architects, women of color, as an undifferentiated category. The concepts "multiracial feminism," "racial ethnic women," and "women of color" homogenize quite different experiences and can falsely universalize experiences across race, ethnicity, sexual orientation, and age.[27] The feminisms created by women of color exhibit a plurality of intellectual and political positions. We speak in many voices, with inconsistencies that are born of our different social locations. Multiracial feminism embodies this plurality and richness. Our intent is not to falsely universalize women of color. Nor do we wish to promote a new racial essentialism in place of the old gender essentialism. Instead, we use these concepts to examine the structures and experiences produced by intersecting forms of race and gender.

It is also essential to acknowledge that race itself is a shifting and contested category whose meanings construct definitions of all aspects of social life.[28] In the United States it helped define citizenship by excluding everyone who was not a white, male property owner. It defined labor as slave or free, coolie or contract, and family as available only to those men whose marriages were recognized or whose wives could immigrate with them. Additionally, racial meanings are contested both within groups and between them.[29]

Although definitions of race are at once historically and geographically specific, they are also transnational, encompassing diasporic groups and crossing traditional geographic boundaries. Thus, while U.S. multiracial feminism calls attention to the fundamental importance of race, it must also locate the meaning of race within specific national traditions.

THE DISTINGUISHING FEATURES OF MULTIRACIAL FEMINISM

By attending to these problems, multiracial feminism offers a set of analytic premises for thinking about and theorizing gender. The following themes distinguish this branch of feminist inquiry.

First, multiracial feminism asserts that gender is constructed by a range of interlocking inequalities, what Patricia Hill Collins calls a "matrix of domination."[30] The idea of a matrix is that several fundamental systems work with and through each other. People experience race, class, gender, and sexuality differently depending upon their social location in the structures of race, class, gender,

and sexuality. For example, people of the same race will experience race differently depending upon their location in the class structure as working class, professional managerial class, or unemployed; in the gender structure as female or male; and in structures of sexuality as heterosexual, homosexual, or bisexual.

Multiracial feminism also examines the simultaneity of systems in shaping women's experience and identity. Race, class, gender, and sexuality are not reducible to individual attributes to be measured and assessed for their separate contribution in explaining given social outcomes, an approach that Elizabeth Spelman calls "pop-bead metaphysics," where a woman's identity consists of the sum of parts neatly divisible from one another.[31] The matrix of domination seeks to account for the multiple ways that women experience themselves as gendered, raced, classed, and sexualized.

Second, multiracial feminism emphasizes the intersectional nature of hierarchies at all levels of social life. Class, race, gender, and sexuality are components of both social structure and social interaction. Women and men are differently embedded in locations created by these cross-cutting hierarchies. As a result, women and men throughout the social order experience different forms of privilege and subordination, depending on their race, class, gender, and sexuality. In other words, intersecting forms of domination produce *both* oppression *and* opportunity. At the same time that structures of race, class, and gender create disadvantages for women of color, they provide unacknowledged benefits for those who are at the top of these hierarchies—whites, members of the upper classes, and males. Therefore, multiracial feminism applies not only to racial ethnic women but also to women and men of all races, classes, and genders.

Third, multiracial feminism highlights the relational nature of dominance and subordination. Power is the cornerstone of women's differences.[32] This means that women's differences are *connected* in systematic ways.[33] Race is a vital el-

women than men. Thus, although an equal number of bathrooms seems fair, equity would mean more women's bathrooms or allowing women to use men's bathrooms for a certain amount of time (Molotch 1988).

The bathroom problem is the outcome of the way gendered bodies are differentially evaluated in Western cultures: Men's social bodies are the measure of what is "human." Gray's *Anatomy,* in use for 100 years, well into the twentieth century, presented the human body as male. The female body was shown only where it differed from the male (Laqueur 1990, 166–67). Denise Riley says that if we envisage women's bodies, men's bodies, and human bodies "as a triangle of identifications, then it is rarely an equilateral triangle in which both sexes are pitched at matching distances from the apex of the human" (1988, 197). Catharine MacKinnon also contends that in Western society, universal "humanness" is male because

> *virtually every quality that distinguishes men from women is already affirmatively compensated in this society. Men's physiology defines most sports, their needs define auto and health insurance coverage, their socially defined biographies define workplace expectations and successful career patterns, their perspectives and concerns define quality in scholarship, their experiences and obsessions define merit, their objectification of life defines art, their military service defines citizenship, their presence defines family, their inability to get along with each other—their wars and rulerships—define history, their image defines god, and their genitals define sex. For each of their differences from women, what amounts to an affirmative action plan is in effect, otherwise known as the structure and values of American society. (1987, 36)*

THE PARADOX OF HUMAN NATURE

Gendered people do not emerge from physiology or hormones but from the exigencies of the social order, mostly, from the need for a reliable division of the work of food production and the social (not physical) reproduction of new members. The moral imperatives of religion and cultural representations reinforce the boundary lines among genders and ensure that what is demanded, what is permitted, and what is tabooed for the people in each gender is well-known and followed by most. Political power, control of scarce resources, and, if necessary, violence uphold the gendered social order in the face of resistance and rebellion. Most people, however, voluntarily go along with their society's prescriptions for those of their gender status because the norms and expectations get built into their sense of worth and identity as a certain kind of human being and because they believe their society's way is the natural way. These beliefs emerge from the imagery that pervades the way we think, the way we see and hear and speak, the way we fantasize, and the way we feel. There is no core or bedrock human nature below these endlessly looping processes of the social production of sex and gender, self and other, identity and psyche, each of which is a "complex cultural construction" (Butler 1990, 36). The paradox of "human nature" is that it is *always* a manifestation of cultural meanings, social relationships, and power politics—"not biology, but culture, becomes destiny" (Butler 1990, 8).

Feminist inquiry has long questioned the conventional categories of social science, but much of the current work in feminist sociology has not gone beyond adding the universal category "women" to the universal category "men." Our current debates over the global assumptions of only two categories and the insistence that they must be nuanced to include race and class are steps in the direction I would like to see feminist research go, but race and class are *also* global categories (Collins 1990; Spelman 1988). Deconstructing sex, sexuality, and gender reveals many possible categories embedded in the social experiences and social practices of what Dorothy Smith calls the "everyday/everynight world" (1990, 31–57). These emergent categories group some people together for comparison with other people without prior assumptions about who is like whom. Categories can be broken up and people regrouped differently into new categories for comparison. This process of discovering categories from similarities and differences in people's behavior or responses can be more meaningful for feminist research than discovering similarities and differences between "females" and "males" or "women" and "men" because the social construction of the conventional sex and gender categories already assumes differences between them and similarities among them. When we rely only on the conventional categories of sex and gender, we end up finding what we looked for—we see what we believe, whether it is that "females" and "males" are essentially different or that "women" and "men" are essentially the same.

REFERENCES

Birrell, Susan J. 1988. Discourses on the gender/sport relationship: From women in sport to gender relations. In *Exercise and sport science reviews.* Vol. 16, edited by Kent Pandolf New York: Macmillan.

Birrell, Susan J., and Sheryl L. Cole. 1990. Double fault: Renée Richards and the construction and naturalization of difference. *Sociology of Sport Journal* 7:1–21.

Boutilier, Mary A., and Lucinda SanGiovanni. 1983. *The sporting woman.* Champaign, IL: Human Kinetics.

Brozan, Nadine. 1978. Training linked to disruption of female reproductive cycle. *New York Times,* 17 April.

Butler, Judith. 1990. *Gender trouble: Feminism and the subversion of identity.* New York and London: Routledge & Kegan Paul.

Carlson, Alison. 1991. When is a woman not a woman? *Women's Sport and Fitness* March:24–29.

Cockburn, Cynthia. 1983. *Brothers: Male dominance and technological change.* London: Pluto.

———. 1985. *Machinery of dominance: Women, men and technical know-how.* London: Pluto.

Collins, Patricia Hill. 1990. *Black feminist thought: Knowledge, consciousness, and the politics of empowerment.* Boston: Unwin Hyman.

Connell, R. W. 1987. *Gender and power.* Stanford, CA: Stanford University Press.

Donato, Katharine M. 1990. Programming for change? The growing demand for women systems analysts. In *Job queues, gender queues: Explaining women's inroads into male occupations,* written and edited by Barbara F. Reskin and Patricia A. Roos. Philadelphia: Temple University Press.

Duff, Robert W., and Lawrence K. Hong, 1984. Self-images of women bodybuilders. *Sociology of Sport Journal* 2:374–80.

Dunning, Eric. 1986. Sport as a male preserve: Notes on the social sources of masculine identity and its transformations. *Theory, Culture and Society* 3: 79–90.

Eitzen, D. Stanley, and Maxine Baca Zinn. 1989. The deathleticization of women: The naming and gender marking of collegiate sport teams. *Sociology of Sport Journal* 6:362–70.

English, Jane. 1982. Sex equality in sports. In *Femininity, masculinity, and androgyny,* edited by Mary Vetterling-Braggin. Boston: Littlefield, Adams.

Epstein, Cynthia Fuchs. 1988. *Deceptive distinctions: Sex, gender and the social order.* New Haven, CT: Yale University Press.

Fausto-Sterling, Anne. 1985. *Myths of gender: Biological theories about women and men.* New York: Basic Books.

Fine, Gary Alan. 1987. *With the boys: Little League baseball and preadolescent culture.* Chicago: University of Chicago Press.

Foucault, Michel. 1978. *The history of sexuality: An introduction.* Translated by Robert Hurley. New York: Pantheon.

Gelman, Susan A., Pamela Collman, and Eleanor E. Maccoby. 1986. Inferring properties from categories versus inferring categories from properties: The case of gender. *Child Development* 57: 396–404.

Gilbert, Sandra M. 1983. Soldier's heart: Literary men, literary women, and the Great War. *Signs: Journal of Women in Culture and Society* 8:422–50.

Glassner, Barry. 1992. Men and muscles. In *Men's lives,* edited by Michael S. Kimmel and Michael A. Messner. New York: Macmillan.

Hargreaves, Jennifer A., ed. 1982. *Sport, culture, and ideology.* London: Routledge & Kegan Paul.

———. 1986. Where's the virtue? Where's the grace? A discussion of the social production of gender relations in and through sport. *Theory, Culture, and Society* 3:109–21.

Hartmann, Heidi I., ed. 1987. *Computer chips and paper clips: Technology and women's employment.* Vol. 2. Washington, DC: National Academy Press.

Hartmann, Heidi I., Robert E. Kraut, and Louise A. Tilly, eds. 1986. *Computer chips and paper clips: Technology and women's employment.* Vol. 1. Washington, DC: National Academy Press.

Haskell, Molly. 1989. Hers: He drives me crazy. *New York Times Magazine,* 24 September, 26, 28.

Hudson, Jackie. 1978. Physical parameters used for female exclusion from law enforcement and athletics. In *Women and sport: From myth to reality,* edited by Carol A. Oglesby. Philadelphia: Lea and Febiger.

Hyde, Janet Shibley. 1990. Meta-analysis and the psychology of gender differences. *Signs: Journal of Women in Culture and Society* 16:55–73.

Jaggar, Alison M. 1983. *Feminist politics and human nature.* Totowa, NJ: Rowman & Allanheld.

Janofsky, Michael. 1992. Yamaguchi has the delicate and golden touch. *New York Times,* 22 February.

Kemper, Theodore D. 1990. *Social structure and testosterone: Explorations of the socio-biosocial chain.* Brunswick, NJ: Rutgers University Press.

Kessler, Suzanne J., 1990. The medical construction of gender: Case management of intersexed infants. *Signs: Journal of Women in Culture and Society* 16:3–26.

Kessler, Suzanne J., and Wendy McKenna. [1978] 1985. *Gender: An ethnomethodological approach.* Chicago: University of Chicago Press.

Kolata, Gina. 1992. Track federation urges end to gene test for femaleness. *New York Times,* 12 February.

Kramer, Patricia E., and Sheila L. Lehman. 1990. Mismeasuring women: A critique of research on computer ability and avoidance. *Signs: Journal of Women in Culture and Society* 16:158–72.

Laqueur, Thomas. 1990. *Making sex: Body and gender from the Greeks to Freud.* Cambridge, MA: Harvard University Press.

Levesque-Lopman, Louise. 1988. *Claiming reality: Phenomenology and women's experience.* Totowa, NJ: Rowman & Littlefield.

MacKinnon, Catharine. 1987. *Feminism unmodified.* Cambridge, MA: Harvard University Press.

Majors, Richard. 1990. Cool pose: Black masculinity in sports. In *Sport, men and the gender order: Critical feminist perspectives,* edited by Michael A. Messner and Donald F. Sabo. Champaign, IL: Human Kinetics.

Mangan, J. A., and Roberta J. Park. 1987. *From fair sex to feminism: Sport and the socialization of women in the industrial and post-industrial eras.* London: Frank Cass.

Messner, Michael A. 1988. Sports and male domination: The female athlete as contested ideological terrain. *Sociology of Sport Journal* 5:197–211.

———. 1992. *Power at play: Sports and the problem of masculinity.* Boston: Beacon Press.

Messner, Michael A., Margaret Carlisle Duncan, and Kerry Jensen. 1993. Separating the men from the girls: The gendered language of televised sports. *Gender & Society* 7:121–37.

Messner, Michael A., and Donald F. Sabo, eds. 1990. *Sport, men, and the gender order: Critical feminist perspectives.* Champaign, IL: Human Kinetics.

Molotch, Harvey. 1988. The restroom and equal opportunity. *Sociological Forum* 3:128–32.

Money, John, and Anke A. Ehrhardt. 1972. *Man & woman, boy & girl.* Baltimore, MD: Johns Hopkins University Press.

Moran, Malcolm. 1992. Title IX: A 20-year search for equity. *New York Times* Sports Section, 21, 22, 23 June.

Naftolin, F., and E. Butz, eds. 1981. Sexual dimorphism. *Science* 211:1263–1324.

Olson, Wendy. 1990. Beyond Title IX: Toward an agenda for women and sports in the 1990s. *Yale Journal of Law and Feminism* 3:105–51.

Perry, Ruth, and Lisa Greber. 1990. Women and computers: An introduction. *Signs: Journal of Women in Culture and Society* 16:74–101.

Prior, Jerilynn C., Yvette M. Yigna, Martin T. Shechter, and Arthur E. Burgess. 1990. Spinal bone loss and ovulatory disturbances. *New England Journal of Medicine* 323:1221–27.

Richards, Renée, with Jack Ames. 1983. *Second serve.* New York: Stein and Day.

Riley, Denise. 1988. *Am I that name? Feminism and the category of women in history.* Minneapolis: University of Minnesota Press.

Scharff, Virginia. 1991. *Taking the wheel: Women and the coming of the motor age.* New York: Free Press.

Slatton, Bonnie, and Susan Birrell. 1984. The politics of women's sport. *Arena Review* 8.

Smith, Dorothy E. 1990. *The conceptual practices of power: A feminist sociology of knowledge.* Toronto: University of Toronto Press.

Spelman, Elizabeth. 1988. *Inessential woman: Problems of exclusion in feminist thought.* Boston: Beacon Press.

Theberge, Nancy. 1987. Sport and women's empowerment. *Women's Studies International Forum* 10:387–93.

Vecsey, George. 1990. Cathy Rigby, unlike Peter, did grow up. *New York Times* Sports Section, 19 December.

Watson, Tracey. 1987. Women athletes and athletic women: The dilemmas and contradictions of managing incongruent identities. *Sociological Inquiry* 57:431–46.

Willis, Paul. 1982. Women in sport in ideology. In *Sport, culture, and ideology,* edited by Jennifer A. Hargreaves. London: Routledge & Kegan Paul.

Wright, Barbara Drygulski et al., eds. 1987. *Women, work, and technology: Transformations.* Ann Arbor: University of Michigan Press.

Yoder, Janice D. 1989. Women at West Point: Lessons for token women in male-dominated occupations. In *Women: A feminist perspective,* edited by Jo Freeman. 4th ed. Palo Alto, CA: Mayfield.

Zimmerman, Jan, ed. 1983. *The technological woman: Interfacing with tomorrow.* New York: Praeger.

Theorizing Difference from Multiracial Feminism

MAXINE BACA ZINN
BONNIE THORNTON DILL

Women of color have long challenged the hegemony of feminisms constructed primarily around the lives of white middle-class women. Since the late 1960s, U.S. women of color have taken issue with unitary theories of gender. Our critiques grew out of the widespread concern about the exclusion of women of color from feminist scholarship and the misinterpretation of our experiences,[1] and ultimately "out of the very discourses, denying, permitting, and producing difference."[2] Speaking simultaneously from "within and against" *both* women's liberation and antiracist movements, we have insisted on the need to challenge systems of domination,[3] not merely as gendered subjects but as women whose lives are affected by our location in multiple hierarchies.

Recently, and largely in response to these challenges, work that links gender to other forms of domination is increasing. In this article, we examine this connection further as well as the ways in which difference and diversity infuse contemporary feminist studies. Our analysis draws on a conceptual framework that we refer to as "multiracial feminism."[4] This perspective is an attempt to go beyond a mere recognition of diversity and difference among women to examine structures of domination, specifically the importance of race in understanding the social construction of gender. Despite the varied concerns and multiple intellectual stances which characterize the feminisms of women of color, they share an emphasis on race as a primary force situating genders differently. It is

the centrality of race, of institutionalized racism, and of struggles against racial oppression that link the various feminist perspectives within this framework. Together, they demonstrate that racial meanings offer new theoretical directions for feminist thought.

TENSIONS IN CONTEMPORARY DIFFERENCE FEMINISM

Objections to the false universalism embedded in the concept "woman" emerged within other discourses as well as those of women of color.[5] Lesbian feminists and postmodern feminists put forth their own versions of what Susan Bordo has called "gender skepticism."[6]

Many thinkers within mainstream feminism have responded to these critiques with efforts to contextualize gender. The search for women's "universal" or "essential" characteristics is being abandoned. By examining gender in the context of other social divisions and perspectives, difference has gradually become important—even problematizing the universal categories, "women" and "men." Sandra G. Harding expresses the shift best in her claim that "there are no gender relations *per se,* but only gender relations as constructed by and between classes, races, and cultures."[7]

Many feminists now contend that difference occupies center stage as *the* project of women studies today.[8] According to one scholar, "difference has replaced equality as the central concern of feminist theory."[9] Many have welcomed the change, hailing it as a major revitalizing force in U.S. feminist theory.[10] But if *some* priorities within mainstream feminist thought have been refocused by attention to difference, there remains an "uneasy alliance"[11] between women of color and other feminists.

If difference has helped revitalize academic feminisms, it has also "upset the apple cart," and introduced new conflicts into feminist studies.[12] For example, in a recent and widely discussed essay, Jane Rowland Martin argues that the current preoccupation with difference is leading feminism into dangerous traps. She fears that in giving privileged status to a predetermined set of analytic categories (race, ethnicity, and class), "we affirm the existence of nothing but difference." She asks, "How do we know that for us, difference does not turn on being fat, or religious, or in an abusive relationship?"[13]

We, too, see pitfalls in some strands of the difference project. However, our perspectives take their bearings from social relations. Race and class difference are crucial, we argue, not as individual characteristics (such as being fat) but insofar as they are primary organizing principles of a society which locates and positions groups within that society's opportunity structures.

Despite the much-heralded diversity trend within feminist studies, difference is often reduced to mere pluralism; a "live and let live" approach where principles of relativism generate a long list of diversities which begin with gender, class, and race and continue through a range of social structural as well as personal characteristics.[14] Another disturbing pattern, which bell hooks refers to as "the commodification of difference," is the representation of diversity as a form of exotica, "a spice, seasoning that livens up the dull dish that is mainstream white culture."[15] The major limitation of these approaches is the failure to attend to the power relations that accompany difference. Moreover, these approaches ignore the inequalities that cause some characteristics to be seen as "normal" while others are seen as "different" and thus, deviant.

Maria C. Lugones expresses irritation at those feminists who see only the *problem* of difference without recognizing *difference*.[16] Increasingly, we find that difference *is* recognized. But this in no way means that difference occupies a "privileged" theoretical status. Instead of using difference to rethink the category of women, difference is often a euphemism for women who differ from the traditional norm. Even in purporting to accept difference, feminist pluralism often creates a social reality that reverts to universalizing women:

> So much feminist scholarship assumes that when we cut through all of the diversity among women created by differences of racial classification, ethnicity, social class, and sexual orientation, a "universal truth" concerning women and gender lies buried underneath. But if we can face the scary possibility that no such certainty exists and that persisting in such a search will always distort or omit someone's experiences, with what do we replace this old way of thinking? Gender differences and gender politics begin to look very different if there is no essential woman at the core.[17]

WHAT IS MULTIRACIAL FEMINISM?

A new set of feminist theories have emerged from the challenges put forth by women of color. Multiracial feminism is an evolving body of theory and practice informed by wide-ranging intellectual traditions. This framework does not offer a singular or unified feminism but a body of knowledge situating women and men in multiple systems of domination. U.S. multiracial feminism encompasses several emergent perspectives developed primarily by women of color: African Americans, Latinas, Asian Americans, and Native Americans, women whose analyses are shaped by their unique perspectives as "outsiders within"— marginal intellectuals whose social locations provide them a particular perspective on self and society.[18] Although U.S. women of color represent many races and ethnic backgrounds—with different histories and cultures—our feminisms cohere in their treatment of race as a basic social division, a structure of power, a focus of political struggle and hence a fundamental force in shaping women's and men's lives.

This evolving intellectual and political perspective uses several terms. While we adopt the label "multiracial," other terms have been used to describe this broad framework. For example, Chela Sandoval refers to "U.S. Third World feminisms,"[19] while other scholars refer to "indigenous feminisms." In their theory text-reader, Alison M. Jagger and Paula M. Rothenberg adopt the label "multicultural feminism."[20]

We use "multiracial" rather than "multicultural" as a way of underscoring race as a power system that interacts with other structured inequalities to shape genders. Within the U.S. context, race, and the system of meanings and ideologies which accompany it, is a fundamental organizing principle of social relationships.[21] Race affects all women and men, although in different ways. Even cultural and group differences among women are produced through interaction within a racially stratified social order. Therefore, although we do not discount the importance of culture, we caution that cultural analytic frameworks that ignore race tend to view women's differences as the product of group-specific values and practices that often result in the marginalization of cultural groups which are then perceived as exotic expressions of a normative center. Our focus on race stresses the social construction of differently situated social groups and their varying degrees of advantage and power. Additionally, this emphasis on race takes on increasing political importance in an era where discourse about race is governed by color-evasive language[22] and a preference for individual rather than group remedies for social inequalities. Our analyses insist upon the primary and pervasive nature of race in contemporary U.S. society while at the same time acknowledging how race both shapes and is shaped by a variety of other social relations.

In the social sciences, multiracial feminism grew out of socialist feminist thinking. Theories about how political economic forces shape women's lives were influential as we began to uncover the social causes of racial ethnic women's

subordination. But socialist feminism's concept of capitalist patriarchy, with its focus on women's unpaid (reproductive) labor in the home failed to address racial differences in the organization of reproductive labor. As feminists of color have argued, "reproductive labor has divided along racial as well as gender lines, and the specific characteristics have varied regionally and changed over time as capitalism has reorganized."[23] Despite the limitations of socialist feminism, this body of literature has been especially useful in pursuing questions about the interconnections among systems of domination.[24]

Race and ethnic studies was the other major social scientific source of multiracial feminism. It provided a basis for comparative analyses of groups that are socially and legally subordinated and remain culturally distinct within U.S. society. This includes the systematic discrimination of socially constructed racial groups and their distinctive cultural arrangements. Historically, the categories of African American, Latino, Asian American, and Native American were constructed as both racially and culturally distinct. Each group has a distinctive culture, shares a common heritage, and has developed a common identity within a larger society that subordinates them.[25]

We recognize, of course, certain pitfalls inherent in an uncritical use of the multiracial label. First, the perspective can be hampered by a biracial model in which only African Americans and Whites are seen as racial categories and all other groups are viewed through the prism of cultural differences. Latinos and Asians have always occupied distinctive places within the racial hierarchy, and current shifts in the composition of the U.S. population are racializing these groups anew.[26]

A second problem lies in treating multiracial feminism as a single analytical framework, and its principle architects, women of color, as an undifferentiated category. The concepts "multiracial feminism," "racial ethnic women," and "women of color" homogenize quite different experiences and can falsely universalize experiences across race, ethnicity, sexual orientation, and age.[27] The feminisms created by women of color exhibit a plurality of intellectual and political positions. We speak in many voices, with inconsistencies that are born of our different social locations. Multiracial feminism embodies this plurality and richness. Our intent is not to falsely universalize women of color. Nor do we wish to promote a new racial essentialism in place of the old gender essentialism. Instead, we use these concepts to examine the structures and experiences produced by intersecting forms of race and gender.

It is also essential to acknowledge that race itself is a shifting and contested category whose meanings construct definitions of all aspects of social life.[28] In the United States it helped define citizenship by excluding everyone who was not a white, male property owner. It defined labor as slave or free, coolie or contract, and family as available only to those men whose marriages were recognized or whose wives could immigrate with them. Additionally, racial meanings are contested both within groups and between them.[29]

Although definitions of race are at once historically and geographically specific, they are also transnational, encompassing diasporic groups and crossing traditional geographic boundaries. Thus, while U.S. multiracial feminism calls attention to the fundamental importance of race, it must also locate the meaning of race within specific national traditions.

THE DISTINGUISHING FEATURES OF MULTIRACIAL FEMINISM

By attending to these problems, multiracial feminism offers a set of analytic premises for thinking about and theorizing gender. The following themes distinguish this branch of feminist inquiry.

First, multiracial feminism asserts that gender is constructed by a range of interlocking inequalities, what Patricia Hill Collins calls a "matrix of domination."[30] The idea of a matrix is that several fundamental systems work with and through each other. People experience race, class, gender, and sexuality differently depending upon their social location in the structures of race, class, gender,

and sexuality. For example, people of the same race will experience race differently depending upon their location in the class structure as working class, professional managerial class, or unemployed; in the gender structure as female or male; and in structures of sexuality as heterosexual, homosexual, or bisexual.

Multiracial feminism also examines the simultaneity of systems in shaping women's experience and identity. Race, class, gender, and sexuality are not reducible to individual attributes to be measured and assessed for their separate contribution in explaining given social outcomes, an approach that Elizabeth Spelman calls "popbead metaphysics," where a woman's identity consists of the sum of parts neatly divisible from one another.[31] The matrix of domination seeks to account for the multiple ways that women experience themselves as gendered, raced, classed, and sexualized.

Second, multiracial feminism emphasizes the intersectional nature of hierarchies at all levels of social life. Class, race, gender, and sexuality are components of both social structure and social interaction. Women and men are differently embedded in locations created by these cross-cutting hierarchies. As a result, women and men throughout the social order experience different forms of privilege and subordination, depending on their race, class, gender, and sexuality. In other words, intersecting forms of domination produce *both* oppression *and* opportunity. At the same time that structures of race, class, and gender create disadvantages for women of color, they provide unacknowledged benefits for those who are at the top of these hierarchies—whites, members of the upper classes, and males. Therefore, multiracial feminism applies not only to racial ethnic women but also to women and men of all races, classes, and genders.

Third, multiracial feminism highlights the relational nature of dominance and subordination. Power is the cornerstone of women's differences.[32] This means that women's differences are *connected* in systematic ways.[33] Race is a vital element in the pattern of relations among minority and white women. As Linda Gordon argues, the very meanings of being a white woman in the United States have been affected by the existence of subordinated women of color; "They intersect in conflict and in occasional cooperation, but always in mutual influence."[34]

Fourth, multiracial feminism explores the interplay of social structure and women's agency. Within the constraints of race, class, and gender oppression, women create viable lives for themselves, their families, and their communities. Women of color have resisted and often undermined the forces of power that control them. From acts of quiet dignity and steadfast determination to involvement in revolt and rebellion, women struggle to shape their own lives. Racial oppression has been a common focus of the "dynamic of oppositional agency" of women of color. As Chandra Talpade Mohanty points out, it is the nature and organization of women's opposition which mediates and differentiates the impact of structures of domination.[35]

Fifth, multiracial feminism encompasses wide-ranging methodological approaches, and like other branches of feminist thought, relies on varied theoretical tools as well. Ruth Frankenberg and Lata Mani identify three guiding principles of inclusive feminist inquiry: "building complex analyses, avoiding erasure, specifying location."[36] In the last decade, the opening up of academic feminism has focused attention on social location in the production of knowledge. Most basically, research by and about marginalized women has destabilized what used to be universal categories of gender. Marginalized locations are well-suited for grasping social relations that remained obscure from more privileged vantage points. Lived experience, in other words, creates alternative ways of understanding the social world and the experience of different groups of women within it. Racially informed standpoint epistemologies have provided new topics, fresh questions, and new understandings of women and men. Women of color have, as Norma Alarcon argues, asserted ourselves as sub-

jects, using our voices to challenge dominant conceptions of truth.[37]

Sixth, multiracial feminism brings together understandings drawn from the lived experiences of diverse and continuously changing groups of women. Among Asian Americans, Native Americans, Latinas, and Blacks are many different national cultural and ethnic groups. Each one is engaged in the process of testing, refining, and reshaping these broader categories in its own image. Such internal differences heighten awareness of and sensitivity to both commonalities and differences, serving as a constant reminder of the importance of comparative study and maintaining a creative tension between diversity and universalization.

DIFFERENCE AND TRANSFORMATION

Efforts to make women's studies less partial and less distorted have produced important changes in academic feminism. Inclusive thinking has provided a way to build multiplicity and difference into our analyses. This has lead to the discovery that race matters for everyone. White women, too, must be reconceptualized as a category that is multiple defined by race, class, and other differences. As Ruth Frankenberg demonstrates in a study of whiteness among contemporary women, all kinds of social relations, even those that appear neutral, are, in fact, racialized. Frankenberg further complicates the very notion of a unified white identity by introducing issues of Jewish identity.[38] Therefore, the lives of women of color cannot be seen as a *variation* on a more general model of white American womanhood. The model of womanhood that feminist social science once held as "universal" is also a product of race and class.

When we analyze the power relations constituting all social arrangements and shaping women's lives in distinctive ways, we can begin to grapple with core feminist issues about how genders are socially constructed and constructed differently. Women's difference is built into our study of gender. Yet this perspective is quite far removed from the atheoretical pluralism implied in much contemporary thinking about gender.

Multiracial feminism, in our view, focuses not just on differences but also on the way in which differences and domination intersect and are historically and socially constituted. It challenges feminist scholars to go beyond the mere recognition and inclusion of difference to reshape the basic concepts and theories of our disciplines. By attending to women's social location based on race, class, and gender, multiracial feminism seeks to clarify the structural sources of diversity. Ultimately, multiracial feminism forces us to see privilege and subordination as interrelated and to pose such questions as, How do the existences and ex-

periences of all people—women and men, different racial-ethnic groups, and different classes—shape the experiences of each other? How are those relationships defined and enforced through social institutions that are the primary sites for negotiating power within society? How do these differences contribute to the construction of both individual and group identity? Once we acknowledge that all women are affected by the racial order of society, then it becomes clear that the insights of multiracial feminism provide an analytical framework, not solely for understanding the experiences of women of color but for understanding *all* women, and men, as well.

NOTES

1. Maxine Baca Zinn, Lynn Weber Cannon, Elizabeth Higginbotham, and Bonnie Thornton Dill, "The Costs of Exclusionary Practices in Women's Studies," *Signs* 11 (winter, 1986): 290–303.

2. Chela Sandoval, "U.S. Third World Feminism: The Theory and Method of Oppositional Consciousness in the Postmodern World," *Genders* (spring, 1991): 1–24.

3. Ruth Frankenberg and Lata Mani, "Cross Currents, Crosstalk: Race, 'Postcoloniality' and the Politics of Location," *Cultural Studies* 7 (May, 1993): 292–310.

4. We use the term "multiracial feminism" to convey the multiplicity of racial groups and feminist perspectives.

5. A growing body of works on difference in feminist thought now exists. Although we cannot cite all of the current work, the following are representative: Michèle Barrett, "The Concept of Difference," *Feminist Review* 26 (July, 1987): 29–42; Christina Crosby, "Dealing With Difference," in *Feminists Theorize the Political,* ed. Judith Butler and Joan W. Scott (New York: Routledge, 1992): 130–43; Elizabeth Fox-Genovese, "Difference, Diversity, and Divisions in an Agenda for the Women's Movement" in *Color, Class, and Country: Experiences of Gender,* ed. Gay Young and Bette J. Dickerson (London: Zed Books, 1994): 232–48; Nancy A. Hewitt, "Compounding Differences," *Feminist Studies* 18 (summer 1992): 313–26; Maria C. Lugones, "On the Logic of Feminist Pluralism," in *Feminist Ethics* ed. Claudia Card (Lawrence: University of Kansas Press, 1991), 35–44; Rita S. Gallin and Anne Ferguson, "The Plurality of Feminism: Rethinking 'Difference,'" in *The Woman and*

International Development Annual (Boulder: Westview Press, 1993), 3: 1–16; and Linda Gordon, "On Difference," *Genders* 10 (spring, 1991): 91–111.

6. Susan Bordo, "Feminism, Postmodernism, and Gender Skepticism," in *Feminism/Postmodernism,* ed. Linda J. Nicholson (London: Routledge, 1990), 133–56.

7. Sandra G. Harding, *Whose Science? Whose Knowledge? Thinking from Women's Lives* (Ithaca: Cornell University Press, 1991), 179.

8. Crosby, 131.

9. Fox-Genovese, 232.

10. Faye Ginsberg and Anna Lowenhaupt Tsing, Introduction to *Uncertain Terms, Negotiating Gender in American Culture,* ed. Faye Ginsberg and Anna Lowenhaupt Tsing (Boston: Beacon Press, 1990), 3.

11. Sandoval, 2.

12. Sandra G. Morgan, "Making Connections: Socialist-Feminist Challenges to Marxist Scholarship," in *Women and a New Academy: Gender and Cultural Contexts,* ed. Jean F. O'Barr (Madison: University of Wisconsin Press, 1989), 149.

13. Jane Rowland Martin, "Methodological Essentialism, False Difference, and Other Dangerous Traps," *Signs* 19 (spring, 1994): 647.

14. Barrett, 32.

15. bell hooks, *Black Looks: Race and Representation* (Boston: South End Press, 1992), 21.

16. Lugones, 35–44.

17. Patricia Hill Collins, Foreword to *Women of Color in U.S. Society,* ed. Maxine Baca Zinn and Bonnie

Thornton Dill (Philadelphia: Temple University Press, 1994), xv.

18. Patricia Hill Collins, "Learning from the Outsider Within: The Sociological Significance of Black Feminist Thought," *Social Problems* 33 (December, 1986): 514–532.

19. Sandoval, 1.

20. Alison M. Jagger and Paula S. Rothenberg, *Feminist Frameworks: Alternative Theoretical Accounts of the Relations between Women and Men.* 3d ed. (New York: McGraw Hill, 1993).

21. Michael Omi and Howard Winant, *Racial Formation in United States: From the 1960s to the 1980s,* 2d ed. (New York: Routledge, 1994).

22. Ruth Frankenberg, *The Social Construction of Whiteness: White Women, Race Matters* (Minneapolis: University of Minnesota Press, 1993).

23. Evelyn Nakano Glenn, "From Servitude to Service Work: Historical Continuities in the Racial Division of Paid Reproductive Labor," *Signs* 18 (autumn, 1992): 3. See also Bonnie Thornton Dill, "Our Mothers' Grief: Racial-Ethnic Women and the Maintenance of Families," *Journal of Family History* 13, no. 4 (1988): 415–31.

24. Morgan, 146.

25. Maxine Baca Zinn and Bonnie Thornton Dill, "Difference and Domination," in *Women of Color in U.S. Society,* 11–12.

26. See Omi and Winant, 53–76, for a discussion of racial formation.

27. Margaret L. Andersen and Patricia Hill Collins, *Race, Class, and Gender: An Anthology* (Belmont, Calif.: Wadsworth, 1992), xvi.

28. Omi and Winant.

29. Nazli Kibria, "Migration and Vietnamese American Women: Remaking Ethnicity," in *Women of Color in U.S. Society,* 247–61.

30. Patricia Hill Collins, *Black Feminist Thought: Knowledge, Consciousness, and the Politics of Empowerment* (Boston: Unwin Hyman, 1990).

31. Elizabeth Spelman, *Inessential Women: Problems of Exclusion in Feminist Thought* (Boston: Beacon Press, 1988).

32. Several discussions of difference make this point. See Baca Zinn and Dill, 10; Gordon, 106; and Lynn Weber, in the "Symposium on West and Fenstermaker's 'Doing Difference,'" *Gender & Society* 9 (August 1995): 515–19.

33. Glenn, 10.

34. Gordon, 106.

35. Chandra Talpade Mohanty, "Cartographies of Struggle: Third World Women and the Politics of Feminism," in *Third World Women and the Politics of Feminism,* ed. Chandra Talpade Mohanty, Ann Russo, and Lourdes Torres (Bloomington: Indiana University Press, 1991), 13.

36. Frankenberg and Mani, 307.

37. Norma Alarcon, "The Theoretical Subject(s) of *This Bridge Called My Back* and Anglo American Feminism," in *Making Face, Making Soul, Haciendo Caras: Creative and Critical Perspectives by Women of Color,* ed. Gloria Anzaldua, (San Francisco: Aunt Lute, 1990), 356.

38. Frankenberg. See also Evelyn Torton Beck, "The Politics of Jewish Invisibility," *NWSA Journal* (fall 1988): 93–102.

3

Children and Gender

Constructions of Difference

BARRIE THORNE

When I first began observing in elementary schools as an ethnographer with gender on my mind, events like the following drew me and my notetaking like a magnet:

> On the playground, a cluster of children played "girls-chase-the-boys" or "boys-chase-the-girls" (they used both names). Boys and girls were by definition on different sides. In the back-and-forth of chasing and being chased, they used gender terms ("I'm gonna get that girl"; "Let's go after those boys") rather than individual names for members of the other side.
>
> In a combined fourth-and-fifth-grade classroom the teacher introduced a math game organized as girls against boys; she would write addition and subtraction problems on the board, and a member of each team would race to be the first to write the correct answer. As the teacher wrote two scorekeeping columns headed "Beastly Boys" and "Gossipy Girls," several boys yelled out, "Noisy girls! Gruesome girls!" while some of the girls laughed. As the game proceeded, the girls sat in a row on top of their desks; sometimes they moved collectively, pushing their hips or whispering, "Pass it on." The boys stood along the wall, several reclining against desks. When members of either group came back victorious from the front of the room, they would do the "giving five" hand-slapping ritual with their team members.

On such occasions—when gender divisions were highlighted and "the girls" and "the boys" were defined as separate, opposing groups—I felt I was at the heart of children's gender relations. But these moments are not the whole of social life in elementary schools; at other times boys and girls interacted in relaxed rather than bounded and antagonistic ways. An example from the same fourth-and-fifth-grade classroom:

> A student teacher had listed various activities on the board and asked students to choose one and sign up for it. Three boys and two girls had chosen to tape record a radio play. The teacher told them they could rehearse in the back of the room. They moved from their desks, settled in chairs at a round table (seated girl-boy-girl-boy-boy), and took turns leaning into the microphone and reading from the script. Now and then they stopped to talk and argue as a group.

I had to press myself to record the details of this situation; it seemed less juicy, less ripe for gendered analysis than the chasing sequence, the math game, or a same-gender group. This disparity in my perception of its relevance led me to ponder our frameworks for thinking about children and gender. These frameworks, which emphasize oppositional dichotomies, neatly fit situations in which boys and girls are organized as separate, bounded groups, and they obscure more relaxed, mixed-gender encounters. What kinds of frameworks can more fully account for the complexity of children's gender relations?

Is it "in the nature" of children that we should gear up different questions for them than we do for adults? Feminist scholarship has mostly centered upon the lives and experiences of adults; it has either ignored children, seen them as objects of adult (primarily women's) labor, or confined discussion of them to questions of "socialization" and "development."[1] In the last two decades our frameworks for thinking about adults and gender have moved beyond unexamined dualisms toward greater complexity. But when we focus on children, we tend to think in more simplistic ways—perhaps one reason for the lingering power of dualisms.[2]

THE DUALISTIC MODEL OF SEX DIFFERENCES

Most of the research on children and gender involves a search either for individual or for group sex differences. Both approaches conceptualize gender in terms of dualisms.

Studies in the "individual sex differences" tradition typically set out to explore possible statistical correlations between individual sex/gender (usually understood as an unproblematic male/female dichotomy) and a specific piece of behavior or measure of personality. The pieces that have been studied range widely, including such personality traits as self-esteem, intellectual aptitudes like verbal or spatial ability, such motivational structure as need for affiliation, and specific behavior, for example, the amount of time spent in rough-and-tumble play. Extensive research has studied whether parents and teachers interact (for example, touch or talk) differently with girls and boys. Sex difference studies specify and gauge behavior (for example, with tests of spatial ability or measures of time spent in rough-and-tumble play or talking with a teacher), aggregate across many individuals, and then look for statistically significant correlations by sex.[3]

The results of sex difference research are always a matter of statistical frequency, for sex/gender differences are never absolutely dichotomous. But where statistically significant differences are found, the language of frequency quickly slides into a portrayal of dualism ("boys engage in more rough-and-tumble play than girls"; "girls have greater verbal ability than boys"; "boys receive more teacher attention"). Many writers have cautioned against translating statistical complexity into a discourse of "the pinks and the blues," the tellingly dichotomous title of a popular television documentary on sex dif-

ference among children.[4] They have noted other related pitfalls in the sex difference approach, such as a bias toward reporting difference rather than similarity and a failure to distinguish statistical significance from the size of an effect.

But dichotomous portrayals may be unavoidable when one's basic strategy is to compare males and females. Individual sex categories[5]—female/male, woman/man, girl/boy—divide the population in half and are marked and sustained by daily social practices of gender display and attribution.[6] Sex difference research treats these categories as relatively unproblematic and continues binary framing with distinctions like similarity versus difference. Recent proposals to use phrases like "sex similarities and differences" or "sex-related differences," provide at best awkward and ambiguous tools for grasping the complexities of gender.

Although the situation is gradually beginning to change, sociologists and anthropologists have largely ceded the study of children to psychologists, who in turn have relegated the study of children to specialists in child development. The social science literature on children and gender reflects this division of labor. The focus has been more on individuals than on social relations, and the favored methods—laboratory experiments, observations organized around preset categories—strip human conduct from the contexts in which it is given meaning.

Group Differences

When psychologists, sociologists, and anthropologists of gender have studied the social relations of children, they have primarily relied on a model of group differences that is founded on the prevalence of gender separation in children's friendships and daily encounters. Every observational study of children's interactions in preschools, elementary schools, and junior high schools in the United States has found a high degree of gender separation in seating choices and in the groups children form.[7] In a study of sixth- and seventh-graders in a middle school whose enrollment was half Black and half white, Schofield found that while racial separation among the students was extensive, gender separation was even greater.[8]

After documenting widespread gender separation in children's social relations, most researchers have compared the separate worlds of boys and girls. The result is a by now familiar litany of generalized contrasts, usually framed as a series of dualisms: boys' groups are larger, and girls' groups are smaller ("buddies" versus "best friends"); boys play more often in public, and girls in more private places; boys engage in more rough-and-tumble play, physical fighting, and overt physical conflict than do girls; boys play more organized team sports, and girls engage in more turn-taking play; within same-gender groups, boys continually maintain and display hierarchies, while girls organize themselves into shifting alliances.[9]

There are problems with this separate worlds approach. Much of the literature, like that on individual sex differences, suffers from androcentrism: the "boys' world" is usually described first (as above) and more extensively; the less richly articulated "girls' world" seems explicitly (as in Lever's study)[10] or implicitly lacking.[11] Even where efforts are made to revalue the "girls' world" (as in Gilligan's reframing of Lever's work)[12] and to give both poles equal weighting, people still construe children's gender relations as polarities. The convention of separate worlds compresses enormous complexity into a series of contrasts: public/private, large/small, competitive/cooperative. It suggests a Victorian world of separate spheres writ small and contemporary.

Gender separation among children is not so total as the separate worlds rendering suggests, and the amount of separation varies by situation. For example, Luria and Herzog found that in a nursery school in Massachusetts two-thirds of playgroups were same-gender (one-third were mixed); 80 percent of playground groups of fifth- and sixth-graders in a public elementary school were same-gender (20 percent were mixed); in a private school, 63 percent of playground groups

were same-gender (37 percent were mixed).[13] For many children in the United States, gender separation is more extensive on school playgrounds than in other daily settings. Girls and boys interact frequently in most elementary school classrooms, since adults organize much of the activity and usually rely on criteria other than gender. Children often report engaging in more cross-gender play in neighborhoods and in families than they do on school playgrounds; in these less populous situations they may have to cross gender and age categories to find playmates, and there are fewer witnesses to tease girls and boys who choose to be together.[14]

The occasions when girls and boys are together are as theoretically and socially significant as when they are apart, yet the literature on children's gender relations has largely ignored interaction between them. In much of the research on children's group life, "gender" has first been located in the separation of boys and girls and then in comparisons of same-gender groups.[15] Comparing groups of girls with groups of boys not only neglects the occasions when they are together but also ignores the complex choreography of separation and integration in children's daily interactions. Frequency counts provide snapshots of single moments, but they cannot teach us about the social processes by which gender is used—or overridden or ignored—as a basis for group formation.[16]

Finally, in relying on a series of contrasts to depict the whole, the separate worlds approach exaggerates the coherence of same-gender interactions and glosses extensive variation among boys and among girls. Characterizations of the "boys' world" suffer from a distortion akin to the "Big Man Bias" in anthropological ethnographies in which male elites are equated with men in general.[17] Larger, bonded groups of boys figure prominently in Joffe's ethnographic description of the "male subculture" of a preschool, Best's description of boys in an elementary school, Everhart's ethnography of a junior high and Cusick's of a high school, and Willis' study of working-class "lads" in a vocational secondary school in England.[18] Other less popular, disruptive, dominant, or socially visible boys—and girls (who remain invisible in the majority of school ethnographies)—appear at the edges of these portrayals, but their standpoints and experiences are voiced only indirectly. (Cusick reports that as a participant-observer he avoided "isolates"; "I was there to do a study not to be a friend to those who had no friends.")[19]

In the fourth-and-fifth-grade class in which I was a participant-observer,[20] a relatively stable group of four to six boys (often joined by a girl who successfully crossed gender boundaries) sat together in the classroom and the lunchroom and moved around the playground as a group, playing the team sports of every season. Because of the group's size, physicality, and social dominance, it *seemed* to be the core of the "boys' world" in that classroom—one more instance of the familiar generalization that boys are organized into "flocks" or "gangs." But other fourth-and-fifth-grade boys did not fit the model. Three of them were loners who avoided sports, preferred to stay indoors, and hung out at the edges of the playground. Three more were involved in an intense dyad-into-triad pattern similar to the social organization often generalized as typical of girls' friendships.[21] Two boys were recent immigrants from Mexico, spoke little English, were marginal in most classroom interaction, and on the playground often joined six to ten other Spanish-speaking, nonbilingual children in an ongoing game of dodgeball that was more mixed in gender and age than any other recurring playground group.

Depictions of girls' social relations have also masked considerable variation. While the fourth-and-fifth-grade girls I observed often used a language of "best friends" (dyads and triads did figure centrally in their social relationships), they also regularly organized into groups of five to seven doing "tricks" on the bars or playing jump rope. Hughes, who observed on an upper-middle-class school playground, and Goodwin, who observed Black children ages ten to thirteen in an urban neighborhood, also found that girls con-

structed larger groups and complex social networks.[22] Girls' social relations are usually depicted as more cooperative than those of boys, but ethnographers have documented patterns of dispute and competition in girls' interactions with one another, including ritual insults that are often said to be typical of boys.[23] Boys' social relations are usually claimed to be more hierarchical than girls', but type of activity affects mode of interaction. The group of neighborhood girls Goodwin studied constructed hierarchies when they played house (a form of pretend play that, tellingly for children's representations of families, involved continual marking of dominance).[24] But when the girls engaged in a task activity like making rings from the rims of glass bottles, their interactions were more collaborative and egalitarian.

FROM DUALISMS TO GENDER AS FLUID AND SITUATED

Instead of scrambling to describe girls (or girls' groups) in contrast to boys', we are beginning to develop more varied and complex ways of thinking about children and gender. This shift of interpretive conventions has been furthered by the work of anthropologists, folklorists, and sociologists, who are more prone than developmental psychologists to start with social relations and to emphasize social contexts and meanings.

Conceptualizing gender in terms of social relations breaks with the relatively static equation of gender with dichotomous difference. An emphasis on social relations is well developed in studies of social class and ethnicity. But what Connell calls "categoricalism" has hounded the study of gender: reliance on relatively unexamined, dichotomous sex (or gender) categories—male/female, woman/man, boy/girl—as tools of analysis.[25] I have already discussed this problem in sex difference research. It is also a problem in the use of gender as an untheorized binary variable,[26] and—coming from a quite different intellectual and political context—in feminist theories that take "women" and "men" as unproblematic categories.[27]

At the level of basic social categories, gender does operate more dualistically than class, race, or ethnicity. Our culture has only two sex categories, and every person is permanently assigned to one or the other with very few attempts to switch. In every situation each individual displays, and others attribute to her or him, characteristics associated with one or the other of the two categories.[28] The workings of social class and race and ethnic categories seem from the start to be far more complex and contingent than gender. Social class and ethnic categories are multiple, sometimes ambiguous, and may vary by situation. A person's social class or ethnicity may not be readily apparent, nor (as is the case with gender) do we always feel a need to know the class or ethnicity of those with whom we interact.

The distinctive features of sex categories lie behind what Wallman calls "the peculiar epistemology of sex"—the deep hold of dualisms on our ways of thinking about gender.[29] But dichotomous sex categories are only one part of the organizational and symbolic processes of gender. The two categories woman and man have multiple and changing meanings, as ethnographies of "femininities" and "masculinities" suggest.[30]

Shifting the level of analysis from the individual to social relations and from sex categories to the variable social organization and symbolic meanings of gender further unravels dichotomous constructions. When the topic is gender, there is no escaping the theme of difference. But the presence, significance, and meanings of differences are refocused when one asks about the social relations that construct differences—and diminish or undermine them.

How is gender made more or less salient in different situations? In specific social contexts, how do the organization and meanings of gender take shape in relation to other socially constructed divisions like age, race, and social class? How do children in varied positions (for example, popular, marginal, or more or less involved in teen culture) navigate and experience a given set of gender relations? By emphasizing variable social contexts and multiple standpoints and meanings, these questions open a more fluid and situated approach to gender.

Social Contexts and the Relative Salience of Gender

Much of the research on children and gender has neglected the importance of social context. Children have been pulled from specificity and fixed by abstract stages of development. Studies of individual sex differences often generalize about girls versus boys without attending to variations in society and culture. A different perspective emerges when one shifts from individuals to group life, with close attention to social contexts.

Earlier I contrasted situations where gender is highly salient with those in which its importance is muted. When children play "boys-chase-the-girls," gender is basic to the organization and symbolism of the encounter. Group gender boundaries are charged with titillating ambiguity and danger,[31] and girls and boys become by definition separate teams or sides.

The idea of *borderwork,* used by Barth to analyze ethnic relations,[32] can also be used to conceptualize social relations maintained across yet based upon and strengthening gender boundaries. When girls and boys are organized as opposing sides in a math contest or in cross-gender chasing, members of both sides may express solidarity within their gender and playful and serious antagonism to the other. But borderwork is also asymmetric. Boys invade girls' games and scenes of play much more than girls invade boys'. Boys control far more playground space than girls. Girls are more often defined as polluting and boys as running the risk of contamination (for example, girls are more often defined as giving "cooties").[33] Difference is related to dominance in children's gender group arrangements, and the workings of power are complex. Girls do not always passively accept their devaluation, but sometimes challenge and derogate boys. They guard their play and respond angrily to invasions; they complain to adults.[34]

Moments of separation and of bounded inter-action evoke perceptions of difference by partici-pants and by the experts who observe them. In everyday life in schools, children and adults talk about the different "natures" of girls and boys pri-marily to justify exclusion or separation and in sit-uations of gender conflict. Two examples from my field notes:

> *A group of sixth-grade girls grabbed the football from the ongoing play of a group of boys [this was one of the few occasions when I saw a group of girls invade a group of boys on the playground]. The boys complained to the playground aide. She responded, "Why won't you let the girls play?" The boys replied, "They can't tackle; when we tackle 'em they cry."*
>
> *During lunchtime an aide who was frazzled by problems of discipline told the third-grade girls and boys they had to sit at separate tables. One girl turned to another and said, half in jest and half in earnest, "The boys are naughty and we're good."*

Gender-marked moments seem to express core truths: that boys and girls are separate and fundamentally different as individuals and as groups. They help sustain a sense of dualism in the face of enormous variation and complex cir-cumstances. But the complexities are also part of the story. In daily school life many situations are organized along lines other than gender, and girls and boys interact in relaxed and non-gender-marked ways. For example, children often play handball and dodgeball in mixed groups; girls and boys sometimes sit together and converse in relaxed ways in classrooms, the cafeteria, or the library. Collective projects, like the radio play de-scribed earlier, often draw girls and boys together and diminish the salience of gender.

Children's gender relations can be understood only if we map the full array of their interactions—occasions when boys and girls are together as well as those when they separate (Goffman coined the apt phrase "with-then-apart" to describe the peri-odic nature of gender segregation).[35] To grasp the fluctuating significance of gender in social life, we must examine encounters where gender seems largely irrelevant as well as those where it is sym-bolically and organizationally central.

Broadening the site of significance to include occasions where gender is both unmarked and marked is one of several analytic strategies that I believe can provide fuller understanding of chil-dren's gender relations. Our conceptual frame-works are whetted on the marked occasions. Extensive gender separation or organizing an event as boys against the girls sets off contrastive thinking and feeds an assumption of gender as di-chotomous difference. By also seeing other con-texts as relevant to gender, we can situate the equation of gender with dualism more accurately and understand something of the hold that con-ceptualization has on us in the thrall of our cul-ture. By developing a sense of the whole and attending to the waning as well as the waxing of gender salience, we can specify not only the so-cial relations that uphold but also those that un-dermine the construction of gender as binary opposition. We can also gain a more complex un-derstanding of the dynamics of power.

Multiple Differences

In specific social contexts, complex interactions among gender and such other social divisions as age, race, ethnicity, social class, and religion are another source of multiplicity. General terms like *intersecting differences* obscure the complex, sometimes contradictory dynamics of concrete situations. The range of possibilities is better evoked by Connell and colleagues, who observe that different social divisions and forms of in-equality may "abrade, inflame, amplify, twist, dampen, and complicate each other."[36]

In the world of elementary schools, age is a more formally institutionalized social division than gender. Being in the first, fourth, or sixth grades determines daily activities and the company one keeps. Different grades may be allocated separate turfs in the lunchroom and the playground, and those who venture out of their age-defined territory may be chastised. In some situations children unite on the basis of age, which then becomes more salient than gender. One day a much disliked teacher who was on yard duty punished a fourth-grader for something he didn't do. He was very upset, and others from his classroom who were playing in the vicinity and witnessed or heard about the incident perceived a great injustice. Girls and boys talked about the situation in mixed clusters and joined as a group to argue with the adult.

Adults (including sociological observers) who work in schools are accorded privileges denied to children. They are not confined to specific lines, seats, and tables; they can move more freely through space; and they have institutionalized authority. Teachers and aides sometimes use their authority to construct and enhance gender divisions among children, as in the cases of the teacher who organized girls and boys into separate teams for classroom contests and the noontime aide who ordered boys and girls to sit at different tables. But adult practices also undermine gender separation between children in schools. In the United States there is a long tradition of mixed-gender public elementary schools, with girls and boys sharing a curriculum and with an ideology of treating everyone the same and of attending to individual needs. Some structural pressures run against separating girls and boys in daily school life, especially in classrooms.[37] Adult practices work in both directions, sometimes separating and sometimes integrating boys and girls. Overall, however, school-based observers have found that less gender separation takes place among children when adults control a situation than when children have more autonomy.[38]

When children have constructed sharp gender boundaries, few of them attempt to cross. But adults claim the privilege of freelancing. In the schools I studied, when boys and girls sat at separate tables in school cafeterias, teachers and aides of both genders sat at either table, and the presence of an adult sometimes created a wedge for more general mixed seating. When the fourth-and-fifth-graders drew names for a winter holiday gift exchange, they decided (in a discussion punctuated by ritual gender antagonism) that girls would give to girls and boys to boys. The teacher decided that she would draw with the boys and suggested that the aide and I (both women) draw with the girls. Our adult status altered the organization of gender.

A mix of age, gender, and ethnicity contributed to the marginalization of two Latino boys in the fourth-and-fifth-grade classroom. The boys were recent immigrants from Mexico and spoke very little English. They sat in a back corner of the classroom and sometimes worked at a side table with a Spanish-speaking aide. The other children treated them as if they were younger, with several girls who sat near them repeatedly monitoring the boys' activities and telling them what to do. When the children were divided by gender, other boys repeatedly maneuvered the Latino boys and another low-status boy into sitting next to girls. These spatial arrangements drew upon a gender meaning—an assumption that being by girls is contaminating—to construct ethnic subordination and marginality.

Gender display may symbolically represent and amplify social class divisions. The students in the two schools I studied were largely working class, but within that loose categorization children's different economic circumstances affected how they looked, especially the girls. It was easier to spot girls from impoverished families than boys because the girls' more varied clothing was less adaptable (as in the case of a mismatched top and bottom) than the T-shirts and jeans the boys wore. Girls' hairstyles were also more varied and complex, providing material for differentiated display of style and grooming, and grooming standards were more exacting for girls than for boys. A fifth-grade girl whose unkempt hair and mismatched old clothing marked her impoverished background was treated like a pariah, while the most popular girl had many well-matched outfits and a well-groomed appearance. The top and bottom rungs of girls' popularity (positions partly shaped by social class) were defined by heterosexual meanings when children teased about a particular boy "liking" or "goin' with" a specific girl. The teasers most frequently named either the most popular girl or the pariah as targets of a boy's liking—the most and least probable and polluting targets of desire.

Attention to the dynamics of social contexts helps situate gender in relationship to other lines of difference and inequality. The meanings of gender are not unitary but multiple, and sometimes contradictory.

Multiple Standpoints

Exploring varied standpoints on a given set of gender relations is another strategy for deconstructing a too coherent, dichotomous portrayal of girls' groups versus boys' groups and for developing a more complex understanding of gender relations. Children who are popular or marginal, those defined as troublemakers or good students, and those who are more or less likely to cross gender boundaries have different experiences of the same situations. Their varied experiences—intricately constructed by and helping to construct gender, social class, ethnicity, age, and individual characteristics—provide multiple vantage points on the complexity of children's social worlds.

An array of social types, including the bully, the troublemaker, the sissy, the tomboy, and the isolate populates both fictional and social science literature on children in schools. If we shift from types to processes, we can get a better hold on the experiences these terms convey. For example, the terms tomboy and sissy take complicated social processes—changing gender boundaries and a continuum of crossing—and reify them into individual essences or conditions (for example, "tomboyism"). Crossing involves definition, activity, and the extent to which a child has a regular place in the other gender's social networks. Boys who frequently seek access to predominantly female groups and activities ("sissies") are more often harassed and teased by both boys and girls. But girls who frequently play with boys ("tomboys") are much less often stigmatized, and they continue to

maintain ties with girls, a probable reason that, especially in the later years of elementary school, crossing by girls is far more frequent than crossing by boys.[39]

When girls are accepted in boys' groups and activities without changing the terms of the interactions (one girl called it being a "buddy"), gender becomes low. Heterosexual idioms, which mark and dramatize gender difference, pose a threat to such acceptance; one can't be a "buddy" and "goin' with" at the same time. The fifth-grade girl who was "buddies" with a group of boys navigated the field of gender relations and meanings very differently than did girls who frequently initiated heterosexual chasing rituals. Unitary notions like the girls' world and girls versus boys are inadequate for this sort of analysis. Instead, one must grapple with multiple standpoints, complex and even contradictory meanings, and the varying salience of gender.

ETHNOGRAPHIES OF SCHOOLING

In developing a contextual and deconstructive approach to understanding gender and children's worlds, I have been influenced by the work of other ethnographers, whose methods bring sensitivity to social contexts and to the construction of meanings. Ethnographers of education who work within "social reproduction theory" (asking how schools reproduce inequalities, mostly of social class and gender) have emphasized students' varying subcultures, some more conforming and some created in opposition to the official structure of schools. In an ethnographic study of working class "lads" in a vocational school in England, Willis gave attention to gender as well as to social class (the primary focus of this tradition anchored in Marxist theories).[40] Resisting the middle-class authority of the school, the lads created an oppositional culture of aggression and joking tied to the working class "masculine" subculture of factory workers. The lads' subculture, different from that of more conforming boys, helped reproduce their class position.

Recent research within this tradition has finally moved girls from the periphery more toward the center of attention. In a study of fifth-graders in U.S. schools, Anyon analyzed strategies related to social class that girls used both to resist and to accommodate institutionalized attempts to enforce femininity.[41] For example, some girls used exaggerated feminine behavior to resist work assignments; those who were "discipline problems" rebelled both against the school and against expectations of them as girls.

Connell and his colleagues, who have studied girls and boys of different social classes in high schools in Australia, use the plural notions *masculinities* and *femininities* to articulate an array of subcultures and individual styles or types of identity.[42] (I find it problematic that they mix, rather than carefully distinguishing, individual and group levels of analysis.) They conceptualize gender and class as "structuring processes" and argue that each school has a "gender regime," constructing, ordering, and arbitrating between different kinds of masculinity and femininity. "The gender regime is in a state of play rather than a permanent condition."[43]

These studies are important in part because they break with the pervasive determinism of conventional "sex-role socialization" literature on gender and schools. Instead of simply "being socialized" (the imagery of children in much feminist literature), girls and boys are granted agency in constructing culture and resisting it as well as in adapting to dominant ideologies. By positing a complex and plural approach to gender, these ethnographies also challenge simplistic dualisms like "the male role versus the female role" or "girls' groups versus boys' groups."

But for all their value, these conceptualizations leave unresolved some of the issues I raised earlier. They analyze gender primarily by emphasizing separation between boys and girls and comparing the dynamics and subcultures of same-gender groups. While the groups and subcultures are multiple, a sense of deep division (separate worlds) between girls and boys persists. How far

such divisions may vary by situation or subculture is not made clear. Dualistic assumptions poke through the multiplicity.

A second problem with Connell's work is that while the plural masculinities and femininities seem useful, the patterns these ethnographers describe sometimes seem more classificatory (an ever-finer grid for fixing gender) than anchored in a close analysis of social processes. By what criteria should a given pattern of interaction be seen as constructing a femininity or a masculinity, that is, as being relevant to the organization and meanings of gender? Some "social reproduction" ethnographers like Everhart largely ignore gender in their analyses of students' everyday interactions.[44] Others, for example, Anyon and Connell and his colleagues, refer the entire field of interaction to notions of gender.[45] This variation points to a more general question. Is gender always relevant? Do some parts of social life transcend it? If our challenge is to trace the threading of gender (and gender inequalities) through the complexity of social life, how can we determine when and how to invoke gendered interpretations?

These difficult questions suggest the need for finer conceptual tuning. In every situation we display and attribute core sex categories: gender does have ubiquitous relevance. But there is wide variation in the organization and symbolism of gender. Looking at social context shifts analysis from fixing abstract and binary differences to examining the social relations and contexts in which multiple differences are constructed, undermined, and given meaning.

This contextual approach to gender—questioning the assumption that girls and boys (and men and women) have different "essential natures" best understood in terms of opposition—clearly resonates with deconstructive, postmodernist tendencies in feminist thought.[46] I reached a deconstructive approach not by way of French theorists, however, but through the contextual and interpretive methods of ethnography.

Feminists have been more deconstructive and aware of multiplicities in thinking about adults than in thinking about children. We refer children's experiences to development and socialization, while granting adults a much broader scene of action. One way around that conceptual double standard is extending to children the frameworks (in this case, a fluid and contextual approach to gender) also used in analyzing the world of adults.

In following that path, however, I have slid across a project that awaits close attention: grappling with differences of age, which, like gender, involve complex interactions of biology and culture. We should turn our critical attention to the dualism adult/child as well as to gender dualisms.

NOTES

1. See Barrie Thorne, "Re-Visioning Women and Social Change: Where Are the Children?" *Gender & Society* 1 (1987): 85–109. The invisibility of children in feminist and sociological thought can be documented by reviewing scholarly journals. Ambert analyzed issues of eight widely-read sociology journals published between 1972 and 1983. At the top of the journals in the proportion of space devoted to children, *Journal of Marriage and Family* had only 3.6 percent and *Sociology of Education* only 6.6 percent of articles on children. The index for the first ten years of the feminist journal *SIGNS* has one entry under "child development," one under "child care," and four under "childbirth." See Anne-Marie Ambert, "Sociology of Sociology: The Place of Children in North American Sociology," in Peter Adler and Patricia A. Adler, eds., *Sociological Studies of Child Development* (Greenwich, Conn.: JAI, 1986) 1:11–31.

2. See M. Z. Rosaldo, "The Use and Abuse of Anthropology: Reflection on Feminism and Cross-Cultural Understanding," *SIGNS* 5 (1980): 389–417.

3. For reviews of some of the research on sex differences see Eleanor Maccoby and Carol Jacklin, *The Psychology of Sex Differences* (Stanford: Stanford University Press, 1974), and Jere E. Brophy and Thomas L. Good, *Teacher-Student Relations* (New York: Holt, Reinhart, 1974).

4. For example, see Carol Jacklin, "Methodological Issues in the Study of Sex-Related Differences," *Developmental Review* 1 (1981): 266–73; Maccoby and Jacklin, *Psychology of Sex Differences;* and Maureen C. McHugh, Randi Daimon Keoske, and Irene Hanson Frieze, "Issues to Consider in Conducting Nonsexist Psychological Research," *American Psychologist* 41 (1986): 879–90.

5. Here is the inevitable footnote on terminology, one more example of the definitional fiddling so prevalent in the social science literature on sex and gender. This perpetual fiddling reflects our ongoing efforts to locate subject matter, to construct appropriate levels of analysis, and to grapple with difficult problems such as how to weigh

and simultaneously grasp the biological and the cultural. I am currently persuaded that: (1) we should conceptually distinguish biological sex, cultural gender, and sexuality (desire), but (2) we should not assume that they are easily separable. One of our central tasks is to clarify their complex, often ambiguous relationships—kept alive in the term "sex/gender system" (a term first put forward in Gayle Rubin, "The Traffic in Women: Notes on the 'Political Economy' of Sex," in Rayna R. Reiter, ed., *Toward an Anthropology of Women* [New York: Monthly Review Press, 1975], 157–210). We should muse about why, after all our careful distinctions, we so easily slip into interchangeable use of *sex, gender,* and *sexual.*

The phrase *sex category* refers to the core, dichotomous categories of individual sex and gender (female/male; girl/boy; woman/man)—dualisms riddled with complexities of biology/culture and age/gender. While these categories appear to be rockbottom and founded in biology—hence "sex" category—they are deeply constructed by cultural beliefs and by social practices of gender display and attribution. *Gender* still seems serviceable as an all-purpose term linked with other words for finer conceptual tuning, e.g., "gender identity," "gender ideology," "the social organization of gender." In my discussion of "sex difference" research I use "sex" rather than "gender" because that has been the (perhaps telling) verbal practice of that tradition.

6. See Suzanne J. Kessler and Wendy McKenna, *Gender: An Ethnomethodological Approach* (New York: John Wiley, 1978); Erving Goffman, "The Arrangement between the Sexes," *Theory and Society* 4 (1977): 301–36; Spencer E. Cahill, "Language Practices and Self-Definition: The Case of Gender Identity Acquisition," *Sociological Quarterly* 287 (1987): 295–311; and Candace West and Don H. Zimmerman, "Doing Gender," *Gender & Society* 1 (1987): 125–51.

7. See reviews in Marlaine E. Lockheed, "Sex Equity in Classroom Organization and Climate," in Susan B. Klein, ed., *Handbook for Achieving Sex Equity through*

Education (Baltimore: Johns Hopkins University Press, 1985), 189–217; and Eleanor Maccoby, "Social Groupings in Childhood: Their Relationship to Prosocial and Antisocial Behavior in Boys and Girls," in Dan Olweus, Jack Block, and Marian Radke-Yarrow, eds., *Development of Antisocial and Prosocial Behavior* (San Diego: Academic, 1985), 263–84.

8. Janet Schofield, *Black and White in School* (New York: Praeger, 1982).

9. See reviews in Daniel N. Maltz and Ruth A. Borker, "A Cultural Approach to Male-Female Miscommunication," in John J. Gumperz, ed., *Language and Social Identity* (New York: Cambridge University Press, 1983), 195–216; Barrie Thorne, "Girls and Boys Together...But Mostly Apart: Gender Arrangements in Elementary Schools," in Willard W. Hartup and Zick Rubin, eds., *Relationships and Development* (Hillsdale, N.J.: Lawrence Erlbaum, 1986), 167–84; and Maccoby, "Social Groupings."

10. Janet Lever, "Sex Differences in the Games Children Play," *Social Problems* 23 (1976): 478–87.

11. The invisibility and marginalization of girls in the extensive British literature on "youth subcultures" was first noted in Angela McRobbie and Jenny Garber, "Girls and Subcultures," in S. Hall and T. Jefferson, eds., *Resistance through Rituals* (London: Hutchinson, 1976).

12. Lever, "Sex Differences"; Carol Gilligan, *In a Different Voice* (Cambridge: Harvard University Press, 1982): 9–11.

13. Zella Luria and Eleanor Herzog, "Gender Segregation across and within Settings" (unpublished paper presented at 1985 annual meeting of the Society for Research in Child Development, Toronto).

14. Most observational research on the gender relations of preadolescent children in the United States has been done in schools. Goodwin's research on children in an urban neighborhood is a notable exception. See Marjorie Harness Goodwin, *Conversational Practices in a Peer Group of Urban Black Children* (Bloomington: Indiana University Press, in press).

15. Two decades ago there was a reverse pattern in research on adult interaction, at least in the literature on sociolinguistics and small groups. "Gender" was assumed to "happen" when men and women were together, not when they were separated. It took feminist effort to bring same-gender relations, especially among women (a virtually invisible topic in traditional research on communication), into that subject matter (see Barrie Thorne, Cheris Kramarae, and Nancy Henley, eds., *Language, Gender and Society* [Rowley, Mass.: Newbury

House, 1983]). These inverse ways of locating gender—defined by the genders separating for children and by their being together for adults—may reflect age-based assumptions. In our culture, adult gender is defined by heterosexuality, but children are (ambivalently) defined as asexual. We load the interaction of adult men and women with heterosexual meaning, but we resist defining children's mixed-gender interaction in those terms. Traditional constructions of children and gender exemplify and ideal of latency.

16. See Barrie Thorne, "An Analysis of Gender and Social Groupings," in Laurel Richardson and Verta Taylor, eds., *Feminist Frontiers* (Reading, Mass.: Addison-Wesley, 1983), 61–63; and idem, "Girls and Boys Together," 170–71.

17. Sherry B. Ortner, "The Founding of the First Sherpa Nunnery, and the Problem of 'Women' as an Analytic Category," in Vivian Patraka and Louise Tilly, eds., *Feminist Re-Visions* (Ann Arbor: University of Michigan Women's Studies Program, 1984).

18. Carole Joffe, "As the Twig Is Bent," in Judith Stacey, Susan Bereaud, and Joan Daniels, eds., *And Jill Came Tumbling After* (New York: Dell, 1974), 79–90; Raphaela Best, *We've All Got Scars* (Bloomington: Indiana University Press, 1983); Robert B. Everhart, *Reading, Writing and Resistance* (Boston: Routledge & Kegan Paul, 1983); Philip A. Cusick, *Inside High School* (New York: Holt, Reinhart and Winston, 1973).

19. Cusick, *Inside High School,* 168.

20. I was a participant-observer in two different elementary schools—for eight months in a largely working class school in California (there were about 500 students, 5 percent Black, 20 percent Hispanic, and 75 percent white), and for three months in a school of similar size, class, and racial/ethnic composition in Michigan. Most of the examples in this paper come from the California school, where I focused primarily on fourth- and fifth-graders. For further reports from this work, see my "Gender and Social Groupings"; "Girls and Boys Together"; and "Crossing the Gender Divide: What 'Tomboys' Can Teach Us about Processes of Gender Separation among Children" (unpublished paper presented at 1985 meeting of the Society for Research on Child Development, Toronto). See also Barrie Thorne and Zella Luria, "Sexuality and Gender in Children's Daily World," *Social Problems* 33 (1986): 176–90.

21. See Thorne and Luria, "Sexuality and Gender," 182–84.

22. Linda A. Hughes, "Beyond the Rules of the Game: Girls' Gaming at a Friends' School (unpublished Ph.D.

diss., University of Pennsylvania Graduate School of Education, 1983); Goodwin, *Conversational Practices.*

23. Marjorie Harness Goodwin and Charles Goodwin, "Children's Arguing," in Susan Philips, Susan Steele, and Christina Tanz, eds., *Language, Gender, and Sex in Comparative Perspective* (Cambridge: Cambridge University Press, 1988).

24. Goodwin, *Conversational Practices.*

25. R. W. Connell, "Theorising Gender," *Sociology* 12 (1985): 260–72. Also see R. W. Connell, *Gender and Power* (Stanford: Stanford University Press, 1987).

26. See Judith Stacey and Barrie Thorne, "The Missing Feminist Revolution in Sociology," *Social Problems* 32 (1985): 301–16.

27. This problem is analyzed in Connell, "Theorising Gender" and *Gender and Power;* Hester Eisenstein, *Contemporary Feminist Thought* (Boston: G. K. Hall, 1984); Jane Flax, "Postmodernism and Gender Relations in Feminist Theory," *SIGNS* 12 (1987): 621–43; Bell Hooks, *Feminist Theory: From Margin to Center* (Boston: South End, 1984); and Sylvia J. Yanagisako and Jane F. Collier, eds., *Gender and Kinship: Essays toward a Unified Analysis* (Stanford: Stanford University Press, 1987).

28. West and Zimmerman, "Doing Gender."

29. Sandra Wallman, "Epistemologies of Sex," in Lionel Tiger and Heather T. Fowler, eds., *Female Hierarchies* (Chicago: Aldine, 1978). Also see Nancy Chodorow, "Feminism and Difference: Gender, Relation, and Difference in Psychoanalytic Perspective," *Socialist Review* 46 (1979): 51–70; Rosaldo, "Use and Abuse of Anthropology"; and Yanagisako and Collier, "Feminism, Gender, and Kinship."

30. See Paul Willis, *Learning to Labor* (New York: Columbia University Press, 1977); and R. W. Connell, D. J. Ashenden, S. Kessler, and G. W. Dowsett, *Making the Difference: Schools, Families, and Social Division* (Boston: Allen & Unwin).

31. On the charged nature of socially constructed boundaries, see Mary Douglas, *Purity and Danger* (New York: Praeger, 1966).

32. Frederik Barth, *Ethnic Groups and Boundaries* (Boston: Little, Brown, 1969).

33. See Thorne, "Girls and Boys Together," 174–75.

34. In an ethnographic study of multiracial school in England, Fuller found that girls of varied social classes and ethnicities had somewhat different ways of responding to boys' efforts to control and devalue them. See Mary Fuller, "Black Girls in a London Comprehensive," in Rosemary Deem, eds., *Schooling for Women's Work* (London: Routledge & Kegan Paul, 19980), 52–65.

35. Goffman, "The Arrangement between the Sexes," 316. The phrase "sex (or gender) segregation among children" has been in widespread use, but as William Hartup suggested in comments at the 1985 meeting of the Society for Research in Child Development, the term *segregation* implies separation far more total and sanctioned than in most social relations among children in the United States.

36. R. W. Connell et al., *Making the Difference,* 182.

37. See David Tyack and Elisabeth Hansot, "Gender in American Public Schools: Thinking Institutionally," *SIGNS* 13 (1988): 741–60. British schools have institutionalized extensive gender separation, described in Sara Delamont, "The Conservative School? Sex Roles at Home, at Work and at School," in Stephen Walker and Len Barton, eds., *Gender, Glass and Education* (Sussex: Falmer, 1983): 93–105.

38. See Luria and Herzog, "Gender Segregation," and Thorne, "Girls and Boys Together."

39. For a fuller analysis, see Thorne, "Crossing the Gender Divide."

40. Willis, *Learning to Labor.*

41. Joan Anyon, "Intersections of Gender and Class: Accommodation and Resistance by Working-Class and Affluent Females to Contradictory Sex-Role Ideologies," in Walker and Len Barton, eds. *Gender, Class and Education,* 1–19.

42. Connell et al., *Making the Difference;* S. Kessler, D. J. Ashenden, R. W. Connell, and G. W. Dowsett, "Gender Relations in Secondary Schooling," *Sociology of Education* 58 (1985): 34–48.

43. Kessler et al., "Gender Relations," 42.

44. Everhart, *Reading, Writing and Resistance.*

45. Anyon, "Intersections of Gender and Class"; Connell et al., *Making the Difference.*

46. On feminist postmodernism, see Flax, "Postmodernism and Gender Relations"; Sandra Harding, *The Science Question in Feminism* (Ithaca: Cornell University Press, 1986); and Toril Moi, *Sexual/Textual Politics* (London: Methuen, 1985).

4

Different Voices, Different Visions

Gender, Culture, and Moral Reasoning

CAROL B. STACK

A great debate stirred my undergraduate college seminar, "Women and Justice." At midsemester, William Jones, an honors student from a rural, Southern, African-American community, stood up and addressed the class. "What," he questioned, "is gender all about?" With some reluctance, he continued. "If Carol Gilligan is right, my brothers and I were raised to be girls as much as boys, and the opposite goes for my sisters. We were raised in a large family with a morality of care as well as justice. We were raised to be responsible to kin, and to be able to face injustices at an early age. Sisters, brothers, it doesn't make a difference. Carol Gilligan should come visit my home town!"

I learn a great deal from teaching. The summer following that course I revisited families I had come to know in rural Carolina counties, bringing William's challenge to Gilligan's scholarship back home. Those observations and the debates that followed in class paralleled my own curiosity, and our collaborative hunch proved true. This chapter reports the results of my own study of the culture of gender, echoing William's question, "What is gender all about?"

Do women and men tend to see moral problems from different horizons? According to some researchers, two moral visions shape our ways of assessing these questions. Carol Gilligan argues in her book, *In a Different Voice,* that "care reasoning," which compels us to respond to those in need, and "justice reasoning," which dictates that we treat others fairly, represent separate moral orientations.[1] In her view, these are not opposites but different modes of apprehending human dilemmas. Gilligan's subsequent research suggests that these moral perspectives originate in the dynamics of early childhood relationships, solidify in adolescence, and are reproduced in the resolution of moral conflicts throughout the life course.[2]

Feminist scholars are indebted to Gilligan and her colleagues, who have brought the voice of care to moral reasoning and to our understanding of the social construction of gender. Nevertheless, as Gilligan's observations confirm, the cross-cultural construction of gender remains relatively unexplored. During the course of my study of African-American return migration to rural Southern homeplaces,[3] moral voices of both justice and care emerged from my interviews with adults and twelve- and thirteen-year-old boys and girls. However, their responses are strikingly different from the gender configurations in Gilligan's published findings.

In my research, I became interested in the vocabulary of gender and gendered discourse surrounding this return migration movement. Influenced by Gilligan's work on moral reasoning, and puzzled by the absence of reference to race and class, I chose to collect working-class adolescent and adult narratives on moral reasoning in addition to my own ethnographic research on return migration, which involved structured observation and the collection of narratives and life histories.[4] I asked these young people and adults about dilemmas similar to the difficult choices examined in Gilligan's studies. The people I interviewed were return migrants—men, women, and children who had moved back to rural Southern homeplaces. The experiences of those I interviewed differ from those of African-Americans who never left the South, and from long-term and recent dwellers in many cities in the United States. Indeed, this work does not generalize from a specific group to all African-Americans.

This study argues that moral reasoning is negotiated with respect to individual or group location within the social structure. Gender is one, but only one, of the social categories—including, among many, class, culture, racial and ethnic formation, and region—that shape the resources within which we construct morality. My goal is to contextualize gender differences in constructing moral lives within the setting of my current research on return migration, as a modest challenge to explanations that fail to situate gender differences.[5] In this chapter I report the responses of fifteen adults and eighty-seven adolescents, borrowing the orientations of "care" and "justice" in order to bring the issue of gendered strategies in moral reasoning into the race, culture, and socioeconomic context.[6]

Situating the construction of gender across race, culture, and historical conditions transforms our thinking about moral reasoning. The creation of gender roles within specific historical and socioeconomic situations is a creative process, one better viewed as mobile than static. Gender construction is negotiated among members of specific communities, for example, as they respond to situations of institutionalized oppression and/ or racial stratification. As an anthropologist concerned with the construction of gender, it has been my hypothesis that gender relationships are improvised against local and global political, economic, and familial affiliations, which are always in transition. My perspective registers serious objections to frameworks built on polarities or fixed oppositions, especially notions that create an illusory sense of "universal" or "essential" gender differences.[7]

Historically, gender as an analytic category has unfolded from early depictions of sex differences and the range of sex roles, to an examination of how gender constructs politics and how politics, class, and race construct gender.[8] Anthropological studies of gender have moved from particular, to universal, and, in this chapter, to contextual. Feminist scholars emerge from this experience with a subtle category of analysis constructed from the concrete, deeply rooted in relationships of power, class, race, and historical circumstance.

Data from my earlier research in urban Black communities in the 1970s,[9] and from my studies of the return migration of African-Americans from the Northeast to the rural South,[10] suggest new notions about the nexus of gender, race, and class relations. Class, racial formation,[11] and economic systems within rural Southern communities create a context in which African-Americans— women and men, boys and girls—experience their relationship to production, employment, class, and material and economic rewards in strikingly similar ways, rather than the divergent ways predicted by theorists of moral reasoning. It is from the vantage point of over twenty years of research on the African-American family that I situate my contributions to Carol Gilligan's discourse on moral voices.[12] I focus on gender as a social relation and suggest that it is negotiated along changing axes of difference.[13]

Although philosophers have debated Gilligan's distinction between care and justice reasoning, as well as her methods of interpreting and coding narratives of moral reasoning, in this chapter I will not challenge such concerns. This present undertaking is narrower in scope. The research does not disentangle methodological issues surrounding Gilligan and her critics,[14] or enter debates on moral reasoning or moral stages of development. It does, however, question the validity of universal gender differences.

On separate occasions several adults and adolescents who had returned home to rural Southern communities worked with me on this research by constructing scenarios of difficult choices they face in their own lives. The dilemmas constructed by local community members approximate Gilligan and colleagues' most current procedures, in which they ask people to talk about a situation where they were unsure what the right thing to do was, and they had to make a choice.[15] I chose to elicit culturally relevant dilemmas rather than employing the classic "Heinz dilemma" (whether Heinz should steal drugs for his dying wife) used by Gilligan. In Gilligan's current, more open-ended approach, people respond to a dilemma of their own making. What is important in this style of research is not the specific nature of the dilemma but what people say about it.

An intriguing aspect of my study of Black return migration is the cyclical migration of children. They accompany parents or extended kin, or journey alone along well-worn paths between their families' home bases in the North and in the South. Many of the parents of these children had participated in cyclical migrations and dual residences. Today, dual patterns of residence are common for young Black children whose kinship ties extend across state lines and regions of the country.[16] Their homes are in both city and countryside; their schooling is divided between public schools in Harlem, Brooklyn, or Washington, D.C., and country schools in the South. Their cyclical patterns of residence are common knowledge to school administrators, teachers, and social workers in their communities. I have been interested in how children experience their own migration, especially in light of the vivid descriptions they have given me of the tough choices they are asked to make. Straddling family ties in the North and South, and loyalties and attachments across the generations, children face real-life dilemmas over where to reside and with whom, and over what defines their responsibility to others. Their dilemmas dramatize cultural aspects of migration.

Several twelve- and thirteen-year-olds helped me construct a dilemma from the real-life situations they had described to me. One child suggested that we put the dilemma in the form of a "Dear Abby" letter, since the "Dear Abby" column is popular reading in the local community. Eighty-seven children of the North-South return migration responded to the following dilemma:

Dear Abby:

I am 12 and my brother is 10. My mother wants us to go and stay with her in New York City, and my grandparents want us to stay here in New Jericho with them. What should we do?

Love, Sally

The way children resolved the "Dear Abby" dilemma and personalized their responses reflects children's experiences as participants in this migration trend. From what children "told" "Dear Abby," and from complementary life histories, we began to understand how these boys and girls perceived their lives and constructed their roles—gender, among others—as family members caught in the web of cultural, economic, and historical forces. Their responses were infused with both a sense of responsibility to those in need and an attempt to treat others fairly.

Jimmy wrote:

I think I should stay with the one that needs my help the most. My grandmother is unable to do for herself and I should stay with her and let my mother come to see me.

Sarah wrote:

I should talk to my parents and try to get them to to understand that my grandparents cannot get around like they used to. I want to make an agreement to let my brother go to New York and go to school, and I'll go to school down here. In the summer I will go and be with my parents and my brother can come down home.

Helen wrote:

I should stay with my grandparents because for one reason, there are many murderers up North, and my grandparents are old and need my help around the house.

A group of adults who had returned to Southern homeplaces, women and men between the ages of twenty-five and forty, designed the "Clyde Dilemma":

Clyde is very torn over a decision he must make. His two sisters are putting pressure on him to leave Washington, D.C., and go back home to take care of his parents. His mother is bedridden and his father recently lost a leg from sugar. One of his sisters has a family and a good job up North, and the other just moved there recently to get married. Clyde's sisters see him as more able to pick up and go back home since he is unmarried and works part-time—although he keeps trying to get a better job. What should Clyde do?

People deeply personalized their responses as they spoke of experiences within their own extended families. James Hopkins recalled, "Three of us rotated to keep my father at home," and he went on to remind me that "you must love a human being, not a dollar." Molly Henderson, who moved back in 1979, said, "Family should take care of family. It's a cycle. Someone has to do it, and it is Clyde's turn." Sam Henderson, Molly's uncle, told me, "You must take care of those who took care of you. Clyde's next in line, it's his turn." And Sam Hampton said, "He has no alternative." Others repeated, "It's not so hard if everybody helps" or "Family is the most important sacrifice we can make."

FINDINGS

My findings pay particular attention to class differences as well as the formation of ethnic and racial consciousness. They contrast dramatically with Gilligan's observations that while girls and women turn equally to justice and care reasoning, boys and men far less often turn to care reasoning, especially as they grow older.[17] All of the responses to the dilemmas were coded and analyzed for fifteen adults and eighty-seven adolescents (forty-two girls, forty-five boys), according to the recoded guidelines of Gilligan and colleagues. Gilligan has a separate category termed "both," which I will call "mixed" (as in a mixture that cannot be separated into constituents). In the final analysis, my results do not differ whether

TABLE 1   Justice and Care Reasoning Among Adolescents, by Gender

	Boys (N = 45)	Girls (N = 42)
Justice only	42% (19)	43% (18)
Care only	31% (14)	31% (13)
Justice and Care	27% (12)	26% (11)

"mixed" is dropped or is counted as both justice and care. As shown in Table 1, the presence of justice as a reason (with or without care) is not different for boys versus girls. Likewise, the presence of care as a reason (with or without justice) is not different for boys versus girls (Pearson Chi-square test). Table 2 shows that the same conclusions are obtained for adult men versus women (Fisher exact test).

The patterns of percentages are virtually identical for boys and girls, with justice higher than care in each group. The percentage was also nearly the same for boys and girls who used both.

The adult women articulated both kinds of reasoning (care and justice) more than men did. There is no real difference between men and women in justice reasoning. Notice that only one (and that one a man) of fifteen of the adults used care reasoning alone.

The contextualization of moral reasoning in this study presents a configuration of gender differences and similarities strikingly different from Gilligan's results. Among African-American families returning to the South, adolescents and adults

TABLE 2   Justice and Care Reasoning Among Adults, by Gender

	Men (N = 7)	Women (N = 8)
Justice only	43% (3)	37.5% (3)
Care only	14% (1)	.0%
Justice and Care	43% (3)	62.5% (5)

are close to identical when their discourse is coded for care and justice reasoning. This suggests that situating gender difference in the context of class and race transforms our thinking about moral reasoning.

MORAL KNOWLEDGE, SOCIAL ACTION, AND GENDER

Two questions arise from these results. First, in contrast to Gilligan's findings, why the convergence between African-American male and female responses? How and why do these similarities exist? Second, what is the relationship between moral reasoning and the ways in which men and women carry out their lives and conduct social actions?

This research substantiates findings from my earlier studies of dependency relationships experienced by both African-American males and females. In many aspects of their relationship to work, to social institutions, and to political conditions, Black women and other women of color affirm the similar circumstances that encircle their lives and the lives of men. In *Talking Back,* an essay on feminist thinking, bell hooks argues the oversimplicity of viewing women as victims and men as dominators; women can be agents of domination, and men and women are both oppressed and dominated.[18] Such realities do not discount the role of sexism in public and private lives or the participation of oppressed men in the domination of others. However, data from my study of return migration suggest that the shared experience that informs the construction of self and the formation of identity among return migrants produces a convergence in the vocabulary of rights, morality, and the social good.

A collective social conscience manifests itself in several strategies across the life course. From an early age girls and boys become aware of the tyranny of racial and economic injustice. By the age of twelve or thirteen, children are aware of the workplace experiences of their parents, of sexual

favors rural women must offer to keep their jobs in Southern mills and processing plants, of threats to the sanity and dignity of kin. Women and men who return to the South are imbued with a sense of both memory and history. Those who return home confront their past, and engage in a collective negotiation with social injustice. They carry back with them a mission or desire to fight for racial justice as they return to what they refer to as "my testing ground." They define themselves as "community" or as "race persons"—those who work for the good of the race.

These men and women also share a care orientation. Those who return to rural Southern communities find refuge across the generations in their Southern families. Both men and women are embedded in their extended families; they similarly experience tensions between their individual aspirations and the needs of kin. These tensions surface as a morality of responsibility; they are voiced loud and clear in the Clyde dilemma, and in life histories I collected during the course of my research.

Parallels in the experiences of men and women with reference to external forces that shape their lives, suggest that under these conditions there is a convergence between Black men and women of all ages in their construction of themselves in relationship to others. The way both men and women describe themselves indicates a sense of identity deeply connected to others—to borrow Wade Nobles's language, an "extended self." Individuals perceive their obligations within the context of a social order anchored in others rather than in an individualist focus on their personal welfare.[19] In more than 1,000 pages of self-narratives that I collected during the course of the study of return migration, people affirmed, with force and conviction, the strength of kinship ties to their rural Southern families. Over and over they emphasized, "Family is the most important sacrifice." Family ties entail intricate dependencies for Black men and women, especially for those on the edge of poverty.

Likewise, the interviews with children revealed a collective social conscience and a profound sensitivity among young people to the needs of their families. The children's voices tell a somber story of the circumstances and material conditions of their lives. Their expectations about where they will live in the coming year conform to the changing needs and demands of other family members, old and young, and family labor force participation.

The construction of gender, as Black and other feminist researchers of color have emphasized, is shaped by the experience of sex, race, class, and consciousness.[20] Future research on the construction of gender must contribute another dimension to the construction of feminist theory. It should provide a critical framework for analysis of gender consciousness, and a cautionary reminder to those theorists who argue that gender is universally shared and experienced.

My treatment of the results of coding data on care and justice reasoning among African-Americans returning to the South has startling results. Taken out of context, and compared with Gilligan's early findings, it would appear that, in contrast to the Harvard studies, gender configures fewer differences in ways of knowing among this specific group of African-Americans. But what is the relationship between ways of knowing and ways of acting?

My five-year study of African-American return migration to the rural South makes it clear that in any study we must examine multiple levels of analysis. Looking beyond the coding, the men and women who received similar scores on justice and care reasoning produced remarkably different gendered strategies for action. In their assumption of the work of kinship, the roles of wage earners and caretakers, and in their political actions, men and women in these rural Southern communities differed.

Particularly striking are gendered strategies of political action. In their battle to subvert an oppressive social order, the men who return as adults to their Southern homeplaces work principally within the local Black power structure, avoiding confrontation with the near-at-hand White power structure. When they challenge existing mores, they confront the Black male hierarchy within local landowning associations or the church. The social order women discover upon their return is a male symbolic order both within the local Black community and in relation to the local white community. Women find themselves struggling between contradictory forces of the old South and their own political missions. They face a race and gender system in which they are drawn into dependencies emerging from male structures in the local Black community. But these women, unlike the men who return, take action to circumvent this race/gender hierarchy as well as the local patronage systems. They create public programs, such as Title XX Day Care and Head Start, by creating an extensive statewide network of support in the public and private sectors. These women build community bases by carrying out their struggle in a public domain outside the jurisdiction of the local public power structure. Male preachers, politicians, and power brokers also reproduce dependency relationships between Blacks and Whites. While men participate in public spheres within their local Black communities, women bypass local black and white male structures, moving within a wider, regionally defined public domain.

There is a disjunction across race, culture, class, and gender between the study of moral voices—what people say—and observations of how people conduct themselves—what they do—as they are situated in familiar places and public spaces. We must always study, side by side, both discourse and course of action. This brings us face to face with the difference between interpretative studies of moral voices and ethnographies of gender that situate moral reasoning in everyday activity. Cross-disciplinary differences in feminist methodologies reinforce the importance within feminist scholarship of "talking back" to one another.

NOTES

1. Carol Gilligan, *In a Different Voice: Psychological Theory and Women's Development* (Cambridge, Mass.: Harvard University Press, 1982).

2. Carol Gilligan and Grant Wiggins, "The Origins of Morality in Early Childhood Relationships," in *The Emergence of Morality,* ed. Jerome Kagan and Sharon Lamb (Chicago: University of Chicago Press, 1987).

3. Carol B. Stack, *The Proving Ground: African-Americans Reclaim the Rural South* (New York: Pantheon, in press).

4. Between 1975 and 1980, 326,000 black individuals returned to a ten-state region of the South.

5. I am grateful to Nancy Chodorow for her view that this chapter addresses gender differentiation and gender strategies rather than gender construction.

6. Carol B. Stack, "The Culture of Gender Among Women of Color," *Signs* 12, no. 1 (Winter 1985): 321–324.

7. Laura Nader, 1989. "Orientalism, Occidentalism, and the Control of Women," *Cultural Dynamics* 2, no. 3 (1989): 323.

8. Joan W. Scott, "Gender: A Useful Category of Historical Analysis," *American Historical Review* 91, no. 5 (December 1986): 1053–1075.

9. Carol B. Stack, *All Our Kin: Strategies for Survival in a Black Community* (New York: Harper & Row, 1974).

10. Stack, *The Proving Ground.*

11. Michael Omi and Howard Winant, *Racial Formation in the United States* (New York: Routledge and Kegan Paul, 1986).

12. Gilligan, *In a Different Voice.*

13. Teresa de Lauretis, "Eccentric Subjects: Feminist Theory and Historical Consciousness," unpublished MS, University of California at Santa Cruz.

14. Linda K. Kerber, Catherine G. Greeno, Eleanor E. Maccoby, Zella Luria, Carol B. Stack, and Carol Gilligan, "In a Different Voice: An Interdisciplinary Forum," *Signs* 12, no. 1 (Winter 1985): 304–333.

15. Jane Atanuchi, private communication.

16. Carol B. Stack and John Cromartie, "The Journeys of Children," unpublished MS.

17. Carol Gilligan, "Women's Place in Man's Life Cycle," *Harvard Educational Review* 49, no. 4 (1979): 413–446; and *In a Different Voice.*

18. bell hooks (Gloria Watkins), *Talking Back: Thinking Feminist, Thinking Back* (Boston: South End Press, 1989), esp. p. 20.

19. Vernon Dixon, "World Views and Research Methodology," in L. M. King, Vernon Dixon, and W. W. Nobles, eds., *African Philosophy: Assumptions and Paradigms for Research on Black Persons* (Los Angeles: Fanon Center, 1976).

20. Bonnie Thornton Dill, "The Dialectics of Black Womanhood," in *Feminism and Methodology,* ed. Sandra Harding (Bloomington: Indiana University Press, 1987).

5

Masculinities
and Globalization

R. W. CONNELL

The current wave of research and debate on masculinity stems from the impact of the women's liberation movement on men, but it has taken time for this impact to produce a new intellectual agenda. Most discussions of men's gender in the 1970s and early 1980s centered on an established concept, the male sex role, and an established problem: how men and boys were socialized into this role. There was not much new empirical research. What there was tended to use the more abstracted methods of social psychology (e.g., paper-and-pencil masculinity/femininity scales) to measure generalized attitudes and expectations in ill-defined populations. The largest body of empirical research was the continuing stream of quantitative studies of sex differences—which continued to be disappointingly slight (Carrigan, Connell, and Lee 1985).

The concept of a unitary male sex role, however, came under increasing criticism for its multiple oversimplifications and its incapacity to handle issues about power (Kimmel 1987; Connell 1987). New conceptual frameworks were proposed that linked feminist work on institutionalized patriarchy, gay theoretical work on homophobia, and psychoanalytic ideas about the person (Carrigan, Connell, and Lee 1985; Hearn 1987). Increasing attention was given to certain studies that located issues about masculinity in a fully described local context, whether a British printing shop (Cockburn 1983) or a Papuan mountain community (Herdt 1981). By the late 1980s, a genre of empirical research based on these ideas was developing, most clearly in sociology but also in anthropology, history, organiza-tion studies, and cultural studies. This has borne fruit in the 1990s in what is now widely recognized as a new generation of social research on masculinity and men in gender relations (Connell 1995; *Widersprueche* 1995; Segal 1997).

Although the recent research has been diverse in subject matter and social location, its characteristic focus is the construction of masculinity in a particular milieu or moment—a clergyman's family (Tosh 1991), a professional sports career (Messner 1992), a small group of gay men (Connell 1992), a bodybuilding gym (Klein 1993), a group of colonial schools (Morrell 1994), an urban police force (McElhinny 1994), drinking groups in bars (Tomsen 1997), a corporate office on the verge of a decision (Messerschmidt 1997). Accordingly, we might think of this as the "ethnographic moment" in masculinity research, in which the specific and the local are in focus. (This is not to deny that this work *deploys* broader structural concepts simply to note the characteristic focus of the empirical work and its analysis.)

The ethnographic moment brought a much-needed gust of realism to debates on men and masculinity, a corrective to the simplifications of role theory. It also provided a corrective to the trend in popular culture where vague discussions of men's sex roles were giving way to the mystical generalities of the mythopoetic movement and the extreme simplifications of religious revivalism.

Although the rich detail of the historical and field studies defies easy summary, certain conclusions emerge from this body of research as a whole. In short form, they are the following.

Plural Masculinities. A theme of theoretical work in the 1980s, the multiplicity of masculinities has now been very fully documented by descriptive research. Different cultures and different periods of history construct gender differently. Striking differences exist, for instance, in the relationship of homosexual practice to dominant forms of masculinity (Herdt 1984). In multicultural societies, there are varying definitions and enactments of masculinity, for instance, between Anglo and Latino communities in the United States (Hondagneu-Sotelo and Messner 1994). Equally important, more than one kind of masculinity can be found within a given cultural setting or institution. This is particularly well documented in school studies (Foley 1990) but can also be observed in workplaces (Messerschmidt 1997) and the military (Barrett 1996).

Hierarchy and Hegemony. These plural masculinities exist in definite social relations, often relations of hierarchy and exclusion. This was recognized early, in gay theorists' discussions of homophobia; it has become clear that the implications are far-reaching. There is generally a hegemonic form of masculinity, the most honored or desired in a particular context. For Western popular culture, this is extensively documented in research on media representations of masculinity (McKay and Huber 1992). The hegemonic form need not be the most common form of masculinity. Many men live in a state of some tension with, or distance from, hegemonic masculinity; others (such as sporting heroes) are taken as exemplars of hegemonic masculinity and are required to live up to it strenuously (Connell 1990a). The dominance of hegemonic masculinity over other forms may be quiet and implicit, but it may also be vehement and violent, as in the important case of homophobic violence.

Collective Masculinities. Masculinities, as patterns of gender practice, are sustained and enacted not only by individuals but also by groups and institutions. This fact was visible in Cockburn's (1983) pioneering research on informal workplace culture, and it has been confirmed over and over: in workplaces (Donaldson 1991), in organized sport (Whitson 1990; Messner 1992), in schools (Connell 1996), and so on. This point must be taken with the previous two: institutions may construct multiple masculinities and define relationships between them. Barrett's (1996) illuminating study of hegemonic masculinity in the U.S. Navy shows how this takes different forms in the different subbranches of the one military organization.

Bodies as Arenas. Men's bodies do not determine the patterns of masculinity, but they are still of great importance in masculinity. Men's bodies are addressed, defined and disciplined (as in sport; see Theberge 1991), and given outlets and pleasures by the gender order of society. But men's bodies are not blank slates. The enactment of masculinity reaches certain limits, for instance, in the destruction of the industrial worker's body (Donaldson 1991). Masculine conduct with a female body is felt to be anomalous or transgressive, like feminine conduct with a male body; research on gender crossing (Bolin 1988) shows the work that must be done to sustain an anomalous gender.

Active Construction. Masculinities do not exist prior to social interaction, but come into existence as people act. They are actively produced, using the resources and strategies available in a given milieu. Thus the exemplary masculinities of sports professionals are not a product of passive disciplining, but as Messner (1992) shows, result from a sustained, active engagement with the demands of the institutional setting, even to the point of serious bodily damage from "playing hurt" and accumulated stress. With boys learning masculinities, much of what was previously taken as socialization appears, in close-focus studies of schools (Walker 1988; Thorne 1993), as the outcome of intricate and intense maneuvering in peer groups, classes, and adult-child relationships.

Contradiction. Masculinities are not homogeneous, simple states of being. Close-focus research on masculinities commonly identifies contradictory desires and conduct; for instance, in Klein's (1993) study of bodybuilders, the contradiction between the heterosexual definition of hegemonic masculinity and the homosexual practice by which some of the bodybuilders finance the making of an exemplary body. Psychoanalysis provides the classic evidence of conflicts within personality, and recent psychoanalytic writing (Chodorow 1994; Lewes 1988) has laid some emphasis on the conflicts and emotional compromises within both hegemonic and subordinated forms of masculinity. Life-history research influenced by existential psychoanalysis (Connell 1995) has similarly traced contradictory projects and commitments within particular forms of masculinity.

Dynamics. Masculinities created in specific historical circumstances are liable to reconstruction, and any pattern of hegemony is subject to contestation, in which a dominant masculinity may be displaced. Heward (1988) shows the changing gender regime of a boys' school responding to the changed strategies of the families in its clientele. Roper (1991) shows the displacement of a production-oriented masculinity among engineering managers by new financially oriented generic managers. Since the 1970s, the reconstruction of masculinities has been pursued as a conscious politics. Schwalbe's (1996) close examination of one mythopoetic group shows the complexity of the practice and the limits of the reconstruction.

If we compare this picture of masculinity with earlier understandings of the male sex role, it is clear that the ethnographic moment in research has already had important intellectual fruits.

Nevertheless, it has always been recognized that some issues go beyond the local. For instance, mythopoetic movements such as the highly visible Promise Keepers are part of a spectrum of masculinity politics; Messner (1997) shows for the United States that this spectrum involves at least eight conflicting agendas for the remaking of masculinity. Historical studies such as Phillips (1987)

on New Zealand and Kimmel (1996) on the United States have traced the changing public constructions of masculinity for whole countries over long periods; ultimately, such historical reconstructions are essential for understanding the meaning of ethnographic details.

I consider that this logic must now be taken a step further, and in taking this step, we will move toward a new agenda for the whole field. What happens in localities is affected by the history of whole countries, but what happens in countries is affected by the history of the world. Locally situated lives are now (indeed, have long been) powerfully influenced by geopolitical struggles, global markets, multinational corporations, labor migration, transnational media. It is time for this fundamental fact to be built into our analysis of men and masculinities.

To understand local masculinities, we must think in global terms. But how? That is the problem pursued in this article. I will offer a framework for thinking about masculinities as a feature of world society and for thinking about men's gender practices in terms of the global structure and dynamics of gender. This is by no means to reject the ethnographic moment in masculinity research. It is, rather, to think how we can use its findings more adequately.

THE WORLD GENDER ORDER

Masculinities do not first exist and then come into contact with femininities; they are produced together, in the process that constitutes a gender order. Accordingly, to understand the masculinities on a world scale, we must first have a concept of the globalization of gender.

This is one of the most difficult points in current gender analysis because the very conception is counterintuitive. We are so accustomed to thinking of gender as the attribute of an individual, even as an unusually intimate attribute, that it requires a considerable wrench to think of gender on the vast scale of global society. Most relevant discussions, such as the literature on women and development, fudge the issue. They treat the entities that extend internationally (markets, corporations, intergovernmental programs, etc.) as ungendered in principle—but affecting unequally gendered recipients of aid in practice, because of bad policies. Such conceptions reproduce the familiar liberal-feminist view of the state as in principle gender-neutral, though empirically dominated by men.

But if we recognize that very large scale institutions such as the state are themselves gendered, in quite precise and specifiable ways (Connell 1990b), and if we recognize that international relations, international trade, and global markets are inherently an arena of gender formation and gender politics (Enloe 1990), then we can recognize the existence of a world gender order. The term can be defined as the structure of relationships that interconnect the gender regimes of institutions, and the gender orders of local society, on a world scale. That is, however, only a definition. The substantive questions remain: what is the shape of that structure, how tightly are its elements linked, how has it arisen historically, what is its trajectory into the future?

Current business and media talk about globalization pictures a homogenizing process sweeping across the world, driven by new technologies, producing vast unfettered global markets in which all participate on equal terms. This is a misleading image. As Hirst and Thompson (1996) show, the global economy is highly unequal and the current degree of homogenization is often overestimated. Multinational corporations based in the three major economic powers (the United States, European Union, and Japan) are the major economic actors worldwide.

The structure bears the marks of its history. Modern global society was historically produced, as Wallerstein (1974) argued, by the economic and political expansion of European states from the fifteenth century on and by the creation of colonial empires. It is in this process that we find the roots of the modern world gender order. Imperialism was, from the start, a gendered process. Its first phase, colonial conquest and settlement, was car-

ried out by gender-segregated forces, and it resulted in massive disruption of indigenous gender orders. In its second phase, the stabilization of colonial societies, new gender divisions of labor were produced in plantation economies and colonial cities, while gender ideologies were linked with racial hierarchies and the cultural defense of empire. The third phase, marked by political decolonization, economic neocolonialism, and the current growth of world markets and structures of financial control, has seen gender divisions of labor remade on a massive scale in the "global factory" (Fuentes and Ehrenreich 1983), as well as the spread of gendered violence alongside Western military technology.

The result of this history is a partially integrated, highly unequal and turbulent world society, in which gender relations are partly but unevenly linked on a global scale. The unevenness becomes clear when different substructures of gender (Connell 1987; Walby 1990) are examined separately.

The Division of Labor. A characteristic feature of colonial and neocolonial economies was the restructuring of local production systems to produce a male wage worker–female domestic worker couple (Mies 1986). This need not produce a "housewife" in the Western suburban sense, for instance, where the wage work involved migration to plantations or mines (Moodie 1994). But it has generally produced the identification of masculinity with the public realm and the money economy and of femininity with domesticity, which is a core feature of the modern European gender system (Holter 1997).

Power Relations. The colonial and postcolonial world has tended to break down purdah systems of patriarchy in the name of modernization, if not of women's emancipation (Kandiyoti 1994). At the same time, the creation of a westernized public realm has seen the growth of large-scale organizations in the form of the state and corporations, which in the great majority of cases are culturally masculinized and controlled by men. In *compra-dor* capitalism, however, the power of local elites depends on their relations with the metropolitan powers, so the hegemonic masculinities of neocolonial societies are uneasily poised between local and global cultures.

Emotional Relations. Both religious and cultural missionary activity has corroded indigenous homosexual and cross-gender practice, such as the native American *berdache* and the Chinese "passion of the cut sleeve" (Hinsch 1990). Recently developed Western models of romantic heterosexual love as the basis for marriage and of gay identity as the main alternative have now circulated globally—though as Altman (1996) observes, they do not simply displace indigenous models, but interact with them in extremely complex ways.

Symbolization. Mass media, especially electronic media, in most parts of the world follow North American and European models and relay a great deal of metropolitan content; gender imagery is an important part of what is circulated. A striking example is the reproduction of a North American imagery of femininity by Xuxa, the blonde television superstar in Brazil (Simpson 1993). In counterpoint, exotic gender imagery has been used in the marketing strategies of newly industrializing countries (e.g., airline advertising from Southeast Asia)—a tactic based on the long-standing combination of the exotic and the erotic in the colonial imagination (Jolly 1997).

Clearly, the world gender order is not simply an extension of a traditional European-American gender order. That gender order was changed by colonialism, and elements from other cultures now circulate globally. Yet in no sense do they mix on equal terms, to produce a United Colours of Benetton gender order. The culture and institutions of the North Atlantic countries are hegemonic within the emergent world system. This is crucial for understanding the kinds of masculinities produced within it.

THE REPOSITIONING OF MEN AND THE RECONSTITUTION OF MASCULINITIES

The positioning of men and the constitution of masculinities may be analyzed at any of the levels at which gender practice is configured: in relation to the body, in personal life, and in collective social practice. At each level, we need to consider how the processes of globalization influence configurations of gender.

Men's bodies are positioned in the gender order, and enter the gender process, through body-reflexive practices in which bodies are both objects and agents (Connell 1995)—including sexuality, violence, and labor. The conditions of such practice include where one is and who is available for interaction. So it is a fact of considerable importance for gender relations that the global social order distributes and redistributes bodies, through migration, and through political controls over movement and interaction.

The creation of empire was the original "elite migration," though in certain cases mass migration followed. Through settler colonialism, something close to the gender order of Western Europe was reassembled in North America and in Australia. Labor migration within the colonial systems was a means by which gender practices were spread, but also a means by which they were reconstructed, since labor migration was itself a gendered process—as we have seen in relation to the gender division of labor. Migration from the colonized world to the metropole became (except for Japan) a mass process in the decades after World War II. There is also migration within the periphery, such as the creation of a very large immigrant labor force, mostly from other Muslim countries, in the oil-producing Gulf states.

These relocations of bodies create the possibility of hybridization in gender imagery, sexuality, and other forms of practice. The movement is not always toward synthesis, however, as the race/ethnic hierarchies of colonialism have been recreated in new contexts, including the politics of the metropole. Ethnic and racial conflict has been growing in importance in recent years, and as Klein (1997) and Tillner (1997) argue, this is a fruitful context for the production of masculinities oriented toward domination and violence. Even without the context of violence, there can be an intimate interweaving of the formation of masculinity with the formation of ethnic identity, as seen in the study by Poynting, Noble, and Tabar (1997) of Lebanese youths in the Anglo-dominant culture of Australia.

At the level of personal life as well as in relation to bodies, the making of masculinities is shaped by global forces. In some cases, the link is indirect, such as the working-class Australian men caught in a situation of structural unemployment (Connell 1995), which arises from Australia's changing position in the global economy. In other cases, the link is obvious, such as the executives of multinational corporations and the financial sector servicing international trade. The requirements of a career in international business set up strong pressures on domestic life: almost all multinational executives are men, and the assumption in business magazines and advertising directed toward them is that they will have dependent wives running their homes and bringing up their children.

At the level of collective practice, masculinities are reconstituted by the remaking of gender meanings and the reshaping of the institutional contexts of practice. Let us consider each in turn.

The growth of global mass media, especially electronic media, is an obvious "vector" for the globalization of gender. Popular entertainment circulates stereotyped gender images, deliberately made attractive for marketing purposes. The example of Xuxa in Brazil has already been mentioned. International news media are also controlled or strongly influenced from the metropole and circulate Western definitions of authoritative masculinity, criminality, desirable femininity, and so on. But there are limits to the power of global mass communications. Some local centers of mass entertainment differ from the Hollywood model, such as the Indian popular film industry centered in Bombay. Further, media research emphasizes that audiences are highly selective in their reception of media messages, and we must allow for popular recognition of the fantasy in mass entertainment. Just as economic globalization can be exaggerated, the creation of a global culture is a more turbulent and uneven process than is often assumed (Featherstone 1995).

More important, I would argue, is a process that began long before electronic media existed, the export of institutions. Gendered institutions not only circulate definitions of masculinity (and femininity), as sex role theory notes. The functioning of gendered institutions, creating specific conditions for social practice, calls into existence specific patterns of practice. Thus, certain patterns of collective violence are embedded in the organization and culture of a Western-style army, which are different from the patterns of precolonial violence. Certain patterns of calculative egocentrism are embedded in the working of a stock market; certain patterns of rule following and domination are embedded in a bureaucracy.

Now, the colonial and postcolonial world saw the installation in the periphery, on a very large scale, of a range of institutions on the North Atlantic model: armies, states, bureaucracies, corporations, capital markets, labor markets, schools, law courts, transport systems. These are gendered institutions and their functioning has directly reconstituted masculinities in the periphery. This has not necessarily meant photocopies of European masculinities. Rather, pressures for change are set up that are inherent in the institutional form.

To the extent that particular institutions become dominant in world society, the patterns of masculinity embedded in them may become global standards. Masculine dress is an interesting indicator: almost every political leader in the world now wears the uniform of the Western business executive. The more common pattern, however, is not the complete displacement of local patterns but the articulation of the local gender order with the gender regime of global-model institutions. Case studies such as Hollway's (1994) account of bureaucracy in Tanzania illustrate the point; there, domestic patriarchy articulated with masculine authority in the state in ways that subverted the government's formal commitment to equal opportunity for women.

We should not expect the overall structure of gender relations on a world scale simply to mirror patterns known on the smaller scale. In the most vital of respects, there is continuity. The world gender order is unquestionably patriarchal, in the sense that it privileges men over women. There is a patriarchal dividend for men arising from unequal wages, unequal labor force participation, and a highly unequal structure of ownership, as well as cultural and sexual privileging. This has been extensively documented by feminist work on women's situation globally (e.g., Taylor 1985), though its implications for masculinity have mostly been ignored. The conditions thus exist for the production of a hegemonic masculinity on a world scale, that is to say, a dominant form of masculinity that embodies, organizes, and legitimates men's domination in the gender order as a whole.

The conditions of globalization, which involve the interaction of many local gender orders, certainly multiply the forms of masculinity in the global gender order. At the same time, the specific shape of globalization, concentrating economic and cultural power on an unprecedented scale, provides new resources for dominance by particular groups of men. This dominance may become institutionalized in a pattern of masculinity that becomes, to some degree, standardized across localities. I will call such patterns *globalizing masculinities,* and it is among them, rather than narrowly within the metropole, that we are likely to find candidates for hegemony in the world gender order.

GLOBALIZING MASCULINITIES

In this section, I will offer a sketch of major forms of globalizing masculinity in the three historical phases identified above in the discussion of globalization.

Masculinities of Conquest and Settlement

The creation of the imperial social order involved peculiar conditions for the gender practices of men. Colonial conquest itself was mainly carried out by segregated groups of men—soldiers, sailors, traders, administrators, and a good many who were all these by turn (such as the Rum Corps in early New South Wales, Australia). They were drawn from the more segregated occupations and milieu in the metropole, and it is likely that the men drawn into colonization tended to be the more rootless. Certainly the process of conquest could produce frontier masculinities that combined the occupational culture of these groups with an unusual level of violence and egocentric individualism. The vehement contemporary debate about the genocidal violence of the Spanish conquistadors—who in fifty years completely exterminated the population of Hispaniola—points to this pattern (Bitterli 1989).

The political history of empire is full of evidence of the tenuous control over the frontier exercised by the state—the Spanish monarchs unable to rein in the conquistadors, the governors in Sydney unable to hold back the squatters and in Capetown unable to hold back the Boers, gold rushes breaking boundaries everywhere, even an independent republic set up by escaped slaves in Brazil. The point probably applies to other forms of social control too, such as customary controls on men's sexuality. Extensive sexual exploitation of indigenous women was a common feature of conquest. In certain circumstances, frontier masculinities might be reproduced as a local cultural tradition long after the frontier had passed, such as the gauchos of southern South America, the cowboys of the western United States.

In other circumstances, however, the frontier of conquest and exploitation was replaced by a frontier of settlement. Sex ratios in the colonizing population changed, as women arrived and locally born generations succeeded. A shift back toward the family patterns of the metropole was likely. As Cain and Hopkins (1993) have shown for the British empire, the ruling group in the colonial world as a whole was an extension of the dominant class in the metropole, the landed gentry, and tended to reproduce its social customs and ideology. The creation of a settler masculinity might be the goal of state policy, as it seems to have been in late-nineteenth-century New Zealand, as part of a general process of pacification and the creation of an agricultural social order (Phillips 1987). Or it might be undertaken through institutions created by settler groups, such as the elite schools in Natal studied by Morrell (1994).

The impact of colonialism on the construction of masculinity among the colonized is much less documented, but there is every reason to think it was severe. Conquest and settlement disrupted all the structures of indigenous society, whether or not this was intended by the colonizing powers (Bitierli 1989). Indigenous gender orders were no exception. Their disruption could result from the pulverization of indigenous communities (as in the seizure of land in eastern North America and southeastern Australia), through gendered labor migration (as in gold mining with Black labor in South Africa; see Moodie 1994), to ideological attacks on local gender arrangements (as in the missionary assault on the *berdache* tradition in North America; see Williams 1986). The varied course of resistance to colonization is also likely to have affected the making of masculinities. This is clear in the region of Natal in South Africa, where sustained resistance to colonization by the Zulu kingdom was a key to the mobilization of ethnic-national masculine identities in the twentieth century (Morrell 1996).

Masculinities of Empire

The imperial social order created a hierarchy of masculinities, as it created a hierarchy of communities and races. The colonizers distinguished "more manly" from "less manly" groups among their subjects. In British India, for instance, Bengali men were supposed effeminate while Pathans and Sikhs were regarded as strong and warlike. Similar distinctions were made in South Africa between Hottentots and Zulus, in North America between Iroquois, Sioux, and Cheyenne on one side, and southern and southwestern tribes on the other.

At the same time, the emerging imagery of gender difference in European culture provided general symbols of superiority and inferiority. Within the imperial "poetics of war" (MacDonald 1994), the conqueror was virile, while the colonized were dirty, sexualized, and effeminate or childlike. In many colonial situations, indigenous men were called "boys" by the colonizers (e.g., in Zimbabwe; see Shire 1994). Sinha's (1995) interesting study of the language of political controversy in India in the 1880s and 1890s shows how the images of "manly Englishman" and "effeminate Bengali" were deployed to uphold colonial privilege and contain movements for change. In the late nineteenth century, racial barriers in colonial societies were hardening rather than weakening, and gender ideology tended to fuse with racism in forms that the twentieth century has never untangled.

The power relations of empire meant that indigenous gender orders were generally under pressure from the colonizers, rather than the other way around. But the colonizers too might change. The barriers of late colonial racism were not only to prevent pollution from below but also to forestall "going native," a well-recognized possibility—the starting point, for instance, of Kipling's famous novel *Kim* ([1901] 1987). The pressures, opportunities, and profits of empire might also work changes in gender arrangements among the colonizers, for instance, the division of labor in households with a large supply of indigenous workers as domestic servants (Bulbeck 1992). Empire might also affect the gender order of the metropole itself by changing gender ideologies, divisions of labor, and the nature of the metropolitan state. For instance, empire figured prominently as a source of masculine imagery in Britain, in the Boy Scouts, and in the cult of Lawrence of Arabia (Dawson 1991). Here we see examples of an important principle: the interplay of gender dynamics between different parts of the world order.

The world of empire created two very different settings for the modernization of masculinities. In the periphery, the forcible restructuring of economics and workforces tended to individualize, on one hand, and rationalize, on the other. A widespread result was masculinities in which the rational calculation of self-interest was the key to action, emphasizing the European gender contrast of rational man/irrational woman. The specific form might be local—for instance, the Japanese "salaryman," a type first recognized in the 1910s, was specific to the Japanese context of large, stable industrial conglomerates (Kinmonth 1981). But the result generally was masculinities defined around economic action, with both workers and entrepreneurs increasingly adapted to emerging market economies.

In the metropole, the accumulation of wealth made possible a specialization of leadership in the dominant classes, and struggles for hegemony in which masculinities organized around domination or violence were split from masculinities organized around expertise. The class compromises that allowed the development of the welfare state in Europe and North America were paralleled by gender compromises—gender reform movements (most notably the women's suffrage movement) contesting the legal privileges of men and forcing concessions from the state. In this context, agendas of reform in masculinity emerged: the temperance movement, compassionate marriage, homosexual rights movements, leading eventually to the pursuit of androgyny in "men's liberation" in the 1970s (Kimmel and Mosmiller 1992). Not all reconstructions of masculinity, however, emphasized tolerance or moved toward androgyny. The vehement masculinity politics of fascism, for instance, emphasized dominance and difference and glorified violence, a pattern still found in contemporary racist movements (Tillner 1997).

Masculinities of Postcolonialism and Neoliberalism

The process of decolonization disrupted the gender hierarchies of the colonial order and, where armed struggle was involved, might have involved a deliberate cultivation of masculine hardness and violence (as in South Africa; see Xaba 1997). Some activists and theorists of liberation struggles celebrated this, as a necessary response to colonial violence and emasculation; women in liberation struggles were perhaps less impressed. However one evaluates the process, one of the consequences of decolonization was another round of disruptions of community-based gender orders and another step in the reorientation of masculinities toward national and international contexts.

Nearly half a century after the main wave of decolonization, the old hierarchies persist in new shapes. With the collapse of Soviet communism, the decline of postcolonial socialism, and the ascendancy of the new right in Europe and North America, world politics is more and more organized around the needs of transnational capital and the creation of global markets.

The neoliberal agenda has little to say, explicitly, about gender: it speaks a gender-neutral language of "markets," "individuals," and "choice." But the world in which neoliberalism is ascendant is still a gendered world, and neoliberalism has an implicit gender politics. The "individual" of neoliberal theory has in general the attributes and interests of a male entrepreneur, the attack on the welfare state generally weakens the position of women, while the increasingly unregulated power of transnational corporations places strategic power in the hands of particular groups of men. It is not surprising, then, that the installation of capitalism in Eastern Europe and the former Soviet Union has been accompanied by a reassertion of dominating masculinities and, in some situations, a sharp worsening in the social position of women.

We might propose, then, that the hegemonic form of masculinity in the current world gender order is the masculinity associated with those who control its dominant institutions: the business executives who operate in global markets, and the political executives who interact (and in many contexts, merge) with them. I will call this *transnational business masculinity*. This is not readily available for ethnographic study, but we can get some clues to its character from its reflections in management literature, business journalism, and corporate self-promotion, and from studies of local business elites (e.g., Donaldson 1997).

As a first approximation, I would suggest this is a masculinity marked by increasing egocentrism, very conditional loyalties (even to the corporation), and a declining sense of responsibility for others (except for purposes of image making). Gee, Hull and Lankshear (1996), studying recent management textbooks, note the peculiar construction of the executive in "fast capitalism" as a person with no permanent commitments, except (in effect) to the idea of accumulation itself. Transnational business masculinity is characterized by a limited technical rationality (management theory), which is increasingly separate from science.

Transnational business masculinity differs from traditional bourgeois masculinity by its increasingly libertarian sexuality, with a growing tendency to commodify relations with women. Hotels catering to businessmen in most parts of the world now routinely offer pornographic videos, and in some parts of the world, there is a well-developed prostitution industry catering for international businessmen. Transnational business masculinity does not require bodily force, since the patriarchal dividend on which it rests is accumulated by impersonal, institutional means. But corporations increasingly use the exemplary bodies of elite sportsmen as a marketing tool (note the phenomenal growth of corporate "sponsorship" of sport in the last generation) and indirectly as a means of legitimation for the whole gender order.

MASCULINITY POLITICS ON A WORLD SCALE

Recognizing global society as an arena of masculinity formation allows us to pose new questions about masculinity politics. What social dynamics in the global arena give rise to masculinity politics, and what shape does global masculinity politics take?

The gradual creation of a world gender order has meant many local instabilities of gender. Gender instability is a familiar theme of poststructuralist theory, but this school of thought takes as a universal condition a situation that is historically specific. Instabilities range from the disruption of men's local cultural dominance as women move into the public realm and higher education, through the disruption of sexual identities that produced "queer" politics in the metropole, to the shifts in the urban intelligentsia that produced "the new sensitive man" and other images of gender change.

One response to such instabilities, on the part of groups whose power is challenged but still dominant, is to reaffirm *local* gender orthodoxies and hierarchies. A masculine fundamentalism is, accordingly, a common response in gender politics at present. A soft version, searching for an essential masculinity among myths and symbols, is offered by the mythopoetic men's movement in the United States and by the religious revivalists of the Promise Keepers (Messner 1997). A much harder version is found, in that country, in the right-wing militia movement brought to world attention by the Oklahoma City bombing (Gibson 1994), and in contemporary Afghanistan, if we can trust Western media reports, in the militant misogyny of the Talibaan. It is no coincidence that in the two latter cases, hardline masculine fundamentalism goes together with a marked anti-internationalism. The world system—rightly enough—is seen as the source of pollution and disruption.

Not that the emerging global order is a hotbed of gender progressivism. Indeed, the neoliberal agenda for the reform of national and international economics involves closing down historic possibilities for gender reform. I have noted how it subverts the gender compromise represented by the metropolitan welfare state. It has also undermined the progressive-liberal agendas of sex role reform represented by affirmative action programs, anti-discrimination provisions, child care services, and the like. Right-wing parties and governments have been persistently cutting such programs, in the name of either individual liberties or global competitiveness. Through these means, the patriarchal dividend to men is defended or restored, without an *explicit* masculinity politics in the form of a mobilization of men.

Within the arenas of international relations, the international state, multinational corporations, and global markets, there is nevertheless a deployment of masculinities and a reasonably clear hegemony. The transnational business masculinity described above has had only one major competitor for hegemony in recent decades, the rigid, control-oriented masculinity of the military, and the military-style bureaucratic dictatorships of Stalinism. With the collapse of Stalinism and the end of the cold war, Big Brother (Orwell's famous parody of this form of masculinity) is a fading threat, and the more flexible, calculative, egocentric masculinity of the fast capitalist entrepreneur holds the world stage.

We must, however, recall two important conclusions of the ethnographic moment in masculinity research: that different forms of masculinity exist together and that hegemony is constantly subject to challenge. These are possibilities in the global arena too. Transnational business masculinity is not completely homogeneous; variations of it are embedded in different parts of the world system, which may not be completely compatible. We may distinguish a Confucian variant, based in East Asia, with a stronger commitment to hierarchy and social consensus, from a secularized Christian variant, based in North America, with more hedonism and individualism and greater tolerance for social conflict. In certain arenas, there is already conflict between the business and political leaderships embodying these forms of masculinity: initially over human rights versus Asian values, and more recently over the extent of trade and investment liberalization.

If these are contenders for hegemony, there is also the possibility of opposition to hegemony. The global circulation of "gay" identity (Altman 1996) is an important indication that nonhegemonic masculinities may operate in global arenas, and may even find a certain political articulation, in this case around human rights and AIDS prevention.

REFERENCES

Altman, Dennis. 1996. Rupture or continuity? The internationalisation of gay identities. *Social Text* 48 (3): 77–94.

Barrett, Frank J. 1996. The organizational construction of hegemonic masculinity: The case of the U.S. Navy. *Gender Work and Organization* 3 (3): 129–42.

BauSteineMaenner, ed. 1996. *Kritische Maennerforschung* [Critical research on men]. Berlin: Argument.

Bitterli, Urs. 1989. *Cultures in conflict: Encounters between European and non-European cultures, 1492–1800,* Stanford, CA: Stanford University Press.

Bolin, Anne. 1988. *In search of Eve: Transexual rites of passage.* Westport, CT: Bergin & Garvey.

Bulbeck, Chilla. 1992. *Australian women in Papua New Guinea: Colonial passages 1920–1960.* Cambridge, U.K.: Cambridge University Press.

Cain, P. J., and A. G. Hopkins. 1993. *British Imperialism: Innovation and expansion, 1688–1914.* New York: Longman.

Carrigan, Tim, Bob Connell, and John Lee. 1985. Toward a new sociology of masculinity. *Theory and Society* 14 (5): 551–604.

Chodorow, Nancy. 1994. *Femininities, masculinities, sexualities: Freud and beyond.* Lexington: University Press of Kentucky.

Cockburn, Cynthia. 1983. *Brothers: Male dominance and technological change.* London: Pluto.

Cohen, Jon. 1991. NOMAS: Challenging male supremacy. *Changing Men* (Winter/Spring): 45–46.

Connell, R. W. 1987. *Gender and power.* Cambridge, MA: Polity.

———. 1990a. An iron man: The body and some contradictions of hegemonic masculinity. In *Sport, men and the gender order: Critical feminist perspectives,* edited by Michael A. Messner and Donald F. Sabo, 83–95. Champaign. IL: Human Kinetics Books.

———. 1990b. The state, gender and sexual politics: Theory and appraisal. *Theory and Society* 19:507–44.

———. 1992. A very straight gay: Masculinity, homosexual experience and the dynamics of gender. *American Sociological Review* 57 (6): 735–51.

———. 1995. *Masculinities.* Cambridge, MA: Polity.

———. 1996. Teaching the boys: New research on masculinity, and gender strategies for schools. *Teachers College Record* 98 (2): 206–35.

Cornwall, Andrea, and Nancy Lindisfarne, eds. 1994. *Dislocating masculinity: Comparative ethnographies.* London: Routledge.

Dawson, Graham. 1991. The blond Bedouin: Lawrence of Arabia, imperial adventure and the imagining of English-British masculinity. In *Manful assertions: Masculinities in Britain since 1800,* edited by Michael Roper and John Tosh, 113–44. London: Routledge.

Donaldson, Mike. 1991. *Time of our lives: Labour and love in the working class.* Sydney: Allen & Unwin.

———. 1997. Growing up very rich: The masculinity of the hegemonic. Paper presented at the conference Masculinities: Renegotiating Genders, June, University of Wollongong, Australia.

Enloe, Cynthia. 1990. *Bananas, beaches and bases: Making feminist sense of international politics.* Berkeley: University of California Press.

Featherstone, Mike. 1995. *Undoing culture: Globalization, postmodernism and identity.* London: Sage.

Foley, Douglas E. 1990. *Learning capitalist culture: Deep in the heart of Tejas.* Philadelphia: University of Pennsylvania Press.

Fuentes, Annette, and Barbara Ehrenreich. 1983. *Women in the global factory.* Boston: South End.

Gee, James Paul, Glynda Hall, and Colin Lankshear. 1996. *The new work order: Behind the language of the new capitalism.* Sydney: Allen & Unwin.

Gender Equality Ombudsman. 1997. *The father's quota.* Information sheet on parental leave entitlements, Oslo.

Gibson, J. William. 1994. *Warrior dreams: Paramilitary culture in post-Vietnam America.* New York: Hill and Wang.

Hagemann-White, Carol, and Maria S. Rerrich, eds. 1988. *FrauenMaennerBilder* (Women, Imaging, Men). Bielefeld: AJZ-Verlag.

Hearn, Jeff. 1987. *The gender of oppression: Men, masculinity and the critique of Marxism.* Brighton, U.K.: Wheatsheaf.

Herdt, Gilbert H. 1981. *Guardians of the flutes: Idioms of masculinity.* New York: McGraw-Hill.

———, ed. 1984. *Ritualized homosexuality in Melanesia.* Berkeley: University of California Press.

Heward, Christine. 1988. *Making a man of him: Parents and their sons' education at an English public school 1929–1950.* London: Routledge.

Hinsch, Bret. 1990. *Passions of the cut sleeve: The male homosexual tradition in China.* Berkeley: University of California Press.

Hirst, Paul, and Grahame Thompson. 1996. *Globalization in question: The international economy and the possibilities of governance.* Cambridge, MA: Polity.

Hollstein, Walter. 1992. *Machen Sie Platz, mein Herr! Teilen statt Herrschen* [Sharing instead of dominating]. Hamburg: Rowohlt.

Hollway, Wendy. 1994. Separation, integration and difference: Contradictions in a gender regime. In *Power/gender: Social relations in theory and practice,* edited by H. Lorraine Radtke and Henderikus Stam, 247–69. London: Sage.

Holter, Oystein Gullvag. 1997. Gender, patriarchy and capitalism: A social forms analysis. Ph.D. diss., University of Oslo, Faculty of Social Science.

Hondagneu-Sotelo, Pierrette, and Michael A. Messner. 1994. Gender displays and men's power: The "new man" and the Mexican immigrant man. In *Theorizing masculinities,* edited by Harry Brod and Michael Kaufman, 200–218. Twin Oaks, CA: Sage.

Ito Kimio. 1993. *Otokorashisa-no-yukue* [Directions for masculinities]. Tokyo: Shinyo-sha.

Jolly, Margaret. 1997. From point Venus to Bali Ha'i: Eroticism and exoticism in representations of the Pacific. In *Sites of desire, economies of pleasure: Sexualities in Asia and the Pacific,* edited by Lenore Manderson and Margaret Jolly, 99–122. Chicago: University of Chicago Press.

Kandiyoti, Deniz. 1994. The paradoxes of masculinity: Some thoughts on segregated societies. In *Dislocating masculinity: Comparative ethnographies,* edited by Andrea Cornwall and Nancy Lindisfarne, 197–213. London: Routledge.

Kaufman, Michael. 1997. Working with men and boys to challenge sexism and end men's violence. Paper presented at UNESCO expert group meeting on Male Roles and Masculinities in the Perspective of a Culture of Peace, September, Oslo.

Kimmel, Michael S. 1987. Rethinking "masculinity": New directions in research. In *Changing men: New directions in research on men and masculinity,* edited by Michael S. Kimmel, 9–24. Newbury Park, CA: Sage.

————. 1996. *Manhood in America: A cultural history.* New York: Free Press.

Kimmel, Michael S., and Thomas P. Mosmiller, eds. 1992. *Against the tide: Pro-feminist men in the United States, 1776–1990, a documentary history.* Boston: Beacon.

Kindler, Heinz. 1993. *Maske(r)ade: Jungen- und Maennerarbeit fuer die Pratis* [Work with youth and men]. Neuling: Schwaebisch Gmuend und Tuebingen.

Kinmonth, Earl H. 1981. *The self-made man in Meiji Japanese thought: From Samurai to salary man.* Berkeley: University of California Press.

Kipling, Rudyard. [1901] 1987. *Kim.* London: Penguin.

Klein, Alan M. 1993. *Little big men: Bodybuilding subculture and gender construction.* Albany: State University of New York Press.

Klein, Uta. 1997. Our best boys: The making of masculinity in Israeli society. Paper presented at UNESCO expert group meeting on Male Roles and Masculinities in the Perspectives of a Culture of Peace, September, Oslo.

Lewes, Kenneth. 1988. *The psychoanalytic theory of male homosexuality.* New York: Simon & Schuster.

MacDonald, Robert H. 1994. *The language of empire: Myths and metaphors of popular imperialism, 1880–1918.* Manchester, U.K.: Manchester University Press.

McElhinny, Bonnie. 1994. An economy of affect: Objectivity, masculinity and the gendering of police work. In *Dislocating masculinity: Comparative ethnographies,* edited by Andrea Cornwall and Nancy Lindisfarne, 159–71. London: Routledge.

McKay, Jim, and Debbie Huber. 1992. Anchoring media images of technology and sport. *Women's Studies International Forum* 15 (2): 205–18.

Messerschmidt, James W. 1997. *Crime as structured action: Gender, race, class, and crime in the making.* Thousand Oaks, CA: Sage.

Messner, Michael A. 1992. *Power at play: Sports and the problem of masculinity.* Boston: Beacon.

————. 1997. *The politics of masculinities: Men in movements.* Thousand Oaks, CA: Sage.

Metz-Goeckel, Sigrid, and Ursula Mueller. 1986. *Der Mann: Die Brigitte-Studie* [The male]. Beltz: Weinheim & Basel.

Mies, Maria. 1986. *Patriarchy and accumulation on a world scale: Women in the international division of labour.* London: Zed.

Moodie, T. Dunbar. 1994. *Going for gold: Men, mines, and migration.* Johannesburg: Witwatersand University Press.

Morrell, Robert. 1994. Boys, gangs, and the making of masculinity in the White secondary schools of Natal, 1880–1930. *Masculinities* 2 (2): 56–82.

————. ed. 1996. *Political economy and identities in KwaZulu-Natal: Historical and social perspectives.* Durban, Natal: Indicator Press.

Nakamura, Akira. 1994. *Watashi-no Danseigaku* [My men's studies]. Tokyo: Kindaibugei-sha.

Oftung, Knut, ed. 1994. *Menns bilder og bilder av menn* [Images of men]. Oslo: Likestillingsradet.

Phillips, Jock. 1987. *A man's country? The image of the Pakeha male, a history.* Auckland: Penguin.

Poynting, S., G. Noble, and P. Tabar. 1997. "Intersections" of masculinity and ethnicity: A study of male Lebanese immigrant youth in Western Sydney. Paper presented at the conference Masculinities: Renegotiating Genders, June, University of Wollongong, Australia.

Roper, Michael. 1991. Yesterday's model: Product fetishism and the British company man, 1945–85. In *Manful assertions: Masculinities in Britain since 1800,* edited by Michael Roper and John Tosh, 190–211. London: Routledge.

Schwalbe, Michael. 1996. *Unlocking the iron cage: The men's movement, gender politics, and the American culture.* New York: Oxford University Press.

Segal, Lynne. 1997. *Slow motion: Changing masculinities, changing men.* 2d ed. London: Virago.

Seidler, Victor J. 1991. *Achilles heel reader: Men, sexual politics and socialism.* London: Routledge.

Shire, Chenjerai. 1994. Men don't go to the moon: Language, space and masculinities in Zimbabwe. In *Dislocating masculinity: Comparative ethnographies,* edited by Andrea Cornwall and Nancy Lindisfarne, 147–58. London: Routledge.

Simpson, Amelia. 1993. *Xuxa: The mega-marketing of a gender, race and modernity.* Philadelphia: Temple University Press.

Sinha, Mrinalini. 1995. *Colonial masculinity: The manly Englishman and the effeminate Bengali in the late nineteenth century.* Manchester, U.K.: Manchester University Press.

Taylor, Debbie. 1985. Women: An analysis. In *Women: A world report,* 1–98. London: Methuen.

Theberge, Nancy. 1991. Reflections on the body in the sociology of sport. *Quest* 43:123–34.

Thorne, Barrie. 1993. *Gender play: Girls and boys in school.* New Brunswick. NJ: Rutgers University Press.

Tillner, Georg. 1997. Masculinity and xenophobia. Paper presented at UNESCO meeting on Male Roles and Masculinities in the Perspective of a Culture of Peace, September, Oslo.

Tomsen, Stephen. 1997. A top night: Social protest, masculinity and the culture of drinking violence. *British Journal of Criminology* 37 (1): 90–103.

Tosh, John. 1991. Domesticity and manliness in the Victorian middle class: The family of Edward White Benson. In *Manful assertions: Masculinities in Britain since 1800,* edited by Michael Roper and John Tosh, 44–73. London: Routledge.

United Nations Educational, Scientific and Cultural Organization (UNESCO). 1997. *Male roles and masculinities in the perspective of a culture of peace: Report of expert group meeting, Oslo, 24–28 September 1997.* Paris: Women and a Culture of Peace Programme, Culture of Peace Unit, UNESCO.

Walby, Sylvia. 1990. *Theorizing patriarchy.* Oxford, U.K.: Blackwell.

Walker, James C. 1988. *Louts and legends: Male youth culture in an inner-city school.* Sydney: Allen & Unwin.

Wallerstein, Immanuel. 1974. *The modern world-system: Capitalist agriculture and the origins of the European world-economy in the sixteenth century.* New York: Academic Press.

Whitson, David. 1990. Sport in the social construction of masculinity. In *Sport, men, and the gender order: Critical feminist perspectives,* edited by Michael A. Messner and Donald F. Sabo, 19–29. Champaign, IL: Human Kinetics Books.

Widersprueche. 1995. Special Issue: Maennlichkeiten. Vol. 56/57.

Williams, Walter L. 1986. *The spirit and the flesh: Sexual diversity in American Indian culture.* Boston: Beacon.

Xaba, Thokozani. 1997. Masculinity in a transitional society: The rise and fall of the "young lions." Paper presented at the conference Masculinities in Southern Africa, June, University of Natal-Durban, Durban.

6

Gender Displays and Men's Power

The "New Man" and the Mexican Immigrant Man

PIERRETTE HONDAGNEU-SOTELO
MICHAEL A. MESSNER

In our discussions about masculinity with our students (many of whom are white and upper-middle class), talk invariably turns to critical descriptions of the "macho" behavior of "traditional men." Consistently, these men are portrayed as "out there," not in the classroom with us. Although it usually remains an unspoken subtext, at times a student will actually speak it: Those men who are still stuck in "traditional, sexist, and macho" styles of masculinity are Black men, Latino men, immigrant men, and working-class men. They are not us; we are the New Men, the Modern, Educated, and Enlightened Men. The belief that poor, working-class, and ethnic minority men are stuck in an atavistic, sexist "traditional male role," while White, educated middle-class men are forging a more sensitive egalitarian "New," or "Modern male role," is not uncommon. Social scientific theory and research on men and masculinity, as well as the "men's movement," too often collude with this belief by defining masculinity almost entirely in terms of gender display (i.e., styles of talk, dress, and bodily comportment), while ignoring men's structural positions of power and privilege over women and the subordination of certain groups of men to other men (Brod, 1983–1984).

In this chapter, we will contrast the gender display and structural positions of power (in both public and domestic spheres of life) of two groups of men: class-privileged White men and Mexican immigrant men. Our task is to explore and explicate some links between contemporary men's gender displays and men's various positions in a social structure of power.

THE "NEW MAN" AS IDEOLOGICAL CLASS ICON

Today there is a shared cultural image of what the New Man looks like: He is a White, college-educated professional who is a highly involved and nurturant father, "in touch with" and expressive of his feelings, and egalitarian in his dealings with women. We will briefly examine two fragments of the emergent cultural image of the contemporary New Man: the participant in the mythopoetic men's movement and the New Father.[1] We will discuss these contemporary images of men both in terms of their larger cultural meanings and in terms of the extent to which they represent any real shift in the ways men live their lives vis-à-vis women and other men. Most important, we will ask if apparent shifts in the gender displays of some White, middle-class men represent any real transformations in their structural positions of power and privilege.

ZEUS POWER AND THE MYTHOPOETIC MEN'S MOVEMENT

A recently emergent fragment of the cultural image of the New Man is the man who attends the weekend "gatherings of men" that are at the heart of Robert Bly's mythopoetic men's movement.

Bly's curious interpretations of mythology and his highly selective use of history, psychology, and anthropology have been soundly criticized as "bad social science" (e.g., Connell, 1992a; Kimmel, 1992; Pelka, 1991). But perhaps more important than a critique of Bly's ideas is a sociological interpretation of why the mythopoetic men's movement has been so attractive to so many predominantly White, college-educated, middle-class, middle-aged men in the United States over the past decade. (Thousands of men have attended Bly's gatherings, and his book was a national bestseller.) We speculate that Bly's movement attracts these men *not* because it represents any sort of radical break from "traditional masculinity" but precisely because it is so congruent with shifts that are already taking place within current constructions of hegemonic masculinity. Many of the men who attend Bly's gatherings are already aware of some of the problems and limits of narrow conceptions of masculinity. A major preoccupation of the gatherings is the poverty of these men's relationships with their fathers and with other men in workplaces. These concerns are based on very real and often very painful experiences. Indeed, industrial capitalism undermined much of the structural basis of middle-class men's emotional bonds with each other as wage labor, market competition, and instrumental rationality largely supplanted primogeniture, craft brotherhood, and intergenerational mentorhood (Clawson, 1989; Tolson, 1977). Bly's "male initiation" rituals are intended to heal and reconstruct these masculine bonds, and they are thus, at least on the surface, probably experienced as largely irrelevant to men's relationships with women.

But in focusing on how myth and ritual can reconnect men with each other and ultimately with their own "deep masculine" essences, Bly manages to sidestep the central point of the feminist critique—that men, as a group, benefit from a structure of power that oppresses women as a group. In ignoring the social structure of power, Bly manages to convey a false symmetry between the feminist women's movement and his men's movement.

He assumes a natural dichotomization of "male values" and "female values" and states that feminism has been good for women in allowing them to reassert "the feminine voice" that had been suppressed. But Bly states (and he carefully avoids directly blaming feminism for this), "the masculine voice" has now been muted—men have become "passive...tamed...domesticated." Men thus need a movement to reconnect with the "Zeus energy" that they have lost. "Zeus energy is male authority accepted for the good of the community" (Bly, 1990, p. 61).

The notion that men need to be empowered *as men* echoes the naïveté of some 1970s men's liberation activists who saw men and women as "equally oppressed" by sexism (e.g., Farrell, 1975). The view that everyone is oppressed by sexism strips the concept of oppression of its political meaning and thus obscures the social relations of domination and subordination. Oppression is a concept that describes a relationship between social groups; for one group to be oppressed, there must be an oppressor group (Freire, 1970). This is not to imply that an oppressive relationship between groups is absolute or static. To the contrary, oppression is characterized by a constant and complex state of play: Oppressed groups both actively participate in their own domination and actively resist that domination. The state of play of the contemporary gender order is characterized by men's individual and collective oppression of women (Connell, 1987). Men continue to benefit from this oppression of women, but, significantly, in the past 25 years, women's compliance with masculine hegemony has been counterbalanced by active feminist resistance.

Men do tend to pay a price for their power: They are often emotionally limited and commonly suffer poor health and a life expectancy lower than that of women. But these problems are best viewed not as "gender oppression," but rather as the "costs of being on top" (Kann, 1986). In fact, the shifts in masculine styles that we see among some relatively privileged men may be interpreted as a sign that these men would like to stop paying these costs, but it does not necessarily signal a desire to cease being "on top." For example, it has become commonplace to see powerful and successful men weeping in public—Ronald Reagan shedding a tear at the funeral of slain U.S. soldiers, basketball player Michael Jordan openly crying after winning the NBA championship. Most recent, the easy manner in which the media lauded U.S. General Schwartzkopf as a New Man for shedding a public tear for the U.S. casualties in the Gulf War is indicative of the importance placed on *styles of masculine gender display* rather than the institutional *position of power* that men such as Schwartzkopf still enjoy.

This emphasis on the significance of public displays of crying indicates, in part, a naive belief that if boys and men can learn to "express their feelings," they will no longer feel a need to dominate others. In fact, there is no necessary link between men's "emotional inexpressivity" and their tendency to dominate others (Sattel, 1976). The idea that men's "need" to dominate others is the result of an emotional deficit overly psychologizes a reality that is largely structural. It does seem that the specific type of masculinity that was ascendent (hegemonic) during the rise of entrepreneurial capitalism was extremely instrumental, stoic, and emotionally inexpressive (Winter & Robert, 1980). But there is growing evidence (e.g., Schwartzkopf) that today there is no longer a neat link between class-privileged men's emotional inexpressively and their willingness and ability to dominate others (Connell, 1991b). We speculate that a situationally appropriate public display of sensitivity such as crying, rather than signaling weakness, has instead become a legitimizing sign of the New Man's power.[2]

Thus relatively privileged men may be attracted to the mythopoetic men's movement because, on the one hand, it acknowledges and validates their painful "wounds," while guiding them to connect with other men in ways that are both nurturing and mutually empowering.[3] On the other hand, and unlike feminism, it does not confront men with the reality of how their own privileges are based on the continued subordination of women and other men. In short, the mythopoetic men's movement may be seen as facilitating the reconstruction of a new form of hegemonic masculinity—a masculinity that is less self-destructive, that has revalued and reconstructed men's emotional bonds with each other, and that has learned to feel good about its own Zeus power.

THE NEW FATHER

In recent years Western culture has been bombarded with another fragment of the popular image of the New Man: the involved, nurturant father. Research has indicated that many young heterosexual men do appear to be more inclined than were their fathers to "help out" with housework and child care, but most of them still see these tasks as belonging to their wives or their future wives (Machung, 1989; Sidel, 1990). Despite the cultural image of the "new fatherhood" and some modest increases in participation by men, the vast majority of child care, especially of infants, is still performed by women (Hochschild, 1989; LaRossa, 1988; Lewis, 1986; Russell, 1983).

Why does men's stated desire to participate in parenting so rarely translate into substantially increased involvement? Lynn Segal (1990) argues that the fact that men's apparent attitudinal changes have not translated into widespread behavioral changes may be largely due to the fact men that may (correctly) fear that increased parental involvement will translate into a loss of their power over women. But she also argues that increased paternal involvement in child care will not become a widespread reality unless and until the structural preconditions—especially economic equality for women—exist. Indeed, Rosanna Hertz (1986) found in her study of upper-middle class "dual career families" that a more egalitarian division of family labor sometimes developed as a rational (and constantly negotiated) response to a need to maintain his career, her career, and the family. In other words, career and pay equality for women was a structural precondition for the development of equality between husbands and wives in the family.

However, Hertz notes two reasons why this is a very limited and flawed equality. First, Hertz's sample of dual-career families in which the women and the men made roughly the same amount of money is still extremely atypical. In two-income families, the husband is far more likely to have the higher income. Women are far more likely than men to work part-time jobs, and among full-time workers, women still earn about 65 cents to the male dollar and are commonly segregated in lower paid, lower status, dead-end jobs (Blum, 1991; Reskin & Roos, 1990). As a result, most women are not in the structural position to be able to bargain with their husbands for more egalitarian divisions of labor in the home. As Hochschild's (1989) research demonstrates, middle-class women's struggles for equity in the home are often met by their husbands' "quiet resistance," which sometimes lasts for years. Women are left with the choice of either leaving the relationship (and suffering not only the emotional upheaval, but also the downward mobility, often into poverty, that commonly follows divorce) or capitulating to the man and quietly working her "second shift" of family labor.

Second, Hertz observes that the roughly egalitarian family division of labor among some upper-middle class dual-career couples is severely shaken when a child is born into the family. Initially, new mothers are more likely than fathers to put their careers on hold. But eventually many resume their careers, as the child care and much of the home labor is performed by low-paid employees, almost always women, and often immigrant women and/or women of color. The construction of the dual-career couple's "gender equality" is thus premised on the family's privileged position within a larger structure of social inequality. In other words, some of the upper-middle class woman's gender oppression is, in effect, bought off with her class privilege, while the man is let off the hook from his obligation to fully participate in child care and housework. The upper-middle class father is likely to be more involved with his children today than his father was with him, and this will likely enrich his life. But given the fact that the day-to-day and moment-to-moment care and nurturance of his children is still likely to be performed by women (either his wife and/or a hired, lower-class woman), "the contemporary revalorisation of fatherhood has enabled many men to have the best of both worlds" (Segal, 1990, p. 58). The cultural image of the New Father has given the middle-class father license to choose to enjoy the emotional fruits of parenting, but his position of class and gender privilege allow him the resources with which he can buy or negotiate his way out of the majority of second shift labor.

In sum, as a widespread empirical reality, the emotionally expressive, nurturant, egalitarian New Man does not actually exist; he is an ideological construct, made up of disparate popular images that are saturated with meanings that express the anxieties, fears, and interests of relatively privileged men. But this is not to say that some changes are not occurring among certain groups of privileged men (Segal, 1990). Some men are expressing certain feelings that were, in the past, considered outside the definition of hegemonic masculinity. Some men are reexamining and changing their relationships with other men. Some men are participating more—very equitably in some cases, but marginally in many others—in the care and nurturance of children. But the key point is that when examined within the context of these men's positions in the overall structure of power in society, these changes do not appear to challenge or undermine this power. To the contrary, the cultural image of the New Man and the partial and fragmentary empirical changes that this image represents serve to file off some of the rough edges of hegemonic masculinity in such a way that the possibility of a happier and healthier life for men is created, while deflecting or resisting feminist challenges to men's institutional power and privileges. But because at least verbal acceptance of the "New Woman" is an important aspect of this reconstructed hegemonic masculinity, the ideological image of the New Man requires a counterimage against which to stand in opposition. Those aspects of traditional hegemonic masculinity that the New Man has rejected—overt physical and verbal displays of domination, stoicism and emotional inexpressivity, overt misogyny in the workplace and at home—are now increasingly projected onto less privileged groups of men: working-class men, gay body-builders, Black athletes, Latinos, and immigrant men.

MEXICAN IMMIGRANT MEN

According to the dominant cultural stereotype, Latino men's "machismo" is supposedly characterized by extreme verbal and bodily expressions of aggression toward other men, frequent drunkenness, and sexual aggression and dominance expressed toward normally "submissive" Latinas. Manuel Peña's (1991) research on the workplace culture of male undocumented Mexican immigrant agricultural workers suggests that there is a great deal of truth to this stereotype. Peña examined the Mexican immigrant male's participation in *charritas coloradas* (red jokes) that characterize the basis of the workplace culture. The most common basis of humor in the *charritas* is sexualized "sadism toward women and symbolic threats of sodomy toward other males" (Paredes, 1966, p. 121).

On the surface, Peña argues, the constant "half-serious, half playful duels" among the men, as well as the images of sexually debased "perverted wenches" and "treacherous women" in the *charritas,* appear to support the stereotype of the Mexican immigrant male group as being characterized by a high level of aggressive masculine posturing and shared antagonisms and hatred directed toward women. But rather than signifying a fundamental hatred of women, Peña argues that these men's public displays of machismo should be viewed as a defensive reaction to their oppressed class status:

As an expression of working-class culture, the folklore of machismo can be considered a realized signifying system [that] points to, but simultaneously displaces, a class relationship and its attendant conflict. At the same time, it introduces a third element, the gender relationship, which acts as a mediator between the signifier (the folklore) and the signified (the class relationship). (Peña, 1991, p. 40)

Undocumented Mexican immigrant men are unable to directly confront their class oppressors, so instead, Peña argues, they symbolically displace their class antagonism into the arena of gender relations. Similar arguments have been made about other groups of men. For instance, David Collinson (1988) argues that Australian male blue-collar workers commonly engage in sexually aggressive and misogynist humor, as an (ultimately flawed) means of bonding together to resist the control of management males (who are viewed, disparagingly, as feminized). Majors and Billson (1992) argue that young black males tend to embody and publicly display a "cool pose," an expressive and often sexually aggressive style of masculinity that acts as a form of resistance to racism. These studies make important strides toward building an understanding of how subordinated and marginalized groups of men tend to embody and publicly display styles of masculinity that at least symbolically resist the various forms of oppression that they face within hierarchies of intermale dominance. These studies all share the insight that the public faces of subordinated groups of men are *personally and collectively constructed performances of masculine gender display.* By contrast, the public face of the New Man (his "sensitivity," etc.) is often assumed to be one-and-the-same with who he "is," rather than being seen as a situationally constructed public gender display.

Yet in foregrounding the oppression of men by men, these studies risk portraying aggressive, even misogynist, gender displays primarily as liberatory forms of resistance against class and racial oppression (e.g., Mirandé, 1982). Though these studies view microlevel gender display as constructed within a context of structured power relations, macrolevel gender relations are rarely viewed as a constituting dynamic within this structure. Rather gender is commonly viewed as . . . an effect of the dominant class and/or race relations. What is obscured, or even drops out of sight, is the feminist observation that masculinity itself is a form of domination over women. As a result, women's actual experiences of oppression and victimization by men's violence are conspicuously absent from these analyses, thus leaving the impression that misogyny is merely a symbolic displacement of class (or race) antagonism. What is needed, then, is an examination of masculine gender display and power within the context of intersecting systems of class, race, and gender relations (Baca Zinn, Cannon, Higginbotham, & Dill, 1986; Collins, 1990). In the following section we will consider recent ethnographic research on Mexican immigrant communities that suggests that gender dynamics help to constitute the immigration process and, in turn, are reconstituted during and following the immigrant settlement process.

THE RHETORIC OF RETURN MIGRATION AS GENDER DISPLAY

Mexican immigrant men who have lived in the United States for long periods of time frequently engage in the rhetoric of return migration. These stated preferences are not necessarily indicative of what they will do, but they provide some telling clues to these men's feelings and perceptions about their lives as marginalized men in the United States. Consider the following statements:[4]

> I've passed more of my life here than in Mexico. I've been here for thirty-one years. I'm not putting down or rejecting this country, but my intentions have always been to return to Mexico . . . I'd like to retire there, perhaps open a little business. Maybe I could buy and sell animals, or open a restaurant. Here I work for a big company, like a

> slave, always watching the clock. Well I'm bored with that.

> I don't want to stay in the U.S. anymore. [Why not?] Because here I can no longer find a good job. Here, even if one is sick, you must report for work. They don't care. I'm fed up with it. I'm tired of working here too. Here one must work daily, and over there with my mother, I'll work for four, maybe five months, and then I'll have a four or five month break without working. My mother is old and I want to be with the family. I need to take care of the rancho. Here I have nothing, I don't have my own house, I even share the rent! What am I doing here?

> I would like to return, but as my sons are born here, well that is what detains me here. Otherwise, I would go back to Mexico . . . Mexico is now in a very inflationary situation. People come here not because they like it, but because the situation causes them to do so, and it makes them stay here for years and years. As the song says, this is a cage made of gold, but it is still a cage.

These statements point to disappointments with migration. In recent years, U.S.-bound migration has become institutionalized in many areas of Mexico, representing a rite of passage for many young, single men (Davis, 1990; Escobar, Gonzalez de la Rocha, & Roberts, 1987). But once in the United States the accomplishment of masculinity and maturity hinges on living up to the image of a financially successful migrant. If a man returns home penniless, he risks being seen as a failure or a fool. As one man explained: "One cannot go back without anything, because people will talk. They'll say 'oh look at this guy, he sacrificed and suffered to go north and he has nothing to show for it.'"

Although most of these men enjoyed a higher standard of living in the United States than in Mexico, working and settling in the United States significantly diminished their patriarchal privileges. Although the men compensated by verbally demonstrating their lack of commitment to staying in the United States, most of these men realized that their lives remained firmly anchored in the United States and that they lacked the ability to return. They could not acquire sufficient savings in the public sphere to fund return migration, and in the domestic sphere, they did not command enough authority over their wives or children, who generally wished to remain in the United States, to coerce the return migration of their families. Although Mexican immigrant men blamed the terms of U.S. production as their reason for wanting to return to Mexico, we believe that their diminished patriarchal privileges significantly fueled this desire to return.[5] Here, we examine the diminution of patriarchy in three arenas: spatial mobility, authority in family decision-making processes, and household labor.

Mexican immigrant men, especially those who were undocumented and lacked legal status privileges, experienced limited spatial mobility in their daily lives and this compromised their sense of masculinity (Rouse, 1990). As undocumented immigrants, these men remained fearful of apprehension by the Immigration Naturalization Service and by the police.[6] In informal conversations, the men often shared experiences with police harassment and racial discrimination. Merely "looking Mexican," the men agreed, was often cause for suspicion. The jobs Mexican immigrant men commonly took also restricted their spatial mobility. As poor men who worked long hours at jobs as gardeners, dishwashers, or day laborers, they had very little discretionary income to afford leisure activities. As one man offered, "Here my life is just from work to the home, from work to the home."

Although the men, together with their families, visited parks, shops, and church, the public spaces open to the men alone were typically limited to street corners and to a few neighborhood bars, pool halls, and doughnut shops. As Rouse (1990) has argued, Mexican immigrant men, especially those from rural areas, resent these constrictions on their public space and mobility and attempt to reproduce public spaces that they knew in Mexico in the context of U.S. bars and pool halls. In a California immigrant community Rouse observed that "men do not come to drink alone or

to meet with a couple of friends...they move from table to table, broadening the circuits of information in which they participate and modulating social relationships across the widest possible range." Although these men tried to create new spaces where they might recapture a public sense of self, the goal was not so readily achieved. For many men, the loss of free and easy mobility signified their loss of publicly accorded status and recognition. One man, a junkyard assembler who had worked in Mexico as a rural *campesino* (peasant), recalled that in his Mexican village he enjoyed a modicum of public recognition: "I would enter the bars, the dances, and when I entered everyone would stand to shake my hand as though I were somebody—not a rich man, true, but I was famous. Wherever you like, I was always mentioned. Wherever you like, everyone knew me back there." In metropolitan areas of California, anonymity replaced public status and recognition.

In Mexico many of these men had acted as the undisputed patriarchs in major family decision-making processes, but in the United States they no longer retained their monopoly on these processes. When families were faced with major decisions—such as whom to seek for legal help, whether or not to move to another town, or the decision to lend money or make a major purchase—spousal negotiation replaced patriarchal exertions of authority. These processes did not go uncontested, and some of the decision-making discussions were more conflictual than harmonious, but collaboration, not domination, characterized them.

This trend toward more egalitarian patterns of shared authority often began with migration. In some families, men initially migrated north alone, and during their absences, the women acted decisively and autonomously as they performed a range of tasks necessary to secure family sustenance. Commentators have referred to this situation as one in which "thousands of wives in the absence of their husbands must 'take the reigns'" (Mummert, 1988, p. 283) and as one in which the wives of veteran migrants experience "a freedom where woman command" (*una libertad donde mujeres mandan*) (Baca & Bryan, 1985). This trend toward more shared decision making continued after the women's migration and was also promoted by migration experiences as well as the relative increase in women's and the decrease in men's economic contributions to the family (Hondagneu-Sotelo, 1992). As the balance of relative resources and contributions shifted, the women assumed more active roles in key decision-making processes. Similar shifts occurred with the older children, who were now often reluctant to subordinate their earnings and their autonomy to a patriarchal family hierarchy. As one man somewhat reluctantly, but resignedly, acknowledged: "Well, each person orders one's self here, something like that . . . Back there [Mexico], no. It was still whatever I said. I decided matters."

The household division of labor is another arena that in some cases reflected the renegotiation of patriarchal relations. Although most families continued to organize their daily household chores along fairly orthodox, patriarchal norms, in some families—notably those where the men had lived for many years in "bachelor communities" where they learned to cook, iron, and make tortillas—men took responsibility for some of the housework. In these cases, men did part of the cooking and housework, they unself-consciously assumed the role of host in offering guests food and beverages, and in some instances, the men continued to make tortillas on weekends and special occasions. These changes, of course, are modest if judged by ideal standards of feminist egalitarianism, but they are significant when compared to patriarchal family organization that was normative before immigration.

This movement toward more egalitarian divisions of labor in some Mexican immigrant households cannot be fully explained by the men's acquisition of household skills in bachelor communities. (We are reminded, for instance, of several middle-class male friends of ours who lived in "bachelor" apartments during college, and after later marrying, conveniently "forgot" how to cook, wash clothes, and do other household chores.) The acquisition of skills appears to be a necessary, but

not a sufficient, condition for men's greater household labor participation in reunited families.

A key to the movement toward greater equality within immigrant families was the change in the women's and men's relative positions of power and status in the larger social structure of power. Mexican immigrant man's public status in the United States is very low, due to racism, insecure and low-paying jobs, and (often) illegal status. For those families that underwent long periods of spousal separation, women often engaged in formal- or informal-sector paid labor for the first time, developed more economic skills and autonomy, and assumed control over household affairs. In the United States nearly all of the women sought employment, so women made significant economic contributions to the family. All of these factors tend to erode men's patriarchal authority in the family and empower women to either directly challenge that authority or at least renegotiate "patriarchal bargains" (Kandiyoti, 1988) that are more palatable to themselves and their children.

Although it is too hasty to proclaim that gender egalitarianism prevails in interpersonal relations among undocumented Mexican immigrants, there is a significant trend in that direction. This is indicated by the emergence of a more egalitarian household division of labor, by shared decision-making processes, and by the constraints on men's and expansion of women's spatial mobility. Women still have less power than men, but they generally enjoy more than they previously did in Mexico. The stereotypical image of dominant macho males and submissive females in Mexican immigrant families is thus contradicted by actual research with these families.

MASCULINE DISPLAYS AND RELATIVE POWER

We have suggested that men's overt public displays of masculine bravado, interpersonal dominance, misogyny, embodied strength, and so forth are often a sign of a lack of institutional power and privilege, vis-à-vis other men. Though it would be a mistake to conclude that Mexican immigrant men are not misogynist (or, following Peña, that their misogyny is merely a response to class oppression), there is considerable evidence that their actual relations with women in families—at least when measured by family divisions of labor and decision-making processes—are becoming more egalitarian than they were in Mexico. We have also argued that for more privileged men, public displays of sensitivity might be read as signs of class/race/gender privilege and power over women and (especially) over other men (see Table 1 for a summary comparison of these two groups)....

In complex, stratified societies where the standards of hegemonic masculinity are that a man should control resources (and other people), men who do not have access to these standards of masculinity thus tend to react with displays of toughness, bravado, "cool pose," or "hombre" (Baca Zinn, 1982). Marginalized and subordinated men, then, tend to overtly display exaggerated embodiments and verbalizations of masculinity that can be read as a desire to express power over others within a context of relative powerlessness. By contrast, many of the contemporary New Man's highly celebrated public displays of sensitivity can be read as a desire to project an image of egalitarianism within a context where he actually enjoys considerable power and privilege over women and other men. Both groups of men are "displaying gender," but the specific forms that their masculine

displays take tend to vary according to their relative positions in (a) the social structure of men's overall power relationship to women and (b) the social structure of some men's power relationships with other men.

CONCLUSION

We have argued for the importance of viewing microlevel gender displays of different groups of men within the context of their positions in a larger social structure of power. Too often critical discussions of masculinity tend to project atavistic hypermasculine, aggressive, misogynist masculinity onto relatively powerless men. By comparison, the masculine gender displays of educated, privileged New Men are too often uncritically applauded, rather than skeptically and critically examined. We have suggested that when analyzed within a structure of power, the gender displays of the New Man might best be seen as strategies to reconstruct hegemonic masculinity by projecting aggression, domination, and misogyny onto subordinate groups of men. Does this mean that all of men's changes today are merely symbolic and ultimately do not contribute to the types of changes in gender relations that feminists have called for? It may appear so, especially if social scientists continue to collude with this reality by viewing shifts in styles of hegemonic masculinity as indicative of

TABLE 1 Comparison of Public and Domestic Gender Displays of White, Class-Privileged Men and Mexican Immigrant Men

	PUBLIC		DOMESTIC	
	Power/Status	*Gender Display*	*Power/Status*	*Gender Display*
White, class-privileged men	High, built into position	"Sensitive," little overt misogyny	High, based on public status/high income	"Quiet control"
Mexican immigrant men	Low (job status, pay, control of work, legal rights, public status)	"Hombre": verbal misogyny, embodied toughness in work/peer culture	Contested, becoming more egalitarian	Exaggerated symbols of power and authority in family

the arrival of a New Man, while viewing marginalized men as Other—as atavistic, traditional men. Instead, a critical/feminist analysis of changing masculinities in the United States might begin with a focus on the ways that marginalized and subordinated masculinities are changing.

This shift in focus would likely accomplish three things: First, it would remove hegemonic masculinity from center stage, thus taking the standpoints of oppressed groups of men as central points of departure. Second, it would require the deployment of theoretical frameworks that examine the ways that the politics of social class, race, ethnicity, and sexuality interact with those of gender (Baca Zinn, Cannon, Higginbotham, & Dill, 1986; Collins, 1990; Harding, 1986; Hondagneu-Sotelo, 1992; Messner, 1990). Third, a sociology of masculinities that starts from the experience of marginalized and subordinated men would be far more likely to have power and politics—rather than personal styles or lifestyles—at its center. This is because men of color, poor and working-class men, immigrant men, and gay men are often in very contradictory positions at the nexus of intersecting systems of domination and subordination. In short, although they are oppressed by class, race, and/or sexual systems of power, they also commonly construct and display forms of masculinity as ways of resisting other men's power over them, as well as asserting power and privilege over women. Thus, to avoid reverting to the tendency to view masculinity simply as a defensive reaction to other forms of oppression, it is crucial in such studies to keep women's experience of gender oppression as close to the center of analysis as possible. This sort of analysis might inform the type of progressive coalition building that is necessary if today's changing masculinities are to contribute to the building of a more egalitarian and democratic world.

NOTES

1. This section of the chapter is adapted from Messner (1993).
2. It is significant, we suspect, that the examples cited of Reagan, Jordan, and Schwartzkopf publicly weeping occurred at moments of *victory* over other men in war and sport.
3. Our speculation on the class and racial bias of the mythopoetic men's movement and on the appeal of the movement to participants is supported, in part, by ongoing (but as yet unpublished) research by sociologist Michael Schwalbe. Schwalbe observes that the "wounds" of these men are very real, because a very high proportion of them are children of alcoholic parents and/or were victims of childhood sexual abuse or other forms of violence. Many are involved in recovery programs.

4. Material in this section is drawn from Hondagneu-Sotelo's study of long-term undocumented immigrant settlers, based on 18 months of field research in a Mexican undocumented immigrant community. See Hondagneu-Sotelo, (1992) *Gendered Transitions: Mexican Experiences of Immigrants.* Berkeley: University of California Press.
5. For a similar finding and analysis in the context of Dominican immigrants in New York City, see Pessar (1986).
6. This constraint was exacerbated by passage of the Immigration Reform and Control Act of 1986, which imposed employer sanctions and doubly criminalized undocumented immigrants' presence at the workplace.

REFERENCES

Baca, R., & Bryan, D. (1985). Mexican women, migration and sex roles. *Migration Today, 13,* 14–18.

Baca Zinn, M. (1982). Chicano men and masculinity. *Journal of Ethnic Studies, 10,* 29–44.

Baca Zinn, M., Cannon, L. W., Higginbotham, E., & Dill, B. T. (1986). The costs of exclusionary practices in woman's studies. *Signs: Journal of Women in Culture and Society, 11,* 290–303.

Blum, L. M. (1991). *Between feminism and labor: The significance of the comparable worth movement.* Berkeley: University of California Press.

Bly, R. (1990). *Iron John: A book about men.* Reading, MA: Addison-Wesley.

Brod, H. (1983–1984). Work clothes and leisure suits: The class basis and bias of the men's movement. *Changing Men, 11,* 10–12, 38–40 (Winter).

Brod, H. (Ed.). (1987). *The making of masculinities: The new men's studies.* Boston: Allen & Unwin.

Clawson. M. A. (1989). *Constructing brotherhood: Class, gender, and fraternalism.* Princeton, NJ: Princeton University Press.

Collins, P. H. (1990). *Black feminist thought: Knowledge, consciousness, and the politics of empowerment.* Boston: Unwin Hyman.

Collinson, D. L. (1988). "Engineering humor": Masculinity, joking and conflict in shop-floor relations. *Organization Studies, 9,* 181–199.

Coltrane, S. (1992). The micropolitics of gender in nonindustrial societies. *Gender & Society, 6,* 86–107.

Connell, R. W. (1987). *Gender and power.* Stanford, CA: Stanford University Press.

Connell, R. W. (1991a). Live fast and die young: The construction of masculinity among young working-class men on the margin of the labour market. *Australian & New Zealand Journal of Sociology, 27,* 141–171.

Connell, R. W. (1991b). *Men of reason: Themes of rationality and change in the lives of the men in the new professions.* Unpublished paper.

Connell, R. W. (1992a). Drumming up the wrong tree. *Tikkun, 7,* 517–530.

Connell, R. W. (1992b). Masculinity, violence, and war. In M. S. Kimmel & M. A. Messner (Eds.), *Men's lives* (2nd ed., pp. 176–182). New York: Macmillan.

Davis, M. (1990). *Mexican voices, American dreams: An oral history of Mexican immigration to the United States.* New York: Henry Holt.

Escobar, A. L., Gonzalez de la Rocha, M., & Roberts, B. (1987). Migration, labor markets, and the international economy: Jalisco, Mexico and the United States. In J. Eades (Ed.), *Migrants, workers, and the social order* (pp. 42–64). London: Tavistock.

Farrell, W. (1975). *The liberated man.* New York: Bantam.

Freire, P. (1970). *Pedagogy of the oppressed.* New York: Herder & Herden.

Harding, S. (1986). *The science question in feminism.* Ithaca, NY: Cornell University Press.

Henley, N. M. (1977). *Body politics: Power, sex, and nonverbal communication.* Englewood Cliffs, NJ: Prentice Hall.

Hertz, R. (1986). *More equal than others: Women and men in dual career marriages.* Berkeley: University of California.

Hochschild. A. (1989). *The second shift: Working parents and the revolution at home.* New York: Viking.

Hondagneu-Sotelo, P. (1992). Overcoming patriarchal constraints: The reconstruction of gender relations among Mexican immigrant women and men. *Gender & Society, 6,* 393–415.

Kandiyoti, D. (1988). Bargaining with patriarchy. *Gender & Society, 2,* 274–290.

Kann, M. E. (1986). The costs of being on top. *Journal of the National Association for Women Deans, Administrators, & Counselors, 49,* 29–37.

Kaufman, M. (Ed.). (1987). *Beyond patriarchy: Essays by men on pleasure, power, and change.* Toronto: Oxford University Press.

Kimmel, M. S. (1992). Reading men: Men, masculinity, and publishing. *Contemporary Sociology, 21,* 162–171.

LaRossa, R. (1988). Fatherhood and social change. *Family Relations, 37,* 451–457.

Lewis, C. (1986). *Becoming a father.* Milton Keynes, UK: Open University Press.

Lyman, P. (1987). The fraternal bond as a joking relation: A case study of the role of sexist jokes in male group bonding. In M. Kimmel (Ed.), *Changing men: New directions in research on men and masculinities* (pp. 148–163). Newbury Park, CA: Sage.

Machung, A. (1989). Talking career, thinking job: Gender differences in career and family expectations of Berkeley seniors. *Feminist Studies, 15.*

Majors, R., & Billson, J. M. (1992). *Cool pose: The dilemmas of black manhood in America.* New York: Lexington.

Martin, P. Y., & Hummer, R. A. (1989). Fraternities and rape on campus. *Gender & Society, 3,* 457–473.

Messner, M. A. (1990). Men studying masculinity: Some epistemological questions in sport sociology. *Sociology of Sport Journal, 7,* 136–153.

Messner, M. A. (1992). *Power at play: Sports and the problem of masculinity.* Boston: Beacon.

Messner, M. A. (1993). "Changing men" and feminist politics in the U.S. *Theory & Society, 22,* 723–737.

Mirandé, A. (1982). Machismo: Rucas, chingasos y chagaderas. *De Colores: Journal of Chicano Expression and Thought, 6*(1/2), 17–31.

Mummert, G. (1988). Mujeres de migrantes y mujeres migrantes de Michoacán: Nuevo papeles para las que se quedan y para las que se van. In T. Calvo & G. Lopez (Eds.), *Movimientos de población en el occident de Mexico* (pp. 281–295). Mexico, DF: Centre d'etudes mexicaines and centroamericaines and El colegio de Mexico.

Paredes, A. (1966). The Anglo-American in Mexican folklore. In R. B. Browne & D. H. Wenkelman (Eds.), *New voices in American studies*. Lafayette, IN: Purdue University Press.

Pelka, F. (1991). Robert Bly and Iron John: Bly romanticizes history, trivializes sexist oppression and lays the blame for men's "grief" on women. *On the Issues, 19,* 17–19, 39.

Peña, M. (1991). Class, gender and machismo: The "treacherous woman" folklore of Mexican male workers. *Gender & Society, 5,* 30–46.

Pessar, P. (1986). The role of gender in Dominican settlement in the United States. In J. Nash & H. Safa (Eds.). *Women and change in Latin America* (pp. 273–294). South Hadley, MA: Bergin & Garvey.

Reskin, B. F., & Roos, P. A. (1990). *Job queues, gender queues: Explaining women's inroads into male occupations*. Philadelphia: Temple University Press.

Rouse, R. (1990, March 14). *Men in space: Power and the appropriation of urban form among Mexican migrants in the United States*. Paper presented at the Residential College, University of Michigan, Ann Arbor.

Russell, G. (1983). *The changing role of fathers*. London: University of Queensland.

Sabo, D. F. (1985). Sport, patriarchy, and male identity: New questions about men and sport. *Arena Review, 9,* 1–30.

Sattel, J. W. (1976). The inexpressive male: Tragedy or sexual politics? *Social Problems, 23,* 469–477.

Segal, L. (1990). *Slow motion: Changing masculinities, changing men*. New Brunswick, NJ: Rutgers University.

Sidel, R. (1990). *On her own: Growing up in the shadow of the American dream*. New York: Penguin.

Tolson, A. (1977). *The limits of masculinity: Male identity and women's liberation*. New York: Harper & Row.

Winter, M. F., & Robert, E. R. (1980). Male dominance, late capitalism, and the growth of instrumental reason. *Berkeley Journal of Sociology, 25,* 249–280.

7

Studying across Difference

Race, Class, and Gender in Qualitative Research

MARGARET L. ANDERSEN

Sociological studies of race have often been distorted by having been centered in the perspectives and experiences of dominant group members. This has resulted both from the exclusion of African American, Latino, and Native American people from the general frameworks of sociology and from the application of ethnocentric concepts to the study of racial-ethnic groups. As Ladner (1973), among others, points out:

> Blacks have always been measured against an alien set of norms. As a result they have been considered to be a deviation from the ambiguous white middle-class model, which itself has not always been clearly defined. This inability or refusal to deal with Blacks as a part and parcel of the varying historical and cultural contributions to the American scene has, perhaps, been the reason sociology has excluded the Black perspective from its widely accepted mainstream theories. (p. xxiii)

Like its sister discipline, women's studies, Black studies seeks to build more inclusive research through incorporating the experiences and perspectives of traditionally excluded groups. One way to accomplish this has been to encourage studies of race and ethnic relations by minority scholars themselves, on the assumption that they are better able to understand the nuances of racial oppression. This assumption is best stated by Blauner and Wellman (1973):

> There are certain aspects of racial phenomena, however, that are particularly difficult, if not impossible, for a member of the oppressing group to grasp empirically and formulate conceptually. These barriers are existential and methodological as well as political and ethical. We refer here to the nuances of culture and group ethos; to the meaning of oppression and especially psychic relations; to what is called the Black, the Mexican-American, the Asian and the Indian experience. (p. 329)

Blauner and Wellman's argument underscores the point that research occurs in the context of power relationships, both between the researcher and research subjects and in the society at large. As they point out:

> Scientific research does not exist in a vacuum. Its theory and practice reflect the structure and values of society. In capitalist America, where massive inequalities in wealth and power exist between classes and racial groups, the processes of social research express both race and class oppression. The control, exploitation, and privilege that are generic components of social oppression exist in the relation of researchers to researched, even though their manifestations may be subtle and masked by professional ideologies. (pp. 314–315)

This position, largely articulated during the early 1970s in sociological writing, poses important questions about the social construction of knowledge about race and ethnic relations. Particularly, the question is raised; How can White scholars contribute to our understanding of the experiences of racial groups? Can dominant groups comprehend the experiences of outsiders and, if so, under what conditions and with which methodological practices?

Doing research in minority communities poses unique methodological problems for members of both minority and majority groups. Baca Zinn (1979), a Chicana sociologist, has described the methodological problems she faces when doing research on Chicano families. She directly acknowledges that her relationships with research subjects are never equal and that, as a researcher, she cannot alter the political context in which research takes place. She argues that minority scholars may generate questions that are different from those asked by majority group researchers. Minority scholars are also less likely to experience distrust, hostility, and exclusion within minority communities. At the same time, however, the accountability and commitment of minority scholars to the communities they study pose unique problems for their research practice. In a different context, Cannon, Higginbotham, and Leung (1988) have shown that qualitative studies are also easily biased by the greater willingness of white middle-class subjects to participate in research. Because dominant groups have less reason to expect they will be exploited by researchers, they are more likely to volunteer as research subjects.

The problems of doing research within minority communities are compounded by the social distance imposed by class and race relations when interviewers are White and middle-class and those being interviewed are not. For White scholars wanting to study race relations, these conclusions in the research literature are daunting. How can White scholars elicit an understanding of race relations as experienced by racial minorities? How can White scholars study those who have been historically subordinated without further producing sociological accounts distorted by the political economy of race, class, and gender?

John Gwaltney, a blind Black anthropologist who studied the experiences and beliefs of people in his hometown community, has written eloquently about the obstacles white researchers should expect when doing research in Black communities. The Black men and women he interviewed strongly expressed their mistrust of White social scientists. They reported, "I wouldn't want to talk to any anthropologist or sociologist or any of those others if they were White because whatever I said they would write down what they felt like, so I might just as well save my breath" (quoted in Gwaltney, 1980, p. xxv). Another said, "We know White folks but they do not know us, and that's just how the Lord planned the thing.... Now they are great ones for begging you to tell them what you really think. But you know, only a fool would really do that" (p. 102). Given these problems, how can White researchers study Black and Latino subjects or, for that matter, how can men study women? Although the focus in this chapter is on studying across racial differences, the theoretical discussion applies to the relationship between any dominant group researcher and his or her minority group subjects.

Feminist scholars have argued that members of subordinated groups have unique viewpoints on their own experiences and on the society as a whole. Known as standpoint theorists, these scholars argue that race, class, and gender are origins of, as well as objects of, sociological knowledge. According to this literature, a feminist standpoint is distinct from a perspective or bias because it "preserve[s] the presence of the active and experiencing subject" (D. E. Smith, 1987, p. 105). Standpoint theorists understand that researchers and their subjects are located in specific social-historical settings. Because there is a social relationship between researchers and their research subjects, research cannot be construed as a process of eliminating the presence of the researcher. Yet, the claim of objectivity often assumes that the researcher has no presence or that to be objective is to remove oneself from the situation at hand. Considering this argument, feminist standpoint theorists have argued that research must be seen in context. Politically engaged standpoints are not simply the result of biological identity. Rather, standpoints are achieved; they are not inherent in one's race, sex, or class. But how are such standpoints accomplished by dominant group members wanting to construct liberating knowledge about race, class, and gender relations?

Standpoint theorists argue that those who maintain an interest in reproducing racist and sexist relations are least able to see the social construction of race, class, and gender relations. Indeed, "there are some perspectives on society from which, however well-intentioned one may be, the real relations of humans with each other and with the natural world are not visible" (Hartsock, 1983, p. 285). Feminist standpoint theorists draw from Marxist theory the idea that material life structures and sets limits on the understanding of social relations; thus the vision of the ruling class, race, and gender is partial, because it not only structures the material relations in which all are forced to participate, but also takes for granted the labor, indeed the very existence, of oppressed groups.

Patricia Hill Collins (1986) argues that the marginality of Black feminist scholars gives them distinctive analyses of race, class, and gender. She sees Black feminist scholars as best generating Black feminist theory, but also suggests that all intellectuals can learn to read their personal and cultural biographies as significant sources of knowledge. As "outsiders within," Black feminist scholars use the tension in their cultural identities to generate new ways of seeing and new sociological insights. Likewise, majority group scholars can develop and utilize tensions in their own cultural identities to enable them to see different aspects of minority group experiences and to examine critically majority experiences and beliefs.

This understanding recasts earlier arguments that only minority scholars can produce knowledge about racial-ethnic groups. It suggests that White scholars doing research on race and ethnicity should examine self-consciously the influence of institutional racism and the way it shapes the formulation and development of their research, rather than assume a color-blind stance. This is a fundamentally different posture from that advocated by the norms of "unbiased, objective" scien-

tific research, in which one typically denies the influence of one's own status (be it race, gender, class, or other social status) in the shaping of knowledge. It requires that we see ourselves as "situated in the action of our research" (Rapp, 1983), examining our own social location, not just that of those we study.

Elsewhere I have argued that White feminist scholars can transform their teaching and thinking through centering their thoughts in the experience of women of color (Andersen, 1988). Feminist scholarship has shown that moving previously excluded groups to the center of our research and teaching produces more representative accounts of society and culture. Building more inclusive ways of seeing requires scholars to take multiple views of their subjects, abandoning the idea that there is a singular reality that social science can discover. Minority group members have insights about and interpretations of their experiences that are likely different from those generated by White scholars. The question is not whether White scholars should write about or attempt to know the experience of people of color, but whether their interpretations should be taken to be the most authoritative (Hooks, 1989). Furthermore, how, in constructing sociological analyses, can dominant group members examine their own racial identities and challenge the societal system of racial stratification in which what they observe is situated?

THE SETTING

These issues are examined, here in the context of a community study of race relations. In this study, I (a White scholar) wanted to know how changes in the political economy of race relations were experienced by African Americans in this community. What meaning do African Americans in this community give to their experience? And how do they define the class, race system in which they live? I studied a small community with a historically rigid racial division of labor and a history of paternalism persistently defining contemporary relations between Whites and Blacks—hardly a social structure conducive to the trust and empathy desirable for building a sociological research project. I entered this project knowing the particular limitations that my own racial status would create.

The community is located on the Eastern Shore of Maryland—a peninsula on the eastern shore of the Chesapeake Bay. The community appears prosperous and alluring and in many ways seems to be an ideal American town. There is a central village green. Church spires are the highest points in the city skyscape, and the main street is dotted with chic boutiques. Those who walk on the streets seem to know each other; they stop to chat and, in their conversations, they inquire about each other's families and exchange news about others in town.

Because this is a waterfront community, it can also be approached by boat. On the shore, one sees expensive waterfront estates—so many of them that one might wonder how so many people became so rich. Many of these estates are invisible from land; from the bay, their long docks can be seen—many with multiple yacht slips. Sailboats fill the rivers and coves surrounding this town, and motor yachts twice the size of the average American home (and full of more than the usual amenities) are common. One of these yachts displays a flag at the bow: "He who dies with the most toys wins!"

Yet there is a dual reality here—one hidden in small, all-Black hamlets that do not, in many cases, even appear on the road maps and that do not front the bay waters, as do the privileged acres of the rich. The dual reality is perhaps no better described than by Frederick Douglass, himself a slave 150 years ago on the estate of Edward Lloyd, the Eastern Shore's largest slaveholder. The sailing ships that contemporary visitors today covet and admire were, to Douglass, symbols of the oppression of Black people. Standing on the shores of the Chesapeake, he wrote, "Those beautiful vessels, robed in white and so delightful to the eyes of freemen, were to me so many shrouded ghosts to terrify and torment me with thoughts of my wretched condition" (Douglass, 1962, p. 125).

Sociological descriptions of the county in which the Eastern Shore lies reveal great inequality in the experiences of Whites and Blacks living here. Slightly more than one-third of Black persons live below the poverty line, compared with less than 5% of White families.[1] (Nationally, 16.1% of Black families in the same year lived in poverty.) Median income for White families here in 1980 was approximately $21,000; for Black families, it was less than $7,500—only 35% of White family income. (Nationally, Black family income in 1980 was 60.2% of White family income.) Inequality between Whites and Blacks in this county is further demonstrated by the skewed character of income distribution. Nearly 40% of Black households in this county have incomes less than $5,000 per year (nationally, this figure is 2.5%), compared with less than 13% for White households. No Black households in this county have incomes higher than $35,000, and only 2% have incomes between $25,000 and $35,000, compared with one-fourth of White households.

The persistence of such striking inequality on the Eastern Shore, with its historical past based on a plantation economy, makes it a region rich for sociological study. Less than 100 miles from Philadelphia, Baltimore, and Washington, D.C., the region seems like an anachronism in that the yachts, fashionable shops, and luxury automobiles are clearly symbolic of contemporary class relations, but the juxtaposition of rurally segregated Black communities and paternalistic relations between Whites and Blacks evokes a strong feeling that the past is still present. The Eastern Shore remains predominantly rural, agricultural, and geographically isolated. It is here that slavery originated in the United States, although slavery is more typically associated with states further south. Until 1790, two-thirds of the slave population lived around the Chesapeake Bay, where tobacco and wheat crops dominated production. In 1660, Maryland was the first state to enact laws defining slavery as a legitimate institution. Now, former plantations are owned by elites and, in some cases, multinational corporations. Patterns of residential segregation are characteristic of the living arrangements between Whites and Blacks.

Two questions framed my research on the Eastern Shore: What has been the experience of African Americans in this community? and What are their understandings of how race relations have changed in their lifetimes? Pursuing the answers to these questions demanded data different from those that could be gathered through secondary sources. My questions were both historical and qualitative, each involving different methodological problems that ultimately will shape what is known from this study. The absence of firsthand accounts reflecting on and describing African American experience in this community limits sociological understanding of the development and persistence of racism. The methodological problems posed by the historical analysis are similar to those posed by contemporary qualitative research. Historians have been overly dependent on historical records left by members of the dominant group, usually elites. Other available historical documents are typically those left by philanthropists or government agencies, documents often characterized by images of Black Americans as pathological (Uya, 1981).

Although I used primary historical evidence from archival and personal documents to understand the historical experience of African Americans in this community, contemporary accounts of race relations through the eyes of Black Americans are rare. This is precisely the kind of information that the literature suggests is most inaccessible to white researchers. Wondering whether I could reliably collect such information, I proceeded to do field research and to conduct extended interviews with low-income, elderly (mostly in their 80s) women, both Black and White, who had little formal schooling. As a White, middle-aged, middle-class researcher, I knew I was crossing not only racial boundaries but also those of class, age, and education. Because of the high degree of racial and class segregation in this community, these boundaries seemed potentially even more clearly marked. Ideally, I could

have hired Black interviewers to conduct these interviews, but without research funding, this was impossible.

INTERVIEWING ACROSS RACE AND CLASS

The subjects for this study were poor elderly women, both Black and White—women whose lives have perhaps been the most distorted by social scientific research. These are women whose experiences have been underrepresented, at best, in the social science literature. More typically, they are excluded and ignored in sociological studies, even though their lives provide a rich portrait of the fabric of social life and, especially, race, class, and gender relations. My interviews with these women reveal that the scientific framework of social science research actually obstructs the formation of relationships essential to achieving an understanding of these women's lives.

The interviews were designed to produce open-ended oral histories of the women's work and family histories and their perceptions of how relations between Whites and Blacks in their community had changed over the course of their lifetimes. Although qualitatively based, interviews are typically guided by the same principles of detachment and neutrality characteristic of quantitative research analyses. As Oakley (1981) has argued, conventional reports of interview data typically include the following information about the interviews: how many there were, how long they were, how they were recorded, and whether the questions followed a standard format. Researchers typically do not report the characteristics of interviewers, nor do they discuss interviewees' feelings about being interviewed, the quality of the interaction between the interviewer and interviewee, or the reception and hospitality extended to the interviewer. Routine methodological instructions tell interviewers to control the interview by directing their questions and the answers of those with whom they are speaking. This method of research procedure is, as Oakley argues, fundamentally hierarchical. It manipulates those being interviewed as objects of study and suggests that there should be minimal human contact and no emotional involvement between the research subject and the researcher. In fact, researchers are warned that the

> *interview is designed to minimize the local, concrete, immediate circumstances of the particular encounter, including the respective personalities of the participants.... As an encounter between these two particular people the typical interview has no meaning; it is conceived in a framework of other, comparable meanings, between other couples, each recorded in such fashion that elements of communication in common can be easily isolated from more idiosyncratic qualities. (Benney & Hughes, 1970, pp. 196–197; quoted in Oakley, 1981, p. 32)*

Oakley concludes that sociologists are routinely instructed to interview research subjects by manipulating them as objects of study. According to conventional methodology, the best data are those that are produced through minimal human contact and minimal interrelationship. Researchers are admonished not to get too emotionally involved with subjects. Such a method assumes the passivity of respondents and forces them to adapt to the situation as defined by the interviewer. Moreover, researchers are told never to inform interviewees of their own beliefs and values.

My research suggests that this conventional methodological approach is counter to that required for White scholars to produce more inclusive and less partial and distorted accounts of race, class, and gender relations. To begin with, it is impossible even to count the exact number of interviews in my project and to report the amount of time they took. Many of the women included in this research refused to be interviewed formally, but were willing to talk with me for hours. One woman asked that the tape recorder be turned off at various places in our conversation. With the tape recorder off, she spoke freely about information she thought should remain confidential, although it revealed important, yet sensitive, information about race and gender relationships in the

community. Another woman told me her long and intriguing life history and talked openly about class and race relations in the community, but refused to be taped. We sat in my car for most of an afternoon, in subfreezing winter temperatures. Other important information and ideas in this project came from many days and hours of informal discussion with these women at the local senior center. Thus the field research for the project and the actual interviews blur, with no exact number of interviews to be reported, but, nonetheless, with these conversations/interviews providing rich data about race and gender relations in this community.

As found in other work on race and ethnic relations, the women in this study were savvy to the potentially exploitive character of academic research. Many told stories about past researchers who had come to study them but who had not, in their eyes, done a very good job. They talked at length about what was wrong with the researchers' approaches, personalities, and attitudes. They scoffed at the presumption of many researchers that they could come to this community and learn about women's lives from a distance. The women also clearly understood that the research was more important to me than it was to them. They knew it would have little effect on them, and it would not change their lives. They made themselves helpers for my purposes, but did not let themselves be exploited. Moreover, within their accounts of previous research projects were clues about the grounds on which they would trust me—despite the clear differences between us.

Several talked at length about how my "personality" made them more trusting, open, and willing to speak with me. These comments made me think about what I was doing—consciously and unconsciously—to elicit their reported trust. Primarily, I did not pose myself as an expert in their lives. Quite the contrary, I introduced myself as someone who was interested in learning about them particularly because their lives were unreported and undervalued by teachers and scholars. Most responded by being honored that someone was going to "write a book about them." One woman reported talking with her daughter following the interview, saying how helpful it had been because now she and her family were talking about their racial histories. She said, "I really liked talking with you. You know it's helpful to us talking about our backlives. It helps you start to think about your backlife. You talk plain and understanding. It helps me think about my backlife."

Most of these women thought of themselves as "just ordinary." When they were reluctant to be interviewed, it was often because they did not understand why anyone would take an interest in them. Defining their experience as important to know and understand, especially in a context where their age, class, gender, and, in some cases, race left them undervalued, increased the cooperation and rapport I was able to generate with them. More important, for many, seeing their life as of interest to a "teacher" affirmed them and made them feel positively valued. Throughout the process of meeting and interviewing them, I was reminded of the humility with which I had to work. I could not assume the role of expert, and I needed to be willing to talk about my life as a woman and as a White person in my conversations with them. It was important that I did not think of them as victims of racial, sexual, and class oppression, but wanted to learn how they valued their own experience. I was actually aided by the fact that I had no research funding and was not representing an agency. Although in some ways the research suffered from my being unable to hire Black interviewers, it also was important to the women that the research was not sponsored by any organization. They particularly wanted assurance that I was not from the Social Security Administration—a key agency in their own feelings of economic dependence and frustration with bureaucracy.

As other field researchers have found, engaging myself in their world was critical to my research. I was an active volunteer in the senior center that these women regularly attended. Although it was difficult for me to contribute as much time as I did, given other demands on my time as a scholar-teacher, my participation in the center reassured the women of my commitment to them. During the interviews, many talked explicitly about the fact that I spent so many hours there and worked with them on their projects. I was careful to disengage from my role as a professional scholar-teacher while at the center, sharing in their activities, including senior exercises, music, and crafts.

My participation in the everyday activities of the women's culture, both in the center and in their homes, greatly facilitated this research. I threaded needles for those with failing eyesight, glued sequins on pipe-cleaner butterflies in preparation for an annual yard sale, delivered sandwiches during the yard sale, helped make Christmas ornaments and pottery, and discussed cooking, knitting, sewing, and crafts. Often, while doing these things, the women provided the most telling comments on their relationships with each other, their pasts, their feelings about their community, their families, and their work. During these times, I also learned how the women felt; their conversations were filled with emotion, humor, gossip, and play.

In sum, what seems to have made these interviews possible was my direct violation of the usual admonitions to social science researchers. During the interviews, I answered questions about myself, my background, my family, and my ideas. In the interviews and during the field research, the women and I exchanged our feelings and ideas about many of the subjects we were discussing. At times, I showed the emotion I felt during very moving moments in their accounts of their experiences.

Other feminist and qualitative research shows that emotion, the engagement of self, and the relationship between the knower and the known all guide research, just as they guide social action. For example, in her book *Street Woman,* on women's crime, Miller (1986) writes of being afraid, intimidated, and uncomfortable, and, as she learned more about the women's lives, angry and depressed. But she concludes, "For reasons I do not know, these emotions, as paralyzing as they could have been, were rather motivating forces with regard to the research" (p. 189). In my project, despite my trepidations about crossing class, race, and age lines, I was surprised by the openness and hospitality with which I was greeted, I am convinced that the sincerity of these women's stories emanated not only from their dignity and honor, but also from my willingness to express how I felt, to share my own race and gender experiences, and to deconstruct the role of expert as I proceeded through this research.

CONCLUSION

Some of the methodological practices that emerged in this research are common to more qualitative research methods. For example, qualitative researchers have typically noted the importance of rapport in establishing good research relations. But, as Reinharz (1983) has suggested, research is an act of self-discovery, as well as a process of learning about others. Self-examination of my own privilege as a White scholar facilitated this research project, allowing me to challenge the arrogance that the stance of White privilege creates. Although the structure of sociology as a profession discourages such engaged work, I am convinced that this self-reflective method of constructing knowledge is more compelling and reliable than standard, detached ways of knowing. I know that my understanding of these women's lives will always be partial, incomplete, and distorted. I also know that the Black women did not likely report the same things to me as they would have to a Black interviewer, but that does not make their accounts any less true. If the task of sociology is to understand the multiple intersections between social structure and biographies, then the many ways in which we see ourselves and our relationships to others should be part of sociological accounts.

Feminist scholars have argued that the reconstruction of knowledge from a feminist standpoint necessitates studying the world from the perspective of women (McIntosh, 1983, 1988). Because androcentric scholarship has imposed on sociological observations categories, concepts, and theories originating in the lives of men from dominant groups, we have created an incomplete and distorted knowledge of social life. Studying women on their own terms is more likely to engage the subjective self—that of both the actor and the researcher. Yet, when our research remains too tightly bound by the framework of scientific methodology, we miss much of the texture and nuance in social relationships.

Feminist discussions of research methodology have focused on discovering the social relationship between the knower and the known, arguing that the attempt at scientific neutrality obfuscates and denies this relationship (Harding, 1986). Contrary to the scientific image of the knower as a neutral and objective party, feminist epistemologists have argued that the relationship between the researcher and her subjects is a social relationship, and is bound by the same patterns of power relations found in other social relationships.

My study with the women of the Eastern Shore, as well as the above discussion, suggests that we should develop research practices that acknowledge and take as central the class, race, and gender relations in which researchers and research subjects are situated. At the same time, we should question assumptions that the knower is the ultimate authority on the lives of those whom she or he studies. We should not assume that White scholars are unable to generate research with people of color as research subjects, but we must be aware that to do so, White scholars must work in ways that acknowledge and challenge White privilege and question how such privilege may shape research experiences. Developing analyses that are inclusive of race, class, and gender also requires that discussions of race, class, and gender be thoroughly integrated into debates about research process and the analysis of data. This requires an acknowledgment of the complex, multiple, and contradictory identities and realities that shape our collective experience. As whites learn to see the world through the experiences of others, a process that is itself antithetical to the views of privileged groups, we can begin to construct more complete and less distorted ways of seeing the complex relations of race, class, and gender.

NOTES

1. Data are taken from 1980 U.S. Census materials. Because the respondents were promised anonymity, data are given in approximate terms so as not to disclose the exact identity of the town.

REFERENCES

Andersen, M. L. (1988). Moving our minds: Studying women of color and re-constructing sociology. *Teaching Sociology, 15,* 123–132.

Baca Zinn, M. (1979). Field research in minority communities: Ethical, methodological and political observations by an insider. *Social Problems, 27,* 209–219.

Blauner R., & Wellman, D. (1973). Toward the decolonization of social research. In J. Ladner (Ed.), *The death of white sociology.* New York: Vintage.

Cannon, L. W., Higginbotham, E., & Leung, M. A. (1988). Race and class bias in qualitative research on women. *Gender & Society, 2,* 449–662.

Collins, P. H. (1986). Learning from the outsider within: The sociological significance of Black feminist thought. *Social Problems, 33,* 14–32.

Douglass, F. (1962). *The life and times of Frederick Douglass.* New York: Collier.

Gwaltney, J. (1980). *Drylongso: A self-portrait of Black America.* New York: Random House.

Harding, S. (1986). *The science question in feminism.* Ithaca, NY: Cornell University Press.

Hartsock, N. (1983). The feminist standpoint: Developing the ground for a specifically feminist historical materialism. In S. Harding & M. Hintakka (Eds.), *Discovering reality. Feminist perspectives on epistemology, metaphysics, methodology, and philosophy of science* (pp. 283–310). Dordrecht, Netherlands: D. Reidel.

Ladner, J. A. (Ed.). (1973). *The death of white sociology.* New York: Random House.

Miller, E. (1986). *Street woman.* Philadelphia: Temple University Press.

McIntosh, P. (1983). *Interactive phases of curriculum revision* (Working Paper). Wellesley, MA: Wellesley College, Center for Research on Women.

Oakley, A. (1981). Interviewing women. In H. Roberts (Ed.), *Doing feminist research* (pp. 30–61). New York: Routledge & Kegan Paul.

Rapp, R. (1983). *Anthropology: The science of man?* Address presented at the University of Delaware.

Reinharz, S. (1983). Experiential analysis: A contribution to feminist research. In G. Bowles & R. R. Duelli-Klein (Ed.), *Theories of woman's studies* (pp. 162–191). New York: Routledge & Kegan Paul.

Smith, D. E. (1987). *The everyday world as problematic: A feminist sociology.* Boston: Northeastern University Press.

Uya, O. E. (1981). Using federal archives: Some problems in doing research. In R. L. Clark (Ed.), *Afro-American history sources for research* (pp. 19–29). Washington, DC: Howard University Press.

PART TWO

Bodies

Section 1   Embodiments of Control and Resistance

Section 2   Violence

The old Freudian dictum that "biology is destiny," that women's and men's different *social* positions and activities are simply reflections of *natural* differences between the sexes, is deeply grounded in our cultural assumptions. But this belief does not stand up to critical scrutiny. First, even when we acknowledge the fact that there are some average differences between women's and men's bodies (e.g., on average, men have a higher muscle-to-fat ratio than women do), average differences are not categorical differences (e.g., some women are more muscular than some men). Second, average bodily differences between women and men do not necessarily translate into particular social structures or practices. In fact, recent research in the sociology of the body shows a dynamic, reciprocal relationship between bodies and their social environments. For example, boys and men have been encouraged and rewarded for "building" muscular bodies, while girls and women have been discouraged or punished for this. Even among today's fitness-conscious young women, most feel that "too much muscle" is antithetical to attractiveness. These social beliefs and practices result in more muscular male bodies and "slimmed" or "toned" female bodies that, together, appear to reflect "natural" differences.

In short, average bodily differences between women and men are at least as much a *result* of social beliefs and practices as they are a cause. In fact, since the early 1970s, many feminists have pointed to patriarchal control over women's bodies (e.g., sexual control, rape, and other forms of violence; medical control of women's reproduction; the imposition of commercial fashions and narrow beauty standards; cultural beliefs about food; and an obsession with thinness) as a major locus of men's control over women. Many feminists argued that social inequalities were predicated on men's assertion of their own will through the objectification and exploitation of women's bodies. This is a powerful observation that informed a great deal of fruitful feminist organizing around issues like girls' and women's eating disorders, rape crisis centers, birth control centers, reproductive rights organizations, and women's shelters against domestic violence. But as the articles in the first section of Part One demonstrate, the view of women as disempowered body-objects and men as empowered body-subjects tends to overgeneralize about a more complex reality. Jane Sprague Zones critically analyzes the cosmetics industry's suppression of diversity among women, and the ways that narrow bodily standards of beauty sometimes result in negative health consequences. Nomy Lamm offers a powerfully personal statement of resistance to the culture of thinness. Lamm discusses how her youthful "punk grrrl" feminism has provided her with a means for resisting the narrow mainstream media constructions of female beauty and for making the revolutionary assertion that her fat body is beautiful. Some similar themes are explored in the article by Gerschick and Miller, whose analysis of physically disabled men reveals how a marginalized group of men relates to dominant conceptions of masculinity that stress physical strength and independence. Finally, Debbie Nathan takes the discussion of body politics to broader institutional and transnational contexts. Her description of abortion around the Texas–Mexico border reveals the dangers and risks associated with abortion when it is limited or outlawed by state or national law.

Men's violence against other men on the streets and in wars has historically been more visible than men's violence against women. Only very recently have we begun to understand the extent of men's violence against women and the more general implications of this violence for gender relations. The articles in the second section of this part explore several dimensions of the relationship between gender and violence. Jack Straton draws on recent studies to dispel the "myth of the battered husband," and Richie and Kanuha discuss the particular issues and barriers that battered women of color have faced in the public health care system. The article by Nancy Matthews discusses the crucial importance of expanding racial diversity in the antirape movement, and, finally, Michael Messner examines male athletes' violence against other men and its broader significance for gender relations.

8

Beauty Myths and Realities and Their Impact on Women's Health

JANE SPRAGUE ZONES

Of all the characteristics that distinguish one human being from the next, physical appearance has the most immediate impact. How a person looks shapes the kinds of responses she or he evokes in others. Physical appearance has similar effects on other social statuses. Those considered beautiful or handsome are more likely to accrue benefits such as attributions of goodness and better character, more desirability as friends and partners, and upward social mobility. Those considered unattractive receive less attention as infants, are evaluated more harshly in school, and earn less money as employees. The significance of physical appearance shifts in intensity as it interacts with other statuses, such as gender, race/ethnicity, age, class, and disability. For groups targeted for social mistreatment, such as women and racial or ethnic minorities, physical appearance has profound implications not only for the creation of first impressions but also for enduring influence on social effectiveness. The power of appearance pushes people to assimilate in order to avoid unwanted attention or to attract desired attention. The pushes and pulls to look "conventionally attractive" constitute assaults on diversity.

In this chapter, I describe and evaluate some of the ways that social concerns with women's appearance affect physical and emotional health status and limit the range of perceived and actual possibilities open to individuals and to groups. My particular focus is on how physical appearance is perceived by and affects women of color, those in various social classes, and women who are older

or disabled. A review of research and literature that reflect women's personal experiences indicates that cultural preoccupation with how we look militates against the appreciation and expression of women's diversity.

I find two major bodies of research on this topic: the experimental social psychology and the body-image literatures. Much of what we know academically about appearance and its social effects is derived from experimental social psychology, mostly studies of the human face. This body of work generally neglects analyses of social status other than gender distinctions that affect interpersonal (usually romantic) attachment. This research, carried out mainly in university settings with primarily white undergraduate students, is paralleled by a smaller number of studies using other populations that yield comparable results. Global measures of physical attractiveness are employed, in which judges rate "stimulus persons" (either human confederates or photographic images of people with "normal" features) along a continuum ranging from very low to very high physical attractiveness (Patzer 1985). The body-image literature comes primarily from clinical psychology and feminist theory. Body-image scholars (Iazzetto 1988) typically cite historical evidence and open-ended interviews with informants to support their arguments. This school is much more attentive than are the experimentalists to the interaction of social statuses and physical appearance and to social and political contexts generally. Both approaches contribute to understanding the real effects of physical appearance. This chapter interweaves these two strands to show commonalities and differences between women in an attempt to understand the power of appearance in women's lives.

COMMONALTIES IN PERCEPTION OF BEAUTY

Many women concur that personal beauty, or "looking good," is fostered from a very early age. It is probably true that the ways in which people assess physical beauty are not naturally determined but socially and culturally learned and therefore "in the eye of the beholder." However, we tend to discount the depth of our *common* perception of beauty, mistakenly assuming that individuals largely set their own standards. At any period in history, within a given geographic and cultural territory, there are relatively uniform and widely understood models of how women "should" look. Numerous studies over time reinforce this notion (Iliffe 1960; Patzer 1985; Perrett, May, and Yoshikawa 1994).

Although there have always been beauty ideals for women (Banner 1983), in modern times the proliferation of media portrayals of feminine beauty in magazines, billboards, movies, and television has both hastened and more broadly disseminated the communication of detailed expectations. There are increasingly demanding criteria for female beauty in western culture, and women are strongly pressured to alter their appearance to conform with these standards.

Naomi Wolf, in her book *The Beauty Myth* (1991), contends that the effect of widespread promulgation of womanly ideals of appearance perpetuates the myth that the "quality called 'beauty' objectively and universally exists. Women must want to embody it and men must want to possess women who embody it. This embodiment is an imperative for women and not for men, which situation is necessary and natural because it is biological, sexual, and evolutionary" (12). Wolf declares that this is all falsehood. Instead, beauty is politically and economically determined, and the myth is the "last, best belief system that keeps male dominance intact" (12). She argues that as women have emerged successfully in many new arenas, the focus on and demand for beauty has become more intense, attacking the private sense of self and creating new barriers to accomplishment. In Wolf's view, the increasing obsession with beauty is a backlash to women's liberation.

BEAUTY'S SOCIAL SIGNIFICANCE FOR INDIVIDUALS

Much of the evidence from studies done by experimental social psychologists shows why people assign such importance to their appearance. They have found that people judged to be physically attractive, both male and female, are assumed to possess more socially desirable personality traits and expected to lead happier lives (Dion, Berscheid, and Walster 1972). Social science research shows that "cute babies are cuddled more than homely ones; attractive toddlers are punished less often. Teachers give special attention to better-looking pupils, strangers offer help more readily to attractive people, and jurors show more sympathy to good-looking victims" (Freedman 1986:7–8). This principle holds in virtually every aspect of our lives from birth to death and across racial and ethnic groups (Patzer 1985:232–33). The effects of these myriad positive responses to and assumptions about people who are considered attractive have self-fulfilling aspects as well. The expectations of others strongly shape development, learning, and achievement: people thought to be attractive become more socially competent and accomplished (Goldman and Lewis 1977).

Appearance-based discrimination targets women more than men. Women's self-esteem and happiness are significantly associated with their physical appearance; no such relationship exists for men as a group (Allgood-Merten, Lewinsohn, and Hops 1990; Mathes and Kahn 1975). Women's access to upward mobility is also greatly affected by physical appearance, which is a major determinant of marriage to a higher status man. By contrast, potential partners evaluate men more for intelligence or accomplishment. The significance of beauty in negotiating beneficial marriages is particularly true for White working-class women (Elder 1969; Taylor and Glenn 1976; Udry 1977; Udry and Eckland 1984). Banner (1983), who has traced the shifting models of beauty and fashion over two hundred years of American history, concludes that although standards of beauty may have changed, and women have greatly improved their access to social institutions, many females continue to define themselves by physical appearance and their ability to attract a partner.

The preoccupation with appearance serves to control and contain women's ambitions and motivations to gain power in larger political contexts. To the degree that many females feel they must dedicate time, attention, and resources to maintaining and improving their looks, they neglect activities to improve social conditions for themselves or others. Conversely, as women become increasingly visible as powerful individuals in shaping events, their looks become targeted for irrelevant scrutiny and criticism in ways with which men in similar positions are not forced to contend (Freedman 1986; Wolf 1991). For example, Marcia Clark, the lead prosecutor in the O. J. Simpson trial, was the focus of unremitting media attention for her dress, hairstyle, demeanor, and private life.

The major difference between discrimination based on appearance and mistreatment based on gender, race, or other social attributes is that individuals are legally protected against the latter (Patzer 1985:11). In an eye-opening review of legal cases related to appearance and employment, Wolf documents the inconsistencies that characterize decisions to dismiss women on the basis of their looks. "Legally, women *don't* have a thing to wear" (1991:42). Requirements of looking both businesslike and feminine represent a moving target that invites failure. In *Hopkins v. Price-Waterhouse,* a woman who brought in more clients than any other employee was denied a partnership because, her employers claimed, she did not walk, talk, or dress in an adequately feminine manner nor did she wear makeup. In another court case, it was ruled "inappropriate for a supervisor" of women to dress "like a woman" (Wolf 1991:39). If one appears businesslike, one cannot be adequately feminine; if one appears feminine, one cannot adequately conduct business.

BEAUTY MYTHS AND THE EROSION OF SELF-WORTH

Perhaps the biggest toll the "beauty myth" takes is in terms of women's identity and self-esteem. Like members of other oppressed groups of which we may also be part, women internalize cultural stereotypes and expectations, perpetuating them by enforced acceptance and agreement. For women, this is intensified by the interaction of irrational social responses to physical appearance not only with gender but with other statuses as well—race, class, age, disability, and the like. Continuous questioning of the adequacy of one's looks drains attention from more worthwhile and confidence-building pursuits.

A number of years ago, novelist Alice Walker was invited to speak at her alma mater, Spelman College, the highly regarded historically Black women's college in Atlanta. She used the opportunity to describe her experience of feeling as if she had reached the extent of her capacities for accomplishment a few years prior. "I seemed to have reached a ceiling in my brain," Walker recalled. She realized that "in my physical self there remained one last barrier to my spiritual liberation, at least in the present phase. My hair." Walker recognized it was not the hair itself but her relationship with it that was the problem. Months of experimentation with different styles followed. From childhood, her hair had endured domination, suppression, and control at the hands of outsiders. "Eventually I knew *precisely* what my hair wanted:…to be left alone by anyone, including me, who did not love it as it was" (Walker 1988:52–53). With that realization, the ceiling at the top of Walker's brain lifted, and her mind and spirit could continue to grow. Many African American women have sought just such a liberation from their hair, and others have celebrated its possibilities (Mercer 1990).

Glassner argues that the dramatically increased attention to fitness, diet, and physical well-being in recent years has been accompanied by a plummeting of satisfaction with our bodies (1988:246). There seems to be little relationship between actual physical attractiveness (conformance to culturally valued standards determined by judges) and individual women's satisfaction with their own appearance (Murstein 1972). Both men and women are unrealistic about how others perceive their bodies, but men tend to assume that people think they look better and women tend to assume that they look worse than they actually are perceived (Fallon and Rozin 1985). A recent poll of United States residents (Cimons 1990) found that fewer than a third of adults were happy with their appearance. Women were twice as likely as men to consider themselves to be fat.

Nagging self-doubts about weight emanate from the difference between projected images of women, many of which depict severely undernourished bodies, and our everyday reality. Half of the readers of *Vogue* magazine wear size 14 or larger (Glassner 1988:12), tormenting themselves with images of models with size 6 or smaller figures in every issue. Female models are 9 percent taller and 16 percent thinner than average women. Even the majority of women runners who are in good physical condition and fall within the ranges of weight and body fat considered desirable describe themselves as overweight (Robinson 1983). Research consistently shows that women not only overestimate their own size (Penner, Thompson, and Coovert 1991; Thompson and Dolce 1989) but they expect men to prefer thinner women than is the actual case (Rozin and Fallon 1988).

Internalizing the oppressive messages and images from outside has the effect of making the situation seem intractable. In Alice Walker's case, the distress that she had internalized from the

ways in which people (or ads or media impressions) had communicated concern or distaste for her hair distracted her from her work, eroded her confidence, and slowed her progress. Competition between women is a prominent feature of internalized sexism, reflecting women's collusion with beauty expectations that are both limiting and unrealistically demanding. Women become each other's critics, keeping each other anxious and in line, thereby maintaining the status quo. In *Memoirs of an Ex-Prom Queen,* one of the enduring feminist novels of the 1970s, Alix Kates Shulman created a teenage protagonist so obsessed with and insecure about her looks that she realizes she actually is beautiful only after she learns that her closest friends hate her for it.

Internalized oppression causes additional harm by redirecting mistreatment from the dominant culture to other members of one's own group (Lipsky 1987). A transcript of a kitchen table conversation between two Black women illustrates how the preferential treatment of lighter-skinned slaves by their masters (who frequently fathered them) during the slavery era has produced continuing conflict among African Americans to the present day (Anderson and Ingram 1994). Tamara, a dark-skinned woman, recounts being ridiculed by family and neighbors as "ugly and black.... That's when I stopped liking black kids altogether. They hated me, and they made me hate my best friend [who was darker]. I remember everything about my childhood. It's like a diary.... I kept telling myself, 'There's got to be a way to get over this. One day this is going to stop.' But it never did. As I grew older, it just got worse.... To this day, I still find myself walking with my head down and trying to cover up my body" (358, 361). The preoccupation with skin color also had hurtful repercussions for Michele, a light-skinned Black woman. "Light-skinned blacks resent it when people say we are trying to be or act white.... On the other hand, society, both black and white, gives us these messages that we are 'better' than darker-skinned Blacks. It's sort of like we're in limbo"

(359). The acting out of internalized oppression between members of a group creates additional pressures to assimilate or avoid visibility, and it disrupts the unity essential for social progress.

QUANTIFYING BEAUTY: CONVENTIONALITY AND COMPUTER ENHANCEMENT

The predominant, nearly universal standard for beauty in American society is to be slender, young, upper-class, and white without noticeable physical imperfections or disabilities. To the extent that a woman's racial or ethnic heritage, class background, age, or other social and physical characteristics do not conform to this ideal, assaults on opportunities and esteem increase. Physical appearance is at the core of racism and most other social oppressions, because it is generally what is used to classify individuals.

Although expectations relative to appearance vary in style and interpretation, there are commonalities in their effects on women. Bordo (1993) makes a strong philosophical case for examining the multiplicity of interpretations of the body. She cautions, however, that we must at the same time recognize the significant leveling effect of "the everyday deployment of mass cultural representations.... First, the representations *homogenize.* In our culture, this means that they will smooth out all racial, ethnic, and sexual 'differences' that disturb Anglo-Saxon, heterosexual expectations and identifications.... Second, these homogenized images *normalize*—that is, they function as models against which the self continually measures, judges, 'disciplines,' and 'corrects' itself" (24–25).

In a number of studies, conventionality has been found to be the most important component of beauty (Webster and Driskell 1983). Judith Langlois and colleagues used a computer to blend likenesses of individuals into composites, mathematically averaging out their features. Undergraduate students judged composites of sixteen or thirty-two faces to be significantly more attractive than individual faces for both male and female images. Composites made from blending thirty-two faces were judged more attractive than those composed of only sixteen (Langlois et al. 1990, 1991). A similar study, using Japanese and Caucasian judges and subjects found that "aesthetic judgements of face shape are similar across different cultural backgrounds" (Perrett, May, and Yoshikawa 1994:239) and that the raters had the highest regard for a computerized caricature that exaggerated the ways that the fifteen most preferred faces differed from the average sixty.

This research is now being applied in the popular media. A computer-generated multiethnic supermodel cover face on a major women's magazine labeled "Who Is the Face of America?" accompanies a story lauding our "radically diversifying demographics" (Gaudoin 1994) when the image projected is one of convergence rather than diversity.

BEAUTY AND THE CHALLENGE OF SOCIAL DIVERSITY

Although significant beauty ideals appear to transcend cultural subgroup boundaries, appearance standards do vary by reference group. Clothing preferred by adolescents, for example, which experiences quick fashion turnover, is considered inappropriate for older people. Body piercing, a current style for young White people in urban areas of the United States, is repellant to most older adults and some ethnic minorities in the same age group. Religious and political ideologies are often identified through appearance. Islamic fundamentalist women wear clothing that covers body and face, an expression of religious sequestering; Amish women wear conservative clothing and distinctive caps; orthodox Jewish women wear wigs or cover their hair; African American women for many years wore natural hairdos to show racial pride; and Native American women may wear tribal jewelry and distinctive clothes that indicate their respect for heritage. In recent years, the disability rights movement has encouraged personal visibility to accompany the tearing down of barriers to access, resulting in a greater variety of appliances (including elegant streamlined wheelchairs) and functional clothing.

Although there are varying and conflicting standards of good looks and appropriate appearance that are held simultaneously by social subgroups, the dominant ideals prevail and are legitimated most thoroughly in popular culture. Webster and Driskell (1983) contend that physical appearance has effects similar to those of other social statuses such as gender, race, age, class, and so on, conferring superiority or inferiority in the social hierarchy. The implications of physical appearance gain in intensity when they are confounded with other statuses. Wendy Chapkis (1986) presents the perspectives of women from many groups—elderly, fat, Black, Asian, lesbian, disabled, and so on—who describe the injuries they have experienced as a result of their combined oppressions. To avoid social harassment and discrimination because of appearance, women frequently alter their looks to appear more conventional, an unwitting attack on diversity. Lisa Diane White, a leader in the Black Women's Health Project's self-help movement, addresses challenges involved in showing diversity. "With the recent upsurge of pride in our African heritage, we like to think that we as Black women feel better about ourselves today than our sisters did in the past.... But I think a lot of us are striving still for standards of beauty and acceptability that aren't our own, and we're suffering the pain inherent in this kind of quest" (quoted in Pinkney 1994:53).

One major way that dominant social forces have dealt with those who diverge is to remove these expressions from view—through ghettoization, anti-immigration policies, special education programs, retirement policies, and so on. The ultimate social insult is to render the oppressed invisible. Social barriers to visibility are expressed as well in pressures to avoid drawing attention to oneself. Those features that render us "different"

are frequently the objects of harassment or unwanted attention. We learn to appear invisible. In the following sections, the gender effects of appearance in combination with other social statuses are described through personal accounts and social research.

Race and Ethnicity

In recent years, there has been a burgeoning of women's literature that provides a rich context for the significance of appearance in women's lives. Analyzing Toni Morrison's *The Bluest Eye,* a novel about a poor black family, Lakoff and Scherr describe how the author shows "ugliness seeping through the skin, becoming conviction." The dominant culture's imposition of white standards of beauty presents an added and impossible burden for women of color. Lakoff and Scherr's interviews with women of color found that as children they grew up feeling ugly and knowing that there was nothing they could do about it. "For these women the American Dream of beauty was a perpetual reminder of what they were not, and could never be" (Lakoff and Scherr 1984:252).

An examination by Patricia Morton (1991) of scholarly portrayals of Black women in American history and social science during this century showed persistent "shaping and endorsement of a distinctive and profoundly disempowering, composite image of Black womanhood…as a natural and permanent slave woman" (ix). The introduction of the black liberation movement with its slogan "Black Is Beautiful" meant to many African American women a welcome contradiction to the assorted ways in which racism had imposed feelings of ugliness. The impossibility of ever achieving the dominant culture's ideal, or even coming close, was deeply daunting. But ethnic pride movements also bring about pressures of their own for their constituents to look a particular way, fulfill a particular ideal (Mercer 1990).

Among White Americans who identify with ethnic minority groups, appearance plays a similar role, sometimes with frightening intensity. A Holocaust survivor continues to dye her hair blonde into old age because it was her light hair color that allowed her to pass as a non-Jew and avoid the Nazi death camps as a young adult. Her current feeling of security, unrelated to actual safety, remains bound up in her ability to pass.

A study of physical features of faces in photographs of "Miss Universe" contestants, half of whom were White, the others Black or Asian, found that Black and Asian beauty pageant contestants possessed most of the patterns of features associated with attractiveness in the white entrants (Cunningham 1986). Even though contestants were selected by their own nations, and judges for the international contest were from the Japanese contest site, the researcher suggests that both western and nonwestern national representatives were selected because they approximated western standards of beauty.

A comparison of U.S. women with women and girls in nonwestern countries shows that American females have a poorer self-image and diet more (Rothblum 1990). A parallel finding from a study by Aune and Aune (1994) found that White American women and men paid more attention to their appearance than African Americans and that, of the three groups, Asian Americans were the least concerned about personal appearance. Western beauty ideals have permeated the "global village," but their psychological effects appear to be greatest at the source. The pursuit of beauty has provided more and more commodities to offer on the world market, and in this industry, the United States is on the surplus side of the trade balance.

Age

Youthful appearance is a major feature of the beauty standard. In American society, peoples' worries about aging center around economic need, disability, dependency, and death, all very significant and frightening issues. Consequently, visible signs of age on face and body often provoke dread. In *The Coming of Age* (1972:297), Simone de Beauvoir remarks that she has "never come across

one single woman, either in life or in books, who has looked upon her own old age cheerfully. In the same way, no one ever speaks of 'a beautiful old woman.'"

Experimental studies corroborate the association of youthful features with attractiveness. Johnson (1985) points out that it is perceived age, not actual age, that is the decisive factor, and he concludes from his research on White women and men that "maintaining or recapturing youthful vigor is an important determinant of judged attractiveness" (160). However, gender differences appear to be related to age. In further studies, female judges found photos of men maintained their level of attractiveness across groups of increasing age, whereas male judges found photos of older women less attractive than those of younger women (Mathes et al. 1985).

Although there are limits to what an individual can do to stave off the physical effects of aging over a lifetime, many products and services claim to prolong youth. Raising fears about aging is a major tool in marketing cosmetics, hair coloring, and cosmetic surgery. Mary Kay Ash, addressing women who sell her cosmetic line, stated that "very young girls with perfect complexions can possibly be naturally beautiful, but at about age 25, things begin to happen. And senility begins at 28" (Rubenstein 1984). Of course, fostering the notion that young adults should begin to consider themselves beset by physical deterioration greatly extends the market for Mary Kay's products.

Wolf (1991:14) argues that aging in women is considered ugly because women become more powerful with age. Stronger attacks are required upon personal worth to undermine the threat posed by accumulation of experience and influence as we grow older.

Disability

Erving Goffman's classic studies of stigma (1963) provided the underpinnings for much of the research on physical appearance. His work focused on the negative social consequences of visible disability and other attributes that are socially devalued. To the extent that individuals have visible physical differences, they are at greater jeopardy of being perceived as and viewing themselves as unattractive.

Alice Walker wrote of being blinded in one eye by a BB pellet at age eight. She changed overnight from being a confident, cute whiz in school to a withdrawn and scared child who did not raise her head. She faced the unwanted curiosity of others because of the noticeable white scar tissue on the eye. At night she pleaded with the eye to clear up. "I tell it I hate and despise it. I do not pray for sight. I pray for beauty" (Walker 1990:284). After the scar tissue's removal at age fourteen, Walker emerged with greater confidence, but the inner scars of self-doubt remained to be battled into adulthood.

A survey of college students with disabilities indicates that they view their visible disabilities as being the primary referent in interactions with others. One student summed it up: "I think the visual impact of a person sitting in a chair with wheels on it is so great as to render all other impressions, such as dress or grooming, virtually insignificant" (Kaiser, Freeman, and Wingate 1984:6). Nevertheless, the authors conclude that people with physical disabilities respond to the labeling process by managing aspects of their appearance over which they can exert some control. Much of the effort goes toward "normalizing" appearance, attempting to make the disability less obvious.

In *Autobiography of a Face,* Lucy Grealy describes the effects of disfiguring cancer surgery that removed much of her jaw at age nine. In adolescence her face constitutes her identity, not unlike other girls her age, but because of the disfigurement, to an even greater extreme: "By equating my face with ugliness, in believing that without it I would never experience the deep, bottomless grief I called ugliness, I separated myself even further from other people, who I thought never experienced grief this deep" (Grealy 1994:180).

Class

Class status has a complex relationship to physical appearance, shaping standards of beauty that may be expensive and dysfunctional and requiring adherence to standards for class membership and identity. Similarly, physical beauty has ramifications for class status: people judged to be physically attractive stay in school longer, get better jobs, and have higher incomes—the three primary components of socioeconomic status.

Devotion of energy to "improvement" of appearance sometimes has dysfunctional results. Sociologist Thorstein Veblen noted a century ago in *The Theory of the Leisure Class* that the major characteristic of envied clothing is that it is impractical for any kind of work. Little did he anticipate the popularity of Levi's 501 denim jeans for people of all classes in the 1990s.

To generate continued profits, the fashion industry promotes frequent and dramatic changes in style that require investment in new clothing and "looks." These fashions come from many sources: media and sports stars (expensive high-top shoes, for example), the ghetto (cornrows, baggy pants, do-rags), as well as Paris fashions (ready-to-wear copies) (Davis 1992). Considerable resources are expended by people of all income levels to give the appearance of currency and affluence.

One researcher reports that appearance is more significant for African American women who are better educated than for those with less education (Udry 1977). Michele, a professional, who identifies herself as light-skinned, describes her repugnance at assumptions she feels Black men often make about her because of her skin color: "They think I'm attractive, some kind of 'catch.'… For instance, I went out with this dude recently. Mr. Fiction Writer, Would-be Lawyer, whatever. We met at a cafe. No sooner had we sat down than he puts his arm out and says, 'Umm, I like that. It's not often I get to go out with a person around the same shade as I am.' I thought, 'Oh, my God, this man is colorstruck.' All he could talk about was color, color, color.... I was so offended. We are just obsessed with shade" (Anderson and Ingram 1994:360).

Color is also used to make insidious class distinctions among Latinos. Richard Rodriguez, a California-raised Chicano, would incur his mother's wrath when he let himself be darkened by the summer sun as a boy. "You know how important looks are in this country. With *los gringos* looks are all that they judge on. But you! Look at you! You're so careless!... You won't be satisfied till you end up looking like *los pobres* who work in the fields, *los braceros* [physical laborers]" (Rodriguez 1990:265).

THE COMMERCIAL IMPERATIVE IN THE QUEST FOR BEAUTY

Standards of beauty are continually evolving and proliferating, and as new standards develop, "bodies are expected to change as well" (Freedman 1986:6). Unlike race, gender, or age, attractiveness may be considered to some extent an "achieved" characteristic subject to change through individual intervention (Webster and Driskell 1983). As Wolf puts it, "The beauty myth is always actually prescribing *behavior* and not appearance" (1991:14; emphasis added). In her study of black and white Baltimore women of various ages, both working class and middle class, Emily Martin found a common theme in ways that women discussed their health, which she summarized as "your self is separate from your body" (1989:77). Participants in Martin's study saw the body as something that must be coped with or adjusted to.

To accommodate expectations for physical appearance, women are exhorted to invest large amounts of time, money, and physical and emotional energy into their physical being. "The closer women come to power, the more physical self-consciousness and sacrifice are asked of them. 'Beauty' becomes the condition for a woman to take the next step" (Wolf 1991:28). Geraldine Fer-

raro, who was the first female candidate for vice president of the United States nominated by a major political party, noted in her autobiography that there were more reports on what she wore than on what she said.

Although there are many compelling theories about how the cultural preoccupation with feminine appearance evolved, it is clear that at present it is held in place by a number of very profitable industries. The average person is exposed to several hundred to several thousand advertisements per day (Moog 1990). To pitch their products, advertisers create messages that cannot immediately be recognized as advertising, selling images in the course of selling products. Two-thirds of the models who appear in magazine ads are teenagers or young adults. Although we are now seeing greater diversity in models, older people, low-income people, and people with disabilities rarely show up in advertisements because they do not project the image that the product is meant to symbolize (Glassner 1988:37). In numerous ways, advertising attacks women's self-esteem so they will purchase products and services in order to hold off bad feelings (Barthel 1988).

Most women's magazines generate much of their revenue from advertisers, who openly manipulate the content of stories. Wolf (1991:81–85) documents incidents in which advertisers canceled accounts because of editorial decisions to print stories unsupportive of their products. *Ms.* magazine, for example, reportedly lost a major cosmetics account after it featured Soviet women on the cover who were not wearing makeup.

Americans spend an estimated $50 billion a year on diets, cosmetics, plastic surgery, health clubs, and related gadgets (Glassner 1988:13). A review of costs of common beauty treatments itemized in a 1982 newspaper story found that a woman of means could easily rack up the bulk of an annual salary to care for her physical appearance. This entailed frequent visits to the hair salon, exercise classes, regular manicures, a home skin-care program with occasional professional facials, a monthly pedicure, professional makeup session and supplies, a trip to a spa, hair removal from various parts of the body, and visits to a psychiatrist to maintain essential self-esteem (Steger 1982). The list did not include the expense of special dietary programs, cosmetic surgery or dentistry, home exercise equipment, or clothing.

As new standards of beauty expectations are created, physical appearance becomes increasingly significant, and as the expression of alternative looks are legitimized, new products are developed and existing enterprises capitalize on the trends. Liposuction, developed relatively recently, has become the most popular of the cosmetic surgery techniques. Synthetic fats have been developed, and there is now a cream claimed to reduce thigh measurements.

Weight Loss

Regardless of the actual size of their bodies, more than half of American females between ages ten and thirty are dieting, and one out of every six college women is struggling with anorexia and bulimia (Iazzetto 1992). The quest to lose weight is not limited to White, middle-class women. Iazzetto cites studies that find this pervasive concern in black women, Native American girls (75 percent trying to lose weight), and high school students (63 percent dieting). However, there may be differences among adolescent women in different groups as to how rigid their concepts of beauty are and how flexible they are regarding body image and dieting (Parker et al. 1995). Studies of primary school girls show more than half of all young girls and close to 80 percent of ten- and eleven-year-olds on diets because they consider themselves "too fat" (Greenwood 1990; Seid 1989). Analyses of the origins, symbolic meanings, and impact of our culture's obsession with thinness (Chernin 1981; Freedman 1989; Iazzetto 1988; Seid 1989) occupy much of the body-image literature.

Concern about weight and routine dieting are so pervasive in the United States that the weight-loss industry grosses more than $33 billion each year. Over 80 percent of those in diet programs are women. These programs keep growing even in the face of 90 to 95 percent failure rates in providing and maintaining significant weight loss. Congressional hearings in the early 1990s presented evidence of fraud and high failure rates in the weight-loss industry, as well as indications of severe health consequences for rapid weight loss (Iazzetto 1992). The Food and Drug Administration (FDA) has reviewed documents submitted by major weight-loss programs and found evidence of safety and efficacy to be insufficient and unscientific. An expert panel urged consumers to consider program effectiveness in choosing a weight-loss method but acknowledged lack of scientific data for making informed decisions (Brody 1992).

Fitness

Whereas in the nineteenth century some physicians recommended a sedentary lifestyle to preserve feminine beauty, in the past two decades of the twentieth century, interest in physical fitness has grown enormously. Nowhere is this change more apparent than in the gross receipts of some of the major fitness industries. In 1987, health clubs grossed $5 billion, exercise equipment $738 million (up from $5 million ten years earlier), diet foods $74 billion, and vitamin products $2.7 billion (Brand 1988). Glassner (1989) identifies several reasons for this surge of interest in fitness, including the aging of the "baby boom" cohort with its attendant desire to allay the effects of aging through exercise and diet, and the institution of "wellness" programs by corporations to reduce insurance, absentee, and inefficiency costs. A patina of health, well-toned but skinny robustness, has been folded into the dominant beauty ideal.

Clothing and Fashion

For most of us, first attempts to accomplish normative attractiveness included choosing clothing that enhanced our self-image. The oppressive effects of corsets, clothing that interfered with movement, tight shoes with high heels, and the like have been well documented (Banner 1983, 1988). Clothing represents the greatest monetary investment that women make in their appearance. Sales for *exercise* clothing alone in 1987 (including leotards, bodysuits, warm-up suits, sweats, and shoes) totaled $2.5 billion (Schefer 1988). To bolster sales, fashion leaders introduce new and different looks at regular intervals, impelling women to invest in what is currently in vogue. Occasionally the designers' new ideas are rejected wholesale, but this is generally a temporary setback. John Molloy's best-selling *Women's Dress for Success Book* (1977) attempted to resolve this problem for women by prescribing a skirted suit "uniform" that women could wear at work much like the standardized clothing that businessmen wear. He was able to demonstrate its utility in allowing women to project themselves as competent and effective in the workplace. Furthermore, to the extent that women who worked outside the home adopted this outfit, they would not become prey to the vagaries and expense of rapidly shifting fashion. The clothing industry orchestrated a wholesale attack on Molloy's strategy, labeling his uniform unfeminine, and another sensible strategy failed (Wolf 1991:43–45).

Cosmetics

The average person in North America uses more than twenty-five pounds of cosmetics, soaps, and toiletries each year (Decker 1983). The cosmetics industry produces over twenty thousand products containing thousands of chemicals, and it grosses over $20 billion annually (Becker 1991; Wolf 1991). Stock in cosmetics manufacturers has been rising 15 percent a year, in large part because of depressed petroleum prices. The oil derivative ethanol is the base for most products (Wolf 1991:82, 307). Profit margins for products are over 50 percent (McKnight 1989). Widespread false claims for cosmetics were virtually unchallenged for fifty years after the FDA became responsible for cosmetic industry oversight in 1938, and even now, the indus-

try remains largely unregulated (Kaplan 1994). Various manufacturers assert that their goods can "retard aging," "repair the skin," or "restructure the cell." "Graphic evidence" of "visible improvement" when applying a "barrier" against "eroding effects" provides a pastiche of some familiar advertising catchphrases (Wolf 1991:109–10).

The FDA has no authority to require cosmetics firms to register their existence, to release their formulas, to report adverse reactions, or to show evidence of safety and effectiveness before marketing their products (Gilhooley 1978; Kaplan 1994). Authorizing and funding the FDA to regulate the cosmetics industry would allow some means of protecting consumers from the use of dangerous products.

Cosmetic Surgery

In interviews with cosmetic surgeons and users of their services, Dull and West (1991) found that the line between reconstructive plastic surgery (repair of deformities caused congenitally or by injury or disease) and aesthetic surgery has begun to blur. Doctors and their patients are viewing unimpaired features as defective and the desire to "correct" them as intrinsic to women's nature, rather than as a cultural imperative.

Because of an oversupply of plastic surgeons, the profession has made efforts to expand existing markets through advertising and by appeals to women of color. Articles encouraging "enhancement of ethnic beauty" have begun to appear, but they focus on westernizing Asian eyelids and chiseling African American noses. As Bordo (1993:25) points out, this technology serves to promote commonality rather than diversity.

Plastic surgery has been moving strongly in the direction of making appearance a bona fide medical problem. This has been played out dramatically in recent times in the controversy regarding silicone breast implants, which provides plastic surgeons with a substantial amount of income. Used for thirty years in hundreds of thousands of women (80 percent for cosmetic augmentation), the effects of breast implants have only recently begun to be studied to determine their health consequences over long periods (Zones 1992). In a petition to the FDA in 1982 to circumvent regulation requiring proof of safety and effectiveness of the implants, the American Society of Plastic and Reconstructive Surgeons stated, "There is a common misconception that the enlargement of the female breast is not necessary for maintenance of health or treatment of disease. There is a substantial and enlarging body of medical information and opinion, however, to the effect that these *deformities* [small breasts] are really a disease which in most patients result in feelings of inadequacy...due to a lack of self-perceived femininity. The enlargement of the underdeveloped female breast is, therefore, often very necessary to insure an improved quality of life for the patient" (Porterfield 1982:4–5; emphasis added).

Cosmetic surgeon James Billie of Arkansas, who claims to have operated on over fifteen thousand beauty contestants in the past ten years, maintains that three-quarters of Miss USA pageant contestants have undergone plastic surgery (Garchik 1992). Cosmetic surgery generates over a third of a billion dollars per year for practitioners, some of whom offer overnight household financing for patients. The hefty interest rates are returned in part to the surgeons by the finance corporation (Krieger 1989). Although cosmetic surgery is the biggest commercial contender in the medical realm, prescription drugs are increasingly lucrative ventures (such as Retin-A to reduce wrinkling skin, and hormones to promote growth in short boys and retard it in tall girls).

HEALTH RISKS IN QUEST OF BEAUTY

Physicians and medical institutions have been quoted as associating beauty with health and ugliness with disease. Dr. Daniel Tostesen of Harvard Medical School, whose research is supported by Shiseido, an expensive cosmetics line, claims that there is a "'subtle and continuous gradation' between health and medical interests on the one

hand, and 'beauty and well-being on the other'" (Wolf 1991:227). The imperative to look attractive, while promising benefits in self-esteem, often entails both serious mental and physical health risks.

Mental Health

For most women, not adhering to narrow, standardized appearance expectations causes insecurity and distraction, but for many, concerns about appearance can have serious emotional impact. Up until adolescence, boys and girls experience about the same rates of depression, but at around age twelve, girls' rates of depression begin to increase more rapidly. A study of over eight hundred high school students found that a prime factor in this disparity is girls' preoccupation with appearance. In discussing the study, the authors concluded that "if adolescent girls felt as physically attractive, effective, and generally good about themselves as their male peers did, they would not experience so much depression" (Allgood-Merten, Lewinsohn, and Hops 1990:61). Another study of the impact of body image on onset and persistence of depression in adolescent girls found that whereas a relatively positive body image does not seem to offer substantial protection against the occurrence of depression, it does seem to decrease the likelihood that depression will be persistent (Rierdan and Koff 1991; Rierdan, Koff, and Stubbs 1989).

Physical Health

Perceived or actual variation from society's ideal takes a physical toll, too. High school and college-age females who were judged to be in the bottom half of their group in terms of attractiveness had significantly higher blood pressure than the young women in the top half. The relationship between appearance and blood pressure was not found for males in the same age group (Hansell, Sparacino, and Ronchi 1982).

Low bodyweight has been heavily promoted as a life-prolonging characteristic. There is evidence to support this contention, but the effect of advocating low weight in collusion with the heavy cultural prescription for a very slender look has led people into cycles of weight loss and regained weight that may act as an independent risk factor for cardiovascular disease (Bouchard 1991). A recent review of the medical literature on weight fluctuation concludes that the potential health benefits of moderate weight loss in obese people, however, is greater than the known risks of "yo-yo dieting" (National Task Force 1994). Women constitute 90 percent of people with anorexia, an eating disorder that can cause serious injury or death. The incidence of anorexia has grown dramatically since the mid-1970s, paralleling the social imperative of thinness (Bordo 1986).

There are direct risks related to using commodities to alter appearance. According to the Consumer Products Safety Commission, more than 200,000 people visit emergency rooms each year as a result of cosmetics-related health problems (Becker 1991). Clothing has its perils as well. In recent years, meralgia paresthetica, marked by sciatica, pain in the hip and thigh region, with tingling and itchy skin, has made an appearance among young women in the form of "skin-tight jean syndrome" (Gateless and Gilroy 1984). In earlier times, the same problems have arisen with the use of girdles, belts, and shoulder bags. The National Safety Council revealed that in 1989 over 100,000 people were injured by their clothing and another 44,000 by their jewelry (Seligson 1992). These figures greatly underestimate actual medical problems.

Approximately 33 to 50 percent of all adult women have used hair coloring agents. Evidence over the past twenty-five years has shown that chemicals used in manufacturing hair dyes cause cancers in animals (Center 1979). Scientists at the National Cancer Institute (NCI) recently reported a significantly greater risk of cancers of the lymph system and of a form of cancer affecting bone marrow, multiple myeloma, in women who use hair coloring (Zahm et al. 1992). In the last twenty years, the incidence of non-Hodgkin's lymphoma in the United States increased by more than 50 percent largely as a result of immune deficiency caused by HIV. However, the NCI researchers conclude that, assuming a causal relationship, hair coloring product use accounts for a larger percentage of non-Hodgkin's lymphoma among women than any other risk factor. These conclusions have been challenged, however, by more recent research (Fackelmann 1994).

Because no cosmetic products require follow-up research for safety and effectiveness, virtually anything can be placed on the market without regard to potential health effects. Even devices implanted in the body, which were not regulated before 1978, can remain on the market for years without appropriate testing. During the decade of controversy over regulating silicone breast implants, the American Society of Plastic and Reconstructive Surgeons vehemently denied any need for controlled studies of the implant in terms of long-term safety. The society spent hundreds of thousands of dollars of its members' money in a public relations effort to avoid the imposition of requirements for such research to the detriment of investing in the expensive scientific follow-up needed (Zones 1992). Although case reports indicate a potential relationship between the implants and connective tissue diseases, recent medical reports discount the association. Definitive research will take more time to assuage women's fears.

Health consequences of beauty products extend beyond their impact on individuals. According to the San Francisco Bay Area Air Quality Management District, aerosols release 25 tons of pollution every day. Almost half of that is from hairsprays. Although aerosols no longer use chlorofluorocarbons (CFCs), which are the greatest cause of depletion of the upper atmosphere ozone layer, aerosol hydrocarbons in hairsprays are a primary contributor to smog and ground pollution.

THE BEAUTY OF DIVERSITY

Both personal transformation and policy intervention will be necessary to allow women to present themselves freely. Governmental institutions, including courts and regulatory agencies, need to accord personal and product liability related to appearance products and services the attention they require to ensure public health and safety. The legal system must develop well-defined case law to assist the court in determining inequitable treatment based on appearance discrimination.

Short of complete liberation from limitations imposed by appearance expectations, women will continue to attempt to "improve" appearance to better social relations. Ultimately, however, this is a futile struggle because of the depth and intensity of feelings and assumptions that have become attached to physical appearance. The predominant advice given to women in the body-image literature is to seek therapeutic assistance to transform damaged self-image into a more positive perspective on oneself. Brown (1985) recommends a social context in which such transformation can take place, as does Schwichtenberg (1989), who suggests that, failing women's unified rejection of costly and potentially dangerous beauty products and processes, women should band together into support networks. Lesbian communities have led the way, showing how mutual support can diminish the effects of the dominant society on women. By using supportive relationships as an arena to experiment with physical presence, women create a manageable and enjoyable social situation. The Black Women's Health Project has successfully modeled the formation of local support groups to encourage members to lead healthier lives. Having a small group as referents reduces the power of commercial interests to define beauty standards. Overweight women have created such resources in the form of national alliances (such as the National Association to Advance Fat Acceptance), magazines (such as *Radiance*), and regional support systems (Iazzetto 1992).

The personal solution to individual self-doubt or even self-loathing of our physical being is to continuously make the decision to contradict the innumerable messages we are given that we are anything less than lovely as human beings. Pinkney (1994) suggests several ways to reshape "a raggedy body image" by improving self-perception: respect yourself, search for the source of the distress, strut your strengths, and embrace the aging process. In a passage from *Beloved,* Toni Morrison demonstrates the way: "Love your hands! Love them. Raise them up and kiss them. Touch others with them, pat them together, stroke them on your face 'cause they don't love that either. *You* got to love it, *you!*" (1994:362).

REFERENCES

Allgood-Merten, Betty, Peter M. Lewinsohn, and Hyman Hops. (1990). "Sex differences and adolescent depression." *Journal of Abnormal Psychology* 99:55–63.

Anderson, Michele, and Tamara Ingram. (1994). "Color, color, color." Pp. 356–61 in Evelyn C. White (ed.), *The Black Women's Health Book,* rev. ed. Seattle: Seal Press.

Aune, R. Kelly, and Krystyna S. Aune. (1994). "The influence of culture, gender and relational status on appearance management." *Journal of Cross-Cultural Psychology* 25(2):258–72.

Banner, Lois W. (1983). *American Beauty.* Chicago: University of Chicago Press.

Barthel, Diane. (1988). *Putting on Appearances: Gender and Advertising.* Philadelphia: Temple University Press.

Beauvoir, Simone de. (1972). *The Coming of Age.* New York: Putnam.

Becker, Hilton. (1991). "Cosmetics: Saving face at what price? *Annals of Plastic Surgery* 26:171–73.

Bordo, Susan. (1986). "Anorexia nervosa: Psychopathology as the crystallization of culture." *Philosophical Forum* 17:73–104.

———. (1993). *Unbearable Weight: Feminism, Western Culture and the Body.* Berkeley: University of California Press.

Bouchard, Claude. (1991). "Is weight fluctuation a risk factor?" *New England Journal of Medicine* 324:1887–89.

Brand, David. (1988). "A nation of health worrywarts?" *Time,* 25 July, 66.

Brody, Jane E. (1992). "Panel criticizes weight-loss programs." *New York Times,* 2 April, A10.

Brown, Laura S. (1985). "Women, weight, and power: Feminist theoretical and therapeutic issues." *Women and Therapy* 4:61–71.

Chapkis, Wendy. (1986). *Beauty Secrets: Women and the Politics of Appearance.* Boston: South End Press.

Chernin, Kim. (1981). *The Obsession: Reflections on the Tyranny of Slenderness.* New York: Harper Colophon Books.

Cimons, Marlene. (1990). "Most Americans dislike their looks, poll finds." *Los Angeles Times,* 19 August, A4.

Cunningham, Michael R. (1986). "Measuring the physical in physical attractiveness: Quasi-experiments on the sociobiology of female facial beauty." *Journal of Personality and Social Psychology* 50: 925–35.

Davis, Fred. (1992). *Fashion, Culture and Identity.* Chicago: University of Chicago Press.

Decker, Ruth. (1983). "The not-so-pretty risks of cosmetics." *Medical Self-Care* (Summer):25–31.

Dion, Karen, Ellen Berscheid, and Elaine Waister. (1972). "What is beautiful is good." *Journal of Personality and Social Psychology* 24:285–90.

Dull, Diana, and Candace West. (1991). "Accounting for cosmetic surgery: the accomplishment of gender." *Social Problems* 38:54–70.

Elder, Glen H., Jr. (1969). "Appearance and education in marriage mobility." *American Sociological Review* 34:519–33.

Fackelmann, K. A. (1994). "Mixed news on hair dyes and cancer risk." *Science News* 145 (5 Feb.):86.

Fallon, April E., and Paul Rozin. (1985). "Sex differences in perceptions of desirable body shape." *Journal of Abnormal Psychology* 94:102–5.

Freedman, Rita. (1986). *Beauty Bound.* Lexington, MA: Lexington Books.

———. (1989). *Bodylove.* New York: Harper and Row.

Garchik, Leah. (1992). "Knife tricks come to the rescue." *San Francisco Chronicle,* 1 September, C5.

Gateless, Doreen, and John Gilroy. (1984). "Tight-jeans meralgia: Hot or cold?" *Journal of the American Medical Association* 252:42–43.

Gaudoin, Tina. (1994). "Is all-American beauty un-American?" *Mirabella* (Sept.):144–46.

Gilhooley, Margaret. (1978). "Federal regulation of cosmetics: An overview." *Food Drug Cosmetic Law Journal* 33:231–38.

Glassner, Barry. (1988). *Bodies: Why We Look the Way We Do (and How We Feel about It).* New York: Putnam.

———. (1989). "Fitness and the postmodern self." *Journal of Health and Social Behavior* 30:180–91.

Goffman, Erving. (1963). *Stigma: Notes on the Management of Spoiled Identity.* Englewood Cliffs, NJ: Prentice-Hall.

Goldman, William, and Philip Lewis. (1977). "Beautiful is good: Evidence that the physically attractive are more socially skillful." *Journal of Experimental and Social Psychology* 13:125–30.

Grealy, Lucy. (1994). *Autobiography of a Face.* Boston: Houghton Mifflin.

Greenwood, M. R. C. (1990). "The feminine ideal: A new perspective." *UC Davis Magazine* (July):8–11.

Hansell, Stephen, J. Sparacino, and D. Ronchi. (1982). "Physical attractiveness and blood pressure: Sex and age differences." *Personality and Social Psychology Bulletin* 8:113–21.

Iazzetto, Demetria. (1988). "Women and body image: Reflections in the fun house mirror." Pp. 34–53 in Carol J. Leppa and Connie Miller (eds.), *Women's Health Perspectives: An Annual Review.* Volcano, CA: Volcano Press.

———. (1992). "What's happening with women and body image?" *National Women's Health Network News*:1, 6, 7.

Iliffe, A. H. (1960). "A study of preferences in feminine beauty." *British Journal of Psychology* 51:267–73.

Johnson, Douglas F. (1985). "Appearance and the elderly." Pp. 152–60 in Jean Ann Graham and Albert M. Kligman (eds.), *The Psychology of Cosmetic Treatments.* New York: Praeger.

Kaiser, Susan B., Carla Freeman, and Stacy B. Wingate. (1984). "Stigmata and negotiated outcomes: The management of appearance by persons with physical disabilities." Annual meeting of the American Sociological Association, San Antonio, TX.

Kaplan, Sheila. (1994). "The ugly face of the cosmetics lobby." *Ms.* (Jan.–Feb.):88–89.

Krieger, Lisa M. (1989). "Fix your nose now, pay later." *San Francisco Examiner,* 30 October, 1.

Lakoff, Robin Tolmach, and Raquel L. Scherr. (1984). *Face Value: The Politics of Beauty.* Boston: Routledge and Kegan Paul.

Langlois, Judith H., Lori A. Roggman, and Loretta A. Rieser-Danner. (1990). "Infants' differential social responses to attractive and unattractive faces." *Developmental Psychology* 26:153–59.

Langlois, Judith H., Jean M. Ritter, Lori A. Roggman, and Lesley S. Vaughn. (1991). "Facial diversity and infant preferences for attractive faces." *Developmental Psychology* 27:79–84.

Lipsky, Suzanne. (1987). *Internalized Racism.* Seattle: Rational Island.

Martin, Emily. (1989). *The Woman in the Body: A Cultural Analysis of Reproduction.* Boston: Beacon Press.

Mathes, Eugene W., and Arnold Kahn. (1975). "Physical attractiveness, happiness, neuroticism, and self-esteem." *Journal of Psychology* 90:27–30.

Mathes, Eugene W., Susan M. Brennan, Patricia M. Haugen, and Holly B. Rice. (1985). "Ratings of physical attractiveness as a function of age." *Journal of Social Psychology* 125:157–68.

McKnight, Gerald. (1989). *The Skin Game: The International Beauty Business Brutally Exposed.* London: Sidgwick and Jackson.

Mercer, Kobena. (1990). "Black hair/style politics." Pp. 247–64 in Russell Ferguson, Martha Gever, Trinh T. Minh-ha, and Cornel West (eds.), *Out There: Marginalization and Contemporary Cultures.* Cambridge: MIT Press.

Molloy, John T. (1977). *The Woman's Dress for Success Book.* New York: Warner Books.

Moog, Carol. (1990). *Are They Selling Her Lips? Advertising and Identity.* New York: William Morrow.

Morrison, Toni. (1994). "We flesh." P. 362 in Evelyn C. White (ed.), *The Black Women's Health Book,* rev. ed. Seattle: Seal Press.

Morton, Patricia. (1991). *Disfigured Images: The Historical Assault on Afro-American Women.* New York: Praeger.

Murstein, Bernard I. (1972). "Physical attractiveness and marital choice." *Journal of Personality and Social Psychology* 22:8–12.

National Task Force on the Prevention and Treatment of Obesity. (1994). "Weight cycling." *Journal of the American Medical Association* 272(15): 1196–1202.

Parker, Sheila, Mimi Nichter, Mark Nichter, Nancy Vuckovic, Colette Sims, and Cheryl Ritenbaugh. (1995). "Body image and weight concerns among African American and white adolescent females: Differences that make a difference." *Human Organization* 54(2):103–13.

Patzer, Gordon L. (1985). *The Physical Attractiveness Phenomena.* New York: Plenum Press.

Penner, Louis A., J. Kevin Thompson, and Dale L. Coovert. (1991). "Size overestimation among anorexics: Much ado about very little?" *Journal of Abnormal Psychology* 100:90–93.

Perrett, D. I., K. A. May, and S. Yoshikawa. (1994). "Facial shape and judgments of female attractiveness." *Nature* 368:239–42.

Pinkney, Deborah Shelton. (1994). "Body check." *Heart and Soul* (Summer):50–55.

Porterfield, H. William. (1982). *Comments of the American Society of Plastic and Reconstructive Surgeons on the Proposed Classification of Inflatable Breast Prosthesis and Silicone Gel-Filled Breast Prosthesis,* submitted to the Food and Drug Administration. Washington, 1 July.

Rierdan, Jill, and Elissa Koff. (1991). "Depressive symptomatology among very early maturing girls." *Journal of Youth and Adolescence* 20: 415–515.

Rierdan, Jill, Elissa Koff, and Margaret L. Stubbs. (1989). "Timing of menarche, preparation, and initial menstrual experience: replication and further analyses in a prospective study." *Journal of Youth and Adolescence* 18:413–26.

Robinson, Jennifer. (1983). "Body image in women over forty." *Melpomene Institute Bulletin* 2:12–14.

Rodriguez, Richard. (1990). "Complexion." Pp. 265–78 in Russell Ferguson, Martha Gever, Trinh T. Minh-ha, and Cornel West (eds.), *Out There: Marginalization and Contemporary Cultures.* Cambridge: MIT Press.

Rothblum, Esther. (1990). "Women and weight: Fad and fiction." *Journal of Psychology* 124:5–24.

Rozin, Paul, and April E. Fallon. (1988). "Body image, attitudes to weight, and misperceptions of figure preferences of the opposite sex: A comparison of men and women in two generations." *Journal of Abnormal Psychology* 97:342–45.

Rubenstein, Steve. (1984). "Cosmetic queen tells her women to think pink." *San Francisco Chronicle,* 3 February, 5.

Schefer, Dorothy. (1988). "Beauty: The real cost of looking good." *Vogue* (Nov.):157–68.

Schwichtenberg, Cathy. (1989). "The 'mother lode' of feminist research: Congruent paradigms in the analysis of beauty culture." Pp. 291–306 in Brenda Dervin, Lawrence Grossberg, Barbara J. O'Keefe, and Ellen Wartella (eds.), *Rethinking Communication.* Newbury Park, CA: Sage.

Seid, Roberta Pollack. (1989). *Never Too Thin: Why Women Are at War with Their Bodies.* New York: Prentice Hall.

Seligson, Susan. (1992). "The attack bra and other vicious clothes." *San Francisco Chronicle,* 13 January, D3–D4.

Shulman, Alix Kates. (1972). *Memoirs of an Ex-Prom Queen.* New York: Bantam Books.

Steger, Pat. (1982). "The making of a BP: How to diet, polish and pay your way to well-groomed perfection." *San Francisco Chronicle,* 3 August, 15.

Taylor, Patricia Ann, and Norval D. Glenn. (1976). "The utility of education and attractiveness for females' status attainment through marriage." *American Sociological Review* 41:484–98.

Thompson, J. Kevin, and Jefferey J. Dolce. (1989). "The discrepancy between emotional vs. rational estimates of body size, actual size, and ideal body ratings: Theoretical and clinical implications." *Journal of Clinical Psychology* 45:473–78.

Udry, J. Richard. (1977). "The importance of being beautiful: a reexamination and racial comparison." *American Journal of Sociology* 83:154–60.

Udry, J. Richard, and Bruce K. Eckland. (1984). "Benefits of being attractive: Differential payoffs for men and women." *Psychological Reports* 54:47–56.

Veblen, Thorstein. [1899] (1973). *The Theory of the Leisure Class.* Boston: Houghton Mifflin.

Walker, Alice. (1988). "Oppressed hair puts a ceiling on the brain." *Ms.* 16(6):52–53.

———. (1990). "Beauty: When the other dancer is the self." Pp. 280–87 in Evelyn C. White (ed.), *The Black Women's Health Book.* Seattle: Seal Press.

Webster, Murray, Jr., and James E. Driskell Jr. (1983). "Beauty as status." *American Journal of Sociology* 89:140–65.

Wolf, Naomi. (1991). *The Beauty Myth: How Images of Beauty Are Used against Women.* New York: William Morrow.

Zahm, Sheila Hoar, Dennis D. Weisenburger, Paula A. Babbitt, et al. (1992). "Use of hair coloring products and the risk of lymphoma, multiple myeloma, and chronic lymphocytic leukemia." *American Journal of Public Health* 82:990–97.

Zones, Jane Sprague. (1992). "The political and social context of silicone breast implant use in the United States." *Journal of Long-Term Effects of Medical Implants* 1:225–41.

9

It's a Big Fat Revolution

NOMY LAMM

I am going to write an essay describing my experiences with fat oppression and the ways in which feminism and punk have affected my work. It will be clear, concise and well thought-out, and will be laid out in the basic thesis paper, college essay format. I will deal with these issues in a mature and intellectual manner. I will cash in on as many fifty-cent words as possible.

I lied. (You probably already picked up on that, huh?) I can't do that. This is my life, and my words are the most effective tool I have for challenging Whiteboyworld (that's my punk-rock cutesy but oh-so-revolutionary way of saying "patriarchy"). If there's one thing that feminism has taught me, it's that the revolution is gonna be on my terms. The revolution will be incited through my voice, my words, not the words of the universe of male intellect that already exists. And I know that a hell of a lot of what I say is totally contradictory. My contradictions can coexist, cuz they exist inside of me, and I'm not gonna simplify them so that they fit into the linear, analytical pattern that I know they're supposed to. I think it's important to recognize that all this stuff does contribute to the revolution, for real. The fact that I write like this cuz it's the way I want to write makes this world just that much safer for me.

I wanna explain what I mean when I say "the revolution," but I'm not sure whether I'll be able to. Cuz at the same time that I'm being totally serious, I also see my use of the term as a mockery of itself. Part of the reason for this is that I'm fully aware that I still fit into dominant culture in many ways. The revolution could very well be enacted against me, instead of for me. I don't want to make myself sound like I think I'm the most oppressed, most punk-rock, most revolutionary person in the world. But at the same time I do think that revolution is a word I should use as often as I can, because it's a concept that we need to be aware of. And I don't just mean it in an abstract, intellectualized way, either. I really do think that the revolution has begun. Maybe that's not apparent to mainstream culture yet, but I see that as a good sign. As soon as mainstream culture picks up on it, they'll try to co-opt it.

For now the revolution takes place when I stay up all night talking with my best friends about feminism and marginalization and privilege and oppression and power and sex and money and real-life rebellion. For now the revolution takes place when I watch a girl stand up in front of a crowd of people and talk about her sexual abuse. For now the revolution takes place when I get a letter from a girl I've never met who says that the zine I wrote changed her life. For now the revolution takes place when the homeless people in my town camp out for a week in the middle of downtown. For now the revolution takes place when I am confronted by a friend about something racist that I have said. For now the revolution takes place in my head when I know how fucking brilliant my girlfriends and I are.

And I'm living the revolution through my memories and through my pain and through my triumphs. When I think about all the marks I have against me in this society, I am amazed that I haven't turned into some worthless lump of shit. Fatkikecripplecuntqueer. In a nutshell. But then I have to take into account the fact that I'm an articulate, white, middle-class college kid, and that provides me with a hell of a lot of privilege and opportunity for dealing with my oppression that may not be available to other oppressed people. And since my personality/being isn't divided up into a privileged part and an oppressed part, I have to deal with the ways that these things interact, counterbalance and sometimes even overshadow each other. For example, I was born with one leg. I guess it's a big deal, but it's never worked into my body image in the same way that being fat has. And what does it mean to be a white woman as opposed to a woman of color? A middle-class fat girl as opposed to a poor fat girl? What does it mean to be fat, physically disabled and bisexual? (Or fat, disabled and *sexual at all*?)

See, of course, I'm still a real person, and I don't always feel up to playing the role of the revolutionary. Sometimes it's hard enough for me to just get out of bed in the morning. Sometimes it's hard enough to just talk to people at all, without having to deal with the political nuances of everything that comes out of their mouths. Despite the fact that I do tons of work that deals with fat oppression, and that I've been working so so hard on my own body image, there are times when I really hate my body and don't want to deal with being strong all the time. Because I am strong and have thought all of this through in so many different ways, and I do have naturally high self-esteem, I've come to a place where I can honestly say that I love my body and I'm happy with being fat. But occasionally, when I look in the mirror and I see this body that is so different from my friends', so different from what I'm told it should be, I just want to hide away and not deal with it anymore. At these times it doesn't seem fair to me that I have to always be fighting to be happy. Would it be easier for me to just give in and go on another diet so that I can stop this perpetual struggle? Then I could still support the fat grrrl revolution without having it affect me personally in every

way. And I know I know I know that's not the answer and I could never do that to myself, but I can't say that the thought never crosses my mind.

And it doesn't help much when my friends and family, who all know how I feel about this, continue to make anti-fat statements and bitch about how fat they feel and mention new diets they've heard about and are just dying to try. "I'm shaped like a watermelon." "Wow, I'm so happy, I now wear a size seven instead of a size nine." "I like this mirror because it makes me look thinner."

I can't understand how they could still think these things when I'm constantly talking about these issues, and I can't believe that they would think that these are okay things to talk about in front of me. And it's not like I want them to censor their conversation around me.... I just want them to not think it. I know that most of this is just a reflection of how they feel about themselves and isn't intended as an attack on me or an invalidation of my work, but it makes it that much harder for me. It puts all those thoughts inside me. Today I was standing outside of work and I caught a glimpse of myself in the window and thought, "Hey, I don't look that fat!" And I immediately realized how fucked up that was, but that didn't stop me from feeling more attractive because of it.

I want this out of me. This is not a part of me, and theoretically I can separate it all out and throw away the shit, but it's never really gone. When will this finally be over? When can I move on to other issues? It will never be over, and that's really fucking hard to accept.

I am living out this system of oppression through my memories, and even when I'm not thinking about them they are there, affecting everything I do. Five years old, my first diet. Seven years old, being declared officially "overweight" because I weigh ten pounds over what a "normal" seven-year-old should weigh. Ten years old, learning to starve myself and be happy feeling constantly dizzy. Thirteen years old, crossing the border from being bigger than my friends to actually being "fat." Fifteen years old, hearing the boys in the next room talk about how fat (and hence unattractive) I am. Whenever I perform, I remember the time when my dad said he didn't like the dance I choreographed because I looked fat while I was doing it. Every time I dye my hair I remember when my mom wouldn't let me dye my hair in seventh grade because seeing fat people with dyed hair made her think they were just trying to cover up the fact that they're fat, trying to look attractive despite it (when of course it's obvious what they should really do if they want to look attractive, right?). And these are big memorable occurrences that I can put my finger on and say, "This hurt me." But what about the lifetime of media I've been exposed to that tells me that only thin people are lovable, healthy, beautiful, talented, fun? I know that those messages are all packed in there with the rest of my memories, but I just can't label them and their effects on my psyche. They are elusive and don't necessarily feel painful at the time. They are well disguised and often even appear alluring and romantic. (I will never fall in love because I cannot be picked up and swung around in circles....)

All my life the media and everyone around me have told me that fat is ugly. Which of course is just a cultural standard that has many, many medical lies to fall back upon. Studies have shown that fat people are unhealthy and have short life expectancies. Studies have also shown that starving people have these same peculiarities. These health risks to fat people have been proven to be a result of continuous starvation—dieting—and not of fat itself. I am not fat due to lack of willpower. I've been a vegetarian since I was ten years old. Controlling what I eat is easy for me. Starving myself is not (though for most of my life I wished it was). My body is supposed to be like this, and I've been on plenty of diets where I've kept off some weight for a period of several months and then gained it all back. Two years ago I finally ended the cycle. I am not dieting anymore because I know that this is how my body is supposed to be, and this is how I want it to be. Being fat does not make me less healthy or less active. Being fat does not make me less attractive.

On TV I see a thin woman dancing with a fabulously handsome man, and over that I hear, "I was never happy until I went on [fill in the blank] diet program, but now I'm getting attention from men, and I feel so good! I don't have to worry about what people are saying about me behind my back, because I know I look good. You owe it to yourself to give yourself the life you deserve. Call [fill in the blank] diet program today, and start taking off the pounds right away!" TV shows me a close-up of a teary-eyed fat girl who says, "I've tried everything, but nothing works. I lose twenty pounds, and I gain back twenty-five. I feel so ashamed. What can I do?" The first time I saw that commercial I started crying and memorized the number on the screen. I know that feeling of shame. I know that feeling of having nowhere left to turn, of feeling like I'm useless because I can't lose all that "unwanted fat." But I know that the unhappiness is not a result of my fat. It's a result of a society that tells me I'm bad.

Where's the revolution? My body is fucking beautiful, and every time I look in the mirror and acknowledge that, I am contributing to the revolution.

I feel like at this point I'm expected to try to prove to you that fat can be beautiful by going into descriptions of "rippling thighs and full smooth buttocks." I won't. It's not up to me to convince you that fat can be attractive. I refuse to be the self-appointed full-figured porno queen. Figure it out on your own.

It's not good enough for you to tell me that you "don't judge by appearances"—so fat doesn't bother you. Ignoring our bodies and "judging only by what's on the inside" is not the answer. This seems to be along the same line of thinking as that brilliant school of thought called "humanism": "We are all just people, so let's ignore trivialities such as race, class, gender, sexual preference, body type and so on." Bullshit! The more we ignore these aspects of ourselves, the more shameful they become and the more we are expected to be what is generally implied when these qualifiers are not given—white, straight, thin, rich, male. It's unrealistic to try to overlook these exterior (and hence meaningless, right?) differences, because we're still being brainwashed with the same shit as everyone else. This way we're just not talking about it. And I don't want to be told, "Yes you're fat, but you're beautiful on the inside." That's just another way of telling me that I'm ugly, that there's no way that I'm beautiful on the outside. Fat does not equal ugly, don't give me that. My body *is* me. I want you to see my body, acknowledge my body. True revolution comes not when we learn to ignore our fat and pretend we're no different, but when we learn to use it to our advantage, when we learn to deconstruct all the myths that propagate fat-hate.

My thin friends are constantly being validated by mainstream feminism, while I am ignored. The most widespread mentality regarding body image at this point is something along these lines: Women look in the mirror and think, "I'm fat," but really they're not. Really they're thin.

Really they're thin. But really I'm fat. According to mainstream feminist theory, I don't even exist. I know that women do often look in the mirror and think that they are fatter than they are. And yes, this is a problem. But the analysis can't stop there. There are women who *are* fat, and that needs to be dealt with. Rather than just reassuring people, "No, you're not fat, you're just curvy," maybe we should be demystifying fat and dealing with fat politics as a whole. And I don't mean maybe, I mean it's a necessity. Once we realize that fat is not "inherently bad" (and I can't even believe I'm writing that—"inherently bad"—it sounds so ridiculous), then we can work out the problem as a whole instead of dealing only with this very minute part of it. All forms of oppression work together, and so they have to be fought together.

I think that a lot of the mainstream feminist authors who claim to be dealing with this issue are doing it in a very wrong way. Susie Orbach, for example, with *Fat Is a Feminist Issue*. She tells us: Don't diet, don't try to lose weight, don't feed the diet industry. But she then goes on to say: But if you eat right and exercise, you will lose weight!

And I feel like, great, nice, it's so very wonderful that that worked for her, but she's totally missing the point. She is trying to help women, but really she is hurting us. She is hurting us because she's saying that there's still only one body that's okay for us (and she's the one to help us get it!). It's almost like that *Stop the Insanity* woman, Susan Powter. One of my friends read her book and said that the first half of it is all about fat oppression and talks about how hard it is to be fat in our society, but then it says: So use my great new diet plan! This kind of thing totally plays on our emotions so that we think, Wow, this person really understands me. They know where I'm coming from, so they must know what's best for me.

And there are so many "liberal" reasons for perpetuating fat-hate. Yes, we're finally figuring out that dieting never works. How, then, shall we explain this horrible monstrosity? And how can we get rid of it? The new "liberal" view on fat is that it is caused by deep psychological disturbances. Her childhood was bad, she was sexually abused, so she eats and gets fat in order to hide herself away. She uses her fat as a security blanket. Or maybe when she was young her parents caused her to associate food with comfort and love, so she eats to console herself. Or maybe, like with me, her parents were always on diets and always nagging her about what she was eating, so food became something shameful that must be hoarded and kept secret. And for a long, long time I really believed that if my parents hadn't instilled in me all these fucked-up attitudes about food, I wouldn't be fat. But then I realized that my brother and sister both grew up in exactly the same environment, and they are both thin. Obviously this is not the reason that I am fat. Therapy won't help, because there's nothing to cure. When will we stop grasping for reasons to hate fat people and start realizing that fat is a totally normal and natural thing that cannot and should not be gotten rid of?

Despite what I said earlier about my friends saying things that are really hurtful to me, I realize that they are actually pretty exceptional. I don't want to make them seem like uncaring, ignorant people. I'm constantly talking about these issues, and I feel like I'm usually able to confront my friends when they're being insensitive, and they'll understand or at least try to. Sometimes when I leave my insular circle of friends I'm shocked at what the "real world" is like. Hearing boys on the bus refer to their girlfriends as their "bitches," seeing fat women being targeted for harassment on the street, watching TV and seeing how every fat person is depicted as a food-obsessed slob, seeing women treated as property by men who see masculinity as a right to power…. I leave these situations feeling like the punk scene, within which most of my interactions take place, is so sheltered. I cannot imagine living in a community where I had nowhere to go for support. I cannot imagine living in the "real world."

But then I have to remember that it's still there in my community—these same fucked-up attitudes are perpetuated within the punk scene as well; they just take on more subtle forms. I feel like these issues are finally starting to be recognized and dealt with, but fat hating is still pretty standard. Of course everyone agrees that we shouldn't diet and that eating disorders are a result of our oppressive society, but it's not usually taken much further than that. It seems like people have this idea that punk is disconnected from the media. That because we are this cool underground subculture, we are immune to systems of oppression. But the punkest, coolest kids are still the skinny kids. And the same cool kids who are so into defying mainstream capitalist "Amerika" are the ones who say that fat is a symbol of capitalist wealth and greed. Yeah, that's a really new and different way of thinking: Blame the victim. Perpetuate institutionalized oppression. Fat people are not the ones who are oppressing these poor, skinny emo boys.

This essay is supposed to be about fat oppression. I feel like that's all I ever talk about. Sometimes I feel my whole identity is wrapped up in my fat. When I am fully conscious of my fat, it

can't be used against me. Outside my secluded group of friends, in hostile situations, I am constantly aware that at any moment I could be harassed. Any slight altercation with another person could lead to a barrage of insults thrown at my body. I am always ready for it. I've found it doesn't happen nearly as often as I expect it, but still I always remain aware of the possibility. I am "the Fat Girl." I am "the Girl Who Talks About Fat Oppression." Within the punk scene, that's my security blanket. People know about me and know about my work, so I assume that they're not gonna be laughing behind my back about my fat. And if they are, then I know I have support from other people around me. The punk scene gives me tons of support that I know I wouldn't get elsewhere. Within the punk scene, I am able to put out zines, play music, do spoken-word performances that are intensely personal to me. I feel really strongly about keeping nothing secret. I can go back to the old cliché about the personal being political, and no matter how trite it may sound, it's true. I went for so long never talking about being fat, never talking about how that affects my self-esteem, never talking about the ways that I'm oppressed by this society. Now I'm talking. Now I'm talking, I'm talking all the time, and people listen to me. I have support.

And at the same time I know that I have to be wary of the support that I receive. Because I think to some people this is just seen as the cool thing, that by supporting me they're somehow receiving a certain amount of validation from the punk scene. Even though I am totally open and don't keep secrets, I have to protect myself.

This is the revolution. I don't understand the revolution. I can't lay it all out in black and white and tell you what is revolutionary and what is not. The punk scene is a revolution, but not in and of itself. Feminism is a revolution; it is solidarity as well as critique and confrontation. This is the fat grrrl revolution. It's mine, but it doesn't belong to me. Fuckin' yeah.

Coming to Terms

Masculinity and Physical Disability

THOMAS J. GERSCHICK
ADAM STEPHEN MILLER

Men with physical disabilities are marginalized and stigmatized in American society. The image and reality of men with disabilities undermines cultural beliefs about men's bodies and physicality. The body is a central foundation of how men define themselves and how they are defined by others. Bodies are vehicles for determining value, which in turn translates into status and prestige. Men's bodies allow them to demonstrate the socially valuable characteristics of toughness, competitiveness, and ability (Messner 1992). Thus, one's body and relationship to it provide a way to apprehend the world and one's place in it. The bodies of men with disabilities serve as a continual reminder that they are at odds with the expectations of the dominant culture. As anthropologist Robert Murphy (1990: 94) writes of his own experiences with disability:

> Paralytic disability constitutes emasculation of a more direct and total nature. For the male, the weakening and atrophy of the body threaten all the cultural values of masculinity: strength, activeness, speed, virility, stamina, and fortitude.

This article seeks to sharpen our understanding of the creation, maintenance, and recreation of gender identities by men who, by birth, accident, or illness, find themselves dealing with a physical disability. We examine two sets of social dynamics that converge and clash in the lives of men with physical disabilities. On the one side, these men must deal with the presence and pressures of hegemonic masculinity, which demands strength. On the other side, societal members perceive people with disabilities to be weak.

For the present study, we conducted in-depth interviews with ten men with physical disabilities in order to gain insights into the psychosocial aspects of men's ability to come to terms with their physical and social condition. We wanted to know how men with physical disabilities respond to the demands of hegemonic masculinity and their marginalization. For instance, if men with disabilities need others to legitimate their gender identity during encounters, what happens when others deny them the opportunity? How do they reconcile the conflicting expectations associated with masculinity and disability? How do they define masculinity for themselves, and what are the sources of these definitions? To what degree do their responses contest and/or perpetuate the current gender order? That is, what are the political implications of different gender identities and practices? In addressing these questions, we contribute to the growing body of literature on marginalized and alternative gender identities.

We will first discuss the general relationship between physical disability and hegemonic masculinity. Second, we will summarize the methods used in this study. Next, we will present and discuss our central findings. Finally, we discuss how the gender identities and life practices of men with disabilities contribute to the politics of the gender order.

HEGEMONIC MASCULINITY
AND PHYSICAL DISABILITY

Recently, the literature has shifted toward understanding gender as an interactive process. Thus, it is presumed to be not only an aspect of what one *is,* but more fundamentally it is something that one *does* in interaction with others (West and Zimmerman 1987). Whereas previously, gender was thought to be strictly an individual phenomenon, this new understanding directs our attention to the interpersonal and institutional levels as well. The lives of men with disabilities provide an instructive arena in which to study the interactional nature of gender and its effect on individual gender identities.

In *The Body Silent,* Murphy (1990) observes that men with physical disabilities experience "embattled identities" because of the conflicting expectations placed on them as men and as people with disabilities. On the one side, contemporary masculinity privileges men who are strong, courageous, aggressive, independent and self-reliant (Connell 1987). On the other side, people with disabilities are perceived to be, and treated as, weak, pitiful, passive, and dependent (Murphy 1990). Thus, for men with physical disabilities, masculine gender identity and practice are created and maintained at the crossroads of the demands of contemporary masculinity and the stigmatization associated with disability. As such, for men with physical disabilities, being recognized as masculine by others is especially difficult, if not impossible, to accomplish. Yet not being recognized as masculine is untenable because, in our culture, everyone is expected to display an appropriate gender identity (West and Zimmerman 1987).

METHODS

This research was based on in-depth interviews with ten men. Despite the acknowledged problem of identity management in interviews, we used this method because we were most interested in the subjective perceptions and experiences of our informants. To mitigate this dynamic, we relied on probing questions and reinterviews. Informants were located through a snowball sample, utilizing friends and connections within the community of people with disabilities. All of our informants were given pseudonyms, and we further protected their identity by deleting nonessential personal detail. The age range of respondents varied from sixteen to seventy-two. Eight of our respondents were white, and two were African American. Geographically, they came from both coasts and the Midwest. All were "mobility impaired," and most were para- or quadriplegics. Given the small sample size and the modicum of diversity within it, this work must necessarily be understood as exploratory.

We interviewed men with physical disabilities for three primary reasons. First, given the diversity of disabilities and our modest resources, we had to bound the sample. Second, mobility impairments tend to be more apparent than other disabilities, such as blindness or hearing loss, and people respond to these men using visual clues. Third, although the literature in this area is scant, much of it focuses on men with physical disabilities.

Due to issues of shared identities, Adam did all the interviews. Interviews were semistructured and tape-recorded. Initial interviews averaged approximately an hour in length. Additionally, we contacted all of our informants at least once with clarifying questions and, in some cases, to test ideas that we had. These follow-ups lasted approximately thirty minutes. Each informant received a copy of his interview transcript to ensure that we had captured his perspective accurately. We also shared draft copies of this chapter with them and incorporated their insights into the current version.

There were two primary reasons for the thorough follow-up. First, from a methodological standpoint, it was important for us to capture the experience of our informants as fully as possible. Second, we felt that we had an obligation to allow them to control, to a large extent, the representation of their experience.

Interviews were analyzed using an analytic induction approach (Denzin 1989; Emerson 1988; Katz 1988). In determining major and minor patterns of masculine practice, we used the responses to a series of questions including, What is the most important aspect of masculinity to you? What would you say makes you feel most manly or masculine? Do you think your conception of masculinity is different from that of able-bodied men as a result of your disability? If so, how and why? If not, why not? Additionally, we presented our informants with a list of characteristics associated with prevailing masculinity based on the work of R. W. Connell (1987, 1990a, 1990b, 1991) and asked them to rate their importance to their conception of self. Both positive and negative responses to this portion of our questionnaire guided our insight into how each man viewed his masculinity. To further support our discussion, we turned to the limited academic literature in this area. Much more helpful were the wide range of biographical and autobiographical accounts of men who have physical disabilities (see, for instance, Murphy 1990; Callahan 1989; Kriegel 1991; Hahn 1989; and Zola 1982).

Finally, in analyzing the data we were sensitive to making judgments about our informants when grouping them into categories. People with disabilities are shoehorned into categories too much as it is. We sought to discover what was common among their responses and to highlight what we perceived to be the essence of their views. In doing so, we endeavored to provide a conceptual framework for understanding the responses of men with physical disabilities while trying to be sensitive to their personal struggles.

DISABILITY, MASCULINITY, AND COMING TO TERMS

While no two men constructed their sense of masculinity in exactly the same way, there appeared to be three dominant frameworks our informants used to cope with their situations. These patterns can be conceived of in relation to the standards inherent in dominant masculinity. We call them the three Rs: *reformulation*, which entailed men's redefinition of hegemonic characteristics on their own terms; *reliance*, reflected by sensitive or hy-

persensitive adoptions of particular predominant attributes; and *rejection*, characterized by the renunciation of these standards and either the creation of one's own principles and practices or the denial of masculinity's importance in one's life. However, one should note that none of our interviewees *entirely* followed any one of these frameworks in defining his sense of self. Rather, for heuristic reasons, it is best to speak of the major and minor ways each man used these three patterns. For example, some of our informants relied on dominant standards in their view of sexuality and occupation but also reformulated the prevailing ideal of independence.

Therefore, we discuss the *primary* way in which these men with disabilities related to hegemonic masculinity's standards, while recognizing that their coping mechanisms reflected a more complex combination of strategies. In doing so, we avoid "labeling" men and assigning them to arbitrary categories.

Reformulation

Some of our informants responded to idealized masculinity by reformulating it, shaping it along the lines of their own abilities, perceptions, and strengths, and defining their manhood along these new lines. These men tended not to contest these standards overtly, but—either consciously or unconsciously—they recognized in their own condition an inability to meet these ideals as they were culturally conceived.

An example of this came from Damon, a seventy-two-year-old quadriplegic who survived a spinal-cord injury in an automobile accident ten years ago. Damon said he always desired, and had, control of his life. While Damon required round-the-clock personal care assistants (PCAs), he asserted that he was still a very independent person:

> *I direct all of my activities around my home where people have to help me to maintain my apartment, my transportation, which I own, and direction in where I go. I direct people how to get there, and I tell them what my needs will be when I am going and coming, and when to get where I am going.*

Damon said that his sense of control was more than mere illusion; it was a reality others knew of as well. This reputation seemed important to him:

People know from Jump Street that I have my own thing, and I direct my own thing. And if they can't comply with my desire, they won't be around.... I don't see any reason why people with me can't take instructions and get my life on just as I was having it before, only thing I'm not doing it myself. I direct somebody else to do it. So, therefore, I don't miss out on very much.

Hegemonic masculinity's definition of independence privileges self-reliance and autonomy. Damon required substantial assistance: indeed, some might term him "dependent." However, Damon's reformulation of the independence ideal, accomplished in part through a cognitive shift, allowed him to think otherwise.

Harold, a forty-six-year-old polio survivor, described a belief and practice akin to Damon's. Also a quadriplegic, Harold similarly required PCAs to help him handle daily necessities: Harold termed his reliance on and control of PCAs "acting through others":

When I say independence can be achieved by acting through other people, I actually mean getting through life, liberty, and the pursuit of happiness while utilizing high-quality and dependable attendant-care services.

As with Damon, Harold achieved his perceived sense of independence by controlling others. Harold stressed that he did not count on family or friends to do favors for him, but *employed* his PCAs in a "business relationship" he controlled. Alternatives to family and friends are used whenever possible because most people with disabilities do not want to burden or be dependent on their families any more than necessary (Murphy 1990).

Social class plays an important role here. Damon and Harold had the economic means to afford round-the-clock assistance. While none of our informants experienced economic hardship, many

people with disabilities depend on the welfare system for their care, and the amount and quality of assistance they receive make it much more difficult to conceive of themselves as independent.

A third man who reformulated predominant demands was Brent, a forty-five-year-old administrator. He told us that his paraplegic status, one that he had lived with since he was five years old, had often cast him as an "outsider" to society. This status was particularly painful in his late adolescence, a time when the "sexual revolution" was sweeping America's youth:

A very important measure of somebody's personhood—manhood—was their sexual ability.... What bothers me more than anything else is the stereotypes, and even more so, in terms of sexual desirability. Because I had a disability, I was less desirable than able-bodied people. And that I found very frustrating.

His experiences led him to recast the hegemonic notion that man's relations with a partner should be predominantly physical. As a result, he stressed the importance of emotional relations and trust. This appeared to be key to Brent's definition of his manhood:

For me, that is my measure of who I am as an individual and who I am as a man—my ability to be able to be honest with my wife. Be able to be close with her, to be able to ask for help, provide help. To have a commitment, to follow through, and to do all those things that I think are important.

As Connell (1990a) notes, this requires a capacity to not only be expressive, but also to have feelings worth expressing. This clearly demonstrates a different form of masculine practice.

The final case of reformulation came from Robert, a thirty-year-old survivor of a motorcycle accident. Able-bodied for much of his life, Robert's accident occurred when he was twenty-four, leaving him paraplegic. Through five years of intensive physical therapy, he regained 95 percent of his original function, though certain effects linger to this day.

Before his accident, Robert had internalized many of the standards of dominant masculinity exemplified by frequenting bars, leading an active sex life, and riding a motorcycle. But, if our research and the body of autobiographical works from men with physical disabilities has shown anything, it is that coming to terms with a disability eventually changes a man. It appeared to have transformed Robert. He remarked that, despite being generally "recovered," he had maintained his disability-influenced value system:

> I judge people on more of a personal and character level than I do on any physical, or I guess I did; but, you know, important things are guys that have integrity, guys that are honest about what they are doing, that have some direction in their life and know... peace of mind and what they stand for.

One of the areas that Robert said took the longest to recover was his sexuality—specifically, his confidence in his sexual ability. While Robert said sexual relations were still important to him, like Brent he reformulated his previous, largely hegemonic notion of male sexuality into a more emotionally and physically egalitarian model:

> I've found a whole different side to having sex with a partner and looking at satisfying the partner rather than satisfying myself; and that has taken the focus off of satisfying myself, being the big manly stud, and concentrating more on my partner. And that has become just as satisfying.

However, reformulation did not yield complete severance from prevailing masculinity's standards as they were culturally conceived. For instance, despite his reformulative inclinations, Robert's self-described "macho" attitude continued in some realms during his recovery. He, and all others we interviewed, represented the complexity of gender identities and practices; no man's masculinity fell neatly into any one of the three patterns.

For instance, although told by most doctors that his physical condition was probably permanent, Robert's resolve was unyielding. "I put my

blinders on to all negative insight into it and just totally focused on getting better," he said. "And I think that was, you know, a major factor on why I'm where I'm at today." This typified the second pattern we identified—reliance on hegemonic masculinity's standards. It was ironic, then, that Robert's tenacity, his never-ending work ethic, and his focused drive to succeed were largely responsible for his almost-complete recovery. While Robert reformulated much of his earlier sense of masculinity, he still relied on this drive.

Perhaps the area in which men who reformulate most closely paralleled dominant masculinity was the emphasis they placed on their occupation. Our sample was atypical in that most of our informants were professionally employed on a full-time basis and could, therefore, draw on class-based resources, whereas unemployment among people with disabilities is very high. Just as societal members privilege men who are accomplished in their occupation, Harold said he finds both "purpose," and success, in his career:

> No one is going to go through life without some kind of purpose. Everyone decides. I wanted to be a writer. So I became a writer and an observer, a trained observer.

Brent said that he drew much of his sense of self, his sense of self-esteem, and his sense of manhood from his occupational accomplishments. Initially, Brent denied the importance of the prevailing ideal that a man's occupational worth was derived from his breadwinner status:

> It is not so important to be the breadwinner as it is to be competent in the world. You know, to have a career, to have my name on the door. That is what is most important. It is that recognition that is very important to me.

However, he later admitted that being the breadwinner still was important to him, although he denied a link between his desires and the "stereotypical" conception of breadwinner status. He maintained that "it's still important to me, because I've always been able to make money."

Independence, both economic and physical, were important to all of our informants.

Rejection of hegemonic ideals also occurred among men who primarily depended on a reformulative framework. Harold's view of relationships with a partner dismissed the sexually powerful ideal: "The fact of the matter is that I'm not all that upset by the fact that I'm disabled and I'm a male. I mean, I know what I can do." We will have more to say about the rejection of dominant conceptions of sexuality later.

In brief summary, the subset of our informants whose primary coping pattern involved reformulation of dominant standards recognized their inability to meet these ideals as they are culturally conceived. Confident in their own abilities and values, and drawing from previous experience, they confronted standards of masculinity on their own terms. In doing so, they distanced themselves from masculine ideals.

Reliance

However, not all of the men with physical disabilities we interviewed depended on a reformulative approach. We found that many of our informants *were* concerned with others' views of their masculinity and with meeting the demands of hegemonic masculinity. They primarily used the second pattern, reliance, which involves the internalization of many more of the ideals of predominant masculinity, including physical strength, athleticism, independence, and sexual prowess. Just as some men depended on reformulation for much of their masculine definition, others, despite their inability to meet many of these ideals, relied on them heavily. As such, these men did not seem to be as comfortable with their sense of manhood; indeed, their inability to meet society's standards bothered them very much.

This subset of our informants found themselves in a double bind that left them conflicted. They embraced dominant conceptions of masculinity as a way to gain acceptance from themselves and from others. Yet, they were continuously reminded in their interactions with others that they

were "incomplete." As a result, the identity behind the facade suffered; there were, then, major costs associated with this strategy.

The tension between societal expectations and the reality of men with physical disabilities was most clearly demonstrated by Jerry, a sixteen-year-old who had juvenile rheumatoid arthritis. While Jerry was physically able to walk for limited distances, this required great effort on his part; consequently, he usually used a wheelchair. He was concerned with the appearance of his awkward walking. "I feel like I look a little, I don't know, more strange when I walk," he said.

The significance of appearance and external perception of manliness is symptomatic of the difficulty men with physical disabilities have in developing an identity and masculinity free of others' perceptions and expectations. Jerry said:

> I think [others' conception of what defines a man] is very important, because if they don't think of you as one, it is hard to think of yourself as one; or, it doesn't really matter if you think of yourself as one if no one else does.

Jerry said that, particularly among his peers, he was not perceived as attractive as the able-bodied teenagers; thus, he had difficulty in male-female relations beyond landing an occasional date. "[The girls believe] I might be a 'really nice person,' but not like a guy per se," he said. "I think to some extent that you're sort of genderless to them." This clearly represents the emasculation and depersonalization inherent in social definitions of disability.

However, Jerry said that he faced a more persistent threat to his autonomy—his independence and his sense of control—from others being "uncomfortable" around him and persisting in offering him assistance he often did not need. This made him "angry," though he usually did not refuse the help out of politeness. Thus, with members of his social group, he participated in a "bargain": they would socialize with him as long as he remained in a dependent position where they could "help" him.

This forced, situational passivity led Jerry to emphasize his autonomy in other areas. For instance, Jerry avoided asking for help in nearly all situations. This was directly tied to reinforcing his embattled manhood by displaying outward strength and independence:

> If I ever have to ask someone for help, it really makes me like feel like less of a man. I don't like asking for help at all. You know, like even if I could use some, I'll usually not ask just because I can't, I just hate asking.... [A man is] fairly self-sufficient in that you can sort of handle just about any situation, in that you can help other people, and that you don't need a lot of help.

Jerry internalized the prevailing masculine ideal that a man should be independent; he relied on that ideal for his definition of manhood. His inability to meet this ideal—partly through his physical condition, and partly from how others treated him—threatened his identity and his sense of manhood, which had to be reinforced even at the expense of self-alienation.

One should not label Jerry a "relier" simply because of these struggles. Being only sixteen years of age—and the youngest participant in our study—Jerry was still developing his sense of masculinity; and, as with many teenagers both able-bodied and disabled, he was trying to fit into his peer group. Furthermore, Jerry will continue to mature and develop his self-image and sense of masculinity. A follow-up interview in five years might show a degree of resolution to his struggles.

Such a resolution could be seen in Michael, a thirty-three-year-old manager we interviewed, who also internalized many of the standards of hegemonic masculinity. A paraplegic from an auto accident in 1977, Michael struggled for many years after his accident to come to terms with his condition.

His struggles had several sources, all tied into his view of masculinity's importance. The first was that, before his accident, he accepted much of the dominant conception of masculinity. A high-school student, farm hand, and football and track star at the time, Michael said that independence,

relations with the women he dated, and physical strength were central to his conception of self.

After his accident, Michael's doctors told him there was a 50-50 chance that he would regain the ability to walk, and he clung to the hope. "I guess I didn't understand it, and had hope that I would walk again," he said. However, he was "depressed" about his situation, "but not so much about my disability, I guess. Because that wasn't real yet."

But coming home three months after his accident didn't alleviate the depression. Instead, it heightened his anxiety and added a new component—vulnerability. In a span of three months, Michael had, in essence, his sense of masculinity and his security in himself completely stripped away. He was in an unfamiliar situation; and far from feeling strong, independent, and powerful, he felt vulnerable and afraid: "No one," he remarked, "can be prepared for a permanent disability."

His reliance on dominant masculinity, then, started with his predisability past and continued during his recovery as a coping mechanism to deal with his fears. The hegemonic standard Michael strove most to achieve was that of independence. It was central to his sense of masculinity before and at the time of our interview. Indeed, it was so important that it frustrated him greatly when he needed assistance. Much like Jerry, he refused to ask for it:

> I feel that I should be able to do everything for myself and I don't like it.... I don't mind asking for things that I absolutely can't do, like hanging pictures, or moving furniture, or having my oil changed in my car; but there are things that I'm capable of doing in my chair, like jumping up one step. That I feel like I should be able to do, and I find it frustrating when I can't do that sometimes. ... I don't like asking for [help I don't think I need]. It kind of makes me mad.

When asked if needing assistance was "unmanly," Michael replied, "There's probably some of that in there." For both Michael and Jerry, the independence ideal often led to risk-taking behavior in order to prove to themselves that they were more than their social definition.

Yet, much like Robert, Michael had reformulated his view of sexuality. He said that his physical sexuality made him "feel the most masculine"—apparently another reliant response with a stereotypical emphasis on sexual performance. However, it was more complicated. Michael said that he no longer concentrated on pleasing himself, as he did when able-bodied, but that he now had a more partner-oriented view of sexuality. "I think that my compensation for my feeling of vulnerability is I've overcompensated by trying to please my partner and leave little room to allow my partner to please me. . . . Some of my greatest pleasure is exhausting my partner while having sex." Ironically, while he focused more on his partner's pleasure than ever before, he did so at his own expense; a sense of balancing the needs of both partners was missing.

Thus, sex served multiple purposes for Michael—it gave him and his partner pleasure; it reassured his fears and his feelings of vulnerability; and it reconfirmed his masculinity. His sexuality, then, reflected both reliance and reformulation.

While independence and sexuality were both extremely important to Scott, a thirty-four-year-old rehabilitation engineer, he emphasized a third area for his sense of manhood—athletics. Scott served in the Peace Corps during his twenties, working in Central America. He described his life-style as "rigorous" and "into the whole sports thing," and used a mountain bike as his primary means of transportation and recreation. He was also an avid hockey player in his youth and spent his summers in softball leagues.

Scott acquired a polio-like virus when he was twenty-five years old that left him permanently paraplegic, a situation that he did not initially accept. In an aggressive attempt to regain his physical ability, and similar to Robert, Scott obsessively attacked his rehabilitation

. . . thinking, that's always what I've done with all the sports. If I wasn't good enough, I worked a little harder and I got better. So, I kept thinking my walking isn't very good now. If I push it, it will get better.

But Scott's athletic drive led not to miraculous recovery, but overexertion. When ordered by his doctors to scale back his efforts, he realized he could not recover strictly through tenacity. At the time of our interview, he was ambivalent about his limitations. He clearly did not feel like a failure: "I think that if I wouldn't have made the effort, I always would have wondered, could I have made a difference?" Following the athlete's code of conduct, "always give 110 percent," Scott attacked his recovery. But when his efforts were not enough—when he did not "emerge victorious"— he accepted it as an athlete would. Yet, his limitations also frustrated him at times, and in different areas.

For example, though his physical capacity was not what it was, Scott maintained a need for athletic competition. He played wheelchair basketball and was the only wheelchair-participant in a city softball league. However, he did not return to hockey, the sport he loved as a youngster; in fact, he refused to even try the sled-based equivalent.

Here was Scott's frustration. His spirit of athleticism was still alive, but he lamented the fact that he could not compete exactly as before:

[I miss] the things that I had. I played hockey: that was my primary sport for so many years. Pretty much, I did all the sports. But, like, I never played basketball; never liked basketball before. Which is why I think I can play now. See, it would be like the equivalent to wheelchair hockey. Some friends of mine have talked to me about it, [but] I'm not really interested in that. Because it wouldn't be real hockey. And it would make me feel worse, rather that better.

In this respect, Scott had not completely come to terms with his limitations. He still wanted to be a "real" athlete, competing in the same sports, in the same ways, with the same rules, with others who shared his desire for competition. Wheelchair hockey, which he derogatorily referred to as "gimp hockey," represented the antithesis of this for him.

Scott's other responses added to this emphasis. What he most disliked about having a disability was "that I can't do the things that I want to be able to do," meaning he could not ride his bike or motorcycle, he could not play "real" hockey, and he was unable to live a freewheeling, spontaneous life-style. Rather, he had to plan ahead of time where he went and how he got there. The frustration caused by having to plan nearly every move was apparent in almost all of our interviews.

However, on the subject of independence, Scott said "I think I'm mostly independent," but complained that there were some situations where he could not meet his expectations and had to depend on his wife. Usually this was not a "major issue," but "there's still times when, yeah, I feel bad about it; or, you know it's the days where she doesn't feel like it, but she kind of has to. That's what bothers me the most, I guess." Thus, he reflected the general desire among men with disabilities not to be a burden of any kind on family members.

Much of the time, Scott accepted being "mostly independent." His reliance on the ideals of athleticism and independence played a significant part in his conception of masculinity and self. However, Scott learned, though to a limited degree, to let go of some of his previous ideals and to accept a different, reformulated notion of independence and competition. Yet, he could not entirely do so. His emphasis on athletics and independence was still strong, and there were many times when athletics and acceptance conflicted.

However, one should stop short of a blanket assessment of men with disabilities who rely on hegemonic masculinity standards. "Always" is a dangerous word, and stating that "men who rely on hegemonic standards are *always* troubled" is a dangerous assumption. An apparent exceptional case among men who follow a reliant pattern came from Aaron, a forty-one-year-old paraplegic. Rather than experiencing inner turmoil and conflict, Aaron was one of the most upbeat individuals we interviewed. Aaron said that, before his 1976 accident, he was "on top of the world," with a successful business, a commitment to athletics that included basketball shoot-

arounds with NBA prospects, and a wedding engagement. Indeed, from the time of his youth, Aaron relied on such hegemonic standards as sexuality, independence, athleticism, and occupational accomplishment.

For example, when asked what masculinity meant to him before his accident, Aaron said that it originally meant sexual conquest. As a teen, he viewed frequent sexual activity as a "rite of passage" into manhood.

Aaron said he had also enjoyed occupational success, and that this success was central to his definition of self, including being masculine. Working a variety of jobs ranging from assembly-line worker to white-collar professional, Aaron said, "I had been very fortunate to have good jobs, which were an important part of who I was and how I defined myself."

According to Aaron, much of his independence ideal came from his father. When his parents divorced, Aaron's father explained to him that, though he was only five, he would have to be "the man of the house." Aaron took this lesson to heart, and strived to fulfill this role both in terms of independence and providing for the family. "My image of manhood was that of a provider," he said, "one who was able to make a contribution to the financial stability of the family in addition to dealing with the problems and concerns that would come up."

His accident, a gunshot wound injuring his spinal cord, left him completely dependent. Predictably, Aaron could not immediately cope with this. "My whole self image itself was real integrally tied up with the things I used to do," he said. "I found my desire for simple pleasures to be the greatest part of the pain I had to bear."

His pain increased when he left the hospital. His fiancee had left him, and within two years he lost "everything that was important to me"—his house, his business, his savings, most of his friends, and even, for a while, his hope.

However, much as with Robert, Aaron's resiliency eventually turned his life around. Just as he hit bottom, he began telling himself that "if you hold on long enough, if you don't quit, you'll get through it." Additionally, he attacked his therapy with the vengeance he had always devoted to athletics. "I'd never been confronted with a situation in my entire life before that I was not able to overcome by the efforts of my own merit," he said. "I took the same attitude toward this."

Further, he reasserted his sexuality. Though he then wore a colostomy bag, he resumed frequent sexual intercourse, taking the attitude that "this is who I was, and a woman was either going to have to accept me as I was, or she's got to leave me f—— alone."

However, he realized after those five years that his hard work would not be rewarded nor would he be miraculously healed. Figuring that "there's a whole lot of life that I need to live, and this wasn't the most efficient way to live it," he bought a new sport wheelchair, found a job, and became involved in wheelchair athletics. In this sense, a complex combination of all three patterns emerged in Aaron as reliance was mixed with reformulation and rejection.

Furthermore, his soul-searching led him to develop a sense of purpose in his life, and a reason for going on:

> [During my recovery] I felt that I was left here to enrich the lives of as many people as I could before I left this earth, and it gave me a new purpose, a new vision, a new mission, new dreams.

Tenacity, the quest for independence, athletics, and sexual activity carried Aaron through his recovery. Many of these ideals, which had their source in his father's teachings, remained with him as he continued to be active in athletics (everything from basketball to softball to scuba diving), to assert his sexuality, and to aim for complete autonomy. To Aaron, independence, both physical and financial, was more than just a personal ideal; it was one that should be shared by all people with disabilities. As such, he aspired to be a role model for others:

> The work that I am involved in is to help people gain control over their lives, and I think it's vitally important that I walk my talk. If . . . we hold our-

> selves out to be an organization that helps people gain control over their lives, I think it's vitally important for me as the CEO of that organization to live my life in a way that embodies everything that we say we're about.

Clearly, Aaron was not the same man he was before his disability. He said that his maturity and his experience with disability "made me stronger," and that manhood no longer simply meant independence and sexual conquest. Manhood also meant

> . . . being responsible for one's actions; being considerate of another's feelings; being sensitive to individuals who are more vulnerable than yourself to what their needs would be; standing up on behalf and fighting for those who cannot speak out for themselves, fight for themselves. It means being willing to take a position and be committed to a position, even when it's inconvenient or costly to take that point of view, and you do it only because of the principle involved.

This dovetailed significantly with his occupation, which was of great importance to him. But as alluded to above, Aaron's emphasis on occupation cannot be seen as mere reliance on the hegemonic conception of occupational achievement. It was more a reformulation of that ideal from self-achievement to facilitating the empowerment of others.

Nevertheless, Aaron's struggle to gain his current status, like the struggle of others who rely on hegemonic masculinity's standards, was immense. Constructing hegemonic masculinity from a subordinated position is almost always a Sisyphean task. One's ability to do so is undermined continuously by physical, social, and cultural weakness. "Understandably, in an effort to cope with this stress (balancing the demands for strength and the societal perception of weakness)," writes political scientist Harlan Hahn, "many disabled men have tended to identify personally and politically with the supposed strength of prevalent concepts of masculinity rather than with their disability" (1989: 3). To relinquish masculinity under these circumstances is to court gender annihilation, which is untenable to some men. Consequently, relying on hegemonic masculinity becomes more understandable (Connell 1990a: 471).

Rejection

Despite the difficulties it presents, hegemony, including that related to gender, is never complete (Janeway 1980, Scott 1985). For some of our informants, resistance took the form of creating alternative masculine identities and subcultures that provided them with a supportive environment. These men were reflected in the final pattern: rejection. Informants who followed this pattern did not so much share a common ideology or set of practices; rather, they believed that the dominant conception of masculinity was wrong, either in its individual emphases or as a practice. One of these men developed new standards of masculinity in place of the ones he had rejected. Another seemingly chose to deny masculinity's importance, although he was neither effeminate or androgynous. Instead, they both emphasized their status as "persons," under the motto of "people first." This philosophy reflected a key tenet of the Disability Rights Movement.

Alex, a twenty-three-year-old, first-year law student, survived an accident that left him an incomplete quadriplegic when he was fourteen. Before that time, he felt he was an outsider at his private school because he eschewed the superficial, athletically oriented, and materialistic atmosphere. Further, he said the timing of the accident, when many of his peers were defining their social roles, added to this outsider perspective, in that it made him unable to participate in the highly social, role-forming process. "I didn't learn about the traditional roles of sexuality, and whatever the rules are for such behavior in our society, until later," he said. "Because of my physical characteristics, I had to learn a different set of rules."

Alex described himself as a "nonconformist." This simple moniker seemed central to his conception of selfhood and masculinity. Alex, unlike men who primarily reformulate these tenets, rejected the attitudinal and behavioral prescriptions of hegemonic masculinity. He maintained that his standards were his own—not society's—and he scoffed at commonly held views of masculinity.

For example, Alex blamed the media for the idea that men must be strong and attractive, stating "The traditional conception is that everyone has to be Arnold Schwartzenegger...[which] probably lead[s] to some violence, unhappiness, and things like that if they [men] don't meet the standards."

As for the importance of virility and sexual prowess, Alex said "There is a part of me that, you know, has been conditioned and acculturated and knows those [dominant] values"; but he sarcastically laughed at the notion of a man's sexual prowess being reflected in "making her pass out," and summed up his feelings on the subject by adding, "You have to be willing to do things in a nontraditional way."

Alex's most profound rejection of a dominant ideal involved the importance of fathering, in its strictest sense of the man as impregnator:

> There's no reason why we (his fiancee and himself) couldn't use artificial insemination or adoption. Parenting doesn't necessarily involve being the male sire. It involves being a good parent.... Parenting doesn't mean that it's your physical child. It involves responsibility and an emotional role as well. I don't think the link between parenthood is the primary link with sexuality. Maybe in terms of evolutionary purposes, but not in terms of a relationship.

Thus, Alex rejected the procreation imperative encouraged in hegemonic masculinity. However, while Alex took pride at overtly rejecting prevailing masculinity as superficial and silly, even he relied on it at times. Alex said he needed to support himself financially and would not ever want to be an emotional or economic "burden" in a relationship. On one level, this is a common concern for most people, disabled or not. But on another level, Alex admitted that it tied in to his sense of masculinity:

> If I was in a relationship and I wasn't working, and my spouse was, what could be the possible reasons for my not working? I could have just been

fired. I could be laid off. Who knows what happened? I guess...that's definitely an element of masculinity, and I guess I am just as influenced by that as, oh, as I guess as other people, or as within my definition of masculinity. What do you know? I have been caught.

A different form of rejection was reflected in Leo, a fifty-eight-year-old polio survivor. Leo, who had striven for occupational achievement since his youth, seemed to value many hegemonic traits: independence, money-making ability, and recognition by peers. But he steadfastly denied masculinity's role in shaping his outlook.

Leo said the most important trait to him was his mental capacity and intelligence, since that allowed him to achieve his occupational goals. Yet he claimed this was not related to the prevailing standard. Rather, it tied into his ambitions from before his disability and his willingness to do most anything to achieve his goals.

Before we label him "a rejector," however, note that Leo was a believer in adaptive technology and personal assistance, and he did not see a contradiction between using personal-care assistants and being independent. This seemed to be a reformulation, just as with Damon and Harold but when we asked Leo about this relation to masculinity, he flatly denied any connection.

Leo explained his renunciation of masculinity by saying "It doesn't mean a great deal...it's not how I think [of things]." He said that many of the qualities on our list of hegemonic characteristics were important to him on an individual level but did not matter to his sense of manhood. Leo maintained that there were "external" and "internal" reasons for this.

The external factors Leo identified were the Women's and Disability Rights Movements. Both provided support and alternatives that allow a person with a disability the freedom to be a person, and not (to use Leo's words) a "strange bird." Indeed, Leo echoed the call of the Disability Rights Movement when he described himself as a "person first." In this way, his humanity took precedence and his gender and his disability became less significant.

Also, Leo identified his background as a contributing factor to his outlook. Since childhood, he held a group of friends that valued intellectual achievement over physical performance. In his youth, Leo said he was a member of a group "on the college route." He remained in academia.

Internally, his view of masculinity came from maturity. He had dealt with masculinity and related issues for almost sixty years and reached a point at which he was comfortable with his gender. According to him, his gender conceptions ranged across all three patterns. This was particularly evident in his sexuality. When younger, he relied on a culturally valued, genital sexuality and was concerned with his potency. He wanted to "be on top," despite the physical difficulties this presented him. At the time of our interview, he had a reformulated sexuality. The Women's Movement allowed him to remain sexually active without worrying about "being on top." He even rejected the idea (but not necessarily the physical condition) of potency, noting that it was "even a funny word—potent—that's power."

Further, his age allowed Leo to let go of many of the expectations he had for himself when younger. For instance, he used to overcompensate with great physical activity to prove his manhood and to be "a good daddy." But, he said, he gradually learned that such overcompensation was not necessary.

The practice of "letting go," as Leo and many of our other informants had done, was much like that described by essayist Leonard Kriegel (1991) who, in a series of autobiographical essays, discussed the metaphor of "falling into life" as a way of coping with a disability and masculinity. Kriegel described a common reaction to coping with disability; that is, attempting to "overcome" the results of polio, in his case, by building his upper-body strength through endless hours of exercise. In the end, he experienced premature arthritis in his shoulders and arms. The metaphor of giving up or letting go of behavioral expectations and gender practices as a way to gain greater strength and control over one's life was prevalent among the men who primarily rejected dominant masculinity. As Hahn notes, this requires a cognitive shift and a change in reference group as well as a source of social support:

> *I think, ironically, that men with disabilities can acquire strength by acknowledging weakness. Instead of attempting to construct a fragile and ultimately phony identity only as males, they might have more to gain, and little to lose, both individually and collectively by forging a self-concept about the concept of disability. Certainly this approach requires the exposure of a vulnerability that has been a primary reason for the elaborate defense mechanisms that disabled men have commonly employed to protect themselves (1989:3).*

Thus, men with disabilities who rejected or renounced masculinity did so as a process of deviance disavowal. They realized that it was societal conceptions of masculinity, rather than themselves, that were problematic. In doing so, they were able to create alternative gender practices.

SUMMARY AND CONCLUSION

The experiences of men with physical disabilities are important, because they illuminate both the insidious power and limitations of contemporary masculinity. These men have insider knowledge of what the subordinated know about both the gender and social order (Janeway 1980). Additionally, the gender practices of some of these men exemplify alternative visions of masculinity that are obscured but available to men in our culture. Finally, they allow us to elucidate a process of paramount importance: How men with physical disabilities find happiness, fulfillment, and a sense of self-worth in a culture that has, in essence, denied them the right to their own identity, including their own masculinity.

Based on our interviews, then, we believe that men with physical disabilities depend on at least three patterns in their adjustment to the double bind associated with the demands of hegemonic masculinity and the stigmatization of being disabled. While each of our informants used one pattern more than the others, none of them depended entirely on any one of the three.

To judge the patterns and practices associated with any form of masculinity, it is necessary to explore the implications for both the personal life of the individual and the effect on the reproduction of the societal gender order (Connell 1990a). Different patterns will challenge, comply, or actively support gendered arrangements.

The reliance pattern is reflected by an emphasis on control, independence, strength, and concern for appearances. Men who rely on dominant conceptions of masculinity are much more likely to internalize their feelings of inadequacy and seek to compensate or overcompensate for them. Because the problem is perceived to be located within oneself rather than within the social structure, this model does not challenge, but rather perpetuates, the current gender order.

A certain distancing from dominant ideals occurs in the reformulation pattern. But reformulation tends to be an independent project, and class-based resources play an important role. As such, it doesn't present a formidable challenge to the gender order. Connell (1990a: 474) argues that this response may even modernize patriarchy.

The rejection model, the least well represented in this article, offers the most hope for change. Linked closely to a sociopolitical approach that defines disability as a product of interactions between individuals and their environment, disability (and masculinity) is understood as socially constructed.

Members of the Disability Rights Movement, as a result, seek to reconstruct masculinity through a three-prong strategy. First, they focus on changing the frame of reference regarding who defines disability and masculinity, thereby changing the social-construction dynamics of both. Second, they endeavor to help people with disabilities be more self-referent when defining their identities. To do that, a third component must be implemented: support structures, such as alternative subcultures, must exist. If the Disability Rights Movement is successful in elevating this struggle to the level of collective practice, it will challenge the legitimacy of the institutional arrangements of the current gender order.

In closing, there is much fruitful work to be done in the area of masculinity and disability. For instance, we should expect men with disabilities to respond differently to the demands associated with disability and masculinity due to sexual orientation, social class, age of onset of one's disability, race, and ethnicity. However, *how* and *why* gender identity varies for men with disabilities merits further study. We hope that this work serves as an impetus for others to take up these issues.

REFERENCES

Callahan, John. 1989. *Don't Worry, He Won't Get Far on Foot.* New York: Vintage Books.

Connell, R. W. 1991. "Live Fast and Die Young: The Construction of Masculinity among Young Working-Class Men on the Margin of the Labor Market." *The Australian and New Zealand Journal of Sociology,* Volume 27, Number 2, August, pp. 141–171.

———. 1990a. "A Whole New World: Remaking Masculinity in the Context of the Environmental Movement." *Gender & Society,* Volume 4, Number 4, December, pp. 452–478.

———. 1990b. "An Iron Man: The Body and Some Contradictions of Hegemonic Masculinity," In *Sport, Men, and the Gender Order,* Michael Messner and Donald Sabo, eds. Champaign, IL: Human Kinetics Publishers, Inc., pp. 83–96.

———. 1987. *Gender and Power: Society, the Person, and Sexual Politics.* Stanford, CA: Stanford University Press.

Denzin, Norman. 1989. *The Research Act: A Theoretical Introduction to Sociological Methods.* Englewood Cliffs, NJ: Prentice-Hall.

Emerson, Robert. 1988. "Introduction." In *Contemporary Field Research: A Collection of Readings,* Robert Emerson, ed. Prospect Heights, IL: Waveland Press, pp. 93–107.

Hahn, Harlan. 1989. "Masculinity and Disability." *Disability Studies Quarterly,* Volume 9, Number 3, pp. 1–3.

Janeway, Elizabeth. 1980. *Powers of the Weak.* New York: Alfred A. Knopf.

Katz, Jack. 1988. "A Theory of Qualitative Methodology: The Social System of Analytic Fieldwork." In *Contemporary Field Research: A Collection of Readings,* Robert Emerson, ed. Prospect Heights, IL: Waveland Press, pp. 127–148.

Kriegel, Leonard. 1991. *Falling into Life.* San Francisco: North Point Press.

Messner, Michael A. 1992. *Power at Play: Sports and the Problem of Masculinity.* Boston: Beacon Press.

Murphy, Robert F. 1990. *The Body Silent.* New York: W. W. Norton.

Scott, James C. 1985. *Weapons of the Weak: Everyday Forms of Peasant Resistance.* New Haven: Yale University Press.

West, Candace, and Don H. Zimmerman. 1987. "Doing Gender." *Gender & Society,* Volume 1, Number 2, June, pp. 125–151.

Zola, Irving Kenneth. 1982. *Missing Pieces: A Chronicle of Living with a Disability.* Philadelphia: Temple University Press.

11

Abortion Stories on the Border

DEBBIE NATHAN

"Your period's late?" The clerk at Ciudad Juarez's Benavides Pharmacy offers a customer syringes of female hormones. "Inject this twice," she advises. Down the street, at the market where El Pasoans and tourists buy party piñatas, herbalists hawk bags of leaves and bark. "Guaranteed to bring on your period if you're less than three months overdue," one vendor says.

In Mexico, with few exceptions, abortion is a crime. State law governing the city of Juarez, for instance, declares that a woman convicted of having an illegal abortion can be imprisoned for as long as five years, and her abortionist for three.

Nevertheless, before the U.S. Supreme Court legalized abortion in 1973, American women flocked to Mexico to end their pregnancies. Black market abortions were easy to get then; and though most still offered today are medically risky, they remain available.

Texas already prohibits Medicaid funding of abortion and restricts techniques used to abort "viable fetuses" older than 20 weeks. After the Supreme Court ruled on the Webster case, Texas was considered one of 22 states likely to further limit or even outlaw abortion. Should this happen, the Mexican border may once again become an abortion underground option for many American women.

Elizabeth Canfield, a Planned Parenthood counselor in Albuquerque, New Mexico, worked from 1968 to 1971 with Clergy Counseling Service for Problem Pregnancies in Los Angeles. The group referred American women to abortionists in Mexican border cities, especially Juarez.

"Juarez had many abortionists," Canfield said. "Most were physicians; others were laypeople trained by doctors. They charged $160 to $200 to do an early abortion, and millions of dollars were being made. Everybody had relationships with the cop on the beat. Enormous payoffs were taking place—they couldn't conceive of the U.S. referrers not wanting a kickback."

A woman who went to Mexico for an abortion entered a James Bond world, Canfield says. "You needed to carry your money inside your bra. You couldn't ever say 'abortion,' just something like 'Liz sent me.'"

"Though some black market abortion providers were very humanitarian," Canfield says, "they were all doing it for the money." Even back-up services, like airlines, cleaned up—whether intentionally or not. She recalls, for instance, one U.S. travel agent who "didn't want to know anything about what we were doing when we made reservations through her. One day she called me and said, 'You won't believe this, but we received an award for selling the most three-day weekends to Mexico.' Her boss kept asking how it was that so many of her clients wanted to go there. She was mortified!" Canfield remembers.

After abortion was legalized in the United States, the Mexican black market dissolved. Mexican women of means, however, can still find doctors who will occasionally provide discreet early abortions, says Dr. Francisco Urango Vallarta, former director of the Autonomous University's medical school in Chihuahua City, about 225 miles beyond the border.

"It's illegal, of course, so no one is going to routinely do the procedure and thus earn a reputation as an abortionist," Urango says. "But occasionally, a doctor will, say, fall behind on his car payments. Then he may do one." The procedure of choice, Urango says, is the dilatation and curettage (D&C) procedure, scraping the pregnant patient's uterus under the pretext of checking for diseases. The D&C automatically causes abortion.

Many Mexican doctors who favor abortion rights but are reluctant to break the law refer their patients to U.S. clinics such as Reproductive Services in El Paso. Reproductive Services does 2,500 abortions annually, and a quarter of the patients are from Mexico. Most are middle- and upper-class women seeking medically safe abortions.

Those Mexican women with neither connections nor money to cross the border must rely on cheap home or drugstore remedies. As indigent American women did in the United States before abortion was legalized, many Mexicans trying to end their pregnancies drink tea made of herbs such as thyme, rue, or cedar bark, sold at herb markets. Or they use synthetic chemicals. At a Mexican pharmacy one doesn't need prescriptions to buy hormone injections and drugs to make the uterus contract so as to expel the fetus. If such measures aren't successful, a Mexican woman may apply caustic chemicals or pay midwives or nurses, nicknamed "stork scarers," to stick catheters through her cervix.

These methods are often ineffective and dangerous. The Mexican Social Security Institute reported almost 60,000 cases of abortion-related complications in 1988. Of those, at least 100 resulted in massive infections or hemorrhaging that led to death. Indeed, in Mexico, illegal abortion is considered the second most common cause of maternal mortality (after childbirth). Even so, the country's federal Health Secretariat estimates that at least 500,000 of the procedures are performed annually.

In Ciudad Juarez, Dr. Carlos Cano Vargas, Assistant Chief of Obstetrics and Gynecology at the city's General Hospital, believes many of the 350 miscarriages his department sees annually are really illegal abortions.

"But it's hard to prove," he says, "because everyone conceals it. The pharmacy drugs leave no traces. Infection can happen after a natural miscarriage too, so that's no proof either. You may see caustic chemical lesions or a catheter, but that's very rare. A woman can be on her death bed and usually won't admit anything. In six years I've seen only two cases of obvious abortions. For every verifiable one in Juarez, there are countless more covered up."

Delia is a pseudonym for a Juarez woman whose abortion would have gone unnoticed last year had it not been botched. The 26-year-old is the mother of three preschoolers; her husband is a "twin plant" factory worker, earning about $40 per week. When their youngest child was six months old, Delia found herself pregnant again. She is taciturn but matter-of-fact while describing what happened next.

"We couldn't afford another child, so I took hormone shots from the drugstore and rue tea from the herb market. Nothing worked. Then a friend told me about a nurse abortionist. For $350,000 pesos (at the time about $200) she put a catheter up me that she was going to remove next day. But at night I got such a high fever that my husband insisted I go to a clinic. If only I'd known how to take out the catheter! Because when the doctor saw it in me he got really mad and called the police. They came and interrogated me, but of course I wouldn't tell them where the nurse was.

"The police made the clinic detain me for three days. Later at the station I was interrogated again for four hours. Finally, the detectives left the room and I just walked out. I hid at my mother's house for a few days but the police never came back."

"Oh yes," Delia said, "it's very common for women here to get abortions. If you know the pharmacist you can get the injections, and there are lots of abortionists. A lot of my friends have had abortions. Most already have children."

Delia's abortion was reported in the local Mexican press—complete with her name and address—on the police blotter page, along with stories about gang leaders, robbers and rapists. She was never indicted, however.

"It is hard to prosecute these cases," shrugs State Police Chief Investigator Saul Oscar Osollo. Delia's was one of only about five abortions reported to the Juarez police each year, he said.

Some Mexican women with botched abortions are luckier than Delia—they make it to El Paso, where health care providers like Reproductive Services do mop-up duty. Once, says clinic director Patti Pagels, "We suctioned a woman's uterus and found rubber bands in it. The patient was from Juarez. We told her we weren't going to report it, but she wouldn't admit having done anything."

Another recent patient, a 17-year-old, "came in already 16 or 17 weeks pregnant. The lab work indicated she was perfectly healthy; but—this is how fast the infection sets in—next day when she returned, a faucet of green, rancid pus was coming out of her vagina. We immediately gave her 2000 milligrams of tetracycline. An hour later she was blue and shivering—she couldn't swallow and her temperature was 104.5. She ended up spending five days on antibiotics at Thomason (El Paso's county hospital)."

"She told us she'd gone to somebody in Juarez who'd stuck something up her. It scared me! I thought, 'What if she hadn't come here? How long would she have waited to tell her parents?'"

"Death from septic abortion is horrible," Pagels says. "My God, nobody should ever have to die like that."

Elizabeth Canfield, recalling her work two decades ago referring American women to Mexican abortionists, predicts that if abortions are outlawed in Texas, women will travel to other states where they remain legal. But if a change in the law results in ready availability of abortion in Mexican cities, Americans along the border may go south as they did in the past.

Canfield keeps in touch with a former Juarez abortionist. "He's now a law enforcement officer," she said. "He told me recently that if things ever get tough again in this country, he'll help us again."

12

The Myth of the "Battered Husband Syndrome"

JACK C. STRATON

The most recurrent backlash against women's safety is the myth that men are battered as often as women. Suzanne Steinmetz (1978) created this myth with her 1977 study of 57 couples, in which four wives were seriously beaten *but no husbands were beaten.* By a convoluted thought process (Pagelow, 1985) she concluded that her finding of zero battered husbands implied that men just don't report abuse and therefore 250,000 American husbands (Steinmetz, 1977) are battered each year by their wives (*Time Magazine,* 1978), a figure that exploded to 12 million in the subsequent media feeding frenzy (Storch, 1978).

Men have never before been shy in making their needs known, so it is peculiar that in 17 years, this supposedly huge contingent of "battered men" has never revealed itself in the flesh. Could it be that it simply does not exist? Indeed, a careful analysis of domestic violence, using everything from common experience to medical studies to U.S. National Crime Survey data, show that only three (Gaquin, 1977/1978) to four (Schwartz, 1987) percent of interspousal violence involves attacks on men by their female partners.

In the myth's latest incarnation, Katherine Dunn (*The New Republic,* August 1, 1994) is unable to counter these hard scientific data so she turns to disputed sociological studies by Murray Straus and associates (Straus & Gelles, 1986; Straus, Gelles, & Schwartz, 1980, p. 36) for "proof" that violence rates are almost equal. She first implies that these studies are unassailable by calling the authors "two of the most respected re-searchers in the field of domestic violence." She then cynically attempts to undercut Straus's critics by labeling them as "advocacy groups." In fact, Straus's critics are unimpeachable scientists of both genders, such as Emerson and Russell Dobash (1981) and Edward Gondolf (1988) who say his studies are *bad science,* with findings and conclusions that are contradictory, inconsistent, and unwarranted (Dobash & Dobash, 1981; Pleck et al., 1978; Pagelow, 1980; Saunders, 1988).

There are three major flaws in Straus's work. The first is that he used a set of questions that cannot discriminate between intent and effect (Dobash, Dobash, Wilson, & Daly, 1992; Jackson, 1988; Newton & Gildman, 1983). This so-called Conflict Tactics Scale (or CTS) equates a woman pushing a man in self-defense to a man pushing a woman down the stairs (Jackson, 1988). It labels a mother as violent if she defends her daughter from the father's sexual molestation. It combines categories such as "hitting" and "trying to hit" despite the important difference between them (Pagelow, 1985, p. 178).

Because it looks at only one year, this study equates a single slap by a woman to a man's 15-year history of domestic terrorism. Even Steinmetz herself says the CTS studies ignore the difference between a slap that stings and a punch that causes permanent injury (Steinmetz, 1980). Indeed, after analyzing the results of the U.S. National Crime Surveys, sociologist Martin Schwartz concluded that 92% of those seeking medical care from a private physician for injuries received in a spousal assault are women (Schwartz, 1987). The NCS study shows that one man is hospitalized for injuries received in a spousal assault for every 46 women hospitalized (Saunders, 1988).

Even if we ignore all of the previously mentioned flaws in Straus's CTS studies, they are bad science on a second set of grounds. Straus interviewed only one partner, but other studies (Szinovacz, 1983; Jouriles & O'Leary, 1985) that independently interviewed both partners found that their accounts of the violence did not match. Also, a study by Richard Gelles and John Harrop (1991) using the CTS failed to find any difference in self-reporting of violence against children by step-parents versus birth-parents—in vivid contrast to the actual findings that a step-parent is up to 100 times more likely to assault a small child than is a birth parent (Daly & Wilson, 1988; Dobash et al., 1992). Any research technique that contains a 10,000 percent systematic error is totally unreliable.

In fact, a third independent case can be made against Straus's study. It excluded incidents of violence that occur after separation and divorce, yet these account for 75.9 percent of spouse-on-spouse assaults, with a male perpetrator 93.3 percent of the time, according to the U.S. Department of Justice (1984). The Straus study relied on self-reports of violence by one member of each household, yet men who batter typically under-report their violence by 50 percent (Edleson & Brygger, 1986). Finally, the CTS does not include sexual assault as a category although more women are raped by their husbands than beaten only (Russell, 1990, p. 90). Adjusting Straus's own statistics to include this reality makes the ratio of male to female spousal violence more than sixteen to one.

Police and court records persistently indicate that women are 90 to 95 percent of the victims of reported assaults (Dobash et al., 1992). Promoters of the idea that women are just as abusive as men suggest that these results may be biased because the victims were self-reporting. But Schwartz's analysis of the 1973–1982 U.S. National Crime

Surveys shows that men who are assaulted by their spouses actually call the police more often than women who were assaulted by their spouses (Schwartz, 1987). In any case, criminal victimization surveys using random national samples are free of any reporting bias. They give similar results:

- The 1973–81 U.S. National Crime Survey, including over a million interviews, found that only 3 to 4% of marital assaults involved attacks on men by their female partners (Gaquin, 1977/1978; Schwartz, 1987).
- The 1981 and 1987 Canadian surveys (Solicitor General of Canada, 1985; Sacco & Johnson, 1990) found that the number of assaults of males was too low to provide reliable estimates.
- The 1982 and 1984 British surveys found that women accounted for all of the victims of marital assaults (Worrall & Pease).

This is not to say that men are not harmed in our society, but most often men are harmed by other men. Eighty-seven percent of men murdered in the U.S. are killed by other men (U.S. Department of Justice, 1991, p. 17). Those doing the killing in every major and minor war in this and previous centuries have mostly been men! Instead of attempting to undercut services for the enormous number of women who are terrorized by their mates, those who claim to care for men had better address our real enemies: ourselves.

Of course we must have compassion for those relatively few men who are harmed by their wives and partners, but it makes logical sense to focus our attention and work on the vast problem of male violence (96 percent of domestic violence) and not get side-tracked by the relatively tiny (4 percent) problem of male victimization. The biggest concern, though, is not the wasted effort on a false issue, it is the fact that batterers, like O. J. Simpson, who think *they* are the abused spouses, are very dangerous during separation and divorce. In one study of spousal homicide, over half of the male defendants were separated from their victims (Bernard et al., 1982). Arming these men with warped statistics to fuel their already warped world view is unethical, irresponsible, and quite simply lethal.

REFERENCES

Bernard, G. W., Vera, H., Vera, M. I., & Newman, G. (1982). Till death do us part: A Study of spouse murder. *Bulletin of the American Academy of Psychiatry and the Law, 10.*

Daly, M., & Wilson, M. (1988). Evolutionary social psychology and family homicide. *Science, 242,* 519–524.

Dobash, R. E., & Dobash, R. P. (1981). The case of wife beating. *Journal of Family Issues, 2,* 439–470.

Dobash, R. E., Dobash, R. P., Wilson, M., & Daly, M. (1992). The myth of sexual symmetry in marital violence. *Social Problems, 39,* 71–91.

Edleson, J., & Brygger, M. (1986). Gender differences in reporting of battering incidences. *Family Relations, 35,* 377–382.

Gaquin, D. A. (1977/1978). Spouse abuse: Data from the National Crime Survey. *Victimology, 2,* 632–643.

Gelles. R. J., & Harrop, J. W. (1991). The risk of abusive violence among children with nongenetic caretakers. *Family Relations, 40,* 78–83.

Gondolf, E. G. (1988). (Letter). *Social Work, 32,* 190.

Jackson, J. (1988). (Letter). *Social Work, 32,* 189–190.

Jouriles, E. N., & O'Leary, K. D. (1985). Interspousal reliability of marital violence. *Journal of Consulting and Clinical Psychology, 53,* 419–421 (as analyzed in Dobash et al., 1992).

Newton, P., & Gildman, G. (1983). *Defining domestic violence: Violent episode or violent act?* Paper presented at the American Sociological Association Conference, Detroit, Illinois.

Pagelow, M. (1980, November). *Double victimization of battered women.* Presented at the meeting of the American Society of Criminology, San Francisco.

Pagelow, M. D. (1985). The "battered husband syndrome": Social problem or much ado about little. In N. Johnson (Ed.), *Marital violence* (Sociological Review Monograph, 31, pp. 172–195). London: Routledge & Kegan Paul.

Pleck, E., Pleck, J. H., Grossman, M., & Bart, P. B. (1978). The Battered Date Syndrome: A comment on Steinmetz' article. *Victimology, 2,* 680–684.

Russell, D. E. H. (1990). *Rape in marriage.* Bloomington, IN: Indiana University Press.

Sacco, V. F., & Johnson, H. (1990). *Patterns of criminal victimization.* Ottawa: Statistics Canada.

Saunders, D. G. (1988). Other "truths" about domestic violence: A reply to McNeely and Robinson-Simpson. *Social Work, 32,* 179–183.

Schwartz, M. D. (1987). Gender and injury in spousal assaults. *Sociological Focus, 20,* 61–75.

Solicitor General of Canada. (1985). Female victims of crime. *Canadian Urban Victimization Survey Bulletin* No. 4. Ottawa: Programs Branch/Research and Statistics Group.

Steinmetz, S. (1977). Wifebeating, husbandbeating: A comparison of the use of physical violence to resolve marital fights. In M. Roy (Ed.), *Battered women* (pp. 63–72). New York: Van Nostrand Reinhold.

Steinmetz, S. K. (1978). The battered husband syndrome. *Victimology, 2,* 499–509.

Steinmetz, S. K. (1980). Women and violence: Victims and perpetrators. *American Journal of Psychotherapy, 34,* 334–350.

Storch, G. (1978, August 7). Claim of 12 million battered husbands takes a beating. *Miami Herald,* p. 16.

Straus, M. A., & Gelles, R. J. (1986). Societal change and change in family violence from 1975 to 1985 as revealed by two national surveys. *Journal of Marriage and the Family, 48,* 465–479.

Straus, M. A., Gelles, R. J., & Steinmetz, S. (1980). *Behind closed doors: Violence in the American family.* New York: Doubleday.

Szinovacz, M. E. (1983). Using couple data as a methodological tool: The case of marital violence. *Journal of Marriage and the Family, 45,* 633–644.

Time Magazine. (1978, March 20). *The battered husbands,* p. 69.

U.S. Department of Justice, Bureau of Justice Statistics. (1984, April). *Family Violence,* p. 4.

U.S. Department of Justice. (1991). *Crime in the United States: Uniform Crime Reports.* Washington, DC: Author.

Worrall, A., & Pease. K. (1986). *Patterns in criminal homicide: Evidence from the 1982 British crime survey.* Philadelphia: University of Pennsylvania Press.

13

Battered Women of Color
in Public Health Care Systems
Racism, Sexism, and Violence

BETH E. RICHIE
VALLI KANUHA

INTRODUCTION

The problems of rape, battering, and other forms of violence against women have existed throughout history. Only recently have these experiences, traditionally accepted as natural events in the course of women's lives, received significant attention as major social problems (Schechter 1985). For many years there was a tendency for both human service providers and public policy research to focus only on the individual lives of women, children, and men who are damaged or lost due to domestic violence. This narrow focus on individual victims and perpetrators involved in domestic violence rather than on an examination of the role social institutions play in the maintenance of violence against women represents one of the major gaps in our analysis of this pervasive social issue. Paradoxically, the very institutions which have been constructed for the protection and care of the public good—such as the criminal justice system, religious organizations, hospitals, and health care agencies—have long sanctioned disparate and unequal attention to women in society (Lewin and Olesen 1985). Only through a critique of these historically patriarchal and often sexist institutions will we comprehend domestic violence as more than individual acts of violence by perpetrators against victims.

Another equally problematic gap in contemporary analysis and study of violence against women exists with regard to race and ethnicity, i.e., how individual and institutional racism affects the lives of women of color who are battered. With a few notable exceptions, there is very little research on the ways that traditional responses of societal institutions to violence against women are complicated by racism and, therefore, how battered women of color are systematically at a disadvantage when seeking help in most domestic violence situations (Rios 1985). The result is that battered women who are African-American, Latina, Asian/Pacific Islander, East Indian, Native-American, and members of other communities of color are vulnerable to abuse not only from their partners, but from insensitive, ineffective institutions as well.

This chapter will address an important factor which is often ignored in our understanding and analysis of domestic violence. While our increasing knowledge of battered women is usually applied in the context that "all women are vulnerable to male violence," the emphasis of this discussion will be on those differential social, economic, and cultural circumstances that render women of color, in particular, vulnerable to male violence at both individual and institutional levels. In addition, this article will focus specifically on the experiences of battered women of color within the health care system, including hospitals, clinics, and public health agencies. As will be described in later sections, many women of color rely significantly on public health institutions not only for ongoing preventive health care and crisis intervention services, but, more importantly, as a viable access point for other services and institutions, e.g., public welfare, housing assistance, legal advice, and so on. Thus the emphasis of this chapter is on the relationship between health care institutions and battered women of color, although similar critiques could be made about the inadequate response of other public institutions (such as religious organizations or the criminal justice system) to battered women of color. Finally, this essay will discuss some effective strategies and programs which address the unique and complex issues affecting women of color who are battered.

BALANCING OUR MULTIPLE LOYALTIES: SPECIAL CONSIDERATIONS FOR WOMEN OF COLOR AND VICTIMS OF DOMESTIC VIOLENCE

In order to understand the special circumstances and tensions experienced by battered women of color it is important to understand the interface of gender inequality, sexism, and racism as they affect women both in their racial/ethnic communities and in society at large. Because of the powerful effects of a violent relationship, many battered women are required, either overtly or covertly, to balance the often conflicting needs and expectations of their batterers, their communities, and the larger society. These conflicting expectations, rules, and loyalties often compromise the strategies which are available to liberate women of color from violent relationships. This discussion will serve as a foundation for examining the compound effects of oppression which many women of color face even prior to entering the health care system for medical treatment of and protection from domestic violence.

Communities of color in this country have historically been devastated by discriminatory and repressive political, social, and economic policies. It is commonplace to associate high infant mortality, school drop-out rates, criminality, drug abuse, and most other indices of social dysfunction with African-American, Latino, Native-American, and other non-European ethnic groups (Perales and Young 1988). Even among the "model minorities," Asians and Pacific Islanders, groups of new immigrants as well as their assimilated relatives have shown increased rates of HIV and AIDS, mental health problems, and other negative cofactors which are in part attributable to their status as non-majority (non-White) people in the United States (Chua-Eoan 1990).

Most everyone, from historians to social scientists to politicians, whether conservative or radical, considers racism to be a significant, if not the primary, cause of this disproportionate level of social deterioration among communities of color (Steinberg 1989). While the dynamics of racism have often been studied from a macro-perspective, comparing the effects of race discrimination on particular ethnic groups vis-à-vis society at large, the differential effects of racism on women versus men of color has not been given due attention. In order to adequately understand any analysis of the combined effects of racism, sexism, and battering, a consideration of gender-based tension within communities of men and women of color, separate from and related to the predominant White society, is required.

There are many stereotypes about women of color which affect not only our understanding of them as women, but particularly our analysis of and sensitivity to them with regard to domestic violence. For example, many portrayals of women of color espouse their inherent strengths as historical, matriarchal heads of households (Rudwick and Rudwick 1971). While this stereotype of women of color as super homemakers, responsible family managers, and unselfish nurturers may be undisputed, such attributions do not mean that all (or most) women of color are therefore empowered and supported in their various family roles or have positions of leadership within their ethnic communities. Many women of color with whom we work state that they face the burden either of having to be overly competent and successful or having to avoid the too-often painful reality of becoming "just an-other one of those horror stories or pitiful statistics on the front page of the newspaper." For women of color who are experiencing domestic violence, the implicit community and societal expectation to be strong and continue to care for themselves and their families results in their denying not only the actual existence of battering in their lives, but the extent and nature of that abuse (Richie 1992). For example, one Korean woman who was repeatedly punched around her head and face by her husband reported that she used cosmetics extensively each day when she went to Mass with her husband, in order to assure protection of her own, as well as her husband's, dignity among their church and neigh-borhood friends. When she went to work as a typist in a White business, she was especially careful not to disclose evidence of her abuse, in order to pro-tect both herself and her husband from her co-workers' judgments that "there was something wrong with Korean people."

While public policy makers are concerned about the rapidly escalating crime rate in this country, many leaders in cities predominated by communities of color are becoming increasingly concerned about the profile of those convicted for crimes, i.e., young boys and men of color. The predominance of men of color in correctional fa-cilities (close to 90 percent of the penal population in some cities) has polarized everyone, from scholars to community leaders to policy makers. While most mainstream legislators and public health officials are reluctant to discuss it publicly, there is a rising belief that men of color are inher-ently problematic and socially deviant. More pro-gressive analysts have ascribed criminal behavior among nonwhite males to historically racist social conditions that are reinforced by criminal, legal, and penal systems which disproportionately arrest and convict men of color at least in part because of their skin color (Kurtz 1990).

There are no equally concerned dialogues about how women of color continue to be victims of crime more often than White women and about the disparate treatment they receive from not only racist, but sexist social systems. An African-American woman who works with battered women as a court advocate states unequivocally that battered women of color are usually treated less respectfully by prosecutors and judges than the White women with whom she works. In addi-tion, when this same court advocate has raised this disparity with her African-American brothers and male friends in her community, she is often de-rided as being "one of those White women's lib-bers" who has betrayed "her own" by working on a problem like domestic violence, which will fur-ther stigmatize and destroy the men of color who are charged with battering. Unfortunately, this dia-lectic of the comparable oppression of women and men of color has resulted in a troubling silence about the needs of women of color and led to counterproductive discussions between women and men of color about the meaning and signifi-cance of domestic violence, specifically, and sex-ism in general.

For a battered woman of color who experi-ences violence at the hands of a man of color from her own ethnic group, a complex and troublesome dynamic is established that is both enhanced and compromised by the woman's relationship to her community. She is battered by another member of her ethnic community, whose culture is vulnerable to historical misunderstanding and extinction by society at large. For the battered woman, this means that she may be discriminated against in her attempt to secure services *while at the same time* feeling protective of her batterer, who might also be unjustly treated by such social institutions as the police and the judicial system. Most battered women of color are acutely aware of how the po-lice routinely brutalize men of color, how hospitals and social services discriminate against men of color, and the ways men of color are more readily labeled deviant than White men. In one Midwest-ern city, anecdotal reports from court and police monitors have shown that men of color awaiting arraignment for domestic violence charges fre-quently arrive in court with bruises supposedly in-flicted by police officers. One Indian woman stated that when she saw her husband in court the morning after a battering incident, he looked just as bad as she did, with black eyes and bruises about his face. Feeling pity for him, she refused to testify, and upon release he told her of being beaten by police while being transported between the jail and the court house. Although the existence of police brutality is unfortunately not a new phenomenon, it is certainly compromised and complicated in the context of domestic violence, *especially* for men and women of color who are seeking help from this already devastating problem. For battered women of color, seeking help for the abuse they are experiencing always requires a tenuous balance between care for and loyalty to themselves, their batterers, and their communities.

The situation is further complicated by the fact that communities of color have needed to prioritize the pressing social, economic, and health problems which have historically plagued their people and neighborhoods. Because of sexism, the particular concerns of women typically do not emerge at the top of the list. The values of family stability, community self-determination, and protection of one's racial and ethnic culture are often seen as incompatible with addressing the needs of battered women within communities of color. Most of us who have worked in the domestic violence movement are well aware of the gross misconceptions that battering is just a woman's issue or that domestic violence in communities of color is not as serious as other problems. The most dangerous consequence, for battered women of color, however, is that they are often entrapped by these misconceptions and misguided loyalties and thus remain in the confines of violent and abusive households (Richie 1985).

While credit for a broad-based societal response to the problem of violence against women must be given to the feminist movement and its successful grassroots organizing in the mid-1970s, another process of "split loyalties" has emerged, compromising the analysis regarding battered women of color. Those women of color who identify themselves as activists, feminists, and organizers within the battered women's movement often face an additional barrier among their feminist peers when raising issues related to the particular dynamics of domestic violence and race/ethnicity (hooks 1984). Many White feminists and the organizations they have created become very threatened when women of color, with their concomitant expanded analysis of battering and racism, have moved into leadership roles. Many women of color in the violence against women movement have challenged the long-standing belief of many White feminists that sexism is the primary, if not the only, cause of women's oppression. In a reform movement which has had such a significant impact on the values, behaviors, and subsequent policies regarding women and violence, the reluctance or inability to integrate an understanding of violence against women with other forms of oppression (such as racism, classism, ageism) in addition to sexism has been disappointing (Davis 1985). A more significant concern, though, is the effect of limited analysis on women and children of color who are seeking refuge and safety from both hostile partners and social institutions outside the battered women's movement.

In summary, our understanding of women of color who are battered must be considered against the political, social, and cultural backdrop of their racial and ethnic communities; within the framework of institutional responses that are historically based in racism and other prejudices; and against the background of the feminist agenda, which has been primarily responsible for galvanizing all of the above to address this pervasive social issue. It is in this context that we turn to an examination of the particular influence, concerns, and barriers of the health care system in dealing with battered women of color.

BATTERED WOMEN OF COLOR: HEALTH PROBLEMS AND HEALTH CARE

Women who are battered are often seriously hurt; their physical and psychological injuries are life-threatening and long-lasting. In one-third of all battering incidents, a weapon is used, and 40 percent result in the need for emergency medical attention (Stark 1977). Research suggests that one-third of all adult female suicide attempts can be associated with battering, and 25 percent of all female homicide victims die at the hands of their husbands or boyfriends (Browne 1987). More women are injured in their homes by their spouses or male partners each year than by accidents or illnesses (FBI 1982).

It is not surprising, therefore, that most battered women report their first attempt to seek help is from a health care institution, even before contacting the police (Stark 1977). This is especially true in communities of color, where police response is likely to be sporadic, at best (Davis 1985). Yet research indicates that of those battered women using the emergency room for acute treatment of injuries related to an abusive incident, only one in ten was identified as battered (McLeer and Amwar 1989). Similar findings have been cited for women using ambulatory care settings. A random sample of women seeking health maintenance visits at neighborhood health clinics revealed that 33 percent were battered women and less than 10 percent received safety information or counseling for domestic violence (Richie 1985). The following story of Yolanda (a pseudonym) illustrates the role of health facilities in the lives of battered women.

> Yolanda is a forty-six-year old who receives primary health care from a neighborhood health clinic. She uses the services of the walk-in clinic two or more times each month, complaining of discomfort, sleeplessness and fatigue. Yolanda never mentions that her boyfriend abuses her, but her clinic visits correspond directly with the pattern of his alcohol binges. The staff of the clinic know about her boyfriend's mistreatment, because he sometimes comes to the clinic drunk and will threaten her if she does not leave with him.

For Yolanda, the clinic symbolizes a safe, public place of refuge. From her experience, she knows it is legitimate to seek assistance when one is sick, and she trusts health authorities to take care of her

needs. Health providers lose an important opportunity for intervention when they do not offer assistance to Yolanda, especially since they have clear evidence that her boyfriend is violent toward her. She, in turn, feels that the violence must be hidden and that it is a source of shame, since her health care providers do not acknowledge it or offer to help.

For many battered women of color, the unresponsiveness of most health care institutions is symbolic of the overall reality of social disenfranchisement and deterioration in poor, nonwhite communities across the United States. While lack of quality, affordable housing is a major problem for many people of color, the majority of the homeless are women of color and their children (Perales and Young 1988). The drug epidemic, particularly crack and heroin use, has had a significant impact on violence against women. There is growing anecdotal evidence to suggest that battered women are often forced to use drugs as part of the pattern of their abuse, yet there is a serious lack of treatment programs for women, particularly poor women with children (Chavkin 1990). The spread of HIV and AIDS among many women of color has been compounded by the HIV infection rate among children of HIV-positive mothers. Many women with HIV report that negotiating for safer sex or clean needles is difficult when they are controlled by violent, coercive partners.

With regard to women and the social problems of drugs, homelessness, and AIDS, most public health officials have been quick to label women as the criminals, rather than the victims of a society that is disintegrating before our very eyes. When we add to the above the battering, rape, and psychological abuse of those same women who are homeless, drug addicted, and HIV-positive, it is clear that the health care system can be either a vehicle for assistance or a significant barrier for women who are seeking protection from a myriad of health and social problems.

The experience of Ana illustrates the interrelatedness that can occur between domestic violence, drug use, HIV infection, and the chronic and acute need for health care. Ana's husband was an injection drug user who had battered her severely throughout their ten-year marriage. He had been very ill for a period of months and had tested positive for HIV. Ana was already pregnant when her husband was tested, but he insisted that she carry through with the pregnancy. She was battered twice in the four months since she had gotten pregnant, and after one incident she was unable to get out of bed for two days. Her husband Daniel reportedly was concerned about the baby and took her to the emergency room of their local hospital. During the triage interview, the ER (Emergency Room) nurse noticed the tension between Ana and Daniel but was uncomfortable addressing it. The nurse later reported that she did not want to offend them by suggesting that they appeared to be having "marriage problems" because they were Hispanic, and she understood that Hispanics were embarrassed about discussing such matters with health professionals. After being admitted for observation, Ana began to complain of increased pains in her abdomen. After five days in the hospital, Ana hemorrhaged and lost her baby. At that time, she discovered that she had been tested for HIV and was seropositive. She returned home to a distraught and angry husband, who blamed the baby's death on her. She was beaten again and returned to the ER once more.

Ana's case illustrates one of the most troubling examples of the interface between health care and violence against women. With the long-standing lack of adequate and accessible prenatal care for poor women of color, pregnant women of color who are battered are especially vulnerable. Research indicates that 20 percent of all women who are battered experience the first incident during pregnancy (McFarlane 1989). The situation for pregnant battered women is further complicated by the troubling legal trend to hold women accountable for any damage inflicted upon a fetus in utero. If a pregnant woman is battered and the fetus is harmed, she may be criminally liable for not leaving the abusive relationship. Not surprisingly, in most recent "fetal death" cases across the

country, the women who are most severely punished are women of color (Pollitt 1990).

As the health care system has labored under increased social and economical stress, specialized programs for women and for certain communities have also been curtailed. For battered women of color this trend has specific and dangerous affects. With a steady increase in immigrants from Central America, South America, and the Caribbean, battered women who do not have legal status in this country are destined to remain invisible and underserved. Because of their undocumented status and other significant barriers (such as language and cultural differences), many battered women of color are denied assistance by the same organizations established to protect them, e.g., public welfare, legal advocacy, and health clinics (Kanuha 1987). One battered women's program specifically targeted to serve Caribbean women and their children reports that battered women who must use hospital services for their injuries often have to borrow Medicaid cards from other women in order to conceal their undocumented status. Staff from this same program describe the difficulty that one undocumented woman had even getting out of the house, much less to the hospital, as her batterer was rightfully suspicious that reports of his criminal behavior would also jeopardize *his* illegal status.

Most hospital-based crisis intervention programs do not have multi-lingual or multi-cultural staff who are trained in and sensitive to the special issues of women of color. For example, reliance on translators to communicate with non-English speaking women effectively compromises the confidentiality and protection of battered women who are immigrants, from small ethnic communities, or who must use their own family members as translators to describe painful and private incidents of violence in the home. There are numerous stories of women of color receiving insensitive treatment by health care staff who attribute domestic violence to stereotypes such as "I've heard you Latins have hot tempers" or "Asian women are so passive, it really explains why they get beaten by their husbands."

Finally, if a battered woman of color is also a lesbian, differently abled, or from any other group that is already stigmatized, her access to quality care from health providers may be further compromised. One battered lesbian who was an African American described a physician who was continually incredulous about her claims that a "pretty girl like her" would be beaten by her female lover. In fact, she stopped going to the hospital for emergency attention, even though she had no other health insurance, because she was angry at such homophobic treatment and therefore became increasingly reluctant to use the services of that hospital.

As long as health care institutions continue to be the primary, and usually first, access point for battered women of color, we must require them to institute ongoing training, education, and specialized programs, and to hire culturally knowledgeable staff to address the particular needs of this special group of women.

THE RESPONSE OF WOMEN OF COLOR

Despite the philosophical and political contradictions and the practical barriers described in the previous sections, women of color have actively and creatively challenged the discriminatory, institutional practices of health care and crisis intervention services. Against extremely difficult economic, cultural, and political odds, battered women of color and their advocates have initiated a broad-based response to violence against women in communities of color. Aspects of this response will be summarized in the remainder of the chapter.

One of the most significant developments in response to domestic violence in communities of color has been the creation of grassroots crisis intervention services by and for women of color. The majority of these programs have been organized autonomously from White women, privileging the analysis and experience of women of color by assuming the cultural, historical, and linguistic norms of Asian/Pacific Islander, Latin, African-American, Native-American and other nonwhite cultures. Typically located in neighborhoods and communities of color, these programs have a strong emphasis on community organization and public education. While many of these programs struggle for financial support and recognition from mainstream public health agencies and feminist organizations, they endure in great part because they are grounded in a community-based approach to problem solving.

The Violence Intervention Program for Latina women and their children in the community of East Harlem and the Asian Womens' Center in Chinatown are good examples of community-based programs in New York City. Refugee Women In Development (REFWID), in Washington, D.C., has a domestic violence component, as does Arco Iris, a retreat center for Native-American women and other women of color who have experienced violence in Arkansas. In Minnesota, women of color have created a statewide battered women's coalition called Black, Indian, Hispanic and Asian Women In Action (BIHA). In California, California Women Of Color Against Domestic Violence organizes and publishes a newsletter, "Out Loud," and women of color from seven southern states have created The Southeast Women Of Color Task Force Against Domestic Violence. Nationally, the members of the Women Of Color Task Force of the National Coalition Against Domestic Violence have provided national leadership training and technical assistance on the issues of battering and women of color, and their task force has served as a model for the development of programs for battered women of color across the country.

In addition to providing crisis intervention and emergency shelter services to battered women, these community-based programs and statewide coalitions for women of color are involved in raising the issue of battering within other contexts of social justice efforts. Representatives of grassroots battered women's programs are often in leadership roles on such issues as reproductive freedom, immigration policy, lesbian rights, criminal justice reform, homelessness, AIDS policy, and other issues that affect women of color. The National Black Women's Health Project in Atlanta is a good example of this.

Finally, in the past several years there has been a proliferation of literature on violence against women by scholars and activists who are women of color. Seal Press's New Leaf Series published Evelyn C. White's *Chain, Chain Change: For Black Women Dealing with Physical and Emotional Abuse* and Myrna Zambrano's *Mejor Sola Que Mal Acompañada.* Another good example of analysis by and for battered women of color is a publication by the Center for Domestic and Sexual Violence in Seattle, *The Speaking Profits Us: Violence Against Women of Color,* a collection of papers edited by Mary Violet Burns. Kitchen Table, Women of Color Press in Albany, New York, has been a leader in publishing writing by women of color, addressing the issue of violence against women in the Freedom Organizing pamphlet series and in many other works (Smith 1985).

By providing direct crisis intervention services, educating communities of color, advocating on broader feminist and social justice issues and publishing culturally relevant resources, Asian/Pacific Islanders, Latinas, Native-Americans, African Americans, Caribbeans, and other women of color have demonstrated a strong commitment to addressing violence against women. Our contributions have significantly enhanced both the conventional research on battered women and the progressive work of the battered women's movement, challenging the accepted analysis that violence against women has equivalent effects on all women. We must continue to develop community-based programs that are culturally relevant and responsive to the complexity of experiences faced by women of color, including inadequate health care, unemployment, homelessness, a failing educational system, and violence. Equally important, we must continue to work within our own cultures to challenge those traditions, assumptions, and values that reinforce male domination and ignore women's needs. In so doing, the struggle to end violence against women of color will include individual liberation as well as social reform. For us, the most compelling motivation for continuing this effort comes from the courage, commitment, and endurance that battered women of color have shown in their personal and collective struggles. On a daily basis they persist in defying the limits that violence, sexism, and racism impose on their lives. Our response must be to let their stories challenge and inspire us—women of color, battered women, White women, and men alike—to work actively to end individual and institutional violence against women.

NOTE

The women described in this essay are referred to anonymously or by pseudonyms to protect their safety and privacy. Their stories are both composites and individual accounts of women with whom the authors have worked.

REFERENCES

Browne, A. 1987. *When Battered Women Kill.* New York: Free Press.

Cazenave, N., and M. Straus. 1979. "Race, Class Network Embeddedness and Family Violence: A Search for Potent Support Systems." *Journal of Comparative Family Studies* 10:281–299.

Chavkin, W. 1990. "Drug Addiction and Pregnancy: Policy Crossroads." *American Journal of Public Health* 80 (4):483–87.

Chua-Eoan, H. 1990. "Strangers in Paradise." *Time* (April). 135:32–35.

Davis, A. 1985. *Violence against Women and the Ongoing Challenge to Racism.* Latham, N.Y.: Kitchen Table Press.

Federal Bureau of Investigation. 1982. *Uniform Crime Reports.* Washington, D.C.: Department of Justice.

Flitcraft, A. 1977. "Battered Women: An Emergency Room Epidemiology with Description of a Clinical Syndrome and Critique of Present Therapeutics." Doctoral Thesis, Yale University School Of Medicine. New Haven: Yale University.

hooks, b. 1984. *Feminist Theory: From Margin to Center.* Boston: South End Press.

Kanuha, V. 1987. "Sexual Assault in Southeast Asian Communities: Issues in Intervention." *Response* 10:3–4.

Kurtz, H. 1990. "Jail City: Behind Bars with New York's 20,000 Inmates." *New York Magazine.* April 23, 1990.

Lewin, E., and F. Olesen, eds. 1985. *Women, Health and Healing: Towards a New Perspective.* New York: Travistock Publications.

McFarlane, J. 1989. "Battering During Pregnancy: Tip of an Iceberg Revealed." *Women and Health* 15 (3):69–84.

McLeer, S., and R. Amwar. 1989. "A Study of Battered Women Presenting in an Emergency Department." *American Journal of Public Health.* 79 (1):65–66.

Perales, C., and L. Young, eds. 1988. *Too Little Too Late: Dealing with the Health Needs of Women in Poverty.* New York: Harrington Press.

Pollitt, K. 1990. "A New Assault on Feminism." *Nation* 250:409–11.

Richie, B. 1985. "Battered Black Women: A Challenge for the Black Community." *Black Scholar* 16:40–44.

Richie, B. 1992. "An Exploratory Study of the Link between Gender Identity Development, Violence Against Women, and Crime among African-American Battered Women." Ph.D. diss., The Graduate School and University Center, City University of New York.

Rios, E. 1985. "Double Jeopardy: Cultural and Systemic Barriers Faced by the Latina Battered Woman." Unpublished paper presented at the New York Women against Rape Conference, New York.

Rudwick, B., A. Meier, and E. Rudwick, eds. 1971. *Black Matriarchy: Myth or Reality.* Belmont, Calif.: Wadsworth Press.

Schechter, S. 1985. *Women and Male Violence.* Boston: South End Press.

Smith, B., ed. 1985. *Home Girls: A Black Feminist Anthology.* Latham, N.Y.: Kitchen Table Press.

Stark, E., A. Flintcraft and W. Frazier. 1977. "Medicine and Patriarchal Violence: The Social Construction of a 'Private Event.'" *International Journal of Health Services.* 9 (3): 461–94.

Steinberg, S. 1989. *The Ethnic Myth: Race, Ethnicity, and Class in America.* Boston: Beacon Press.

White, E. 1985. *Chain, Chain Change: For Black Women Dealing with Physical and Emotional Abuse.* Seattle: Seal Press.

Zambrano, M. 1985. *Mejor Sola Que Mal Acompañada: Para la Mujer Golpeada/ For the Latina in an Abusive Relationship.* Seattle: Seal Press.

14

Surmounting a Legacy

The Expansion of Racial Diversity in a Local Anti-Rape Movement

NANCY A. MATTHEWS

The anti-rape movement in Los Angeles originated from collectivist feminism and feminist social work networks. Between 1973 and 1980, five grassroots-led rape crisis organizations were started, including the Los Angeles Commission on Assaults Against Women (LACAAW), the Pasadena YWCA Rape Crisis Center and Hotline, the East Los Angeles Rape Hotline (ELA), the Center for the Pacific-Asian Family, and the San Fernando Valley Rape Crisis Service. While the bilingual, Latina-run East Los Angeles hotline and the multilingual Pacific-Asian hotline brought some women of color into the movement, very few Black women were involved, and the predominantly Black areas of the county (South Central Los Angeles) were virtually unserved. Since 1980, when the California Office of Criminal Justice Planning began funding rape crisis services, the state has promoted a relatively conservative, social service approach to this work. Yet ironically, during these years, state money also furthered one of the more progressive goals of the American anti-rape movement, to become multiracial and multicultural and to expand services to all women.

This article examines the problem of racial and ethnic diversity in the Los Angeles anti-rape movement, shows how racial diversity in the local movement was facilitated by the state's involvement in establishing two new Black rape crisis centers in the mid-1980s, and explores the consequences for race relations in the anti-rape movement in the United States.

FEMINISM, RACE, AND RAPE

The predominance of Whites, problematic for the American feminist movement as a whole, also affected the anti-rape movement. Despite collectivist feminist roots in the civil rights movement and the new left of the 1960s, the women's liberation movement in the United States remained dominated by White and middle-class women (Ferree and Hess 1985). Evans (1979) attributes this narrowness to the historic conjunction of the birth of feminism within the new left just when the Black movement was becoming separatist.

Many Black women who were interested in feminism in the early 1970s agreed with Black Panther Kathleen Cleaver that Black and White women would have to work in separate organizations, coming together in coalitions, because the problems each group of women faced were different enough that they could not be solved in the same organizations (Giddings 1984, p. 311). Thus the early anti-rape movement in the United States arose in a context of the distrust Black women felt of White feminism and the beginnings of Black feminism. This legacy, combined with the general level of racism in American society, has made multiracial organizing, feminist or otherwise, difficult.

Long before the anti-rape movement, the issues of race and rape were linked in the United States. From the 1880s through the 1950s, lynchings of Black men were justified on the basis of their threat to White women's virtue. Although Ida B. Wells investigated over 700 lynchings and found that accusations of rape had been made in less than one-third, the myth of Black men's proclivity for rape became ingrained in our culture (Davis 1981; Giddings 1984; Hooks 1981) and was manipulated to keep both Black men and White women in their places. Lynching, rather than rape, became the focus of Black women's activism against violence.

Incidents that linked race and rape caused further disjuncture between White feminists and Blacks in the current feminist movement in the United States. First, as the nationalist phase of the Black movement crested, several male leaders, most notably Eldridge Cleaver in *Soul on Ice* (1968), called for the raping of White women as a political act. Second, Susan Brownmiller, in her eagerness to prove the seriousness of rape, echoed the racist justification of lynching in her pathbreaking book *Against Our Will* (1975), perpetuating the "myth of the Black rapist" (Davis 1981). Rather than confront the issue of rape, even when Black women were raped by Black men, a special issue of *Ebony* magazine on Black-on-Black crime omitted rape (Bart and O'Brien 1985, p. 90).

In 1973, Roz Pulitzer, a Black member of the Manhattan (New York) Women's Political Caucus, which was lobbying on rape issues, said she did not expect Black women to get very involved in the issue. Like Kathleen Cleaver, she felt that "the splits between the concerns of White women and our concerns was so great that strategically we had to have a Black organization to give the women's movement credibility in our own communities. Every group must go through its period of self-identity" (New York Radical Feminists 1974, p. 243). However, Pulitzer, who had been instrumental in forming a Mayor's Task Force on Rape in New York City in 1973, hoped that Black women would take what White women had learned and use it to set up rape counseling and public education in the Black community.

In Los Angeles, it took more than 10 years to happen, and when it did, the impetus came not from grass-roots Black feminist groups, but Black community organizations responding to the state's call for proposals. This study of the expansion of racial diversity in the Los Angeles anti-rape movement is based primarily on oral-history interviews with participants since its beginning in the early 1970s through 1988 and with officials in the California Office of Criminal Justice Planning (OCJP). I conducted 35 interviews between 1987 and 1989 with women who were known as leaders, formal and informal. The interviews took from one to three hours and covered the participant's experience in rape crisis work, her account and perceptions of historical events, and explanations of how the organizations worked. Movement documents, in particular the monthly minutes of the Southern California Rape Hotline Alliance from 1979 to 1988, supplemented the oral accounts.

WOMEN OF COLOR AND THE LOS ANGELES ANTI-RAPE MOVEMENT

The early 1980s were a period of increasing awareness of racial and ethnic issues in the U.S. anti-rape movement. Although there were relatively few women of color in the movement in California, the formation of the Southern California Rape Hotline Alliance and the statewide Coalition of Rape Crisis Centers brought them together and provided the forum in which to raise issues about doing rape crisis work among Black, Latina and Chicana, Asian, and Native American women. The Coalition's Women of Color Caucus brought together women of color in southern California.

The East Los Angeles Rape Hotline, founded in 1976, was the earliest, and one of the few anti-rape organizations that was not predominantly White. It was founded by Latina women concerned about providing bilingual and culturally appropriate services in the largely Latino, Chicano, and Mexicano area of east Los Angeles county. As one of the few bilingual hotlines of any kind, it was kept busy with all kinds of community services, not just rape crisis work. Its connection to the other local anti-rape organizations waxed and waned over the years until 1979, when the Alliance grew and the statewide Coalition provided a forum for meeting other women of color in the movement.

Another ethnically based rape hotline also existed by the late 1970s, although it was less connected to the Los Angeles anti-rape movement. In 1978, Nilda Rimonte started a project to provide rape crisis services to Pacific and Asian immigrant women in Los Angeles. Although Rimonte participated in the Alliance regularly, the Center for the Pacific-Asian Family, as the hotline she founded was called, was not a grassroots organization to the same extent as other hotlines. Because it was set up to serve many language groups (Vietnamese, Korean, Laotian, Cambodian, Filipino, and others), counselors were generally staff members. They also ran a battered women's shelter, so the rape hotline was only one project of the organization. Nevertheless, Rimonte was a central figure in raising ethnic and racial issues in the California anti-rape movement.

By 1982, racism had become a central issue in the movement and in groups' disputes with the state funding agency. Santa Cruz Women Against Rape was defunded (Mackle, Pernell, Shirchild, Baratta, and Groves 1982) and later that year, the East Los Angeles Rape Hotline was audited by the OCJP. Although the organization was told that the OCJP planned "to very carefully scrutinize all rape crisis centers receiving funds" (Alliance Minutes, June 12, 1982), the fact that it was singled out seemed to carry racist overtones. Hotlines had also begun to treat racism as a serious topic in counselor training and the Women of Color Caucus had begun meeting regularly.

The National Coalition Against Sexual Assault (NCASA) had also begun to pay attention to racial diversity. Beverly Smith, a nationally known Black feminist, was a keynote speaker at its 1984 conference and tried to transform the historic connection between race and rape into a positive one by comparing the two crimes rather than setting them in opposition to each other. She made the analogy that "lynching is to racism as rape is to sexism," suggesting that the cultural context makes such acts possible (Roth and Baslow 1984, p. 56).

By 1983, the Women of Color Caucus had made a connection between OCJP funding criteria and problems of rape crisis centers serving Third World people. According to Alliance minutes of January 15, 1983, Emilia Bellone and Teresa Contreras noted that state allocations were based primarily on the number of victims served by particular programs. In addition, the state allocated funds for "new and innovative" programs, encouraging new grant proposals, while money was most needed for basic services, community education, and outreach. An Alliance committee prepared a position paper asking the OCJP to revise its funding allocation criteria. Their central criticism was that using the number of victims served as the only criterion caused "inequities in the distribution of funds, which especially handicaps ethnic minority rape crisis centers":

> One concern stems from the fact that in order to provide rape crisis services in ethnic minority communities, a great deal of time and effort has to go into doing strong outreach and community education. Although in recent years there has been a marked increase in awareness and information about sexual assault for the general public, much of this has not permeated ethnic minority communities. Many factors affect this—language barriers, racism, distrust of educators and the media, etc. (Position Paper 1983, p. 1)

The paper goes on to point out several related problems: traditional coping strategies among some cultures that discourage going outside the family for help, the need for materials to be translated to reach nonassimilated people, and the extra hours of work required both for outreach in ethnic communities and to provide adequate services to individual survivors. They linked class issues with those of race and ethnicity:

Typically, more time must be spent with a survivor who has fewer personal resources. These survivors tend to be ethnic minority women. Often, a non-assimilated ethnic minority survivor requires translating and interpreting, transportation, overnight shelter for herself and possibly children, and counseling to significant others in addition to the usual counseling and advocacy services. So, if a rape crisis center serves a predominantly ethnic minority population, the "average" number of hours of service provided to each survivor is much higher than for a center that serves a predominantly White population. (Position Paper 1983, p. 2)

Grant proposals for "innovative" programs had been the only strategy centers had to increase funding for special outreach. A major issue for the East Los Angeles Rape Hotline was how to include families, especially the men, in their services, which was essential in order to gain legitimacy in the Latino community. In 1983, through a grant for innovative projects from the OCJP, they produced a *fotonovela* about a family in which a teenage girl has been sexually assaulted by her uncle. The story line upholds the cultural value placed on the family, but modifies it so that the young girl's integrity is not sacrificed. They also had an innovative theater program for education in rape prevention. These programs were successful for reaching their community, but were costly to the organization in the time spent creating new programs, and did not solve the problem of more money for basic services.

Although the Alliance committee that wrote the position paper did not get a direct response, Marilyn Peterson, the Branch Manager of the Sexual Assault Program at the OCJP began pursuing avenues of additional money for "high crime" and "minority" areas. The OCJP studied the rates of rape reported by police agencies and rape crisis centers in communities across the state, assuming that the rate of underreporting was consistent. They then surveyed the availability of services in the community by district attorneys' offices, law enforcement, hospitals, family service agencies, and so on. In addition to a high crime rate, the

poverty rate was factored in, because areas with few resources tend to have fewer social services. According to Peterson, the survey was a necessary formality—a bureaucratic justification for what she already knew was needed. The target money was awarded to some of the existing rape crisis centers in Los Angeles, but its most significant effect in the county was the establishment of two new programs located in predominantly Black areas, South Central Los Angeles and Compton. Women in these areas could theoretically use one of the existing hotlines, but geographical distance made providing in-person services such as hospital accompaniment more difficult. The primarily White hotlines did sparse outreach to the Black community. Furthermore, women of color in the anti-rape movement were developing a theory of service provision that recognized that women in crisis were most likely to feel comfortable and use services if they were provided by someone like themselves (Dubrow et al. 1986; Kanuha 1987; Lum 1988; Rimonte 1985). This notion reflects the influence of the peer-counseling roots of rape crisis work as well as increasing awareness of cultural issues. For outreach to succeed, it was important for services like rape crisis to be *of* the community, which the White hotlines were not. Thus homogeneous organizations of different ethnic groups were more effective.

CONSEQUENCES OF FUNDING:
A DIFFERENT APPROACH

The first of the new hotlines, the Rosa Parks Sexual Assault Crisis Center, began in late 1984, in anticipation of the target funding. Avis Ridley-Thomas, who was instrumental in its founding, was at the nexus of several networks that led to the founding of Rosa Parks. She had been working for the new Victim Witness Assistance Program out of the city attorney's office since 1980. Because of her work there, she had been recommended by Assembly woman Maxine Waters to be on the State Sexual Assault Services Advisory Committee (SAC), which advised the OCJP on funding for rape crisis services, training for pros-ecutors, and funding for research. Ridley-Thomas became chair of the committee, which at first had very little money to give out. Hers was another voice, in addition to those of the Alliance mem-bers, raising the issue of underfunding of minor-ity areas. It was clear from her knowledge of South Central Los Angeles that this area had the highest rate of reported sexual assault in the state and no community-provided services.

A longtime activist in the Black community, she tried to organize women's groups to take on rape crisis services as a project, but none that she approached felt they could do that in addition to their other work. She and her husband, Mark Ridley-Thomas, who was the director of the local branch of the Southern Christian Leadership Con-ference (SCLC), applied for and received an OCJP grant to start a rape crisis service. Thus Avis Ridley-Thomas's position in the funding agency, her involvement in service provision to victims, and her relationship to SCLC converged to create a place for the new service.

The Compton YWCA was the second new or-ganization to start a rape crisis program in a pre-dominantly Black community. When the OCJP called for proposals for target funding, the city's police chief encouraged the YWCA director, Elaine Harris, to apply for it. Compton, one of the small cities that compose Los Angeles county, is located south of South Central Los Angeles. Al-though the rate of home ownership is high, so are the poverty and crime rates. As in many of the eco-nomically abandoned areas of the county, gangs are an important source of social identity for young people, which, combined with their involvement in drug dealing, has created a violent environment. The Compton YWCA has struggled to be a com-munity resource in this context. In addition to tra-ditional programs ranging from fitness to music, it offers a minority women's employment program, a job board, a support group for single parents, a food program for needy families, drug diversion counseling, and a support group for families of in-carcerated people. With crime and violence a ma-

jor social and political issue in the community, the organization had a cooperative relationship with the police, which led to the application for target funding. The YWCA had numerous resources, in-cluding experience with grant proposal writing, that could be enlisted in starting the Sexual Assault Crisis Program.

How these two new rape crisis programs were started differed markedly from the existing anti-rape organizations, which had consequences for the nature of the movement and relationships be-tween the new organizations and the older ones in the Alliance and the Coalition. All of the older or-ganizations had been founded out of some kind of grassroots process and with some connection to the wider feminist movement of the 1970s. The stands on feminism differed among the older orga-nizations, but because they were founded in the midst of vibrant feminist activism, they associated what they were doing with the women's move-ment at some level. The Rosa Parks and Compton programs, by contrast, were founded with substan-tial state funding and without strong links to con-temporary feminism.

Their parent organizations were not simply so-cial service agencies. Both SCLC and the YWCA were progressive organizations with grass-roots or-igins, but had long since become established and "becalmed" (Zald and Ash 1966), with hierarchical leadership and bureaucratic structures. The women who were hired to direct the sexual assault pro-grams were social service administrators, not ac-tivists. Nevertheless, many of the women who worked in the new organizations were drawn by the opportunity to work with Black women. As Joan Crear, a staff member at Rosa Parks, said:

> Personally, I got involved because I was very much interested in women's issues, in particular Black women, and I didn't feel that there was a forum in my community for them. I know there was resis-tance to the whole notion of violence, women's issues, feminism, and I wanted to work in an envi-ronment that advocated on behalf of Black women. As for the Rosa Parks Center, it seemed like a good place to start, and I envisioned the center as a

place where eventually, while we're funded to deal with sexual assault, that it's very difficult to separate sexual assault from just what it means to be a woman in the universe, so it gave me an avenue to do that kind of work.

Similarly, Monica Williams, director of the Compton YWCA program, said:

I had a genuine concern for women's issues and rights and moreover, I think I had a real concern for living, since I live in this community [Compton] now, a real concern for Black women. I think our image has always been of strong and persevering and you can take it all, and it doesn't make a difference, and I started to notice that most of the women who were assaulted, that it wasn't a priority for them, that they couldn't see that they were hurting, too. And that usually their first concern was their children, or their home or their husband, or how'm I going to make ends meet, so for me it's just, it's a challenge.

Drawn by their interest in combining working with Black women and working for the Black community, and influenced by the articulated feminism of the women they met through the Alliance, these women began to see themselves as feminists, but the primary interpretive framework in their organizations was community service.

The community action framework, very much a part of the mission of both parent organizations, provided a rationale within which to fit rape crisis services, which replaced the feminist impetus of the older groups. SCLC linked the rape crisis service with their philosophy of nonviolence. The YWCA had a long history of programs to help women and girls in crisis, and many Ys around the country sponsored rape crisis services. Additionally, the emphasis of the target grants on racial and ethnic inequity in service and funding resonated with the national YWCA imperative adopted in 1970 and used in much of their literature: "to thrust our collective power as a women's movement toward the elimination of racism wherever it exists and by any means necessary."

Despite these ideological frames, the new centers were more influenced by the OCJP's definition of rape crisis work than the older anti-rape organizations. Founded with OCJP grants, they had not gone through the grass-roots stage of scraping together precious resources from their communities and therefore did not have independent community roots. As a consequence of their dependence on the OCJP, they were more bureaucratized from the beginning and less suspicious of the OCJP, in contrast to the contentious history that members of the Alliance had with the agency, but similar to the feelings of many less radical rape crisis people around the state. (See Rodriguez [1988] and Schecter [1982] for accounts of similar splits in the battered women's shelter movement between those who resisted conventional bureaucratic organization and those who accepted it.)

Nevertheless, the community context in which the new services were provided posed contradictions with the state's bureaucratic concerns and practices. The special grants that led to the founding of Rosa Parks and Compton were intended to adjust for problems in the delivery of services, such as "hazardous working conditions, an absence of complementary service providers or agencies, high cost of providing services, lack of alternative funding sources, geographical and/or economic conditions; and unmet need for culturally and/or ethnically appropriate services" (OCJP Guidelines 1987, p. 33). These new organizations were therefore encouraged to design programs that met the basic guidelines *and* the specific needs of their communities. The sponsoring organizations, the YWCA and SCLC, were both practiced at responding to their communities and developed rape crisis programs with emphases that differed from other anti-rape programs. For example, the Rosa Parks staff set up support groups to deal with the intertwined problems of incest and alcoholism.

The ways the Compton women served their community despite standardized guidelines was an even sharper contrast. There, rape crisis workers confronted the reality of gangs on a daily basis as part of the context of the community they served.

For example, to avoid confrontations among participants, they had to monitor what colors the young women wore to educational and support group meetings. Some of the women they counseled were survivors of gang-related rapes. Because basic survival was often the presenting problem of the women served, they evolved a broader approach to support and counseling. As the director said:

A woman may come in or call in for various reasons. She has no place to go, she has no job, she has no support, she has no money, she has no food, she's been beaten, and after you finish meeting all those needs, or try to meet all those needs, then she may say, by the way, during all this, I was being raped. So the immediate needs have to be met. So that makes our community different than other communities. A person wants their basic needs first. It's a lot easier to discuss things when you're full. So that we see people who, when they come in with their children, and their children are running around and the person is on edge, we may find out that she just hasn't eaten in a few days. And we may have to pool together money and give her everybody's lunch, or take them to lunch, and days later, maybe months later, the person will say, by the way, I did come in because I was raped, but since you brought up . . . the other things, I do need a place to stay, and I do need a job, and I can't go to the police. So . . . needs are different.

Approaching rape crisis work in such a holistic way did not conform to the requirements of the bureaucracy that provided the funding. In spite of this director's positive view of the OCJP, she also expressed frustration that very labor-intensive work was often not counted toward funding:

A lot of what we do cannot be documented. That there's no place on that form for this woman called and she's standing outside with three kids and she don't have no place to go. [Because the form asks about] rape! So you know you just, it's almost like you end up having this group that's so concerned that it's very difficult for us when a woman calls and says she's battered, not to tell her to come here for counseling, even though that's not what we're supposed to do. When she says, but

I'm right up the street, I don't want to go to the shelter, I just want to talk to somebody, and a staff person like Irma or Roslyn will spend hours with this person and afterwards come in and say, god she's feeling better, and I think this, and I'm going to take her over to the shelter, and . . . it fits no place. It's just something you did. It was an "information and referral."

These "special service delivery problems," as the OCJP *Guidelines* (1987) puts it, are also different from the kind of issues other rape crisis centers face, largely because of this center's location in a relatively impoverished community in which services are scarce.

NEED FOR INNOVATIVE OUTREACH

The challenge of successful outreach to ethnically and racially diverse communities was one of the issues that prompted the Alliance position paper. Getting clients was more than a simple issue of publicity and involved changing the cultural ethic about seeking help. The ELA and Pacific-Asian rape hotlines had faced this problem for years, and women at the hotlines in the Black communities tackled it anew. Despite the high rates of sexual assault in these communities, there was no mobilized citizens' group demanding services. Once the services were funded, women from both Rosa Parks and Compton had to work on legitimizing the idea of seeking a support group or therapy from the outside, a relatively new idea in the Black community. Joan Crear of Rosa Parks explained:

In our community confidentiality, whether it's rape or anything else, is really the key; a community where things don't go outside your family; you know, have a history of family taking care, says don't tell. . . . [I]n terms of picking up and using a hotline, when we're doing education, it's not just about rape, it's about . . . you can call us, we won't tell anybody, we'll keep your secrets. Also in a community where you talk about gang violence, you have people that are afraid. It's really difficult when I talk to a teenager and she's been raped by a gang member. I don't want to . . . tell her to tell the police necessarily, 'cause she's scared for her brother, you know, and she's scared for her family.

Ethnographic studies of Black communities have illuminated the extent of informal networks among members of even the poorest communities that provide both material and emotional support (e.g., Liebow 1967; Stack 1974), but the pursuit of more formal support through counseling is new. Avis Ridley-Thomas, founder of Rosa Parks, talked about the pressure to "strain up"—be tough and take the hard knocks—which militates against seeking outside help with emotional or psychological problems. Williams elaborated:

> *I think we work on empowerment a lot more because of the community we serve. That it's difficult for a person to sit in a group and talk about their rape and the rapist and go through all of the psychological changes without first understanding that they have some other problems too. So that what's been helpful is for Black women to see other Black women to say I understand what it's like, to have to worry about the kids and him.... [T]he former sources of support are gone. That now you see more of us putting children in childcare and daycare, whereas before we had mothers and sister and aunts, and you know, the extended family. So that now, we're kind of [little rueful laugh] socialized a little more, so that we're running into the same things that other people are running into. We say we're stressed. Before we just said life was tough.*

The emergence of an ethic to protect victim's rights was a bridge by which rape crisis services came to Black communities. Competition between the Sexual Assault and Victim-Witness Programs within OCJP led Marilyn Peterson to look for creative ways to increase rape crisis funding, and the target grants were one such strategy that succeeded. Despite this internal competition, victims' rights was a significant factor in Black communities' receptivity to rape crisis services.

The movement for victim's rights helped legitimize the culture of therapy. Because people of color are more likely to be victims of violent crime in the United States, much of the outreach by the newly established victim-witness programs

in the early 1980s was to Blacks, according to Avis Ridley-Thomas. Seeking help for emotional traumas became more acceptable, not only in state supported services, but also in grass-roots victim's groups. While these groups are only loosely connected to the rape crisis organizations, they contributed to a climate in which reaching and helping sexual assault victims was less alien than it might have been earlier.

RACISM, HOMOPHOBIA, AND FEMINISM

The dynamics of interpersonal racism in the Los Angeles anti-rape movement are intertwined in a complex way with differences of political perspective and homophobia. Although the anti-rape movement had become more diverse, the dominant subculture within the local movement is (White) feminism, strongly influenced by a lesbian perspective. The combination of feminist jargon and political viewpoints and the high number of lesbians in leadership positions create an alienating environment for many of the Black women in the anti-rape movement. Although White activists are ideologically predisposed to accept women of color because they believe it is right, their theory about what women of color should be—that is, they should be radical because they are oppressed—does not always fit with reality. Black women hired to work in rape crisis centers have tended to identify with the social service orientation, thus the more conservative side of the movement, which creates tension with the more politically radical women who have dominated the Alliance.

Racial and political differences are compounded by homophobia. Homosexuality is even more hidden in the American Black community than in the general society. Blacks are not alone in the anti-rape movement in their discomfort with the openly lesbian presence; dissension has also surfaced in the statewide Coalition, often between centers outside the major urban areas, which tend to be more conservative, and those from Los Angeles and the Bay Area. However, locally, because a substantial number of the White women are lesbians and most of the Black women are heterosexual, the overlap of racial and sexuality differences exaggerates the schism. Both sides feel they have a moral cause for offense when someone from the other side is inadvertently racist or homophobic.

Despite the fact that all of the centers include these topics in their volunteer and staff training, these tensions affect both interpersonal interactions and organizational processes. Differences in life-style lead to divergent concerns. For example, several Black women mentioned that they wished there were support in the Alliance for dealing with husbands and families while working in rape crisis. This concern for intimate others was shared by heterosexual White women, but not by lesbians, because their partners were less likely to be threatened by their work with survivors of male violence. Lesbians, expecting Black women to be homophobic, sometimes have challenged and tested their sexuality. Even differences of style separated women: for example, the convention of dressing up in the Black community and of dressing down in White feminist circles.

Black women, like some Chicana women earlier, have also felt marginalized by being outside the shared reference system of White feminists. As Teresa Contreras of ELA put it:

> I'm fairly sure that some of us felt threatened by the jargon, the politics, the feminist politics, and the real assertiveness of the women involved in the rape crisis movement, and their confrontational style was totally contrary to the Chicano style.

In interviews, some Black women noted that they did not really understand what "feminism" was and yet felt expected to know and support its precepts. Being thrown into the Alliance and the Coalition where this was the political vocabulary could be intimidating and alienating. Over time, however, some have come to put the name "feminist" to their own positions. Joan Crear, for example, was tentatively identifying herself as a feminist at the time I interviewed her, after working in the anti-rape movement for over two years. She said:

> It has become important for me to say "I'm a feminist" to other women in my community, but I work on a definition where it doesn't sound like it's such a big thing, because I believe that most women, or a lot of women are under... some of the things that feminism encompasses.... [F]or me it means to want to be or to demand to share power in relationships, so I don't know if that's an appropriate term, because when I think about sharing power within relationships I have to look at that in terms of sharing power with my children, my boss, whether male or female, and so it means...I take responsibility for things that happen in my life.... I see myself as an adult woman, as an adult.

Not all women of color live in South Central or East Los Angeles, so the existence of the ethnically based rape crisis centers is only one step toward serving all women and having a multiracial movement. The predominantly White hotlines in Los Angeles are still concerned about recruiting women of color, but face a dilemma when that goal conflicts with maintaining their integrity on feminism and homophobia. But according to Rochelle Coffey, director of the Pasadena hotline, the existence of the Black hotlines has helped give the predominantly White hotlines credibility with women of color in other parts of the county.

CONCLUSION

Whether states co-opt or facilitate social movements is historically contingent on particular political forces (Tilly 1978), and in the historical period described here, both processes occurred. Without state funding, the new Black anti-rape organizations might not exist. But their founding also resulted in the further infusion of a bureaucratic orientation into the anti-rape movement, because the new organizations bear the stamp of their origins. However, there is also a new source of resistance, in addition to the feminists, to the state's demands. The commitment of Rosa Parks and Compton to "serve their community" means that they make demands back to the state to shift its policies so that service is possible.

Despite conflicts, women in the Alliance, Black and White, lesbian and heterosexual, work together. The predictions from the early 1970s that women of color would need to establish their own organizations in order to become active in feminist causes seems to be borne out. Racially and ethni- cally homogeneous organizations have contrib- uted more to diversifying the movement than integration within organizations. They success- fully work together in mixed coalitions when they have powerful common interests, but independent bases.

REFERENCES

Bart, Pauline and Patricia H. O'Brien. 1985. *Stopping Rape: Successful Survival Strategies.* New York: Pergamon.

Brownmiller, Susan. 1975. *Against Our Will: Men, Women, and Rape.* New York: Bantam.

Cleaver, Eldridge. 1968. *Soul on Ice.* New York: Dell.

Davis, Angela. 1981. *Women, Race, and Class.* New York: Random House.

Dubrow, Gail et al. 1986. "Planning to End Violence Against Women: Notes from a Feminist Confer- ence at UCLA." *Women and Environments* 8:4–27.

Evans, Sara. 1979. *Personal Politics.* New York: Vin- tage Books.

Ferree, Myra Marx and Beth B. Hess. 1985. *Contro- versy and Coalition: The New Feminist Movement,* Boston: Twayne.

Giddings, Paula. 1984. *When and Where I Enter: The Impact of Black Women on Race and Sex in Amer- ica.* New York: Bantam.

hooks, bell. 1981. *Ain't I a Woman: Black Women and Feminism.* Boston: South End Press.

Kanuha, Valli. 1987. "Sexual Assault in Southeast Asian Communities: Issues in Intervention." *Re- sponse* 10:4–6.

Liebow, Elliot. 1967. *Tally's Corner.* Boston: Little, Brown.

Lum, Joan. 1988. "Battered Asian Women." *Rice* (March):50–52.

Mackle, Nancy, Deanne Pernell, Jan Shirchild, Con- suelo Baratta, and Gail Groves. 1982. "Dear Aegis: Letter from Santa Cruz Women Against Rape." *Aegis: Magazine on Ending Violence Against Women* 35:28–30.

New York Radical Feminists. 1974. *Rape: The First Sourcebook for Women,* edited by Noreen Connell and Cassandra Wilson. New York: New American Library.

Office of Criminal Justice Planning. 1987. *California Sexual Assault Victim Services and Prevention Pro- gram Guidelines.* Sacramento: State of California.

Rimonte, Nilda. 1985. Protocol for the Treatment of Rape and Other Sexual Assault. Los Angeles County Commission for Women.

Rodriguez, Noelie Maria. 1988. "Transcending Bureau- cracy: Feminist Politics at a Shelter for Battered Women." *Gender & Society* 2:214–27.

Roth, Stephanie and Robin Baslow. 1984. "Compro- mising Positions at Anti-Rape Conference." *Aegis: Magazine on Ending Violence Against Women* 38: 56–58.

Schecter, Susan. 1982. *Women and Male Violence: The Visions and Struggles of the Battered Women's Movement.* Boston: South End Press.

Southern California Rape Hotline Alliance. 1982. Minutes.

———. 1983. "Position Paper." Drafted by Emilia Bel- lone and Nilda Rimonte for the Committee to De- velop OCJP Position Paper.

Stack, Carol. 1974. *All Our Kin: Strategies for Survival in a Black Community.* New York: Harper & Row.

Tilly, Charles. 1978. *From Mobilization to Revolution.* Reading, MA: Addison-Wesley.

Zald, Mayer N. and Roberta Ash. 1966. "Social Move- ment Organizations: Growth, Decay and Change." *Social Forces* 44:327–41.

15

When Bodies Are Weapons

MICHAEL A. MESSNER

In many of our most popular spectator sports, winning depends on the use of violence. To score and win, the human body is routinely turned into a weapon to be used against other bodies, causing pain, serious injury, and even death. How do we interpret the social meaning of this violence? Is it socially learned behavior that serves to legitimize masculine power over women? Commentators—both apologists and critics—have made sweeping statements about sports and violence, but their analyses rarely take into account the meanings of violence in sports to the athletes themselves. We can begin to understand the broader social meanings of violence in sports by listening to the words of former athletes.

With the possible exception of the boxer in the ring, perhaps the one position in modern sports that requires the most constant physical aggressiveness is that of lineman in U.S. football. While TV cameras focus primarily on those few who carry, throw, catch, and kick the ball, the majority of the players on the field are lined up a few inches apart from each other. On each play they snarl, grunt, and curse; at the snap of the ball they slam their large and heavily armored bodies into each other. Blood, bruises, broken bones, and concussions often result.

Marvin Upshaw, now thirty-six years old, was a lineman in professional football for nine years. He seemed a bit stung when I asked him how he could submit to such punishment for so many years:

> You know, a lot of people look at a lineman and they say, "Oh, man, you gotta be some kinda ani-

> mal *to get down there and beat on each other like that.*" But it's just like a woman giving birth. Everybody says, you know, "That's a great accomplishment; she must be really beautiful." And I do, too—I think it's something that's an act of God, that's unreal. But she hasn't done nothing that she wasn't built for. See what I'm saying? Now here I am, 260, 270 pounds, and that's my position. My physical self helped me.... That's what I'm built for. Just like a truck carrying a big Caterpillar: you see the strain, but that's what it's built for. So as far as that being a real big accomplishment, it is, but it's not. That's all you were built for.

BORN OR BUILT?

Upshaw's comparisons of the aggressive uses of his body in football with a woman giving birth and with a truck are telling. These comparisons exemplify one of the major paradoxes in men's construction of meaning surrounding the use of their bodies as weapons. On the one hand, many of the men I interviewed explained their aggression and violence as natural: to them, repeated bone-crunching collisions with other men are simply "an act of God," "like a woman giving birth." On the other hand, they know that their bodies are, like trucks, "built" by human beings to do a specific job. Time after time I have heard former athletes, almost in the same breath, talk of their "natural" and "God-given" talent *and* of the long hours, days, and years of training and sacrifice that went into developing their bodies and their skills. "I was a natural," said MacArthur Lane, a former professional football star. "Just about ev-

ery hour of the day when I wasn't sleeping or eating, I'd be on the playground competing."

Similarly, Jack Tatum, who in his years with the Oakland Raiders was known as the Assassin for his fierce and violent "hits" on opposing receivers, described himself as a "natural hitter." But his descriptions of his earliest experiences in high school football tell a different story. Though he soon began to develop a reputation as a fierce defensive back, hitting people bothered him at first:

> When I first started playing, if I would hit a guy hard and he wouldn't get up, it would bother me. [But] when I was a sophomore in high school, first game, I knocked out two quarterbacks, and people loved it. The coach loved it. The more you play, the more you realize that it is just a part of the game— somebody's gonna get hurt. It could be you, it could be him—most of the time it's better if it's him.

Tatum's words suggest that the routine use of violence against others to achieve an athletic goal doesn't come naturally at all, but may require a good deal of encouragement from others. Recent studies of young ice hockey players corroborate this: the combination of violent adult athletic role models and rewards from coaches, peers, and the community for the willingness to successfully use violence creates a context in which violence becomes normative behavior. Young males who earn reputations as aggressive "hitters" often gain a certain status in the community and among their peers, thus anchoring (at least temporarily) what otherwise might be insecure masculine identities.

TWO INFAMOUS "HITS"

What happens when legitimate ("legal") aggression results in serious injury, as it so often does in sports? Both Jack Tatum and Ray Fosse, a former professional baseball player, were involved in frighteningly violent collisions, each of which resulted in serious injury. In each incident, the play was "legal"—no penalty was issued by officials. Each incident also stimulated a lively public con-

troversy concerning violence in sports. These two men's remembrances are instructive in connecting the athlete's experiences of violence in sports with the larger social meanings surrounding such public incidents.

By the time Jack Tatum got to the pros, he had become the kind of fearsome hitter that coaches dream of. Though he took pride in the fact that he was not a "dirty" player (i.e., his hits were within the rules), he was perhaps too good at his craft. Intimidation was the name of the game, but there was growing concern within football and in the sports media that Jack Tatum's "knockouts" were too brutal. In 1978, Tatum delivered one of his hits to an opposing wide receiver, Darryl Stingley. Stingley's neck was broken in two places, and he would never walk again. Suddenly, Tatum was labeled as part of a "criminal element" in the National Football League. Tatum was confused, arguing that this had been a "terrible accident," but was nevertheless simply a "routine play" which was "within the rules."

> I guess the thing that mystified me was that I could play for nine years and one guy gets hurt and then everybody comes down on me, you know. It's just like for nine years I've been playing the game the wrong way. But I've made All-Pro, I've been runner-up for Rookie of the Year, I've got all the honors playing exactly the same way. So, you know, it just kind of mystified me as to why there was just all of a sudden this stuff because a guy got hurt. It wasn't the first time a guy got paralyzed in football, so it really wasn't that unusual.

Ray Fosse received a violent hit from Pete Rose in the 1970 Major League Baseball All-Star game, while 60 million people watched on television. In the twelfth inning, Pete Rose was steaming around third base; he needed only to touch home plate in order to score the winning run. Fosse's job as catcher was to block the plate with his body and hope that the ball arrived in time for him to catch it and tag Rose out. Rose arrived a split second before the ball, and, looking a lot like a football player delivering a hit, drove his body

straight at Fosse and touched the plate safely. Fosse's shoulder was separated, and despite his youth he never fully regained the powerful home-run swing he had demonstrated earlier that summer. Again, a serious injury had resulted from a technically legal play. Rose was seen by some as a hero, but others criticized him, asking if it was right for him to hurt someone else simply to score a run in what was essentially an exhibition game. Rose seemed as mystified by these questions as Jack Tatum had been. "I play to win," responded Rose. "I just did what I had to do."

When I interviewed Fosse years later, well into his retirement, he lamented the effect of the injury but saw it not as the result of a decision by Pete Rose but rather as "part of the game." It was fate that had broken his body—not a person. In fact, he felt nothing but respect for Rose:

> I never once believed that he hit me intentionally. He's just a competitor, and I only wish that every other major-league ball player played as hard as he did. . . . But I would say that that was the beginning of a lot of pain and problems for me. . . .

There is clearly a contextual morality in Tatum's and Fosse's constructions of meaning surrounding these two violent collisions. The rules of the game provide a context that frees the participants from the responsibility for moral choices. As long as the participants play by the rules, they not only feel that they should be free from moral criticism, but also understand that they are entitled to "respect"—that form of emotionally distant connection with others that is so important to traditional masculine identity. Flagrant rule-violators, most athletes believe, are "violent" and deserve to be penalized; others, like Tatum and Rose, are "aggressive competitors" deserving of respect. But this distinction is shaken when serious injury results from "legal" actions, and public scrutiny raises questions about the athletes' personal morality. Both Tatum and Fosse appear mystified by the public perspective on events in terms of individual choice or morality. They just play by the rules.

THE PRICE ATHLETES PLAY

There is another painful paradox in today's organized combat sports. Top athletes, who are popularly portrayed as models of good physical conditioning and health, suffer from a very high incidence of permanent injuries, alcoholism, drug abuse, obesity, and heart problems when they retire. The way athletes are taught to regard their bodies as machines and weapons with which to annihilate opponents often results in their using violence against their own bodies. Partly for this reason, former professional football players in the United States have an average life-expectancy of about fifty-six years—roughly fifteen years shorter than the overall average life-expectancy of U.S. males. Football, of course, is especially brutal, but baseball has had its share of casualties, too. Ray Fosse's interview with me seemed to be an almost endless chronicle of injuries and surgeries. "When someone got injured," he explained, "we had a saying: 'Throw dirt on it, spit on it, go play.'"

Not only professional athletes parade their injuries this way. Nearly every former athlete I interviewed, amateur or professional, told at least one story of an injury that disabled him, at least for a time. Many had incurred serious injuries that had permanently harmed their health. Although most wore these injuries with pride, like badges of masculine status, athletes also grudgingly acknowledged that their healthy bodies were a heavy price to pay for glory. But for them to question their decisions to "give up" their bodies would ultimately mean questioning the entire system of rules through which they had successfully established relationships and a sense of identity. Instead, former athletes usually rationalized their own injuries as "part of the game." They claimed that their pain contributed to the development of their character and ultimately gained them the respect of others.

Clearly, heavy personal costs are paid by those who participate in violent organized sports. And, because of poverty, institutionalized racism

and lack of other career options, it is poor and ethnic minority males who are disproportionately channeled into athletic careers—and especially into the more dangerous positions within the combat sports. Males from more privileged backgrounds often play sports in school, but because they face a wider range of educational and career choices they often choose to leave sports at a relatively early age. Young men from poor and non-White backgrounds face a constricted range of options. Lacking other resources and choices, they may see sports as the one legitimate context in which a youngster from a disadvantaged background can establish a sense of masculine identity in the world.

SPORTS VIOLENCE
AND GENDER RELATIONS

With the twentieth century decline in the practical need for physical strength in work and in warfare, representations of the muscular male body as strong, virile, and powerful have taken on increasingly important ideological significance in gender relations. Indeed, the body plays such a central role in the construction of contemporary gender relations because it is so closely associated with the natural. Yet, to develop their bodies for competition, athletes spend a tremendous amount of time exercising and weight-training, and sometimes even use illegal and dangerous drugs, such as steroids. Though an athletic body is popularly thought of as natural, it is nevertheless the product of social practice.

The embodiment of culturally dominant forms of masculinity entails the imbedding of force and skill in the body. Through this process, men's power over women comes to appear as though it is natural. Sports are an important organizing institution for the embodiment of dominant masculinity. Sports suppress natural (sex) similarities, construct differences, and then, largely through the media, weave a structure of symbol and interpretation around these differences which naturalizes them. Several theorists have suggested that the major

ideological salience of sports as mediated spectacle may lie not so much in violence as it does in the opportunity sports give male spectators to identify with the muscular male body. Morse, in a fascinating analysis of the use of slow-motion instant replays in football, argues that the visual representation of violence is transformed by slow motion replays into gracefulness (Morse 1983). The salient social meanings of these images of male power and grace lie not in identification with violence, Morse argues, but rather, in narcissistic and homoerotic identification with the male body. Perhaps the violence represents a denial of the homoeroticism in sports.

Violence in sports may play another important social role—that of constructing differences among men. Whereas males from lower socioeconomic and ethnic minority backgrounds disproportionately pursue careers in violent sports, privileged men are likelier, as Woody Guthrie once suggested, to commit violence against others "with fountain pens." But with the exception of domestic violence against women and children, physical violence is rarely a part of the everyday lives of these men. Yet violence among men may still have important ideological and psychological meaning for men from privileged backgrounds. There is a curious preoccupation among middle-class males with both movie characters who are working-class tough guys, and with athletes who are fearsome "hitters" and who heroically "play hurt." These tough guys of the culture industry are both heroes, who "prove" that "we men" are superior to women, and the "other" against whom privileged men define themselves as "modern." The "tough guys" are, in a sense, contemporary gladiators sacrificed so that elite men can have a clear sense of where they stand in the intermale pecking order. Ironically, although many young black males are attracted to sports as a milieu in which they can find respect, to succeed in sports they must become intimidating, aggressive, and violent. Television images—like that of Jack Tatum "exploding" Darryl Stingley—become symbolic "proof" of the racist belief that Black males are naturally more violent and aggressive. Their marginalization as men—signified by their engaging in the very violence that makes them such attractive spectacles—contributes to the construction of culturally dominant (White, upper- and middle-class) masculinity.

REFERENCES

Morse, M. 1983. "Sport on Television: Replay and Display," pp. 44–66. In *Regarding Television: Critical Approaches,* ed. E. A. Kaplan. Los Angeles: University Publications of America.

PART THREE

Sexualities

Section 1   Sexual Relations, Intimacy, and Power

Section 2   Sexuality and Identity

The women's movement reawakened during the late 1960s and early 1970s during a sexual revolution that was telling youth "if it feels good, do it!" In this context an initial impulse of second-wave feminism was for women to reclaim sexual pleasure for themselves. But soon some feminists began to argue that "sexual liberation" had simply freed men to objectify and exploit women more. As studies began to illuminate the widespread realities of rape, sexual harassment in workplaces, and sexual exploitation of women in prostitution, it became more and more clear that for women, sexuality was a realm of danger rather than pleasure. As a result, by the mid- to late 1970s, feminist activism focused more and more on antirape and antipornography efforts.

By the mid-1980s, other feminists—often younger women, women of color, and lesbian and bisexual women—began to criticize the radical feminist preoccupation with the centrality of male heterosexuality and pornography in women's oppression. And by the early 1990s many younger feminists sought to reclaim sexual pleasure as a realm of empowerment for women. In the first article in this section, Deborah Tolman argues that cultural factors that frame adolescent girls' sexuality as dangerous tend to divert them from discovering and using their sexual desires in empowering ways. Next, Susan Bordo takes the recent explosion of discourse about the widespread use of the drug Viagra to reflect on the problems and limits of a culture that equates men's penises with power tools that need to be "turned on" by a "potency pill." Matthew Gutmann's analysis of Mexican men's recent growth in "self-consciousness about sexuality" offers a fascinating window into the complex interweavings of notions of "potency" with masculine identities and relationships. Finally, Cynthia Enloe's research demonstrates how female prostitutes on U.S. military bases are doing more than "sex work"—they are also serving as mediators between foreign soldiers and local men. In short, the commodification of women's sexuality provides key linkages in men's worlds—even across national and cultural boundaries.

The articles in the second section of Part Two explore the area of sexual identity. It is widely accepted among scholars today that the idea that there are distinct sexual "types" of people like "the homosexual" and "the heterosexual" is a very modern construction. But it is also well known that social constructions have real consequences. Modern medical and scientific discourse may have created "the homosexual" with the goal of controlling "deviant" character types and normalizing "the heterosexual," but starting mostly in the 1970s men and women who identified as "gay" and "lesbian" drew strength from their shared identities. And from this strength, they challenged prevailing cultural attitudes, customs, and laws.

In addition to challenging prejudice and discrimination, the existence of a movement of gay, lesbian, and bisexual people potentially raises critical questions about "normal" heterosexual practices. For instance, Marilyn Frye's article on "Lesbian 'Sex'" starts with empirical observations made by some sexologists that point to low levels of sexual activity by lesbian couples. She then shifts the inquiry away from the question of "how often," to the more difficult question of what does it mean to be "doing it?"—and Frye creatively redirects this question toward taken-for-granted assumptions about "straight sex." The next two articles reflect on these same issues in different ways. Michael Messner draws partly on autobiography to reflect on the social processes involved in a young male's construction of himself as "100% heterosexual," and Arlene Stein draws on her research in the San Francisco Bay Area to reflect on the ways that the successes of the lesbian community in the 1970s and 1980s ultimately helped to undermine any sense of a unified lesbian identity, especially with many younger women of the 1990s. Finally, Yen Le Espiritu's study illustrates the ways that Filipina immigrants in the United States sometimes define themselves in opposition to their conception of White women as sexually "immoral." Espiritu's analysis reveals the complex and contradictory interweavings of identities that are constructed in contexts of unequal power by race, gender, sexuality, and national origin.

16

Doing Desire

Adolescent Girls' Struggles for/with Sexuality

DEBORAH L. TOLMAN

In order to perpetuate itself, every oppression must corrupt or distort those various sources of power within the culture of the oppressed that can provide energy for change. For women, this has meant suppression of the erotic as a considered source of power and information within our lives. (Lorde 1984, 53)

Recent research suggests that adolescence is the crucial moment in the development of psychological disempowerment for many women (e.g., Brown and Gilligan 1992; Gilligan 1990). As they enter adolescence, many girls may lose an ability to speak about what they know, see, feel, and experience evident in childhood as they come under cultural pressure to be "nice girls" and ultimately "good women" in adolescence. When their bodies take on women's contours, girls begin to be seen as sexual, and sexuality becomes an aspect of adolescent girls' lives; yet "nice" girls and "good" women are not supposed to be sexual outside of heterosexual, monogamous marriage (Tolman 1991). Many girls experience a "crisis of connection," a relational dilemma of how to be oneself and stay in relationships with others who may not want to know the truth of girls' experiences (Gilligan 1989). In studies of adolescent girls' development, many girls have demonstrated the ironic tendency to silence their own thoughts and feelings for the sake of relationships, when what they think and feel threatens to be disruptive (Brown and Gilligan 1992). At adolescence, the energy needed for

resistance to crushing conventions of femininity often begins to get siphoned off for the purpose of maintaining cultural standards that stand between women and their empowerment. Focusing explicitly on embodied desire, Tolman and Debold (1993) observed similar patterns in the process of girls learning to look at, rather than experience, themselves, to know themselves from the perspective of men, thereby losing touch with their own bodily feelings and desires. It is at this moment in their development that many women will start to experience and develop ways of responding to their own sexual feelings. Given these realities, what are adolescent girls' experiences of sexual desire? How do girls enter their sexual lives and learn to negotiate or respond to their sexuality?

Despite the real gains that feminism and the sexual revolution achieved in securing women's reproductive rights and increasing women's sexual liberation (Rubin 1990), the tactics of silencing and denigrating women's sexual desire are deeply entrenched in this patriarchal society (Brown 1991). The Madonna/whore dichotomy is alternately virulent and subtle in the cultures of adolescents (Lees 1986; Tolman 1992). Sex education curricula name male adolescent sexual desire; girls are taught to recognize and to keep a lid on the sexual desire of boys but not taught to acknowledge or even to recognize their own sexual feelings (Fine 1988; Tolman 1991). The few feminist empirical studies of girls' sexuality suggest that sexual desire is a complicated, important experience for adolescent girls about which little is known. In an ethnographic study, Fine noticed that adolescent girls' sexuality was acknowledged by adults in school, but in terms that denied the sexual subjectivity of girls; this "missing discourse of desire" was, however, not always absent from the ways girls themselves spoke about their sexual experiences (Fine 1988). Rather than being "educated," girls' bodies are suppressed under surveillance and silenced in the schools (see also Lesko 1988). Although Fine ably conveys the existence of girls' discourse of desire, she does not articulate that discourse. Thompson collected 400 girls' narratives about sexuality, romance, contraception and pregnancy (Thompson 1984, 1990) in which girls' desire seems frequently absent or not relevant to the terms of their sexual relationships. The minority of girls who spoke of sexual pleasure voiced more sexual agency than girls whose experiences were devoid of pleasure. Within the context of girls' psychological development, Fine's and Thompson's work underscore the need to understand what girls' experiences of their sexual desire are like.

A psychological analysis of this experience for girls can contribute an understanding of both the possibilities and limits for sexual freedom for women in the current social climate. By identifying how the culture has become anchored in the interior of women's lives—an interior that is birthed through living in the exterior of material conditions and relationships—this approach can keep distinct women's psychological responses to sexual oppression and also the sources of that oppression. This distinction is necessary for avoiding the trap of blaming women for the ways our minds and bodies have become constrained.

METHODOLOGICAL DISCUSSION

Sample and Data Collection

To examine this subject, I interviewed 30 girls who were juniors in an urban and a suburban public high school ($n = 28$) or members of a gay and lesbian youth group ($n = 2$). They were 16.5 years old on average and randomly selected. The girls in the larger study are a heterogeneous group, representing different races and ethnic backgrounds (Black, including Haitian and African American; Latina, including Puerto Rican and Colombian; Euro-American, including Eastern and Western European), religions (Catholic, Jewish, and Protestant), and sexual experiences. With the exception of one Puerto Rican girl, all of the girls from the suburban school were Euro-American; the racial/ethnic diversity in the sample is represented by the urban school. Interviews with school personnel confirmed that the student population of the urban school was almost exclusively poor or working class and the students in the suburban school were middle and upper-middle class. This information is important in that my focus is on how girls' social environments shape their understanding of their sexuality. The fact that girls who live in the urban area experience the visibility of and discourse about violence, danger and the consequences of unprotected sex, and that the suburban girls live in a community that offers a veneer of safety and stability, informs their experiences of sexuality. Awareness of these features of the social contexts in which these girls are developing is essential for listening to and understanding their narratives about sexual experiences.

The data were collected in one-on-one, semi-structured clinical interviews (Brown and Gilligan 1992). This method of interviewing consists of following a structured interview protocol that does not direct specific probes but elicits narratives. The interviewer listens carefully to a girl, taking in her voice, and responding with questions that will enable the girl to clarify her story and know she is being heard. In these interviews, I asked girls direct questions about desire to elicit descriptions and narratives. Most of the young women wove their concerns about danger into the narratives they told.

Analytic Strategy

To analyze these narratives, I used the Listening Guide—an interpretive methodology that joins hermeneutics and feminist standpoint epistemology (Brown et al. 1991). It is a voice-centered, relational method by which a researcher becomes a listener, taking in the voice of a girl, developing an interpretation of her experience. Through multiple readings of the same text, this method makes audible the "polyphonic and complex" nature of voice and experience (Brown and Gilligan 1992, 15). Both speaker and listener are recognized as individuals who bring thoughts and feelings to the text, acknowledging the necessary subjectivity of both participants. Self-consciously embedded in a standpoint acknowledging that patriarchal culture silences and obscures women's experiences, the method is explicitly psychological and feminist in providing the listener with an organized way to respond to the coded or indirect language of girls and women, especially regarding topics such as sexuality that girls and women are not supposed to speak of. This method leaves a trail of evidence for the listener's interpretation, and thus leaves room for other interpretations by other listeners consistent with the epistemological stance that there is multiple meaning in such stories. I present a way to understand the stories these young women chose to tell me, our story as I have heard and understood it. Therefore, in the interpretations that follow I include my responses, those of an adult woman, to these girls' words, providing information about girls' experiences of sexual desire much like countertransference informs psychotherapy.

Adolescent Girls' Experiences of Sexual Desire

The first layer of the complexity of girls' experiences of their sexual desire was revealed initially

in determining whether or not they felt sexual feelings. A majority of these girls (two-thirds) said unequivocally that they experienced sexual desire; in them I heard a clear and powerful way of speaking about the experience of feeling desire that was explicitly relational and also embodied. Only three of the girls said they did not experience sexual feelings, describing silent bodies and an absence of or intense confusion about romantic or sexual relationships. The remaining girls evidenced confusion or spoke in confusing ways about their own sexual feelings. Such confusion can be understood as a psychic solution to sexual feelings that arise in a culture that denigrates, suppresses, and heightens the dangers of girls' sexuality and in which contradictory messages about women's sexuality abound.

For the girls who said they experienced sexual desire, I turned my attention to how they said they responded to their sexual feelings. What characterized their responses was a sense of struggle; the question of "doing desire"—that is, what to do when they felt sexual desire—was not straightforward for any of them. While speaking of the power of their embodied feelings, the girls in this sample described the difficulties that their sexual feelings posed, being aware of both the potential for pleasure and the threat of danger that their desire holds for them. The struggle took different shapes for different girls, with some notable patterns emerging. Among the urban girls, the focus was on how to stay safe from bodily harm, in and out of the context of relational or social consequences, whereas among the suburban girls the most pronounced issue was how to maintain a sense of themselves as "good" and "normal" girls (Tolman 1992). In this article, I will offer portraits of three girls. By focusing on three girls in depth, I can balance an approach to "variance" with the kind of case study presentation that enables me to illustrate both similarities and differences in how girls in the larger sample spoke about their sexual feelings. These three girls represent different sexual preferences—one heterosexual, one bisexual, and one lesbian.[1] I have chosen to forefront the difference of sexual preference because it has been for some women a source of empowerment and a route to community; it has also been a source of divisiveness among feminists. Through this approach, I can illustrate *both* the similarities and differences in their experiences of sexual desire, which are nested in their individual experiences as well as their social contexts. Although there are many other demarcations that differentiate these girls—social class, race, religion, sexual experience—and this is not the most pervasive difference in this sample,[2] sexual preference calls attention to the kinds of relationships in which girls are experiencing or exploring their sexual desire and which take meaning from gender arrangements and from both the presence and absence of institutionalization (Fine 1988; Friend 1993). Because any woman whose sexuality is not directly circumscribed by heterosexual, monogamous marriage is rendered deviant in our society, all adolescent girls bear suspicion regarding their sexuality, which sexual preference highlights. In addition, questions of identity are heightened at adolescence.

Rochelle Doing Desire

Rochelle is a tall, larger, African American girl who is heterosexual. Her small, sweet voice and shy smile are a startling contrast to her large body, clothed in white spandex the day of our interview. She lives in an urban area where violence is embedded in the fabric of everyday life. She speaks about her sexual experience with a detailed knowledge of how her sexuality is shaped, silenced, denigrated, and possible in relationships with young men. As a sophomore, she thought she "had to get a boyfriend" and became "eager" for a sexual relationship. As she describes her first experience of sexual intercourse, she describes a traditional framing of male-female relationships:

> I felt as though I had to conform to everything he said that, you know, things that a girl and a guy were supposed to do, so like, when the sex came, like, I did it without thinking, like, I wish I would have waited . . . we started kissing and all that stuff and it just happened. And when I got, went home, I

> was like, I was shocked, I was like, why did I do that? I wish I wouldn't a did it.

Did you want to do it?

> Not really. Not really. I just did it because, maybe because he wanted it, and I was always like tryin' to please him and like, he was real mean, mean to me, now that I think about it, I was like kind of stupid, cause like I did everything for him and he just treated me like I was nothing and I just thought I had just to stay with him because I needed a boyfriend so bad to make my life complete but like now it's different.

Rochelle's own sexual desire is absent in her story of defloration—in fact, she seems to be missing altogether. In a virtual caricature of dominant cultural conventions of femininity, Rochelle connects her disappearance at the moment of sex—"it just happened"—to her attempts to fulfill the cultural guidelines for how to "make [her] life complete." She has sex because "he wanted it," a response that holds no place for whether or not she feels desire. In reflecting on this arrangement, Rochelle now feels she was "stupid . . . to do everything for him" and in her current relationship, things are "different." As she explains: "I don't take as much as I did with the first guy, cause like, if he's doin' stuff that I don't like, I tell him, I'll go, I don't like this and I think you shouldn't do it and we compromise, you know. I don't think I can just let him treat me bad and stuff."

During the interview, I begin to notice that desire is not a main plot line in Rochelle's stories about her sexual experiences, especially in her intimate relationships. When I ask her about her experiences of sexual pleasure and sexual desire, she voices contradictions. On one hand, as the interview unfolds, she is more and more clear that she does not enjoy sex: "I don't like sex" quickly becomes "I hate sex . . . I don't really have pleasure." On the other hand, she explains that

> there are certain times when I really really really enjoy it, but then, that's like, not a majority of the times, it's only sometimes, once in a while . . . if I was to have sex once a month, then I would enjoy it . . . if I like go a long period of time without

havin' it then, it's really good to me, cause it's like, I haven't had something for a long time and I miss it. It's like, say I don't eat cake a lot, but say, like every two months, I had some cake, then it would be real good to me, so that's like the same thing.

Rochelle conveys a careful knowledge of her body's hunger, her need for tension as an aspect of her sexual pleasure, but her voiced dislike of sex suggests that she does not feel she has much say over when and how she engages in sexual activity.

In describing her experiences with sexuality, I am overwhelmed at how frequently Rochelle says that she "was scared." She is keenly aware of the many consequences that feeling and responding to her sexual desire could have. She is scared of being talked about and getting an undeserved reputation: "I was always scared that if I did that (had sexual intercourse) I would be portrayed as, you know, something bad." Even having sex within the confines of a relationship, which has been described by some girls as a safe haven for their sexuality (Rubin 1990; Tolman 1992), makes her vulnerable; she "could've had a bad reputation, but luckily he wasn't like that"; he did not choose to tell other boys (who then tell girls) about their sexual activity. Thinking she had a sexually transmitted disease was scary. Because she had been faithful to her boyfriend, having such a disease would mean having to know that her boyfriend cheated on her and would also make her vulnerable to false accusations of promiscuity from him. Her concern about the kind of woman she may be taken for is embedded in her fear of using contraception: "When you get birth control pills, people automatically think you're having sex every night and that's not true." Being thought of as sexually insatiable or out of control is a fear that many girls voice (Tolman 1992); this may be intensified for African American girls, who are creating a sexual identity in a dominant cultural context that stereotypes Black women as alternately asexual and hypersexual (Spillers 1984).

Rochelle's history provides other sources of fear. After her boyfriend "flattened [her] face," when she realized she no longer wanted to be with

him and broke off the relationship, she learned that her own desire may lead to male violence. Rochelle confided to me that she has had an abortion, suffering such intense sadness, guilt, and anxiety in the wake of it that, were she to become pregnant again, she would have the baby. For Rochelle, the risk of getting pregnant puts her education at risk, because she will have to sacrifice going to college. This goal is tied to security for her; she wants to "have something of my own before I get a husband, you know, so if he ever tries leavin' me, I have my own money." Given this wall of fears, I am not surprised when Rochelle describes a time when simply feeling desire made her "so scared that I started to cry." Feeling her constant and pervasive fear, I began to find it hard to imagine how she can feel any other feelings, including sexual ones.

I was thus caught off guard when I asked Rochelle directly if she has felt desire and she told me that she does experience sexual desire; however, she explained "most of the time, I'm by myself when I do." She launched, in breathless tones, into a story about an experience of her own sexual desire just the previous night:

Last night, I had this crank call.... At first I thought it was my boyfriend, cause he likes to play around, you know. But I was sitting there talking, you know, and thinking of him and then I found out it's not him, it was so crazy weird, so I hang the phone up and he called back, he called back and called back. And then I couldn't sleep, I just had this feeling that, I wanted to have sex so so bad. It was like three o'clock in the morning. And I didn't sleep the rest of the night. And like, I called my boyfriend and I was tellin' him, and he was like, what do you want me to do, Rochelle, I'm sleeping! [Laughs.] I was like, okay, okay, well I'll talk to you later, bye. And then, like, I don't know, I just wanted to, and like, I kept tossin' and turnin'. And I'm trying to think who it was, who was callin' me, cause like, it's always the same guy who always crank calls me, he says he knows me. It's kinda scary.... I can't sleep, I'm like, I just think about it, like, oh I wanna have sex so bad, you know, it's like a fever, drugs, something like that. Like last night, I don't know, I think if I woulda had the car and stuff, I probably woulda left the house. And went over to his house, you know. But I couldn't, cause I was babysitting.

When I told her that it sounds a little frightening but it sounds like there's something exciting about it, she smiled and leaned forward, exclaiming, "Yeah! It's like sorta arousing." I was struck by the intensity of her sexual feelings and also by the fact that she is alone and essentially assured of remaining alone due to the late hour and her responsibilities. By being alone, not subject to observation or physical, social, emotional, or material vulnerability, Rochelle experienced the turbulent feelings that are awakened by this call in her body. Rochelle's desire has not been obliterated by her fear; desire and fear both reverberate through her psyche. But she is not completely alone in this experience of desire, for her feelings occur in response to another person, whom she at first suspects is her boyfriend speaking from a safe distance, conveying the relational contours of her sexual desire. Her wish to bring her desire into her relationship, voiced in her response of calling her boyfriend, is in conflict with her fear of what might happen if she did pursue her wish—getting pregnant and having a baby, a consequence that Rochelle is desperate to avoid.

I am struck by her awareness of both the pleasure and danger in this experience and how she works the contradiction without dissociating from her own strong feelings. There is a brilliance and also a sadness in the logic her body and psyche have played out in the face of her experiences with sexuality and relationships. The psychological solution to the dilemma that desire means for her, of feeling sexual desire only when she cannot respond as she says she would like to, arises from her focus on these conflicts as personal experiences, which she suffers and solves privately. By identifying and solving the dilemma in this way, Rochelle is diminished, as is the possibility of her developing a critique of these conflicts as not just personal problems but as social inequities that emerge in her personal relationships and on her body. Without this perspective, Rochelle is less likely to become empowered through her own desire to identify that the ways in which she must curtail herself and be curtailed by others are socially constructed, suspect, and in need of change.

Megan Doing Desire

Megan, a small, freckled, perky Euro-American, is dressed in baggy sweats, comfortable, unassuming, and counterpointed by her lively engagement in our interview.[3] She identifies herself as "being bisexual" and belongs to a gay youth group; she lives in a city in which wealth and housing projects coexist. Megan speaks of knowing she is feeling sexual desire for boys because she has "kind of just this feeling, you know? Just this feeling inside my body." She explains: "My vagina starts to kinda like act up and it kinda like quivers and stuff, and like I'll get like tingles and and, you can just feel your hormones (laughing) doing something weird, and you just, you get happy and you just get, you know, restimulated kind of and it's just, and Oh! Oh!" and "Your nerves feel good." Megan speaks about her sexual desire in two distinct ways, one for boys and one for girls. In our interview, she speaks most frequently about her sexual feelings in relation to boys. The power of her own desire and her doubt about her ability to control herself frighten her: "It scares me when I'm involved in a sexual situation and I just wanna go further and further and cause it just, and it scares me that, well, I have control, but if I even just let myself not have control, you know?. . . I'd have sex and I can't do that." Megan knows that girls who lose control over their desire like that can be called "sluts" and ostracized.

When asked to speak about an experience of sexual desire, Megan chooses to describe the safety of a heterosexual, monogamous relationship. She tells me how she feels when a boyfriend was "feeling me up"; not only is she aware of and articulate about his bodily reactions and her own, she narrates the relational synergy between her own desire and his:

I just wanted to go on, you know? Like I could feel his penis, you know, 'cause we'd kinda lied down you know, and, you just really get so into it and intense and, you just wanna, well you just kinda keep wanting to go on or something, but it just feels good.... His penis being on my leg made, you know, it hit a nerve or something, it did something because it just made me start to get more horny or whatever, you know, it just made me want to do more things and stuff. I don't know how, I can't, it's hard for me to describe exactly how I felt, you know like, (intake of breath)... when he gets more excited then he starts to do more things and you can kind of feel his pleasure and then you start to get more excited.

With this young man, Megan knows her feelings of sexual desire to be "intense," to have a momentum of their own, and to be pleasurable. Using the concrete information of his erection, she describes the relational contours of her own embodied sexual desire, a desire that she is clear is her own and located in her body but that also arises in response to his excitement.

Although able to speak clearly in describing a specific experience she has had with her desire, I hear confusion seep into her voice when she notices that her feelings contradict or challenge societal messages about girls and sexuality:

It's so confusing, 'cause you have to like say no, you have to be the one to say no, but why should you be the one to, cause I mean maybe you're enjoying it and you shouldn't have to say no or anything. But if you don't, maybe the guy'll just keep going and going, and you can't do that because then you would be a slut. There's so [much] like, you know, stuff that you have to deal with and I don't know, just I keep losing my thought.

Although she knows the logic offered by society—that she must "say no" to keep him from "going and going," which will make her "a slut"—Megan identifies what is missing from that logic, that "maybe you're"—she, the girl—"the one who is enjoying it." The fact that she may be experiencing sexual desire makes the scripted response—to silence his body—dizzying. Because she does feel her own desire and can identify the potential of her own pleasure, Megan asks

the next logical question, the question that can lead to outrage, critique, and empowerment: "Why should you have to be the one to [say no]?" But Megan also gives voice to why sustaining the question is difficult; she knows that if she does not conform, if she does not "say no"—both to him and to herself—then she may be called a slut, which could lead to denigration and isolation. Megan is caught in the contradiction between the reality of her sexual feelings in her body and the absence of her sexual feelings in the cultural script for adolescent girls' sexuality. Her confusion is an understandable response to this untenable and unfair choice: a connection with herself, her body, and sexual pleasure or a connection with the social world.

Megan is an avid reader of the dominant culture. Not only has she observed the ways that messages about girls' sexuality leave out or condemn her embodied feelings for boys, she is also keenly aware of the persuasiveness of cultural norms and images that demand heterosexuality:

Every teen magazine you look at is like, guy this, how to get a date, guys, guys, guys, guys, guys. So you're constantly faced with I have to have a boyfriend, I have to have a boyfriend, you know, even if you don't have a boyfriend, just [have] a fling, you know, you just want to kiss a guy or something. I've had that mentality for so long.

In this description of compulsory heterosexuality (Rich 1983), Megan captures the pressure she feels to have a boyfriend and how she experiences the insistence of this demand, which is ironically in conflict with the mandate to say no when with a boy. She is aware of how her psyche has been shaped into a "mentality" requiring any sexual or relational interests to be heterosexual, which does not corroborate how she feels. Compulsory heterosexuality comes between Megan and her feelings, making her vulnerable to a dissociation of her "feelings" under this pressure.

Although she calls herself bisexual, Megan does not describe her sexual feelings for girls very much in this interview. In fact, she becomes so confused that at one point she says she is not sure if her feelings for girls are sexual:

> *I mean, I'll see a girl I really really like, you know, because I think she's so beautiful, and I might, I don't know. I'm so confused.... But there's, you know, that same mentality as me liking a guy if he's really cute, I'm like, oh my God, you know, he's so cute. If I see a woman that I like, a girl, it's just like wow, she's so pretty, you know. See I can picture like hugging a girl; I just can't picture the sex, or anything, so, there's something being blocked.*

Megan links her confusion with her awareness of the absence of images of lesbian sexuality in the spoken or imagistic lexicon of the culture, counterpointing the persuasiveness of heterosexual imagery all around her. Megan suggests that another reason that she might feel "confused" about her feelings for girls is a lack of sexual experience. Megan knows she is feeling sexual desire when she can identify feelings in her own body—when her "vagina acts up"—and these feelings occur for her in the context of a sexual relationship, when she can feel the other person's desire. Because she has never been in a situation with a girl that would allow this embodied sexual response, she posits a connection between her lack of sexual experience with girls and her confusion.

Yet she has been in a situation where she was "close to" a girl and narrates how she does not let her body speak:

> *There was this one girl that I had kinda liked from school, and it was really weird 'cause she's really popular and everything. And we were sitting next to each other during the movie and, kind of her leg was on my leg and I was like, wow, you know, and that was, I think that's like the first time that I've ever felt like sexual pleasure for a girl. But it's so impossible, I think I just like block it out, I mean, it could never happen.... I just can't know what I'm feeling.... I probably first mentally just say no, don't feel it, you know, maybe. But I never start to feel, I don't know. It's so confusing. 'Cause finally it's all right for me to like a girl, you know? Before*

> *it was like, you know, the two times that I really, that it was just really obvious that I liked them a lot, I had to keep saying no no no no, you know, I just would not let myself. I just hated myself for it, and this year now that I'm talking about it, now I can start to think about it.*

Megan both narrates and interprets her dissociation from her embodied sexual feelings and describes the disciplinary stance of her mind over her body in how she "mentally" silences her body by saying "no," preempting her embodied response. Without her body's feelings, her embodied knowledge, Megan feels confused. If she runs interference with her own sexual feelings by silencing her body, making it impossible for her to feel her desire for girls, then she can avoid the problems she knows will inevitably arise if she feels sexual feelings she "can't know"—compulsory heterosexuality and homophobia combine to render this knowledge problematic for her. Fearing rejection, Megan keeps herself from feelings that could lead to disappointment, embarrassment or frustration, leaving her safe in some ways, yet also psychologically vulnerable.

Echoing dominant cultural constructions of sexual desire, Megan links her desire for girls with feelings of fear: "I've had crushes on some girls ... you can picture yourself kissing a guy but then if you like a girl a lot and then you picture yourself kissing her, it's just like, I can't, you know, oh my God, no (laughs), you know it's like scary ... it's society ... you never would think of, you know, it's natural to kiss a girl." Megan's fear about her desire for girls is different from the fears associated with her desire for boys; whereas being too sexual with boys brings the stigma of being called a "slut," Megan fears "society" and being thought of as "unnatural" when it comes to her feelings for girls. Given what she knows about the heterosexual culture in which she is immersed—the pressure she feels to be interested in "guys" and also given what she knows about homophobia—there is an inherent logic in Megan's confused response to her feelings for girls.

Melissa Doing Desire

Melissa, dressed in a flowing gypsy skirt, white skin pale against the lively colors she wears, is clear about her sexual desire for girls, referring to herself as "lesbian"; she is also a member of a gay/lesbian youth group. In speaking of her desire, Melissa names not only powerful feelings of "being excited" and "wanting," but also more contained feelings; she has "like little crushes on like millions of people and I mean, it's enough for me." Living in a world defined as heterosexual, Melissa finds that "little crushes" have to suffice, given a lack of opportunity for sexual exploration or relationship: "I don't know very many people my age that are even bisexual or lesbians...so I pretty much stick to that, like, being hugely infatuated with straight people. Which can get a little touchy at times ...realistically, I can't like get too ambitious, because that would just not be realistic."

At the forefront of how Melissa describes her desire is her awareness that her sexual feelings make her vulnerable to harm. Whereas the heterosexual girls in this study link their vulnerability to the outcomes of responding to their desire—pregnancy, disease, or getting a bad reputation—Melissa is aware that even the existence of her sexual desire for girls can lead to anger or violence if others know of it: "Well I'm really lucky that like nothing bad has happened or no one's gotten mad at me so far, that, by telling people about them, hasn't gotten me into more trouble than, it has, I mean, little things but not like, anything really awful. I think about that and I think it, sometimes, I mean, it could be more dangerous." In response to this threat of violence, Melissa attempts to restrain her own desire: "Whenever I start, I feel like I can't help looking at someone for more than a few seconds, and I keep, and I feel like I have to make myself not, stare at them or something." Another strategy is to express her desire covertly by being physically affectionate with other girls, a behavior that is common and acceptable; by keeping her sexuality secret, she can "hang all over [girls] and stuff and they wouldn't

even think that I meant anything by it." I am not surprised that Melissa associates feeling sexual desire with frustration; she explains that she "find(s) it safer to just think about the person than what I wanna do, because if I think about that too much and I can't do it, then that'll just frustrate me," leading her to try to intervene in her feelings by "just think[ing] about the person" rather than about the more sexual things she "want(s) to do." In this way, Melissa may jeopardize her ability to know her sexual desire and, in focusing on containing what society has named improper feelings, minimize or exorcise her empowerment to expose that construction as problematic and unjust.

My questions about girls' sexual desire connect deeply with Melissa's own questions about herself; she is in her first intimate relationship, and this interview proves an opportunity to explore and clarify painful twinges of doubt that she had begun to have about it. This relationship began on the initiative of the other girl, with whom she had been very close, rather than out of any sexual feelings on Melissa's part. In fact, Melissa was surprised when her friend had expressed a sexual interest, because she had not "been thinking that" about this close friend. After a history of having to hold back her sexual desire, of feeling "frustrated" and being "hugely infatuated with straight people," rather than having the chance to explore her sexuality, Melissa's response to this potential relationship was that she "should take advantage of this situation." As the interview progresses, Melissa begins to question whether she is sexually attracted to this girl or "it's just sort of like I just wanted something like this for so long that I'm just taking advantage of the situation."

When I ask Melissa questions about the role of her body in her experience of sexual desire, her confusion at first intensifies:

Is that [your body] part of what feels like it might be missing?

(eight-second pause) It's not well, sometimes, I mean I don't know how, what I feel all the time. It's hard like, because I mean I'm so confused about

this. And it's hard like when it's actually happening to be like, ok, now how do I feel right now? How do I feel right now? How am I gonna feel about this?...I don't know, 'cause I don't know what to expect, and I haven't been with anyone else so I don't know what's supposed to happen. So, I mean I'm pretty confused.

The way she speaks about monitoring her body suggests that she is searching for bodily feelings, making me wonder what, if anything, she felt. I discern what she does not say directly; that her body was silent in these sexual experiences. Her hunger for a relationship is palpable: "I really wanted someone really badly, I think, I was getting really sick of being by myself.... I would be like God, I really need someone." The desperation in her voice, and the sexual frustration she describes, suggest that her "want" and "need" are distinctly sexual as well as relational.

One reason that Melissa seems to be confused is that she felt a strong desire to be "mothered," her own mother having died last year. In trying to distinguish her different desires in this interview, Melissa began to distinguish erotic feelings from another kind of wanting she also experienced: she said that "it's more of like but I kind of feel like it's really more of like a maternal thing, that I really want her to take care of me and I just wanna touch someone and I just really like the feeling of just how I mean I like, when I'm with her and touching her and stuff. A lot, but it's not necessarily a sexual thing at this point." In contrast to her feelings for her girlfriend, Melissa describes feeling sexually attracted to another girl. In so doing, Melissa clarifies what is missing in these first sexual adventures, enabling her to know what had bothered her about her relationship with her girlfriend:

I don't really think I'm getting that much pleasure, from her, it's just, I mean it's almost like I'm getting experience, and I'm sort of having fun, it's not even that exciting, and that's why I think I don't really like her...because my friend asked me this the other day, well, I mean does it get, I mean when you're with her does it get really, I don't remember the word she used, but just really, like

what was the word she used? But I guess she meant just like, exciting [laughing]. But it doesn't, to me. It's weird, because I can't really say that, I mean I can't think of like a time when I was really excited and it was like really, sexual pleasure, for me, because I don't think it's really like that. I mean not that I think that this isn't good because, I don't know, I mean, I like it, but I mean I think I have to, sort of realize that I'm not that much attracted to her, personally.

Wanting both a relationship and sexual pleasure, a chance to explore closeness and her sexual curiosity, and discovering that this 'relationship leaves out her sexual desire, Melissa laments her silent body: "I sort of expect or hope or whatever that there would be some kind of more excited feeling just from feeling sexually stimulated or whatever. I would hope that there would be more of a feeling than I've gotten so far." Knowing consciously what she "knows" about the absence of her sexual feelings in this relationship has left her with a relational conflict of large proportions for her: "I'm not that attracted to her and I don't know if I should tell her that. Or if I should just kind of pretend I am and try to...anyway." I ask her how she would go about doing that—pretending that she is. She replies, "I don't think I could pretend it for too long." Not being able to "pretend" to have feelings that she knows she wants as part of an intimate relationship, Melissa faces a dilemma of desire that may leave her feeling isolated and lonely or even fraudulent.

ADOLESCENT GIRLS' SEXUAL DESIRE AND THE POSSIBILITIES OF EMPOWERMENT

All of the girls in this study who said they felt sexual desire expressed conflict when describing their responses to their sexual feelings—conflict between their embodied sexual feelings and their perceptions of how those feelings are, in one way or another, anathema or problematic within the social and relational contexts of their lives. Their experiences of sexual desire are strong and pleasurable, yet they speak very often not of the power of desire but of how their desire may get them into trouble. These girls are beginning to voice the internalized oppression of their women's bodies; they knew and spoke about, in explicit or more indirect ways, the pressure they felt to silence their desire, to dissociate from those bodies in which they inescapably live. Larger societal forces of social control in the form of compulsory heterosexuality (Rich 1983), the policing of girls' bodies through school codes (Lesko 1988), and media images play a clear part in forcing this silence and dissociation. Specific relational dynamics, such as concern about a reputation that can easily be besmirched by other girls and by boys, fear of male violence in intimate relationships, and fear of violent repercussion of violating norms of heterosexuality are also audible in these girls' voices.

To be able to know their sexual feelings, to listen when their bodies speak about themselves and about their relationships, might enable these and other girls to identify and know more clearly the sources of oppression that press on their full personhood and their capacity for knowledge, joy, and connection. Living in the margins of a heterosexual society, the bisexual and lesbian girls voice an awareness of these forces as formative of the experiences of their bodies and relationships; the heterosexual girls are less clear and less critical about the ways that dominant constructions of their sexuality impinge on their embodied and relational worlds. Even when they are aware that societal ambivalence and fears are being played out on their minds and bodies, they do not speak of a need for collective action, or even the possibility of engaging in such activities. More often, they speak of the danger of speaking about desire at all. By dousing desire with fear and confusion, or simple, "uncomplicated" denial, silence, and dissociation, the girls in this study make individual psychological moves whereby they distance or disconnect themselves from discomfort and danger. Although disciplining their bodies and curbing their desire is a very logical and understandable way to stay physically, socially, and emotionally safe, it also heightens the chance that girls and women may lose track of the fact that an inequitable social system, and not a necessary situation, renders women's sexual desire

a source of danger, rather than one of pleasure and power in their lives. In "not knowing" desire, girls and women are at risk for not knowing that there is nothing wrong with having sexual feelings and responding to them in ways that bring joy and agency.

Virtually every girl in the larger study told me that no woman had ever talked to her about sexual desire and pleasure "like this"—in depth, listening to her speak about her own experiences, responding when she asked questions about how to masturbate, how to have cunnilingus, what sex is like after marriage. In the words of Rubin: "The ethos of privacy and silence about our personal sexual experience makes it easy to rationalize the refusal to speak [to adolescents]" (1990, 83; Segal 1993). Thompson (1990) found that daughters of women who had talked with them about pleasure and desire told narratives about first intercourse that were informed by pleasure and agency. The recurrent strategy the girls in my study describe of keeping their desire under wraps as a way to protect themselves also keeps girls out of authentic relationships with other girls and women. It is within these relationships that the empowerment of women can develop and be nurtured through shared experiences of both oppression and power, in which collectively articulated critiques are carved out and voiced. Such knowledge of how a patriarchal society systematically keeps girls and women from their own desire can instigate demand and agency for social change. By not talking about sexual desire with each other or with women, a source for empowerment is lost. There is a symbiotic interplay between desire and empowerment: to be empowered to desire one needs a critical perspective, and that critical perspective will be extended and sustained through knowing and experiencing the possibilities of desire and healthy embodied living. Each of these girls illustrates the phenomenon observed in the larger study—the difficulty for girls in having or sustaining a critical perspective on the culture's silencing of their sexual desire. They are denied full access to the power of their own desire and to structural supports for that access.

Common threads of fear and joy, pleasure and danger, weave through the narratives about sexual desire in this study, exemplified by the three portraits. Girls have the right to be informed that gaining pleasure and a strong sense of self and power through their bodies does not make them bad or unworthy. The experiences of these and other adolescent girls illustrate why girls deserve to be educated about their sexual desire. Thompson concludes that "to take possession of sexuality in the wake of the anti-erotic sexist socialization that remains the majority experience, most teenage girls need an erotic education" (1990, 406). Girls need to be educated about the duality of their sexuality, to have safe contexts in which they can explore both danger and desire (Fine 1988) and to consider why their desire is so dangerous and how they can become active participants in their own redemption. Girls can be empowered to know and act on their own desire, a different educational direction than the simplistic strategies for avoiding boys' desire that they are offered. The "just say no" curriculum obscures the larger social inequities being played out on girls' bodies in heterosexual relationships and is not relevant for girls who feel sexual feelings for girls. Even adults who are willing or able to acknowledge that girls experience sexual feelings worry that knowing about their own sexual desire will place girls in danger (Segal 1993). But keeping girls in the dark about their power to choose based on their own feelings fails to keep them any safer from these dangers. Girls who trust their minds and bodies may experience a stronger sense of self, entitlement, and empowerment that could enhance their ability to

make safe decisions. One approach to educating girls is for women to speak to them about the vicissitudes of sexual desire—which means that women must let themselves speak and know their own sexual feelings, as well as the pleasures and dangers associated with women's sexuality and the solutions that we have wrought to the dilemma of desire: how to balance the realities of pleasure and danger in women's sexuality.

Asking these girls to speak about sexual desire, and listening and responding to their answers and also to their questions, proved to be an effective way to interrupt the standard "dire consequences" discourse adults usually employ when speaking at all to girls about their sexuality. Knowing and speaking about the ways in which their sexuality continues to be unfairly constrained may interrupt the appearance of social equity that many adolescent girls (especially white, middle-class young women) naively and trustingly believe, thus leading them to reject feminism as unnecessary and mean-spirited and not relevant to their lives. As we know from the consciousness-raising activities that characterized the initial years of second-wave feminism, listening to the words of other girls and women can make it possible for girls to know and voice their experiences, their justified confusion and fears, their curiosities. Through such relationships, we help ourselves and each other to live in our different female bodies with an awareness of danger, but also with a desire to feel the power of the erotic, to fine-tune our bodies and our psyches to what Audre Lorde has called the "yes within ourselves" (Lorde 1984, 54).

NOTES

1. The bisexual girl and the lesbian girl were members of a gay/lesbian youth group and identify themselves using these categories. As is typical for members of privileged groups for whom membership is a given, the girls who feel sexual desire for boys and not for girls (about which they were asked explicitly) do not use the term "heterosexual" to describe themselves. Although I am aware of the debate surrounding the use of these cat-

egories and labels to delimit women's (and men's) experience, because my interpretive practice is informed by the ways society makes meaning of girls' sexuality, the categories that float in the culture as ways of describing the girls are relevant to my analysis. In addition, the bisexual and lesbian girls in this study are deeply aware of compulsory heterosexuality and its impact on their lives.

2. Of the 30 girls in this sample, 27 speak of a desire for boys and not for girls. This pattern was ascertained by who appeared in their desire narratives and also by their response to direct questions about sexual feelings for girls, designed explicitly to interrupt the hegemony of heterosexuality. Two of the 30 girls described sexual desire for both boys and girls and one girl described sexual desire for girls and not for boys.

3. Parts of this analysis appear in Tolman (1994).

REFERENCES

Brown, L. 1991. Telling a girl's life: Self authorization as a form of resistance. In *Women, girls and psychotherapy: Reframing resistance,* edited by C. Gilligan, A. Rogers, and D. Tolman. New York: Haworth.

Brown, L., E. Debold, M. Tappan, and C. Gilligan. 1991. Reading narratives of conflict for self and moral voice: A relational method. In *Handbook of moral behavior and development: Theory, research, and application,* edited by W. Kurtines and J. Gewirtz. Hillsdale, NJ: Lawrence Erlbaum.

Brown, L., and C. Gilligan. 1992. *Meeting at the crossroads: Women's psychology and girls' development.* Cambridge, MA: Harvard University Press.

Fine, Michelle. 1988. Sexuality, schooling and adolescent females: The missing discourse of desire. *Harvard Educational Review* 58:29–53.

Friend, Richard. 1993. Choices, not closets. In *Beyond silenced voices,* edited by M. Fine and L. Weis. New York: State University of New York Press.

Gilligan, Carol. 1989. Teaching Shakespeare's sister. In *Making connections: The relational world of adolescent girls at Emma Willard School,* edited by C. Gilligan, N. Lyons, and T. Hamner. Cambridge, MA: Harvard University Press.

———. 1990. Joining the resistance: Psychology, politics, girls and women. *Michigan Quarterly Review* 29:501–36.

Lees, Susan. 1986. *Losing out: Sexuality and adolescent girls.* London: Hutchinson.

Lesko, Nancy. 1988. The curriculum of the body: Lessons from a Catholic high school. In *Becoming feminine: The politics of popular culture,* edited by L. Roman. Philadelphia: Falmer.

Lorde, Audre. 1984. The uses of the erotic as power. In *Sister outsider: Essays and speeches.* Freedom, CA: Crossing Press.

Miller, Jean Baker. 1976. *Towards a new psychology of woman.* Boston: Beacon Press.

Rich, Adrienne. 1983. Compulsory heterosexuality and lesbian existence. In *Powers of desire: The politics of sexuality,* edited by A. Snitow, C. Stansell, and S. Thompson. New York: Monthly Review Press.

Rubin. Lillian. 1990. *Erotic wars: What happened to the sexual revolution?* New York: HarperCollins.

Segal, Lynne. 1993. Introduction. In *Sex exposed: Sexuality and the pornography debate,* edited by L. Segal and M. McIntosh. New Brunswick, NJ: Rutgers University Press.

Spillers, Hortense. 1984. Interstices: A small drama of words. In *Pleasure and danger: Exploring female sexuality,* edited by C. Vance. Boston: Routledge and Kegan Paul.

Thompson, Sharon. 1984. Search for tomorrow: On feminism and the reconstruction of teen romance. In *Pleasure and danger: Exploring female sexuality,* edited by C. Vance. Boston: Routledge and Kegan Paul.

———. 1990. Putting a big thing in a little hole: Teenage girls' accounts of sexual initiation. *Journal of Sex Research* 27:341–61.

Tolman, Deborah L. 1991. Adolescent girls, women and sexuality: Discerning dilemmas of desire. *Women, girls and psychotherapy: Reframing resistance,* edited by C. Gilligan, A. Rogers, and D. Tolman. New York: Haworth.

———. 1992. Voicing the body: A psychological study of adolescent girls' sexual desire. Unpublished dissertation, Harvard University.

———. 1994. Daring to desire: Culture and the bodies of adolescent girls. In *Sexual cultures: Adolescents, communities and the construction of identity,* edited by J. Irvine. Philadelphia: Temple University Press.

Tolman, Deborah, and Elizabeth Debold. 1993. Conflicts of body and image: Female adolescents, desire, and the no-body. In *Feminist treatment and therapy of eating disorders,* edited by M. Katzman, P. Fallon, and S. Wooley. New York: Guilford.

17

Pills and Power Tools

SUSAN BORDO

Viagra. "The Potency Pill," as *Time* magazine's cover describes it. Since it went on sale, it has had "the fastest takeoff of a new drug" that the RiteAid drugstore chain has ever seen. It is all over the media. Users are jubilant, claiming effects that last through the night, youth restored, better "quality" erections. "This little pill is like a package of dynamite," says one.

Some even see Viagra as a potential cure for social ills. Bob Guccione, publisher of *Penthouse,* hails the drug as "freeing the American male libido" from the emasculating clutches of feminism. This diagnosis does not sit very comfortably with current medical wisdom, which has declared impotence to be a physiological problem. I, like Guccione, am skeptical of that declaration—but would suggest a deeper meditation on what has put the squeeze on male libido.

Think, to begin with, of the term *impotence.* It rings with disgrace, humiliation—and it was not the feminists who invented it. Writer Philip Lopate, in an essay on his body, says that merely to say the word out loud makes him nervous. Yet remarkably, *impotence*—rather than the more forgiving, if medicalized, *erectile dysfunction*—is still a common nomenclature among medical researchers. *Frigidity,* with its suggestion that the woman is cold, like some barren tundra, went by the board a while ago. But *impotence,* no less loaded with ugly gender implications, remains. Lenore Tiefer, who researches medical terminology, suggests that we cannot let go of *impotence* because to do so would force us to also let go of *potency* and the cultural mythology that equates male sexuality with power. But to hold on to that mythology, men must pay a steep price.

Impotence. Unlike other disorders, impotence implicates the whole man, not merely the body part. He is impotent. Would we ever say about a man with a headache "He is a headache?" Yet this is just what we do with impotence, as Warren Farrell notes in *Why Men Are the Way They Are.* "We make no attempt to separate impotence from the total personality." Then, we expect the personality to perform like a machine.

That expectation of men is embedded throughout our culture. Think of our slang terms, so many of which encase the penis, like a cyborg, in various sorts of metal or steel armor. Big rig. Blow torch. Bolt. Cockpit. Crank. Crowbar. Destroyer. Dipstick. Drill. Engine. Hammer. Hand tool. Hardware. Hose. Power tool. Rod. Torpedo. Rocket. Spear. Such slang—common among teenage boys—is violent in what it suggests the machine penis can do to another, "softer" body. But the terms are also metaphorical protection against the failure of potency. A human organ of flesh and blood is subject to anxiety, ambivalence, uncertainty. A torpedo or rocket, on the other hand, would never let one down.

Contemporary urologists have taken the metaphor of man the machine even further. Erectile functioning is "all hydraulics," says Irwin Goldstein of the Boston University Medical Center, scorning a previous generation of researchers who stressed psychological issues. But if it is all a matter of fluid dynamics, why keep the term *impotent,* whose definitions (according to *Webster's Un-*

abridged) are "want of power," "weakness," "lack of effectiveness, helplessness" and (appearing last) "lack of ability to engage in sexual intercourse." In keeping the term *impotence,* the drug companies, it seems, get to have it both ways: reduce a complex human condition to a matter of chemistry while keeping the old shame machine working, helping to assure the flow of men to their doors.

We live in a culture that encourages men to think of their sexuality as residing in their penises and that gives men little encouragement to explore the rest of their bodies. The beauty of the male body has finally been brought out of the cultural closet by Calvin Klein, Versace, and other designers. But notice how many of those new underwear ads aggressively direct our attention to the (often extraordinary) endowments of the models. Many of the models stare coldly, challengingly at the viewer, defying the viewer's gaze to define them in any way other than how they have chosen to present themselves: powerful, armored, emotionally impenetrable. "I am a rock," their bodies seem to proclaim. Commercial advertisements depict women stroking their necks, their faces, their legs, lost in sensual reverie, taking pleasure in touching themselves—all over. Similar poses with men are very rare. Touching oneself languidly, lost in the sensual pleasure of the body, is too feminine, too "soft," for a real man. Crotch-grabbing, thrusting, putting it "in your face"—that is another matter.

There is a fascinating irony in the fact that although it is women whose bodies are most sexually objectified by this culture, women's bodies are permitted much greater sexual expression in our cultural representations than men's. In sex scenes, the moaning and writhing of the female partner have become the conventional cinematic code for heterosexual ecstasy and climax. The male's participation largely gets represented via caressing hands, humping buttocks, and—on rare occasions—a facial expression of intense concentration. She is transported to another world; he is the pilot of the ship that takes her there. When men are shown being transported themselves, it is usually being played for comedy (as in Al Pacino's shrieks in *Frankie and Johnny,* Eddie Murphy's moaning in *Boomerang,* Kevin Kline's contortions in *A Fish Called Wanda*), or it is coded to suggest that something is not quite normal with the man—he is sexually enslaved, for example (as with Jeremy Irons in *Damage*). Men's bodies in the movies are action-hero toys, power tools—wind them up and watch them perform.

Thankfully, the equation between penis and power tool is now being questioned in other movies. Earlier this year, *The Full Monty* brought us a likable group of unemployed workers in Sheffield, England, who hatch the moneymaking scheme of displaying all in a male strip show and learn what it is like to be what feminist theorists call "the object of the gaze." Paul Thomas Anderson's *Boogie Nights* told the story of the rise and fall (so to speak) of a mythically endowed young porn star, Dirk Diggler, who does fine so long as he is the most celebrated stallion in the stable but loses his grip in the face of competition. On the surface, the film is about a world far removed from the lives of most men, a commercial underground where men pray for "wood" and lose their jobs unless they can achieve erection on command. On a deeper level, however, the world of the porn actor is simply the most literalized embodiment—and a perfect metaphor—for a masculinity that demands constant performance from men.

Even before he takes up a career that depends on it, Diggler's sense of self is constellated around his penis; he pumps up his ego by looking in the mirror and—like a coach mesmerizing the team before a game—intoning mantras about his superior gifts. That works well, so long as he believes it. But unlike a real power tool, the motor of male self-worth cannot simply be switched on and off. In the very final shot of the movie, we see Diggler's fabled organ itself. It is a prosthesis, actually (a fact that annoyed several men I know until I pointed out that it was no more a cheat than implanted breasts passing for the real thing). But prosthesis or not and despite its dimensions, it is no masterful tool. It points downward, weighted with expectation, with shame, looking tired and used.

Beginning with the French film *Ridicule* (in which an aristocrat, using his penis as an instrument of vengeance, urinates on the lap of another man), we have seen more unclothed penises in films this year than ever before. But what is groundbreaking about *Boogie Nights* is not that it displays a nude penis, but that it so unflinchingly exposes the job that the mythology of unwavering potency does on the male body. As long as the fortress holds, the sense of power may be intoxicating; but when it cracks—as it is bound to do at some point—the whole structure falls to pieces. Those of whom such constancy is expected (or who require it of themselves) are set up for defeat and humiliation.

Unless, of course, he pops his little pill whenever "failure" threatens. I have no desire to withhold Viagra from the many men who have been deprived of the ability to get an erection by accidents, diabetes, cancer, and other misfortunes to which the flesh—or psyche—is heir. I would just like CNN and *Time* to spend a fraction of the time they devote to describing "how Viagra cures" to looking at how our culture continues to administer the poison for whose effects we now claim a cure. Let us note, too, that the official medical definition of erectile dysfunction (like the definitions of depression and attention deficit disorder) has broadened coincident with the development of new drugs. Dysfunction is no longer defined as "inability to get an erection" but inability to get an erection that is adequate for "satisfactory sexual performance." Performance. Not pleasure. Not feeling. Performance.

Some of what we now call impotence may indeed be physiological in origin; some may be grounded in deep psychic fears and insecurities. But sometimes, too, a man's penis may simply be instructing him that his feelings are not in synch with the job he is supposed to do—or with the very fact that it's a "job." So, I like Philip Lopate's epistemological metaphor for the penis much better than the machine images. Over the years, he has come to appreciate, he writes, that his penis has its "own specialized form of intelligence." The penis knows that it is not a torpedo, no matter what a culture expects of it or what drugs are relayed to its blood vessels. If we accept that, the notion that a man requires understanding and tolerance when he does not "perform" would go by the wayside ("It's OK. It happens" still assumes that there is something to be excused.) So, too, would the idea that there ought to be one model for understanding nonarousal. Sometimes, the penis's "specialized intelligence" should be listened to rather than cured.

Viagra, unfortunately, seems to be marketed—and used—with the opposite message in mind. Now men can perform all night! Do their job no matter how they feel! (The drug does require some degree of arousal, but minimal.) The hype surrounding the drug encourages rather than deconstructs the expectation that men perform like power tools with only one switch—on or off. Until this expectation is replaced by a conception of manhood that permits men and their penises a full range of human feeling, we will not yet have the kind of "cure" we really need.

18

Male Discretion and Sexual Indiscretion in Working Class Mexico City

MATTHEW C. GUTMANN

SEX EDUCATIONS

Alfredo Pérez's wandering father, like many men of the older generations according to Alfredo, was absent for most of his son's life. Before his father died, however, Alfredo Pérez found him and, as he recounts,

"I took my wife and children to see him. He asked me to forgive him. I told him, 'Don't worry about it, Papa. I'm no one to judge you, only God.' A week later he died. I went to see him one Saturday, and by the next Saturday they told me he had died. When he died, well, we went to the burial and to the vigil. A lot of people began looking at me. I saw my sisters, and they said to me, 'Look, we want to introduce you to Papa's son.' So a man said to me, 'Glad to meet you, my name is Alfredo Pérez.' And then another, 'How are you, my name is Alfredo Pérez.' I met five Alfredos, all with the same last name, all my half brothers—Alfredo Pérez, Alfredo Pérez, Alfredo Pérez, each one."

Like his many namesake brothers, Alfredo Pérez was born in Mexico City, and he has lived there all his life. He describes himself as a carpenter, though like most men in the *clases populares* in Mexico, Alfredo counts carpentry as just one of many skills he has acquired over the years, and not one for which he has regularly found employment. Alfredo spent decades doing factory jobs, driving trucks, and occasionally hammering nails, and today he likes to look back on his working life and how he has kept trim over all these years. He had wild years with alcohol and affairs, he tells me, but those days are long past. Now his family is what counts.

"I've been married for thirty-two years, and we've had our ups and downs. I fight with her, we say things to each other. But she respects me, and I her. Even though we fight and we stop talking for a day or two, afterwards we're happy. And that's the way we will go through life, God willing. But the fine thing is to have some children who respect and admire you. I see now how they respect and admire and love me, and it's a *semilla* [seed] that I planted and taught to grow straight and tall." For Alfredo, one's self-identification as a man is closely connected with insemination, financial maintenance, and moral authority, all of which are in turn largely predicated on men's relationships with women.

People in Colonia Santo Domingo speak of men like Alfredo's father as more common in the past. If many Mexican male identities used to be wrapped up in adultery, polygamy, and siring many children, especially male children, today these are less central concerns. These issues are still important to varying degrees to some men, but in the *colonia* many younger men in particular have begun thinking more reflexively about their bodies than their fathers ever did, and today there is a growing sense that sexuality is as much a possibility as it is an ultimatum, that there are multiple sexualities—not just two—and that sexuality can and does change. In short, men in Santo Domingo are participants in what Sedgwick (1990:1) calls "the long crisis of modern sexual definition."

These men today express greater self-consciousness about sexuality, not in the sense that they talk more about sex, but that their manner of talking about sex is different. Two key factors have contributed to these transformations: one, the greater accessibility and widespread use of modern methods of birth control in the past twenty years in Mexico City; and two, in a less obvious but still significant fashion, the open challenge of homosexuality as a major form of sexual life and expression.[1] Both these factors have had direct and indirect ramifications on the construction of contemporary, modern sexualities in Mexican society.

Adult men have rarely died from childbirth in Mexico or anywhere else, of course, but the separation of sex from pregnancy, childbirth, and child rearing has had a profound impact on them as well as on women, and altered more than just fertility rates for men and women.[2] Sexuality increasingly has the ability to culturally transform personal and family life. And more than ever before, sexuality, potentially at least, can similarly be transformed, including sexuality in relation to romantic love.[3] Sexuality in this context is less and less tied to biological imperatives and more associated with desire, which is subjective and transitory. Yet this analysis of desire must always follow from its contextualization, because, as Lancaster (1992: 270) insists, "[d]esire is thus always part of the cultural, economic, and ideological world of social relations and social conflicts."[4]...

In my formal interviews with residents of Santo Domingo I asked men and women who was responsible for teaching their children about sexuality. After several interviews I also began asking people with whom they had discussed sex when they were young. Most had never discussed sexuality with either of their parents. All but a few said that they themselves felt a responsibility to teach their own children more about sex, though people differed, not clearly along gender lines, as to who should do it. Some thought both parents should handle the task together; others believed mothers

should talk with their daughters and fathers with their sons. Several parents admitted that they preferred to wait until their children came to them with questions based on what they had heard or learned at school or elsewhere rather than initiate discussions on the topic.

In Santo Domingo mothers report that they do commonly talk with their daughters about menstruation. Sometimes in these discussions women explain that with their periods the girls have also reached an age when they can become pregnant, and mothers may impart to their daughters whatever they know about the functioning of the female reproductive system. Few fathers and fewer mothers, it seems, talk with their boys about these issues. Thus if there is great ignorance among all youth regarding sexuality, however uninformed girls may be about sex, it seems probable that boys know even less and have even fewer adults with whom they can discuss their concerns regarding their bodies and reproduction.

Based on interviews in Santo Domingo, on discussions with students at the José Vasconcelos Junior High School in the *colonia,* and on figures compiled in the 1988 (Mexican) *National Survey on Sexuality and the Family among Youth,*[5] most young men speak with male friends or with their fathers about sexuality. Around 40 percent of high school students, according to the *National Survey,* had spoken about the subject with male teachers. As for young women, most receive information about sexuality from their mothers and some from female friends and (for high school students) from female teachers.

At least some discussion about sex and bodies is beginning to occur—in contrast to what took place in earlier generations. This situation contributes to an expanding awareness of the distinctions between sex and procreation and a retreat from the perceived difference between what Adrienne Rich identifies as "fathering" and "mothering" (in the United States):

To "father" a child suggests above all to beget, to provide the sperm which fertilizes the ovum. To "mother" a child implies a continuing presence, lasting at least nine months, more often for years. (1976:xi–xii)

While parenting and fathering practices vary significantly across space and time, in Mexico historically there has been a greater cultural significance for men than women regarding insemination, and therefore a closer identification for men than for women between the act of generative sex and social status. Recent studies have called attention to women's bearing and caring for children as distinguishing social markers in Mexico and have discussed how some women utilize the culturally esteemed status of motherhood to further their involvement in political activities (see Logan 1984; Nader 1986; and Martin 1990). But all this is a long way from identifying coitus with mothering.

Perhaps it is significant that there is no direct translation into Spanish for the English expressions *fathering* and *mothering*. Simply to render the former as *ser padre* clarifies nothing, since this phrase may be understood as either "to be a father" or "to be a parent." That is, even to state "to be a father" implies in Spanish (in its own linguistically biased manner) "to be a parent," just as being a parent in Spanish is lexically also being a father. This does not mean that Mexicans or other Spanish speakers are in any fundamental sense restricted in what they do by the peculiarities of their native tongue, but it does indicate that in Spanish some cultural concepts are expressed in more linguistically convoluted ways than are other concepts.[6]

PROCREATION

The importance of "blood ties" between parents and children came up unexpectedly in my discussion with the *muchachos* on the street one day. I happened to mention that one of my brothers had died fourteen years earlier. I told the youths that Andrew was not my brother by blood, but that nonetheless my mother continued to grieve for him, her stepson, as she would have for me. I told them that my mother still sometimes cried when she thought about my brother.

"I say if you had died instead," responded Esteban, "she would cry more because you were her son, right?"

"Maybe. I don't know."

"Sure, she loves your brother, but not like she loves you," said Celso.

"You can't compare a child born from your insides [*entrañas*], who you know is yours, who belongs to you," Jaime added.

I tried to take the discussion away from Andrew by saying, "If you have four children maybe you're going to love one more than the others."

"I think so," said Enrique.

"I don't think so," said Jaime.

"I say no, Mateo, because I have two children and I love them both the same," countered Celso.

Enrique, ever the diplomat, tried to resolve the debate, "What happens is that there are different factors. Maybe your mother cries for the boy because he spent a lot of time with her, he won her affection, he knew how to treat her with respect. Maybe the *muchacho* behaved better toward her than you did."

"That's what my mother sometimes says," I confided, and the *muchachos* smiled sympathetically.

Gabriel talked to me a lot about his four children. It was not until I'd known him for several months that I realized that the oldest two are stepchildren from his wife's previous marriage. Gabi says he loves each child equally and seeks love from each in return. For Gabi, ignoring the ties of blood is a point of pride.

In his late thirties, the skeptical Gabriel has worked for years as a skilled mechanic on the curb of the same side street in Santo Domingo. By fixing cars and *combis* on the street, Gabriel not only avoids costly garage rental but is also able to engage passersby in conversation. He is known among friends as a free spirit, and religion and spirituality are precisely the issues that animate him most. He is especially interested in the Aztecs and has a collection of posters and pamphlets about them. He has taken Nahuatl classes from time to time, and he uses Nahua names for his two youngest children. For Gabriel, it does not matter how children come into the world. When they come into his life, a man must relate to them as a father; this is what adults do, he says. It is of little consequence from whose loins or seed they come. Gabriel's ideas may be exceptional in the *colonia,* but they are not unique....

I asked Toño, a single man of twenty-seven, about whether having children, especially boys, was important to him. "For me," he replied, "having a lot of kids to prove you're macho is *una chingadera* [equivalent to "a lot of bullshit"]. Those ideas are forty years old." Though not everyone would agree with Toño's assessment, he touches upon a sentiment that is more widespread than certain dominant images would lead us to believe: that Mexican men have to confirm their virility through fathering many children (in Rich's sense), especially male children.

Nor has the valorization of those who are fruitful and multiply been an issue solely for men as inseminators. Pronatal policies have been given boosts not only by Catholic Church doctrine, but also by the heart of the modern, liberal elite in Mexico. Following the lead of its not-so-distant neighbor to the north, on 13 April 1922 *Excelsior,* Mexico's newspaper of record, launched a campaign to celebrate the tenth of May every year as Mother's Day. Every year from 1922 until 1953, the newspaper awarded a prize to *la madre más prolífica,* the most prolific mother. Beginning in 1953, the Mexican widow who had made the most sacrifices to educate her children was honored. Mothers who had given birth to only girls were not allowed to compete. In 1968, the prize was given to the mother who since 1910 "had given more sons to the defense of the Fatherland, either as revolutionaries or as members of the National Army" (Acevedo 1982:60–62).

Efforts such as those by the publisher of *Excelsior* in 1922 may have been in part a response to popular will. Margarita Melville (personal communication) reports that her grandmother was active in a 1922 campaign to celebrate Mother's Day in Mexico City, and thus it is possible that the pub-

lisher was also supporting a preexisting demand. And, after all, if there were not a deep affection for mothers in Mexico, *Excelsior* never would have proposed celebrating Mother's Day, and the holiday never would have been accepted as it has been. Yet the more critical question would seem to be, how do ventures that are at least in part orchestrated by elite social classes create, reshape, and channel, and not simply reflect, the desires of so many nonelites? Returning to Gramsci's formulation of contradictory consciousness, the initiation of Mother's Day celebrations in Mexico provides one case of how uncritical consciousness came to be accepted and spread.

The other aspect of contradictory consciousness relates to consciousness that arises from and is reflected in the practical transformation of the real world.[7] If fatherhood in the minds of people in Santo Domingo is less associated with profligate behavior than the stereotypes would indicate, or at least if such behavior is becoming more proscribed, then these changes should be evident in the practical, everyday experiences of men in the *colonia.*...

The point was brought home to me when I went one day in early spring to the butcher shop on Huehuetzin Street to get some meat for Liliana. Although meat is a little more expensive there than it is in the supermarket, Guillermo and his brother always grind the beef twice when they know it will be fed to an infant. As I was leaving I thanked Guillermo and said something to the effect of "OK, gotta go cook this up with some pasta and—" Before I had time to add "vegetables," Guillermo interrupted me and said, "No, not pasta. That's just going to make her fat. *Sabes, el padre no sólo los engendra sino también tiene que atender a su alimentación* [You know, the father doesn't just procreate, he's also got to make sure they eat right]." Guillermo felt that since I was a new father he had the right and responsibility to give me advice when warranted. By wording his counsel of fatherly love and care in contrast to the familiar image of Man the Procreator, Guillermo was, probably consciously, positioning himself in opposition to a history, or at least a story, of Mexican men.

MALE POTENCY

I would recommend that at least once a week men have sexual relations, since, for example in boxing, it stimulates masculine responses which are very necessary for combat. It's false that abstention is necessary or positive. If you have sexual contact, even twice, before the fight, you feel more like a man and your masculinity surges forth.

Bernardo Vargas, psychologist for the
Pachuca futbol *team (quoted in* Escenas
de pudor y liviandad, *by Carlos Monsiváis)*

At least one history of Mexican men has told of them desiring not simply offspring in general but male heirs in particular, and of using their issue as irrefutable confirmation of the potency of their seed. In retrospect I realize that I sometimes baited men for statements that might confirm this "well-known" male cultural standard. I asked César one day, "Come on, tell the truth. Doesn't it bother you that you don't have a son?"

"No, I've never had a preference," he responded, content with his two teenage daughters.

"Because, that's the notion that—"

"Yeah, it's that machismo, that 'If it's not a boy, you leave the house.' No, no. I have always told my woman—she knows, my family knows—that whatever God brings us, great! I never asked for a boy, but there are a lot of folks who do prefer boys."

"Still?"

"Yes, still. I have a brother-in-law, and he just had a son. He told his woman that if it hadn't been a boy, she shouldn't have bothered to find him. I think that this kind of person is sick in the head, because we are already living in a modern age, and we should realize that it's not what one wants. Because if you want a boy, it's so easy to say, 'I want you to have a boy,' but then the whole world would be full of boys! It's like they say, 'Go to the corner, at an intersection, and when the moon is full, do this, and do that, so you'll get a boy.'

That's a lie. Nature is so pretty that she provides us with everything we need. If she wants a boy, then a boy; if not, a girl."

I was determined, however, to find men who esteemed their male children more than their female, and were not too "modern" to say so. Elena told me that her husband, Carlos, had always wanted a boy, as did she, but that they had three girls. Yet when I talked to Carlos he said he was happier with girls, because they were easier to control. Then Diego Trujillo and his wife, both active in the Christian Base Communities, told me about their children: first a girl, the oldest, then another two girls, and then a boy. "Finally!" I exclaimed. Diego looked at me with a puzzled expression and politely responded, "No, we don't feel that way." Perhaps in my zeal to uncover the renowned preference for sons among Mexican men, I had left informants wondering instead, "Is this how they think in the United States?"[8]

In my own defense, I think that Diego probably understood just what I was getting at: an insulting image of Mexican men and their alleged need for male offspring. Therefore, I took his comments as more than a simple affirmation of his feelings and those of his wife about their personal situation. He was also attempting to refute inaccurate, idealized, and often racist beliefs held in the United States about Mexican men, at least the "traditional" ones.

Men and women speak easily of men who want to keep their wives pregnant all the time. But, curiously, among the people I know in Colonia Santo Domingo, no man wants to identify himself as such, nor does any woman want to label her husband in this way. (This is yet another instance of people approving stereotyped characterizations of others while insisting that those generalizations do not apply to themselves.) Referring to men other than her husband or brothers, Lupita the nurse summarized:

"The husbands who are Mexican machos say, 'I want to have children all the time.' And they want to have the woman pregnant while they are on the *otro lado* [other side—that is, the United

States] doing whatever. And when women who have a lot of children, when they have a cesarean birth, they are asked if they want a tubal ligation. The woman who has a Mexican husband says, 'No, because my husband will get angry. Don't sterilize me until God lets me do it.' People get upset as well if you put in IUDs."

The impact of feminist ideas and practices is decidedly mixed in Colonia Santo Domingo, as was revealed in a seemingly exceptional story that Daniel told me about birth control and abortion. During his wife's second pregnancy, Dani told me, she wanted to get an abortion. Daniel was adamant that every life is sacred and that this one had already begun, despite the fact that he is an avowed agnostic and someone who openly ridicules the Catholic Church. On hearing Daniel's story, it was easy for me to conclude, "Here's a guy who's forcing his wife to bear his progeny." Before I had a chance to broach this idea with him, however, Daniel added slyly, "So you know what I did then? I went out and got myself cut"—that is, he got a vasectomy, something that puts him in a rather exclusive category among my friends in Santo Domingo. This was Dani's way of making short- and long-term deals with his wife. Dani's feelings and actions also illustrate that contradictory male identities—in this case, those relating to male sexualities—are to be found not only when comparing groups of men in the population as a whole, but within individual men as well.

URGES AND *AVENTURAS*

After I had spent several months in Mexico, my research suddenly assumed an explicitly sexual character in a very personal way when my wife and daughter returned to the United States for a couple of weeks. Before leaving, Michelle talked casually one day with Angela and Norma about her planned trip. Angela asked if she was worried about leaving me alone for so long, hinting not so subtly at the opportunity this would present me for *aventuras* (adventures)—in other words, adultery. When Michelle responded that she trusted me and

was not concerned, Angela countered, "Well, sure, but do you trust the women?" Michelle had not understood the real threat, Angela counseled: men cannot help themselves when sexual opportunity presents itself.

The day after Michelle and Liliana left, I bumped into Norma and another neighbor, Lupita, at the *sobre ruedas* (open-air market) that is set up on Coyamel Street each Wednesday. After asking if Michelle and Liliana had gotten off all right, Norma turned to me and, forefinger pointing to her eye, said, "¡Te estamos vigilando! [We're keeping an eye on you!]". Lupita added, with the same gesture, that she too would mount a vigilant lookout. It was mainly a joke by these two married women who had already become like family. But it was also a warning to the husband of one of their absent friends that no fooling around would be tolerated—or go unreported. Implicit, again, was the message that men will try to get away with whatever they can sexually, unless they believe they might get caught.

What is interesting is not that the actual frequency of cheating is that high (or low, for that matter), but the insights all this provided into what many women and men in Santo Domingo view as an innate core of male sexuality. As Angela told me later when I asked about her comments to Michelle, "¿A quién le dan pan que llore? [Who cries (i.e., does something inappropriate) when they're given bread?]" Everyone knows what you do with bread: you eat it. The stereotype of men in Mexico being subject to uncontrollable bodily urges and needs is widely held in Santo Domingo—which just proves that some stereotypes about sexual identities in the region are shared by those living there.[9]

Many men tell of having had affairs with women other than their wives. *"No soy santo,"* confides Alfredo, "I'm no saint." The justification for adultery on the part of men is often that men have peculiar "natural desires." Further, men sometimes snickered to me that *"el hombre llega hasta donde la mujer lo diga* [men will get away with whatever women let them]." One of the most common expressions for an extramarital affair is *cana al aire*—literally, "a gray hair to the air," the image being that when you find a gray hair you pull it out quickly and fling it away; you do it, and it is over.

Such "flings" are said to be distinguished by their purely sexual as opposed to romantic content. One woman described to me how when her husband was younger he would often disappear on Friday night and not return until Sunday night. She would tell their children that he was working, to protect them, she said. Taxi drivers have an especially wide reputation for casual rendezvous with women fares. After waxing most poetic on the qualities of his wife, one *taxista* told me that he and she have an agreement that *aventuritas* are fine so long as they are not discussed between them later. "Twenty-one years is a long time to be married," he told me, suggesting that the underlying rationale was boredom in the marital bedroom. He also insisted that she has the same freedom to find lovers as he. After all, he reasoned to me, otherwise it would not be fair.

Affairs are discussed and joked about casually by many people in Santo Domingo. On boarding a *combi* driven by my friend Rafael, I asked how his infant son was doing. He said the boy of four months was doing great. There was one thing, though, that concerned my friend.

"What's bothering you?" I inquired. It was noisy on the minibus and we had to shout to make ourselves heard.

"Every day the boy looks more like people from the 'other side' [the United States]," he screamed.

"How?"

"He's got bright green eyes. I don't even think he's mine!"

He laughed heartily. The other passengers seemed oblivious to this self-disparaging and semi-lewd commentary. His was not the storybook image of a shamefaced and cuckolded husband.

Marcos told me that his wife, Delia, has been joking for years that Lolo, a neighborhood boy of fourteen, is her second husband. It all started when

Delia's sister spread a rumor that Lolo had slept with Delia, Marcos related. "Sometimes I chew Lolo out," he continued, "telling him that I had to go to Tepito to buy my girls shoes when he should be the one doing it."

The documentary record leaves open to question the extent to which such banter is new. For example, the use of the term *cabrón,* which can figuratively refer to a cuckold, is widespread, but by no means necessarily tied to this one meaning or even to a negative quality.[10] Regardless of the history of jokes about infidelity, humorous quips about adultery today take place in a shifting context. Men continue to have affairs; this is nothing new. What has reportedly changed is the number of women who do so, and the fact that some are quite open about having lovers. A particularly promiscuous woman in Santo Domingo has even earned a nickname, La Tasqueña, for her amorous liaisons. La Tasqueña is married to a man who spends ten or eleven months a year in Detroit and returns for only short stays to Santo Domingo to visit her and their two children. Whenever her legal husband is in the United States, she has a series of men (one at a time) living with her, each of whom moves out temporarily when the legal husband returns to the *colonia.* Her nickname derives from an episode that occurred several years ago during one of her legal husband's infrequent visits. She was very late returning to the house one night, and when she finally arrived she complained that she had missed all the *combis* from the Tasqueña metro stop. The problem was that her neighbors had seen her elsewhere and knew this was a ruse to cover up her date that night.

Thus one of the creative responses of some women to men's adultery has been to take lovers of their own. Women's activities as varied as community organizing and paid work have led to far greater opportunities to meet other men and to have affairs with them. To whatever extent sexual "needs" were ever associated with men alone, this seems far less the case today in Santo Domingo.

In refutation of the commonplace that many or most Latin American men have their first sexual escapades with prostitutes, none of the men I interviewed from Colonia Santo Domingo save one admitted to ever having been to a prostitute. Nor had any men taken their sons to prostitutes "to become men." Once again, it is possible that my friends and informants were simply covering up sexual escapades from their pasts. More probable, I think, is that paying for sexual services is today more common in some areas of Mexico City—for instance, around the Centro Histórico—than it is in others. Then, too, it is possible that for many of my friends, paying for sex implies an unmanly inability to attract women sexually.

Going to prostitutes may be more of a tradition among young men from the middle and upper classes. In the survey on sexuality among high school students cited earlier, 20.5 percent of the well-to-do boys reported that their first sexual relation was with a prostitute (Consejo Nacional de Población 1988:120). Men from upper middle class homes also speak of the convention whereby the father hires a maid with whom his sons can have their first sexual encounters. Making caustic references to "the excesses of the feminist movement," one lawyer sarcastically told me that young men are often raped by these older and more sexually aggressive *muchachas,* adding, "I know this from personal experience." The lawyer's comments regarding feminism and rape bore witness to a defensive posture assumed by many men in his milieu today. Still, for this man and others of his class background and generation, it was taken for granted that males would lose their virginity prior to marrying whereas females should be virgins until their wedding night.

Female virginity continues to be an important issue for many men, but this double standard is far less an issue among younger men and women, especially as knowledge about and use of birth control by teens becomes more widespread. But the matter is contested—among teens, and between teens and their parents. As part of this gendered and generational confrontation over virginity, a particularly bizarre rumor about adolescent sexual behavior in the United States was making its way

through the Pedregales in 1993. Some people had heard, and were convinced, that many girls in the United States have their hymens surgically removed so that the first time they have sexual intercourse they will not experience so much pain. This example, among others, was put forth to my wife, Michelle, to demonstrate that women in the United States have much more sexual freedom and know how to better enjoy themselves sexually.

NORTHERN PENETRATIONS

Due especially to factors such as migration and television, cultural boundaries that coincide with geographic divisions are far less prevalent today than at any time in the past. This is true both within Mexico and, of fundamental importance, across the international border with the United States. As Rouse notes,

> the growing institutionalization of migration to the United States...means that more of the Mexican population is oriented to developments outside the country and that this orientation is becoming steadily more pronounced. (1991:16)

The numbers of human beings involved in international migration is staggering. A recent study suggests that "14.8 percent of Mexico's labor force is, at one time or another, employed in the United States—legally or otherwise" (California Chamber of Commerce 1993:14). If these figures are correct, the experience of living and working in the United States is common to one out of every seven adult Mexicans. The impact of this transnational migration on cultural standards and manners within Mexico is evident in the realm of sexuality.

Because of migration and the fact that English has a certain cachet among youth throughout Mexico, and no doubt as a partial result of commercial dumping by the U.S. apparel industry, T-shirts with slogans in English are popular and commonly worn in Colonia Santo Domingo. Some merely appear bizarrely out of place, like one with the words "I love Ollie [North]!" over the Stars and Stripes. Others seem grotesque until you realize that surely most people haven't the foggiest idea what they mean. An eleven-year-old girl walking next to her older brother wears a T-shirt reading, "If I weren't giving head, I'd be dead...."

According to recent figures, at least 3 million households in Mexico City have televisions (perhaps 95 percent of all homes), which are watched daily, and 59 percent of all families in Mexico City have videocassette recorders (García Canclini 1991:164). When we moved into Santo Domingo in mid-1992, in one neighboring household there were four televisions and four VCRs for seven adults and one child. Also of special relevance to the discussion of sexual practices and role models is the fact that every day in Mexico City and throughout the country new and old television programs originating in the United States and dubbed into Spanish are broadcast on major channels. During a random week (24–30 July 1993), the following U.S. television shows were seen: *Murphy Brown, Los años maravillosos* (The Wonder Years), *Beverly Hills 90210, Miami Vice, Los intocables* (The Untouchables), *Bonanza,* and *Alf,* as well as the cartoon shows *Los Simpsons, Las tortugas ninja* ([Teenage Mutant] Ninja Turtles), and *Los verdaderos casafantasmas* (The Real Ghostbusters). That same week, viewers of the major television stations could watch such classic cinematic fare as *Body Double, Absence of Malice, The Bigamist, My Man Godfrey, The Fugitive,* and *The Mummy.*

To call attention to the cultural, economic, and political power of the United States as well as the Catholic Church in Mexico, Arizpe (1993: 378) refers to those bodies as the Regional Caciques. Most of my friends in Santo Domingo are acutely aware of how Mexican and other Latin American men and women are portrayed in U.S. television and cinema. Questions related to sexual roles and machismo, illegal immigrants and racism are noted and judged by audiences throughout Mexico. This does not mean, however, that all reactions are the same, as certain analysts of the "culture industry" would have it. Frequently there is debate over the meaning of episodes on the TV, as some more than others are able to transcend oversimplified representations and messages.

Regardless of the extent to which U.S. television and film do or do not accurately reflect aspects of sexual experiences occurring in the United States, they are reference points orienting international viewers' attention to alternate sexual lifestyles and relations. Following the opening in Mexico of the Hollywood movie *Pretty Woman* (released there as *La mujer bonita*), knee-high leather (or simulated leather) boots such as those worn by Julia Roberts in the film enjoyed enormous popularity for several years among young women in the *clases populares* in Mexico City. Whether or not these boots were directly associated with Roberts's occupation in the movie (she plays a prostitute) or with the story's outcome (she goes off with a handsome young billionaire), such highly gendered fashions are increasingly tied to direct U.S. influences.

Young women in Colonia Santo Domingo also began watching the Miami-based Spanish-language talk show *Cristina* as soon as it appeared on Mexico's Channel 2 at the end of 1992. "Look at what fifteen-year-old girls in the United States are talking about! They know it all!" seventeen-year-old Carmen exclaimed to me one day. Interestingly, Mexican intellectuals are likely to label *Cristina* a "U.S. program" or a "Cuban-American program," whereas young working class women, its main viewing audience in Santo Domingo, seldom care about where it comes from and simply refer to it as "my show."

As I was talking about witches one day with Martha, a friend who sells diapers in bulk in the open-air markets, she said to me, "You know what? There aren't as many witches in Mexico as there used to be. And do you know where they're coming from now? Your country." She smiled and related that she had seen a lot of (U.S.) witches on a *Cristina* program. I suggested that maybe they were part of the North American Free Trade Agreement.

WHEN THE MAN'S AN ASS

In Santo Domingo in the 1990s, if, with respect to women, virginity is less an issue and adultery more of one when compared with the situation twenty years earlier, divorce rates remain approximately the same. In Mexico City, 2 percent of women older than twelve reported their civil status as divorced in the 1990 census, whereas in the country overall the figure was 1 percent (INEGI 1992:22). The fact that of the women I know in Santo Domingo far more than one in fifty says she is divorced leads me to believe that many of these women had common-law marriages, and thus splitting up did not officially constitute divorce. Or perhaps some of them are still legally married yet call themselves divorced because they no longer live with their legal spouses. For whatever reasons, many of them have never gotten formally divorced.

Attitudes about divorce are changing, especially on the part of women, and in some instances this in turn has had dramatic effects on their men. In an interview in June 1991, Marco Rascón, president of the citywide Asamblea de Barrios, told me that divorces were on the rise among the influential organization's membership. He attributed the initiative in most cases to women militants who were no longer willing to tolerate husbands who opposed their wives' political efforts. Increasingly, according to Rascón, conflicts of this type were resolved either in divorce or in the husbands' following their wives and becoming Asamblea activists themselves. Nevertheless, the *muchachos* I talked with on the street were intrigued when they learned that my parents divorced when I was quite young, and they asked me a lot of questions about what it was like to grow up in that situation, indicating that divorce for them still carried a somewhat exotic flavor.

Rosa, a deeply religious and devout Catholic, repeated a story to me that her granddaughter had told her: "Oh, Grandma, in school they assigned us to write about the worst thing that has ever happened to us in our lives, and I put that for me the worst was my parents' divorce." But, Rosa con-

fided to me, "I told her, 'Don't be an ass. It's the best thing that has ever happened to you.'" Rosa never thought highly of her former son-in-law, and for her, church stricture or not, there were some times when divorce was the best way out of a bad situation.

Men in Santo Domingo enjoy complaining about being married, some saying that marriage is to be endured (usually for the sake of the children). Numerous others, both newlyweds and those who have been married for many years, snipe at wives and marriage. But these attacks should not always be taken at face value. In many ways complaints of this kind by men in Santo Domingo are similar to *albures*. Ostensibly and superficially about sex, *albures* are more frequently double-entendre jokes and quips that use sex to comment on other topics and issues.

When they make wisecracks about the miseries of marriage, men likewise frequently use familiar codes, albeit often sexist ones, to vent their rage at life's iniquities and to blame especially loved ones for keeping them in their sorry state of affairs. If pressed on the issue, even some of the most ornery insulters of wives will tell you they pray they will die before their spouses, because they would not know how to live alone. Although male dependency upon wives to feed and clothe them doubtless focuses important aspects of women's subordination to men, such unvarnished sentiments on the part of men are not merely venal attempts at control, nor are they expressed without contradiction.

In the same way that men use *albures* and complain about marriage, those who are caught for their *aventuras* commonly raise the excuse that appearances can be deceptive and that extramarital flings do not necessarily mean what they might appear to mean. (And most of my male friends in Santo Domingo who admit to affairs say that they were eventually caught.) Needless to say, most of my male friends have a more difficult time sifting through the layers of meaning when a question of women's delinquencies arises. Juan came into the kitchen of his home one day as Angela and I were talking about adulterous friends and neighbors. Angela looked up and said to Juan, "Now, tell Mateo whether a man would forgive a woman for such an offense. Would you forgive her?"

"Men almost never forgive such women, and when they do it's because they really love them—" Juan started to respond.

"Or 'because he's an ass!' That's Juan's expression," Angela shot back.

"Men like it," Juan continued, "when their wives say to them, 'Look, I bought you this and—'"

"I bought you a sombrero!" Angela interrupted, making reference to covering the "horns" growing on a cuckolded man's head.

LA CASA CHICA

In Oscar Lewis's (1961) affectionate portrait of Mexican working class family life, *The Children of Sánchez,* he discusses many sexual practices in the capital in the 1950s. Overly confident in the re silience of cultural practices, I was sure when I began fieldwork in 1992 that one of these, *la casa chica* (the small house), was still an entrenched social institution. After all, Jesús Sánchez, whose children are the subject of Lewis's book, usually seemed to have a mistress or second wife, depending upon how you defined the relationship, whom he maintained in *la casa chica* (or *segundo frente* [second front]).

A concept and a practice regarding male gender identities in Mexico that social scientists have more often assumed than studied, *la casa chica* is usually thought of as the arrangement whereby a Mexican man keeps a woman other than his wife in a residence separate from his main (*casa grande*) household. It is generally discussed as a modern form of urban polygamy that is common in all social strata in Mexico and is by no means the prerogative of only wealthy men.[11]

Information on *la casa chica* was initially easy to come by. One man in a Christian Base Community in Colonia Ajusco spoke to me disparagingly of a brother of his who maintained *three* different households simultaneously, and did this

on a factory worker's wages. A few weeks later, Luciano was welding a pipe in our apartment. Neighbors had already told me Luciano had a *casa chica,* so I was especially looking forward to talking with him. I asked Luciano about his family, and he told me that he and his wife were *separados* (separated). They had not lived together for years, he said. When I asked where he was living then, he replied, "Not far from here." But though he no longer shared a home with his "wife"—a couple of times Luciano fumbled over what to call her— because the house and the land were in his name, getting divorced was out of the question; in a divorce he would risk losing all the property.

On another occasion I mentioned to a friend, Margarita, that I was surprised I had not encountered the famous *casa chica* in Santo Domingo. Margarita paused a moment and then said to me carefully, "*¿Sabes qué? Carmela es la casa chica.* [You know what? Carmela is *la casa chica.*]" Carmela, a woman in her late thirties whom I had previously met in the *colonia,* had lived for twelve years with the man she always referred to as her husband. But, it turned out, this man was legally married to (though separated from) another woman with whom he had four children, the youngest then thirteen. Carmela's "husband" had legally adopted her son from an earlier relationship, and she and this man later had a daughter who was then nine.

After a few months of fieldwork, I was getting quite wary of what *la casa chica* meant to different people, and how everyone referred to the "husbands" and "wives" of those involved in *las casas chicas.* By the time Rafael told me in December that his brother was living in their home with his *casa chica,* I had also grown a little weary of the term.

"Is he married to another woman?" I asked Rafael.

"Yes, he's been married for years," came the reply. "Of course, they haven't been together since he's been with this new woman, but he's still married to the first one."

Then a neighbor happened to mention a remarkable but more "classical" *casa chica* arrangement a couple of blocks from where we lived in Santo Domingo.

"You know the tire-repair place on the corner? Well, a guy used to live over it with two sisters. He lived with them both!"

"In the same house?" I asked suspiciously.

"No."

"But each sister knew about the other one?"

"They knew about it and each tried to outdo the other, trying to get him to realize that she was better. He lived with the two sisters, two days with one, two with the other."

"What were they thinking?"

"Their mother was the really stupid one. She used to say that he was her *doble yerno* [double son-in-law]. If the mother thought this, what could you expect from the daughters?"

Yet how the phrase *la casa chica* is used in daily discourse is often quite removed from such classical patterns. Rafael works in maintenance at the National University (UNAM), which borders Colonia Santo Domingo. He once told me that 60 percent of his fellow employees at the university have *casas chicas*. Astonished, I questioned him further. "Yes, I am talking about women as well as men." It soon became apparent that Rafael was talking about people having extramarital affairs; for him *casa chica* was a catchy analogue.

So too, although Margarita refers to Carmela as "*la casa chica*," and although by Carmela's own account the man she lives with cheated on her early in their relationship, this man has been faithful to Carmela for seven years and he is her "husband." As for Luciano's arrangement, a few weeks after fixing our pipes, and after we had gotten to know each other better, he told me that for several years he had lived with a woman other than his "first wife." He and the second woman now have two children together. In responding to questions about "your spouse" in the survey I conducted, Luciano always answered with regard to this second woman.

Most of the *casas chicas* that I know of in Mexico City that conform to a pattern of urban polygamy—where a man shuttles between two (or more) households and the "wives" are often ignorant of each other—are maintained by well-paid workers or men from the middle and upper classes. Other than the rather extraordinary arrangement of the man married to two sisters, and the factory worker with three "wives," generally the only workers who can afford this kind of setup are truckers or migrants to the United States, or men who have high-paying jobs in the electrical, telephone, or petroleum industries.

So what, then, *is* the meaning of *la casa chica,* and what shape does it take in the lives of people in Colonia Santo Domingo? At least in some instances, rather than referring to urban polygamy, *la casa chica* is used to describe second (or later) marriages. In other words, it frequently refers to serial monogamy, and if adultery occasionally occurs, it does so within *this* context. The approach many people take to *la casa chica* is in part a product of Catholic doctrine and antidivorce sanctions. Mexican working class men as well as women have learned to manipulate the cultural rituals and social laws of machismo, not unlike the sixteenth-century rural French, who were, as Natalie Davis (1983:46) writes, a people with "centuries of peasant experience in manipulating popular rituals and the Catholic law on marriage."

This is especially true for the poor, who cannot as easily arrange and afford church annulments of their marriages. Men are culturally expected to financially maintain their (first) "wives" forever, just as these women expect to be supported—not that this situation always obtains. That is, for many men and women *la casa chica* is the best resolution to a situation in which legal divorce is out of the question. It is the way serial monogamy is practiced by many people in a society in which one often must be "married" to one's first spouse for life. The fact that few women and men necessarily intend in this manner to subvert Catholic rules regarding marriage-for-life does not take away from the creative (and subversive) quality of their actions—one of the ways, to paraphrase Ortner (1989–90:79), in which arenas of nonhegemonic practice can become the bases of a significant challenge to hegemony.

In addition to prohibitions against divorce emanating from the Catholic Church, there are other factors that impinge on the situation. After divorce, first wives can more easily prevent fathers from seeing their children. And men such as Luciano can also lose property rights if their de facto divorces become de jure, and if they marry other women and end up living elsewhere.

The traditional *casa chica* arrangement in which one man lives simultaneously with more than one woman and "family" may or may not persist in the upper echelons of Mexican society. But it is not common in Colonia Santo Domingo, at least not in this sense of urban polygamy. At the same time, none of my analysis regarding serial monogamy minimizes the traumatic financial and emotional impact caused by men who do desert their wives and children, regardless of whether these men take up with other women.[12] My argument is instead threefold: first, that the expression *la casa chica* is used in a variety of ways in *colonias populares,* many of which have little to do with adultery as this latter term is defined by men and women involved in these unions; second, that these multiple meanings of *la casa chica* are illustrations of a cultural practice that has emerged in the context of Catholic laws on marriage; and third, that this cultural practice should be seen as part of a manipulative popular response to the church's ban on divorce.

Popular approaches to the *casa chica* in Santo Domingo are thus exemplary of Gramsci's notion of contradictory consciousness, as the unpredictable exigencies of the living enter into lively contest with the oppressive traditions and sycophantic bromides of dead generations. And, therefore, as Herzfeld (1987:84) makes clear in another context, in instances such as the daily references and practices to the *casa chica* we should, rather than merely bearing witness to an "enforced passivity" induced from on high, especially and instead see "the quality of active social invention" in defiance of official discourse and control.

LOS SOLTEROS: MASTURBATION, CELIBACY, AND ASEXUALITY

During the same period in January when my wife and daughter were away and I was temporarily *"un hombre abandonado* [an abandoned man],*"* as some neighbors joked, I expected to hear comments from men about my temporary single status, opportunities for adultery, and much more. Reality proved not so much disappointing as unexpected.

During this time, I spent a Saturday afternoon, as I often did, having a couple of drinks on the corner with a few friends. Marcos, Gabriel, Marcial, Pablo, and Marcelo were all there drinking *anís,* on the rocks or straight, out of plastic cups. Eventually the discussion wound around to the fact that I was alone for a couple of weeks. There were initially some mild inquiries as to whether I would go out looking for some *jovencitas* (young women), but then the comments took an abrupt turn.

"You do know what we say about single guys, don't you?" asked Marcelo. "'*Los solteros son chaqueteros* [Single guys are meat beaters]' and '*No le aprietes el cuello al ganso* [Don't squeeze the goose's neck].'" Everyone laughed, especially when they made me repeat the phrases back to make sure I had learned them correctly. Then they insisted that I copy them down. "You should put them in your book," Marcos recommended.

Masturbating men may not conjure up as romantic an image as a *mujeriego* (womanizer). But I imagine this representation is infinitely more accurate, if mundane, in describing the sex lives of most single men in Santo Domingo than portraits of rapacious young Mexican men always on the prowl for female conquest.[13] Although I briefly hesitated to do so, I checked with Angela the next day to see if she was familiar with the expressions about masturbation I had heard and to make sure I had copied them correctly. She approved my transcriptions and then mentioned that she and her sisters often lament the bachelor status of a nephew by saying to each other, "*Le jala la cabeza al gallo*

[He yanks the cock's head]." So much for my worry about embarrassing this grandmother.

Eventually I discovered that in Colonia Santo Domingo one of the most popular ways to describe a single man is to refer to him as a masturbating man. Roberto, a muffler repairman near where I lived, introduced me to his cousin Mario one day. Noting that his cousin was unmarried, Roberto added, "He's a *maraquero* [another slang expression for a man who masturbates]." No joke was made about the cousin being free to run around with a lot of women because of his single status. On another occasion, when we were discussing parents' roles in teaching their children about sexuality, Roberto told me that he and his wife both consider it important to teach their three boys about masturbation, so that they come to see it as part of a transitional stage and a good way to deal with "*estrés* [stress]." He did caution, however, that masturbation could be overdone and that it was only a stage through which one should pass in adolescence.

The assumption that all men love to have as many orgasms as possible is a view about male sexuality that is widely shared by men and women in Santo Domingo. This premise is basic to understanding the connections between men, masturbation, and womanizing, and to examining many of the sexual justifications and intimations heard in the *colonia*.

Héctor and I were walking through the famous La Merced market one overcast afternoon. We had already visited the Sonora market, where herbs, spices, Buddha statues, and love potions are sold. As we passed by a doorway marked "#4" leading to a series of indoor stalls, Héctor pulled my arm and said he wanted to show me something. He found a stall selling sweets made of squash, nuts, and other delicacies, and bought two pieces of *queso de tuna* (tuna-cactus cheese), a sweet made of the nopal cactus that looks like a light brown hockey puck, only smaller. I bit into one as we went back out on the street and continued walking.

After I had finished about half, Héctor smiled, pointed to the remaining portion, and mis-chievously informed me that *queso de tuna* has a marvelous side effect. About four the next morning, he told me, I would have an erection so hard that it would wake me up. Héctor must have also been sure that I would then want to wake Michelle and have the best sex of my life, because he added, "in the morning you can tell me if it worked." I asked him the obvious question: why hadn't he bothered to mention this little supposed attribute of *queso de tuna* before I ate it? He just laughed, sure that I was really grateful for having been given a food that would unleash my essential male sexual proclivities.

But the view that *all* men have the same sexuality fails to account for multiple sexualities—homosexual, heterosexual, bisexual—and it overlooks androgyny and *a*sexuality. It also overlooks changes in sexuality experienced throughout individuals' lives, from childhood through adolescence, early adulthood, middle age, and old age. And this outlook skirts around significant variations based on class, generation, and family histories.

After a man I know in Santo Domingo confessed to me, "I'll tell you honestly, sex has just never been as important to me as it seems to be for a lot of other guys," I decided to seek out a professional celibate, a Catholic priest, to talk more about male sexuality and asexuality. So I went back to see Padre Víctor Verdín of the Christian Base Communities, at the Iglesia de la Resurrección. I asked him, "For you, the church is your family in a way. But have you never thought that you might be missing something by not having a regular family? It's a naïve question, but a serious one."

"That's a little question, all right! Look, at the level of ideas, a lot of the time I have known that celibacy is right, in terms of leaving you time for others. You have to have a heart which is open to all, and your family is people and your personal relation is an intellectual one with God. But emotionally, in the heart and feelings, I lingered a long time and still I don't think I've got it, really experiencing with serenity and peace an acceptance that there will be tremendous incoherencies, a giant emptiness. It hasn't been easy. There are theories of Freudian sublimation, and in this sense, yes, you can cope. But one goes through various crises. Sometimes what hurts is parenthood. Sometimes it's the lack of tenderness. Sometimes you miss the sexual relation. Sometimes it's everything all at once."

Padre Víctor is a man nonetheless, by which I do not mean here simply that he is biologically male, but that he is a social male. Because of this fact, sexual tensions with women are not obviated by his office: "With women, you have to exercise certain obvious discretion, most of all so that no one misinterprets a certain closeness, or a certain friendliness. People are very sensitive, including in how you greet them, and you have to be careful to avoid ambiguous signs. In this culture, that's the way it is."[14]

Yet in the culture to which Padre Víctor refers, physical intimacy is "the way it is" for some more than others. And, really, there is only so much one man can do about the fact that men's and women's sexualities are increasingly open to ambiguity and misunderstanding. Sex is changing in important if uncalculated ways partly in response to pressures such as those the good padre and his iconoclastic church bring to bear on pregnant teenagers and their lovers. Throughout this Catholic land, youth continue to reach puberty knowing precious little about their and others' bodies. Yet birth control in some form is the standard procedure, albeit a women's procedure. Divorce restrictions remain in place, though they are routinely and creatively dodged, by some through *la casa chica*. Homophobia is a code of boyish insults, whereas sexual experimentation by young men with young men and by young women with young women is increasingly seen as legitimate. Though men are still acting like men, women too are experiencing urges and *aventuras*. The sexual contradictions of a generation have effectively transformed very little and quite a lot.

NOTES

1. I draw in this chapter on Giddens's (1992) insights regarding sexuality, love, and eroticism in modern societies. The term *homosexuality* is used guardedly here to refer to sex between men and sex between women. In Santo Domingo, however, unlike the United States, people usually mean by *homosexual* only the man who is penetrated by another (not necessarily "homosexual") man in anal intercourse. For more on these meanings and practices and certain similarities with regard to sex between men in different parts of Latin America and among Chicanos, see Lancaster 1992 and Almaguer 1991.

2. Unfortunately, no demographic studies have been conducted on fertility rates for men in Mexico. In fact, discussions are just now beginning in the field of demography worldwide as to what the concept of male fertility might even mean (Eugene Hammel, personal communication).

3. As Parker (1991:92) notes in his study of sexual culture in contemporary Brazil, "It is clear that in the modern period sexuality, focused on reproduction, has become something to be managed not merely by the Catholic church or by the state, but by individuals themselves."

4. Lancaster (1992:270) continues: "It is not simply that these relations and conflicts act on some interior and preexisting sexuality 'from the outside' but that they constitute it 'from the inside' as well. Which is to say (contrary to common sense): sexual history is possible only to the extent that desire is thoroughly historicized, and sexual anthropology only to the extent that its subject is effectively relativized."

5. The National Survey was compiled from 10,142 questionnaires completed by high school students, who in Mexico come overwhelmingly from middle and upper middle class backgrounds. See Consejo Nacional de Población 1988.

6. The notion of linguistic constraints on culture is given a classic expression in the Sapir-Whorf Hypothesis: "Human beings…are very much at the mercy of the particular language which has become the medium of expression for their society" (Sapir 1929 [1949]:162). See Tambiah (1990:111–39) for a recent and sensible effort to analyze the question of cross-cultural translation and the commensurability of cultures.

7. For a similar approach to questions of hegemony, borrowing from (Giddens's formulation of "practical

consciousness," see Cowan's (1990) nuanced development of Grimscian theories in her study of gender practices in a Greek Macedonian community.

8. In March 1993, on a beach at Puerto Escondido in Oaxaca, I finally met a man who in the course of a long conversation about his life told me, "I have five kids: four daughters and a baby—*un hijo* [a son]!" He shouted those last words, clearly delighted with the maleness of the new arrival. This man and I also talked about the coincidence of both of us having lived and worked in Chicago and Houston for many years. Might his experiences in the United States have made him especially "pro-boy," or was he simply happy for the variation of a boy amid all those girls? My hunch is that the latter is closer to the truth.

9. Many other ethnographers who have worked in various regions of Mexico report similar sentiments regarding male sexuality. To evoke similar popular beliefs around San Luis Potosí, Behar (1993:290) writes that "men's need for sex is insatiable." Based on fieldwork in Oaxaca, Matthews (1987:228) calls attention to "an important female view of men as being, by nature, lustful, possessing an insatiable sexual appetite. They are like animals in that they seek their own satisfaction and are not concerned with the needs of others." At the same time, such opinions should not be taken to mean that women do not share similar urges. Matthews (1987:225) also speaks of "an important male view of women as being sexually uncontrolled." We may compare these last summations with Brandes's (1980:77) research in Andalusia, Spain, where "women are seductresses, possessed of insatiable, lustful appetites."

10. In this sense, *cabrón* has a usage similar to that of the U.S. English *son of a bitch;* they can be employed as both insults and compliments. For current usage by Mexicans of the term *Sancho,* a nickname for men being cuckolded, see Conover 1987:177–78.

11. For a recent mention of the practice, though not the name, of the *casa chica,* see Bossen 1988:272 on middle class households in Guatemala City. See also Diaz 1970:60 and Fromm and Maccoby 1970:149.

12. Given my interest in fathers and fathering, I was in contact with more men who lived with their families, even if they were not necessarily active in parenting, than I was with those who had abandoned their wives and children. Single mothers were nonetheless common enough in the *colonia.*

13. In my fieldwork in Santo Domingo I was privy to very few discussions about female masturbation.

14. Within the discipline of anthropology there has been an interesting and important dialogue regarding the possibility, and appropriateness, of male ethnographers working with women (see, for example, Gregory 1984; Herzfeld 1985:48; Brandes 1987; and Gilmore 1991:29, n. 2.). I believe that the anthropological study of male identities, of men *as men,* is considerably weakened when the only sources of information are men. In the same way that we have criticized as male bias an understanding of women of whatever culture that is based solely upon what men say about women (see Scheper-Hughes 1983), so too we must not depend on what only men say about themselves. Indeed, I found that on certain sensitive topics, such as domestic violence, rather than being more difficult to discuss these issues with women, it was often much easier to speak with them than it was to get men to think reflexively and report honestly about their experiences and ideas.

REFERENCES

Acevedo, Marta. 1982. *El 10 de mayo.* Mexico City: SEP.

Almaguer, Tomás. 1991. "Chicano Men: A Cartography of Homosexual Identity and Behavior." *differences* 3(2):75–100.

Arizpe, Lourdes. 1993. "Una sociedad en movimiento." In *Antropologia breve de México.* Lourdes Arizpe, ed. Pp. 373–98. Mexico City: Academia de la Investigación Científica.

Behar, Ruth. 1993. *Translated Woman: Crossing the Border with Esperanza's Story.* Boston: Beacon.

Bossen, Laurel. 1988. "Wives and Servants: Women in Middle-Class Households, Guatemala City." In *Urban Life: Readings in Urban Anthropology.* 2nd edition. George Gmelch and Walter P. Zenner, eds. Pp. 265–75. Prospect Heights, IL: Waveland.

Brandes, Stanley. 1980. *Metaphors of Masculinity: Sex and Status in Andalusian Folklore.* Philadelphia: University of Pennsylvania Press.

———. 1987. "Sex Roles and Anthropological Research in Rural Andalusia." *Women's Studies* 13:357–72.

California Chamber of Commerce. 1993. *North American Free Trade Guide: The Emerging Mexican Market and Opportunities in Canada under*

NAFTA. Sacramento: California Chamber of Commerce.

Conover, Ted. 1987. *Coyotes: A Journey through the Secret World of America's Illegal Aliens.* New York: Vintage.

Consejo Nacional de Población. 1988. *Encuesta nacional sobre sexualidad y familia en jóvenes de educación media superior, 1988. (Avances de investigación.)* Mexico City.

Cowan, Jane K. 1990. *Dance and the Body Politic in Northern Greece.* Princeton, NJ: Princeton University Press.

Diaz, May N. 1970. *Tonalá: Conservatism, Responsibility, and Authority in a Mexican Town.* Berkeley: University of California Press.

Fromm, Erich, and Michael Maccoby. 1970. *Social Character in a Mexican Village: A Sociopsychoanalytic Study.* Englewood Cliffs, NJ: Prentice Hall.

García Canclini, Néstor. 1991. "Conclusiones: ¿Para qué sirve el festival?" In *Públicos de arte y política cultural: Un estudio del II Festival de la ciudad de México.* Néstor García Canclini et al., eds. Pp. 159–75. Mexico City: Universidad Autónoma Metropolitana.

Giddens, Anthony. 1992. *The Transformation of Intimacy: Sexuality, Love and Eroticism in Modern Societies.* Stanford, CA: Standford University Press.

Gilmore, David D. 1991. "Commodity, Comity, Community: Male Exchange in Rural Andalusia." *Ethnology* 30(1):17–30.

Gregory, James R. 1984. "The Myth of the Male Ethnographer and the Woman's World." *American Anthropologist* 86(2):316–27.

Herzfeld, Michael. 1985. *The Poetics of Manhood: Contest and Identity in a Cretan Mountain Village.* Princeton, NJ: Princeton University Press.

———. 1987. *Anthropology through the Looking-Glass: Critical Ethnography in the Margins of Europe.* Cambridge: Cambridge University Press.

Instituto Nacional de Estadística, Geografía e Informática. 1990. *Estados Unidos Mexicanos: Resumen general, XI censo general de población y vivienda.* Mexico City: INEGI.

———. 1992. *La mujer en México.* Mexico City: INEGI.

Lancaster, Roger. 1992. *Life Is Hard: Machismo, Danger, and the Intimacy of Power in Nicaragua.* Berkeley: University of California Press.

Logan, Kathleen. 1984. *Haciendo Pueblo: The Development of a Guadalajaran Suburb.* University: University of Alabama Press.

Martin, JoAnn. 1990. "Motherhood and Power: The production of a Woman's Culture of Politics in a Mexican Community." *American Ethnologist* 17 (3):470–90.

Matthews, Holly F. 1987. "Intracultural Variation in Beliefs about Gender in a Mexican Community." *American Behavioral Scientist* 31(2):219–33.

Nader, Laura. 1986. "The Subordination of Women in Comparative Perspective." *Urban Anthropology* 15(3–4):377–97.

Ortner, Sherry B. 1989–90. "Gender Hegemonies." *Cultural Critique* 14:35–80.

Rich, Adrienne. 1976. *Of Women Born: Motherhood as Experience and Institution.* New York: W. W. Norton.

Rouse, Roger. 1991. "Mexican Migration and the Social Space of Postmodernism." *Diaspora* 1(1):8–23.

Sapir, Edward. 1929. (1949) "The Status of Linguistics as a Science." In *Selected Writings of Edward Sapir,* David G. Mandelbaum, ed. Pp. 160–66. Berkeley: University of California Press.

Scheper-Hughes, Nancy. 1983. "Introduction: The Problem of Bias in Androcentric and Feminist Anthropology." *Women's Studies* 10:109–16.

Scheper-Hughes, Nancy. 1992. *Death without Weeping: The Violence of Everyday Life in Brazil.* Berkeley: University of California.

Schmidt, Henry C. 1978. *The Roots of* Lo Mexicano: *Self and Society in Mexican Thought, 1900–1934.* College Station: Texas A&M Press.

Schneider, David, and Raymond Smith. 1973. *Class Differences and Sex Roles in American Kinship and Family Structure.* Englewood Cliffs, NJ: Prentice-Hall.

Sedgwick, Eve Kosofsky. 1990. *Epistemology of the Closet.* Berkeley: University of California Press.

Tambiah, Stanley J. 1990. *Magic, Science, Religion, and the Scope of Rationality.* Cambridge: Cambridge University Press.

19

It Takes More Than Two

The Prostitute, the Soldier, the State, and the Entrepreneur

CYNTHIA ENLOE

Since U.S. occupation troops in Japan are unalterably determined to fraternize, the military authorities began helping them out last week by issuing a phrase book. Sample utility phrases: "You're very pretty"... "How about a date?"... "Where will I meet you?" And since the sweet sorrow of parting always comes, the book lists no less than 14 ways to say goodbye.

Time, July 15, 1946

On a recent visit to London, I persuaded a friend to play hooky from work to go with me to Britain's famous Imperial War Museum. Actually, I was quite embarrassed. In all my trips to London, I had never visited the Imperial War Museum. But now, in the wake of the Gulf War, the time seemed ripe. Maybe the museum would help put this most recent military conflict in perspective, mark its continuities with other wars, and clarify its special human, doctrinal, and technological features. I was in for a disappointment.

Only selective British experiences of the "great" wars were deemed worthy of display. Malaya, Aden, Kenya, the Falklands—these British twentieth-century war zones didn't rate display cases. In fact, Asia, Africa, and the West Indies didn't seem much on the curators' minds at all. There were two formal portraits of turbaned Indian soldiers who had won military honors for their deeds, but there were no displays to make visible to today's visitors how much the British military had relied on men and women from its colonies to fight both world wars. I made a vow

on my next trip to take the train south of London to the Gurkha Museum.

The only civilians who received much attention in the Imperial War Museum were British. Most celebrated were the "plucky" cockney Londoners who coped with the German blitz by singing in the Underground. Women were allocated one glass case showing posters calling on housewives to practice domestic frugality for the cause. There was no evidence, however, of the political furor set off when white British women began to date—and have children with—African-American GIs.

Our disappointment with the museum's portrayal of Britain's wars served to make us trade hunches about what a realistic curatorial approach might be. What would we put on display besides frontline trenches (which at least showed the rats), cockney blitz-coping lyrics, and unannotated portraits of Sikh heroes?

Brothels. In my war museum there would be a reconstruction of a military brothel. It would show rooms for officers and rooms for rank and file soldiers. It would display separate doors for White soldiers and Black soldiers. A manikin of the owner of the business (it might be a disco rather than a formal brothel) would be sitting watchfully in the corner—it could be a man or a woman, a local citizen or a foreigner. The women serving the soldiers might be White European, Berber, Namibian, or Puerto Rican; they might be Korean, Filipina, Japanese, Vietnamese, African-American, or Indian. Depending on the era and locale, they could be dressed in sarongs, saris, or miniskirts topped with T-shirts memorializing resort beaches, soft drinks, and aircraft carriers.

In this realistic war museum, visitors would be invited to press a button to hear the voices of the women chart the routes by which they came to work in this brothel and describe the children, siblings, and parents they were trying to support with their earnings. Several of the women might compare the sexual behavior and outlook of these foreign men with those of the local men they had been involved with. Some of the women probably would add their own analyses of how the British, U.S., French, or United Nations troops had come to be in their country.

Museum goers could step over to a neighboring tape recorder to hear the voices of soldiers who patronized brothels and discos while on duty abroad. The men might describe how they imagined these women were different from or similar to the women from their own countries. The more brazen might flaunt their sexual prowess. They might compare their strength, chivalry, or earning power with that of the local men. Some of the soldiers, however, would describe their feelings of loneliness, their uncertainty of what it means to be a man when you're a soldier, their anxieties about living up to the sexual performance expectations of their officers and buddies.

War—and militarized peace—are occasions when sexual relations take on particular meanings. A museum curator—or a journalist, novelist, or political commentator—who edits out sexuality, who leaves it on the cutting-room floor, delivers to the audience a skewed and ultimately unhelpful

account of just what kinds of myths, anxieties, inequalities, and state policies are required to fight a war or to sustain a militarized form of peace.

A letter from a former CIA analyst, now an academic, suggests one reason why prostitution is so invisible, not only in military museums, but also in "serious" official discussions of security. He noted that in a recent book I had surmised from a Rand Corporation report that Soviet commanders had banned prostitution from their bases in Afghanistan during the counterinsurgency of the 1980s. He warned me not to jump to conclusions. While working as a CIA analyst in the 1970s, he had conducted a classified study of morale and discipline among Soviet forces. During the course of the study, he had interviewed an émigré who had been a conscript on a remote Soviet air force base in Russia's Far North. In reply to the analyst's inquiry about the presence of women on the base, the former conscript recalled that there had been approximately one hundred. What were their functions? *Prostituki!* The U.S. analyst found this pertinent and included the information in his report. But when the official CIA version came out, this was the only information excised by his superiors from the original draft. The analyst, looking back, speculated: "Since the U.S. military represses its bases' dependency on sexual access to local women, the organizational incentive is to avoid mentioning the Soviet problems for fear of drawing attention to the issue in the U.S. The tendency," he went on to explain, "to use information about the USSR as a means of discussing U.S. problems was something I commonly encountered in the CIA."[1]

It is for this reason that feminist ethnographies and oral histories are so vital. They help us to make sense of militaries' dependence on—yet denial of—particular presumptions about masculinity to sustain soldiers' morale and discipline. Without sexualized rest and recreation, would the U.S. military command be able to send young men off on long, often tedious sea voyages and ground maneuvers? Without myths of Asian or Latina women's compliant sexuality, would many American men be able to sustain their own identities, their visions of themselves as manly enough to act as soldiers?

Women who have come to work as prostitutes around U.S. bases tell us that a militarized masculinity is constructed and reconstructed in smoky bars and sparsely furnished rented rooms. If we confine our curiosity only to the boot camp and the battlefield—the focus of most investigations into the formations of militarized masculinity—we will be unable to explain just how masculinity is created and sustained in the peculiar ways still imagined by officials to be necessary to sustain a modern military organization.

We will also miss just how much governmental authority is being expended to insure that a peculiar definition of masculinity is sustained. Military prostitution differs from other forms of industrialized prostitution in that there are explicit steps taken by state institutions to protect the male customers without undermining their perceptions of themselves as sexualized men.

"Close to 250,000 men a month paid three dollars for three minutes of the only intimacy most were going to find in Honolulu."[2] These figures come from records kept in Hawaii during 1941 and 1944. Historians have these precise figures because Honolulu brothel managers, most of whom were White women, had to submit reports to Hawaii's military governor. American soldiers' sexual encounters with local prostitutes were not left to chance or to the market; they were the object of official policy consideration among the military, the police, and the governor's staff. Two hundred and fifty prostitutes paid $1.00 per year to be registered merely as "entertainers" with the Honolulu Police Department because the federal government had passed the May Act in 1941, making prostitution illegal, to assuage the fears of many American civilians that mobilizing for war would corrupt the country's sexual mores.[3] Hawaii's military governor disagreed. He had police and military officers on his side. They saw a tightly regulated prostitution industry as necessary to bolster male soldiers' morale, to prevent sexu-

ally transmitted diseases, and to reassure the Hawaiian White upper class that wartime would not jeopardize their moral order. The navy and the army set up prophylaxis distribution centers along Honolulu's Hotel Street, the center of the city's burgeoning prostitution industry. The two departments collaborated with the local police to try to ensure that licensed prostitutes kept their side of the bargain: in return for the license, women servicing soldiers and sailors up and down Hotel Street had to promise to have regular medical examinations, not to buy property in Hawaii, not to own an automobile, not to go out after 10:30 at night, and not to marry members of the armed forces. The objective was to keep prostitutes quite literally in their place.

The effort was only partially successful. Women working in the most successful brothels, White women, many of whom came by ship from San Francisco to work as prostitutes, made enough money to violate the official rules and buy homes outside Honolulu. They kept $2 of the $3 from each customer. Out of their earnings they paid $100 per month to the brothel manager for room and board, plus extra for laundry and $13 for each required monthly venereal disease test.

Before the war, most Hotel Street brothels had two doors, one for White male customers and one for men of color, most of whom were Asian men who worked on the island's pineapple and sugar plantations. Brothel managers believed this segregation prevented violent outbursts by White men who objected to the women they were paying for servicing men of any other race. As the wartime influx of White soldiers and sailors tilted the brothels' business ever more toward a White clientele, most managers decided that any risk of offending White male customers was bad business; they did away with the second door and turned away men of color altogether.

Opening time for the typical Honolulu brothel during the war years was 9 A.M. It operated on an efficient assembly-line principle. From prostitutes and soldiers recalling the arrangement, we learn that most of the brothels used what was called a 'bull-ring' setup consisting of three rooms. "In one room a man undressed, in a second the prostitute engaged her customer, in a third a man who had finished put his clothes back on."[4] Prostitutes learned to tailor their services to the sexual sophistication of their military clients. They offered oral sex to the more nervous and inexperienced men. A senior military police officer in the middle of the war speculated before an audience of local citizen reformers that those sailors who performed oral sex with the Honolulu prostitutes were those men most likely to engage in homosexual behavior once they were back on board ship. The U.S. military's policymakers tried to think of everything.

Today British and Belize officials work hard together to develop a complex policy to ensure a steady but safe supply of military prostitutes for the British troops stationed in that small ex-colony perched on the edge of Latin America.[5] A new nine-hundred-man batallion arrives every six months. British soldiers have special brothels designated for their patronage, although they slip out of the carefully woven policy net to meet local women in bars and discos in Belize City. Most of the women who work in the officially approved brothels are Latinas, rather than Afro-Belize women; many have traveled across the border from war-torn Guatemala to earn money as prostitutes.

The government-to-government agreement requires that every brothel worker, with the cooperation of the owners, have a photo identification card and undergo weekly medical examinations by a Belizean doctor. Prostitutes are required to use condoms with their military customers, although it is not clear how many women may be paid extra by their customers to break the condom rule. If a soldier-patron does show symptoms of a sexually transmitted disease or tests positive for HIV, it is assumed that the prostitute is to blame. The infected soldier gives his British superiors the name of the prostitute who he believes infected him. On the basis of the soldier's word as well as on test results, on a first "offense" the woman is reprimanded by the brothel owner; on a second offense she is fined; on a third she is fired.

British-born soldiers and their Nepali Gurkha comrades, both in Belize under a Belize-British defense pact, have rather different racial/sexual preferences. Whereas the former are likely to frequent both Latina and Afro-Belize women, the Gurkhas reportedly prefer Latina women, which means that the Gurkhas are more likely to stick to the government-approved prostitutes. The fact that any Gurkha troops go to prostitutes at all, however, contradicts the long-standing British portrayal of Nepali militarized masculinity: though White British men's masculinity is presumed by their officers to require a diet of local sex while overseas, Nepali men's masculinity is constructed as more disciplined, faithful when home and celibate while on assignment abroad.[6] With the end of the Cold War and the relaxation of political tensions between Belize and Guatemala, the future of the government-to-government prostitution agreement has become uncertain. But in early 1992, Britain's Chief of Defence Staff, Field Marshal Sir Richard Vincent, made it known publicly that the Conservative government of John Major was hoping that the British troop rotation in Belize could be continued. Though no longer needed to defend Belize, the British army, according to the field marshal, now finds Belize's climate and topography especially attractive for jungle warfare training.[7] Do the field marshal and his superiors back in London perhaps also find the Belize government's willingness to cooperate in the control of local women's sexuality a military attraction?

The United States fashioned a rather different policy to regulate soldiers' relationships with prostitutes around major U.S. bases such as Clark and Subic Bay in the Philippines. Like the British, the Americans supported compulsory medical examinations of women working as prostitutes. Similarly, women without the license issued with these examinations were prevented from working by the local—in this case Filipino—municipal authorities. U.S. soldiers who contracted sexually transmitted diseases (STDs) were not required to report the woman whom they believe gave them the disease. Nonetheless, it was the practice of the

Angeles City and Olongapo health authorities to pass on to U.S. base officials the names of sex workers who had contracted STDs. The base commanders then ordered that the photographs of infected Filipinas be pinned upside down on the public notice board as a warning to the American men.[8]

Apparently believing that "stable" relationships with fewer local women would reduce the chances that their personnel would become infected, base commanders allowed Filipinas hired out by bar owners to stay with their military boyfriends on the base. U.S. officials occasionally sent out a "contact" card to a club owner containing the name of a Filipina employee whom the Americans suspected of having infected a particular sailor or air force man. However, they refused to contribute to the treatment of prostitutes with sexually transmitted diseases or AIDS and turned down requests that they subsidize Pap smears for early cancer detection for the estimated one hundred thousand women working in the entertainment businesses around Clark and Subic.

The closing of both Clark Air Force Base and Subic Naval Base in 1992 forced many Filipinas in precarious states of health into the ranks of the country's unemployed. Their few options included migrating to Okinawa or Guam, or even to Germany, to continue working as prostitutes for U.S. military men. They may also have been vulnerable to recruiters procuring Filipina women for Japan's entertainment industry, an industry that is increasingly dependent on young women from abroad.[9] Olongapo City's businessman mayor, with his own entertainment investments now in jeopardy, has been in the forefront of promoters urging that Subic Bay's enormous facilities be converted into private enterprises, although the Filipino military is also eager to take over at least part of the operations for its own purposes. Military base conversion is always an intensely gendered process. Even if women working the entertainment sector are not at the conversion negotiation table, they will be on many of the negotiators' minds. For instance, the above-mentioned mayor, among

others, has urged not only that privatized ship maintenance be developed at Subic Bay, but also that tourism development be high on the new investment list.[10] In the coming years, the politics of prostitution in Olongapo City may take on a civilian look, but many of the tourists attracted may be slightly older American men trying to relive their earlier militarized sexual adventures with Filipina women.

There is no evidence thus far that being compelled by the forces of nature and nationalism to shut down two of their most prized overseas bases has caused U.S. military planners to rethink their prostitution policies. Shifting some of the Philippines operations to Guam or Singapore or back home to the United States does not in itself guarantee new official presumptions about the kinds of sexual relations required to sustain U.S. military power in the post–Cold War world. The governments of Singapore and the United States signed a basing agreement in Tokyo in mid-1992. But, despite popular misgivings about the implications of allowing U.S. Navy personnel to use the small island nation for repairs and training, the basing agreement itself was kept secret. Thus, Singapore citizens, as well as U.S. citizens, are left with little information about what policing formulas, public health formulas, and commercial zoning formulas have been devised by the two governments to shape the sexual relations between American and Singapore men and the women of Singapore.[11]

The women who have been generous enough to tell their stories of prostitution have revealed that sexuality is as central to the complex web of relationships between civil and military cultures as are more talked-about security doctrines and economic quid pro quo. Korean and Filipino women interviewed by Sandra Sturdevant and Brenda Stoltzfus for their oral history collection *Let the Good Times Roll* also remind us of how hard it is sometimes to map the boundaries between sexual relations and economics.[12] They found that the local and foreign men who own the brothels, bars, and discos catering to soldiers are motivated by profit. These men weigh the market value of a woman's virginity, her "cherry," as well as her age. They constantly reassess their male clients' demands. Thus, by the early 1990s, bar owners and procurers concluded that AIDS-conscious U.S. soldiers were competing to have sex with younger and younger Filipinas, and so the proprietors sought to supply them, driving down the value of the sexual services supplied by "older" women—women in their early twenties.[13]

Over the decades, U.S. Navy veterans stayed in the Philippines and set up bars and discos, both because they liked living outside the United States (often with Filipina wives) and because they could make a comfortable livelihood from sexualized entertainment. Australian men immigrated to launch their own businesses in the base towns and eventually made up a large proportion of the owners of the military-dependent entertainment industry.[14] Local military personnel, especially officers, also used their status and authority in the rural areas to take part in the industry. Some men in the Philippines military have been known to supplement their salaries by acting as procurers of young rural women for the tourist and military prostitution industries.[15] Similarly, among the investors and managers of Thailand's large prostitution industry are Thai military officers.[16] Militarized, masculinized sexual desire, by itself, isn't sufficient to sustain a full-fledged prostitution industry. It requires (depends on) rural poverty, male entrepreneurship, urban commercialized demand, police protection, and overlapping governmental economic interest to ensure its success.

Yet military prostitution is not simply an economic institution. The women who told their stories to Sturdevant and Stoltzfus were less concerned with parsing analytical categories—what is "economic," what is "social," and what is "political"—than with giving us an authentic account of the pressures, hopes, fears, and shortages they had to juggle every day in order to ensure their physical safety, hold onto some self-respect, and make ends meet for themselves and their children.

The stories that prostitutes tell also underscore something that is overlooked repeatedly in discussions of the impact of military bases on local communities: local women working in military brothels and discos mediate between two sets of men, the foreign soldiers and the local men—some of whom are themselves soldiers, but many of whom are civilians. Outside observers rarely talk about these two sets of men in the same breath. But the women who confided in Stoltzfus and Sturdevant knew that they had to be considered simultaneously. The Korean and Filipina women detailed how their relationships with local male lovers and husbands had created the conditions that initially made them vulnerable to the appeals of the labor-needy disco owners. Unfaithfulness, violent tempers, misuse of already low earnings, neglectful fathering—any combination of these behaviors by their local lovers and husbands might have launched these women into military prostitution. Children, too, have to be talked about. Most of the women servicing foreign soldiers sexually have children, some fathered by local men and others fathered by the foreign soldiers. Prostitution and men's ideas about fathering: the two are intimately connected in these women's lives.

In deeply militarized countries such as the Philippines, South Korea, Honduras, and Afghanistan, a woman working in prostitution may have to cope with local as well as foreign soldiers who need her services to shore up their masculinity. Because it is politically less awkward to concentrate on foreign soldiers' exploitation of local women, local soldiers' militarized and sexualized masculinity is frequently swept under the analytical rug, as if it were nonexistent or harmless. And in fact the local soldiery may have more respect for local women, may have easier access to noncommercialized sex, or may have too little money to spend to become major customers of local prostitutes. But none of those circumstances should be accepted as fact without a close look.

For instance, Anne-Marie Cass, an Australian researcher who spent many months in the late 1980s both with the Philippine government's troops and with insurgent forces, found that

Filipino male soldiers were prone to sexualizing their power. Cass watched as many of them flaunted their sexualized masculinity in front of their female soldier trainees, women expected from respectable families to be virgins. She also reported that many Filipino soldiers "expect to and receive rides on civilian transport, and drinks and the services of prostitutes in discos and bars without payment."[17]

This is not, of course, to argue that local men are the root of the commercialized and militarized sex that has become so rife, especially in countries allied to the United States. Without local governments willing to pay the price for the lucrative R and R business, without the U.S. military's strategies for keeping male soldiers content, without local and foreign entrepreneurs willing to make their profits off the sexuality of poor women—without each of these conditions, even an abusive, economically irresponsible husband would not have driven his wife into work as an Olongapo bar girl. Nonetheless, local men must be inserted into the political equation; the women who tell their stories make this clear. In fact, we need to widen our lens considerably if we are to fully understand militarized prostitution. Here is a list—probably an incomplete list—of the men we need to be curious about, men whose actions may contribute to the construction and maintenance of prostitution around any government's military base:

- husbands and lovers
- bar and brothel owners, local and foreign
- local public health officials
- local government zoning board members
- local police officials
- local mayors
- national finance ministry officials
- national defense officials
- male soldiers in the national forces
- local civilian male prostitution customers
- local male soldier-customers
- foreign male soldier-customers
- foreign male soldiers' buddies
- foreign base commanders
- foreign military medical officers
- foreign national defense planners
- foreign national legislators

Among these men there may be diverse forms of masculinity. Women in Okinawa, Korea, and the Philippines described to Sturdevant and Stoltzfus how they had to learn what would make American men feel manly during sex; it was not always what they had learned would make their Korean, Japanese, or Filipino sexual partners feel manly.

Sexual practice is one of the sites of masculinity's—and femininity's—daily construction. That construction is international. It has been so for generations. Tourists and explorers, missionaries, colonial officials and health authorities, novelists, development technocrats, businessmen, and soldiers have long been the internationalizers of sexualized masculinity. Today the U.S. military's "R and R" policy and the industry it has spawned function only if thousands of poor women are willing and able to learn those sexual acts that U.S. military men rely on to bolster their sense of masculinity. Thus, bar owners, military commanders, and local finance ministry bureaucrats depend on local women to be alert to the historically evolving differences between masculinities.

Korean women have been among the current historical investigators of militarized prostitution. Korean women petitioners, together with a small, supportive group of Japanese feminists and Japanese historians, recently pressed the Japanese government to admit that the Japanese military had a deliberate policy of conscripting Korean, Thai, and Burmese women into prostitution during World War II.[18] In the past, Japanese officials insisted that any Asian women pressed into servicing Japanese soldiers sexually during the war were organized and controlled by civilian businessmen. The military itself was institutionally immune. Senior officers had simply accepted the prostituted women as part of the wartime landscape. This defense is strikingly similar to that employed by U.S. officials when asked about the Pentagon's current prostitution policy. Their Japanese counterparts, however, have had to give up their long-time defense in the face of convincing bureaucratic evidence uncovered by Yoshiaki Yoshimi, a professor of history at Chuo University. In the Self-Defense Agency's library he found a document entitled "Regarding the Recruitment of Women for Military Brothels" dating from the late 1930s, when the Japanese army was moving southward into China. It ordered the military to build "facilities for sexual comfort." The official rationale was that brothels would stop Japanese soldiers from raping Chinese and other women along the route of the army's invasion. Eventually, an estimated 100,000 to 200,000 Asian women were forcibly conscripted to work as *Karayuki-san,* "comfort women," in these military brothels.[19]

Although the uncovering of the document evoked a formal apology from Prime Minister Kiichi Miyazawa, the issue is not resolved. Kim Hak Sun, one of the survivors of the "comfort women" program, and other elderly Korean women are calling on their government and the Japanese government to reach a settlement that will include monetary compensation for the hardships they suffered.[20]

Furthermore, the internationalizing dynamics which have shaped military prostitution in the past grind on. Thus, the uncovering of 1930s and 1940s Japanese policy on prostitution led to a spate of articles in the U.S. media at a time when many Americans were in search of evidence that they were morally superior to, albeit economically lagging behind, Japan. Thus the story was set in a Pearl Harbor context by many U.S. readers, even if not intentionally by its authors. It could have been quite a different story. The research by Yoshiaki Yoshimi, Nakahara Michiko, and other Japanese historians about their country's military's prostitution policies could have been written—and read—so as to draw attention to U.S., British, French, and other militaries' past and present prostitution policies.

This possibility was what inspired Rita Nakashima Brock to write to the *New York Times* in the wake of the discovery of the Tokyo document.

A researcher studying the sex industries in Southeast Asia, she is also an Asian-American woman who spent her childhood on U.S. military bases in the United States, Germany, and Okinawa. She recalls that, as a girl, "I faced the assumption that any woman who looked Asian was sexually available to soldiers. I was often called 'geisha-girl' or 'Suzy Wong' (soldiers usually couldn't tell Japanese from Chinese). Every base I ever lived on . . . had a thriving red-light district near it." When she was older, Brock began to wonder about official military policies that led to the prostitution she had witnessed as a child. "A former Navy chaplain who served in Japan during the post–World War II occupation told me that when he protested the American base commander's efforts to set up prostitution centers using Japanese women, he was reassigned stateside."[21]

Thanh-Dam Truong, a Vietnamese feminist who has investigated the political economy of Thailand's prostitution industry, also reminds us to view sexuality historically. Thai women working in prostitution, she discovered, had to learn new sexual skills in the 1980s that they hadn't needed in the 1960s because by the 1980s their male customers, now mainly local and foreign civilians, had acquired new tastes, new insecurities, and new grounds for competing with other men.[22] Similarly, around the U.S. Navy base at Subic Bay in the late 1980s, bar owners, still dependent on military customers, introduced "foxy boxing." These entrepreneurs believed that having women wrestle and box each other on stage would make the American sailors in the audience more eager for sex with the Filipina employees. Women, in turn, learned that they would be paid for their performance only if at the end of a bout they could show bruises or had drawn blood.[23] At about the same time, women in the bars were instructed by their employers to learn how to pick up coins with their vaginas. This, too, was designed as a new way to arouse the American customers.[24]

Each group of men involved in militarized sexuality is connected to other groups by the women working in the base town bars. But they also may be connected to each other quite directly. At least some Filipino male soldiers are adopting what they see as an American form of militarized masculinity. The men most prone to adopting such attitudes are those in the Scout Rangers, the elite fighting force of the Philippine Constabulary. They act as though Rambo epitomizes the attributes that make for an effective combat soldier: "a soldier in khaki or camouflage, sunglasses or headbands, open shirt, bare head, and well armed, lounging in a roofless jeep traveling down a Davao City street, gun held casually, barrel waving in the air."[25] One consequence of this form of borrowed masculinized intimidation is that local prostitutes servicing Filipino soldiers perform sexual acts that they otherwise would refuse to perform.

A woman who comes to work in a foreign military brothel or disco finds that she must negotiate among all of these male actors. She has direct contact, however, with only some of them. She never hears what advice the foreign base commander passes on to his troops regarding the alleged unhealthiness or deviousness of local women. She never hears what financial arrangements local and foreign medical officials devise to guarantee the well-being of her soldier-customers. She rarely learns what a soldier who wants to marry her and support her children is told by his military chaplain or superior officer. She is not invited into the conference room when U.S., British, or French legislators decide it is politically wise not to hold hearings on their government's military prostitution policy. The Latina woman working as a prostitute in Belize or the Filipina woman working in the Philippines or Okinawa makes her assessments using only what information she has.

Much of that information comes from the women with whom she works. The women who told their stories to Sturdevant and Stoltzfus did not romanticize the sistership between women working in the bars. The environment is not designed to encourage solidarity. Women *have* engaged in collective actions—for instance, bar

workers in Olongapo protested against being forced to engage in boxing matches for the entertainment of male customers. But, despite growing efforts by local feminists to provide spaces for such solidarity, collective action remains the exception. Most women rely on a small circle of friends to accumulate the information necessary to walk the minefield laid by the intricate relationships between the various groups of men who define the military prostitution industry. The women teach each other how to fake orgasms, how to persuade men to use a condom, how to avoid deductions from their pay, how to meet soldier-customers outside their employers' supervision, and how to remain appealing to paying customers when they are older and their valued status as a "cherry girl" is long past.

Women are telling their prostitution stories at a time when the end of the Cold War and the frailty of an industrialized economy are combining to pressure governments in North America and Europe to "downsize" their military establishments. The U.S. Department of Defense has announced the closing of military bases at home and abroad. One of the apparent lessons of the Gulf War in the eyes of many American strategists is that the United States now has the administrative capacity to deploy large numbers of troops overseas rapidly without maintaining a costly and often politically risky base in the region. Simultaneously, Mount Pinatubo spewed its deadly ash so thickly over Clark Air Force Base that even this facility, which until 1991 the Bush administration had deemed vital to American national security, was classified as uneconomical. The Philippine Senate, for its part, rejected Corazón Aquino's requests that the Subic Bay Navy Base agreement be renewed.

Base closings have their own sexual consequences. U.S. military and civilian men and their Filipina lovers had to discuss the possibility of marriage, perhaps each with quite different fears and expectations. There were reports of a number of quick marriages.[26] In March 1992 Pat Ford, National Public Radio's reporter in the

Philippines, described the departure of the last U.S. ship from Subic Bay. Filipina women from Olongapo's bars cried and hugged their sailor boyfriends and customers at the gates of the base.[27] What sexual expectations would the American men take home with them? Perhaps the Filipinas' tears and hugs prompted many men to imagine that they had experienced not commercialized sex but rather relationships of genuine affection. What were women shedding tears for? Perhaps for the loss of some temporary emotional support. Or maybe for the loss of their livelihoods. How many women who have lost their jobs around Subic Bay will seek out the employment agencies that, for a fee, will send them to Kuwait to work as maids?[28] Despite the efforts of the Filipino anti-base campaign, the government had no operative base conversion plan ready to launch that would put women's health and autonomy high on its list of objectives.[29]

It might be tempting to listen to Asian women's stories as if they were tales of a bygone era. That would, I think, be a mistake. Large bases still exist in South Korea and Guam. Over forty thousand American military personnel were stationed in Japan (including Okinawa) at the end of 1991; even more will be redeployed from Clark and Subic Bay. In early 1992, the U.S. government made agreements with officials in Australia, Singapore, and Malaysia to use facilities in their countries for repairs, communications, and training. Even with some cutbacks, the number of American men going through those bases on long tours and on shorter-term

maneuvers will be in the thousands. Governments in Seoul, Tokyo, and Manila have made no moves to cancel the R and R agreements they have with Washington, agreements that spell out the conditions for permitting and controlling the sort of prostitution deemed most useful for the U.S. military. The no-prostitution formula adopted to fight the Gulf War—a no-prostitution formula not initiated by Washington policymakers, but rather imposed on the United States by a Saudi regime nervous about its own Islamic legitimacy—has not been adopted anywhere else. What discussions have U.S. military planners had with their counterparts in Singapore, Canberra, and Kuala Lumpur about morale, commerce, health, and masculinity?

Listening to women who work as prostitutes is as important as ever. For political analysts, listening to them can provide information necessary for creating a more realistic picture of how fathering, child-rearing, man-to-man borrowing, poverty, private enterprise, and sexual practice play vital roles in the construction of militarized femininity and masculinity. For nonfeminist anti-base campaigners, listening to these women will shake the conventional confidence that has come from relying only on economic approaches to base conversion. Marriage, parenting, male violence, and self-respect will all have to be accepted as serious political agenda items if the women now living on wages from prostitution are to become actors, and not mere symbols, in movements to transform foreign military bases into productive civilian institutions. Listening is political.

NOTES _____

An earlier version of this chapter appeared as an introductory essay in Saundra Sturdevant and Brenda Stoltzfus, *Let the Good Times Roll: The Sale of Women's Sexual Labor around U.S. Military Bases in the Philippines, Okinawa and the Southern Part of Korea* (New York: New Press, 1992). This is a wonderful collection of oral histories by Filipina and Korean women working as prostitutes around U.S. bases in the Philippines, South Korea, and Guam.

1. Letter from a former CIA analyst and Defense Department consultant, August 20, 1991.
2. Beth Bailey and David Farber, *The First Strange Place: The Alchemy of Race and Sex in World War II Hawaii* (New York: Free Press, 1992), 95.

3. Ibid., 102–3. The material that follows is based on Bailey and Farber, 95–107.

4. Ibid., 102–3.

5. The information on Belize is contained in a manuscript by Stephanie C. Kane, "Prostitution and the Military: Planning AIDS Intervention in Belize" (Department of American Studies and African-American Studies, State University of New York at Buffalo, 1991); information on the Gurkhas is form correspondence from Stephanie Kane, December 11, 1991.

6. Tamang, "Nepali Women as Military Wives."

7. "Troops Want to Stay in Belize," *Carib News* (New York:), March 17, 1992.

8. The information on Subic Bay and Clark bases is derived from Anne-Marie Cass, "Sex and the Military: Gender and Violence in the Philippines" (Ph.D. diss., Department of Sociology and Anthropology, University of Queensland, Brisbane, Australia, 1992), 206–209; and Saundra Sturdevant and Brenda Stoltzfus, *Let the Good Times Roll: The Sale of Women's Sexual Labor around U.S. Military Bases in the Philippines, Okinawa and the Southern Part of Korea* (New York: New Press, 1992).

9. For descriptions and analyses of the lives of Filipino women and men who have migrated to Japan, including many women who went there for exploitative work in the entertainment industry catering to male customers—see Randolf S. David, "Filipino Workers in Japan: Vulnerability and Survival," *Kasarinlan: A Philippine Quarterly of Third World Studies* (Quezon City: University of the Philippines) 6, no. 3 (1991): 9–23; Rey Ventura, *Underground in Japan,* London, Jonathan Cape, 1992.

10. Rigoberto Tiglao, "Open for Offers" *Far Eastern Economic Review,* October 15, 1992, 62–63.

11. I am grateful to Suzaina Abdul Kadii, of the University of Wisconsin political science graduate program, for her analysis of the U.S.–Singaporean basing agreement process: conversation with the author, Madison, Wisconsin, October 29, 1992.

12. Sturdevant and Stoltzfus, *Let the Good Times Roll.*

13. Cass, "Sex and the Military," 210.

14. Ibid., 205.

15. Ibid., 215.

16. The most complete account of the Thai military's role in Thailand's prostitution industry is Thanh-Dam Truong, *Sex, Money and Morality: Prostitution and Tourism in Southeast Asia* (London: Zed Press, 1990). I am also indebted to Alison Cohn for sharing her as yet unpublished research in Thailand with me at Clark University, Worcester, MA, February–April, 1992. For an investigation of Indonesia's prostitution business, a system which is not organized around either foreign tourists or foreign soldiers but is deeply affected by Indonesia's militarized national politics, see Saraswati Sunindyo's forthcoming Ph.D. dissertation (Department of Sociology, University of Wisconsin, Madison). Saraswati Sunindyo has also written a collection of poetry, entitled *Yakin* (typescript, 1992), which describes some of her own responses to conducting research in a coastal town's government-owned hotel, which was shared by a number of Indonesian women working as prostitutes servicing Indonesian military officers, civil servants, businessmen, farmers, and schoolboys.

17. Cass, "Sex and the Military."

18. Nakahara Michiko, "Forgotten Victims: Asian and Women Workers on the Thai-Burma Railway," *AMPO: Japan-Asia Quarterly* 23, no. 2 (1991): 21–25; Yoshiaki Yoshimi, "Japan Battles Its Memories" (Editorial), *New York Times,* March 11, 1992; Sanger, "Japan Admits"; David E. Sanger, "History Scholar in Japan Exposes a Brutal Chapter," *New York Times,* January 27, 1992.

19. Sanger, "History Scholar."

20. Ibid. See also: George Hicks, "Ghosts Gathering: Comfort Women Issue Haunts Tokyo as Pressure Mounts," *Far Eastern Economic Review,* February 18, 1993, 32–37.

21. Rita Nakashima Brock, "Japanese Didn't Invent Military Sex Industry" (Letter to the Editor), *New York Times,* February 23, 1992.

22. Truong, "Sex, Money and Morality."

23. Cass, "Sex and the Military," 210.

24. Sturdevant and Stoltzfus, *Let the Good Times Roll.* In a slide and tape show produced by Sturdevant and Stoltzfus, Filipinas describe being ashamed at having to perform demeaning acts. "Pussy Cat III," 726 Gilman St., Berkeley, CA 94710.

25. Anne-Marie Cass, "Sexuality, Gender and Violence in the Militarized Society of the Philippines" (Paper presented at the annual conference of the Australian Sociological Association, Brisbane, December 12–16, 1990), 6.

26. Donald Goertzen, "Withdrawal Trauma," *Far Eastern Economic Review,* January 30, 1992, 10.

27. Pat Ford, "Weekend Edition," National Public Radio, March 21, 1992.

28. I am grateful to Lauran Schultz for bringing to my attention the *Philippine Journal of Public Administration* 34, no. 4 (October 1990), a special issue devoted to articles on the current conditions of Filipina women, in-

cluding women as migrants. See, in particular, Bievenda M. Amarles, "Female Migrant Labor: Domestic Helpers in Singapore," 365–389; Prosperina Domingo Tapales, "Women, Migration and the Mail-Order Bride Phenomenon: Focus on Australia," 311–322.

29. American Friends Service Committee Peace Education Division and the Alliance for Philippine Concerns, *Swords into Plowshares: Economic Conversion and the U.S. Bases in the Philippines* (Philadelphia, PA: American Friends Service Committee, 1991). See also Sheila Coronel, "With Hope and Tears, U.S. Closes Philippine Base," *New York Times,* November 25, 1992; P. N. Abinales, "Searching for the Philippine Eden—the Post-Bases Era," *Kasarinlan: A Philippine Quarterly of Third World Studies* 7, no. 4 (1992): 8–12.

20

Lesbian "Sex"[1]

MARILYN FRYE

The reasons the word "sex" is in quotation marks in my title are two: one is that the term "sex" is an inappropriate term for what lesbians do, and the other is that whatever it is that lesbians do that (for lack of a better word) might be called "sex" we apparently do damned little of it. For a great many lesbians, the gap between the high hopes we had some time ago for lesbian sex and the way things have worked out has turned the phrase "lesbian sex" into something of a bitter joke. I don't want to exaggerate: many lesbians are having gratifying erotic lives. But there is much grumbling among us about "lesbian bed death," especially in long-term relationships.[2] I want to explore the meanings of the relative dearth of what (for lack of a better word) we call lesbian "sex."...

Recent discussions of lesbian "sex" frequently cite the findings of a study on couples by Blumstein and Schwartz,[3] which is perceived by most of those who discuss it as having been done well, with a good sample of couples—lesbian, male homosexual, heterosexual non-married and heterosexual married couples. These people apparently found that lesbian couples "have sex" far less frequently than any other type of couple, that lesbian couples are less "sexual" as couples and as individuals than anyone else. In their sample, only about one third of lesbians in relationships of two years or longer "had sex" once a week or more; 47% of lesbians in long-term relationships "had sex" once a month or less, while among heterosexual married couples only 15% had sex once a month or less. And they report that lesbians seem to be more limited in the range of their "sexual" techniques than are other couples.

When this sort of information first came into my circle of lesbian friends, we tended to see it as conforming to what we know from our own experience. We were not surprised to hear that we "had" less "sex" than anyone else or that in our long-term relationships we "had sex" a great deal less frequently than other sorts of couples....

But it was brought to our attention during our ruminations on this that what 85% of long-term heterosexual married couples do more than once a month takes on the average 8 minutes to do.[4]

Although in my experience lesbians discuss their "sex" lives with each other relatively little (a point to which I will return), I know from my own experience and from the reports of a few other lesbians in long-term relationships, that what we do that, on average, we do considerably less frequently, takes on the average, considerably more than 8 minutes to do. Maybe about 30 minutes at the least. Sometimes maybe about an hour. And it is not uncommon that among these relatively uncommon occurrences, an entire afternoon or evening is given over to activities organized around doing it. The suspicion arises that what 85% of heterosexual married couples are doing more than once a month and what 47% of lesbians couples are doing less than once a month is not the same thing....

I remember that one of my first delicious tastes of old gay lesbian culture occurred in a bar where I was chatting with some other lesbians I was just getting acquainted with. One was talking about being busted out of the Marines for being gay. She had been put under suspicion somehow, and was sent off to the base psychiatrist to be questioned, her perverted tendencies to be assessed. He wanted to convince her she had only been engaged in a little youthful experimentation and wasn't really gay. To this end, he questioned her about the extent of her experience. What he asked was, "How many times have you had sex with a woman?" At this, we all laughed and giggled: what an ignorant fool he was! What does he think he means by "times"? What will we count? What's to *count*?

Another of my friends years later, discussing the same conundrum, said that she thought maybe every time you got up to go to the bathroom, that marked a "time." The joke about "how many times" is still good for a chuckle from time to time in my life with my lover. I have no memory of any such topic providing any such merriment in my years of sexual encounters and relationships with men. It would have been very rare indeed that we would not have known how to answer the question "How many times did you do it?"

If what heterosexual married couples do that the individuals report under the rubric "sex" or "have sex" is something that in most instances can easily be individuated into countable instances, this is more evidence that it is not what long-term lesbian couples do...or, for that matter, what short-term lesbian couples do.[5]

What violence did the lesbians do their experience by answering the same question the heterosexuals answered, as though it had the same meaning for them? How did the lesbians figure out how to answer the questions "How frequently?" or "How many times?" My guess is, for starters, that different individuals figured it out differently, to some degree. Some might have counted a two- or three-cycle evening as one "time" they "had sex"; some might have counted that as two or three "times." Some may have counted as "times" only the times both partners had orgasms; some may

have counted as "times" occasions on which at least one had in orgasm; some may not have orgasms or have them rarely and may not have figured orgasms into the calculations; perhaps they counted as a "time" every episode in which both touched the other's vulva more than fleetingly and not for something like a health examination. For some, to count every reciprocal touch of the vulva would have made them count as "having sex" more than most people with work to do would dream of having time for; how do we suppose those individuals counted "times"? Is there any good reason why they should not count all those as "times"? Does it depend on how fulfilling it was? (Was anybody else counting by occasions of fulfillment?)

We have no idea how individual lesbians individuated their so-called "sexual acts" or encounters; we have no idea what it means when they said they did it less than once a month. But this raises questions for how the heterosexuals individuated and counted *their* sexual acts or encounters.... I think that if the heterosexual woman counted "times" according to the standard meaning of "have sex" in English, they counted not according to their own experience of orgasm or even arousal, but according to their partners' orgasms and ejaculations....

So, do lesbian couples really "have sex" any less frequently than heterosexual couples? My own view is that lesbian couples "have sex" a great deal less frequently than heterosexual couples: I think, in fact, we don't "have sex" at all. By the criteria that I'm betting most of the heterosexual people used in reporting the frequency with which they have sex, lesbians don't have sex.... (I'm willing to draw the conclusion that heterosexual women don't have sex either, that what they report is the frequency with which their partners had sex.)

It has been said before by feminists that the concept of "having sex" is a phallic concept; that it pertains to heterosexual intercourse, in fact, primarily to heterosex*ist* intercourse, that is, male-dominant-female-subordinate-copulation-whose-

completion-and-purpose-is-the-male's-ejaculation.
.... For some of us, myself included, the move
from heterosexual relating to lesbian relating was
occasioned or speeded up or brought to closure by
our recognition that what we had done under the
heading "having sex" had indeed been male-
dominant-female-subordinate-copulation-whose-
completion-and-purpose-is-the-male's-ejaculation,
and it was not worthy of doing. Yet now, years
later, we are willing to answer questionnaires that
ask us how frequently we "have sex," and are dissatisfied with ourselves and with our relationships
because we don't "have sex" enough. We are so
dissatisfied that we keep a small army of therapists in business trying to help us "have sex"
more.

We quit having sex years ago, and for excellent and compelling reasons. What exactly is our
complaint now?

In all these years I've been doing and writing
feminist theory, I have not until very recently
written, much less published, a word about sex. I
did not write, though it was suggested to me that I
do so, anything in the SM debates; I left entirely
unanswered an invitation to be the keynote
speaker at a feminist conference about women's
sexuality (which by all reports turned out to be an
excellent conference). I was quite unable to think
of anything but vague truisms to say, and very few
of those. Feminist theory is grounded in experience; I have always written feminist political and
philosophical analysis from the bottom up, starting with my own encounters and adventures, frustrations, pain, anger, etc.... When I put to myself
the task of theorizing about sex and sexuality, it
was as though I had no experience, as though
there was no ground on which and from which to
generate theory. But, if I understand the terminology rightly, I have in fact been what they
call "sexually active" for about a quarter of a
century.... Surely I have experience. But I seem
not to have experiential knowledge of the sort I
need.

Reflecting on all that history, I realize that in
many of its passages this experience has been a
muddle. Acting, being acted on, choosing, desiring, pleasure and displeasure all akimbo—not
coherently determining each other. Even in its
greatest intensity it has for the most part been
somehow rather opaque to me, not fully in my
grasp. My "experience" has in general the character more of a buzzing blooming confusion than
of experience. And it has occurred in the midst of
almost total silence on the part of others about
their experience. The experience of others has for
the most part also been opaque to me; they do not
discuss or describe it in detail at all....

I once perused a large and extensively illustrated book on sexual activity by and for homosexual men. It was astounding to me for one thing in
particular, namely, that its pages constituted a
huge lexicon of specific vocabulary: words for
acts and activities, their sub-acts, preludes and
denouements, their stylistic variation, their se-
quences. Gay male sex, I realized then, is articulate. It is articulate to a degree that, in my world,
lesbian "sex" does not remotely approach. Lesbian "sex" as I have known it most of the time I
have known it is utterly inarticulate. Most of my
lifetime, most of my experience in the realms
commonly designated as "sexual" has been pre-
linguistic, noncognitive. I have, in effect, no linguistic community, no language, and therefore in
one important sense, no knowledge....

Meanings should arise from our bodily self-
knowledge, bodily play, tactile communication,
the ebb and flow of intense excitement, arousal,
tension, release, comfort, discomfort, pain and
pleasure (and I make no distinctions here among
bodily, emotional, intellectual, aesthetic). But
such meanings are more completely muted, less
coalesced into discrete elements of a coherent pattern of meanings (of an experience) than any other
dimensions of our lives. In fact, there are for many
of us virtually no meanings in this realm because
nothing of it is crystallized in a linguistic matrix.[9]

What we have for generic words to cover this
terrain are the words "sex," "sexual" and "sexuality." In our efforts to liberate ourselves from the
stifling woman-hating denial that women even

have bodily awareness, arousal, excitement, orgasms and so on, many of us actively took these words for ourselves, and claimed that we do "do sex" and we are sexual and we have sexuality. This has been particularly important to lesbians because the very fact of "sex" being a phallocentric term has made it especially difficult to get across the idea that lesbians are not, for lack of a penis between us [as Alix Dobkin put it in a song lyric], making do with feeble and partial and pathetic half-satisfactions.... But it seems to me that the attempt to encode our lustiness and lustfulness, our passion and our vigorous carnality in the words "sex," "sexual" and "sexuality" has backfired. Instead of losing their phallocentricity, these words have imported the phallocentric meanings into and onto experience which is not in any way phallocentric. A web of meanings which maps emotional intensity, excitement, arousal, bodily play, orgasm, passion and relational adventure back onto a semantic center in male-dominant-female-subordinate-copulation has been so utterly inadequate as to leave us speechless, meaningless, and ironically, according to the Blumstein and Schwartz report, "not as sexual" as couples or as individuals as any other group.

Our lives, the character of our embodiment, cannot be mapped back on to that semantic center. When we try to synthesize and articulate it by the rules of that mapping, we end up trying to mold our loving and passionate carnal intercourse into explosive 8-minute events. But that is the timing and the ontology of an alienated and patriarchal penis, not of the lesbian body. When the only things that count as "doing it" are those passages of our interactions which most closely approximate a paradigm that arose from the meanings of the rising and falling penis, no wonder we discover ourselves to "do it" rather less often than do pairs with one or more penises present. Interpreting our desires and determining our acts by the rules of that semantic map, we have tended to discount, discontinue, never try, or never even imagine acts, activities, practices, rituals, forms of play, ways of touching, looking, talking, which might be woven into a fabric of our erotic experience....

My positive recommendation is this: Instead of starting with a point (a point in the life of a body unlike our own) and trying to make meanings along vectors from that point, we would do better to start with a wide field of our passions and bodily pleasures and make meanings that weave a web across it. I suggest that we begin the creation of a vocabulary that can encode and expand our meanings by adopting a very wide and general concept of "doing it." Let it be an open, generous, commodious concept encompassing all the acts and activities by which we generate with each other pleasures and thrills, tenderness and ecstasy, passages of passionate carnality of whatever duration or profundity. Everything from vanilla to licorice, from puce to tangerine, from velvet to ice, from cuddles to cunts, from chortles to tears. Starting from there, we can let our experiences generate a finer-tuned descriptive vocabulary that maps and expresses the differences and distinctions among the things we do, the kinds of pleasures we get, the stages and styles of our acts and activities, the parts of our bodies centrally engaged in the different kinds of "doing it," and so on. Our vocabulary will arise among us as we explain and explore and define our pleasures and our preferences across this field, teaching each other what the possibilities are and how to make them real.

The vocabulary will arise among us, of course, only if we talk with each other about what we're doing and why, and what it feels like. Language is social. So is "doing it."...

NOTES

1. This essay was first published in *Sinister Wisdom,* vol. 35 (Summer/Fall 1988). It was first presented as a paper at the meeting of the Society for Women in Philosophy, Midwestern Division, November 13–15, 1987. It was occasioned by Claudia Card's paper "What Lesbians Do," which was published under the title "Intimacy and Responsibility: What Lesbians Do," as the Institute for Legal Studies, University of

Wisconsin-Madison Law School Working Papers Series 2, No. 10. Carolyn Shafer has contributed a lot to my thinking here, and I am indebted also to conversations with Sue Emmert and Terry Grant. For more writing by lesbians on sex, see *An Intimate Wilderness: Lesbian Writers on Sexuality,* edited by Judith Barrington (Portland, OR: Eighth Mountain Press, 1991).

2. When I speak of "we" and "our communities," I actually don't know exactly who that is. I know only that such issues are being discussed in my own circles and in communities other than mine as well (as witness, e.g., discussion in the pages of the *Lesbian Connection*). If what I say here resonates for you, so be it. If not, at least you can know it resonates for some range of lesbians and some of them probably are your friends or acquaintances.

3. Philip Blumstein and Pepper Schwartz, *American Couples* (NY: William Morrow and Company, 1983).

4. Dotty Calabrese gave this information in her workshop on long-term lesbian relationships at the Michigan Womyn's Music Festival, 1987. (Thanks to Terry Grant for this reference.)

5. In their questionnaire, Blumstein and Schwartz use the term "have sexual relations." In the text of their book, they use "have sex."

6. It was brought to my attention by Carolyn Shafer. See pp. 156–7 of my book *The Politics of Reality* (Freedom, CA: The Crossing Press, 1983).

7. *Websters' First New Intergalactic Wickedary of the English Language* (Boston: Beacon Press, 1987).

8. I use the word 'encoding' as it is used in the novel *Native Tongue,* by Suzette Haden Elgin (NY: Daw Books, Inc., 1984). She envisages women identifying concepts, feelings, types of situations, etc., for which there are no words in English (or any other language), and giving them intuitively appropriate names in a women-made language called Laadan.

9. Carolyn Shafer has speculated that one significant reason why lesbian SM occasioned so much excitement, both positive and negative, is that lesbians have been starved for language—for specific, detailed, literal, particular, bodily talk with clear non-metaphorical references to parts of our bodies and the ways they can be stimulated, to acts, postures, types of touch. Books about SM like *Coming to Power* (Boston: Alyson Publications, 1982) feed that need, and call forth more words in response.

21

Becoming 100% Straight

MICHAEL A. MESSNER

In 1995, as part of my job as the President of the North American Society for the Sociology of Sport, I needed to prepare a one-hour long Presidential Address for the annual meeting of some 200 people. This presented a challenge to me: how might I say something to my colleagues that was challenging, at least somewhat original, and above all, not boring. Students may think that their professors are especially boring in the classroom, but believe me, we are usually much worse at professional meetings. For some reason, many of us who are able to speak to our students in the classroom in a relaxed manner, and using relatively jargon-free language, seem at these meetings to become robots, dryly reading our papers—packed with impressively unclear jargon—to our yawning colleagues.

Since I desperately wanted to avoid putting 200 sport studies scholars to sleep, I decided to deliver a talk which I entitled "studying up on sex." The title, which certainly did get my colleagues' attention, was intended as a play on words—a double entendre. "Studying up" has one, generally recognizable colloquial meaning, but in sociology, it has another. It refers to studying "up" in the power structure. Sociologists have perhaps most often studied "down"—studied the poor, the blue or pink-collar workers, the "nuts, sluts and perverts," the incarcerated. The idea of "studying up" rarely occurs to sociologists unless and until we are living in a time when those who are "down" have organized movements that challenge the institutional privileges of elites. So, for instance, in the wake of labor movements, some sociologists

like C. Wright Mills studied up on corporate elites. And recently, in the wake of racial/ethnic civil rights movements, some scholars like Ruth Frankenberg have begun to study the social meanings of "whiteness." Much of my research, inspired by feminism, has involved a studying up on the social construction of masculinity in sport. Studying up, in these cases, has raised some fascinating new and important questions about the workings of power in society.

However, I realized, when it comes to understanding the social and interpersonal dynamics of sexual orientation in sport, we have barely begun to scratch the surface of a very complex issue. Although sport studies has benefited from the work of scholars like Helen Lenskyj, Brian Pronger and others who have delineated the experiences of lesbians and gay men in sports, there has been very little extension of these scholars' insights into a consideration of the social construction of heterosexuality in sport. In sport, just as in the larger society, we seem obsessed with asking "how do people become gay?" Imbedded in this question is the assumption that people who identify as heterosexual, or "straight," require no explanation, since they are simply acting out the "natural" or "normal" sexual orientation. It's the "sexual deviants" who require explanation, we seem to be saying, while the experience of heterosexuals, because we are considered normal, seems to require no critical examination or explanation. But I knew that a closer look at the development of sexual orientation or sexual identity reveals an extremely complex process. I decided to challenge myself and my colleagues by arguing that although we have begun to "study up" on corporate elites in sport, on whiteness, on masculinity, it is now time to extend that by studying up on heterosexuality.

But in the absence of systematic research on this topic, where could I start? How could I explore, raise questions about, and begin to illuminate the social construction of heterosexuality for my colleagues? Fortunately, I had for the previous two years been working with a group of five men (three of whom identified as heterosexual, two as gay) who were mutually exploring our own biographies in terms of our earlier bodily experiences that helped to shape our gender and sexual identities. We modeled our project after that of a German group of feminist women, led by Frigga Haug, who created a research method which they call "memory work." In short, the women would mutually choose a body part, such as "hair," and each of them would then write a short story, based on a particularly salient childhood memory that related to their hair (for example, being forced by parents to cut your hair, deciding to straighten one's curly hair, in order to look more like other girls, etc.). Then, the group would read all of the stories, discuss them one-by-one, with the hope of gaining some more general understanding of, and raising new questions about, the social construction of "femininity." What resulted from this project was a fascinating book called *Female Sexualization,* which my men's group used as an inspiration for our project.

As a research method, memory work is anything but conventional. Many sociologists would argue that this is not really a "research method" at all, because the information that emerges from the project can't be used very confidently as a generalizable "truth," and especially because in this sort of project, the researcher is simultaneously part of what is being studied. How, my more scientifically oriented colleagues might ask, is the researcher to maintain his or her objectivity in this project? My answer is that in this kind of research, objectivity is not the point. In fact, the strength of this sort of research is the depth of understanding that might be gained through a systematic group analysis of one's experience, one's *subjective* orientation to social processes. A clear understanding of the subjective aspect of social life—one's bodily feelings, emotions, and reactions to others—is an invaluable window that allows us to see and ask new sociological questions about group interaction and social structure. In short, group memory work can provide an important, productive, and fascinating insight into aspects of social reality, though not a complete (or completely reliable) picture.

So, as I pondered the lack of existing research on the social construction of heterosexuality in sport, I decided to draw on one of my own stories from my memory work men's group. Some of my most salient memories of embodiment are sports memories. I grew up the son of a high school coach, and I eventually played point guard on my dad's team. In what follows, I juxtapose one of my stories with that of a gay former Olympic athlete, Tom Waddell, whom I had interviewed several years earlier for a book that I wrote on the lives of male athletes.

TWO SEXUAL STORIES

Many years ago I read some psychological studies that argued that even for self-identified heterosexuals, it is a natural part of their development to have gone through "bisexual" or even "homosexual" stages of life. When I read this, it seemed theoretically reasonable, but it did not ring true in my experience. I have always been, I told myself, 100% heterosexual! The group process of analyzing my own autobiographical stories challenged this conception I had developed of myself, and also shed light on the way that the institutional context of sport provided a context for the development of my definition of myself as "100% straight." Here is one of the stories.

When I was in the 9th grade, I played on a "D" basketball team, set up especially for the smallest of high school boys. Indeed, though I was pudgy with baby fat, I was a short 5'2", still pre-pubescent with no facial hair and a high voice that I artificially tried to lower. The first day of practice, I was immediately attracted to a boy I'll call Timmy, because he looked like the boy who played in the Lassie TV show. Timmy was short, with a high voice, like me. And like me, he had no facial hair yet. Unlike me, he was very skinny. I liked Timmy right away, and soon we were together a lot. I noticed things about him that I didn't notice about other boys: he said some words a certain way, and it gave me pleasure to try to talk like him. I remember liking the way the light hit his boyish, nearly hairless body. I thought about him when we weren't together. He was in the school band, and at the football games, I'd squint to see where he was in the mass of uniforms. In short, though I wasn't conscious of it at the time, I was infatuated with Timmy—I had a crush on him. Later that basketball season, I decided—for no reason that I could really articulate then—that I hated Timmy. I aggressively rejected him, began to make fun of him around other boys. He was, we all agreed, a geek. He was a faggot.

Three years later, Timmy and I were both on the varsity basketball team, but had hardly spoken a word to each other since we were freshmen. Both of us now had lower voices, had grown to around 6 feet tall, and we both shaved, at least a bit. But Timmy was a skinny, somewhat stigmatized reserve on the team, while I was the team captain and starting point guard. But I wasn't so happy or secure about this. I'd always dreamed of dominating games, of being the hero. Halfway through my senior season, however, it became clear that I was not a star, and I figured I knew why. I was not aggressive enough.

I had always liked the beauty of the fast break, the perfectly executed pick and roll play between two players, and especially the long twenty-foot shot that touched nothing but the bottom of the net. But I hated and feared the sometimes brutal contact under the basket. In fact, I stayed away from the rough fights for rebounds and was mostly a perimeter player, relying on my long shots or my passes to more aggressive teammates under the basket. But now it became apparent to me that time was running out in my quest for greatness: I needed to change my game, and fast. I decided one day before practice that I was gonna get aggres-

sive. While practicing one of our standard plays, I passed the ball to a teammate, and then ran to the spot at which I was to set a pick on a defender. I knew that one could sometimes get away with setting a face-up screen on a player, and then as he makes contact with you, roll your back to him and plant your elbow hard in his stomach. The beauty of this move is that your own body "roll" makes the elbow look like an accident. So I decided to try this move. I approached the defensive player, Timmy, rolled, and planted my elbow deeply into his solar plexus. Air exploded audibly from Timmy's mouth, and he crumbled to the floor momentarily.

Play went on as though nothing had happened, but I felt bad about it. Rather than making me feel better, it made me feel guilty and weak. I had to admit to myself why I'd chosen Timmy as the target against whom to test out my new aggression. He was the skinniest and weakest player on the team.

At the time, I hardly thought about these incidents, other than to try to brush them off as incidents that made me feel extremely uncomfortable. Years later, I can now interrogate this as a *sexual* story, and as a *gender* story unfolding within the context of the heterosexualized and masculinized institution of sport. Examining my story in light of research conducted by Alfred Kinsey a half-century ago, I can recognize in myself what Kinsey saw as a very common **fluidity and changeability of sexual desire over the lifecourse.** Put simply, Kinsey found that large numbers of adult, "heterosexual" men had previously, as adolescents and young adults, experienced sexual desire for males. A surprisingly large number of these men had experienced sexual contact to the point of orgasm with other males during adolescences or early adulthood. Similarly, my story invited me to consider what is commonly called the "**Freudian theory of bisexuality.**" Sigmund Freud shocked the post-Victorian world by suggesting that all people go through a stage, early in life, when they are attracted to people of the same sex. Adult experiences, Freud argued, eventually led most people to shift their sexual desire to what Freud called an appropriate "love object"—a person of the opposite sex. I also considered my experience in light of what lesbian feminist author Adrienne Rich called **institution of compulsory heterosexuality.** Perhaps the extremely high levels of homophobia that are often endemic in boys' and men's organized sports led me to deny and repress my own homoerotic desire through a direct and overt rejection of Timmy, through homophobic banter with male peers, and through the resultant stigmatization of the feminized Timmy. And eventually, I considered my experience in light of what the radical theorist Herbert Marcuse called the **sublimation of homoerotic desire** into an aggressive, violent act as serving to construct a clear line of demarcation between self-and-other. Sublimation, according to Marcuse, involves the driving underground, into the unconscious, of sexual desires that might appear dangerous due to their socially stigmatized status. But sublimation involves more than simple repression into the unconscious—it involves a transformation of sexual desire into something else—often into aggressive and violent acting out toward others, acts that clarify boundaries between one's self and others and therefore lessen any anxieties that might be attached to the repressed homoerotic desire.

Importantly, in our analysis of my story, my memory group went beyond simply discussing the events in psychological terms. My story did suggest some deep psychological processes at work, perhaps, but it also revealed the importance of social context—in this case, the context of the athletic team. In short, my rejection of Timmy and the joining with teammates to stigmatize him in ninth grade stands as an example of what sociologist R. W. Connell calls a **moment of engagement with hegemonic masculinity,** where I actively took up the male group's task of constructing heterosexual/masculine identities in the context of sport. The elbow in Timmy's gut three years later can be seen as a punctuation mark that occurred precisely because of my fears that I might be failing at this goal.

It is helpful, I think, to compare my story with gay and lesbian "coming out" stories in sport. Though we have a few lesbian and bisexual coming out stories among women athletes, there are very few gay male coming out stories. Tom Waddell, who as a closeted gay man finished sixth in the decathlon in the 1968 Olympics, later came out and started the Gay Games, an athletic and cultural festival that draws tens of thousands of people every four years. When I interviewed Tom Waddell over a decade ago about his sexual identity and athletic career, he made it quite clear that for many years sports *was* his closet. Tom told me,

> *When I was a kid, I was tall for my age, and was very thin and very strong. And I was usually faster than most other people. But I discovered rather early that I liked gymnastics and I liked dance. I was very interested in being a ballet dancer... [but] something became obvious to me right away—that male ballet dancers were effeminate, that they were what most people would call faggots. And I thought I just couldn't handle that...I was totally closeted and very concerned about being male. This was the fifties, a terrible time to live, and everything was stacked against me. Anyway, I realized that I had to do something to protect my image of myself as a male—because at that time homosexuals were thought of primarily as men who wanted to be women. And so I threw myself into athletics—I played football, gymnastics, track and field...I was a* jock—*that's how I was viewed, and I was comfortable with that.*

Tom Waddell was fully conscious of entering sports and constructing a masculine/heterosexual athletic identity precisely because he feared being revealed as gay. It was clear to him, in the context of the 1950s, that being revealed as gay would undercut his claims to the status of manhood. Thus, though he described the athletic closet as "hot and stifling," he remained in the closet until several years after his athletic retirement. He even knowingly played along with locker room discussions about sex and women, knowing that this was part of his "cover":

> *I wanted to be viewed as male, otherwise I would be a dancer today. I wanted the male, macho image of an athlete. So I was protected by a very hard shell. I was* clearly *aware of what I was doing...I*

often felt compelled to go along with a lot of locker room garbage because I wanted that image—and I know a lot of others who did too.

Like my story, Waddell's story points to the importance of the athletic institution as a context in which peers mutually construct and re-construct narrow definitions of masculinity—and heterosexuality is considered to be a rock-solid foundation of this conception of masculinity. But unlike my story, Waddell's story may invoke what sociologist Erving Goffman called a "dramaturgical analysis": Waddell seemed to be consciously "acting" to control and regulate others' perceptions of him by constructing a public "front stage" persona that differed radically from what he believed to be his "true" inner self. My story, in contrast, suggests a deeper, less consciously strategic repression of my homoerotic attraction. Most likely, I was aware on some level of the dangers of such feelings, and was escaping the dangers, disgrace, and rejection that would likely result from being different. For Waddell, the decision to construct his identity largely within sport was a decision to step into a fiercely heterosexual/masculine closet that would hide what he saw to be his "true" identity. In contrast, I was not so much stepping into a "closet" that would hide my identify—rather, I was stepping out into an entire world of heterosexual privilege. My story also suggests how a *threat* to the promised privileges of hegemonic masculinity—my failure as an athlete—might trigger a momentary sexual panic that could lay bare the constructedness, indeed, the *instability* of the heterosexual/masculine identity.

In either case—Waddell's or mine—we can see how, as young male athletes, heterosexuality and masculinity were not something we "were," but something we were *doing*. It is very significant, I think, that as each of us was "doing heterosexuality," neither of us was actually "having sex" with women (though one of us desperately wanted to!). This underscores a point made by some recent theorists, that heterosexuality should not be thought of simply as sexual acts between women

and men; rather, **heterosexuality is a constructed identity, a performance, and an institution** that is not necessarily linked to sexual acts. Though for one of us it was more conscious than for the other, we were both "doing heterosexuality" as an ongoing practice through which we sought (a) to avoid stigma, embarrassment, ostracism, or perhaps worse if we were even suspected of being gay; and (b) to link ourselves into systems of power, status, and privilege that appear to be the birthright of "real men" (i.e., males who are able to successfully compete with other males in sport, work, and sexual relations with women). In other words, each of us actively scripted our own sexual/gender performances, but these scripts were constructed within the constraints of a socially organized (institutionalized) system of power and pleasure.

QUESTIONS FOR FUTURE RESEARCH

As I prepared to tell my above sexual story publicly to my colleagues at the sport studies conference, I felt extremely nervous. Part of the nervousness was due to the fact that I knew some of my colleagues would object to my claim that telling personal stories can be a source of sociological insights. But a larger part of the reason for my nervousness was due to the fact that I was revealing something very personal about my sexuality in such a public way. Most of us aren't used to doing this, especially in the context of a professonal conference. But I had learned long ago, especially from feminist women scholars, and from gay and lesbian scholars, that biography is linked to history, and that part of "normal" academic discourse has been to hide "the personal" (including the fact that the researcher is himself or herself a person, with values, feelings, and, yes, biases) behind a carefully constructed facade of "objectivity." Rather than trying to hide—or be ashamed of—one's subjective experience of the world, I was challenging myself to draw on my experience of the world as a resource. Not that I should trust my experience as the final word on "reality"— white, heterosexual males like myself have made the mistake for centuries of calling their own experience "objectivity," and then punishing anyone who does not share their world view as "deviant." Instead, I hope to use my experience as an example of how those of us who are in dominant sexual/racial/gender/class categories can get a new perspective on the "constructedness" of our identities by juxtaposing our subjective experiences against the recently emerging world views of gay men and lesbians, women, and people of color.

Finally, I want to stress that, juxtaposed, my and Tom Waddell's stories do not shed much light on the question of why some individuals "become gay" while others "become" heterosexual or bisexual. Instead, I'd like to suggest that this is a dead-end question, and that there are far more important and interesting questions to be asked:

- How has heterosexuality, as an institution and as an enforced group practice, constrained and limited all of us—gay, straight, and bi?

- How has the institution of sport been an especially salient institution for the social construction of heterosexual masculinity?
- Why is it that when men play sports they are almost always automatically granted masculine status, and thus assumed to be heterosexual, while when women play sports, questions are raised about their "femininity" and their sexual orientation?

These kinds of questions aim us toward an analysis of the workings of power within institutions—including the ways that these workings of power shape and constrain our identities and relationships—and point us toward imagining alternative social arrangements that are less constraining for everyone.

REFERENCES

Haug, Frigga. 1987. *Female Sexualization: A Collective Work of Memory.* London: Verso.

Katz, Jonathan Ned. 1995. *The Invention of Heterosexuality.* New York: Dutton.

Messner, Michael A. 1992. *Power at Play: Sports and the Problem of Masculinity.* Boston: Beacon Press.

———. 1994. "Gay Athletes and the Gay Games: An interview with Tom Waddell," in M. A. Messner & D. F. Sabo (Eds.), *Sex, Violence and Power in Sports: Rethinking Masculinity* (pp. 113–119). Freedom, CA: The Crossing Press.

Pronger, Brian. 1990. *The Arena of Masculinity: Sports, Homosexuality, and the Meaning of Sex.* New York: St. Martin's Press.

22

Seventies Questions for Nineties Women

ARLENE STEIN

In 1991 news circulated in San Francisco that Amelia's, a lesbian bar which had been located on a busy street in the Mission District for thirteen years, was preparing to close. Bars had come and gone before, reflecting shifts in sexual politics and population. Maud's, the city's longest-running lesbian bar, had closed down two years earlier in the Haight District on the other side of town. Amelia's was the last lesbian bar in San Francisco, so its closure seemed particularly poignant. It marked, some suggested, the end of an era, the end of a time when the community possessed a spatial center. "In the old days," Robin Ward told me, referring to the 1970s, "one could go to a particular place"—a cafe, women's center, or bar—"to find the lesbian community." Fifteen years later, when she broke up with a longtime lover, she went out searching for that community and couldn't find it.

Yet even while Robin and others lamented what they saw as the loss of a "home base" for lesbians, women continued to pour into San Francisco and other cities and towns in search of sexual freedom and community. A columnist in the *San Francisco Examiner* observed that "more lesbians than ever live in San Francisco but the last lesbian bar is set to close." Some explained this in economic terms: unlike gay men, they suggested, lesbians lacked the capital necessary to support a commercial infrastructure. But the owner of Amelia's, a longtime participant in San Francisco's lesbian scene, put it best: "It's a victim of the lesbian community becoming more diverse," she said. "There is an absence of a lesbian community in the presence of a million lesbians."[1] Paradoxically, it was the growth and diversification of lesbian communities, rather than their decline, that destroyed the neighborhood bar.

In the early 1990s, in major urban centers across the nation one could find lesbian parenting groups, support groups for women with cancer and other life-threatening diseases, lesbian sex magazines, organizations for lesbian "career women" and lesbians of color, and mixed organizations in which out lesbians played visible roles. Gay/lesbian newspapers contained notices advertising hiking clubs for lesbians and their dogs, support groups for adult children of alcoholics, "leather and lace" motorcycle clubs, groups for lesbian-identified transsexuals, and many others. A multiplicity of lesbian groupings emerged, each representing a smaller subculture and special interest. There was no longer any hegemonic logic or center; lesbian culture seemed *placeless*. It had become more and more difficult to speak of "lesbian" identity, community, culture, politics, or even sexuality in singular terms. "I don't think there is one lesbian community," said Sunny Connelly, reflecting on nearly twenty years of change. "The community is getting bigger and smaller. Some of the infrastructure is going, bars are closing. In that way it's getting smaller. In the sense that more women are able to feel good about leading lesbian lives, it's getting bigger. But it's spreading out and becoming decentralized, which is good and bad."

Laments about the loss of lesbian community spoke to the loss of a center, of a sense of certainty and unity. For a brief period in the early 1970s, there was a burst of extraordinary solidarity, a feeling that lesbians shared a common oppression and a collective sense of identity. Lesbianism seemed to offer a settled, stable source of identification, affording membership in a bounded group with a common history, which offered both a refuge in a male and heterosexual world and a base for political action against male domination and compulsory heterosexuality. Lesbians were thought to possess one shared culture, "one true self," which was hidden inside a multiplicity of more superficial or artificially imposed "selves." Their common historical experiences and shared cultural codes were believed to provide them, as "one people," with unchanging frames of reference and meaning that continued beneath the vicissitudes of their actual history. This "oneness," underlying all other, more superficial differences, was thought to be the truth, the essence.[2]

But as the lives of the baby boom cohort became more settled, a younger cohort of women emerged, stamping their own generational sensibility upon the contours of lesbian culture and calling into question these earlier notions of collective identity. Like those before them, they constructed their lesbian identities in opposition as much to their lesbian predecessors as to the dominant heterosexual culture. Unlike their older sisters, however, who believed that together they could forge a unified sense of what it meant to be "a lesbian," young women coming of age in the 1990s had to establish lesbian identities at a time when many of the apparent certainties of the past had disappeared.

QUESTIONS OF IDENTITY REVISITED

As a 1970s-influenced feminist studying women psychoanalysts from the 1930s, Nancy Chodorow found that a lack of attunement to gender characterized her interviewees' interpretation of their professional lives. Early women psychoanalysts were highly accomplished individuals who defied standard expectations of women. They had, it seemed, every reason to be conscious of themselves as women. But they were not. This indicates, observes Chodorow, the "variable and situated quality of gender."[3] For some women, and at some historical moments, consciousness of oneself as having a "gender" is more central than for other women at other times.

As a 1980s-influenced researcher looking at the experience of baby boom lesbians, who came of age in the 1970s, I was struck by how salient were their gender and sexual identities. Could the same be said of women coming out today? How, I wondered, do "nineties women"—young lesbians coming of age now—make sense of "seventies questions"? How do they understand their sexual identities, and does this understanding vary significantly from that of their baby boom predecessors? With these broad queries in mind, I interviewed ten lesbian-identified women, ranging in age from nineteen to twenty-nine, whose median year of birth was 1967, asking many of the same questions I had posed to women of the baby boom.

I imagined that I would find that for these younger women, sexual identifications do not play as central a role as they did for the older cohort. Twenty years of feminism, I surmised, had to some extent normalized lesbianism, making it less stigmatized and therefore less central to their lives. However, with some qualifications, I did not find this to be the case. Though the small number of interviews makes any claims speculative, it appears that among those coming out as lesbians today, as for their predecessors, sexuality is typically a highly salient, central aspect of the self. Becoming a lesbian entails placing oneself outside the dominant heterosexual culture, and all that that implies. Young women in particular, who must construct a sense of personhood as they establish a sexual understanding of themselves, face a complicated and frequently difficult task.

However, while the *salience* of lesbian identification among younger women did not seem significantly different from that of baby boomers at the same age, the *meaning* of this identification did. For example, among baby boomers, talk of "community" embodied the belief that lesbians all shared some basic common ground: a common marginality and a shared project of liberation. They believed that out of the diversity of women's lives and experiences they could construct a collective sense of what it meant to be a lesbian, developing subcultures that could nurture that vision. In contrast, when asked whether they considered themselves members of a "lesbian community," most of the younger women equated the idea of "community" with the imposition of "rules" and with the construction of idealized conceptions of lesbianism with which they could not fully identify.

Speaking of her knowledge of feminist theory and culture, twenty-four-year-old Lucia Hicks told me,

> *I went through a period where I identified with "sisterhood is powerful" and all. I learned about it in school. I think that there are some really positive things I can take from that. But as I get older, I think that that whole era was simplistic in a lot of ways. There are a lot of rules. When you read the literature from that period there are a lot of ways of being in the world, and not being in the world. And you fit that picture, or you don't. And that's a little too simplistic for me.*

Though criticizing feminism for its alleged simplicity, Lucia is quick to acknowledge that the existence of lesbian feminist culture—books, ideas, music, and simply lesbian visibility—made her own coming out much easier. "I have to attribute my coming out in part to getting a grasp on feminism," she said. While keeping their distance from lesbian feminism, she and other younger women have also been profoundly influenced by it. "My sense is that a lot of younger dykes don't reject lesbian feminism, but they do take it for granted, not in a bad way. They just don't have to particularly announce it," said Lucia. "They just live it." This sensibility is evident in *Go Fish,* a 1994 film about a circle of lesbian friends in Chicago, which enjoyed mass distribution. The story

starts from the assumption of an inherent acceptability, and even respectability, of lesbian lives. There are no painful coming out stories, the hallmark of lesbian narratives of the 1970s and 1980s. There are no painstaking justifications for lesbianism. It is the perspective of filmmakers who are in their twenties today, who have come of age two decades after Stonewall.

Nineties women have little hope of constructing a unified, collective sense of what it means to be a lesbian or a feminist. They are leery of attempts to define the "lesbian community," doubting if any one image could possibly represent the complexity of lesbian experiences. Twenty-five-year-old Judy Thomas told me, "What I am is in many ways contradictory.... I feel that I'm postfeminist, which isn't to say that I don't think we live in a male-dominated world. I just don't know whether the way to undermine it is to establish new expectations of what we should be. Everything is out there to be sliced and diced and put under the fine microscope." Judy's sense of indeterminacy and contradiction is related to shifts in the relationship between margin and mainstream. To become a lesbian in the 1970s was to stand outside the dominant culture. To affirm and celebrate lesbian lives, feminists were compelled to create an alternative culture. Lesbians of the baby boom went outside the music industry to make a women's music defined against commercial imperatives and "cock rock." They produced films, literature, and theories to make sense of their lives, to make themselves visible. Thanks to these efforts, nineties women have greater access than any previous generation to cultural images, narratives, and other resources that mirror their desires. Today, young women can learn about lesbian lives in women's studies courses, feminist fiction, and, increasingly, in mass-produced popular culture, such as the television show *Roseanne,* or the music of k. d. lang.

Because of these expanded opportunities, women of the postfeminist generation do not feel as strong a sense of loyalty to "feminist" or "women's" culture. They believe that they should be represented in mainstream culture, and they long for that representation. When I asked her what types of music she listened to, nineteen-year-old Ann Carlson answered, "I like 'cock rock' and women's music. I like both. But I like mainstream women's music the best." Rather than listen to "out" lesbian musicians recording on alternative women's music labels, "I like music that speaks to women but isn't only about women.... Tracy Chapman, Melissa Etheridge, Michelle Shocked. They don't use pronouns, proper nouns. To us that's cool. And we notice that men don't listen to that music." Ann subverts the feminist critique of masculinist music by embracing cock rock as a symbol of power *and* women's music as a reminder of her feminist roots. At the same time, however, she prefers "mainstream women's music": women musicians who employ lesbian and feminist imagery but perform for a mass audience. These performers' sexual ambiguity allows for the double appeal of the music—to the subculture, as well as to the mass audience. It permits audience members such as Ann to listen to music they consider to be "lesbian" and know that millions of other people are also listening to it. For her, the ambiguity is part of the appeal.[4] But the pluralization and "mainstreaming" of lesbian images are themselves ambiguous signs of progress: the increasing importance of mass-produced lesbian culture means that while lesbian images are much more plentiful than they ever were before, their production is much more reliant upon the whims of Hollywood and the culture industries, and thus lesbian lives are being commodified.[5] Nonetheless, many younger lesbians welcome this mainstreaming.

Other important differences between the seventies and nineties cohorts concern their views of the sexualization of women's bodies. While the older women claimed power by renouncing lipstick, coquettishness, and sexually explicit representations and by opposing the commercialization of beauty and sex, by 1990 many younger lesbians were asserting their sexual power by reclaiming these practices and withholding access from the conventional male beholder. As the decade wore on, the debates that emerged in bars, in coffee houses, and in the pages of community newspapers often appeared as a generational clash: Were the full-color spreads, in the glossy fashion magazines from *Elle* to *Vanity Fair,* that touted the joys of "lesbian chic" furthering lesbian visibility, or were they creating new, idealized, airbrushed versions of a genteel sapphism? Were younger women, who were pioneering a new roving club scene and unabashedly embracing sexual imagery, the rightful heirs of lesbian feminism or evidence of its demise?

When I first arrived in the Bay Area in 1981, lesbian bars, clubs, and social events were frequented by women who embraced lesbian feminist antistyle—workshirts, jeans, and "sensible shoes." But through the next few years, many lesbians began to dress up. In night clubs and on the street it was not unusual to see younger women flaunt high heels, short skirts, and other trappings of femininity, often consciously evolving the butch-femme codes of the 1950s. Twenty-eight-year-old Jill Dinkins wears her "butch" identity proudly. Whenever she goes out with her girlfriend, they adopt sharply differentiated gender styles. Jill wears leather jackets, short-cropped hair, and men's vests; her girlfriend has long hair and wears makeup and skirts.

As Jill describes these forms of self-presentation, they sound very different from the butch-femme roles practiced by earlier working-class lesbians. For her, adopting a role is more a matter of play than necessity. "I like to play with power and sexuality. It's all a game." She and other nineties women selectively and self-consciously take on elements of butch-femme style. Some interpret the roles in an essentialized way, as showing their "true" nature and refusing the constraints of straight society, but for many these roles are more ambiguous and less naturalized than in the past. They are an aesthetic practice, a self-reflexive performance.[6]

This commitment to individual choice often also extends to sexual practices. Members of the nineties cohort tend to be much more tolerant of "slippages" of identity in general—of inconsistencies among identity, desires, and sexual practices—than their baby boom predecessors. Judy Thomas, who felt attracted to women and girls at a very early age, and who calls herself a "lesbian virgin" because she has never had a heterosexual experience, told me that she was toying with the idea of sleeping with a man, "just for the experience," and that she did not see this as a threat to her lesbian identity. She related a story about her best friend, a lesbian, who recently told her that she was having an affair with a man, fearing Judy's response. She reassured her friend that this news was not a threat to their friendship. "I was so shocked that she even asked me," she said. If there is a greater tolerance for inconsistencies of identity, this may be related to the greater propensity of younger lesbians to speak openly about their sexual practices.

Certainly, the sexual practices and politics of feminist lesbians were more diverse in private than was publicly admitted. As my interviewees suggested, frank sexual talk was muted in the interest of constructing lesbian solidarity. Recall Cindy Ross's description of lesbian sexuality in the 1970s: "Nobody knew what anyone else was doing." For nineties women, particularly members of urban lesbian subcultures, the gap between theorizing and practicing sexuality has seemingly narrowed. The belief that lesbian sexuality is radically different from and superior to other forms of sexuality, and that sexuality and desire are only peripheral aspects of the lesbian experience, is no longer widely held. As Jill Dinkins told me, "I've heard many conversations about sex recently in social settings. Not necessarily in a lovey-dovey manner, or in a clinical manner, but in an experimental sense. That's what a lot of young women are going through right now. They're not modeling themselves after older women." Nineties women were more likely to know about different types of sexual practices and to be aware of sexual and relational problems such as "lesbian bed death," the tendency for long-term lovers' sexual interests to wane. They are also far more likely than their baby boom predecessors to consider sexual fringe groups, such as sadomasochists, to be a legitimate part of the lesbian community. Most striking, perhaps, is the tolerance for—and even celebration of—bisexuality.

Women of the baby boom, I have argued, often suppressed their bisexuality in the interest of identifying as lesbian and challenging compulsory heterosexuality. Today, anecdotal evidence suggests that many young women, particularly on college campuses, have come to openly identify as bisexual rather than exclusively lesbian. Twenty-two-year-old Cindy Yerkovich explained that while she is attracted to men, she feels most comfortable with and sexually fulfilled by women. The label that best expresses who she is is "bi-dyke," signifying that her "sexual orientation is bisexual but [her] identity is lesbian." Cindy, who has long hair and a traditionally feminine appearance, said that she fights against the tendency to place her and others "in boxes": "A lot of stuff that has come down on me has been really looksist. People will call me bisexual not knowing whether I've ever slept with a man. Just because I have long hair. It bugs me that people assume I'm bisexual just because I pass. Gay people assume that I'm bisexual, if they don't assume that I'm straight." When I asked my younger interviewees if they were currently friends with or would choose to be friends with a bisexual woman, or how they would feel if a lesbian friend decided to become involved with a man on either a short-term or long-term basis, their responses tended, on the whole, to be quite positive. Some even suggested that lesbians and bisexual women have much in common by virtue of their "queerness."

Sometimes Cindy calls herself "queer," signifying a fluid sense of sexual orientation and a refusal to fully embrace the term "lesbian." For her, the term signifies a loose but distinguishable set of political and intellectual movements that are quite distinct from an "ethnic" style of lesbian/gay identity politics. *Queer* signifies the possibility of constructing a nonnormative sexuality that includes all who feel disenfranchised by dominant sexual norms.[7] Thus, on the Kinsey scale, Cindy says, "queer means anything that is not a 1 or completely heterosexual.... I think that 1s are just as abnormal as 6s, whatever abnormal means. Queer implies ambiguity. It implies that you can't define things in terms of us and them—it's not that easy. I don't want to define my identity in terms of exclusion." She and others who have been influenced by the queer critique insist that the refusal of lesbian/gay identity, rather than its affirmation, is the radical act. "We have a lesbian identity, a lesbian culture now. It's established. We don't have to fight to establish it. Now's the time to question what we've taken for granted." The presence of people with ambiguous sexual desires, such as bisexuals, challenges the faith in sexual object choice as a master category of sexual and social identity and offers the greatest potential to disrupt the normative heterosexual/homosexual binary.[8]

Armed with poststructuralist and postmodern theories of gender and sexuality, some also suggest that cross-gender practices such as butch-femme and drag are subversive acts that undermine the illusion of a coherently gendered self, therefore providing an alternative to a politics grounded in identity. They quote Judith Butler's claim: gender identities are "performative acts" that are always on uncertain ground.[9] The lengths to which we must go, through dress, demeanor, and all manner of social practices, to prove our masculinity or femininity attest to their tenuousness. Once differences *within* the categories— "woman" and "man," "heterosexual" and "homosexual"—are exposed, the old dichotomous conceptions are called into question.

In major cities, young "queers" infiltrated straight bars, carrying on "kiss-ins" designed to upset "normal" heterosexuality. Relying largely on the decentralized, cultural activism of street posturing, their styles and tactics were a pastiche of images and elements from popular culture, communities of color, AIDS activism, hippies, MTV, feminism, and early gay liberation.[10] At the 1993 march on Washington, marchers chanted in front of the White House: "We're here; we're gay; can Bill come out and play?"[11] Queer activists traveled to shopping malls, proclaiming, "We're here, we're queer, and we're not going shopping." They rejected civil rights strategies in favor of a politics of carnival, transgression, and antiassimilation, blending the in-your-face stance of gay liberationists with a parodic sense of the limits of identity politics.

Describing a short-lived but influential organization that embodied these ideas, one analyst wrote: "In its resistance to social codes (sexual, gender, race, class) that impose unitary identities, in rebelling against forces imposing a repressive coherence and order, Queer Nation affirms an abstract unity of differences without wishing to fix and name these."[12] In other words, the preference for the label *queer* represents "an aggressive impulse of generalization; it rejects a minoritizing logic of toleration or simple political interest-representation in favor of a more thorough resistance to regimes of the normal." Such generalization suggests the difficulty in defining the population whose interests are at stake in queer politics."[13]

My conversations with young lesbians indicate that while relatively few—only the most highly educated and theory-savvy—claim the term *queer* wholeheartedly, many more, if not most, identify with the indeterminacy and irony at the heart of the queer project. They oppose the construction of an identity founded upon exclusions and are uncertain about the content of the category *lesbian*. Yet they tend to qualify their allegiance to "queerness" by retaining a critique of gender inequality. Judy Thomas, who works for a predominantly gay male organization in San Francisco, cautioned that among the men she works with "there is a complete lack of knowledge about lesbians."

I don't think straight men know us, or gay men.... There is a very profound fear or kind of terror toward women that have any kind of sense of self, and there is a terrible resistance on the part of men to look at their own sexism. Some of my friends say that there's not a whole lot of common ground [between gay men and lesbians]. I don't really believe that, actually. But I do know that sexism is alive and well and living in gay male communities, just the same as racism is alive and well and living in my life, and my friends' lives.

Judy and her peers inherit a world in which women still lag far behind men with respect to all common measures of structural equality—pay equity, child care provisions, and the like—while at the same time feminist ideas have made considerable cultural headway. They were far from convinced that their loyalties stood with men. Indeed, among political activists in San Francisco and other cities, gay men and women often coexisted uneasily: ACT UP and Queer Nation chapters in many cities were marred by gender (and racial) conflicts.[14] The new "co-sexual" queer culture could not compensate for real, persistent, structural differences in style, ideology, and access to resources among men and women. This recurrent problem underscored that while the new queer politics asserted the sexual difference that could not be assimilated into feminism, gender, too, resisted being completely subsumed within sexuality.

Even as they integrate feminism into their daily lives, young lesbians seem to reject the view that lesbianism is *the* feminist act and the belief that any sexual identity is more authentic and unmediated than any other. Talk of "lesbian community," "lesbian identity," or "women's culture" and the global theories that underlie such language hold little appeal. When asked whether she identifies as a member of a lesbian community, Jill Dinkins replied: "I feel a sense of community with my friends who are lesbians. But I don't feel a sense of community with all lesbians. We agree on some things: that we love women, and that we want to live our lives as openly as we can. But we disagree on a lot of things: worldviews, political concerns, you name it." Jill spoke of refusing ghettoization, of acknowledging internal group differences, and of affirming individual choice of style and political and sexual expression. In this sense, she is "postfeminist," if that term describes women and men who, while holding their distance from feminist

identities or politics, have been profoundly influenced by them.[15] She and other nineties women simultaneously locate themselves inside and outside the dominant culture, and they feel a loyalty to a multiplicity of different projects—some of them feminist oriented, others more queer identified. They recognize that while marginalized groups construct symbolic fictions of their experience as a means of self-validation, and thus compulsory heterosexuality necessitates the construction of lesbian/gay identities, nevertheless such identities are constraining as well as enabling.

NECESSARY FICTIONS

There is no doubt in my mind that the feminist movement has radically changed, in an important way, everybody's concept of lesbianism, straight or gay. There's not a dyke in the world today (in or out of the bars) who can have the same conversation that she could have had ten years ago. It seeps through the water system, you know?

> Amber Hollibaugh, in Hollibaugh and Moraga, "What We're Rollin' Around in Bed With" (1981)

A veteran activist and early gay liberationist told me a story about going on a shopping expedition with several older relatives to a suburban mall outside of San Francisco. The year was 1990. When they arrived at the mall, she and her relatives encountered some young "queers," dressed in ripped t-shirts and buzz-cut hairdos; they were chanting and holding a "kiss-in," an action designed to break the calm of compulsory heterosexuality and generally cause a stir. She looked at the young queer activists and saw her younger self. "I've always felt stifled by people who want to put me into a kind of strait jacket. There's a part of me that always wants to throw things in for shock value and stir them up a bit."[16]

Twenty years earlier, she had joined gay liberation and feminism out of a similar impulse to "smash the categories" and deconstruct reified notions of gender and sexuality. She judges her generation's efforts to be a qualified success: "We made homosexuality much more visible, we created a presence for gay life in this country. But we were young, naive, and very bold." Though they problematized heterosexuality, activists of her generation failed to problematize the constructed, indeed fragile, nature of their own collective self-concepts. "We wanted to turn everything upside down. Sometimes we failed to see that we were very much a part of the system we were trying to change. Sometimes we asked for too much. We ended up demanding too much of people."

Lesbians of the baby boom passionately affirmed their sexual identities, insisting, at least initially, that such identities are open-ended, evolving, and often situational. They found inadequate the conventional view that sexual identity is, for all intents and purposes, consolidated early in life. It could not account for the experiences of housewives who had never harbored desires for women, but who in the boundary-breaking times of the 1960s and 1970s left their husbands and took up with women. As Jeffrey Weeks put it, sexuality is "provisional, even precarious, dependent upon, and constantly challenged by an unstable relation of unconscious forces, changing social and personal meanings, and historical contingencies."[17]

Having revealed the contingent character of sexuality, however, many women of this generation, particularly those who had been touched by feminist ideas, began to seek stability, closure, and certainty, keeping a watchful eye on the boundaries of the "lesbian community." Over time, the impulse toward consistency won out. They sought congruence between individual and collective identities, even while placing great value upon achieving authenticity, being "true" to oneself. They believed that by achieving a stable sense of identity, they could maintain a sense of coherence and commitment despite external flux, instability, and change and their own passage through different periods of life. They downplayed internal differences: different desires, different self-conceptions, and different varieties of lesbian identification.

By externalizing difference and developing a gender separatism that policed the boundaries

around the lesbian group, lesbian feminists came to reinforce the differences—between insider and outsider, normal and abnormal, male and female, heterosexual and homosexual—that they had originally sought to erase. This had the unintended effect of strengthening the notion of sexual minorities as "other," which left the "center"—heterosexuality—intact. The problem with this "ethnic" conception of homosexuality, writes Barbara Ehrenreich, is that "it denies the true plasticity of human sexuality and, in so doing, helps heterosexuals evade what they fear. And what heterosexuals really fear is not that 'they'—an alien subgroup with perverse tastes in bedfellows—are getting an undue share of power and attention, but that 'they' might well be us."[18]

Perhaps the eventual resurgence of essentialism and sexual binaries, both of which lesbian feminists had initially attacked, was inevitable, given the contradictions within feminists' reconceptualizing of lesbianism in the 1970s. They downplayed desire in the interest of political identity, while making sexual consistency and commitment a test of membership. They imagined lesbianism as an identification that transcended sexuality and, at the same time, defined women according to their sexual relationships. They tried both to undo the old categories and to form stable, consistent sexual identities, to embrace a universalizing conception of identity and unify lesbians as a minority group. But ultimately, they failed to escape dominant conceptions that saw sexuality in binary terms, as either heterosexual *or* homosexual, thus neglecting the diversity within each category and the variability of the boundaries separating them.

It appears that social movements organized around sexual identities are caught in a troubling paradox. "We are," observes Jeffrey Weeks, "increasingly aware that sexuality is about flux and change, that what we call 'sexual' is as much a product of language and culture as of nature. But we earnestly strive to fix it, stabilize it, say who we are by telling of our sex."[19] Perhaps stability and predictability are basic human needs, particularly for those of us living through rapid social transformations, whose identities are accordingly under great pressure to change. Yet the effort spent on keeping collective sexual identities intact may do no more than expose their ultimate instability and impermanence.

The history of lesbianism is the history of the progressive growth of knowledge, reflexivity, and group self-consciousness. Whereas knowledge accumulated about sexuality, as about human life in general, was once believed to clarify our understanding of the world, we have found instead that this knowledge has actually come to undermine our sense of certainty. The more we know, the less we can take for granted. Our capacity to reflect upon everything around us now actually threatens the stability of our institutions, and the resulting uncertainty has become a constituent element of modern institutions.[20] In particular, the more we know, the more we've come to see sexuality as fleeting, unstable, and up for grabs. Queer politics and poststructuralist-inspired queer theory may represent the latest stage in the development of greater and greater reflexivity and indeterminacy.

Today's queer activists enact a new universalizing move, a new attempt to smash the categories; while not unlike the early lesbian/gay liberation impulse, theirs seems more keenly aware of the provisional nature of *all* identities. As they wrestle with the tensions between identity and difference, they too have had heated boundary disputes. "They are trying to combine contradictory impulses: to bring together people who have been made to feel perverse, queer, odd, outcast, different, and deviant, and to affirm sameness by defining a common identity on the fringes," two veteran gay liberation activists note.[21] But at least these young activists seem to be highly sensitive to the contradictory nature of their project. Problematizing homosexuality along with heterosexuality, they are wary of engaging in fights over who belongs in the lesbian/gay/queer community and skeptical about "the possibility and desirability of a clear criterion of belonging."[22]

So while the contested nature of lesbianism is familiar, there is also something new; in Biddy Martin's words, "the irreducibly complex and contested status of identity has itself been made

more visible."[23] This is deeply troubling to many women, particularly those who once held out the hope of constructing a unified lesbian feminist movement. The element of uncertainty here is bound to be unsettling: in contrast, carving out a sense of space, forming a community, and drawing boundaries, however precarious they may be, promote a sense of security. Indeed, the persistence of institutionalized and culturally reproduced normative heterosexuality, as well as the heterosexism that accompanies it, makes it necessary to continue the construction of a sense of difference based on (homo)sexual object choice.

As long as individuals are defined as different and inferior on the basis of their sexual desires or practices, they will need to develop a sense of collective identity and maintain institutions that counter stigma. This seems particularly true today, as a powerful and well-organized right wing in the United States mobilizes to deny lesbian and gay rights, along with the economic and political rights of other marginalized groups.[24] Without an organized and self-conscious movement, these rights cannot be defended. A collective identity requires that boundaries be established by setting forth at least minimal criteria for claiming that identity. The alternative is a vague pluralism that speaks only of "difference" and views all differences as equal and good. This "hundred lifestyles" strategy, which calls for "a pluralism of sexual choice," as Margaret Cerullo says, "doesn't represent an adequate response to the one lifestyle that has all the power"—heterosexuality.[25]

Today many of us, queer and not-so-queer, are searching for a way of talking about (and acting on) sexual identities and politics that avoids the twin pitfalls: an identity politics that refuses difference or a politics of difference without collective identity.[26] As individuals we are members of social groups yet remain ultimately irreducible to categories. "We are," writes Shane Phelan, "specific individuals as well as members of multiple groups."[27] As lesbians, we share differences *and* commonalities. We need to affirm what we share in common without feeling compelled to deny what makes each of us unique.

Individual differences will always exist. We have seen that even among self-identified lesbians, sexualities vary widely. For example, for some women, sexual object choice is open to choice and change. Others experience their sexual desires as relatively fixed. As long as we live in a society in which heterosexuality is normative, women who have early homosexual desires or experiences will develop a more deeply felt sense of difference than those who do not. But this difference is not of paramount significance and should not be used to determine who does and does not belong in our communities. Instead, we need to tolerate ambiguity. We need to question assumptions about who and what constitutes the lesbian community, deliberately courting greater uncertainty rather than seeking closure. This politics is already emerging in practice.

I have described how women of the baby boom, as they enter middle age, are combining commitment to lesbian communities with a greater sense of individualism. They are reconstituting lesbian identity in new, decentered ways as their responsibilities to work and family increase. Many younger women coming of age and coming out today are also reconstituting lesbian identity, in ways that tolerate inconsistency and ambiguity. They simultaneously locate themselves inside and outside the dominant culture as they pursue a wide range of projects. Their strategic deployment of lesbian/gay identities is balanced against their recognition of the limits of such identities.

In the decentered conception of identity that is emerging, individuals are comfortable in multiple contexts. They embody what Kathy Ferguson calls "mobile subjectivities," which are temporal, always in motion, and contingent. Identities, she suggests, are "deceptive homogenizations" that always conceal "some turbulence." If we simply identify on the basis of race, class, or sexuality, we cannot make sense of the used-to-be-working-class-now-professional, the woman of mixed race parentage who appears white, the divorced-mother-now-lesbian, or the former-lesbian-turned-straight. Many

of us experience ourselves *between* rather than *within* existing categories of identification.

As part of this process, "coming out" may be losing its appeal as the guiding narrative of lesbian self-development. The coming out story may no longer be the central narrative of lesbian existence. Bonnie Zimmerman notes that lesbian writers today, as opposed to twenty years ago, have a different focus: "How I came out—how I discovered my real self—no longer engages our attention. We are out, and it's time to get on with our lives."[28] Coming out was once seen as a linear, developmental, goal-driven process, but today it is more likely to be conceptualized as an ongoing, dynamic social interaction, a process of self-creation that is both collective and individual, a "becoming" rather than a "coming out."[29] This decentered model of identity formation mirrors the decentering of lesbian culture and communities, making it possible for us to imagine lesbian identities and communities that are more inclusive, less demanding, less confining, and more able to satisfy our desires for choice and autonomy.

If we understand the permanently unsettled nature of identities and group boundaries, we will be less apt to see this decentering as a sign that the lesbian feminist project has failed. Indeed, it may present new democratic potential. Many women who felt excluded by totalizing conceptions of lesbian identity may find that they can finally participate on their own terms. For example, those who experience their sexuality as fluid may claim lesbian identifications or not, as they find such identifications useful. Women who choose to move from homosexuality to heterosexuality (and back again, perhaps) may not experience that move as quite so threatening to their sense of self.

Sexual identities are fictions. But they are, as Jeffrey Weeks puts it, "necessary fictions." Lesbianism is now conceived as a collective and increasingly public basis of identity. Today, its emerging forms are broadening the range of possibilities for women. The future will undoubtedly bring yet new and different possibilities.

NOTES

1. Rob Morse, editorial, *San Francisco Examiner,* 12 November 1991, p. A3. For similar trends in other cities, see Kelly Harmon and Cindy Kirschman, "Women Behind Bars: Lesbians Lock Horns over the Changing Generational Face of the Lesbian Bar Business," *Advocate,* 31 December 1991, pp. 36–38.

2. This derives from Stuart Hall's work on Black identities (1989).

3. Nancy Chodorow, "Seventies Questions for Thirties Women," in Chodorow 1989, 217.

4. In the early 1990s, a few women were able to "cross over" and achieve mainstream success as out lesbians, integrating their sexuality into their art without allowing it to become either *the* salient fact or else barely acknowledged. k. d. lang and Melissa Etheridge, who had previously coded their sexuality as "androgyny," came out as lesbians, to great fanfare within lesbain/gay circles and to even greater commercial success. On the phenomenon of the "crossover" artist in popular music, see my "Crossover Dreams: Lesbianism and Popular Music since the 1970s" (Stein 1994).

5. For a more detailed explanation of the political implications of this mainstreaming, see Stein 1994. On the recent commodification of lesbian culture, see Clark 1993.

6. For a longer version of this argument, see Stein 1992a.

7. On queer theory and politics, see Allan Bérubé and Jeffrey Escoffier, "Queer/Nation," *Outlook,* Winter 1991, pp. 12–14; Duggan 1992; Fuss 1991; Hark 1994.

8. Seidman 1993, 122.

9. Butler 1990.

10. Gamson 1995.

11. Phelan 1994, 153.

12. Seidman 1993, 133.

13. Warner 1991, 16

14. On the checkered history of recent queer organizing, see Dan Levy, "Queer Nation in S.F. Suspends Activities," *San Francisco Chronicle,* 27 December 1991, p. 21; Michele DeRanleau, "How the Conscience of an Epidemic Unraveled," *San Francisco Examiner,* 1 October 1990, p. 24.

15. For a discussion of postfeminism that articulates this sense of continuity along with change, see Stacey 1990. As Mannheim [1928] 1952 suggests, the transition from one generation to another takes place continuously, through interaction between the two.

16. Martha Shelley, interview with author, 1990.

17. Weeks, 1985, 186.

18. Barbara Ehrenreich, quoted in the *Guardian* (U.K.), 4 May 1993, p. 5. See also de Lauretis 1991.

19. Weeks 1985, 186.

20. Giddens 1991.

21. Bérubé and Escoffier, "Queer/Nation," p. 14.

22. Gamson 1995, 20.

23. Martin 1992, 100.

24. On recent right-wing challenges to lesbian/gay rights, see Patton 1993; S. Johnston 1994.

25. Cerullo 1987, 71.

26. This is close to Stuart Hall's (1989) conception. Similarly, North American feminists have drawn upon the vocabulary of poststructralism to problematize any simple notion of the category "woman" or "woman's experience" as the point of departure for late-twentieth-century sexual politics. See, for example, Scott 1989; Butler 1990.

27. Phelan 1994, 11.

28. Zimmerman 1990, 210.

29. Phelan 1994. Perhaps what is needed, as Rust 1993 suggests, is a social constructionism that "allows for the possibility that individuals who are creating their identities will introduce their own goals" (71). Identity is here conceptualized as more open-ended and evolving, not as "what is, only what is becoming," and often as situational (Cass 1984, 120). Psychoanalytic support for this view is offered by Schafer 1973, who argues that "empirically self-sameness is usually a rather inconstant idea in that it can change markedly in content with a significant change in mood and circumstance" and that in part it changes because one views oneself and one's identity at different times, for different reasons, and from different vantage points (52); see also Lacan 1982, who restores to prominence the Freud who discovered the bisexuality and polymorphous perversity of children, emphasizing that repressed versions remain in the unconscious and constantly destabilize the ego's wish to keep these lost possibilities at bay.

23

"Americans Have a Different Attitude"

Family, Sexuality, and Gender in Filipina American Lives

YEN LE ESPIRITU

I want my daughters to be Filipino especially on sex. I always emphasize to them that they should not participate in sex if they are not married. We are also Catholic. We are raised so that we don't engage in going out with men while we are not married. And I don't like it to happen to my daughters as if they have no values. I don't like them to grow up that way, like the American girls.

Filipina immigrant mother

I found that a lot of the Asian American friends of mine, we don't date like White girls date. We don't sleep around like White girls do. Everyone is really mellow at dating because your parents were constraining and restrictive.

Second generation Filipina daughter

Drawing from my research on Filipino American families in San Diego, California, this paper explores the ways in which racialized immigrants claim through gender the power denied them through racism. Gender shapes immigrant identity and allows racialized immigrants to assert cultural superiority over the dominant group. For Filipino immigrants who come from a homeland that was once a U.S. colony, cultural reconstruction has been a way to counter the cultural Americanization of the Philippines, to resist the assimilative and alienating demands of U.S. society, and to re-

affirm to themselves their self-worth in the face of colonial, racial, and gendered subordination.

The opening narratives above, made by a Filipina immigrant mother and a second generation Filipina daughter, suggest that the virtuous Filipina daughter is partially constructed on the conceptualization of white women as sexually immoral. They also reveal the ways in which women's sexuality—and their enforced "morality"—is fundamental to the structuring of social inequalities. Historically, the sexuality of racialized women has been systematically demonized and denigrated by dominant or oppressor groups to justify and bolster nationalist movements, colonialism, and/or racism. But as the above narratives indicate, racialized groups also castigate the morality of white women as a strategy of resistance—a means to assert a morally superior public face to the dominant society. But this strategy is not without costs. The elevation of Filipina chastity (particularly that of young women) has the effect of reinforcing masculinist and patriarchal power in the name of a greater ideal of national/ethnic self-respect. Because the control of women is one of the principal means of asserting moral superiority, young women in immigrant families face numerous restrictions on their autonomy, mobility, and personal decision making.

STUDYING FILIPINOS IN SAN DIEGO

The information on which this article is based come mostly from original research: in-depth interviews that I conducted with about one hundred Filipinos in San Diego. As in other Filipino communities along the Pacific Coast, the San Diego community grew dramatically in the twenty-five years following passage of the 1965 Immigration Act. In 1990, there were close to 96,000 Filipinos in San Diego County. Although they comprised only 4 percent of the county's general population, they constituted close to 50 percent of the Asian American population (Espiritu 1995). Many post-1965 Filipinos have come to San Diego as professionals—most conspicuously as health care workers. A 1992 analysis of the socio-economic characteristics of recent Filipino immigrants in San Diego indicated that they were predominantly middle class, college-educated, and English-speaking professionals who were much more likely to own rather than rent their homes (Rumbaut 1994).

Using the "snowball" sampling technique, I started by interviewing Filipino Americans whom I knew and then asking them to refer me to others who might be willing to be interviewed. In other words, I chose participants not randomly but rather through a network of Filipino American contacts whom the first group of respondents trusted. To capture as much as possible the diversity within the Filipino American community, I sought and selected respondents of different backgrounds and with diverse viewpoints. The interviews, tape-recorded in English, ranged from three to ten hours each and took place in offices, coffee shops, and homes. My questions were open-ended and covered three general areas: family and immigration history, ethnic identity and practices, and community development among San Diego's Filipinos. The interviewing process varied widely: some respondents needed to be prompted with specific questions, while others spoke at great length on their own. Some chose to cover the span of their lives; others focused on specific events that were particularly important to them.

CONSTRUCTING THE DOMINANT GROUP: THE MORAL FLAWS OF WHITE AMERICANS

In this section, I argue that female morality—defined as women's dedication to their families and sexual restraints—is one of the few sites where economically and politically dominated groups can construct the dominant group as "other" and themselves as superior. Because womanhood is idealized as the repository of tradition, the norms which regulate women's behaviors become a means of determining and defining group status and boundaries. As a consequence, the burdens and complexities of cultural (re)presentation fall most heavily on immigrant women and their daughters. Below, I show that Filipino immigrants claim moral distinctiveness for their community by (re)presenting "Americans" as morally flawed and themselves as family-oriented model minorities and their wives and daughters as paragons of morality.

Family-Oriented Model Minorities: "White Women Will Leave You…"

Many of my respondents constructed their "ethnic" culture as principled and the "American" culture as deviant. Most often, this morality narrative revolves around family life and family relations. When asked what set Filipinos apart from other Americans, my respondents—of all ages and class backgrounds—repeatedly contrasted the close-knit Filipino families to what they perceived to be the more impersonal quality of U.S. family relations. In the following narratives, "Americans" are characterized as lacking in strong family ties and collective identity, less willing to do the work of family and cultural maintenance, and less willing to abide by patriarchal norms in husband/wife relations:

> Our [Filipino] culture is different. We are more close-knit. We tend to help one another. Americans, ya know, they are all right, but they don't help each other that much. As a matter of fact, if the parents are old, they take them to a convalescent home and let them rot there. We would never

do that in our culture. We would nurse them; we would help them until the very end (Filipino immigrant, 60 years old).

Our (Filipino) culture is very communal. You know that your family will always be there, that you don't have to work when you turn 18, you don't have to pay rent when you are 18, which is the American way of thinking. You also know that if things don't work out in the outside world, you can always come home and mommy and daddy will always take you and your children in (second generation Filipina, 33 years old).

Asian parents take care of their children. Americans have a different attitude. They leave their children to their own resources. They get baby sitters to take care of their children or leave them in day care. That's why when they get old, their children don't even care about them (Filipina immigrant, 46 years old).

Implicit in the negative depiction of U.S. families—as uncaring, selfish, and distant—is the allegation that White women are not as dedicated to their families as Filipina women. Several Filipino men who married White women recalled being warned by their parents and relatives that white women will leave you." As one man related, "My mother said to me, 'Well, you know, don't marry a White person because they would take everything that you own and leave you.'" For some Filipino men, perceived differences in attitudes about women's roles between Filipina and non-Filipina women influenced their marital choice. A Filipino American navy man explained why he went back to the Philippines to look for a wife:

My goal was to marry a Filipina. I requested to be stationed in the Philippines to get married to a Filipina. I'd seen the women here and basically they are spoiled. They have a tendency of not going along together with their husband. They behave differently. They chase the male, instead of the male, the normal way of the traditional way is for the male to go after the female. They have sex without marrying. They want to do their own things. So my idea was to go back home and marry somebody who has never been here. I tell my son

the same thing: if he does what I did and finds himself a good lady there, he will be in good hands.

Another man who had dated mostly White women in high school recounted that when it came time for him to marry, he "looked for the kind of women that I'd met in the Philippines."

It is important to note the gender implications of these claims. That is, while both men and women identify the family system as a tremendous source of cultural pride, it is women—through their unpaid housework and kin work—who shoulder the primary responsibility for maintaining family closeness. Because the moral status of the community rests on women's labor, women, as wives and daughters, are not only applauded for but are expected to dedicate themselves to the family. Writing on the constructed image of ethnic family and gender, di Leonardo (1984) reminds us that "a large part of stressing ethnic identity amounts to burdening women with increased responsibilities for preparing special foods, planning rituals, and enforcing 'ethnic' socialization of children" (p. 222). A twenty-three-year-old Filipina spoke about the reproductive work that her mother performed and expected her to learn:

In my family, I was the only girl, so my mom expected a lot from me. She wanted me to help her to take care of the household. I felt like there was a lot of pressure on me. It's very important to my mom to have the house in order: to wash the dishes, to keep the kitchen in order, vacuuming, and dusting and things like that. She wants me to be a perfect housewife. It's difficult. I have been married now for about four months and my mother asks me every now and then what have I cooked for my husband. My mom is also very strict about families getting together on holidays and I would always help her to organize that. Each holiday, I would try to decorate the house for her, to make it more special.

The burden of unpaid reproductive and kin work is particularly stressful for women who work outside the home. In the following narrative, a Filipina wife and mother described the pulls of family and work that she experienced when she went back to school to pursue a doctoral degree in nursing:

> The Filipinos, we are very collective, very connected. Going through the doctoral program, sometimes I think it is better just to forget about my relatives and just concentrate on school. All that connectedness, it steals parts of myself because all of my energies are devoted to my family. And that is the reason why I think Americans are successful. The majority of the American people they can do what they want. They don't feel guilty because they only have a few people to relate to. For us Filipinos, it's like roots under the tree, you have all these connections. The Americans are more like the trunk. I am still trying to go up to the trunk of the tree but it is too hard. I want to be more independent, more like the Americans.

It is important to note that this Filipina interprets her exclusion and added responsibilities as only racial when they are largely gendered. For example, when she says, "the American people they can do what they want," she ignores the differences in the lives of white men and white women—the fact that most white women experience similar pulls of family, education, and work.

Racialized Sexuality and (Im)morality: "In America…Sex Is Nothing"

Sexuality, as a core aspect of social identity, is fundamental to the structuring of gender inequality (Millett 1970). Sexuality is also a salient marker of Otherness and has figured prominently in racist and imperialist ideologies (Gilman 1985; Stoler 1991). Filipinas—both in the Philippines and in the United States—have been marked as desirable but dangerous "prostitutes" and/or submissive "mail order brides" (Halualani 1995; Egan 1996). These stereotypes emerged out of the colonial process, especially the extensive U.S. military presence in the Philippines. Until the early 1990s, the Philippines housed—at times unwillingly—some of the United States' largest overseas airforce and naval bases (Espiritu 1995, 14). Many Filipino nationalists have charged that "the prostitution problem" in the Philippines

stemmed from U.S. and Philippine government policies that promoted a sex industry—brothels, bars, massage parlors—for servicemen stationed or on leave in the Philippines (Coronel and Rosca 1993; Warren 1993). In this context, *all* Filipinas were racialized to be sexual commodities, usable and expendable. The sexualized racialization of Filipina women is captured in Marianne Villanueva's short story "Opportunity" (1991). As the protagonist Nina, a "mail order bride" from the Philippines, enters the lobby to meet her American fiancé, the bellboys snicker and whisper *puta*, whore: a reminder that U.S. economic and cultural colonization of the Philippines always forms a backdrop to any relations between Filipinos and Americans (Wong 1993, 53).

In an effort to counter the pervasive hypersexualization of Filipina women, many of my respondents constructed American society—and white American women in particular—to be much more sexually promiscuous than Filipino. In the following narrative, a mother who came to the United States in her thirties contrasted the controlled sexuality of Filipinas in the Philippines with the perceived promiscuity of White women in the United States:

> In the Philippines, we always have chaperons when we go out. When we go to dances, we have our uncle, our grandfather, and auntie all behind us to make sure that we behave in the dance hall. Nobody goes necking outside. You don't even let a man put his hand on your shoulders. When you were brought up in a conservative country, it is hard to come here and see that it is all freedom of speech and freedom of action. Sex was never mentioned in our generation. I was thirty already when I learned about sex. But to the young generation in America, sex is nothing.

Similarly, another immigrant woman criticized the way young American women are raised, "Americans are so liberated. They allow their children, their girls, to go out even when they are still so young." In contrast, she stated that "the Filipino way, it is very important, the value of the woman, that she is a virgin when she gets married."

In this section on the "moral flaws of White Americans," I have suggested that the ideal "Filipina" is partially constructed on the community's conceptualization of White women. The former was everything which the latter was not: the one was sexually modest and dedicated to her family; the other sexually promiscuous and uncaring. Embodying the moral integrity of the idealized ethnic community, immigrant women, particularly young daughters, are expected to comply with male-defined criteria of what constitutes "ideal" feminine virtues. While the sexual behavior of adult women is confined to a monogamous and heterosexual context, that of young women is denied completely (c.f. Dasgupta and DasGupta 1996, 229–231). In the next section, I detail the ways in which Filipino immigrant parents, under the rubric of "cultural preservation," police their daughters' behaviors in order to safeguard their sexual innocence and virginity.

THE CONSTRUCTION(S) OF THE "IDEAL" FILIPINA: "BOYS ARE BOYS AND GIRLS ARE DIFFERENT..."

As the designated "keepers of the culture" (Billson 1995), the behaviors of immigrant women come under intensive scrutiny from both women and men of their own groups and from U.S.-born Americans (Gabbacia 1994, xi). In a study of the Italian Harlem community, 1880–1950, Robert Anthony Orsi (1985, 135), reports that "all the community's fears for the reputation and integrity of the domus came to focus on the behavior of young women." Because women's moral and sexual loyalties were deemed central to the maintenance of group status, changes in female behavior, especially of growing daughters, were interpreted as signs of moral decay and ethnic suicide, and were carefully monitored and sanctioned (Gabbacia 1994, 113).

Although immigrant families have always been preoccupied with passing on culture, language, and traditions to both male and female children, it is daughters who have the unequal burden of protecting and preserving the family name. Because sons do not have to conform to the image of an "ideal" ethnic subject as daughters do, they often receive special day-to-day privileges denied to daughters (Waters 1996, 75–76; Haddad and Smith 1996, 22–24). This is not to say that immigrant parents do not place undue expectations on their sons; it is rather that these expectations do not pivot around the sons' sexuality or dating choices. In contrast, parental control over the movement and action of daughters begins the moment she is perceived as a young adult and sexually vulnerable. It regularly consists of monitoring her whereabouts and rejecting dating (Wolf 1997). For example, the immigrant parents I interviewed seldom allowed their daughters to date, to stay out late, to spend the night at a friend's house, or to take an out-of-town trip.

Many of the second generation women I spoke to complained bitterly about these parental restrictions. They particularly resent what they see as gender inequity in their families: the fact that their parents place far more restrictions on their activities and movements than on their brothers. Some decried the fact that even their *younger* brothers had more freedom than they did: "It was really hard growing up because my parents would let my younger brothers do what they wanted but I didn't get to do what I wanted even though I was the oldest. I had a curfew and my brothers didn't. I had to ask if I could go places and they didn't. My parents never even asked my brothers when they were coming home."

When questioned about this "double standard," parents responded by pointing to the fact that "girls are different:"

> I have that Filipino mentality that boys are boys and girls are different. Girls are supposed to be protected, to be clean. In the early years, my daughters have to have chaperons and curfews. And they know that they have to be virgins until they get married. The girls always say that is not fair. What is the difference between their brothers and them? And my answer always is, "In the Philippines, you know, we don't do that. The girls stay

home. The boys go out." It was the way that I was raised. I still want to have part of that culture instilled in my children. And I want them to have that to pass on to their children.

Even among self-described western-educated and "tolerant" parents, many continue to ascribe to "the Filipino way" when it comes to raising daughters. As one college-educated father explains:

Because of my Western education, I don't raise my children the way my parents raised me. I tended to be a little more tolerant. But at times, especially in certain issues like dating, I find myself more towards the Filipino way in the sense that I have only one daughter so I tended to be a little bit stricter. So the double standard kind of operates: it's alright for the boys to explore the field but I tended to be overly protective of my daughter. My wife feels the same way because the boys will not lose anything, but the daughter will lose something, their virginity, and it can be also a question of losing face, that kind of thing.

Although many parents generally discourage dating or forbid their daughters to date, they still fully expect these young women to fulfill their traditional roles as women: to get married and have children. A young Filipina recounted the mixed messages she received from her parents:

This is the way it is supposed to work. Okay, you go to school. You go to college. You graduate. You find a job. Then you find your husband, and you have children. That's the whole time line. But my question is, if you are not allowed to date, how are you supposed to find your husband? They say "no" to the whole dating scene because that is secondary to your education, secondary to your family. They do push marriage, but at a later date. So basically my parents are telling me that I should get married and I should have children but that I should not date.

The restrictions on girls' movement sometimes spill over to the realms of academics. Dasgupta and DasGupta (1996, 230) recount that in the Indian American community, while young men were expected to attend faraway competitive colleges, many of her female peers were encour-

aged by their parents to go to the local colleges so that they could live at or close to home. Similarly, Wolf (1997, 467) reports that some Filipino parents pursued contradictory tactics with their children's, particularly their daughters', education by pushing them to achieve academic excellence in high school, but then "pulling the emergency brake" when they contemplated college by expecting them to stay at home, even if it means going to a less competitive college, if at all.

The above narratives suggest that the process of parenting is gendered in that immigrant parents tend to restrict the autonomy, mobility, and personal decision making of their daughters more so than of their sons. I argue that these parental restrictions are attempts to construct a model of Filipina womanhood that is chaste, modest, nurturing, and family-oriented. This is not to say that parent-daughter conflicts exist in all Filipino immigrant families. Certainly, Filipino parents do not respond in a uniform way to the challenges of being racial-ethnic minorities. I met parents who have had to change some of their ideas and practices in response to their inability to control their children's movements and choices:

I have three girls and one boy. I used to think that I wouldn't allow my daughters to go dating and things like that, but there is no way I could do that. I can't stop it. It's the way of life here in America. Sometimes you kind of question yourself, if you are doing what is right. It is hard to accept but you got to accept it. That's the way they are here.

My children are born and raised here, so they do pretty much what they want. They think they know everything. I can only do so much as a parent.... When I try to teach my kids things, they tell me that I sound like an old record. They even talk back to me sometimes....

These narratives, made by a professional Filipino immigrant father and a working-class Filipino immigrant mother respectively, call attention to the shifts in the generational power caused by the migration process and to the possible gap between what parents say they want for their children and their ability to control the young. On the other hand, the interview data do suggest that intergenerational conflicts are socially recognized occurrences in the Filipino community(ies). Even when respondents themselves had not experienced intergenerational tensions, they could always recall a cousin, a girlfriend, or a friend's daughter who had.

SANCTIONS AND REACTIONS: "THAT IS NOT WHAT A DECENT FILIPINO GIRL SHOULD DO…"

I do not wish to suggest that immigrant communities are the only ones who regulate their daughter's mobility and sexuality. Feminist scholars have long documented the construction, containment, and exploitation of women's sexuality in various societies (Maglin and Perry 1996). We also know that the cultural anxiety over unbounded female sexuality is most apparent with regard to adolescent girls (Tolman and Higgins 1996, 206). The difference, I believe, is in the ways that immigrant and non-immigrant families sanction girls' sexuality. Non-immigrant parents rely on the gender-based good girl/bad girl dichotomy to control sexually assertive girls (Tolman and Higgins 1996, 206). In the dominant cultural accounts of women's sexuality, "good girls" are passive, threatened sexual objects while "bad girls" are active, desiring sexual agents (Tolman and Higgins 1996). As Dasgupta and DasGupta write (1996, 236), "the two most pervasive images of women across cultures are the goddess and whore, the good and bad women." This good girl/bad girl cultural story conflates femininity with sexuality, increases women's vulnerability to sexual coercion, and justifies women's containment in the domestic sphere.

Immigrant families, on the other hand, have an extra disciplining mechanism: they can discipline their daughters as racial/national subjects as well as gendered ones. That is, as self-appointed guardians of "authentic" cultural memory, immigrant parents can opt to regulate their daughters' independent choices by linking them to cultural ignorance or betrayal. As both parents and children recounted, young women who disobeyed parental strictures were often branded "non-ethnic," "untraditional," "radical," "selfish," and not "caring about the family." Parents were also quick to warn their daughters about "bad" Filipinas who had gotten pregnant outside of marriage. Filipina Americans who veered from acceptable behaviors were deemed "Americanized"—women who have adopted the sexual mores and practices of white women. As one Filipino immigrant father described the "Americanized" Filipinas: "They are spoiled because they have seen the American way. They go out at night. Late at night. They go out on dates. Smoking. They have sex without marrying."

From the perspective of the second generation daughters, these charges are stinging. Largely unacquainted with the "home" country, U.S.-born children depend on their parents' tutelage to craft and affirm their ethnic self and thus are particularly vulnerable to charges of cultural ignorance or betrayal (Espiritu, 1994). The young women I interviewed were visibly pained—with many breaking down and crying—when they recounted their parents' charges. This deep pain—stemming in part from their desire to be validated as Filipina—existed even among the more "rebellious" daughters. As a 24-year-old daughter explained:

> My mom is very traditional. She wants to follow the Filipino customs, just really adhere to them, like what is proper for a girl, what she can and can't do, and what other people are going to think of her if she doesn't follow that way. When I pushed these restrictions, when I rebelled and stayed out later than allowed, my mom would always say, "That is not what a decent Filipino girl should do. You should come home at a decent hour. What are people going to think of you?" And that would get me really upset, you know, because I think that my character is very much the way it should be for a Filipina. I wear my hair long, I wear decent make-up. I dress properly, conservative. I am family oriented. It hurts me that she doesn't see that I am decent, that I am proper and that I am not going to bring shame to the family or anything like that.

This narrative suggests that even when parents are unable to control the behaviors of their children, their (dis)approval remained strong and powerful in shaping the emotional lives of their daughters (see Wolf 1997). Although better-off parents can and do exert greater controls over their children's behaviors than poorer parents (Wolf 1992; Kibria 1993), I would argue that *all* immigrant parents—regardless of class backgrounds—possess this emotional hold on their children. Therein lies the source of their power.

These emotional pains withstanding, many young Filipinas I interviewed contest and negotiate parental restrictions in their daily lives. Faced with parental restrictions on their mobility, young Filipinas struggle to gain some control over their own social lives, particularly over dating. In many cases, daughters simply misinform their parents of their whereabouts or date without their parents' knowledge. They also rebel by vowing to create more egalitarian relationships with their own husbands and children. A thirty-year-old Filipina who is married to a white American explained why she chose to marry outside her culture:

> In high school, I dated mostly Mexican and Filipino. It never occurred to me to date a white or black guy. I was not attracted to them. But as I kept growing up and my father and I were having all these conflicts, I knew that if I married a Mexican or a Filipino, they would be exactly like my father. And so I tried to date anyone that would not remind me of my dad. A lot of my Filipina friends that I grew up with had similar experiences. So I knew that it wasn't only me. I was determined to marry a white person because he would treat me as an individual.

Another Filipina who was labeled "radical" by her parents indicated that she would be more open-minded in raising her own children: "I see myself as very traditional in upbringing but I don't see myself as constricting on my children one day and I wouldn't put the gender roles on them. I wouldn't lock them into any particular way of behaving." It is important to note that even as these Filipinas desired new gender norms and practices

for their own families, the majority hoped that their children would remain connected to the Filipino culture. My respondents also reported more serious reactions to parental restrictions, recalling incidents of someone they knew who had run away, joined gangs, or attempted suicide.

CONCLUSION

In this paper, I have shown that many Filipino immigrants use the largely gendered discourse of morality as one strategy to decenter whiteness and to locate themselves above the dominant group, demonizing it in the process. Like other immigrant groups, Filipinos praise the United States as a land of significant economic opportunity but simultaneously denounce it as a country inhabited by corrupted and individualistic people of questionable morals. In particular, they criticize American family life, American individualism, and American women (c.f. Gabbacia, 1994, 113). Enforced by distorting powers of memory and nostalgia, this rhetoric of moral superiority often leads to patriarchal calls for cultural "authenticity" which locates family honor and national integrity in its female members. Because the policing of women's bodies is one of the main means of asserting moral superiority, young women face numerous restrictions on their autonomy, mobility, and personal decision making. This practice of cultural (re)construction reveals how deeply the conduct of private life can be tied to larger social structures.

The construction of White Americans as the "other" and American culture as deviant serves a dual purpose: It allows immigrant communities to reinforce patriarchy through the sanctioning of women's (mis)behavior *and* to present an unblemished, if not morally superior, public face to the dominant society. Strong in family values, heterosexual morality, and a hierarchical family structure, this public face erases the Filipina "bad girl" and ignores competing (im)moral practices in the Filipino communities. Through the oppression of Filipina women and the castigation of White women's morality, the immigrant community attempts to exert its moral superiority over the dominant Western culture and to reaffirm to itself its self-worth in the face of economic, social, political, and legal subordination. In other words, the immigrant community uses restrictions on women's lives as one form of resistance to racism. Though significant, this form of cultural resistance severely restricts women's lives, particularly those of the second generation, and casts the family as a site of potentially the most intense conflict and oppressive demands in immigrant lives.

REFERENCES

Billson, Janet Mancini. 1995. *Keepers of the Culture: The Power of Tradition in Women's Lives.* New York: Lexington Books.

Coronel, Sheila and Ninotchka Rosca. 1993. "For the Boys: Filipinas Expose Years of Sexual Slavery by the U.S. and Japan." *Ms.,* November/December p. 11+.

Dasgupta, Shamita Das and DasGupta, Sayantani. 1996. "Public Face, Private Face: Asian Indian Women and Sexuality." Pp. 226–243 in *Women, Sex, and Power in the Nineties,* edited by Nan Bauer Maglin and Donna Perry. New Brunswick, NJ: Rutgers University Press.

Di Leonardo, Micaela. 1984. *The Varieties of Ethnic Experience: Kinship, Class, and Gender among California Italian-Americans.* Ithaca and London: Cornell University Press.

Eastmond, Marita. 1993. "Reconstructing Life: Chilean Refugee Women and the Dilemmas of Exile." Pp. 35–53 in *Migrant Women: Crossing Boundaries and Changing Identities,* edited by Gina Buijs. Oxford: Berg.

Egan, Timothy. 1996. "Mail-Order Marriage, Immigrant Dreams and Death." *New York Times,* 26 May, p. 12+.

Espiritu, Yen Le. 1994. "The Intersection of Race, Ethnicity, and Class: The Multiple Identities of Second Generation Filipinos." *Identities* 1(2–3): 249–273.

———. 1995. *Filipino American Lives.* Philadelphia: Temple University Press.

Gabbacia, Donna. 1994. *From the Other Side: Women, Gender, and Immigrant Life in the U.S., 1820–1990.* Bloomington and Indianapolis: Indiana University Press.

Gilman, Sander L. 1985. *Difference and Pathology: Stereotypes of Sexuality, Race, and Madness.* Ithaca: Cornell University Press.

Haddad Yvonne Y. and Jane I. Smith. 1996. "Islamic Values among American Muslims." Pp. 19–40 in *Family and Gender among American Muslims: Issues Facing Middle Eastern Immigrants and Their Descendants,* edited by Barbara C. Aswad and Barbara Bilge. Philadelphia: Temple University Press.

Halualani, Rona Tamiko. 1995. "The Intersecting Hegemonic Discourses of an Asian Mail-Order Bride Catalog: Philipina 'Oriental Butterfly' Dolls for Sale." *Women's Studies in Communication* 18(1): 45–64.

Kibria, Nazli. 1993. *Family Tightrope: The Changing Lives of Vietnamese Immigrant Community.* Princeton, NJ: Princeton University Press.

Maglin, Nan Bauer and Donna Perry. 1996. "Introduction." Pp. xiii–xxvi in *"Bad Girls/Good Girls": Women, Sex, and Power in the Nineties,* edited by Nan Bauer Maglin and Donna Perry.

Millet, Kate. 1970. *Sexual Politics.* Garden City, NY: Doubleday.

Rumbaut, Ruben. 1994. "The Crucible Within: Ethnic Identity, Self-Esteem, and Segmented Assimilation Among Children of Immigrants." *International Migration Review,* 28(4):748–794.

Stoler, Ann Laura. 1991. "Carnal Knowledge and Imperial Power: Gender, Race, and Morality in Colonial Asia." Pp. 51–101 in *Gender at the Crossroads of Knowledge: Feminist Anthropology in the Postmodern Era,* edited by Micaela di Leonardo. Berkeley: University of California Press.

Tolman, Deborah L. and Tracy E. Higgins. 1996. "How Being a Good Girl Can Be Bad for Girls." Pp. 205–225 in *"Bad Girls/Good Girls": Women, Sex, and Power in the Nineties,* edited by Nan Bauer Maglin and Donna Perry. New Brunswick, NJ: Rutgers University Press.

Villanueva, Marianne. 1991. *Ginseng and Other Tales from Manila.* Corvallis, OR: Calyx.

Warren, Jenifer. 1993. "Suit Asks Navy to Aid Children Left in Philippines." *Los Angeles Times,* 5 March, p. A3+.

Waters, Mary C. 1996. "The Intersection of Gender, Race, and Ethnicity in Identity Development of Caribbean American Teens." Pp. 65–81 in *Urban Girls: Resisting Stereotypes, Creating Identities,* edited by Bonnie J. Ross Leadbeater and Niobe Way. New York and London: New York University Press.

Wolf, Diane L. 1992. *Factory Daughters: Gender, Household Dynamics, and Rural Industrialization in Java.* Berkeley: University of California Press.

———. 1997. "Family Secrets: Transnational Struggles among Children of Filipino Immigrants." *Sociological Perspectives* 40(3):457–482.

Wong, Sau-ling. 1993. *Reading Asian American Literature: From Necessity to Extravagance.* Princeton, NJ: Princeton.

PART FOUR

Identities

Our sense of who we are as women and men is not likely to remain the same over the span of our lives, but how are our identities formed and contested? How do our gendered identities change as they feed into our identities as members of religious groups, nations, or social movements? There is nothing automatic about identities. Identities are fluid rather than primordial, socially constructed rather than inherited, and they shift with changing social contexts. As the world grows more complex and interconnected, our identities, or self-definitions, respond to diverse, and sometimes competing, pulls and tugs.

Identities are both intensely private and vociferously public. Identities are also fundamentally about power and alliances. Racial-ethnic, religious, national, and sexual identities, for example, are at the core of today's social movements and political conflicts. Intertwined with these emergent and contested identities are strong ideas—stated or implicit—of what it is to be feminine and masculine. Most of the articles in this section rely on strong, first-person narratives as a vehicle to reflect how gender interacts with the creation and contestation of multifacted identities. Together, the authors suggest some of the ways that identities are actively shaped and defined in contradistinction to other identities, and to the ways in which identities are sometimes imposed from above, or resisted. In this view, identities involve a process of simultaneously defining and erasing difference, and of claiming and constructing spheres of autonomy.

Feminist identity neither falls from the sky, nor is it dictated from above. Rather, it emerges through struggle, and is likely to assume many different shapes and forms. In the first article, Slavenka Drakulic challenges some of the assumptions about Eastern European women and feminism made by a U.S. feminist. Drakulic suggests that feminist identities are cultivated through struggle, autonomy, and processes that include discussion and reflection, and she gives voice to all of those who have fought against the imposition of identity by outsiders, especially outsiders of privilege. Her reaction to a U.S. feminist's attempt to impose U.S. definitions of "women's issues" resonates with the experiences of many women of color and women from developing nations.

The following article, by Michael S. Kimmel, explores some of the connections between Jewish cultural traits, nonhegemonic masculinities, and oppositional identities of resistance. Jewish men, he argues, are typically seen as "too emotional," "too literate," as outsiders in a WASP-dominated world. Yet marginalized masculinities, to use R. W. Connell's term, may in fact encourage identities that challenge sexism and "any power that is illegitimately constituted."

As numerous commentators have pointed out elsewhere, there is no clear-cut correlation between behavior and identity. This point is probably best illustrated by the examples of homosexually active people who do not identity as gays or lesbians, and heterosexually active individuals who align themselves with gay and lesbian groups. The next article in the section considers some of the ways that sexuality interacts with feminist identity. Anastasia Higginbotham, a young feminist, narrates how feminism has prompted dramatic changes in the way she perceives her sexuality, and she discusses some of the implications of adopting bisexual identity. In all of these articles, gender emerges as both constitutive and responsive to racial-ethnic, national, sexual, and feminist identities.

Too often, racism is only recognized by looking at the disadvantaged. In her short, insightful piece, Peggy McIntosh illuminates the privileges accorded to Whites and to men in systems of race and gender relations. Her analysis of "white privilege as an invisible package of unearned assets" which can be cashed in daily is sure to provoke thoughtful discussion about the invisible markers of identity.

In the following article, the renowned scholar and public intellectual Manning Marable explores how Black men in America have struggled to define themselves outside of the arenas of negative stereotypes imposed on them by the dominant society. Slavery, institutionalized racism, and contemporary economic restructuring have distorted, he argues, the images and identities of Black men. Marable argues that Black men cannot fully challenge racial and gender inequalities without also challenging the negative myths and images imposed on them by others.

24

A Letter from the United States
The Critical Theory Approach

SLAVENKA DRAKULIC

"Dear Slavenka," her letter began; a two-page, single-spaced letter written on a computer. (By the way, I don't remember receiving a handwritten letter from the United States in the last couple of years.) *"I am writing to you about the interview I did with you in New York, in April, right after the Socialist Scholars' Conference (in a luncheonette near Gloria Steinem's apartment, if you remember)...."*

I remember—indeed I do. We were sitting on red plastic chairs, leaning over a plastic table, holding plastic cups with insipid American coffee, and B asked me about the position of women in Eastern Europe after the "velvet revolution." I also remember a kind of geographical map appearing in my mind: Poland, Czechoslovakia, East Germany, Hungary, Bulgaria, Romania, Yugoslavia too—we are talking about perhaps 70 million women there, living in different regions and cultures, speaking different languages, yet all reduced to a common denominator, the system they were living under.

It was after I spoke at the plenary session at that conference that B approached me. The big midtown auditorium at CUNY was almost filled. I was to give a paper on the same subject: women in Eastern Europe. But before I started my speech, I took out one sanitary napkin and one Tampax and, holding them high in the air, I showed them to the audience. "I have just come from Bulgaria," I said, "and believe me, women there don't have either napkins or Tampaxes—they never had them, in fact. Nor do women in Poland, or Czechoslovakia, much less in the Soviet Union or Romania.

This I hold as one of the proofs of why communism failed, because in the seventy years of its existence it couldn't fulfil the basic needs of half the population."

The audience were startled at first; they hadn't expected this, not at a scholarly conference where one could expect theories, analyses, conclusions—words, words, words. Then, people started applauding. For me, the sight of a sanitary napkin and a Tampax was a necessary precondition for understanding what we are talking about: not the generally known fact that women wait in long lines for food or that they don't have washing machines—one could read about this in *Time* or *Newsweek*—but that besides all the hardship of living in Eastern Europe, if they can't find gauze or absorbent cotton, they have to wash bloody cloth pads every month, again and again, as their mothers and grandmothers and great-grandmothers did hundreds of years ago. For them, communism has changed nothing in that respect.

But I wasn't sure that my audience grasped this fact, after all: first, because they were mostly men and, by some caprice of Mother Nature, men usually don't have to wash bloody cloth pads every month; second, because they were leftists. I know them, the American men (and women) of the left. Talking to them always makes me feel like the worst kind of dissident, a right-wing freak (or a Republican, at best), even if I consider myself an honest social democrat. For every mild criticism of life in the system I have been living under for the last forty years they look at me suspiciously, as if I were a CIA agent (while my folks, communists back home, never had any doubts about it—perhaps this is the key difference between Eastern and Western comrades?) But one can hardly blame them. It is not the knowledge about communism that they lack—I am quite sure they know all about it—it's the experience of living under such conditions. So, while I am speaking from "within" the system itself, they are explaining it to me from without. I do not want to claim that you have to be a hen to lay an egg, only that a certain disagreement between these two starting positions is normal. But they don't go for that; they need to be right. They see reality in schemes, in broad historical outlines, the same as their brothers in the East do. I love to hear their great speeches or read their long analyses after brief visits to our poor countries, where they meet with the best minds the establishment can offer (probably speaking English!). I love the way they get surprised or angry when the food is too greasy, there is no hot water in their hotel, they can't buy Alka Seltzer or aspirin, or their plane is late. But best of all I love the innocence of their questions. Sitting in that luncheonette on Seventy-fifth Street with B, I resented the questions she asked me, the way she asked them, as if she didn't understand that menstrual pads and Tampax are both a metaphor for the system and the reality of women living in Eastern Europe. Or as if she herself were not a woman—slim, tall, smart-looking and, surprisingly, dressed with style. Feeling the slick plastic cup in my hand, it came to my mind that her questions are like that—cold, artificial, slippery, not touching my reality.

"I am sorry to have taken so long to get in touch with you. I was in Berlin for a while this summer," the letter continued. *"I am doing a bigger project now on women and Eastern Europe—trying to put together an anthology on this topic. There is already a publisher who has expressed interest. I hope it will be more than a description of events, but some kind of analysis about women and democracy, the public sphere, civil society, modernization, etc. A kind of Critical Theory approach . . ."*

I picked up this letter from my mailbox on my way to the office (together with an American Express bill, which I didn't want to open right away because I knew it would upset me). "She spent several weeks in Berlin," I thought, reading it in the streetcar, "and here she is, making an anthology!" How easy, how incredibly easy it is for her; she even has an editor. Women in Eastern Europe hardly existed as a topic, especially for leftists. And now, what is wanted is no less than a Critical Theory approach! I admit this letter upset me much more than the American Express bill would have. Following her instructions, I am to write *"some article specifically on women in Yugoslavia, dealing with the kinds of interventions women have made in the public discourse, eg, about abortion, women's control over women's bodies, what sorts of influence women have had in the public discourse on these topics, and what sorts of influence the non-feminist media have had on women's issues now."*

Reading all this, I couldn't help laughing out loud. A few people turned their heads in surprise, but I didn't stop laughing. Women's influence in the public discourse? For God's sake, what does she mean? There is hardly any public discourse, except the one about politics. Women don't have any influence, they barely even have a voice. All media are non-feminist, there are no feminist media. All that we could talk about is the absence of influence, of voice, of debate, of a feminist movement. *"Do the women in Yugoslavia argue for an 'essentialism,' i.e., that women are different from men or is it a matter of choice?"* I read in her letter, with utter amazement. With each of her words, the United States receded further and further, almost disappearing from my horizon. Argue what? Argue where? Somehow, in spite of her good intentions, I felt trapped by this letter, the views she expressed in it, like a white mouse in an experimental laboratory. Sitting in her office at the university, with a shelf full of books on Marxism, feminism, or Critical Theory within reach, B asks me about discussion on *"essentialism"* in Yugoslavia. I can imagine her, in her worn-out jeans and fashionable T-shirt, with her trimmed black hair, looking younger than she is (aerobics, macrobiotics), sitting at her computer and typing this letter, these very words that—when I read them in a streetcar in Zagreb ten days later—sound so absurd that I laugh even more, as if I were reading some very good news. *"No, dear B, we don't discuss this matter,"* I will answer in my letter. *"It is not a matter of choice, it is simply not a matter at all, see? And I cannot answer your questions, because they are all wrong."*

But if she doesn't understand us, who will? What is the way to show her what our life—the life of women and feminists—looks like? Maybe instead of answers, I could offer her something else. Suppose that my mind is an album of myriads of pictures, photos, images, paintings, snapshots, collages. And suppose I could show her some of them...

It is the autumn of 1978 and eight of us are sitting in Rada's room on Victims of Fascism Square in Zagreb. It is a little chilly because a balcony door is open, but it has to be that way. Rada hates smoking and yet we all smoke in the excitement—even Rada herself. This is because we have just come back from Beograd, from the first international feminist conference, "Comrade Woman," where we met the well-known Western European feminists Alice Schwarzer, Christine Delphy, and Dacia Maraini for the first time. We thought they were too radical when they told us that they were harassed by men on our streets. We don't even notice it, we said. Or when they talked about wearing high-heeled shoes as a sign of women's subordination. We didn't see it quite like that; we wore such shoes and even loved them. I remember how we gossiped about their greasy hair, no bra, no make-up. But all that didn't stop us from deciding to form our own group, the first feminist group in Yugoslavia. We didn't know how to organize; it even seemed impossible. First we talked. Then we published some articles—nothing big, of course. In a matter of days we were attacked by the official women's organization, Women's Conference, by politicians, university professors, famous columnists—for importing foreign ideology.

So we discover that a feminist is not only a man-eater here, she is an enemy of the state. Some of us received threatening letters. Some got divorced, accused of neglecting their families. A maniac broke into my friend's apartment (convinced that he could understand her!); a writer wrote a porno story about two of us, feminists. Women themselves accused us of being elitist. A man wanted to chain me in the main square; someone spat on my door every night, for years. ...On the other hand, more and more women were joining in, attending our monthly meetings, participating in discussions, forming their own groups—a hundred, perhaps, at the beginning. But it was lonely being one of a few feminists twelve years ago. Sitting in Rada's room and making plans, it's good that we didn't know it then.

Twelve years later, when I was in Warsaw in 1990, Jola took me to another similar room. In fact, it looked like a replica of Rada's, even if this one was not in an ambassador's apartment, with original paintings, antiques, and Ming vases all around. It was in a skyscraper somewhere on the outskirts of town, but the atmosphere was the same: nine young women and their expectations. I ask them why they joined the group. One—a teacher, tall, married, no children—answers jokingly: "Because my husband always interrupts when I talk. It's hard to recognize discrimination when you live with it." They don't know how to organize yet, but they do know that feminism is about prejudices, about woman's self. Three of them had already participated in organizing the first demonstration against the anti-abortion law proposed in the Polish Parliament in May 1989. One came for the first time this very evening. When you think about feminism in Poland, you can count the women on your fingers: Ana, Malgorzata, Stanka, Barbara, Renata, people in this room. "You might laugh at us, but we *are* the Polish Feminist Union," says Jola. "It's hard. Women don't take the initiative here; they wait for somebody to solve their problems—that's very typical for Polish women."

That evening, in her apartment, still in Warsaw, Ana takes down a book from her shelf—a rather thick, ordinary paperback. It looks old, because it's worn out and somehow shabby. But it's not ordinary. I can tell by the way she handles it so carefully, like something unique. "This is the book I told you about," she says, holding out the *Anthology of Feminist Texts,* a collection of early American feminist essays, "the only feminist book translated into the Polish language," the only such book to turn to when you are sick and tired of reading about man-eater/man-killer feminists from the West, I think, looking at it, imagining how many women have read this one copy. "Sometimes I feel like I live on Jupiter, among Jupiterians, and then one day, quite by chance, I discover that I belong to another species. And I discover it in this book. Isn't that wonderful?"

She reminds me of Klara. In Klara's bedroom in Budapest there is a small shelf with about twenty such books. She has collected more because she is an English translator, and she travels to London from time to time. "I read these books when I'm tired and depressed from my everyday life, from the struggle to survive and keep my head above water in spite of everything. Then I just close the door—leaving my job, two kids, the high prices, outside, no men—and read Kate Millett, Betty Friedan, Susan Brownmiller. It's like reading science fiction, an escape from reality. It's so difficult to be a woman here."

I see that when I visit the novelist Erzsébet. She is a thin, quiet woman, and even though she has written four novels, she doesn't sound self-assured at all. We talk. Her husband—a journalist and novelist, too—sits there, drinking vodka and pretending he is not interested in a discussion about women in Hungary. "I'm lucky," she says. "I didn't have to work." When I ask her what she thinks of feminism, she pauses. "I don't understand what these women want," she responds, glancing shyly at her husband. At this point, he just can't stand it anymore. "You want to know

who, in my opinion, was the first feminist?" he asks me, as if his argument is so strong that it will persuade me forever against feminism, his face already red from vodka and barely concealed anger. "I'll tell you who she was—Sappho from Lesbos." I see Erzsébet blushing, nervously playing with her glass. But she doesn't utter a word.

In a dark, smoky writer's club in Sofia, Kristina sits opposite me. She looks disappointed. Her words are bitter as she tells me about a questionnaire she sent out some time ago. "I wrote a hundred letters, asking women if they think we need a feminist organization in Bulgaria. Everyone answered, yes, we do. But I also asked them whether they were prepared to join such an organization, and imagine, only ten out of a hundred women answered positively." I tell her about the eight of us in Zagreb, about Jola and her group in Warsaw, about Enikö and her group of thirty students in Szeged—the first feminist group in Hungary. They were seven at the beginning. "Ten women out of a hundred?" I say. "But I think you're doing splendidly." "You think so?" she says, cheering up a bit. "Then maybe it's worth trying."

"Dear B," I will write in my letter to the United States, *"we live surrounded by newly opened porno shops, porno magazines, peep-shows, stripteases, unemployment, and galloping poverty. In the press they call Budapest 'the city of love, the Bangkok of Eastern Europe.' Romanian women are prostituting themselves for a single dollar in towns on the Romanian-Yugoslav border. In the midst of all this, our anti-choice nationalist governments are threatening our right to abortion and telling us to multiply, to give birth to more Poles, Hungarians, Czechs, Croats, Slovaks. We are unprepared, confused, without organization or movement yet. Perhaps we are even afraid to call ourselves feminists. Many women here see the movement as a 'world without men,' a world of lesbians, that they don't understand and cannot accept. And we definitely don't have answers for you. A Critcal Theory approach? Maybe in ten years. In the meantime, why don't you try asking us something else?"*

25

Judaism, Masculinity, and Feminism

MICHAEL S. KIMMEL

In the late 1960s, I organized and participated in several large demonstrations against the war in Vietnam. Early on—it must have been 1967 or so—over 10,000 of us were marching down Fifth Avenue in New York urging the withdrawal of all U.S. troops. As we approached one corner, I noticed a small but vocal group of counter-demonstrators, waving American flags and shouting patriotic slogans. "Go back to Russia!" one yelled. Never being particularly shy, I tried to engage him. "It's my duty as an American to oppose policies I disagree with. This is patriotism!" I answered. "Drop dead, you commie Jew fag!" was his reply.

Although I tried not to show it, I was shaken by his accusation, perplexed and disturbed by the glib association of communism, Judaism, and homosexuality. "Only one out of three," I can say to myself now, "is not especially perceptive." But yet something disturbing remains about that linking of political, religious, and sexual orientations. What links them, I think, is a popular perception that each is not quite a man, that each is less than a man. And while recent developments may belie this simplistic formulation, there is, I believe, a kernel of truth to the epithet, a small piece I want to claim, not as vicious smear, but proudly. I believe that my Judaism did directly contribute to my activism against that terrible war, just as it currently provides the foundation for my participation in the struggle against sexism.

What I want to explore here are some of the ways in which my Jewishness has contributed to becoming an anti-sexist man, working to make this world a safe environment for women (and men) to fully express their humanness. Let me be clear that I speak from a cultural heritage of Eastern European Jewry, transmuted by three generations of life in the United States. I speak of the culture of Judaism's effect on me as an American Jew, not from either doctrinal considerations—we all know the theological contradictions of a biblical reverence for women, and prayers that thank God for not being born one—nor from an analysis of the politics of nation states. My perspective says nothing of Middle-Eastern machismo; I speak of Jewish culture in the diaspora, not of Israeli politics.

The historical experience of Jews has three elements that I believe have contributed to this participation in feminist politics. First, historically, the Jew is an *outsider*. Wherever the Jew has gone, he or she has been outside the seat of power, excluded from privilege. The Jew is the symbolic "other," not unlike the symbolic "otherness" of women, gays, racial and ethnic minorities, the elderly and the physically challenged. To be marginalized allows one to see the center more clearly than those who are in it, and presents grounds for alliances among marginal groups.

But the American Jew, the former immigrant, is "other" in another way, one common to many ethnic immigrants to the United States. Jewish culture is, after all, seen as an ethnic culture, which allows it to be more oppressive and emotionally rich than the bland norm. Like other ethnic subgroups, Jews have been characterized as emotional, nurturing, caring. Jewish men hug and kiss, cry and laugh. A little too much. A little too loudly. Like ethnics.

Historically, the Jewish man has been seen as less than masculine, often as a direct outgrowth of this emotional "respond-ability." The historical consequences of centuries of laws against Jews, of anti-Semitic oppression, are a cultural identity and even a self-perception as "less than men," who are too weak, too fragile, too frightened to care for our own. The cruel irony of ethnic oppression is that our rich heritage is stolen from us, and then we are blamed for having no rich heritage. In this, again, the Jew shares this self-perception with other oppressed groups who, rendered virtually helpless by an infantilizing oppression, are further victimized by the accusation that they are, in fact, infants and require the beneficence of the oppressor. One example of this cultural self-hatred can be found in the comments of Freud's colleague and friend Weininger (a Jew) who argued that "the Jew is saturated with femininity. The most feminine Aryan is more masculine than the most manly Jew. The Jew lacks the good breeding that is based upon respect for one's own individuality as well as the individuality of others."

But, again, Jews are also "less than men" for a specific reason as well. The traditional emphasis on literacy in Jewish culture contributes in a very special way. In my family, at least, to be learned, literate, a rabbi, was the highest aspiration one could possibly have. In a culture characterized by love of learning, literacy may be a mark of dignity. But currently in the United States literacy is a cultural liability. Americans contrast egghead intellectuals, divorced from the real world, with men of action—instinctual, passionate, fierce, and masculine. Senator Albert Beveridge of Indiana counseled in his 1906 volume *Young Man and the World* (a turn of the century version of *Real Men Don't Eat Quiche*) to "avoid books, in fact, avoid all artificial learning, for the forefathers put America on the right path by learning from completely natural experience." Family, church and synagogue, and schoolroom were cast as the enervating domains of women, sapping masculine vigor.

Now, don't get me wrong. The Jewish emphasis on literacy, on mind over body, does not ex-

empt Jewish men from sexist behavior. Far from it. While many Jewish men avoid the Scylla of a boisterous and physically harassing misogyny, we can often dash ourselves against the Charybdis of a male intellectual intimidation of others. "Men with the properly sanctioned educational credentials in our society," writes Harry Brod, "are trained to impose our opinions on others, whether asked for or not, with an air of supreme self-confidence and aggressive self-assurance." It's as if the world were only waiting for our word. In fact, Brod notes, "many of us have developed mannerisms that function to intimidate those customarily denied access to higher educational institutions, especially women."[1] And yet, despite this, the Jewish emphasis on literacy has branded us, in the eyes of the world, less than "real" men.

Finally, the historical experience of Jews centers around, hinges upon our sense of morality, our ethical imperatives. The preservation of a moral code, the commandment to live ethically, is the primary responsibility of each Jew, male or female. Here, let me relate another personal story. Like many other Jews, I grew up with the words "Never Again" ringing in my ears, branded indelibly in my consciousness. For me they implied a certain moral responsibility to bear witness, to remember—to place my body visibly on the side of justice. This moral responsibility inspired my participation in the anti-war movement, and my active resistance of the draft *as a Jew*. I remember family dinners in front of the CBS Evening News, watching Walter Cronkite recite the daily tragedy of the war in Vietnam. "Never again," I said to myself, crying myself to sleep after watching napalm fall on Vietnamese villagers. Isn't this the brutal terror we have sworn ourselves to preventing when we utter those two words? When I allowed myself to feel the pain of those people, there was no longer a choice; there was, instead, a moral imperative to speak out, to attempt to end that war as quickly as possible.

In the past few years, I've become aware of another war. I met and spoke with women who had been raped, raped by their lovers, husbands, and fathers, women who had been beaten by those husbands and lovers. Some were even Jewish women. All those same words—Never Again—flashed across my mind like a neon meteor lighting up the darkened consciousness. Hearing that pain and that anger prompted the same moral imperative. We Jews say "Never Again" to the systematic horror of the Holocaust, to the cruel war against the Vietnamese, to Central American death squads. And we must say it against this war waged against women in our society, against rape and battery.

So in a sense, I see my Judaism as reminding me every day of that moral responsibility, the *special* ethical imperative that my life, as a Jew, gives to me. Our history indicates how we have been excluded from power, but also, as men, we have been privileged by another power. Our Judaism impels us to stand against any power that is illegitimately constituted because we know only too well the consequences of that power. Our ethical vision demands equality and justice, and its achievement is our historical mission.

NOTE

[1] Harry Brod, "Justice and a Male Feminist" in *The Jewish Newspaper* (Los Angeles) June 6, 1985, p. 6.

26

Chicks Goin' at It

ANASTASIA HIGGINBOTHAM

Aside from the occasional dream of being chased by a man throwing hot dogs at me, I consider myself a fairly well-adjusted feminist. Yes, I sometimes imagine myself alone, late at night, surrounded by candles; the scent of incense fills the air as I scribble on little slips of paper, "Howard Stern—AWAY," while a small doll, cut off at the waist and doused in gasoline, awaits its grim fate.... Still, for all intents and purposes, I think I coexist quite reasonably with the phallo-explosive media and institutions that surround me. Oh, there was that time I talked all through Thanksgiving dinner about why I consider the clitoris to be the jewel of human anatomy and the source of my strength and magic as a woman and feminist. But everyone was telling stories and I just wanted to participate.

I know now that I've overcome the angry stage. When the evening news made me cry and fraternity boys made me vomit. When I thought men who hate women were cowering assholes with too much testosterone and too little brain power. When I thought the fight to bring patriarchy to a screeching, jubilant halt was the only fight worth my time or anyone else's.

But, oh, I've changed from that bitter girl of seventeen. I'm now a bitter woman of twenty-three. I don't watch the news, and I'm convinced that men who hate women are indeed cowering assholes with an exorbitant amount of testosterone and very little brain power, if any. I know that the fight to end patriarchy, to devour it, to deplete and dismember it in favor of a system that does not achieve cosmic orgasm through the oppression of others is a just and valiant fight. And I will continue to pursue this glorious end as long as my soul wanders the earth. Fraternity boys still make me vomit. But now I imagine vomiting on them rather than because of them. I've become a gastric avenger of sorts.

I wasn't always a feminist. In fact, I used to think feminists were sexually undesirable and perpetually angry. (Boy, was I wrong. Feminists are perpetually desirable, and I am sexually angry.) Prior to my feminist epiphany, I felt I was nothing more than big hair with a fellatio fetish, the worst part about this being that I thought I was pretty cool. In the time that has passed since then, I have grown from girl to woman, but more dramatically, I have been transformed from masochist to feminist.

The big hair, accompanied by moderately big breasts and a dancer's ass, all bundled into a squeezy purple dress, attracted all sorts of attention—all sorts dangerous. For one thing, I could have brought my high school to its knees on charges of sexual misconduct. My most serious encounter nearly led to an affair with a teacher who, despite the inappropriateness of his forty-seven-year-old affections for a fifteen-year-old girl, won me over somehow. Being near him made my stomach churn, my throat ache, my eyes blur. Though I wish it had been a temporary virus, I realize now it was probably terror, and at the time it seemed quite romantic. Another of my faculty suitors had a nasty habit of pressing his bulging manhood against my back as I sat in his class furiously taking notes to prove I was smart. They were charmers, all right.

It's appalling to me now, but at the time it felt normal and hardly bothered me. In fact, I thrived on making them all hard and then laughing in their faces at the obvious fact that they could never have me. I thought I was god's gift to men because I could play glam, sweetheart and harlot all in one shot. I had my pick, and like your typical fallen angel-to-be, I chose poorly.

I lost my virginity, or rather, rid myself of its intolerable presence. Virginity implied immaturity, stupidity and a dearth of passion—as such, I wanted no part of it. To me, virginity represented all the qualities of "girliness," none of which merited any respect at all from anyone, anywhere.

Furthermore, coming from a long line of passionate women, I felt drawn to the pleasures of flesh. But more than sexual contact, I wanted the hard edges that come from having a lot of sex with many lovers. My role models were the prostitutes in old Westerns who played poker with mean cowboys (and won). They swore in low, husky voices, were cynical but funny, carried guns in their garter belts and never needed men. I wanted to be scarred by love the way these women were. For what it's worth, I was successful in achieving my goal.

I began having vaginal intercourse—I'd already done everything else—with one of the men who, in middle school, had thrown my brother over a wall to prove his seventh-grade masculinity. Though he was never violent with me, I had yet to recognize a separation between sex/iness, violence and the romantic intrigue of scars. For example, I recall an incident in which my friends and I discussed going to see *The Accused.* They shared my sexually curious desire to see "the gang rape," as I said to them with a mischievous grin, "I heard they show it."

I left the movie theater the following weekend in tears, completely traumatized (scarred, in fact). I spent the next two days in exactly the same condition, crying for that woman, crying for myself and convinced that I would inevitably find myself pinned to a table by hovering, raping, evil men. My fear of rape and of men culminated in frequent nightmares about incest, murder and, of course, more rape.

The problem was not that I suffered an abusive childhood or bad luck, because I didn't. It was also not that I was weak or ill-prepared for life as a young adult in a world full of "adult" bookstores. It was simply that I was born a girl in a society that devalues women and girls. Bam. That easy. And because I lacked the words to describe my demons, I had no power to address them.

I know all kinds of words now. Words like revolution, equality, dignity, reproductive freedom. I've mistressed phrases like subvert the patriarchy, run with the wolves, and take back the night. Words of empowerment. The one word all phallocrats most fear (and well they should), I wear like a badge of honor, my pride, my work, my glowing, spiked tiara. That word is "feminist."

I became a feminist through other forms of activism—race education (my own) and gay rights. One shining moment of radicalization occurred in my Speech 105 class. I'd given a speech on gay, lesbian and bisexual rights—you know the ones I'm talking about. The right to not be beaten up, the right to not be thrown out of the house/church/military, the right to not die from a disease the ruling class chooses to ignore, that is, until they're the ones to get it, blah, blah, blah. Unreasonable demand after unreasonable demand.

So, I've just finished my tribute to queers everywhere, when a student raises his hand to ask me (the only question I received at all), "When you say 'homosexuals,' do you mean guys? Or chicks goin' at it, too?" Chicks goin' at it. Obviously, my rhetoric had sung its way into his tender, eager-to-be-enlightened heart. My calling into the world of gay activism.

Then there was the time I bought these hunky purple hiking boots, a look I'd admired from atop my three-and-a-half-inch heels for some time. I enhanced my purchase by wearing them with dresses, the nonclinging kind, and the most alarming thing happened. I began to walk differently. I no longer wobbled. I took bigger steps, surer steps, harder steps. A friend of mine wears boots anytime she waits tables to combat wobbliness in the face of the inevitable harassment endured by women in the service industry. It's clear to me now that every feminist, indeed every woman, needs a good, solid pair of boots. It's not just a symbolic assault on the patriarchy, it's a fashion statement. Like short hair.

I know because I cut the hell out of my long, curly hair. My mother loved it; my boyfriend hated it. (Duh.) He said it made him feel like he was making love to a boy. I found this particularly amusing since he had very long, very female hair, which provided just the touch I needed to reach orgasm with him. I suddenly realized why he was so upset. I apologized for not having warned him and told him I hoped that he would never cut his own hair. "I know exactly what you mean," I said.

So now we have the boots, the hair, the lesbian fantasy (more on this later), and, in my effort to dive headlong into the stereotypical/archetypal image of a feminist, I offer what was my next, triumphant step toward full-blown feminist liberation. Susan B. Anthony did it. Mary Ann Shadd Cary did it. Ida B. Wells did it, and so did Margaret Sanger. Heck, all the kids were doin' it. On the campus of Vanderbilt University, a place that quite resembles an old southern plantation crawling with J. Crew models and debutantes, I started a feminist newspaper with two womenfriends. The initiation, my rebirth—feminist at last.

We took on woman haters, Limbaugh lovers, date rapers, and the ever-popular, oh-so-predictable brothers (and sisters) of backlash. We lost sleep, I lost a three-year dean's list streak, we nearly went insane, and it was still some of the best fun I ever had in my life. Every heartbeat, every bit of energy, our very souls, we spent for that paper and for each other.

In my prefeminist incarnation, I was incapable of this kind of close relationship with women. Vanity, competition and superficial alliances more accurately describe my friendships with women then. But imagine my surprise as I took this intimacy even one step further when I ended up in bed with a dear friend and coeditor.

We only slept—that day. But we wrapped our bodies around one another and stayed that way, from early one Saturday afternoon to late in the evening. Some of the time I slept, some of the time I contemplated the curve of her hip, some of the time I imagined how we looked, lying there, me with this warm grin crawling across my face. We only slept. Anything more would have been redundant, excessive. I'd been introduced to a feeling I never knew existed. That moment of revelation satisfied me more than any sex ever could.

It also came as a shock to me, for about a minute. Then I put it into my own historical context. I had wondered whether or not I might be lesbian ever since the time the sound of k.d. lang's voice over my headphones made me blush. Plus, I consistently fantasized about women in order to get through sex with men. For, contrary to the much-publicized, rather unfortunate words of Naomi Wolf, the male body is neither home nor shelter to me. It's more like a really itchy blanket with some holes in it. And while I, too, have seen the word "love" trigger an erection, I have also seen the word "rape" inspire much of the same.

And though I know that my rejection of men is not what led me to the arms of women, my experiences with them certainly provided me with the impetus to go looking for something (and someone) else. Sleeping with men required more compromise and more effort than I was willing to make. Sleeping with women felt like just another extension of my sexuality and identity. It is also something I aspired to as a die-hard advocate for women. That's what troubled me.

My bedroom, as you might well expect, was full of politics. Ever since the moment I inherited the fiery skull of knowledge, my head and my bed swarmed with the power dynamics of sex: Who leads, who follows, when is it rape, when is it just bad sex and why do I so desperately hate it these days? But women, I thought, sex with women must be different.

It tormented me for months. I had these massive crushes on my best friend and my boss, and suddenly I was in angst over whether or not to tattoo a pink triangle on my forehead. But I worried (and still do occasionally) that I was taking on lesbianism out of loyalty to a cause, fearful that my capacity to sleep with the bad guys was bad for

PR. Was I trying too hard to sleep with my politics? After all, with all my issues there was hardly room for anyone else in the bed. Why not take advantage? Or, worse yet, was I a wanna-be? A baby dyke? A lesbian chic groupie, flashing in the pan, wanting my fifteen minutes of fame on the cover of *Newsweek*? Or was I truly falling more in love with women, with spirited feminists and with my own womanhood than I had ever been with anyone?

Um...yes.

I figure you can fantasize about sleeping with women only so much before it stops being a fantasy and starts becoming a reality. And while I still have a bed full of feminist ideologies—combined with the world of women-loving women—I find they practically serve as erotica. "Tell me again in your sexiest voice how pathetic the Senate Judiciary Committee is while I light some candles and slip into my sleeveless 'Patriarchy Bites!' T-shirt." Rrowll.

Now, instead of arguing over the well-known fact (known by delinquent assholes) that "some women *like* hard-core S/M porn, eh, eh, whine, whine," I can argue over who knows more lines from *Thelma and Louise.* "You said you and me wuz gonna git outta town and for once jus' really let our hair down. Well, darlin', look out, 'cause my hair is comin' down."

So I'll tell you the truth: I still don't know if all of this makes me a lesbian. I'm definitely bisexual. And I only recently claimed that label for myself without fear of it implying indecisiveness, internalized all-out-lesbian homophobia or the perception that I'm just plain easy. I've known both straight and gay people who shunned it (the word, the deed and the person) for each of the biphobic reasons I just expressed. In the wake of this paranoia, on my part and theirs, I've allowed myself to conclude a few things.

I'm a Libra for goddess' sake. You better believe I'm indecisive! It's the only thing I know for sure at all! I can't even determine whether I'm right-handed or left-handed, just in case my left hand one day decides to assert itself. I'd feel terri-

ble having given up on it before it was ready to come out—if you know what I mean. Needless to say, I only assumed I was straight all those years because nothing led me to believe otherwise. Hallelujah, I believe otherwise!

As far as fearing status as a true-blue lesbian, I'll tell ya, I came out two or three times in front of large audiences before it was even relevant to my personal life. In the heat of many a debate, we needed a lesbian, I took the bulldyke by the horns and BAM: instant lesbian. Short hair, raging feminist, swearing in front of faculty? As if they didn't already think it.

My campus environment proved just slightly less than fascist when it came to gay rights. I mean, it's not as if we had drag queens and biker dykes screamin' across the delicately manicured lawn. (If only we had! The mere thought makes my heart leap.) The atmosphere was more than hostile to even the most meager queer on campus. How can I say this without offending anyone? Do the words Bible-bangin' freaks all carryin' plastic fetuses in their backpacks mean anything to you? The only lesbians we had were these badass, underappreciated grad students and a philosophy professor. I think all the other lesbians transferred.

Besides, my alliance with lesbians, as a women-loving woman and feminist, has always been core to my political activism and identity. Feminists are routinely "accused" of being lesbians or manhaters (as if the two are synonymous). Straight feminists often scramble to defy this stereotype by proclaiming their unfailing love for men and their affinity for bikini waxes. Some subtly distance themselves from lesbians by wearing buttons that claim "straight but not narrow." This is bullshit to me. If being called a lesbian is an insult to me, then I am an insult to lesbians. Any feminist who fears being called lesbian, or who fears association with a movement demanding civil rights for gays, lesbians and bisexuals, is not worthy of being called feminist.

The only other reason that could prevent me from embracing my bisexual identity is the implication to others that I might be easy. Ain't no might about it. I am easy. But, as long as I'm safe, what the hell?

My favorite term (other than plain old "queer") is "bisexual lesbian." It just works for me. I don't expect a man to understand me; I don't applaud him if he does. My heart and my mind belong with other women-loving women.

So here I am. I have birthed of myself a wild and unruly feminist. I feast as often as possible with my womensisters under new and full moons. I am seriously in love with Susan B. Anthony, and I have the dearest little crush on Gloria Steinem (especially during her big hair stage—probably some kind of narcissistic throwback to my past). I don't think I could be prouder of the cause that fuels my existence. I certainly didn't expect this much support, encouragement and spiritual nour-ishment outside of the womb, but what a lovely surprise!

I offer my feminist flamboyance as a personal attack on the patriarchy. And to further hack at the roots of patriarchal power, I would like to co-opt a statement made by Sarah Grimké in 1838. (If there had been a Miss Feminist America Pageant in 1838, this answer to world peace would surely have taken the crown.) She wrote: "All I ask our brethren is, that they will take their feet from off our necks and permit us to stand upright on that ground which God designed us to occupy."[1] I'd like to reiterate (without the "God" part—whole other story), since apparently SOMEBODY wasn't in class that day. Give it up, would you? I'm so over it.

NOTE

1. Gerda Lerner, *The Creation of Feminist Consciousness: From the Middle Ages to Eighteen-seventy* (New York: Oxford University Press, 1993), p. 162.

27

White Privilege

Unpacking the Invisible Knapsack

PEGGY McINTOSH

Through work to bring materials from Women's Studies into the rest of the curriculum, I have often noticed men's unwillingness to grant that they are over-privileged, even though they may grant that women are disadvantaged. They may say they will work to improve women's status, in the society, the university, or the curriculum, but they can't or won't support the idea of lessening men's. Denials which amount to taboos surround the subject of advantages which men gain from women's disadvantages. These denials protect male privilege from being fully acknowledged, lessened or ended.

Thinking through unacknowledged male privilege as a phenomenon, I realized that since hierarchies in our society are interlocking, there was most likely a phenomenon of White privilege which was similarly denied and protected. As a White person, I realized I had been taught about racism as something which puts others at a disadvantage, but had been taught not to see one of its corollary aspects, White privilege, which puts me at an advantage.

I think Whites are carefully taught not to recognize White privilege, as males are taught not to recognize male privilege. So I have begun in an untutored way to ask what it is like to have White privilege. I have come to see White privilege as an invisible package of unearned assets which I can count on cashing in each day, but about which I was 'meant' to remain oblivious. White privilege is like an invisible weightless knapsack of special provisions, maps, passports, codebooks, visas, clothes, tools and blank checks.

Describing White privilege makes one newly accountable. As we in Women's Studies work to reveal male privilege and ask men to give up some of their power, so one who writes about having White privilege must ask, "Having described it, what will I do to lessen or end it?"

After I realized the extent to which men work from a base of unacknowledged privilege, I understood that much of their oppressiveness was unconscious. Then I remembered the frequent charges from women of color that White women whom they encounter are oppressive. I began to understand why we are justly seen as oppressive, even when we don't see ourselves that way. I began to count the ways in which I enjoy unearned skin privilege and have been conditioned into oblivion about its existence.

My schooling gave me no training in seeing myself as an oppressor, as an unfairly advantaged person, or as a participant in a damaged culture. I was taught to see myself as an individual whose moral state depended on her individual moral will. My schooling followed the pattern my colleague Elizabeth Minnich has pointed out: Whites are taught to think of their lives as morally neutral, normative, and average, and also ideal, so that when we work to benefit others, this is seen as work which will allow "them" to be more like "us."

I decided to try to work on myself at least by identifying some of the daily effects of White privilege in my life. I have chosen those conditions which I think in my case *attach somewhat more to skin-color privilege* than to class, religion, ethnic status, or geographical location, though of course all these other factors are intricately intertwined. As far as I can see, my African American co-workers, friends and acquaintances with whom I come into daily or frequent contact in this particular time, place, and line of work cannot count on most of these conditions.

1. I can if I wish arrange to be in the company of people of my race most of the time.
2. If I should need to move, I can be pretty sure of renting or purchasing housing in an area which I can afford and in which I would want to live.
3. I can be pretty sure that my neighbors in such a location will be neutral or pleasant to me.
4. I can go shopping alone most of the time, pretty well assured that I will not be followed or harassed.
5. I can turn on the television or open to the front page of the paper and see people of my race widely represented.
6. When I am told about our national heritage or about "civilization," I am shown that people of my color made it what it is.
7. I can be sure that my children will be given curricular materials that testify to the existence of their race.
8. If I want to, I can be pretty sure of finding a publisher for this piece on White privilege.
9. I can go into a music shop and count on finding the music of my race represented, into a supermarket and find the staple foods which fit with my cultural traditions, into a hairdresser's shop and find someone who can cut my hair.
10. Whether I use checks, credit cards, or cash, I can count on my skin color not to work against the appearance of financial reliability.
11. I can arrange to protect my children most of the time from people who might not like them.
12. I can swear, or dress in second hand clothes, or not answer letters, without having people attribute these choices to the bad morals, the poverty, or the illiteracy of my race.

13. I can speak in public to a powerful male group without putting my race on trial.
14. I can do well in a challenging situation without being called a credit to my race.
15. I am never asked to speak for all the people of my racial group.
16. I can remain oblivious of the language and customs of persons of color who constitute the world's majority without feeling in my culture any penalty for such oblivion.
17. I can criticize our government and talk about how much I fear its policies and behavior without being seen as a cultural outsider.
18. I can be pretty sure that if I ask to talk to "the person in charge," I will be facing a person of my race.
19. If a traffic cop pulls me over or if the IRS audits my tax return, I can be sure I haven't been singled out because of my race.
20. I can easily buy posters, postcards, picture books, greeting cards, dolls, toys, and children's magazines featuring people of my race.
21. I can go home from most meetings of organizations I belong to feeling somewhat tied in, rather than isolated, out-of-place, outnumbered, unheard, held at a distance, or feared.
22. I can take a job with an affirmative action employer without having co-workers on the job suspect that I got it because of race.
23. I can choose public accommodation without fearing that people of my race cannot get in or will be mistreated in the places I have chosen.
24. I can be sure that if I need legal or medical help, my race will not work against me.
25. If my day, week, or year is going badly, I need not ask of each negative episode or situation whether it has racial overtones.
26. I can choose blemish cover or bandages in "flesh" color and have them more or less match my skin.

I repeatedly forgot each of the realizations on this list until I wrote it down. For me White privilege has turned out to be an elusive and fugitive subject. The pressure to avoid it is great, for in facing it I must give up the myth of meritocracy. If these things are true, this is not such a free country; one's life is not what one makes it; many doors open for certain people through no virtues of their own.

In unpacking this invisible knapsack of White privilege, I have listed conditions of daily experience which I once took for granted. Nor did I think of any of these perquisites as bad for the holder. I now think that we need a more finely differentiated taxonomy of privilege, for some of these varieties are only what one would want for everyone in a just society, and others give licence to be ignorant, oblivious, arrogant and destructive.

I see a pattern running through the matrix of White privilege, a pattern of assumptions which were passed on to me as a White person. There was one main piece of cultural turf; it was my own turf, and I was among those who could control the turf. *My skin color was an asset for any move I was educated to want to make.* I could think of myself as belonging in major ways, and of making social systems work for me. I could freely disparage, fear, neglect, or be oblivious to anything outside of the dominant cultural forms. Being of the main culture, I could also criticize it fairly freely.

In proportion as my racial group was being made confident, comfortable, and oblivious, other groups were likely being made inconfident, uncomfortable, and alienated. Whiteness protected me from many kinds of hostility, distress, and violence, which I was being subtly trained to visit in turn upon people of color.

For this reason, the word "privilege" now seems to me misleading. We usually think of privilege as being a favored state, whether earned or conferred by birth or luck. Yet some of the conditions I have described here work to systematically overempower certain groups. Such privilege simply *confers dominance* because of one's race or sex.

I want, then, to distinguish between earned strength and unearned power conferred systemically. Power from unearned privilege can look like strength when it is in fact permission to escape or to dominate. But not all of the privileges on my list are inevitably damaging. Some, like the expectation that neighbors will be decent to you, or that your race will not count against you in court, should be the norm in a just society. Others, like the privilege to ignore less powerful people, distort the humanity of the holders as well as the ignored groups.

We might at least start by distinguishing between positive advantages which we can work to spread, and negative types of advantages which unless rejected will always reinforce our present hierarchies. For example, the feeling that one belongs within the human circle, as Native Americans say, should not be seen as privilege for a few. Ideally it is an *unearned entitlement.* At present, since only a few have it, it is an *unearned advantage* for them. This paper results from a process of coming to see that some of the power which I originally saw as attendant on being a human being in the U.S. consisted in *unearned advantage* and *conferred dominance.*

I have met very few men who are truly distressed about systemic, unearned male advantage and conferred dominance. And so one question for me and others like me is whether we will be like them, or whether we will get truly distressed, even outraged, about unearned race advantage and conferred dominance and if so, what we will do to lessen them. In any case, we need to do more work in identifying how they actually affect our daily lives. Many, perhaps most, of our White students in the U.S. think that racism doesn't affect them because they are not people of color; they do not see "whiteness" as a racial identity. In addition, since race and sex are not the only advantaging systems at work, we need similarly to examine the daily experience of having age advantage, or ethnic advantage, or physical ability, or advantage related to nationality, religion, or sexual orientation.

Difficulties and dangers surrounding the task of finding parallels are many. Since racism, sexism, and heterosexism are not the same, the advantaging associated with them should not be seen as the same. In addition, it is hard to disentangle aspects of unearned advantage which rest more on social class, economic class, race, religion, sex and ethnic identity than on other factors. Still, all of the oppressions are interlocking, as the Combahee River Collective Statement of 1977 continues to remind us eloquently.

One factor seems clear about all of the interlocking oppressions. They take both active forms which we can see and embedded forms which as a member of the dominant group one is taught not to see. In my class and place, I did not see myself as a racist because I was taught to recognize racism only in individual acts of meanness by members of my group, never in invisible systems conferring unsought racial dominance on my group from birth.

Disapproving of the systems won't be enough to change them. I was taught to think that racism could end if White individuals changed their attitudes. (But) a "white" skin in the United States opens many doors for Whites whether or not we approve of the way dominance has been conferred on us. Individual acts can palliate, but cannot end, these problems.

To redesign social systems we need first to acknowledge their colossal unseen dimensions. The silences and denials surrounding privilege are the key political tool here. They keep the thinking about equality or equity incomplete, protecting unearned advantage and conferred dominance by making these taboo subjects. Most talk by Whites about equal opportunity seems to me now to be about equal opportunity to try to get into a position of dominance while denying that *systems* of dominance exist.

It seems to me that obliviousness about White advantage, like obliviousness about male advantage, is kept strongly inculturated in the United States so as to maintain the myth of meritocracy, the myth that democratic choice is equally available to all. Keeping most people unaware that freedom of confident action is there for just a small number of people props up those in power, and serves to keep power in the hands of the same groups that have most of it already.

Though systemic change takes many decades, there are pressing questions for me and I imagine for some others like me if we raise our daily consciousness on the perquisites of being light-skinned. What will we do with such knowledge? As we know from watching men, it is an open question whether we will choose to use unearned advantage to weaken hidden systems of advantage, and whether we will use any of our arbitrarily awarded power to try to reconstruct power systems on a broader base.

28

The Black Male
Searching beyond Stereotypes

MANNING MARABLE

What is a Black man? Husband and father. Son and brother. Lover and boyfriend. Uncle and grandfather. Construction worker and sharecropper. Minister and ghetto hustler. Doctor and mineworker. Auto mechanic and presidential candidate.

What is a Black man in an institutionally racist society, in the social system of modern capitalist America? The essential tragedy of being Black and male is our inability, as men and as people of African descent, to define ourselves without the stereotypes the larger society imposes upon us, and through various institutional means perpetuates and permeates within our entire culture. Our relations with our sisters, our parents and children, and indeed across the entire spectrum of human relations are imprisoned by images of the past, false distortions that seldom if ever capture the essence of our being. We cannot come to terms with Black women until we understand the half-hidden stereotypes that have crippled our development and social consciousness. We cannot challenge racial and sexual inequality, both within the Black community and across the larger American society, unless we comprehend the critical difference between the myths about ourselves and the harsh reality of being Black men.

CONFRONTATION WITH WHITE HISTORY

The conflicts between Black and White men in contemporary American culture can be traced directly through history to the earliest days of chattel slavery. White males entering the New World were ill adapted to make the difficult transition from Europe to the American frontier. As recent historical research indicates, the development of what was to become the United States was accomplished largely, if not primarily, by African slaves, men and women alike. Africans were the first to cultivate wheat on the continent; they showed their illiterate masters how to grow indigo, rice, and cotton; their extensive knowledge of herbs and roots provided colonists with medicines and preservatives for food supplies. It was the Black man, wielding his sturdy axe, who cut down most of the virgin forest across the southern colonies. And in times of war, the White man reluctantly looked to his Black slave to protect him and his property. As early as 1715, during the Yemassee Indian war, Black troops led British regulars in a campaign to exterminate Indian tribes. After another such campaign in 1747, the all-White South Carolina legislature issued a public vote of gratitude to Black men, who "in times of war, behaved themselves with great faithfulness and courage, in repelling the attacks of his Majesty's enemies." During the American Revolution, over two thousand Black men volunteered to join the beleaguered Continental Army of George Washington, a slaveholder. A generation later, two thousand Blacks from New York joined the state militia's segregated units during the War of 1812, and Blacks fought bravely under Andrew Jackson at the Battle of New Orleans. From Crispus Attucks to the 180,000 Blacks who fought in the Union Army during the Civil War, Black men gave their lives to preserve the liberties of their White male masters.

The response of White men to the many sacrifices of their sable counterparts was, in a word, contemptuous. Their point of view of Black males was conditioned by three basic beliefs. Black men were only a step above the animals—possessing awesome physical power but lacking in intellectual ability. As such, their proper role in White society was as laborers, not as the managers of labor. Second, the Black male represented a potential political threat to the entire system of slavery. And third, but by no means last, the Black male symbolized a lusty sexual potency that threatened White women. This uneven mixture of political fears and sexual anxieties was reinforced by the White males' crimes committed against Black women, the routine rape and sexual abuse that all slave societies permit between the oppressed and the oppressor. Another dilemma, seldom discussed publicly, was the historical fact that some White women of social classes were not reluctant to request the sexual favors of their male slaves. These inherent tensions produced a racial model of conduct and social context that survived the colonial period and continued into the twentieth century. The White male–dominated system dictated that the only acceptable social behavior of any Black male was that of subservience—the loyal slave, the proverbial Uncle Tom, the ever-cheerful and infantile Sambo. It was not enough that Black men must cringe before their White masters; they must express open devotion to the system of slavery itself. Politically, the Black male was unfit to play even a minor role in the development of democracy. Supreme Court Chief Justice Roger B. Tawney spoke for his entire class in 1857: "Negroes [are] beings of an inferior order, and altogether unfit to associate with the White race, either by social or political relations; and so far inferior that they have no rights which the White man was bound to respect." Finally, Black males disciplined for various crimes against White supremacy—such as escaping from the plantation, or murdering their masters—were often punished in a sexual manner. On this point, the historical record is clear. In the colonial era, castration of Black males was required by the legislatures of North and South Carolina, Virginia, Pennsylvania, and New Jersey. Black men were castrated simply for striking a White man or for attempting to learn to read and write. In the late nineteenth century, hundreds of Black male victims of lynching were first sexually mutilated before being executed. The impulse to castrate Black males was popularized in White literature and folklore, and even today, instances of such crimes are not entirely unknown in the rural South.

The relations between Black males and White women were infinitely more complex. Generally, the vast majority of White females viewed Black men through the eyes of their fathers and husbands. The Black man was simply a beast of burden, a worker who gave his life to create a more comfortable environment for her and her children. And yet, in truth, he was still a man. Instances of interracial marriage were few and were prohibited by law even as late as the 1960s. But the fear of sexual union did not prohibit many White females, particularly indentured servants and working-class women, from soliciting favors from Black men. In the 1840s, however, a small group of white middle-class women became actively involved in the campaign to abolish slavery. The founders of modern American feminism—Susan B. Anthony, Elizabeth Cady Stanton, and Lucretia Mott—championed the cause of emancipation and defended Blacks' civil rights. In gratitude for their devotion to Black freedom, the leading Black abolitionist of the period, Frederick Douglass, actively promoted the rights of White women against the White male power structure. In 1848, at the Seneca Falls, New York, women's rights convention, Douglass was the only man, Black or White, to support the extension of voting rights to all women. White women looked to Douglass for leadership in the battle against sexual and racial discrimination. Yet curiously, they were frequently hostile to the continued contributions of Black women to the cause of freedom. When the brilliant orator Sojourner Truth, second only to Douglass as a leading figure in the abolitionist movement, rose to lecture before an 1851 women's convention in Akron, Ohio, White women cried out, "Don't let her speak!" For these White liberals, the destruction of slavery was simply a means to expand democratic rights to White women: the goal was defined in racist terms. Black men like Douglass were useful allies only so far as they promoted White middle-class women's political interests.

The moment of truth came immediately following the Civil War, when Congress passed the Fifteenth Amendment, which gave Black males the right to vote. For Douglass and most Black leaders, both men and women, suffrage was absolutely essential to preserve their new freedoms. While the Fifteenth Amendment excluded females from the electoral franchise, it nevertheless represented a great democratic victory for all oppressed groups.

For most White suffragists, however, it symbolized the political advancement of the Black male over White middle-class women. Quickly their liberal rhetoric gave way to racist diatribes. "So long as the Negro was lowest in the scale of being, we were willing to press his claims," wrote Elizabeth Cady Stanton in 1865. "But now, as the celestial gate to civil rights is slowly moving on its hinges, it becomes a serious question whether we had better stand aside and see 'Sambo' walk into the kingdom first." Most White women reformists concluded that "it is better to be the slave of an educated White man than of a degraded, ignorant black one." They warned Whites that giving the vote to the Black male would lead to widespread rape and sexual assaults against White women of the upper classes. Susan B. Anthony vowed "I will cut off this right arm of mine before I will ever work for or demand the ballot for the Negro and not the [White] woman." In contrast, Black women leaders like Sojourner Truth and Frances E. Watkins Harper understood that the enfranchisement of Black men was an essential step for the democratic rights of all people.

The division between White middle-class feminists and the civil rights movement of Blacks, beginning over a century ago, has continued today in debates over affirmative action and job quotas. White liberal feminists frequently use the rhetoric of racial equality but often find it difficult to support public policies that will advance Black males over their own social group. Even in the 1970s, such liberal women writers as Susan Brownmiller continued to resurrect the myth of the "Black male-as-rapist" and sought to define White women in crudely racist terms. The weight of White history, from White women and men alike, has been an endless series of stereotypes used to frustrate the Black man's images of himself and to blunt his constant quest for freedom.

CONFRONTING THE BLACK WOMAN

Images of our suffering—as slaves, sharecroppers, industrial workers, and standing in unemployment lines—have been intermingled in our relationship with the Black woman. We have seen her straining under the hot southern sun, chopping cotton row upon row and nursing our children on the side. We have witnessed her come home, tired and weary after working as a nurse, cook, or maid in White men's houses. We have seen her love of her children, her commitment to the church, her beauty and dignity in the face of political and economic exploitation. And yet, so much is left unsaid. All too often the Black male, in his own silent suffering, fails to communicate his love and deep respect for the mother, sister, grandmother, and wife who gave him the courage and commitment to strive for freedom. The veils of oppression, and the illusions of racial stereotypes, limit our ability to speak the inner truths about ourselves and our relationships to Black women.

The Black man's image of the past is, in most respects, a distortion of social reality. All of us can feel the anguish of our great-grandfathers as they witnessed their wives and daughters being raped by their White masters, or as they wept when their families were sold apart. But do we feel the double bondage of the Black woman, trying desperately to keep her family together and yet at times distrusted by her own Black man? Less than a generation ago, most Black male social scientists argued that the Black family was effectively destroyed by slavery; that the Black man was much less than a husband or father; and that the result was a "Black matriarchy" that crippled the economic, social, and political development of the Black community. Back in 1965, Black scholar C. Eric Lincoln declared that the slavery experience had "stripped the Negro male of his masculinity" and "condemned him to a eunuch-like existence in a culture that venerates masculine primacy." The rigid rules of Jim Crow applied more to Black men than to their women, according to Lincoln: "Because she was frequently the White man's mistress, the Negro woman occasionally flaunted the rules of segregation.... The Negro [male] did not earn rewards for being manly, courageous, or assertive, but for being accommodating—for fulfilling the stereotype of what he has been forced to be." The social by-product of Black demasculinization, concluded Lincoln, was the rise of Black matriarchs, who psychologically castrated their husbands and sons. "The Negro female has had the responsibility of the Negro family for so many generations that she accepts it, or assumes it, as second nature. Many older women have forgotten why the responsibility developed upon the Negro woman in the first place, or why it later became institutionalized," Lincoln argues. "And young Negro women do not think it absurd to reduce the relationship to a matter of money, since many of them probably grew up in families where the only income was earned by the mothers: the fathers may not have been in evidence at all." Other Black sociologists perpetuated these stereotypes, which only served to turn Black women and men against each other instead of focusing their energies and talents in the struggle for freedom.

Today's social science research on Black female–male relations tells us what our common sense should have indicated long ago—that the essence of Black family and community life has been a positive, constructive, and even heroic experience. Andrew Billingsley's *Black Families in White America* illustrates that the Black "extended family" is part of our African heritage that was never eradicated by slavery or segregation. The Black tradition of racial cooperation, the collectivist rather than individualistic ethos, is an outgrowth of the unique African heritage that we still maintain. It is clear that the Black woman was the primary transmitter and repositor of the cultural heritage of our people and played a central role in the socialization and guidance of Black male and female children. But this fact does not by any way justify the myth of a "Black matriarchy." Black women suffered from the economic exploitation and racism Black males experienced—but they also were trapped by institutional sexism and all of the various means of violence that have been used to oppress all women, such as rape, "wife beating," and sterilization. The majority of the Black poor throughout history have been overwhelmingly female; the lowest paid major group within the labor force in America is black women, not men.

In politics, the sense of the Black man's relations with Black women are again distorted by stereotypes. Most of us can cite the achievement of the great Black men who contributed to the freedom of our people: Frederick Douglass, W. E. B. DuBois, Marcus Garvey, Martin Luther King, Jr., Malcolm X, Paul Robeson, Medgar Evers, A. Philip Randolph. Why then are we often forgetful of Harriet Tubman, the fearless conductor on the Underground Railroad, who spirited over 350 slaves into the North? What of Ida B. Wells, newspaper editor and antilynching activist; Mary Church Terrell, educator, member of the Washington, D.C., Board of Education from 1895 to 1906, and civil rights leader; Mary McLeod Bethune, college president and director of the Division of Negro Affairs for the National Youth Administration; and Fannie Lou Hamer, courageous desegregation leader in the South during the 1960s? In simple truth, the cause of Black freedom has been pursued by Black women and men equally. In Black literature, the eloquent appeals to racial equality penned by Richard Wright, James Baldwin, and Du Bois are paralleled in the works of Zora Neale Hurston, Alice Walker, and Toni Morrison. Martin Luther King, Jr., may have expressed for all of us our collective vision of equality in his "I Have a Dream" speech at the 1963 March on Washington—but it was the solitary act of defiance by the Black woman, Rosa Parks, that initiated the great Montgomery bus boycott in 1955 and gave birth to the modern civil rights movement. The struggle of our foremothers and forefathers transcends the barrier of gender, as Black women have tried to tell their men for generations. Beyond the stereotypes, we find a common heritage of suffering, and a common will to be free.

THE BLACK MAN CONFRONTS HIMSELF

The search for reality begins and ends with an assessment of the actual socioeconomic condition of Black males within the general context of the larger society. Beginning in the economic sphere, one finds that the illusion of Black male achievement in the marketplace is undermined by statistical evidence. Of the thousands of small businesses initiated by Black entrepreneurs each year, over 90 percent go bankrupt within thirty-six months. The Black businessman suffers from redlining policies of banks, which keep capital outside his hands. Only one out of two hundred Black businessmen have more than twenty paid employees, and over 80 percent of all Black men who start their own firms must hold a second job, working sixteen hours and more each day to provide greater opportunities for their families and communities. In terms of actual income, the gap between the Black man and the White man has increased in the past decade. According to the Bureau of Labor Statistics, in 1979 only forty-six thousand Black men earned salaries between $35,000 and $50,000 annually. Fourteen thousand Black men (and only two thousand Black women) earned $50,000 to $75,000 that year. And in the highest income level, $75,000 and above, there were four thousand Black males compared to five hundred and forty-eight thousand White males.

This racial stratification is even sharper at the lower end of the income scale. Using 1978 poverty statistics, only 11.3 percent of all White males under fourteen years old live in poverty, while the figure for young Black males is 42 percent. Between the ages of fourteen and seventeen, 9.6 percent of White males and 38.6 percent of Black males are poor. In the age group eighteen to twenty-one years, 7.5 percent of White males and 26.1 percent of all Black males are poor. In virtually every occupational category, Black men with identical or superior qualifications earn less than their White male counterparts. Black male furniture workers, for example, earn only 69 percent of White males' average wages; in printing and publishing, 68 percent; in all nonunion jobs, 62 percent.

Advances in high-technology leave Black males particularly vulnerable to even higher unemployment rates over the next decades. Millions of Black men are located either in the "old line" industries such as steel, automobiles, rubber, and textiles, or in the public sector—both of which have experienced severe job contractions. In agriculture, to cite one typical instance, the disappearance of Black male workers is striking. As late as forty years ago, two out of every five Black men were either farmers or farm workers. In 1960, roughly 5 percent of all Black men were still employed in agriculture, and another 3 percent owned their own farms. By 1983, however, less than 130,000 Black men worked in agriculture. From 1959 to 1974, the number of Black-operated cotton farms in the South dropped from 87,074 to 1,569. Black tobacco farmers declined in number from 40,670 to barely 7,000 during the same period. About three out of four Black men involved in farming today are not self-employed.

From both rural and urban environments, the numbers of jobless Black adult males have soared since the late 1960s. In 1969, for example, only 2.5 percent of all Black married males with families were unemployed. This percentage increased to about 10 percent in the mid-1970s, and with the recession of 1982–1984 exceeded 15 percent. The total percentage of all Black families without a single income earner jumped from 10 percent in 1968 to 18.5 percent in 1977—and continued to climb into the 1990s.

These statistics fail to convey the human dimensions of the economic chaos of Black male joblessness. Thousands of jobless men are driven into petty crime annually, just to feed their families; others find temporary solace in drugs or alcohol. The collapse of thousands of black households and the steady proliferation of female-headed, single-parent households is a social consequence of the systematic economic injustice inflicted upon Black males.

Racism also underscores the plight of Black males within the criminal justice system. Every year in this country there are over 2 million arrests of Black males. About three hundred thousand Black men are currently incarcerated in federal and state prisons or other penal institutions. At least half of the Black prisoners are less than thirty years of age, and over one thousand are not even old enough to vote. Most Black male prisoners were unemployed at the time of their arrests; the others averaged less than $8,000 annual incomes during the year before they were jailed. And about 45 percent of the thirteen hundred men currently awaiting capital punishment on death row are Afro-Americans. As Lennox S. Hinds, former National Director of the National Conference of Black Lawyers has stated, "Someone Black and poor tried for stealing a few hundred dollars has a 90 percent likelihood of being convicted of robbery with a sentence averaging between 94 to 138 months. A White business executive who embezzled hundreds of thousands of dollars has only a 20 percent likelihood of conviction with a sentence averaging about 20 to 48 months." Justice is not "color blind" when Black males are the accused.

What does the economic and social destruction of Black males mean for the Black community as a whole? Dr. Robert Staples, associate professor of sociology at the University of California–San Francisco, cites some devastating statistics of the current plight of younger Black males:

Less than twenty percent of all Black college graduates in the early 1980s are males. The vast majority of young Black men who enter college drop out within two years.

At least one-fourth of all Black male teenagers never complete high school.

Since 1960, Black males between the ages of 15 to 20 have committed suicide at rates higher than that of the general White population. Suicide is currently the third leading cause of death, after homicides, and accidents, for Black males aged 15 to 24.

About half of all Black men over age 18 have never been married [or are] separated, divorced or widowed.

Despite the fact that several million Black male youths identify a career in professional athletics as a desirable career, the statistical probability of any Black man making it to the pros exceeds 20,000 to one.

One half of all homicides in America today are committed by Black men—whose victims are other Black men.

The typical Black adult male dies almost three years before he can even begin to collect Social Security.

Fred Clark, a staff psychologist for the California Youth Authority, states that the social devastation of an entire generation of Black males has made it extremely difficult for eligible Black women to locate partners. "In Washington, D.C., it is estimated that there is a one to twelve ratio of Black [single] males to eligible females," Clark observes. "Some research indicates that the female is better suited for surviving alone than the male. There are more widowed and single Black females than males. Males die earlier and more quickly than females when single. Single Black welfare mothers seem to live longer than single unemployed Black males."

Every socioeconomic and political indicator illustrates that the Black male in America is facing an unprecedented crisis. Despite singular examples of successful males in electoral politics, business, labor unions, and the professions, the overwhelming majority of Black men find it difficult to acquire self-confidence and self-esteem within the chaos of modern economic and social life. The stereotypes imposed by White history and by the lack of knowledge of our own past often convince many younger Black males that their struggle is too overwhelming. Black women have a responsibility to comprehend the forces that destroy the lives of thousands of their brothers, sons, and husbands. But Black men must understand that they, too, must overcome their own inherent and deeply ingrained sexism, recognizing that Black women must be equal partners in the battle to uproot injustice at every level of the society. The strongest ally Black men have in their battle to achieve Black freedom is the Black woman. Together, without illusions and false accusations, without racist and sexist stereotypes, they can achieve far more than they can ever accomplish alone.

REFERENCES

Clark, K. 1965. *Dark Ghetto.* New York: Harper and Row.

Davis, A. Y. 1981. *Women, Race and Class.* New York: Random House.

Billingsley, A. 1968. *Black Families in White America.* Englewood Cliffs, NJ: Prentice-Hall.

Lincoln, C. E. 1965. "The Absent Father Haunts the Negro Family." *New York Times Magazine,* Nov. 28.

Marable, M. 1983. *How Capitalism Underdeveloped Black America.* Boston: South End Press.

PART FIVE

Families

Section 1   Constructing Motherhood and Fatherhood

Section 2   Work and Families

Family life is shrouded in myth. No matter how much families change, they are idealized as natural or biological units based on the timeless functions of love, motherhood, and childbearing. Family evokes warmth, caring, and unconditional love in a refuge set apart from the public world. In this image, family and society are separate. Relations *inside* the family are idealized as nurturant, and those *outside* the family are seen as competitive. This ideal assumes a gendered division of labor; a husband/father associated with the public world and a wife/mother defined as the heart of the family. Although this image bears little resemblance to present family situations, it is still recognizable in our cultural ideals.

In the past two decades, feminist thought has been in the forefront of efforts to demythologize the family. Feminist thinkers have demonstrated that family forms are socially and historically constructed, not monolithic universals that exist for all times and all peoples and that the arrangements governing family life are not the inevitable result of unambiguous differences between women and men. Feminist thinkers have drawn attention to disparities in family life and to the contradictions within families between love and power and between family images on the one hand and lived family experiences on the other. They have directed attention to the close connection between families and other structures and institutions in society.

Early feminist critiques of the family characterized it as a primary site of women's oppression and argued in support of women's increased participation in the labor force as a means of attaining greater autonomy. But this analysis did not apply well to women of color or working-class women generally because it falsely universalized the experiences of White middle-class women who had the option of staying home to raise their children. More recently, feminist thought has begun to create a more complex understanding of the relationship between family and work by examining differences among women and taking men's experiences into account.

Questioning motherhood has been a central theme in recent feminist studies. A series of articles in the first section of this part explores both symbolic meanings and concrete realities of motherhood. They uncover experiences that are not simply gendered but shaped by other lines of difference as well. In her study of mother love and infant-death on Alto do Cruzeiro, Nancy Scheper-Hughes discovers an ambiguous form of mothering that is far removed from the essentialized and mythical portrait. Instead, the local context produces differences that seem impossible and even unthinkable. Next, Patricia Hill Collins takes race and class into account in rethinking motherhood. Distinctive sociohistorical realities engender more generalized and collective mothering relationships for Black women.

A growing U.S. market for domestic and childcare workers is redefining motherhood for many Latinas. In the next article, Pierrette Hondagneu-Sotelo and Ernestine Avila reveal an arrangement in which immigrant mothers work in the United States while their children remain in Mexico or Central America. Calling this adaptation "transnational mothering," their study shows how global patterns of family dispersal produce variations in the meanings and priorities of motherhood. In the following essay, Judith K. Witherow describes how the yardstick for measuring mothers' worth denies the reality of Native American experience. She offers a different view of what is and is not important in a mother. Finally, we move to fatherhood as Ralph LaRossa confronts the idea that fathering in the United States has undergone dramatic changes.

The second section of this part takes up questions about work and family, giving us new insights about women's and men's experiences in public and private spheres. First, in a study of women and men in southern Spain, David Gilmore exposes the false dichotomy of public and private power. We cannot assume that men's public activities automatically give them freedom and power, nor that women's domestic activities render them powerless. Looking carefully at what goes on within and between households reveals a female infrastructure of control that challenges conventional wisdom about gender and power.

By now it is a truism that families throughout the world have been affected by the movement of women into the work force. But on closer look, women's new work patterns are part of a much larger upheaval in the relationship between work and family. The next two articles address the shaping power of larger economic forces on women's family roles. The impact of shifting economies on women and their families varies considerably by class. Patricia Fernández Kelly's comparison of industrial housework among Mexican American and Cuban women shows how the class context gives rise to different work and family patterns. While Cuban women's employment enhances their families' middle-class status, Mexican American women must rely on their work for survival. Next, Nazli Kibria discovers wide-ranging class differentiation in how Bangladeshi women workers view and experience their income and their bargaining power. Finally, research by Elizabeth Higginbotham and Lynn Weber raises intriguing questions about the role of the family in the upward mobility of Black and White professional women.

29

(M)Other Love

Culture, Scarcity, and Maternal Thinking

NANCY SCHEPER-HUGHES

Maternal practices begin in love, a love which for most women is as intense, confusing, ambivalent, poignantly sweet as any they will experience.

Sara Ruddick (1980:344)

...The subject of my study is love and death on the Alto do Cruzeiro, specifically *mother* love and *child* death. It is about the meanings and effects of deprivation, loss, and abandonment on the ability to love, nurture, trust, and have and keep faith in the broadest senses of these terms. It treats the individual and the personal as well as the collective and cultural dimensions of maternal practices in an environment hostile to the survival and well-being of mothers and infants. I argue that a high expectancy of child death is a powerful shaper of maternal thinking and practice as evidenced, in particular, in delayed attachment to infants sometimes thought of as temporary household "visitors." This detachment can be mortal at times, contributing to the severe neglect of certain infants and to a "failure" to mourn the death of very young babies. I am *not* arguing that mother love, as we understand it, is deficient or absent in this threatened little human community but rather that its life history, its course, is different, shaped by overwhelming economic and cultural constraints. And so I trace the gradual unfolding of maternal love and attentive, "holding" care once the risk of loss (through chaotic and unpredictable early death) seems to have passed. This discussion is embedded in an examination of the cultural construction of emotions,

and it attempts to overcome the distinctions between "natural" and "socialized" affects, between "deep" private feelings and "superficial" public sentiments, between conscious and unconscious emotional expressions. In its attempts to show how emotion is shaped by political and economic context as well as by culture, this discussion can be understood as a "political economy" of the emotions....

Mother love is anything *other* than natural and instead represents a matrix of images, meanings, sentiments, and practices that are everywhere socially and culturally produced. In place of a poetics of motherhood, I refer to the pragmatics of motherhood, for, to paraphrase Marx, these shantytown women create their own culture, but they do not create it just as they please or under circumstances chosen by themselves....

What I discovered while working as a medic in the Alto do Cruzeiro during the 1960s was that while it was possible, and hardly difficult, to rescue infants and toddlers from premature death from diarrhea and dehydration by using a simple sugar, salt, and water solution (even bottled Coca-Cola worked fine in a pinch), it was more difficult to enlist mothers themselves in the rescue of a child they perceived as ill-fated for life or as better off dead. More difficult still was to coax some desperate young mothers to take back into the bosom of the family a baby they had already come to think of as a little winged angel, a fragile bird, or a household guest or visitor more than as a permanent family member. And so Alto babies "successfully" rescued and treated in the hospital rehydration clinic or in the creche and returned home were sometimes dead before I had the chance to make a follow-up house call. Eventually I learned to inquire warily before intervening: "Dona Maria, do you think we should try to save this child?" or, even more boldly, "Dona Auxiliadora, is this a child worth keeping?" And if the answer was no, as it sometimes was, I learned to keep my distance.

Later, I learned that the high expectancy of death and the ability to face death with stoicism and equanimity produced patterns of nurturing that differentiated those infants thought of as "thrivers" and as "keepers" from those thought of as born "already wanting to die." The survivors and keepers were nurtured, while the stigmatized or "doomed" infants were allowed to die *à míngua*, "of neglect." Mothers sometimes stepped back and allowed nature to take its course. This pattern I first (and rather unfortunately) labeled "ethnoeugenic selective neglect." Today I simply call it "mortal neglect." Both are unhappy terms, and it is little wonder that some critics have been offended by what they saw as a lapse in cultural relativism or as a failure of solidarity with my female "subjects." An earlier notion of "benign neglect" perhaps comes closer to the women's own perceptions of their actions. Nevertheless, translated to the North American context, "benign neglect" conjures up images of unkempt and unsupervised, yet otherwise happy and carefree, older street urchins riding subway trains on hot summer nights in New York City. The mortally neglected infants and babies I am referring to here are often (although not always) prettily kept: washed, such hair as they have combed, and their emaciated little bodies dusted with sweet-smelling talcum powders. When they die, they usually do so with candles propped up in tiny waxen hands to light their way to the afterlife. At least some of these little "angels" have been freely "offered up" to Jesus and His Mother, although "returned" to whence they came is closer to the popular idiom....

LORDES AND ZEZINHO: THE AMBIGUITIES OF MOTHER LOVE

In 1966 I was called on for a second time to help Lordes, my young neighbor, deliver a child, this one a fair and robust little tyke with a lusty cry. But while Lordes showed great interest in the newborn, she ignored Zé, who spent his days miserably curled up in a fetal position and lying on a piece of urine-soaked cardboard beneath his mother's hammock. The days passed and with Lordes's limited energy and attention given over to the newborn, Zezinho's days seemed numbered. I finally decided to intervene. In taking Zé away from Lordes and bringing him to the relative safety of the creche, I repeated the words that Alto women often used when deciding to rescue a *criança condenada* (condemned child) from a relative or neighbor. "Give me that child," I said, "for he'll never escape death in your house!" Lordes did not protest, but the creche mothers laughed at my efforts on behalf of such a hopeless case. Zezinho himself resisted the rescue with a perversity matching my own. He refused to eat, and he wailed pitifully whenever anyone approached him. The creche mothers advised to leave Zezinho alone. They said that they had seen many babies like this one, and "if a baby *wants* to die, it *will* die." There was no sense in frustrating him so, for here was a child who was completely "lifeless," without any "fight" at all. His eyes were already sinking to the back of his head, a sign that he had already begun his journey into the next life. It was very wrong, the creche mothers warned, to fight with death.

Their philosophy was alien to me, and I continued to do battle with the boy, who finally succumbed: he began to eat, although he never did more than pick at his food with lack of interest. Indeed, it did seem that Zé had no *gosto,* no "taste" for life. As he gained a few kilos, Zé's huge head finally had something to balance on. His wispy, light hair began to grow in, and his funny, wizened, old man face grew younger once his first two teeth (long imprisoned in shrunken gums) erupted. Gradually, too, Zezinho developed an odd and ambivalent attachment to his surrogate mother, who, when frustrated, was known to angrily force-feed him. Then the power struggle was on in earnest; once when Zé spit his *mingau* in my face, I turned him over and swatted him soundly on his skinny, leathery backside. He wouldn't even give the satisfaction of crying. Throughout all, Zé's legs remained weak and bowed, and long before he could stand upright, he would drag them behind him in a funny sort of hand crawl. Once he became accustomed to it, Zé liked being held, and he would wrap his spindly arms tightly around my neck and his legs around my waist. He reminded one of a frightened Brazilian spider monkey. His anger at being loosed from that uncomfortable, stranglehold position was formidable. Zé even learned to smile, although it more resembled a pained grimace. Withal, I was proud of my "success" and of proving the creche mothers wrong. Zé *would* live after all!

There were many other little ones in the creche like Zezinho, but none had arrived quite so wasted as he, and none ever engaged me in quite the same way. But as the time approached to return Zé to his mother, my first doubts began to surface. Could it be true, as the creche mothers hinted, that Zé would never be "quite right," that he would always live in the shadows "looking" for death, a death I had tricked once but would be unable to forestall forever? Such "fatalistic" sentiments were not limited to the creche mothers by any means. A visiting pediatrician from the American Midwest took a dim view of the creche. At first I could not understand his negative reactions. What could be wrong? Each of the thirty-some creche babies wore hand-laundered cotton diapers with the monogram UPAC stitched onto each. There were handmade canvas cot-cribs and even a playpen donated by the German sisters of the local convent. In the midst of the tour of the facilities, the doctor turned away and wearily rested his head on his elbow against the wall. "What do you think you are doing?" he asked.

I had to shake myself out of my own accommodation to see what the American pediatrician was noting: that the diapers, so white from having been beaten against stones and bleached by the sun to sterilize them, were covering fleshless little bottoms. The high point of the day was the weighing-in ritual, and we would cheer when a ten-month-old would weigh in at a fraction over his "normal" six or seven kilos: "*Gordinho* [fatty]!" or "*Guloso* [greedy]," we would say in mocking jest but also in encouragement. The "toddlers" in their playpens sat on their mats passively, without crying but also without playing. They moved themselves away from the brightly colored plastic toys, unfamiliar objects altogether. The creche had something of the grotesque about it, for it was a child care center, a place where healthy, active babies should have been howling and laughing and fighting among themselves. From the visiting doctor's clinical perspective, virtually all the creche babies were seriously physically and "developmentally delayed" and likely to remain so, carrying their early damage into what could only become highly compromised adult lives.

What *was* I doing, indeed? Could Zé ever be "right" again? Could he develop normally after the traumas he had been through? Worse, perhaps, were the traumas yet to come, as I would soon be returning him to Lordes in her miserable lean-to on the trash-littered Vultures' Path. Would he have been better off dead after all that I had put him through? And what of Lordes? Was this fair to her? She barely had enough to sustain herself and her newborn. But Lordes did agree to take Zezinho back, and she seemed more interested in him now that he looked a bit more human than spider monkey. Meanwhile, my own interest in the child began to wane. I was beginning to "let go." By this time I was becoming better socialized to Alto life. Never again would I put so much effort where the odds were so poor.

When I returned to Bom Jesus and the Alto in 1982 among the women who formed my original research sample was Lordes, no longer living in her lean-to but still in desperate straits and still fighting to put together some semblance of a life for her five living children, the oldest of whom was Zé, now a young man of seventeen. Zé struck me as a slight, quiet, reserved young man with an ironic, inward-turning smile and a droll sense of humor. He had long, thin, yet obviously strong, arms; I could see that they had always served him well, compensating for legs still somewhat bowed. Much was made of my reunion with Lordes and Zé, and the story was told again and again of how I had whisked Zé away from Lordes when he was all but given up for dead and had force-fed him like a fiesta turkey. Zé laughed the hardest of all at these "survivor tales" and at his own near-miss with death at the hands of an "indifferent" mother who often forgot to feed and bathe him. Zé and his mother obviously enjoyed a close and affectionate relationship, and while we spoke, Zé draped his arm protectively around his little mother's shoulders. There was no bitterness or resentment, and when I asked Zé alone and in private who had been his best friend in life, the one person he could always count on for support, he took a long drag on his cigarette and replied without a trace of irony, "Mãezinha [my little mother], of course!" For her part, Lordes gave "homage" to her son as her *filho eleito,* her "elect," or favorite, son, her "arms and legs," she called him, more important to her than the shadowy, older man with whom she was then living and more beloved than any other of her living children. . . .

OUR LADY OF SORROWS

> *Mother, behold your Son; Son, behold*
> *your Mother.*
> *John 19:25*

. . . On my next return to Bom Jesus in 1987 I was told the news immediately: "Go find Lordes—she has suffered a terrible tragedy. She is mad with grief." I found Lordes at home disconsolate, plunged into a profound mourning. With tears coursing freely down her suddenly, prematurely aged cheeks, Lordes explained that her favorite son, "her arms and legs," had been brutally mur-

dered on the night of the feast of São Pedro by his lover's ex-husband. Zé had been fooled; he never knew that his girlfriend had a husband. Lordes struck her breast in grief.

"If only my Zé were alive today, my life would not be one of suffering and misery. Not one of my other children turned out like him. On the day he died he left my house filled with enough groceries for a month. It was as if he knew he would be leaving me. I couldn't eat for weeks after the murder, and it pained me to look at all the food he had left me: yams, manioc, pimientos, beans. . . . These other wretched children of mine, they only know how to drive me crazy by asking for things. As soon as Zé was old enough to work, he said to me, 'Little Mama, now you are free. You will never have to worry again. You won't have to depend on some worthless bum to feed and protect you. I will see that you always have enough to eat and a bed to sleep on. I will be your protector.' And he was! He was like a mother to me! He never forgot me, even after he found a woman of his own. How many mothers can say that about their son?". . .

MOTHER LOVE AND CHILD DEATH

Love is always ambivalent and dangerous. Why should we think that it is any less so between a mother and her children? And yet it has been the fate of mothers throughout history to appear in strange and distorted forms. Mothers are sometimes portrayed as larger than life, as all-powerful, and sometimes as all-destructive. Or mothers are represented as powerless, helplessly dependent, and angelic. Historians, anthropologists, philosophers, and the "public" at large are influenced by old cultural myths and stereotypes about childhood innocence and maternal affection as well as their opposites. The "terrible" power attributed to mothers is based on the perception that the infant cannot survive for very long without considerable nurturing love and care, and normally that has been the responsibility of mothers. The infant's life is a vulnerable thing and depends to a great extent on the mother's good will. Sara Ruddick has captured the contradictions well in noting that mothers, while so totally in control of the lives and well-being of their infants and small babies, are themselves under the dominion and control of others, usually of men. Simultaneously powerful and powerless, it is no wonder that artists, scholars, and psychoanalysts can never seem to agree whether "mother" was the primary *agent* or the primary *victim* of various domestic tragedies. And so myths of a savagely protective "maternal instinct" compete at various times and places with the myth of the equally powerful, devouring, "infanticidal" mother.

Whenever we try to pierce the meanings of lives very different from our own, we face two interpretive risks. On the one hand, we may be tempted to attribute our own ways of thinking and feeling to "other" mothers. Any suggestion of radically different existential premises (such as those, for example, that guide selective neglect in Northeast Brazil) is rejected out of hand as impossible, unthinkable. To describe some poor women as aiding and abetting the deaths of certain of their infants can only be seen as "victim blaming." But the alternative is to cast women as passive "victims" of their fate, as powerless, without will, agency, or subjectivity. Part of the difficulty lies in the confusion between *causality* and *blame.* There must be a way to look dispassionately at the problem of child survival and conclude that a child died from mortal neglect, even at her or his mother's own hands, without also blaming the mother—that is, without holding her personally and morally accountable.

Related to this is the persistent idea that mothers, *all* mothers, *must* feel grief, a "depth of sorrow," in reaction to infant death. Women who do not show an "appropriate" grief are judged by psychoanalytic fiat to be "repressing" their "natural" maternal sentiments, to be covering them over with a culturally prescribed but *superficial* stoicism, or they may be seen as emotionally ravaged, "numbed" by grief, and traumatized by shock. But it was indifference, not numbing or

shock, that I often observed. The traumatized individual does not shrug her shoulders and say cheerily, "It's better the baby should die than either you or me" and quickly become pregnant because little babies are interchangeable and easily replaced.

One may experience discomfort in the face of profound human differences, some of which challenge our cultural notions of the "normal" and the "ethical." But to attribute "sameness" across vast social, economic, and cultural divides is a serious error for the anthropologist, who must begin, although cautiously, from a respectful assumption of difference. Here we want to direct our gaze to the ways of seeing, thinking, and feeling that represent these women's experience of being-in-the-world and, as faithful Catholics, their being-beyond-this-world. This means avoiding the temptation of all "essentializing" and "universalizing" discourses, whether they originate in the biomedical and psychological sciences or in philosophical or cultural feminism.

On the other hand, there is the danger of over-distancing ourselves from those we are trying to understand so as to suggest that there is no common ground at all. This is found in some deconstructionist and postmodernist theories of gender politics where the categories of "woman" and "mother" are rigorously problematized and deconstructed out of existence. Less radically, one can see the "overproduction of difference" in the writings of those modern social historians who have suggested that mother love is an invention of the "modern" world and that until very recently in human history women scarcely knew how to love their children. The language of these historians can be extreme and off-putting....

So perhaps there is a middle ground between the two rather extreme approaches to mother love—the sentimentalized maternal "poetics" and the mindlessly automatic "maternal bonding" theorists, on the one hand, and the "absence of love" theorists, on the other. Between these is the reality of maternal thinking and practice grounded in specific historical and cultural realities and bounded by different economic and demographic constraints. Maternal practices always begin as a response to "the historical reality of a biological child in a particular social world."

Seen in the context of a particular social world and historical reality, the story of Lordes and Zé conveys the ambiguities of mothering on the Alto do Cruzeiro where mortal selective neglect and intense maternal attachment coexist. Alto mothers, like Lordes, do sometimes turn away from certain ill-fated babies and abandon them to an early death in which their own neglect sometimes plays a final and definitive part. But maternal indifference does not always lead to death, and should an infant or a toddler show, like Zé, that he has a hidden "talent" for life, his mother may greet the "doomed" child's surprising turnabout with grateful joy and deep and lasting affection. And these same "neglectful" mothers can exclaim, like Lordes, that they live only for their grown children, some of whom only survived in spite of them. In so doing, these women are neither hypocritical nor self-delusional. . . .

HOLDING ON AND LETTING GO— THE PRAGMATICS OF MOTHERING

. . . Sara Ruddick has suggested that although some economic and social conditions, such as extreme poverty or social isolation, can erode maternal affection, they do not kill that love. Her understanding of mother love carried resonances of Winnicott as she referred to the metaphysical attitude of "holding"—holding *on,* holding *up,* holding *close,* holding *dear.* Maternal thinking, she suggested, begins with a stance of protectiveness, "an attitude governed, above all, by the priority of keeping over acquiring, of conserving the fragile, of maintaining whatever is at hand and necessary to the child's life" (1980:350). . . .

But what of mothering in an environment like the Alto where the risks to child health and safety are legion, so many, in fact, that mothers must necessarily concede to a certain "humility," even "passivity," toward a world that is in so many respects beyond their control? Among the mothers of the Alto maternal thinking and practice are often guided by another, quite opposite metaphysical stance, one that can be called, in light of the women's own choice of metaphors, "letting go." If holding has the double connotations of loving, maternal care (to have and to hold), on the one hand, and of retentive, restraining holding on or holding back, on the other, letting go also has a double valence. In its most negative sense, letting go can be thought of as letting loose destructive maternal power, as in child-battering and other forms of physical abuse. But malicious child abuse is extremely rare on the Alto do Cruzeiro, where babies and young children are often idealized as "innocents" who should not be physically disciplined or restrained. But letting go in the form of abandonment is not uncommon on the Alto, and the occasional neonate is found from time to time where he or she was let go in a backyard rubbish heap. And the abandonment of newborns by their overwrought mothers is so common in the maternity wing of the local hospital that a copybook is kept hanging on a cord just outside the nursery in which the data on abandonments and informal adoptions are recorded. There is no stigma in leaving an infant behind, although the birth mother is required by the nursing staff to remain in the hospital until a prospective adoptive parent can be found. The mother rarely has to wait more than a few days. Once an adoptive parent or couple appears—and there is no regulation of the process save for the few instances in which the nurse on duty takes a personal dislike to a potential adoptive parent—the birth mother need only sign her name (or affix her mark) after a statement declaring that she has freely given up her infant son or daughter born on such a date and time at the hospital. The adoptive parent is free to register the infant as her own birth child at the *cartório civil,* and most do so. In 1986 twelve newborns, eight males and four females, were left behind in the nursery by their mothers. In 1987 ten newborns, seven girls and three boys, were abandoned. Although all the birth mothers were poor, some of them wretchedly so, and only six could sign their own names, as many of them were older (thirty and older) as younger mothers (sixteen to twenty-nine), and almost an equal number were living with a spouse or lover as those who reported themselves to be "single," "separated," or "abandoned."

But here I want to reflect on another meaning of letting go. Among the women of the Alto to let go also implies a metaphysical stance of calm and reasonable resignation to events that cannot easily be changed or overcome. This is expressed in the women's frequent exhorting of each other, especially in times of great difficulty, to "let it go," "let it pass," "let it be": *Deixe, menina—deixe isso, deixe as coisas como são para ver como ficam.* In other words, "Leave it be, girl; leave things alone, and see how they turn out for themselves."... It is present each time Alto mothers say that their infants are "like birds," nervous and flighty creatures that are here today and gone tomorrow. A perfectly good mother can in good faith and with a clear conscience let go of an infant who "wants" to escape life, just as one may set free into the heavens a miserable wild bird that was beating its wings against its cage.

"What does it mean, *really*," I asked Doralice, an older woman of the Alto who often intervenes in poor households to rescue young and vulnerable mothers and their threatened infants, "to say that infants are like birds?"

"It means that...well, there is another expression you should know first. It is that all of us, our lives, are like burning candles. At any moment we can suddenly 'go out without warning [*a qualquer momento apaga*].' But for the infant this is even more so. The grownup, the adult, is very attached to life. One doesn't want to leave it with ease or without a struggle. But infants are not so connected, and their light can be extinguished very easily. As far as they are concerned, *tanto faz,* alive or dead, it makes no real difference to them. There is not that strong *vontade* to live that marks the big person. And so we say that 'infants are like little birds,' here one moment, flying off the next. That is how we like to think about their deaths, too. We like to imagine our dead infants as little winged angels flying off to heaven to gather noisily around the thrones of Jesus and Mary, bringing pleasure to them and hope for us on earth."

And so a good part of learning how to mother on the Alto includes knowing when to let go of a child who shows that he wants to die. The other part is knowing just when it is safe to let oneself go enough to love a child, to trust him or her to be willing to enter the *luta* that is this life on earth....

NOTES

1. Ruddick, Sarah. 1980. "Maternal Thinking." *Feminist Studies* 6:342–364.

30

The Meaning of Motherhood in Black Culture and Black Mother–Daughter Relationships

PATRICIA HILL COLLINS

"What did your mother teach you about men?" is a question I often ask students in my courses on African-American women. "Go to school first and get a good education—don't get too serious too young," "Make sure you look around and that you can take care of yourself before you settle down," and "Don't trust them, want more for yourself than just a man," are typical responses from Black women. My students share stories of how their mothers encouraged them to cultivate satisfying relationships with Black men while anticipating disappointments, to desire marriage while planning viable alternatives, to become mothers only when fully prepared to do so. But, above all, they stress their mothers' insistence on being self-reliant and resourceful.

These daughters, of various ages and from diverse social class backgrounds, family structures and geographic regions, had somehow received strikingly similar messages about Black womanhood. Even though their mothers employed diverse teaching strategies, these Black daughters had all been exposed to common themes about the meaning of womanhood in Black culture.[1]

This essay explores the relationship between the meaning of motherhood in African-American culture and Black mother–daughter relationships by addressing three primary questions. First, how have competing perspectives about motherhood intersected to produce a distinctly Afrocentric ideology of motherhood? Second, what are the enduring themes that characterize this Afrocentric ideology of motherhood? Finally, what effect might this

Afrocentric ideology of motherhood have on Black mother–daughter relationships?

COMPETING PERSPECTIVES ON MOTHERHOOD

The Dominant Perspective: Eurocentric Views of White Motherhood

The cult of true womanhood, with its emphasis on motherhood as woman's highest calling, has long held a special place in the gender symbolism of White Americans. From this perspective, women's activities should be confined to the care of children, the nurturing of a husband, and the maintenance of the household. By managing this separate domestic sphere, women gain social influence through their roles as mothers, transmitters of culture, and parents for the next generations.[2]

While substantial numbers of White women have benefited from the protections of White patriarchy provided by the dominant ideology, White women themselves have recently challenged its tenets. On one pole lies a cluster of women, the traditionalists, who aim to retain the centrality of motherhood in women's lives. For traditionalists, differentiating between the experience of motherhood, which for them has been quite satisfying, and motherhood as an institution central in reproducing gender inequality, has proved difficult. The other pole is occupied by women who advocate dismantling motherhood as an institution. They suggest that compulsory motherhood be outlawed and that the experience of motherhood can only be satisfying if women can also choose not to be mothers. Arrayed between these dichotomous positions are women who argue for an expanded, but not necessarily different, role for women—women can be mothers as long as they are not *just* mothers.[3]

Three themes implicit in White perspectives on motherhood are particularly problematic for Black women and others outside of this debate. First, the assumption that mothering occurs within the confines of a private, nuclear family household where the mother has almost total responsibility for child-rearing is less applicable to Black families. While the ideal of the cult of true womanhood has been held up to Black women for emulation, racial oppression has denied Black families sufficient resources to support private, nuclear family households. Second, strict sex-role segregation, with separate male and female spheres of influence within the family, has been less commonly found in African-American families than in White middle-class ones. Finally, the assumption that motherhood and economic dependency on men are linked and that to be a "good" mother one must stay at home, making motherhood a full-time "occupation," is similarly uncharacteristic of African-American families.[4]

Even though selected groups of White women are challenging the cult of true womanhood and its accompanying definition of motherhood, the dominant ideology remains powerful. As long as these approaches remain prominent in scholarly and popular discourse, Eurocentric views of White motherhood will continue to affect Black women's lives.

Eurocentric Views of Black Motherhood

Eurocentric perspectives on Black motherhood revolve around two interdependent images that together define Black women's roles in White and in African-American families. The first image is that of the Mammy, the faithful, devoted domestic servant. Like one of the family, Mammy conscientiously "mothers" her White children, caring for them and loving them as if they were her own.

Mammy is the ideal Black mother for she recognizes her place. She is paid next to nothing and yet cheerfully accepts her inferior status. But when she enters her own home, this same Mammy is transformed into the second image, the too-strong matriarch who raises weak sons and "unnaturally superior" daughters.[5] When she protests, she is labeled aggressive and unfeminine, yet if she remains silent, she is rendered invisible.

The task of debunking Mammy by analyzing Black women's roles as exploited domestic workers and challenging the matriarchy thesis by demonstrating that Black women do not wield disproportionate power in African-American families has long preoccupied African-American scholars.[6] But an equally telling critique concerns uncovering the functions of these images and their role in explaining Black women's subordination in systems of race, class, and gentler oppression. As Mae King points out, White definitions of Black motherhood foster the dominant group's exploitation of Black women by blaming Black women for their characteristic reactions to their own subordination.[7] For example, while the stay-at-home mother has been held up to all women as the ideal, African-American women have been compelled to work outside the home, typically in a very narrow range of occupations. Even though Black women were forced to become domestic servants and be strong figures in Black households, labeling them Mammys and matriarchs denigrates Black women. Without a countervailing Afrocentric ideology of motherhood, White perspectives on both White and African-American motherhood place Black women in a no-win situation. Adhering to these standards brings the danger of the lowered self-esteem of internalized oppression, one that, if passed on from mother to daughter, provides a powerful mechanism for controlling African-American communities.

African Perspectives on Motherhood

One concept that has been constant throughout the history of African societies is the centrality of motherhood in religions, philosophies, and social institutions. As Barbara Christian points out, "There is no doubt that motherhood is for most African people symbolic of creativity and continuity."[8]

Cross-cultural research on motherhood in African societies appears to support Christian's claim.[9] West African sociologist Christine Oppong suggests that the Western notion of equating household with family be abandoned because it obscures women's family roles in African cultures.[10] While the archetypal White, middle-class nuclear family conceptualizes family life as being divided into two oppositional spheres—the "male" sphere of economic providing and the "female" sphere of affective nurturing—this type of rigid sex role segregation was not part of the West African tradition. Mothering was not a privatized nurturing "occupation" reserved for biological mothers, and the economic support of children was not the exclusive responsibility of men. Instead, for African women, emotional care for children and providing for their physical survival were interwoven as interdependent, complementary dimensions of motherhood.

In spite of variations among societies, a strong case has been made that West African women occupy influential roles in African family networks.[11] First, since they are not dependent on males for economic support and provide much of their own and their children's economic support, women are structurally central to families.[12] Second, the image of the mother is one that is culturally elaborated and valued across diverse West African societies. Continuing the lineage is essential in West African philosophies, and motherhood is similarly valued.[13] Finally, while the biological mother-child bond is valued, child care was a collective responsibility, a situation fostering cooperative, age-stratified, woman-centered "mothering" networks.

Recent research by Africanists suggests that much more of this African heritage was retained among African-Americans than had previously been thought. The retention of West African culture as a culture of resistance offered enslaved Africans and exploited African-Americans alternative ideologies to those advanced by dominant groups. Central to these reinterpretations of African-American institutions and culture is a reconceptualization of Black family life and the role of women in Black family networks.[14] West African perspectives may have been combined with the changing political and economic situations framing African-American communities to produce certain enduring themes characterizing an Afrocentric ideology of motherhood.

ENDURING THEMES OF AN AFROCENTRIC IDEOLOGY OF MOTHERHOOD

An Afrocentric ideology of motherhood must reconcile the competing worldviews of these three conflicting perspectives of motherhood. An ongoing tension exists between efforts to mold the institution of Black motherhood for the benefit of the dominant group and efforts by Black women to define and value their own experiences with motherhood. This tension leads to a continuum of responses. For those women who either aspire to the cult of true womanhood without having the resources to support such a lifestyle, or who believe the stereotypical analyses of themselves as dominating matriarchs, motherhood can be oppressive. But the experience of motherhood can provide Black women with a base of self-actualization, status in the Black community, and a reason for social activism. These alleged contradictions can exist side by side in African-American communities, families, and even within individual women.

Embedded in these changing relationships are four enduring themes that I contend characterize an Afrocentric ideology of motherhood. Just as the issues facing enslaved African mothers were quite different from those currently facing poor Black women in inner cities, for any given historical moment the actual institutional forms that these themes take depend on the severity of oppression and Black women's resources for resistance.

Bloodmothers, Othermothers, and Women-Centered Networks

In African-American communities, the boundaries distinguishing biological mothers of children from other women who care for children are often fluid and changing. Biological mothers or bloodmothers are expected to care for their children. But African and African-American communities have also recognized that vesting one person with full responsibility for mothering a child may not be wise or possible. As a result, "othermothers," women who assist bloodmothers by sharing mothering responsibilities, traditionally have been central to the institution of Black motherhood.[15]

The centrality of women in African-American extended families is well known.[16] Organized, resilient, women-centered networks of bloodmothers and othermothers are key to this centrality. Grandmothers, sisters, aunts, or cousins acted as othermothers by taking on childcare responsibilities for each other's children. When needed, temporary child care arrangements turned into long-term care or informal adoption.[17]

In African-American communities, these women-centered networks of community-based childcare often extend beyond the boundaries of biologically related extended families to support "fictive kin."[18] Civil rights activist Ella Baker describes how informal adoption by othermothers functioned in the Southern, rural community of her childhood:

> My aunt who had thirteen children of her own raised three more. She had become a midwife, and a child was born who was covered with sores. Nobody was particularly wanting the child, so she took the child and raised him...and another mother decided she didn't want to be bothered with two children. So my aunt took one and raised him...they were part of the family.[19]

Even when relationships were not between kin or fictive kin, African-American community norms were such that neighbors cared for each other's children. In the following passage, Sara Brooks, a Southern domestic worker, describes the importance of the community-based childcare that a neighbor offered her daughter. In doing so, she also shows how the African-American cultural value placed on cooperative childcare found institutional support in the adverse conditions under which so many Black women mothered:

> She kept Vivian and she didn't charge me nothin either. You see, people used to look after each other, but now it's not that way. I reckon it's because we all was poor, and I guess they put theirself in the place of the person that they was helpin.[20]

Othermothers were key not only in supporting children but also in supporting bloodmothers who, for whatever reason, were ill-prepared or had little desire to care for their children. Given the pressures from the larger political economy, the emphasis placed on community-based childcare and the respect given to othermothers who assume the responsibilities of childcare have served a critical function in African-American communities. Children orphaned by sale or death of their parents under slavery, children conceived through rape, children of young mothers, children born into extreme poverty, or children who for other reasons have been rejected by their bloodmothers have all been supported by othermothers who, like Ella Baker's aunt, took in additional children, even when they had enough of their own.

Providing as Part of Mothering

The work done by African-American women in providing the economic resources essential to Black family well-being affects motherhood in a contradictory fashion. On the one hand, African-American women have long integrated their activities as economic providers into their mothering relationships. In contrast to the cult of true womanhood, in which work is defined as being in opposition to and incompatible with motherhood, work for Black women has been an important and valued dimension of Afrocentric definitions of Black motherhood. On the other hand, African-American women's experiences as mothers under oppression were such that the type and purpose of work Black women were forced to do had a great impact on the type of mothering relationships bloodmothers and othermothers had with Black children.

While slavery both disrupted West African family patterns and exposed enslaved Africans to the gender ideologies and practices of slaveowners, it simultaneously made it impossible, had they wanted to do so, for enslaved Africans to implement slaveowner's ideologies. Thus, the separate spheres of providing as a male domain and affective nurturing as a female domain did not develop within African-American families.[21] Providing for Black children's physical survival and attending to their affective, emotional needs continued as interdependent dimensions of an Afrocentric ideology of motherhood. However, by changing the conditions under which Black women worked and the purpose of the work itself, slavery introduced the problem of how best to continue traditional Afrocentric values under oppressive conditions. Institutions of community-based childcare, informal adoption, greater reliance on othermothers, all emerge as adaptations to the exigencies of combining exploitative work with nurturing children.

In spite of the change in political status brought on by emancipation, the majority of African-American women remained exploited agricultural workers. However, their placement in Southern political economics allowed them to combine childcare with field labor. Sara Brooks describes how strong the links between providing and caring for others were for her:

> When I was about nine I was nursin my sister Sally—I'm about seven or eight years older than Sally. And when I would put her to sleep, instead of me goin somewhere and sit down and play, I'd get my little old hoe and get out there and work right in the field around the house.[22]

Black women's shift from Southern agriculture to domestic work in Southern and Northern towns and cities represented a change in the type of work done, but not in the meaning of work to women and their families. Whether they wanted to or not, the majority of African-American women had to work and could not afford the luxury of motherhood as a noneconomically productive, female "occupation."

Community Othermothers and Social Activism

Black women's experiences as othermothers have provided a foundation for Black women's social activism. Black women's feelings of responsibility for nurturing the children in their own extended family networks have stimulated a more generalized ethic of care where Black women feel accountable to all the Black community's children.

This notion of Black women as community othermothers for all Black children traditionally allowed Black women to treat biologically unrelated children as if they were members of their own families. For example, sociologist Karen Fields describes how her grandmother, Mamie Garvin Fields, draws on her power as a community othermother when dealing with unfamiliar children.

> She will say to a child on the street who looks up to no good, picking out a name at random, "Aren't you Miz Pinckney's boy?" in that same reproving tone. If the reply is, "No, ma'am, my mother is Miz Gadsden," whatever threat there was dissipates.[23]

The use of family language in referring to members of the Black community also illustrates this dimension of Black motherhood. For example, Mamie Garvin Fields describes how she became active in surveying the poor housing conditions of Black people in Charleston.

> I was one of the volunteers they got to make a survey of the places where we were paying extortious rents for indescribable property. I said "we," although it wasn't Bob and me. We had our own home, and so did many of the Federated Women. Yet we still fell like it really was "we" living in those terrible places, and it was up to us to do something about them.[24]

To take another example, while describing her increasingly successful efforts to teach a boy who had given other teachers problems, my daughter's kindergarten teacher stated, "You know how it can be—the majority of children in the learning disabled classes are *our children*. I know he didn't belong there, so I volunteered to take him." In these statements, both women invoke the language of family to describe the ties that bind them as Black women to their responsibilities to other members of the Black community as family.

Sociologist Cheryl Gilkes suggests that community othermother relationships are sometimes behind Black women's decisions to become community activists.[25] Gilkes notes that many of the Black women community activists in her study became involved in community organizing in response to the needs of their own children and of those in their communities. The following comment is typical of how many of the Black women in Gilkes' study relate to Black children: "There were a lot of summer programs springing up for kids, but they were exclusive . . . and I found that most of *our kids* (emphasis mine) were excluded."[26] For many women, what began as the daily expression of their obligations as community othermothers, as was the case for the kindergarten teacher, developed into full-fledged roles as community leaders.

Motherhood as a Symbol of Power

Motherhood, whether bloodmother, othermother, or community othermother, can be invoked by Black women as a symbol of power. A substantial portion of Black women's status in African-American communities stems not only from their roles as mothers in their own families but from their contributions as community othermothers to Black community development as well.

The specific contributions Black women make in nurturing Black community development form the basis of community-based power. Community othermothers work on behalf of the Black community by trying, in the words of late nineteenth century Black feminists, to "uplift the race," so that vulnerable members of the commu-

nity would be able to attain the self-reliance and independence so desperately needed for Black community development under oppressive conditions. This is the type of power many African-Americans have in mind when they describe the "strong, Black women" they see around them in traditional African-American communities.

When older Black women invoke this community othermother status, its results can be quite striking. Karen Fields recounts an incident described to her by her grandmother illustrating how women can exert power as community othermothers:

> One night . . . as Grandmother sat crocheting alone at about two in the morning, a young man walked into the living room carrying the portable TV from upstairs. She said, "Who are you looking for this time of night?" As Grandmother [described] the incident to me over the phone, I could hear a tone of voice that I know well. It said, "Nice boys don't do that." So I imagine the burglar heard his own mother or grandmother at that moment. He joined in the familial game just created: "Well, he told me that I could borrow it." "Who told you?" "John." "Um um, no John *lives* here. You got the wrong house."[27]

After this dialogue, the teenager turned around, went back upstairs and returned the television.

In local Black communities, specific Black women are widely recognized as powerful figures, primarily because of their contributions to the community's well-being through their roles as community othermothers. Sociologist Charles Johnson describes the behavior of an elderly Black woman at a church service in rural Alabama of the 1930s. Even though she was not on the program, the woman stood up to speak. The master of ceremonies rang for her to sit down but she refused to do so claiming, "I am the mother of this church, and I will say what I please." The master of ceremonies later explained to the congregation—"Brothers, I know you all honor Sister Moore. Course our time is short but she has acted as a mother to me . . . Any time old folks get up I give way to them."[28]

IMPLICATIONS FOR BLACK MOTHER–DAUGHTER RELATIONSHIPS

In her discussion of the sex-role socialization of Black girls, Pamela Reid identifies two complementary approaches in understanding Black mother–daughter relationships.[29] The first, psychoanalytic theory, examines the role of parents in the establishment of personality and social behavior. This theory argues that the development of feminine behavior results from the girls' identification with adult female role models. This approach emphasizes how an Afrocentric ideology of motherhood is actualized through Black mothers' activities as role models.

The second approach, social learning theory, suggests that the rewards and punishments attached to girls' childhood experiences are central in shaping women's sex-role behavior. The kinds of behaviors that Black mothers reward and punish in their daughters are seen as key in the socialization process. This approach examines specific experiences that Black girls have while growing up that encourage them to absorb an Afrocentric ideology of motherhood.

African-American Mothers as Role Models

Feminist psychoanalytic theorists suggest that the sex-role socialization process is different for boys and girls. While boys learn maleness by rejecting femaleness via separating themselves from their mothers, girls establish feminine identities by embracing the femaleness of their mothers. Girls identify with their mothers, a sense of connection that is incorporated into the female personality. However, this mother-identification is problematic because, under patriarchy, men are more highly valued than women. Thus, while daughters identify with their mothers, they also reject them, since in patriarchal families, identifying with adult women as mothers means identifying with persons deemed inferior.[30]

While Black girls learn by identifying with their mothers, the specific female role with which Black girls identify may be quite different than that modeled by middle-class White mothers. The presence of working mothers, extended family othermothers, and powerful community othermothers offers a range of role models that challenge the tenets of the cult of true womanhood.

Moreover, since Black mothers have a distinctive relationship to White patriarchy, they may be less likely to socialize their daughters into their proscribed role as subordinates. Rather, a key part of Black girls' socialization involves incorporating the critical posture that allows Black women to cope with contradictions. For example, Black girls have long had to learn how to do domestic work while rejecting definitions of themselves as Mammies. At the same time they've had to take on strong roles in Black extended families without internalizing images of themselves as matriarchs.

In raising their daughters, Black mothers face a troubling dilemma. To ensure their daughters' physical survival, they must teach their daughters to fit into systems of oppression. For example, as a young girl in Mississippi, Black activist Ann Moody questioned why she was paid so little for the domestic work she began at age nine, why Black women domestics were sexually harassed by their White male employers, and why Whites had so much more than Blacks. But her mother refused to answer her questions and actually became angry whenever Ann Moody stepped out of her "place."[31] Black daughters are raised to expect to work, to strive for an education so that they can support themselves, and to anticipate carrying heavy responsibilities in their families and communities because these skills are essential for their own survival as well as for the survival of those for whom they will eventually be responsible.[32] And yet mothers know that if daughters fit too well into the limited opportunities offered Black women, they become willing participants in their own subordination. Mothers may have ensured their daughters' physical survival at the high cost of their emotional destruction.

On the other hand, Black daughters who offer serious challenges to oppressive situations may not physically survive. When Ann Moody became involved in civil rights activities, her mother first begged her not to participate and then told her not to come home because she feared the Whites in Moody's hometown would kill her. In spite of the dangers, many Black mothers routinely encourage their daughters to develop skills to confront oppressive conditions. Thus, learning that they will work, that education is a vehicle for advancement, can also be seen as ways of preparing Black girls to resist oppression through a variety of mothering roles. The issue is to build emotional strength, but not at the cost of physical survival.

This delicate balance between conformity and resistance is described by historian Elsa Barkley Brown as the "need to socialize me one way and at the same time to give me all the tools I needed to be something else."[33] Black daughters must learn how to survive in interlocking structures of race, class, and gender oppression while rejecting and transcending those very same structures. To develop these skills in their daughters, mothers demonstrate varying combinations of behaviors devoted to ensuring their daughters' survival— such as providing them with basic necessities and ensuring their protection in dangerous environments to helping their daughters go farther than mothers themselves were allowed to go.

The presence of othermothers in Black extended families and the modeling symbolized by community othermothers offer powerful support for the task of teaching girls to resist White perceptions of Black womanhood while appearing to conform to them. In contrast to the isolation of middle-class White mother/daughter dyads, Black women-centered extended family networks foster an early identification with a much wider range of models of Black womanhood, which can lead to a greater sense of empowerment in young Black girls.

Social Learning Theory and Black Mothering Behavior

Understanding this goal of balancing the needs of ensuring their daughters' physical survival with the vision of encouraging them to transcend the boundaries confronting them sheds some light on some of the apparent contradictions in Black mother-daughter relationships. Black mothers are often described as strong disciplinarians and overly protective parents; yet these same women manage to raise daughters who are self-reliant and assertive.[34] Professor Gloria Wade-Gayles offers an explanation for this apparent contradiction by suggesting that Black mothers "do not socialize their daughters to be passive or irrational. Quite the contrary, they socialize their daughters to be independent, strong and self-confident. Black mothers are suffocatingly protective and domineering precisely because they are determined to mold their daughters into whole and self-actualizing persons in a society that devalues Black women."[35]

Black mothers emphasize protection either by trying to shield their daughters as long as possible from the penalties attached to their race, class, and gender or by teaching them how to protect themselves in such situations. Black women's autobiographies and fiction can be read as texts revealing the multiple strategies Black mothers employ in preparing their daughters for the demands of being Black women in oppressive conditions. For example, in discussing the mother–daughter relationship in Paule Marshall's *Brown Girl, Brownstones*, Rosalie Troester catalogues some of these strategies and the impact they may have on relationships themselves:

> Black mothers, particularly those with strong ties to their community, sometimes build high banks around their young daughters, isolating them from the dangers of the larger world until they are old and strong enough to function as autonomous women. Often these dikes are religious, but sometimes they are built with education, family, or the restrictions of a close-knit and homogeneous community…this isolation causes the currents between Black mothers and daughters to run deep and the relationship to be fraught with an emotional intensity often missing from the lives of women with more freedom.[36]

Black women's efforts to provide for their children also may affect the emotional intensity of Black mother–daughter relationships. As Gloria Wade-Gayles points out, "Mothers in Black women's fiction are strong and devoted…but…they are rarely affectionate."[37] For far too many Black mothers, the demands of providing for children are so demanding that affection often must wait until the basic needs of physical survival are satisfied.

Black daughters raised by mothers grappling with hostile environments have to confront their feelings about the difference between the idealized versions of maternal love extant in popular culture and the strict, assertive mothers so central to their lives.[38] For daughters, growing up means developing a better understanding that offering physical care and protection is an act of maternal love. Ann Moody describes her growing awareness of the personal cost her mother paid as a single mother of three children employed as a domestic worker. Watching her mother sleep after the birth of another child, Moody remembers:

> For a long time I stood there looking at her. I didn't want to wake her up. I wanted to enjoy and preserve that calm, peaceful look on her face, I wanted to think she would always be that happy…Adline and Junior were too young to feel the things I felt and know the things I knew about Mama. They couldn't remember when she and Daddy separated. They had never heard her cry at night as I had or worked and helped as I had done when we were starving.[39]

Renita Weems's account of coming to grips with maternal desertion provides another example of a daughters efforts to understand her mother's behavior. In the following passage, Weems struggles with the difference between the stereotypical image of the super strong Black mother and her own alcoholic mother, who decided to leave her children:

> My mother loved us. I must believe that. She worked all day in a department store bakery to buy shoes and school tablets, came home to curse out neighbors who wrongly accused her children of any impropriety (which in an apartment complex usually meant stealing), and kept her house cleaner than most sober women.[40]

Weems concludes that her mother loved her because she provided for her to the best of her ability.

Othermothers often play central roles in defusing the emotional intensity of relationships between bloodmothers and their daughters and in helping daughters understand the Afrocentric ideology of motherhood. Weems describes the women teachers, neighbors, friends, and othermothers that she turned to for help in negotiating a difficult mother/daughter relationship. These women, she notes, "did not have the onus of providing for me, and so had the luxury of talking to me."[41]

June Jordan offers one of the most eloquent analyses of a daughter's realization of the high personal cost Black women have paid as bloodmothers and othermothers in working to provide an economic and emotional foundation for Black children. In the following passage, Jordan captures the feelings that my Black women students struggled to put into words:

> As a child I noticed the sadness of my mother as she sat alone in the kitchen at night…Her woman's work never won permanent victories of any kind. It never enlarged the universe of her imagination or her power to influence what happened beyond the front door of our house. Her woman's work never tickled her to laugh or shout or dance. But she did raise me to respect her way of offering love and to believe that hard work is often the irreducible factor for survival, not something to avoid. Her woman's work produced a reliable home base where I could pursue the privileges of books and music. Her woman's work invented the potential for a completely different kind of work for us, the next generation of Black women: huge, rewarding hard work demanded by the huge, new ambitions that her perfect confidence in us engendered.[42]

Jordan's words not only capture the essence of the Afrocentric ideology of motherhood so central to the well-being of countless numbers of Black women. They simultaneously point the way into the future, one where Black women face the challenge of continuing the mothering traditions painstakingly nurtured by prior generations of African-American women.

NOTES

1. The definition of culture used in this essay is taken from Leith Mullings, "Anthropological Perspectives on the Afro-American Family," *American Journal of Social Psychiatry* 6 (1986): 11–16. According to Mullings, culture is composed of "the symbols and values that create the ideological frame of reference through which people attempt to deal with the circumstances in which they find themselves" (13).

2. For analyses of the relationship of the cult of true womanhood to Black women, see Leith Mullings, "Uneven Development: Class, Race and Gender in the United States Before 1900," in *Women's Work, Development and the Division of Labor by Gender,* ed. Eleanor Leacock and Helen Safa (South Hadley, MA: Bergin & Garvey, 1986), pp. 41–57; Bonnie Thornton Dill, "Our Mothers' Grief: Racial Ethnic Women and the Maintenance of Families," Research Paper 4, Center for Research on Women (Memphis, TN: Memphis State University, 1986); and Hazel Carby, *Reconstructing Womanhood: The Emergence of the Afro-American Woman Novelist* (New York: Oxford University Press, 1987), esp. chapter 2.

3. Contrast, for example, the traditionalist analysis of Selma Fraiberg, *Every Child's Birthright: In Defense of Mothering* (New York: Basic Books, 1977) to that of Jeffner Allen, "Motherhood: The Annihilation Of Women," in *Mothering, Essays in Feminist Theory,* ed. Joyce Trebilcot (Totawa, NJ: Rowan & Allanheld, 1983). See also Adrienne Rich. *Of Woman Born: Motherhood as Experience and Institution* (New York: Norton, 1976). For an overview of how traditionalists and feminists have shaped the public policy debate on abortion, see Kristin Luker, *Abortion and the Politics of Motherhood* (Berkeley, CA: University of California, 1984).

4. Mullings, "Uneven Development"; Dill. "Our Mother's Grief"; and Carby, *Reconstructing Womanhood.* Feminist scholarship is also challenging Western notions of the family. See Barrie Thorne and Marilyn Yalom, eds., *Rethinking the Family* (New York: Longman, 1982).

5. Since Black women are no longer heavily concentrated in private domestic service, the Mammy image may be fading. In contrast, the matriarch image, popularized in Daniel Patrick Moynihan's, *The Negro Family: The Case for National Action* (Washington, D.C.: U.S. Government Printing Office, 1965), is reemerging in public debates about the feminization of poverty and the urban underclass. See Maxine Baca Zinn, "Minority Families in Crisis: The Public Discussion," Research Paper 6, Center for Research on Women (Memphis, TN: Memphis State University, 1987).

6. For an alternative analysis of the Mammy image, see Judith Rollins, *Between Women: Domestics and Their Employers* (Philadelphia: Temple University, 1985). Classic responses to the matriarchy thesis include Robert Hill, *The Strengths of Black Families* (New York: Urban League, 1972); Andrew Billingsley, *Black Families in White America* (Englewood Cliffs, NJ: Prentice-Hall, 1968); and Joyce Ladner, *Tomorrow's Tomorrow,* (Garden City, NY: Doubleday, 1971). For a recent analysis, see Linda Burnham, "Has Poverty Been Feminized in Black America?" *Black Scholar* 16 (1985): 15–24.

7. Mae King, "The Politics of Sexual Stereotypes," *Black Scholar* 4 (1973):12–23.

8. Barbara Christian, "An Angle of Seeing: Motherhood in Buchi Emecheta's *Joys of Motherhood* and Alice Walker's *Meridian,"* in *Black Feminist Criticism,* ed. Barbara Christian (New York: Pergamon, 1985), p. 214.

9. See Christine Oppong, ed., *Female and Male in West Africa* (London: Allen & Unwin, 1983); Niara Sudarkesa, "Female Employment and Family Organization in West Africa," in *The Black Woman Cross-Culturally,* ed. Filomina Chiamo Steady (Cambridge, MA: Schenkman, 1981), pp. 49-64; and Nancy Tanner, "Matrifocality in Indonesia and Africa and Among Black Americans," in *Woman, Culture, and Society,* ed. Michelle Rosaldo and Louise Lamphere (Stanford, CA: Stanford University Press, 1974), pp. 129–56.

10. Christine Oppong, "Family Structure and Women's Reproductive and Productive Roles: Some Conceptual and Methodological Issues," in *Women's Roles and Population Trends in the Third World,* ed. Richard Anker, Myra Buvinic, and Nadia Youssef (London: Croom Heim, 1982), pp. 133–50.

11. The key distinction here is that, unlike the matriarchy thesis, women play central roles in families and this centrality is seen as legitimate. In spite of this centrality, it is important not to idealize African women's family roles. For an analysis by a Black African feminist, see

Awa Thiam, *Black Sisters, Speak Out: Feminism and Oppression in Black Africa* (London: Pluto, 1978).

12. Sudarkasa, "Female Employment."

13. John Mbiti, *African Religions and Philosophies* (New York: Anchor, 1969).

14. Niara Sudarkasa, "Interpreting the African Heritage in Afro-American Family Organization," in *Black Families,* ed. Harriette Pipes McAdoo (Beverly Hills, CA: Sage, 1981), pp. 37–53; and Deborah Gray White, *Ar'n't I a Woman? Female Slaves in the Plantation South* (New York: W. W. Norton, 1985).

15. The terms used in this section appear in Rosalie Riegle Troester's "Turbulence and Tenderness: Mothers, Daughters, and 'Othermothers' in Paule Marshall's *Brown Girl, Brownstones,"* *SAGE: A Scholarly Journal on Black Women* 1 (Fall 1984):13–16.

16. See Tanner, "Matrifocality"; see also Carrie Allen McCray, "The Black Woman and Family Roles," in *The Black Woman,* ed. LaFrances Rogers-Rose (Beverly Hills, CA: Sage, 1980), pp. 67–78; Elmer Martin and Joanne Mitchell Marlin, *The Black Extended Family* (Chicago: University of Chicago Press, 1978); Joyce Aschenbrenner, *Lifelines, Black Families in Chicago* (Prospect Heights, IL: Waveland, 1975); and Carol B. Stack, *All Our Kin* (New York: Harper & Row, 1974).

17. Martin and Martin, *The Black Extended Family*; Stack, *All Our Kin*; and Virginia Young, "Family and Childhood in a Southern Negro Community," *American Anthropologist* 72 (1970):269–88.

18. Stack, *All Our Kin.*

19. Ellen Cantarow, *Moving the Mountain: Women Working for Social Change* (Old Westbury, NY: Feminist Press, 1980), p. 59.

20. Thordis Simonsen, ed., *You May Plow Here, The Narrative of Sara Brooks* (New York: Touchstone, 1986), p. 181.

21. White, *Ar'n't I a Woman?*; Dill, "Our Mothers' Grief"; Mullings, "Uneven Development."

22. Simonsen, *You May Plow Here,* p. 86.

23. Mamie Garvin Fields and Karen Fields, *Lemon Swamp and Other Places, A Carolina Memoir* (New York: Free Press, 1983), p. xvii.

24. Ibid, p. 195.

25. Cheryl Gilkes, "'Holding Back the Ocean with a Broom,' Black Women and Community Work," in *The Black Woman,* ed. Rogers-Rose, 1980, pp. 217–31, and "Going Up for the Oppressed: The Career Mobility of Black Women Community Workers," *Journal of Social Issues* 39 (1983):115–39.

26. Gilkes, " 'Holding Back the Ocean.'" p. 219.

27. Fields and Fields, *Lemon Swamp,* p. xvi.

28. Charles Johnson, *Shadow of the Plantation* (Chicago: University of Chicago Press, 1934, 1979), p. 173.

29. Pamela Reid, "Socialization of Black Female Children," in *Women: A Developmental Perspective,* ed. Phyllis Berman and Estelle Ramey (Washington, DC: National Institutes of Health, 1983).

30. For works in the feminist psychoanalytic tradition, see Nancy Chodorow, "Family Structure and Feminine Personality," in *Woman, Culture, and Society,* ed. Rosaldo and Lamphere, 1974; Nancy Chodorow, *The Reproduction of Mothering* (Berkeley, CA: University of California, 1978); and Jane Flax, "The Conflict Between Nurturance and Autonomy in Mother-Daughter Relationships and Within Feminism," *Feminist Studies* 4 (1978):171–89.

31. Ann Moody, *Coming of Age in Mississippi* (New York: Dell, 1968).

32. Ladner, *Tomorrow's Tomorrow;* Gloria Joseph, "Black Mothers and Daughters: Their Roles and Functions in American Society," in *Common Differences*, ed. Gloria Joseph and Jill Lewis (Garden City, NY: Anchor, 1981), pp. 75–126; Lena Wright Myers, *Black Women, Do They Cope Better?* (Englewood Cliffs, NJ: Prentice-Hall, 1980).

33. Elsa Barkley Brown, "Hearing Our Mothers' Lives," paper presented at fifteenth anniversary of African-American and African Studies at Emory College, Atlanta, 1986. This essay appeared in the Black Women's Studies issue of *SAGE: A Scholarly Journal on Black Women,* vol. 6, no. 1:4–11.

34. Joseph, "Black Mothers and Daughters"; Myers, 1980.

35. Gloria Wade-Gayles, "The Truths of Our Mothers' Lives: Mother-Daughter Relationships in Black Women's Fiction," *SAGE: A Scholarly Journal on Black Women* 1 (Fall 1984):12.

36. Troester, "Turbulence and Tenderness," p. 13.

37. Wade-Gayles, "The Truths," p. 10.

38. Joseph, "Black Mothers and Daughters."

39. Moody, *Coming of Age,* p. 57.

40. Renita Weems, "'Hush. Mama's Gotta Go Bye Bye': A Personal Narrative," *SAGE: A Scholarly Journal on Black Women* 1 (Fall 1984):26.

41. Ibid, p. 27.

42. June Jordan, *On Call, Political Essays* (Boston: South End Press, 1985), p. 145.

31

"I'm Here, but I'm There"

The Meanings of Latina Transnational Motherhood

PIERRETTE HONDAGNEU-SOTELO
ERNESTINE AVILA

While mothering is generally understood as practice that involves the preservation, nurturance, and training of children for adult life (Ruddick 1989), there are many contemporary variants distinguished by race, class, and culture (Collins 1994; Dill 1988, 1994; Glenn 1994). Latina immigrant women who work and reside in the United States while their children remain in their countries of origin constitute one variation in the organizational arrangements, meanings, and priorities of motherhood. We call this arrangement "transnational motherhood," and we explore how the meanings of motherhood are rearranged to accommodate these spatial and temporal separations. In the United States, there is a long legacy of Caribbean women and African American women from the South, leaving their children "back home" to seek work in the North. Since the early 1980s, thousands of Central American women, and increasing numbers of Mexican women, have migrated to the United States in search of jobs, many of them leaving their children behind with grandmothers, with other female kin, with the children's fathers, and sometimes with paid caregivers. In some cases, the separations of time and distance are substantial; 10 years may elapse before women are reunited with their children. In this article we confine our analysis to Latina transnational mothers currently employed in Los Angeles in paid domestic work, one of the most gendered and racialized occupations.[1]

We examine how their meanings of motherhood shift in relation to the structures of late-20th-century global capitalism.

Motherhood is not biologically predetermined in any fixed way but is historically and socially constructed. Many factors set the stage for transnational motherhood. These factors include labor demand for Latina immigrant women in the United States, particularly in paid domestic work; civil war, national economic crises, and particular development strategies, along with tenuous and scarce job opportunities for women and men in Mexico and Central America; and the subsequent increasing numbers of female-headed households (although many transnational mothers are married). More interesting to us than the macro determinants of transnational motherhood, however, is the forging of new arrangements and meanings of motherhood.

Central American and Mexican women who leave their young children "back home" and come to the United States in search of employment are in the process of actively, if not voluntarily, building alternative constructions of motherhood. Transnational motherhood contradicts both dominant U.S., White, middle-class models of motherhood, and most Latina ideological notions of motherhood. On the cusp of the millennium, transnational mothers and their families are blazing new terrain, spanning national borders, and improvising strategies for mothering. It is a brave odyssey, but one with deep costs....

RETHINKING MOTHERHOOD

Feminist scholarship has long challenged monolithic notions of family and motherhood that relegate women to the domestic arena of private/public dichotomies and that rely on the ideological conflation of family, woman, reproduction, and nurturance (Collier and Yanagisako 1987, 36).[2] "Rethinking the family" prompts the rethinking of motherhood (Glenn 1994; Thorne and Yalom 1992), allowing us to see that the glorification and exaltation of isolationist, privatized mothering is historically and culturally specific.

The "cult of domesticity" is a cultural variant of motherhood, one made possible by the industrial revolution, by breadwinner husbands who have access to employers who pay a "family wage," and by particular configurations of global and national socioeconomic and racial inequalities. Working-class women of color in the United States have rarely had access to the economic security that permits a biological mother to be the only one exclusively involved with mothering during the children's early years (Collins 1994; Dill 1988, 1994; Glenn 1994). As Evelyn Nakano Glenn puts it, "Mothering is not just gendered, but also racialized" (1994, 7) and differentiated by class. Both historically and in the contemporary period, women lacking the resources that allow for exclusive, full-time, round-the-clock mothering rely on various arrangements to care for children. Sharing mothering responsibilities with female kin and friends as "other mothers" (Collins 1991), by "kin-scription" (Stack and Burton 1994), or by hiring child care (Uttal 1996) are widely used alternatives.

Women of color have always worked. Yet, many working women—including Latina women—hold the cultural prescription of solo mothering in the home as an ideal. We believe this ideal is disseminated through cultural institutions of industrialization and urbanization, as well as from preindustrial, rural peasant arrangements that allow for women to work while tending to their children. It is not only White, middle-class ideology but also strong Latina/o traditions, cultural practices, and ideals—Catholicism, and the Virgin Madonna figure—that cast employment as oppositional to mothering. Cultural symbols that model maternal femininity, such as *La Virgen de Guadalupe,* and negative femininity, such as *La Llorona* and *La Malinche,* serve to control Mexican and Chicana women's conduct by prescribing idealized visions of motherhood.[3]

Culture, however, does not deterministically dictate what people do.[4] Many Latina women must work for pay, and many Latinas innovate income-earning strategies that allow them to simultaneously earn money and care for their children. They sew garments on industrial sewing machines at home (Fernández Kelly and Garcia 1990) and incorporate their children into informal vending to friends and neighbors, at swap meets, or on the sidewalks (Chinchilla and Hamilton 1996). They may perform agricultural work alongside their children or engage in seasonal work (Zavella 1987); or they may clean houses when their children are at school or alternatively, incorporate their daughters into paid house cleaning (Romero 1992, 1997). Engagement in "invisible employment" allows for urgently needed income and the maintenance of the ideal of privatized mothering. The middle-class model of mothering is predicated on mother-child isolation in the home, while women of color have often worked with their children in close proximity (Collins 1994), as in some of the examples listed above. In both cases, however, mothers are with their children. The long distances of time and space that separate transnational mothers from their children contrast sharply to both mother-child isolation in the home or mother-child integration in the workplace.

Performing domestic work for pay, especially in a live-in job, is often incompatible with providing primary care for one's own family and home (Glenn 1986; Rollins 1985; Romero 1992, 1997).[5] Transnational mothering, however, is neither exclusive to live-in domestic workers nor to single mothers. Many women continue with transnational mothering after they move into live-out paid domestic work, or into other jobs. Women with income-earning husbands may also become transnational mothers.[6] The women we interviewed do not necessarily divert their mothering to the children and homes of their employers but instead reformulate their own mothering to accommodate spatial and temporal gulfs.

Like other immigrant workers, most transnational mothers came to the United States with the intention to stay for a finite period of time. But as time passes and economic need remains, prolonged stays evolve. Marxist-informed theory maintains that the separation of work life and family life constitutes the separation of labor maintenance costs from the labor reproduction costs (Burawoy 1976; Glenn 1986). According to this framework, Latina transnational mothers work to maintain themselves in the United States and to support their children—and reproduce the next generation of workers—in Mexico or Central America. One precursor to these arrangements is the mid-20th-century Bracero Program, which in effect legislatively mandated Mexican "absentee fathers" who came to work as contracted agricultural laborers in the United States. Other precursors, going back further in history, include the 18th- and 19th-centuries' coercive systems of labor, whereby African American slaves and Chinese sojourner laborers were denied the right to form residentially intact families (Dill 1988, 1994).

Transnational mothering is different from some of these other arrangements in that now women with young children are recruited for U.S. jobs that pay far less than a "family wage." When men come north and leave their families in Mexico—as they did during the Bracero Program and as many continue to do today—they are fulfilling familial obligations defined as breadwinning for the family. When women do so, they are embarking not only on an immigration journey but on a more radical gender-transformative odyssey. They are initiating separations of space and time from their communities of origin, homes, children, and—

sometimes—husbands. In doing so, they must cope with stigma, guilt, and criticism from others. A second difference is that these women work primarily not in production of agricultural products or manufacturing but in reproductive labor, in paid domestic work, and/or vending. Performing paid reproductive work for pay—especially caring for other people's children—is not always compatible with taking daily care of one's own family. All of this raises questions about the meanings and variations of motherhood in the late 20th century.

TRANSNATIONAL MOTHERHOOD AND PAID DOMESTIC WORK

Just how widespread are transnational motherhood arrangements in paid domestic work? Of the 153 domestic workers surveyed, 75 percent had children. Contrary to the images of Latina immigrant women as breeders with large families—a dominant image used in the campaign to pass California's Proposition 187—about half (47 percent) of these women have only one or two children. More significant for our purposes is this finding: Forty percent of the women with children have at least one of their children "back home" in their country of origin.

Transnational motherhood arrangements are not exclusive to paid domestic work, but there are particular features about the way domestic work is organized that encourage temporal and spatial separations of a mother-employee and her children. Historically and in the contemporary period, paid domestic workers have had to limit or forfeit primary care of their families and homes to earn income by providing primary care to the families and homes of employers, who are privileged by race and class (Glenn 1986; Rollins 1985; Romero 1992). Paid domestic work is organized in various ways, and there is a clear relationship between the type of job arrangement women have and the likelihood of experiencing transnational family arrangements with their children. To understand the variations, it is necessary to explain how the employment is organized.

Although there are variations within categories, we find it useful to employ a tripartite taxonomy of paid domestic work arrangements. This includes live-in and live-out nanny-housekeeper jobs, and weekly housecleaning jobs.

Weekly house cleaners clean different houses on different days according to what Romero (1992) calls modernized "job work" arrangements. These contractual-like employee-employer relations often resemble those between customer and vendor, and they allow employees a degree of autonomy and scheduling flexibility. Weekly employees are generally paid a flat fee, and they work shorter hours and earn considerably higher hourly rates than do live-in or live-out domestic workers. By contrast, live-in domestic workers work and live in isolation from their own families and communities, sometimes in arrangements with feudal remnants (Glenn 1986). There are often no hourly parameters to their jobs, and as our survey results show, most live-in workers in Los Angeles earn below minimum wage. Live-out domestic workers also usually work as combination nanny-housekeepers, generally working for one household, but contrary to live-ins, they enter daily and return to their own home in the evening. Because of this, live-out workers better resemble industrial wage workers (Glenn 1986).

Live-in jobs are the least compatible with conventional mothering responsibilities. Only about half (16 out of 30) of live-ins surveyed have children, while 83 percent (53 out of 64) of live-outs and 77 percent (45 out of 59) of house cleaners do. As Table I shows, 82 percent of live-ins with children have at least one of their children in their country of origin. It is very difficult to work a live-in job when your children are in the United States. Employers who hire live-in workers do so because they generally want employees for jobs that may require round-the-clock service. As one owner of a domestic employment agency put it,

They (employers) want a live-in to have somebody at their beck and call. They want the hours that are most difficult for them covered, which is like six thirty in the morning 'till eight when the kids go to

school, and four to seven when the kids are home, and it's homework, bath, and dinner.

According to our survey, live-ins work an average of 64 hours per week. The best live-in worker, from an employer's perspective, is one without daily family obligations of her own. The workweek may consist of six very long workdays. These may span from dawn to midnight and may include overnight responsibilities with sleepless or sick children, making it virtually impossible for live-in workers to sustain daily contact with their own families. Although some employers do allow for their employees' children to live in as well (Romero 1996), this is rare. When it does occur, it is often fraught with special problems, and we discuss these in a subsequent section of this article. In fact, minimal family and mothering obligations are an informal job placement criterion for live-in workers. Many of the agencies specializing in the placement of live-in nanny-housekeepers will not even refer a woman who has children in Los Angeles to interviews for live-in jobs. As one agency owner explained, "As a policy here, we will not knowingly place a nanny in a live-in job if she has young kids here." A job seeker in an employment agency waiting room acknowledged that she understood this job criterion more broadly, "You can't have a family, you can't have anyone (if you want a live-in job)."

The subminimum pay and the long hours for live-in workers also make it very difficult for these workers to have their children in the United States. Some live-in workers who have children in the same city as their place of employment hire their own nanny-housekeeper—often a much younger, female relative—to provide daily care for their children, as did Patricia, one of the interview respondents whom we discuss later in this article. Most live-ins, however, cannot afford this alternative; ninety-three percent of the live-ins surveyed earn below minimum wage (then $4.25 per hour). Many live-in workers cannot afford to bring their children to Los Angeles, but once their children are in the same city, most women try to leave live-in work to live with their children.

TABLE 1   Domestic Workers: Wages, Hours Worked and Children's Country of Residence

	LIVE-INS ($n = 30$)	LIVE-OUTS ($n = 64$)	HOUSE CLEANERS ($n = 59$)
Mean hourly wage	$3.79	$5.90	$9.40
Mean hours worked per week	64	35	23
Domestic workers with children	($n = 16$)	($n = 53$)	($n = 45$)
All children in the United States (%)	18	58	76
At least one child "back home"	82	42	24

At the other end of the spectrum are the house cleaners that we surveyed, who earn substantially higher wages than live-ins (averaging $9.46 per hour as opposed to $3.79) and who work fewer hours per week than live-ins (23 as opposed to 64). We suspect that many house cleaners in Los Angeles make even higher earnings and work more hours per week, because we know that the survey undersampled women who drive their own cars to work and who speak English. The survey suggests that house cleaners appear to be the least likely to experience transnational spatial and temporal separations from their children.

Financial resources and job terms enhance house cleaners' abilities to bring their children to the United States. Weekly housecleaning is not a bottom-of-the-barrel job but rather an achievement. Breaking into housecleaning work is difficult because an employee needs to locate and secure several different employers. For this reason, relatively well-established women with more years of experience in the United States, who speak some English, who have a car, and who have job references predominate in weekly housecleaning. Women who are better established in the United States are also more likely to have their children here. The terms of weekly housecleaning employment—particularly the relatively fewer hours worked per week, scheduling flexibility, and relatively higher wages—allow them to live with, and care for, their children. So, it is not surprising that 76 percent of house cleaners who are mothers have their children in the United States.

Compared with live-ins and weekly cleaners, live-out nanny-housekeepers are at an intermedi-

ate level with respect to the likelihood of transnational motherhood. Forty-two percent of the live-out nanny-housekeepers who are mothers reported having at least one of their children in their country of origin. Live-out domestic workers, according to the survey, earn $5.90 per hour and work an average workweek of 35 hours. Their lower earnings, more regimented schedules, and longer workweeks than house cleaners, but higher earnings, shorter hours, and more scheduling flexibility than live-ins explain their intermediate incidence of transnational motherhood.

The Meanings of Transnational Motherhood

How do women transform the meaning of motherhood to fit immigration and employment? Being a transnational mother means more than being the mother to children raised in another country. It means forsaking deeply felt beliefs that biological mothers should raise their own children, and replacing that belief with new definitions of motherhood. The ideal of biological mothers raising their own children is widely held but is also widely broken at both ends of the class spectrum. Wealthy elites have always relied on others—nannies, governesses, and boarding schools—to raise their children (Wrigley 1995), while poor, urban families often rely on kin and "other mothers" (Collins 1991).

In Latin America, in large, peasant families, the eldest daughters are often in charge of the daily care of the younger children, and in situations of extreme poverty, children as young as five or six may be loaned or hired out to well-to-do families as "child-servants," sometimes called *criadas* (Gill 1994).[7] A middle-aged Mexican woman that we interviewed, now a weekly house cleaner, homeowner, and mother of five children, recalled her own experience as a child-servant in Mexico: "I started working in a house when I was 8…they hardly let me eat any food…. It was terrible, but I had to work to help my mother with the rent." This recollection of her childhood experiences reminds us how our contemporary notions of motherhood are historically and socially circumscribed, and also correspond to the meanings we assign to childhood (Zelizer 1994).

This example also underlines how the expectation on the child to help financially support her mother required daily spatial and temporal separations of mother and child. There are, in fact, many transgressions of the mother-child symbiosis in practice—large families where older daughters care for younger siblings, child-servants who at an early age leave their mothers, children raised by paid nannies and other caregivers, and mothers who leave young children to seek employment—but these are fluid enough to sustain ideological adherence to the prescription that children should be raised exclusively by biological mothers. Long-term physical and temporal separation disrupts this notion. Transnational mothering radically rearranges mother-child interactions and requires a concomitant radical reshaping of the meanings and definitions of appropriate mothering.

Transnational mothers distinguish their version of motherhood from estrangement, child abandonment, or disowning. A youthful Salvadoran woman at the domestic employment waiting room reported that she had not seen her two eldest boys, now ages 14 and 15 and under the care of her own mother in El Salvador, since they were toddlers. Yet, she made it clear that this was different from putting a child up for adoption, a practice that she viewed negatively, as a form of child abandonment. Although she had been physically separated from her boys for more than a decade, she maintained her mothering ties and financial obligations to them by regularly sending home

money. The exchange of letters, photos, and phone calls also helped to sustain the connection. Her physical absence did not signify emotional absence from her children. Another woman who remains intimately involved in the lives of her two daughters, now ages 17 and 21 in El Salvador, succinctly summed up this stance when she said, "I'm here, but I'm there." Over the phone, and through letters, she regularly reminds her daughters to take their vitamins, to never go to bed or to school on an empty stomach, and to use protection from pregnancy and sexually transmitted diseases if they engage in sexual relations with their boyfriends.

Transnational mothers fully understand and explain the conditions that prompt their situations. In particular, many Central American women recognize that the gendered employment demand in Los Angeles has produced transnational motherhood arrangements. These new mothering arrangements, they acknowledge, take shape despite strong beliefs that biological mothers should care for their own children. Emelia, a 49-year-old woman who left her five children in Guatemala nine years ago to join her husband in Los Angeles explained this changing relationship between family arrangements, migration, and job demand:

> One supposes that the mother must care for the children. A mother cannot so easily throw her children aside. So, in all families, the decision is that the man comes (to the U.S.) first. But now, since the man cannot find work here so easily, the woman comes first. Recently, women have been coming and the men staying.

A steady demand for live-in housekeepers means that Central American women may arrive in Los Angeles on a Friday and begin working Monday at a live-in job that provides at least some minimal accommodations. Meanwhile, her male counterpart may spend weeks or months before securing even casual day laborer jobs. While Emelia, formerly a homemaker who previously earned income in Guatemala by baking cakes and pastries in her home, expressed pain and sadness at not being with her children as they grew, she was also proud of her accomplishments. "My children," she stated, "recognize what I have been able to do for them."

Most transnational mothers, like many other immigrant workers, come to the United States with the intention to stay for a finite period of time, until they can pay off bills or raise the money for an investment in a house, their children's education, or a small business. Some of these women return to their countries of origin, but many stay. As time passes, and as their stays grow longer, some of the women eventually bring some or all of their children. Other women who stay at their U.S. jobs are adamant that they do not wish for their children to traverse the multiple hazards of adolescence in U.S. cities or to repeat the job experiences they themselves have had in the United States. One Salvadoran woman in the waiting room at the domestic employment agency—whose children had been raised on earnings predicated on her separation from them—put it this way:

> I've been here 19 years, I've got my legal papers and everything. But I'd have to be crazy to bring my children here. All of them have studied for a career, so why would I bring them here? To bus tables and earn minimum wage? So they won't have enough money for bus fare or food?

Who Is Taking Care of the Nanny's Children?

Transnational Central American and Mexican mothers may rely on various people to care for their children's daily, round-the-clock needs, but they prefer a close relative. The "other mothers" on which Latinas rely include their own mothers, *comadres* (co-godmothers) and other female kin, the children's fathers, and paid caregivers. Reliance on grandmothers and comadres for shared mothering is well established in Latina culture, and it is a practice that signifies a more collectivist, shared approach to mothering in contrast to a more individualistic, Anglo-American approach (Griswold del Castillo 1984; Segura and Pierce

1993). Perhaps this cultural legacy facilitates the emergence of transnational motherhood.

Transnational mothers express a strong preference for their own biological mother to serve as the primary caregiver. Here, the violation of the cultural preference for the biological mother is rehabilitated by reliance on the biological grandmother or by reliance on the ceremonially bound comadres. Clemencia, for example, left her three young children behind in Mexico, each with their respective *madrina,* or godmother.

Emelia left her five children, then ranging in ages from 6 to 16, under the care of her mother and sister in Guatemala. As she spoke of the hardships faced by transnational mothers, she counted herself among the fortunate ones who did not need to leave the children alone with paid caregivers:

> One's mother is the only one who can really and truly care for your children. No one else can.... Women who aren't able to leave their children with their mother or with someone very special, they'll wire money to Guatemala and the people (caregivers) don't feed the children well. They don't buy the children clothes the mother would want. They take the money and the children suffer a lot.

Both Central American and Mexican woman stated preferences for grandmothers as the ideal caregivers in situations that mandated the absence of the children's biological mother. These preferences seem to grow out of strategic availability, but these preferences assume cultural mandates. Velia, a Mexicana who hailed from the border town of Mexicali, improvised an employment strategy whereby she annually sent her three elementary school-age children to her mother in Mexicali for the summer vacation months. This allowed Velia, a single mother, to intensify her housecleaning jobs and save money on day care. But she also insisted that "if my children were with the woman next door (who babysits), I'd worry if they were eating well, or about men (coming to harass the girls). Having them with my mother allows me to work in peace." Another woman specified more narrowly, insisting that only maternal grandmothers could provide adequate caregiving. In a conversation in a park, a Salvadoran woman offered that a biological mother's mother was the one best suited to truly love and care for a child in the biological mother's absence. According to her, not even the paternal grandmother could be trusted to provide proper nurturance and care. Another Salvadoran woman, Maria, left her two daughters, then 14 and 17, at their paternal grandmother's home, but before departing for the United States, she trained her daughters to become self-sufficient in cooking, marketing, and budgeting money. Although she believes the paternal grandmother loves the girls, she did not trust the paternal grandmother enough to cook or administer the money that she would send her daughters.

Another variation in the preference for a biological relative as a caregiver is captured by the arrangement of Patricia, a 30-year-old Mexicana who came to the United States as a child and was working as a live-in, caring for an infant in one of southern California's affluent coastal residential areas. Her arrangement was different, as her daughters were all born, raised, and residing in the United States, but she lived apart from them during weekdays because of her live-in job. Her three daughters, ages 1½, 6, and 11, stayed at their apartment near downtown Los Angeles under the care of their father and a paid nanny-housekeeper, Patricia's teenage cousin. Her paid caregiver was not an especially close relative, but she rationalized this arrangement by emphasizing that her husband, the girls' father, and therefore a biological relative, was with them during the week.

> Whenever I've worked like this, I've always had a person in charge of them also working as a live-in. She sleeps here the five days, but when my husband arrives he takes responsibility for them.... When my husband arrives (from work) she (cousin/paid caregiver) goes to English class and he takes charge of the girls.

And another woman who did not have children of her own but who had worked as a nanny for her aunt stated that "as Hispanas, we don't believe in bringing someone else in to care for our children." Again, the biological ties help sanction the shared child care arrangement.

New family fissures emerge for the transnational mother as she negotiates various aspects of the arrangement with her children, and with the 'other mother' who provides daily care and supervision for the children. Any impulse to romanticize transnational motherhood is tempered by the sadness with which the women related their experiences and by the problems they sometimes encounter with their children and caregivers. A primary worry among transnational mothers is that their children are being neglected or abused in their absence. While there is a long legacy of child-servants being mistreated and physically beaten in Latin America, transnational mothers also worry that their own paid caregivers will harm or neglect their children. They worry that their children may not receive proper nourishment, schooling and educational support, and moral guidance. They may remain unsure as to whether their children are receiving the full financial support they send home. In some cases, their concerns are intensified by the eldest child or a nearby relative who is able to monitor and report the caregiver's transgression to the transnational mother.

Transnational mothers engage in emotion work and financial compensation to maintain a smoothly functioning relationship with the children's daily caregiver. Their efforts are not always successful, and when problems arise, they may return to visit if they can afford to do so. After not seeing her four children for seven years, Carolina abruptly quit her nanny job and returned to Guatemala in the spring of 1996 because she was concerned about one adolescent daughter's rebelliousness and about her mother-in-law's failing health. Carolina's husband remained in Los Angeles, and she was expected to return. Emelia, whose children were cared for by her mother and sister, with the assistance of paid caregivers, regularly responded to her sister's reminders to send gifts, clothing, and small amounts of money to the paid caregivers. "If they are taking care of my children," she explained, "then I have to show my gratitude."

Some of these actions are instrumental. Transnational mothers know that they may increase the likelihood of their children receiving adequate care if they appropriately remunerate the caregivers and treat them with the consideration their work requires. In fact, they often express astonishment that their own Anglo employers fail to recognize this in relation to the nanny-housekeeper work that they perform. Some of the expressions of gratitude and gifts that they send to their children's caregivers appear to be genuinely disinterested and enhanced by the transnational mothers' empathy arising out of their own similar job circumstances. A Honduran woman, a former biology teacher, who had left her four sons with a paid caregiver, maintained that the treatment of nannies and housekeepers was much better in Honduras than in the United States, in part, because of different approaches to mothering:

> We're very different back there.... We treat them (domestic workers) with a lot of affection and respect, and when they are taking care of our kids, even more so. The Americana, she is very egotistical. When the nanny loves her children, she gets jealous. Not us. We are appreciative when someone loves our children, and bathes, dresses, and feeds them as though they were their own.

These comments are clearly informed by the respondent's prior class status, as well as her simultaneous position as the employer of a paid nanny-housekeeper in Honduras and as a temporarily unemployed nanny-housekeeper in the United States. (She had been fired from her nanny-housekeeper job for not showing up on Memorial Day, which she erroneously believed was a work holiday.) Still, her comments underline the importance of showing appreciation and gratitude to the caregiver, in part, for the sake of the children's well-being.

Transnational mothers also worry about whether their children will get into trouble during adolescence or if they will transfer their allegiance and affection to the "other mother." In general, transnational mothers, like African American mothers who leave their children in the South to work up North (Stack and Button 1994), believe that the person who cares for the children has the right to discipline. But when adolescent youths are paired with elderly grandmothers, or ineffective disciplinary figures, the mothers may need to intervene. Preadolescent and adolescent children who show signs of rebelliousness may be brought north because they are deemed unmanageable by their grandmothers or paid caregivers. Alternatively, teens who are in California may be sent back in hope that it will straighten them out, a practice that has resulted in the migration of Los Angeles-based delinquent youth gangs to Mexican and Central American towns. Another danger is that the child who has grown up without the transnational mother's presence may no longer respond to her authority. One woman at the domestic employment agency, who had recently brought her adolescent son to join her in California, reported that she had seen him at a bus stop, headed for the beach. When she demanded to know where he was going, he said something to the effect of "and who are you to tell me what to do?" After a verbal confrontation at the bus kiosk, she handed him $10. Perhaps the mother hoped that money will be a way to show caring and to advance a claim to parental authority.

Motherhood and Breadwinning

Milk, shoes, and schooling—these are the currency of transnational motherhood. Providing for children's sustenance, protecting their current well-being, and preparing them for the future are widely shared concerns of motherhood. Central American and Mexican women involved in transnational mothering attempt to ensure the present and future well-being of their children through U.S. wage earning, and as we have seen, this requires long-term physical separation from their children.

For these women, the meanings of motherhood do not appear to be in a liminal stage. That is, they do not appear to be making a linear progression from a way of motherhood that involves daily, face-to-face caregiving toward one that is defined primarily through breadwinning. Rather than replacing caregiving with breadwinning definitions of motherhood, they appear to be expanding their definitions of motherhood to encompass breadwinning that may require long-term physical separations. For these women, a core belief is that they can best fulfill traditional caregiving responsibilities through income earning in the United States while their children remain "back home."

Transnational mothers continue to state that caregiving is a defining feature of their mothering experiences. They wish to provide their children with better nutrition, clothing, and schooling, and most of them are able to purchase these items with dollars earned in the United States. They recognize, however, that their transnational relationships incur painful costs. Transnational mothers worry about some of the negative effects on their children, but they also experience the absence of domestic family life as a deeply personal loss. Transnational mothers who primarily identified as homemakers before coming to the United States identified the loss of daily contact with family as a sacrifice ventured to financially support the children. As Emelia, who had previously earned some income by baking pastries and doing catering from her home in Guatemala, reflected,

> The money (earned in the U.S.) is worth five times more in Guatemala. My oldest daughter was then 16, and my youngest was 6 (when I left). Ay, it's terrible, terrible, but that's what happens to most women (transnational mothers) who are here. You sacrifice your family life (for labor migration).

Similarly, Carolina used the word *sacrifice* when discussing her family arrangement, claiming that her children "tell me that they appreciate us (parents), and the sacrifice that their papa and mama make for them. That is what they say."

The daily indignities of paid domestic work—low pay, subtle humiliations, not enough food to eat, invisibility (Glenn 1986; Rollins 1985;

Romero 1992)—means that transnational mothers are not only stretching their U.S.-earned dollars further by sending the money back home but also, by leaving the children behind, they are providing special protection from the discrimination the children might receive in the United States. Gladys, who had four of her five children in El Salvador, acknowledged that her U.S. dollars went further in El Salvador. Although she missed seeing those four children grow up, she felt that in some ways, she had spared them the indignities to which she had exposed her youngest daughter, whom she brought to the United States at age 4 in 1988. Although her live-in employer had allowed the four-year-old to join the family residence, Gladys tearfully recalled how that employer had initially quarantined her daughter, insisting on seeing vaccination papers before allowing the girl to play with the employer's children. "I had to battle, really struggle," she recalled, "just to get enough food for her (to eat)." For Gladys, being together with her youngest daughter in the employer's home had entailed new emotional costs.

Patricia, the mother who was apart from her children only during the weekdays when she lived in with her employer, put forth an elastic definition of motherhood, one that included both meeting financial obligations and spending time with the children. Although her job involves different scheduling than most employed mothers, she shares views similar to those held by many working mothers:

> It's something you have to do, because you can't just stay seated at home because the bills accumulate and you have to find a way.... I applied at many different places for work, like hospitals, as a receptionist—due to the experience I've had with computers working in shipping and receiving, things like that, but they never called me.... One person can't pay all the bills.

Patricia emphasized that she believes motherhood also involves making an effort to spend time with the children. According to this criterion, she explained, most employers were deficient, while she was compliant. During the middle of the week, she explained, "I invent something, some excuse for her (the employer) to let me come home, even if I have to bring the (employer's) baby here with me…just to spend time with my kids."

Transnational mothers echoed these sentiments. Maria Elena, for example, whose 13-year-old son resided with his father in Mexico after she lost a custody battle, insisted that motherhood did not consist of only breadwinning: "You can't give love through money." According to Maria Elena, motherhood required an emotional presence and communication with a child. Like other transnational mothers, she explained how she maintained this connection despite the long-term geographic distance: "I came here, but we're not apart. We talk (by telephone)…. I know (through telephone conversations) when my son is fine. I can tell when he is sad by the way he speaks." Like employed mothers everywhere, she insisted on a definition of motherhood that emphasized quality rather than quantity of time spent with the child: "I don't think that a good mother is one who is with her children at all times…. It's the quality of time spent with the child." She spoke these words tearfully, reflecting the trauma of losing a custody battle with her ex-husband. Gladys also stated that being a mother involves both breadwinning and providing direction and guidance. "It's not just feeding them, or buying clothes for them. It's also educating them, preparing them to make good choices so they'll have a better future."

Transnational mothers seek to mesh caregiving and guidance with breadwinning. While breadwinning may require their long-term and long-distance separations from their children, they attempt to sustain family connections by showing emotional ties through letters, phone calls, and money sent home. If at all financially and logistically possible, they try to travel home to visit their children. They maintain their mothering responsibilities not only by earning money for their children's livelihood but also by communicating and advising across national borders, and across the boundaries that separate their children's place of

residence from their own places of employment and residence.

Bonding with the Employers' Kids and Critiques of "Americana" Mothers

Some nanny-housekeepers develop very strong ties of affection with the children they care for during long workweeks. It is not unusual for nanny-housekeepers to be alone with these children during the workweek, with no one else with whom to talk or interact. The nannies, however, develop close emotional ties selectively, with some children, but not with others. For nanny-housekeepers who are transnational mothers, the loving daily caregiving that they cannot express for their own children is sometimes transferred to their employers' children. Carolina, a Guatemalan woman with four children between the ages of 10 and 14 back home, maintained that she tried to treat the employers' children with the same affection that she had for her own children "because if you do not feel affection for children, you are not able to care for them well." When interviewed, however, she was caring for two-year-old triplets—for whom she expressed very little affection—but she recalled very longingly her fond feelings for a child at her last job, a child who vividly reminded her of her daughter, who was about the same age:

> When I saw that the young girl was lacking in affection, I began to get close to her and I saw that she appreciated that I would touch her, give her a kiss on the cheek…. And then I felt consoled too, because I had someone to give love to. But, I would imagine that she was my daughter, ah? And then I would give pure love to her, and that brought her closer to me.

Another nanny-housekeeper recalled a little girl for whom she had developed strong bonds of affection, laughingly imitating how the preschooler, who could not pronounce the "f" sound, would say "you hurt my peelings, but I don't want to pight."

Other nanny-housekeepers reflected that painful experiences with abrupt job terminations had taught them not to transfer mother love to the children of their employers. Some of these women reported that they now remained very measured and guarded in their emotional closeness with the employers' children, so that they could protect themselves for the moment when that relationship might be abruptly severed.

I love these children, but now I stop myself from becoming too close. Before, when my own children weren't here (in the United States), I gave all my love to the children I cared for (then toddler twins). That was my recompensation (for not being with my children). When the job ended, I hurt so much. I can't let that happen again.

I love them, but not like they were my own children because they are not! They are not my kids! Because if I get to love them, and then I go, then I'm going to suffer like I did the last time. I don't want that.

Not all nanny-housekeepers bond tightly with the employers' children, but most of them are critical of what they perceive as the employers' neglectful parenting and mothering. Typically, they blame biological mothers (their employers) for substandard parenting. Carolina recalled advising the mother of the above-mentioned little girl, who reminded her of her own child, that the girl needed to receive more affection from her mother, whom she perceived as self-absorbed with physical fitness regimes. Carolina had also advised other employers on disciplining their children. Patricia also spoke adamantly on this topic, and she recalled with satisfaction that when she had advised her current employer to spend more than 15 minutes a day with the baby, the employer had been reduced to tears. By comparison to her employer's mothering, Patricia cited her own perseverance in going out of her way to visit her children during the week:

If you really love your kids, you look for the time, you make time to spend with your kids.... I work all week and for some reason I make excuses for

her (employer) to let me come (home)...just to spend time with my kids.

Her rhetoric of comparative mothering is also inspired by the critique that many nanny-housekeepers have of female employers who may be out of the labor force but who employ nannies and hence do not spend time with their children.

I love my kids, they don't. It's just like, excuse the word, shitting kids.... What they prefer is to go to the salon, get their nails done, you know, go shopping, things like that. Even if they're home all day, they don't want to spend time with the kids because they're paying somebody to do that for them.

Curiously, she spoke as though her female employer is a wealthy woman of leisure, but in fact, both her current and past female employers are wealthy business executives who work long hours. Perhaps at this distance on the class spectrum, all class and racially privileged mothers look alike. "I work my butt off to get what I have," she observed, "and they don't have to work that much."

In some ways, transnational mothers who work as nanny-housekeepers cling to a more sentimentalized view of the employers' children than of their own. This strategy allows them to critique their employers, especially homemakers of privilege who are occupied with neither employment nor daily caregiving for their children. The Latina nannies appear to endorse motherhood as a full-time vocation in contexts of sufficient financial resources, but in contexts of financial hardship such as their own, they advocate more elastic definitions of motherhood, including forms that may include long spatial and temporal separations of mother and children.

As observers of late-20th-century U.S. families (Skolnick 1991; Stacey 1996) have noted, we live in an era wherein no one normative family arrangement predominates. Just as no one type of mothering unequivocally prevails in the White middle class, no singular mothering arrangement prevails among Latina immigrant women. In fact, the exigencies of contemporary immigration seem to multiply the variety of mothering arrangements. Through our research with Latina immigrant women who work as nannies, housekeepers, and house cleaners, we have encountered a broad range of mothering arrangements. Some Latinas migrate to the United States without their children to establish employment, and after some stability has been achieved, they may send for their children or they may work for a while to save money, and then return to their countries of origin. Other Latinas migrate and may postpone having children until they are financially established. Still others arrive with their children and may search for employment that allows them to live together with their children, and other Latinas may have sufficient financial support—from their husbands or kin—to stay home full-time with their children.

In the absence of a universal or at least widely shared mothering arrangement, there is tremendous uncertainty about what constitutes "good mothering," and transnational mothers must work hard to defend their choices. Some Latina nannies who have their children with them in the United States condemn transnational mothers as "bad women." One interview respondent, who was able to take her young daughter to work with her, claimed that she could never leave her daughter. For this woman, transnational mothers were not only bad mothers but also nannies who could not be trusted to adequately care for other people's children. As she said of an acquaintance, "This woman left her children (in Honduras)…she was taking care (of other people's children), and I said, 'Lord, who are they (the employers) leaving their children with if she did that with her own children!'"

Given the uncertainty of what is "good mothering," and to defend their integrity as mothers when others may criticize them, transnational mothers construct new scales for gauging the quality of mothering. By favorably comparing themselves with the negative models of mothering that they see in others—especially those that they are able to closely scrutinize in their employers' homes—transnational mothers create new definitions of good-mothering standards. At the same time, selectively developing motherlike ties with other people's children allows them to enjoy affectionate, face-to-face interactions that they cannot experience on a daily basis with their own children.

DISCUSSION: TRANSNATIONAL MOTHERHOOD

In California, with few exceptions, paid domestic work has become a Latina immigrant women's job. One observer has referred to these Latinas as "the new employable mothers" (Chang 1994), but taking on these wage labor duties often requires Latina workers to expand the frontiers of motherhood by leaving their own children for several years. While today there is a greater openness to accepting a plurality of mothering arrangements—single mothers, employed mothers, stay-at-home mothers, lesbian mothers, surrogate mothers, to name a few—even feminist discussions generally assume that mothers, by definition, will reside with their children.

Transnational mothering situations disrupt the notion of family in one place and break distinctively with what some commentators have referred to as the "epoxy glue" view of motherhood (Blum and Deussen 1996; Scheper-Hughes 1992). Latina transnational mothers are improvising new mothering arrangements that are borne out of women's financial struggles, played out in a new global arena, to provide the best future for themselves and their children. Like many other women of color and employed mothers, transnational mothers rely on an expanded and sometimes fluid number of family members and paid caregivers. Their caring circuits, however, span stretches of geography and time that are much wider than typical joint custody or "other mother" arrangements that are more closely bound, both spatially and temporally.

…Although not addressed directly in this article, the experiences of these mothers resonate with current major political issues. For example, transnational mothering resembles precisely what immigration restrictionists have advocated through California's Proposition 187 (Hondagneu-Sotelo 1995).[8] While proponents of Proposition 187 have never questioned California's reliance on low-waged Latino immigrant workers, this restrictionist policy calls for fully dehumanized immigrant workers, not workers with families and family needs (such as education and health services for children). In this respect, transnational mothering's externalization of the cost of labor reproduction to Mexico and Central America is a dream come true for the proponents of Proposition 187.

Contemporary transnational motherhood continues a long historical legacy of people of color being incorporated into the United States through coercive systems of labor that do not recognize family rights. As Bonnie Thornton Dill (1988), Evelyn Nakano Glenn (1986), and others have pointed out, slavery and contract labor systems were organized to maximize economic productivity and offered few supports to sustain family life. The job characteristics of paid domestic work, especially live-in work, virtually impose transnational motherhood for many Mexican and Central American women who have children of their own.

The ties of transnational motherhood suggest simultaneously the relative permeability of borders, as witnessed by the maintenance of family ties and the new meanings of motherhood, and the impermeability of nation-state borders. Ironically, just at the moment when free trade proponents and pundits celebrate globalization and transnationalism, and when "borderlands" and "border crossings" have become the metaphors of preference for describing a mind-boggling range of conditions, nation-state borders prove to be very real obstacles for many Mexican and Central American women who work in the United States and who, given the appropriate circumstances, wish to be with their children. While demanding the right for women workers to live with their children may provoke critiques of sentimentality, essentialism, and the glorification of motherhood, demanding the right for women workers to choose their own motherhood arrangements would be the beginning of truly just family and work policies, policies that address not only inequalities of gender but also inequalities of race, class, and citizenship status.

NOTES

1. No one knows the precise figures on the prevalence of transnational motherhood just as no one knows the myriad consequences for both mothers and their children. However, one indicator that hints at both the complex outcomes and the frequencies of these arrangements is that teachers and social workers in Los Angeles are becoming increasingly concerned about some of the deleterious effects of these mother-child separations and reunions. Many Central American women who made their way to Los Angeles in the early 1980s, fleeing civil wars and economic upheaval, pioneered transnational mothering, and some of them are now financially able to bring the children whom they left behind. These children, now in their early teen years, are confronting the triple trauma of simultaneously entering adolescence—with its own psychological upheavals; a new society—often in an inner-city environment that requires learning to navigate a new language, place and culture; and they are also entering families that do not look like the ones they knew before their mothers' departure, families with new siblings born in the United States, and new step-fathers or mother's boyfriends.

2. Acknowledgment of the varieties of family and mothering has been fueled, in part, by research on the growing numbers of women-headed families, involving families of all races and socioeconomic levels—including Latina families in the United States and elsewhere (Baca Zinn 1989; Fernández Kelly and Garcia 1990), and by recognition that biological ties do not necessarily constitute family (Weston 1991).

3. *La Virgen de Guadalupe,* the indigenous virgin who appeared in 1531 to a young Indian boy and for whom a major basilica is built, provides the exemplary maternal model, *la mujer abnegada* (the self-effacing woman), who sacrifices all for her children and religious faith. *La Malinche,* the Aztec woman that served Cortes as a translator, a diplomat, and a mistress, and *La Llorona* (the weeping one), a legendary solitary, ghostlike figure reputed either to have been violently murdered by a

jealous husband or to have herself murdered her children by drowning them, are the negative and despised models of femininity. Both are failed women because they have failed at motherhood. *La Malinche* is stigmatized as a traitor and a whore who collaborated with the Spanish conquerors, and *La Llorona* is the archetypal evil woman condemned to eternally suffer and weep for violating her role as a wife and a mother (Soto 1986).

4. A study comparing Mexicanas and Chicanas found that the latter are more favorably disposed to homemaker ideals than are Mexican-born women. This difference is explained by Chicanas' greater exposure to U.S. ideology that promotes the opposition of mothering and employment and to Mexicanas' integration of household and economy in Mexico (Segura 1994). While this dynamic may be partially responsible for this pattern, we suspect that Mexicanas may have higher rates of labor force participation because they are also a self-selected group of Latinas; by and large, they come to the United States to work.

5. See Romero (1997) for a study focusing on the perspective of domestic workers' children. Although most respondents in this particular study were children of day workers, and none appear to have been children of transnational mothers, they still recall significant costs stemming from their mothers' occupation.

6. This seems to be more common among Central American women than Mexican women. Central American women may be more likely than are Mexican women to have their children in their country of origin, even if their husbands are living with them in the United States because of the multiple dangers and costs associated with undocumented travel from Central America to the United States. The civil wars of the 1980s, continuing violence and economic uncertainty, greater difficulties and costs associated with crossing multiple national borders, and stronger cultural legacies of socially sanctioned consensual unions may also contribute to this pattern for Central Americans.

7. According to interviews conducted with domestic workers in La Paz, Bolivia in the late 1980s, 41 percent got their first job between the age of 11 and 15, and one-third got their first job between the ages of 6 and 8. Some parents received half of the child-servant's salary (Gill 1994, 64). Similar arrangements prevailed in preindustrial, rural areas of the United States and Europe.

8. In November 1994, California voters passed Proposition 187, which legislates the denial of public school education, health care, and other public benefits to undocumented immigrants and their children. Although currently held up in the courts, the facility with which Proposition 187 passed in the California ballots rejuvenated anti-immigrant politics at a national level. It opened the door to new legislative measures in 1997 to deny public assistance to legal immigrants.

REFERENCES

Blum, Linda, and Theresa Deussen. 1996. Negotiating independent motherhood: Working-class African American women talk about marriage and motherhood. *Gender & Society* 10:199–211.

Burawoy, Michael. 1976. The functions and reproduction of migrant labor: Comparative material from Southern Africa and the United States. *American Journal of Sociology* 81:1050–87.

Chang, Grace. 1994. Undocumented Latinas: Welfare burdens or beasts of burden? *Socialist Review* 23:151–85.

Chinchilla, Norma Stoltz, and Nora Hamilton. 1996. Negotiating urban space: Latina workers in domestic work and street vending in Los Angeles. *Humbolt Journal of Social Relations* 22:25–35.

Collier, Jane Fishburne, and Sylvia Junko Yanagisako. 1987. *Gender and kinship: Essays toward a unified analysis.* Stanford, CA: Stanford University Press.

Collins, Patricia Hill. 1991. *Black feminist thought. Knowledge, consciousness, and the politics of empowerment.* New York: Routledge.

———. 1994. Shifting the center: Race, class, and feminist theorizing about motherhood. In *Mothering: Ideology, experience, and agency,* edited by Evelyn Nakano Glenn, Grace Chang, and Linda Rennie Forcey. New York: Routledge.

Dill, Bonnie Thornton. 1988. Our mothers' grief. Racial-ethnic women and the maintenance of families. *Journal of Family History* 13:415–31.

———. 1994. Fictive kin, paper sons and compadrazgo: Women of color and the struggle for family survival. In *Women of color in U.S. society,* edited by Maxine Baca Zinn and Bonnie Thornton Dill. Philadelphia: Temple University Press.

Fernández Kelly, M. Patricia, and Anna Garcia. 1990. Power surrendered, power restored: The politics of work and family among Hispanic garment workers in California and Florida. In *Women, politics & change,* edited by Louise A. Tilly and Patricia Gurin. New York: Russell Sage.

Gill, Lesley. 1994. *Precarious dependencies: Gender-class and domestic service in Bolivia.* New York: Columbia University Press.

Glenn, Evelyn Nakano. 1986. *Issei, Nisei, warbride: Three generations of Japanese American women in domestic service.* Philadelphia: Temple University Press.

———. 1994. Social constructions of mothering: A thematic overview. In *Mothering: Ideology, experience, and agency,* edited by Evelyn Nakano Glenn, Grace Chang, and Linda Rennie Forcey. Now York: Routledge.

Griswold del Castillo, Richard. 1984. *La Familia: Chicano families in the urban Southwest, 1848 to the present.* Notre Dame, IN: University of Notre Dame Press.

Hondagneu-Sotelo, Pierrette. 1995. Women and children first: New directions in anti-immigrant politics. *Socialist Review* 25:169–90.

Rollins, Judith. 1985. *Between women: Domestics and their employers.* Philadelphia: Temple University Press.

Romero, Mary. 1992. *Maid in the U.S.A.* New York: Routledge.

———. 1996. Life as the maid's daughter: An exploration of the everyday boundaries of race, class and gender. In *Feminisms in the academy: Rethinking the disciplines,* edited by Abigail J. Steward and Donna Stanon. Ann Arbor: University of Michigan Press.

———. 1997. Who takes care of the maid's children? Exploring the costs of domestic service. In *Feminism and families,* edited by Hilde L. Nelson. New York: Routledge.

Ruddick, Sara. 1989. *Maternal thinking: Toward a politics of peace.* Boston: Beacon.

Scheper-Hughes, Nancy. 1992. *Death without weeping: The violence of everyday life in Brazil.* Berkeley: University of California Press.

Segura, Denise A. 1994. Working at motherhood: Chicana and Mexican immigrant mothers and em-

ployment. In *Mothering: Ideology, experience, and agency,* edited by Evelyn Nakano Glenn, Grace Chang, and Linda Rennie Forcey. New York: Routledge.

Segura, Denise A., and Jennifer L. Pierce. 1993. Chicana/o family structure and gender personality: Chodorow, familism, and psychoanalytic sociology revisited. *Signs: Journal of Women in Culture and Society* 19:62–79.

Skolnick, Arlene S. 1991. *Embattled paradise: The American family in an age of uncertainty.* New York: Basic Books.

Soto, Shirlene. 1986. Tres modelos culturales: La Virgin de Guadalupe, la Malinche, y la Llorona. *Fem* (Mexico City), no. 48:13–16.

Stacey, Judith. 1996. *In the name of the family: Retaining family values in the postmodern age.* Boston: Beacon.

Stack, Carol B., and Linda M. Burton. 1994. Kinscripts: Reflections on family, generation, and culture. In *Mothering: Ideology, experience, and agency,* edited by Evelyn Nakano Glenn, Grace Chang, and Linda Rennie Forcey. New York: Routledge.

Thorne, Barrie, and Marilyn Yalom. 1992. *Rethinking the family: Some feminist questions.* Boston: Northeastern University Press.

Uttal, Lynet. 1996. Custodial care, surrogate care, and coordinated care: Employed mothers and the meaning of child care. *Gender & Society* 10: 291–311.

Weston, Kath. 1991. *Families we choose: Lesbians, gays, kinship.* New York: Columbia University Press.

Wrigley. 1995. *Other people's children.* New York: Basic Books.

Zavella, Patricia. 1987. *Women's work and Chicano families: Cannery workers of the Santa Clara Valley.* Ithaca, NY: Cornell University Press.

Zelizer, Viviana. 1994. *Pricing the priceless child: The social value of children.* Princeton, NJ: Princeton University Press.

Zinn, Maxine Baca. 1989. Family, race and poverty in the eighties. *Signs: Journal of Women in Culture and Society* 14:856–69.

32

Native American Mother

JUDITH K. WITHEROW

Some months ago I saw an article in the newspaper about a Mother of the Year contest. Fantastic, I thought! Here's my chance to make up for a whole lot of things. Simple, too, because I always figured I had the best mother in the world. Then I started reading the necessary qualifications and found that not one of them applied to her. This woman that I had always loved was a complete failure according to these rules:

"First, that she be a successful mother, as evidenced by the character and the achievements of her children. Second, that she be an active member of a religious body. Third, that she embody those traits highly regarded in mothers: cheerfulness, courage, patience, affection, kindness, understanding, a good homemaking ability. Fourth, that she exemplify in her life and her conduct the precepts of the golden rule. Fifth, that she have a sense of responsibility in civic affairs and that she be active in service for public benefit. Sixth, that she be qualified to represent the Mother of America in all responsibilities attached to her role as national mother, if selected."

Where did they find this yardstick for measuring a woman's worth? From the same measure that has always stipulated that this be a one-culture country, and either you assimilate or you pay the consequences. Why must *everything* be based on White, middle-class standards? I keep asking myself these questions, but apparently there are no simple answers. All I know for sure is that we as a people no longer wish to deny our Native American background—not when we see the alternatives that serve as its replacement. Not being able to enter my mother in this contest may seem of small importance, but it's just another in a long list of ways to discriminate. Therefore, I would like to give another version of what is and what isn't important in a mother.

First, that she be a successful mother, as evidenced by the character and the achievements of her children. I can only presume this means college-educated or outstanding in some other "reputable" field of endeavor. This first qualification alone is wrong for many reasons. The sole responsibility for the character and achievement of the children is placed on the mother. The role of the father is of no apparent significance and zoutside influences are totally ignored. What bothers me most is that it's only the finished product that counts. What the mother may have had to sacrifice in raising her children is of no relevance. She can only attain the status of Successful Mother through the achievements of *others*.

Suppose, in your culture, that the emphasis was placed on your ability to live off the land. Just surviving would be a great achievement. Anyone who is aware of the socioeconomic condition of native Americans could attest to this; we have it the worst of any race. In my family we are all highly skilled in ways pertaining to our natural background. I am proud to be considered an expert markswoman. I also fish and hunt as good, or better, than anyone I know. These I consider achievements. Society does not. They are at best considered leisure activities or, at worst, barbaric practices. It is not taken into account that a segment of this society still lives off the land. Fishing and hunting are natural means of survival, although man's continued interference with the environment will soon destroy even this option. What is so wrong in preferring meat that has not been shot full of hormones? Or what is so cruel about giving a wild animal an even chance when you are hunting? Are either of these things taken into consideration in your slaughterhouses? We have a natural respect for all living things. It is wrong to misuse anything the Earth Mother has provided for you. These things, I believe, constitute character. Would a contest judge agree?

Second, that she be an active member of a religious body. At face value, this would seem to mean your standard organized church. Possibly just serving as a Sunday school teacher would constitute being an "active member." Culture aside, we all know what role we as women have been allowed to play in any church. This country has always been big on pushing Christianity. It has gotten us a foothold in just about every other country. There has always been this overwhelming project to Americanize and Christianize. The terrible thing is that it works so well. You are given religion, and in turn you lose your identity in your own culture. What it gives you is a false sense of being accepted by this all-encompassing religion. In reality, it is only another ploy on your road to assimilation. Therefore, it would not be enough to just be in awe of the moon, the sun, the earth, and all of its elements. Nor would the Earth Mother, or any other deity, be acceptable in this land where a white, male God reigns supreme.

Third, that she embody those traits highly regarded in mothers: cheerfulness, courage, patience, affection, kindness, understanding, a good homemaking ability. These are highly commendable traits, but they won't "put meat on the table." My memories are of a woman carrying water from a creek to wash clothes by hand; a woman constantly in search of dead trees to chop up for firewood; a woman wise in the use of teas and herbs, because unless it was an emergency, doctors were an unaffordable luxury. Superstition played a large part in some of the cures. Two examples: If you

stepped on a nail, you greased it and put it above the door. Then if the evil spirits came in, they would slip back out. The wound was also treated with poultices so you were doubly protected. Another cure was for whooping cough. When my mother was a baby, her brother came down with it, and they were afraid if she caught it she would die. So they had a neighbor bring his black stallion over, and had it blow its breath in her face. She's never had the disease, and I have no explanation why it worked. I also know willow bark is good for curing headaches. I know society sneers at cures like these. Well, when we see things like DES and Flagyl and many other things, we can't help but wonder if our ways really are uncivilized.

I would say she had most of the traits mentioned earlier—courage, patience, and so on. However, if you can raise six children to adulthood under the worst of conditions, whether you did it cheerfully or not is of little importance. When you don't have running water or electricity in your house, you can bet you don't have much else either. So being a good homemaker in the shacks we grew up in would have been some neat trick!

Fourth, that she exemplify in her life and her conduct the precepts of the golden rule: "Do unto others as you have them do unto you." Here she would definitely qualify. She would never deliberately hurt anyone, even when it was over some things we considered justifiable. She can make any number of excuses to explain why someone acted a certain way. Maybe her pride won't allow her to admit that such things as racism and classism do exist.

Even the destruction of a family home didn't harden her. A small fire had started in the house, and the fire department was called. The firemen came in, and with their hatchets set about destroying everything in the house. Only two rooms had partially burned, and we decided to clean out what the firemen had destroyed, and build back. No sooner had this been completed and we were ready for rebuilding when someone else came in with gasoline and burned the house to the ground.

This list could go on forever, because every day some sort of harassment or discrimination occurs. The older people like my mother may accept it as the natural order of things, unlike this generation, which is learning to question every aspect of this society. So much for the "golden rule."

Fifth, that she have a sense of responsibility in civic affairs and that she be active in service for public benefit. These two are really hilarious. If you are hungry and in rags, civic or public services will not be high on your list of "things to do." Anyway, your race alone might exclude you from "responsibility in civic affairs." It still happens. Having a poor woman volunteering her services would upset the "natural order" even though she would be able to say where those services could really be used. So a working woman is really discriminated against: she can't afford to volunteer, but she won't get paid either.

Sixth, that she be qualified to represent the Mother of America in all responsibilities attached to her role as national mother, if selected. How could anyone not tamed and trained in this society's ways ever hope to qualify? I wouldn't want to qualify. It seems to me everyone is too hung up on certificates and stuff like that. Sure, I would have liked it for my mother; that is, I would have, until I gave it some thought. There is no way I would expose her to so much phoniness. She may have been unacceptable in this contest, but in *my* world she is without comparison.

Maybe I haven't expressed all of her attributes properly. Maybe no one else would see them as such. But this business of accepting only one life-style as proper is unreal. Somewhere along the way, the true values in life have been lost.

33

Fatherhood and Social Change

RALPH LaROSSA

The consensus of opinion in American society is that something has happened to American fathers. Long considered minor players in the affairs of their children, today's fathers often are depicted as major parental figures, people who are expected to—people who presumably want to—*be there* when their kids need them. "Unlike their own fathers or grandfathers," many are prone to say.

But, despite all the attention that the so-called "new fathers" have been receiving lately, only a few scholars have systematically conceptualized the changing father hypothesis, and no one to date has marshalled the historical evidence needed to adequately test the hypothesis (Demos, 1982; Hanson & Bozett, 1985; Hanson & Bozett, 1987; Lamb, 1987; Lewis, 1986; Lewis & O'Brien, 1987; McKee & O'Brien, 1982; Pleck, 1987; Rotundo, 1985).

Given that there is not much evidence to support the hypothesis, (a) how do we account for the fact that many, if not most, adults in America believe that fatherhood has changed, and (b) what are the consequences—for men, for women, for families—resulting from the apparent disparity between beliefs and actuality? The purpose of this article is to answer these two questions.

THE ASYNCHRONY BETWEEN THE CULTURE AND CONDUCT OF FATHERHOOD

The institution of fatherhood includes two related but still distinct elements. There is the *culture of fatherhood* (specifically the shared norms, values, and beliefs surrounding men's parenting), and

there is the *conduct of fatherhood* (what fathers do, their paternal behaviors). The distinction between culture and conduct is worth noting because although it is often assumed that the culture and conduct of a society are in sync, the fact is that many times the two are not synchronized at all. Some people make a habit of deliberately operating outside the rules, and others do wrong because they do not know any better (e.g., my 4-year-old son). And in a rapidly changing society like ours, countervailing forces can result in changes in culture but not in conduct, and vice-versa.

The distinction between culture and conduct is especially relevant when trying to assess whether fatherhood has changed because the available evidence on the history of fatherhood suggests that the *culture of fatherhood has changed more rapidly than the conduct.* For example, E. Anthony Rotundo (1985) argues that since 1970 a new style of American fatherhood has emerged, namely "Androgynous Fatherhood." In the androgynous scheme,

> *A good father is an active participant in the details of day-to-day child care. He involves himself in a more expressive and intimate way with his children, and he plays a larger part in the socialization process that his male forebears had long since abandoned to their wives. (p. 17)*

Rotundo (1985) is describing not what fathers lately have been doing but what some people would *like* fathers to *begin* doing. Later on he says that the new style is primarily a middle-class phenomenon and that "even within the upper-middle class ... there are probably far more men who still practice the traditional style of fathering than the new style." He also surmises that "there are more *women* who *advocate* 'Androgynous Fatherhood' than there are *men* who *practice* it" (p. 20). Similarly, Joseph Pleck (1987) writes about the history of fatherhood in the United States and contends that there have been three phases through which modern fatherhood has passed. From the early 19th to mid-20th centuries there was the father as distant breadwinner. Then, from 1940 to 1965 there was the father as sex role model. Finally, since around 1966 there has emerged the father as nurturer. Pleck's "new[est] father," like Rotundo's "androgynous father" is an involved father. He is also, however, more imagined than real. As Pleck acknowledges from the beginning, his analysis is a history of the "dominant *images* [italics added] of fatherhood" (p. 84).

Rotundo and Pleck are clear about the fact that they are focusing on the culture of fatherhood, and they are careful about drawing inferences about the conduct of fatherhood from their data. Others, however, have not been as careful. John Mogey, for example, back in 1957, appears to have mistaken cultural for behavioral changes when, in talking about the emerging role of men in the family, he asserts that the "newer" father's "behavior is best described as participation, the reintegration of fathers into the conspicuous consumption as well as the child rearing styles of family life" (Mogey, as cited in Lewis, 1986, p. 6). Ten years later, Margaret Mead (1967), too, extolled the arrival of the new father:

> We are evolving a new style of fatherhood, in which young fathers share very fully with mothers in the care of babies and little children. In this respect American men differ very much from their own grandfathers and are coming to resemble much more closely men in primitive societies. (p. 36)

And recently there appeared in my Sunday newspaper the comment that "[Modern men] know more about the importance of parenting. They're aware of the role and of how they are doing it. Fifty years ago, fathers didn't think much about what kind of job they were doing" (Harte, 1987, p. 4G).

Neither Mogey nor Mead nor the newspaper presented any evidence to support their views. One can only guess that they were reporting what they assumed—perhaps hoped—was true generally (i.e., true not only for small "pockets" of fathers here and there), for, as was mentioned before, no one to date has carried out the kind of historical study needed to test the changing father hypothesis. If, however, the professional and lay public took seriously the thesis that fathers have changed and if others writing for professional and popular publications have echoed a similar theme, then one can easily understand how the notion that today's fathers are "new" could become implanted in people's minds. Indeed, there is a good chance that this is exactly what has happened. That is to say, Rotundo (1985) and Pleck (1987) probably are correct: there has been a shift in the culture of fatherhood—the way fathers and mothers think and feel about men as parents. But what separates a lot of fathers and mothers from Rotundo and Pleck is that, on some level of consciousness, the fathers and mothers also believe (incorrectly) that there has been a proportionate shift in the conduct of fatherhood.

I say on "some" level of consciousness because, on "another" level of consciousness, today's fathers and mothers *do* know that the conduct of fatherhood has not kept pace with the culture. And I include the word "proportionate" because, while some researchers have argued that there have been changes in paternal behavior since the turn of the century, no scholar has argued that these changes have occurred at the same rate as the ideological shifts that apparently have taken place. These two points are crucial to understanding the consequences of the asynchrony between culture and conduct, and they will soon be discussed in more detail. But first another question: If the behavior of fathers did not alter the ideology of fatherhood, then what did?

The answer is that the culture of fatherhood changed primarily in response to the shifts in the conduct of motherhood. In the wake of declines in the birth rate and increases in the percentage of mothers in the labor force, the culture of motherhood changed, such that it is now more socially acceptable for women to combine motherhood with employment outside the home (Margolis, 1984). The more it became apparent that today's mothers were less involved with their children, on a day-to-day basis, than were their own mothers or grandmothers, the more important it became to ask the question: Who's minding the kids? Not appreciating the extent to which substitute parents (day-care centers, etc.) have picked up the slack for mothers, many people (scholars as well as the lay public) assumed that fathers must be doing a whole lot more than before and changed their beliefs to conform to this assumption. In other words, mother–child interaction was erroneously used as a "template" to measure father–child interaction (Day & Mackey, 1986).

Generally speaking, culture follows conduct rather than vice-versa (Stokes & Hewitt, 1976). Thus, the fact that the culture of fatherhood has changed more rapidly than the conduct of fatherhood would seem to represent an exception to the rule. However, it may not be an exception at all. What may be happening is that culture *is* following conduct, but not in a way we normally think it does. Given the importance that American society places on mothers as parents, it is conceivable that the conduct of motherhood has had a "cross-fertilizing" effect on the culture of fatherhood. There is also the possibility that the conduct of fatherhood is affecting the culture of fatherhood, but as a stabilizer rather than a destabilizer. As noted, research suggests that androgynous fatherhood as an ideal has failed to become widespread. One reason for this may be that the conduct of fatherhood is arresting whatever "modernizing" effect the conduct of motherhood is having. Put differently, the conduct of fatherhood and the conduct of motherhood may, on a societal level, be exerting contradictory influences on the culture of fatherhood.

THE CONDUCT OF FATHERHOOD VERSUS THE CONDUCT OF MOTHERHOOD

Contending that the conduct of fatherhood has changed very little over the course of the 20th century flies in the face of what many of us see every day: dads pushing strollers, changing diapers, playing in the park with their kids. Also, what about the men who publicly proclaim that they have made a conscientious effort to be more involved with their children than their own fathers were with them?

What cannot be forgotten is that appearances and proclamations (both to others and ourselves) can be deceiving; everything hinges on how we conceptualize and measure parental conduct. Michael Lamb (1987) notes that scholars generally have been ambiguous about what they mean by parental "involvement," with the result that it is difficult to compare one study with the next, and he maintains that if we ever hope to determine whether or not fathers have changed, we must arrive at a definition that is both conceptually clear and comprehensive. The definition which he thinks should be used is one that separates parental involvement into three components: engagement, accessibility, and responsibility. *Engagement* is time spent in one-on-one interaction with a child (whether feeding, helping with homework, or playing catch in the backyard). *Accessibility* is a less intense degree of interaction and is the kind of involvement whereby the parent is doing one thing (cooking, watching television) but is ready or available to do another (respond to the child, if the need arises). *Responsibility* has to do with who is accountable for the child's welfare and care. Responsibility includes things like making sure that the child has clothes to wear and keeping track of when the child has to go to the pediatrician.

Reviewing studies that allow comparisons to be made between contemporary fathers' involvement with children and contemporary mothers' involvement with children, Lamb (1987) estimates that in two-parent families in which mothers are unemployed, fathers spend about one fifth to one quarter as much time as mothers do in an engagement status and about a third as much time as mothers do just being accessible to their children. In two-parent families with employed mothers, fathers spend about 33% as much time as mothers do in an engagement status and 65% as much time being accessible. As far as responsibility is concerned, mothers appear to carry over 90% of the load, regardless of whether they are employed or not. Lamb also notes that observational and survey data indicate that the behavioral styles of fathers and mothers differ. Mother–child interaction is dominated by caretaking whereas father–child interaction is dominated by play.

> *Mothers actually play with their children more than fathers do but, as a proportion of the total amount of child–parent interaction, play is a much more prominent component of father–child interaction, whereas caretaking is more salient with mothers. (p. 10)*

In looking for trends, Lamb relies on one of the few studies which allows historical comparisons to be made—a 1975 national survey that was repeated in 1981 (Juster, 1985). No data apparently were collected on parents' accessibility or responsibility levels, but between 1975 and 1981, among men and women aged 18 to 44, there was a 26% increase in fathers' engagement levels and a 7% increase in mothers'. Despite these shifts, paternal engagement was only about one third that of mothers, increasing from 29% in 1975 to 34% in 1981 (Lamb, 1987).

While there is nothing intrinsically wrong with talking about percentage changes, one should be careful about relying on them and them alone. If, for example, one examines the tables from which Lamb drew his conclusions (Juster, 1985), one finds that the number of hours per week that the fathers spent in child care was 2.29 hours in 1975, compared to 2.88 hours in 1981, which is an increase of about 35 minutes per week or 5 minutes per day. The mothers in the sample, on the other hand, spent 7.96 hours per week in child

care in 1975, compared to 8.54 hours per week in child care in 1981, which also is an increase of about 35 minutes per week or 5 minutes per day. Thus, in absolute terms, fathers and mothers increased their child care by the same amount.

Bear in mind also that we are still talking about only one component of parental involvement, namely engagement. The two national surveys provide little, if any, information about changes in the accessibility and responsibility levels of fathers and mothers. Perhaps I am being overly cautious, but I cannot help but feel that until we gather historical data which would allow us to compare all three components of fatherhood, we should temper our excitement about surveys which suggest changes in the conduct of fatherhood over time. (For a tightly reasoned alternative viewpoint, see Pleck, 1985.)

Comparisons over time are difficult to make not only because so few scholars have chosen to study the history of fatherhood, but also because the studies carried out over the years to measure family trends provide scant information about fatherhood, per se. For instance, during a recent visit to the Library of Congress, I examined the Robert and Helen Lynd archival collection which I had hoped would include copies of the interview schedules from their two Middletown studies. It had occurred to me that if I could review the raw data from the studies, then I could perhaps plot paternal involvement trends from 1924 to 1935 to 1978, the times of the first, second, and third data collections in the Middletown series (Lynd & Lynd, 1929, 1937; Caplow, Bahr, Chadwick, Hill, & Williamson, 1982). Unfortunately, only four sample interviews from the earlier studies were in the archives. The rest apparently were destroyed. It is a shame that the Middletown data were not saved because the most recent book in the series presents a table which shows an increase in the weekly hours that fathers spent with their children between 1924 and 1987 (Caplow et al., 1982). There is no indication whether this represents an increase in engagement or accessibility or both. Had I been able to look at the interviews themselves, however, I might have been able to discern subtle variations.

What about the dads who are seen interacting with their kids in public (see Mackey & Day, 1979)? A thoughtful answer to this question also must address how we conceptualize and measure paternal involvement. Does the paternal engagement level of fathers in public square with the paternal engagement level of fathers in private, or are we getting an inflated view of fatherhood from public displays? If we took the time to scrutinize the behavior of fathers and mothers in public would we find that, upon closer examination, the division of child care is still fairly traditional. When a family with small children goes out to eat, for example, who in the family—mom or dad—is more accessible to the children; that is to say, whose dinner is more likely to be interrupted by the constant demands to "put ketchup on my hamburger, pour my soda, cut my meat"? And how can one look at a family in public and measure who is responsible for the children? How do we know, for instance, who decides whether the kids need clothes; indeed, how do we know who is familiar with the kids' sizes, color preferences, and tolerance levels for trying on clothes? The same applies to studies of paternal involvement in laboratory settings (see Parke, 1981). What can a study of father–child interaction in, say, a hospital nursery tell us about father–child interaction in general? The fact that fathers are making their presence known in maternity wards certainly is not sufficient to suggest that the overall conduct of fathers has changed in any significant way. Finally, the fact that fathers can be seen in public with their children may not be as important as the question, How much time do fathers spend *alone* with their children? One recent study found that mothers of young children spent an average of 44.45 hours per week in total child-interaction time (which goes beyond engagement), while fathers spent an average of 29.48 hours per week, a 1.5 to 1 difference. If one looked, however, at time spent alone with children, one discovered

that 19.56 hours of mothers' child-interaction time, compared with 5.48 hours of fathers' child-interaction, was solo time, a 3.6 to 1 difference. Moreover, while fathers' total interaction time was positively affected by the number of hours their wives worked, fathers' solo time was not affected at all (Barnett & Baruch, 1987).

As for the public proclamations, almost all the books and articles which tout the arrival of "new" fatherhood are written not by a cross-section of the population but by upper-middle class professionals. Kort and Friedland's (1986) edited book, for instance, has 57 men writing about their pregnancy, birth, and child-rearing experiences. But who are these men? For the most part, they are novelists, educators, sculptors, real estate investors, radio commentators, newspaper editors, publishers, physicians, performers, psychologists, social workers, and attorneys. Not exactly a representative sample. As Rotundo (1985) notes, androgynous fatherhood as an ideal has caught the attention of the upper-middle class more than any other group, but that even in this group, words seem to speak louder than actions.

While the perception of fathers in public and the Kort and Friedland (1986) book may not accurately represent what fathers in general are *doing*, they can most certainly have an effect of what people *think* fathers are doing and should be doing. Which brings us back to the question, What are the consequences that have resulted from the apparent disparity between beliefs and actuality?

THE CONSEQUENCES OF ASYNCHRONOUS SOCIAL CHANGE

Thirty years ago, E. E. LeMasters (1957) made the point that parenthood (and not marriage, as many believe) is the real "romantic complex" in our society, and that even middle-class couples, who do more than most to plan for children, are caught unprepared for the responsibilities of parenthood. Later on, he and John DeFrain (1983) traced America's tendency to romanticize parenthood to a number of popular folk beliefs or myths, some of which are: raising children is always fun, children are forever sweet and cute, children will invariably turn out well if they have "good" parents, and having children will never disrupt but in fact will always improve marital communication and adjustment. Needless to say, anyone who is a parent probably remembers only too vividly the point at which these folk beliefs began to crumble in her/his mind.

The idea that fathers have radically changed —that they now are intimately involved in raising their children—qualifies also as a folk belief, and it too is having an impact on our lives and that of our children. On the positive side, people are saying that at least we have made a start. Sure, men are not as involved with their children as some of us would like them to be, but, so the argument goes, the fact that we are talking about change represents a step in the right direction. (Folk beliefs, in other words, are not necessarily negative. The myth that children are always fun, for example, does have the positive effect of making children more valued than they would be if we believed the opposite: that they are always a nuisance.) But what about the negative side of the myth of the changing father? Is there a negative side? My objective is to focus here on this question because up to now scholars and the media have tended to overlook the often unintentional but still very real negative consequences that have accompanied asynchronous change in the social institution of fatherhood.

I am not saying that professionals have been oblivious to the potentially negative consequences of "androgynization" on men's lives, for one could point to several articles and chapters which have addressed this issue (e.g., Benokraitis, 1985; Berger, 1979; Lamb, Pleck, & Levine, 1987; Lutwin & Siperstein, 1985; Pleck, 1979; Scanzoni, 1979). Rather, the point being made is that scholars and the media, for the most part, have overlooked the difficulties associated with a *specific* social change, namely the asynchronous change in the social institution of fatherhood.

The Technically Present But Functionally Absent Father

The distinction between engagement and accessibility outlined by Lamb (1987) is similar to the distinction between *primary time* and *secondary time* in our study of the transition to parenthood (LaRossa & LaRossa, 1981). The social organization of a family with children, especially young children, parallels the social organization of a hospital in that both are *continuous coverage social systems* (Zerubavel, 1979). Both are set up to provide direct care to someone (be it children or patients) on a round-the-clock or continuous basis. And both the family and the hospital, in order to give caregivers a break every now and then, will operate according to some formal or informal schedule such that some person or persons will be "primarily" involved with the children or patients (on duty) while others will be "secondarily" involved (on call or accessible).

Like Lamb, we also found that the fathers' levels of engagement, accessibility, and responsibility were only a fraction of the mothers', and that fathers tended to spend a greater part of their care giving time playing with their children. Moreover, we found that the kinds of play that fathers were likely to be involved in were the kinds of activities that could be carried out at a secondary (semi-involved) level of attention, which is to say that it was not unusual for fathers to be primarily involved in watching television or doing household chores while only secondarily playing with their children.

When asked why they wanted to be with their children, the fathers often would answer along the lines that a father has to "put in some time with his kids" (LaRossa, 1983, p. 585). Like prisoners who "do time" in prison many fathers see themselves as "doing time" with their children. If, on some level of consciousness, fathers have internalized the idea that they should be more involved with their children, but on another level of consciousness they do not find the idea all that attractive, one would expect the emergence of a hybrid style: the technically present but functionally absent father (cf. Feldman & Feldman, 1975, cited in Pleck, 1983).

The technically present but functionally absent father manifests himself in a variety of ways. One father in our study prided himself on the fact that he and his wife cared for their new baby on an alternating basis, with him "covering" the mornings and his wife "covering" the afternoons. "We could change roles in a night," he said; "it wouldn't affect us." But when this father was asked to describe a typical morning spent alone with his infant son, he gave the distinct impression that he saw fatherhood as a *job* and that while he was "there" in body, he was someplace else in spirit.

> *I have the baby to be in charge of, [which has] really been no problem for me at all. But that's because we worked out a schedule where he sleeps a pretty good amount of that time. . . . I generally sort of have to be with him in the sense of paying attention to his crying or dirty diapers or something like that for any where between 30 to 45 minutes, sometimes an hour, depending. But usually I can have two hours of my own to count on each morning to do my own work, so it's no problem. That's just the breaks that go with it.*

Another example: Recently, there appeared an advertisement for one of those minitelevisions, the kind you can carry around in your pocket. Besides promoting the television as an electronic marvel, the man who was doing the selling also lauded how his mini-TV had changed his life: "Now when I go to my son's track meets, I can keep up with other ball games" (Kaplan, 1987, p. 32a). The question is: Is this father going to the track meets to see his son race, or is he going simply to get "credit" from his son for being in the stands? One more example: A newspaper story about a father jogging around Golden State Park in San Francisco who is so immersed in his running that he fails to notice his 3-year-old daughter—whom he apparently had brought with

him—crying "Daddy, Daddy" along the side of the running track. When he finally notices her, he stops only long enough to tell his daughter that it is not his job to watch her, but her job to watch for him (Gustatis, 1982).

What will be the impact of the mixed messages that these children—and perhaps countless others—are getting from their fathers? Research capable of measuring and assessing the complexity of these encounters is needed to adequately answer this question (Pleck, 1983).

Marital Conflict in Childbearing and Child-Rearing Families

Because our study was longitudinal, we were able to trace changes over time; and we found that from the third, to the sixth, to the ninth month postpartum, couples became more traditional, with fathers doing proportionately less child care (LaRossa & LaRossa, 1981). It was this traditionalization process that provided us with a close-up view of what happens when the bubble bursts; that is, what happens when the romanticized vision of dad's involvement starts to break down.

One father, first interviewed around the third month after his daughter's birth, wanted to communicate that he was not going to be an absentee father like some of his friends were:

> *I've got a good friend of mine, he's the ultimate male chauvinist pig. He will not change a diaper. . . . [But] I share in changing the diapers, and rocking the baby, and in doing those kinds of things. . . . I love babies.*

During the sixth month interview, however, it was revealed that he indeed had become very much the absentee father. In fact, almost every evening since the first interview he had left the house after dinner to play basketball, or participate in an amateur theater group, or sing in the local choir.

Since what he was doing contradicted what he said he would do, he was asked by his wife to "account" for his behavior. *Accounts* are demanded of social actors whose behavior is thought to be out of line. By submitting an account, which in common parlance generally takes the form of an excuse or justification, and having it honored or accepted by the offended party, a person who stands accused can manage to create or salvage a favorable impression (Scott & Lyman, 1968). Because the wife did not honor the accounts that her husband offered, the father was put in the position of either admitting he was wrong (i.e., apologizing) or coming up with more accounts. He chose the latter, and in due course offered no fewer than 20 different explanations for his conduct, to include "I help out more than most husbands do" and "I'm not good at taking care of the baby." At one dramatic point during the second interview, the husband and wife got into a verbal argument over how much of the husband's contribution to child care was "fact" and how much was "fancy." (He, with his head: "I *know* I was [around a lot]." She, with her heart: "[To me] it just doesn't *feel* like he was.")

This couple illustrates what may be happening in many homes as a result of the asynchrony between the culture and conduct of fatherhood. In the past, when (as best we can tell) both the culture and conduct of fatherhood were more or less traditional, fathers may not have been asked to account for their low paternal involvement. If the culture said that fathers should not be involved with their children and if fathers were not involved with their children, then fathers were perceived as doing what they should be doing. No need for an explanation. Today, however, the culture and conduct of fatherhood appear to be out of sync. The culture has moved toward (not to) androgyny much more rapidly than the conduct. On some level of consciousness, fathers and mothers believe that the behavior of fathers will measure up to the myth. Usually, this is early in the parental game, before or just after the birth of the first child. In time, however, reality sets in, and on another level of consciousness it becomes apparent that mom is doing more than planned because dad is doing less than planned. The wife challenges the legitimacy of the (more unequal than she had foreseen) division of child care, demanding an explanation from her husband, which may or may not be offered, and if offered may or may not be honored, and so on.

In short, one would expect more conflict in marriage today centered around the legitimacy of the division of child care than, say, 40 years ago because of the shift in the culture of fatherhood that has occurred during this time. Some may say, "Great, with more conflict there will be needed change." And their point is valid. But what must be kept in mind is that conflict also can escalate and destroy. Given that at least one recent study has reported that the most likely conflict to lead a couple to blows is conflict over children (Straus, Gelles, & Steinmetz, 1980), family researchers and practitioners would be well advised to pay attention to the possibility that violence during the transition to parenthood may be one negative consequence of asynchronous social change.

Fathers and Guilt

Several years ago, Garry Trudeau (1985), who writes *Doonesbury,* captured to a tee the asynchrony between the culture and conduct of fatherhood when he depicted a journalist-father sitting at his home computer and working on an autobiographical column on "The New Fatherhood" for the Sunday section of the newspaper. "My editor feels there's a lot of interest in the current, more involved generation of fathers," the journalist tells his wife who has just come in the room. "He asked me to keep an account of my experiences." Trudeau's punch line is that when Super Dad is asked by his wife to watch his son because she has to go to a meeting, he says no because if he did, he would not meet his deadline. In the next day's *Doonesbury,* Trudeau fired another volley at the new breed of fathers. Now the son is standing behind his computer-bound father and ostensibly is asking for his father's attention. But again Super Dad is too busy pecking away at his fatherhood diary to even look up: "Not now, son. Daddy's busy" (March 24 & 25).

Trudeau's cartoons, copies of which sit on my wall in both my office and my den, are a reminder to me not to be so caught up in writing about what it means to be a father (thus contributing to the culture of fatherhood) that I fail to *be* a father. The fact, however, that I took the time to cut the cartoons out of the newspaper (and make not one but two copies) and the fact that Trudeau, who is himself a father, penned the cartoons in the first place is indicative of a feeling that many men today experience, namely ambivalence over their performance as fathers.

To feel "ambivalent" about something is to feel alternately good and bad about it. The plethora of autobiographical books and articles written by fathers in the past few years conveys the impression that men do feel and, perhaps most importantly, should feel good about their performance as fathers. A lot of men do seem to be proud of their performance, what with all the references to "new" fatherhood and the like. At the same time, however, men are being almost constantly told—and can see for themselves, if they look close enough—that their behavior does not square with the ideal, which means that they are being reminded on a regular basis that they are *failing* as fathers. Failing not when compared with their own fathers or grandfathers perhaps, but failing when compared with the image of fatherhood which has become part of our culture and which they, on some level of consciousness, believe in.

This is not to suggest that in the past men were totally at ease with their performance as fathers, that they had no doubts about whether they were acting "correctly." For one thing, such an assertion would belie the fact that role playing is, to a large degree, improvisational, that in everyday life (vs. the theater) scripts almost always are ill defined and open to a variety of interpretations (Blumer, 1969). Perhaps more importantly, asserting that men in the past were totally at ease with their performance as fathers would ignore the fact that, contrary to what many think, some of our fathers and grandfathers were ambivalent about the kind of job they were doing. In a study just begun on the history of fatherhood in America, I have come across

several cases of men in the early 1900s expressing concern over the quality of their paternal involvement. In 1925, for example, one father wrote to a psychologist to ask whether he was *too involved* with his 2-year-old son. Apparently, he had taught the boy both the alphabet and how to count, and he now wondered whether he had forced his son to learn too much too soon (LaRossa, 1988).

So, what *is* the difference between then and now? I would say it is a difference in degree not kind. I would hypothesize that, given the asynchrony between the culture and conduct of fatherhood, the number of fathers who feel ambivalent and, to a certain extent, guilty about their performance as fathers has increased over the past three generations. I would also hypothesize that, given it is the middle class which has been primarily responsible for the changes in the culture of fatherhood, it is the middle-class fathers who are likely to feel the most ambivalent and suffer from the most guilt.

There is a certain amount of irony in the proposition that middle-class men are the ones who are the most likely to experience ambivalence and guilt, in that middle-class men are also the ones who seem to be trying the hardest to act according to the emerging ideal. As noted, the testimonials from the so-called androgynous fathers almost invariably are written by middle-class professionals. But it is precisely because these middle-class professionals are trying to conform to the higher standards that one would expect that they would experience the most ambivalence and guilt. Like athletes training for the Olympics, androgynous-striving fathers often are consumed with how they are doing as fathers and how they can do better. For example:

> Should I play golf today, or should I spend more time playing with Scott and Julie? Should I stay late in the office to catch up or should I leave early to go home and have dinner with the children? There is an endless supply of these dilemmas each day. (Belsky, 1986, p. 64)

Some may argue that the parental anxiety that men are beginning to experience is all for the better, that they now may start feeling bad enough about their performance to really change. This argument does have merit. Yes, one positive outcome of asynchronous social change is that ultimately men may become not only more involved with their children but also more sensitive to what it is like to be a mother. After all, for a long time women have worried about *their* performance as parents. It should not be forgotten, however, that the guilt which many women experience as mothers (and which has been the subject of numerous novels, plays, and films) has not always been healthy for mothers—or families. In sum, when it comes to parenthood, today it would appear that both men and women can be victims as well as benefactors of society's ideals.

CONCLUSION

Fatherhood is different today than it was in prior times but, for the most part, the changes that have occurred are centered in the culture rather than in the conduct of fatherhood. Whatever changes have taken place in the behavior of fathers, on the basis of what we know now, seem to be minimal at best. Also, the behavioral changes have largely occurred within a single group—the middle class.

The consequences of the asynchrony between the (comparatively speaking) "modern" culture of fatherhood and the "less modern" or "traditional" conduct of fatherhood are (a) the emergence of the technically present but functionally absent father, (b) an increase in marital conflict in childbearing and child-rearing families, and (c) a greater number of fathers, especially in the middle class, who feel ambivalent and guilty about their performance as fathers.

A number of recommendations seem to be in order. First, more people need to be made aware of the fact that the division of child care in America has not significantly changed, that—despite the beliefs that fathers are a lot more involved with their children—mothers remain, far and away, the primary child caregivers. The reason for publicizing this fact is that if our beliefs represent what we want (i.e., more involved fathers) and we

mistakenly assume that what we want is what we have, our complacency will only serve to perpetuate the culture-conduct disjunction. Thus, scholars and representatives of the media must commit themselves to presenting a balanced picture of "new fatherhood."

Second, and in line with the above, men must be held responsible for their actions. In our study of the transition to parenthood, we found that the language that couples use to account for men's lack of involvement in infant care does not simply reflect the division of infant care, it constructs that division of infant care. In other words, the accounts employed by new parents to excuse and justify men's paternal role distance serves as a social lubricant in the traditionalization process (LaRossa & LaRossa, 1981). Thus, when men say things like "I'm not good at taking care of the baby" or "I can't be with Junior now, I have to go to the office, go to the store, go to sleep, mow the lawn, pay the bills, and so forth" the question must be raised, are these reasons genuine (i.e., involving insurmountable role conflicts) or are they nothing more than rationalizations used by men to do one thing (not be with their children) but believe another ("I like to be with my children")? If they are rationalizations, then they should not be honored. Not honoring rationalizations "delegitimates" actions and, in the process, puts the burden of responsibility for the actions squarely on the person who is carrying out the actions. Only when men are forced to seriously examine their commitment to fatherhood (vs. their commitment to their jobs and avocations) can we hope to bring about the kinds of changes that will be required to alter the division of child care in this country (LaRossa, 1983).

What kinds of changes are we talking about? Technically present but functionally absent fathers are products of the society in which we live. So also, the traditionalization process during the transition to parenthood and the conflict and guilt it apparently engenders cannot be divorced from the socio-historical reality surrounding us and of which we are a part. All of which means that if we hope to alter the way men relate to their children, we cannot be satisfied with individualistic solutions which see "the problem" as a private, therapeutic matter best solved through consciousness raising groups and the like. Rather, we must approach it as a public issue and be prepared to alter the institutional fabric of American society (cf. Mills, 1959). For example, the man-as-breadwinner model of fatherhood, a model which emerged in the 19th and early 20th centuries and which portrays fathers primarily as breadwinners whose wages make family consumption and security possible, remains dominant today (Pleck, 1987). This model creates structural barriers to men's involvement with their children, in that it legitimates inflexible and highly demanding job schedules which, in turn, increase the conflict between market work and family work (Pleck, 1985). More flex-time jobs would help to relieve this conflict. So would greater tolerance, on the part of employers, of extended paternity leaves (Levine, 1976). I am not suggesting that the only reason that men are not as involved with their children is that their jobs keep them from getting involved. The fact that many

women also contend with inflexible and highly demanding job schedules and still are relatively involved with their children would counter such an assertion. Rather, the point is that the level of achievement in market work expected of men in America generally is higher than the level of achievement in market work expected of women and that this socio-historical reality must be entered into any equation which attempts to explain why fathers are not more involved.

When we will begin to see significant changes in the conduct of fatherhood is hard to say. The past generally provides the data to help predict the future. But, as the historian John Demos (1982) once noted, "Fatherhood has a very long history, but virtually no historians" (p. 425). Hence, our ability to make informed predictions about the future of fatherhood is severely limited. Hopefully, as more empirical research—historical and otherwise—on fatherhood is carried out, we will be in a better position to not only see what is coming but to deal with what is at hand.

REFERENCES

Barnett, R. C., & Baruch, G. K. (1987). Determinants of fathers' participation in family work. *Journal of Marriage and the Family, 49,* 29–40.

Belsky, M. R. (1986). Scott's and Julie's Daddy. In C. Kort & R. Friedland (Eds.), *The father's book: Shared experiences* (pp. 63–65). Boston: G. K. Hall.

Benokraitis, N. (1985). Fathers in the dual-earner family. In S. M. H. Hanson & F. W. Bozett (Eds.), *Dimensions of fatherhood* (pp. 243–268). Beverly Hills, CA: Sage Publications.

Berger, M. (1979). Men's new family roles—Some implications for therapists. *Family Coordinator, 28,* 638–646.

Blumer, H. (1969). *Symbolic interactionism: Perspective and method.* Englewood Cliffs, NJ: Prentice Hall.

Caplow, T. with Bahr, H. M., Chadwick, B. A., Hill, R., & Williamson, M. H. (1982). *Middletown families: Fifty years of change and continuity.* Minneapolis: University of Minnesota Press.

Day, R. D., & Mackey, W. C. (1986). The role image of the American father: An examination of a media

myth. *Journal of Comparative Family Studies, 17,* 371–388.

Demos, J. (1982). The changing faces of fatherhood: A new exploration in American family history. In S. H. Cath, A. R. Gurwitt, & J. M. Ross (Eds.), *Father and child: Developmental and clinical perspectives* (pp. 425–445). Boston: Little, Brown.

Gustatis, R. (1982, August 15). Children sit idle while parents pursue leisure. *Atlanta Journal and Constitution,* pp. 1D, 4D.

Hanson, S. M. H., & Bozett, F. W. (1985). *Dimensions of fatherhood.* Beverly Hills, CA: Sage Publications.

Hanson, S. M. H., & Bozett, F. W. (1987). Fatherhood: A review and resources. *Family Relations, 36,* 333–340.

Harte, S. (1987, June 21). Fathers and sons. Narrowing the generation gap: Atlanta dads reflect a more personal style of parenting. *Atlanta Journal and Constitution,* pp. 4G, 6G.

Juster, F. T. (1985). A note on recent changes in time use. In F. T. Juster & F. P. Stafford (Eds.), *Time, goods, and well-being* (pp. 313–332). Ann Arbor, MI: Institute for Social Research.

Kaplan, D. (1987, Early Summer). The great $39.00 2" TV catch. *DAK Industries Inc.,* p. 32A.

Kort, C., & Friedland, R. (Eds.), (1986). *The father's book: Shared experiences.* Boston: G. K. Hall.

Lamb, M. E. (1987). Introduction: The emergent American father. In M. E. Lamb (Ed.), *The father's role: Cross-cultural perspectives* (pp. 3–25). Hillsdale, NJ: Lawrence Erlbaum.

Lamb, M. E., Pleck, J. H., & Levine, J. A. (1987). Effects of increased paternal involvement on fathers and mothers. In C. Lewis & M. O'Brien (Eds.), *Reassessing fatherhood: New observations on fathers and the modern family* (pp. 109–125). Beverly Hills, CA: Sage Publications.

LaRossa, R. (1983). The transition to parenthood and the social reality of time. *Journal of Marriage and the Family, 45,* 579–589.

LaRossa, R. (1988, November). *Toward a social history of fatherhood in America.* Paper presented at the Theory Construction and Research Methodology Workshop, Annual Meeting of National Council of Family Relations, Philadelphia, PA.

LaRossa, R., & LaRossa, M. M. (1981). *Transition to parenthood: How infants change families.* Beverly Hills, CA: Sage Publications.

LeMasters, E. E. (1957). Parenthood as crisis. *Marriage and Family Living, 19,* 352–355.

LeMasters, E. E., & DeFrain, J. (1983). *Parents in contemporary America: A sympathetic view* (4th ed.). Homewood, IL: Dorsey.

Levine, J. A. (1976). *Who will raise the children?* New York: Bantam.

Lewis, C. (1986). *Becoming a father.* Milton Keynes, England: Open University Press.

Lewis, C., & O'Brien, M. (1987). *Reassessing fatherhood: New observations on fathers and the modern family.* Beverly Hills, CA: Sage Publications.

Lutwin, D. R., & Siperstein, G. N. (1985). Househusband fathers. In S. M. H. Hanson & F. W. Bozett (Eds.), *Dimensions of fatherhood* (pp. 269–287). Beverly Hills, CA: Sage Publications.

Lynd, R. S., & Lynd, H. M. (1929). *Middletown: A study in American culture.* New York: Harcourt & Brace.

Lynd, R. S., & Lynd, H. M. (1937). *Middletown in transition: A study in cultural conflicts.* New York: Harcourt & Brace.

Mackey, W. C., & Day, R. D. (1979). Some indicators of fathering behaviors in the United States: A crosscultural examination of adult male-child interaction. *Journal of Marriage and the Family, 41,* 287–297.

Margolis, M. L. (1984). *Mothers and such: Views of American women and why they changed.* Berkeley: University of California Press.

McKee, L., & O'Brien, M. (Eds.), (1982). *The father figure.* London: Tavistock.

Mead, M. (1967). Margaret Mead answers: How do middle-class American men compare with men in other cultures you have studied? *Redbook, 129,* 36.

Mills, C. W. (1959). *The sociological imagination.* London: Oxford University Press.

Parke, R. D. (1981). *Fathers.* Cambridge, MA: Harvard University Press.

Pleck, J. H. (1979). Men's family work: Three perspectives and some data. *Family Coordinator, 28,* 481–488.

Pleck, J. H. (1983). Husbands' paid work and family roles: Current research issues. In H. Z. Lopata & J. H. Pleck (Eds.), *Research in the interweave of social roles, Vol. 3, Families and jobs* (pp. 251–333). Greenwich, CT: JAI Press.

Pleck, J. H. (1985). *Working wives/Working husbands.* Beverly Hills, CA: Sage Publications.

Pleck, J. H. (1987). American fathering in historical perspective. In M. S. Kimmel (Ed.), *Changing men: New directions in research on men and masculinity* (pp. 83–97). Beverly Hills, CA: Sage Publications.

Rotundo, E. A. (1985). American fatherhood: A historical perspective. *American Behavioral Scientist, 29,* 7–25.

Scanzoni, J. (1979). Strategies for changing male family roles: Research and practice implications. *Family Coordinator, 28,* 435–442.

Scott, M. B., & Lyman, S. M. (1968). Accounts. *American Sociological Review, 33,* 46–62.

Stokes, R., & Hewitt, J. P. (1976). Aligning actions. *American Sociological Review, 41,* 838–849.

Straus, M., Gelles, R. J., & Steinmetz, S. K. (1980). *Behind closed doors: Violence in the American family.* New York: Anchor/Doubleday.

Trudeau, G. B. (1985, March 24 & March 25). *Doonesbury.* United Press Syndicate.

Zerubavel, E. (1979). *Patterns of time in hospital life: A sociological perspective.* Chicago: University of Chicago Press.

34

Men and Women in Southern Spain
"Domestic Power" Revisited[1]

DAVID D. GILMORE

Anthropologists have begun to challenge standard assumptions about gender in southern Europe. Initiated by feminists compensating for male bias in data collection, recent studies[2] have revitalized Mediterranean ethnography by transcending sexual stereotypes of woman as reticent, passive, and submissive, and man as active, powerful, and assertive. Disavowing the alleged "invisibility" of peasant women and providing new insight into women's daily routines both in and out of doors, these studies take us far beyond the crude sex-based oppositions such as honor/shame, kinship/friendship, and public/private, with their often hidden androcentric biases.

The argument is that if we look at what goes on within and among households rather than public policy-making, women are neither so recessive nor so powerless as male anthropologists and their informants have stated. My topic here is the question of "domestic power" and who has it. Data are taken from two rural communities in western Andalusia (Seville Province). "Fuenmayor" and "El Castillo"[3] are located some ten miles apart on either side of the national highway linking the provincial capitals of Seville and Cordoba. No comparison is intended here; the two examples are treated as a single case study.

RURAL TOWNS

Fuenmayor is an agricultural town of about 8,000 people in the alluvial Guadalquivir River Basin. Its economy is based on dry cultivation of Mediterranean staple crops such as olives, wheat, and sunflowers. El Castillo is about half the size of its neighbor, with about 4,000 people. The two towns represent matched "twins" sharing similar market adaptations, history, and mutual participation in a generally shared ritual cycle. As in the larger town, the Castilleros are almost all involved in rainfall agriculture. The smaller community has somewhat more land under garden irrigation and so has a slightly higher per capita income.

El Castillo also has a vestigial cottage industry of esparto-grass manufacturing, producing tiny quantities of sandals, mats, and bridles, but this is hardly thriving today with the competition of mass-produced goods. In contrast, Fuenmayor has one of the few liquor mills in the *comarca* (ecological zone), producing small amounts of bottled anisette and cheap brandy. Sometimes this contrasting specialization gives rise to jokes about drunks versus cobblers, but otherwise the two towns enjoy friendly relations and their people mingle freely, intermarrying without comment.

Both towns are class-stratified, with relatively minor differences in wealth being the source of much discussion and concern. The main difference is that El Castillo does not have a significant resident gentry (*señoritos*) because its municipal territory is more subdivided. In addition, El Castillo has no aristocratic absentee landowners as does Fuenmayor, whose municipal territory includes a huge latifundium[4] owned by a Madrid-based duke. So, while the people of Fuenmayor recognize three resident social classes—the gentry, the peasants (*mayetes*), and the landless laborers (*jornaleros*)—the Castilleros proudly say they are more egalitarian, with only peasants and farm workers present. "We are more together," they say, glossing over the fact that there are a few wealthy peasant families who hire labor.

Today, both communities are Left-leaning, with strong Communist and Socialist representation, although in keeping with the generally more sophisticated quality of Fuenmayor's political life, most of the current regional leaders come from Fuenmayor. In most other respects, also, the two towns are similar, especially in their lingering observation of traditional sex and gender distinctions. In what follows I discuss primarily the men and women of the working classes: smallholding peasants and rural proletarians. The gentry of Fuenmayor and the relatively few rich farmers of El Castillo form an important contrast that I will address later.

The rigid sexual segregation typical of Andalusian agrotowns prevailed in these two towns until the 1970s, which represents our ethnographic present. As throughout the region, men are expected to remain outside the home, either at work, or, when unemployed or after hours, at the neighborhood tavern. Men who linger at home are morally suspect; their manhood is questionable. Community gossip is relentless on this score. Men who avoid the male camaraderie of the bars at night are often likened to "motherhens," and "brooding cows." Very concerned about their manly image, most men avoid spending too much time indoors.

In El Castillo, there is one exception to this. Some men have organized an "eating club," which meets alternately in each club member's home. The man in question prepares a feast with his wife's help and invites all the others to the festivities. This, however, is somewhat of an anomaly, and even the Castilleros say openly that this is daring and "modern."

Men and women in both towns say that men "belong" in the streets, women in the home. A good woman is "mistress of her house": chaste, housebound, secluded, a careful housekeeper and a devoted mother. A good man, conversely, although he is a concerned husband and father and a good provider, is not expected to be deeply involved in domestic activities. As we have seen,

any retreat away from the hurly-burly and the often exhausting male rivalries of the extra-domestic world is, for a self-respecting man, a cultural solecism as damaging to reputation as a woman's immodesty. Thus, while women are "forced" to avoid the public places, one may say equally that men are "forced" to give up the tranquility and comfort of the home for the greater part of the day.

Depending upon individual personality, this spatial "gender schema" can be said to be equally repressive for both sexes. One is tempted to add that the association of "public" with freedom and power, and of "private" with deprivation and oppression, is an ethnocentric imposition upon a much richer reality.

CONJUGAL DECISION MAKING

Prenuptial Example

In Andalusia, the engagement is usually a long, drawn-out process often involving years. Consequently, such decisions often presage future directions and set the stage for marital relations to come. The following incident involves fiances (*novios*) from El Castillo. It involves the most important decision a couple can make: when to marry.

Eulogio, a man of about 30, and Carmen, 28, had been engaged for four years—a relatively long period, but not unusual by any means. Carmen decided it was time to marry: she had compiled her *ajuar* or trousseau; her parents had finally rebuilt and furnished an upstairs apartment in the parental home for the newlyweds. Besides, she was impatient for the big day. However, Eulogio resisted setting a date, and the wedding was becoming a bone of contention. A trucker with a growing business transporting comestibles to and from Seville, he felt he needed more time to amass capital before marriage. As he put it to friends, a man wants to gain financial independence before, not after, marriage—a common sentiment finding wide approval among his friends and confidants. So a basic disagreement erupted, setting the stage for a battle of wills, directly observed by Eulogio's male friends.

The unfolding of their rather stormy nuptial story is revealing for two reasons: first, because of the personal characteristics of the fiances, and second, because of the fact that within Eulogio's circle of bachelor friends, he was considered an exemplary "strong man," whose relations with his fiancee were watched closely for evidence of the hoped-for male domestic prerogative. That is, Eulogio was considered somewhat of a test case in the sense of masculine "right," a model for other as-yet unmarried men in his circle. Whether or not he would prevail over a woman was therefore regarded among his fellows as an augury. As elsewhere in Spain, El Castillo men pay lip service to an ideology of patriarchal privilege—at least in their bachelor days.

Eulogio was a gregarious man, tall and athletic, a successful risk-taker in business, stentorian in conversation, somewhat boastful, generous, "correct" in his dealings with men. Up to that point, too, he had appeared dominant in courtship (he appeared to be in charge, at least in public). In his teens, he had been a leader of his *pandilla,* or youthful clique, had achieved noncommissioned officer's rank in the army, and was considered to have leadership qualities. Independence and self-assurance were his hallmarks, consciously cultivated and acknowledged among both men and women in El Castillo. Contrariwise, Carmen was a small, demure, physically unimpressive woman, who gave no indication, at least among men, of any outstanding qualities of character.

When Eulogio told his friends that his wedding would be postponed for another year because, as he put it, *he dicho* ("I have spoken"), there was general agreement that Carmen would simply have to wait. Yet within a month, Eulogio astonished his friends by sheepishly confiding that the wedding date had been set, that Carmen had gotten her way on an early marriage and that there was "no remedy." What had caused this dramatic turnaround? One day I sat in a bar with a number of mutual friends who were discussing the fiasco.

The men earnestly debated Eulogio's demise. One bachelor, Geraldo, expressed shock over his friend's craven capitulation. How was it possible, he asked, that a big strong man like Eulogio could relent so easily, put up so weak a struggle, and be so dominated by a small and apparently demure woman? "Who rules," Geraldo asked plaintively, "the man or the woman?"

The verb used here is *mandar,* "to command or dictate," a commonly heard term in discussions of politics. This concept of *manda,* or rule, has historically played an important role in masculine self-image in Andalusia, especially among rural farm workers. For these men to maintain their honor they must rule themselves, be their own master; hence they are manly. To be "ruled," by which is meant to be controlled by or dependent upon others, is to be dominated, with almost a ring of emasculation about it. One who is ruled is *manso,* "tame," the same term used in the farm context for a steer, a castrated bull (Marvin 1984:65). The "rule" concept finds symbolic expression in all walks of life, political, sexual, and interpersonal. Hence its use is effectively important in contexts in which male self-image is involved. Geraldo's question therefore had resonance beyond the call to colors in the battle of the sexes. It brought a reflective response from another, older man.

This man, Carlos, himself married, had the advantage of personal experience in such matters and also knew the fiances better than the rest. As such men often do in Andalusian bars, Carlos gave a little speech, beginning with the standard pontifical prelude: "look man, what happens is the following" (*lo que paza e' lo ziguiente*). Listening attentively, the others found his subsequent comments both amusing and profoundly true.

Carlos spoke candidly about the balance of power between the sexes. He allowed that the man rules in Spain, except, he added ironically, "when he doesn't." This latter occurs in most matters that are important to the woman. The reason for this is that the man is preoccupied by other matters and cannot give his full attention to details to which his wife, or fiancee, devotes all her energies. The final say in such matters, according to Carlos, is held not by the man or the woman, but by the support they can muster from interested kin. In this sense, the woman will prevail in domestic matters because she has the unfailing support of her mother, whose role in life is to protect her daughter and to advance her interests, while the man stands alone. The women, then, in tandem, can almost always "wear the man down." Carlos thus introduced two important principles: the inherent power of women in conjugal matters as a result of the divided attention and solitariness of men; and more telling, the considerable role played by the infamous *bête noire* of Andalusian husbands, the mother-in-law (*suegra*), in terrorizing her son-in-law. The invocation of the mother-in-law drew sighs of recognition and self-pity from most men present.

Carlos added that personality is of course very important here. For the man to prevail against wife and *suegra* he must be unusually "strong," meaning stubborn. However, even if he is strong and his wife is "submissive" (*floja*), his *suegra* is always strong, and the alliance of women is too potent to resist without an intolerable exhaustion of male energies. Equally important is the fact that the husband is rarely at home, leaving the field open to usurpation by wife and *suegra,* who are deeply invested in matters of the home. In any case, it is clear that "power" in this case, at least from the male perspective, was wielded by a woman, or perhaps more accurately, women in domestic alliance, since the ability to prevail in an important decision was "unexpected," unequivocal, and independent of "right" as men see it. Although my informants would be surprised to hear the word power used in this seemingly trivial context, they would nevertheless agree that important decisions affecting a man's life are often beyond his control and in the hands of manipulative or scheming women.

As Carlos was finishing his peroration about the power of the *novia* allied with the dreadful mother-in-law, one of the most popular local poets and comedians, a man known to everyone by his nickname "Juanito el Chocho," walked into the bar. Overhearing our conversation, the poet joined in by performing a credible pantomime of his "pugilistic" *suegra,* replete with right hooks and up-percuts. These comical convulsions culminated in a crescendo of obscene gestures indicating "she has me by the ass." Finally, before wandering off to the bar to reward his own performance with a drink, he sang a *copla* from one of his own epics, entitled "La Vida del Hombre" ("Man's Life")—a typical way of concluding such discussions by invoking the summary power of wit. After catching the lyrics, the other men joined in:

Yo pelé con mi novia	I had a fight with my novia
Y mi suegra se enteró.	And my mother-in-law (to be) found out.
Me pegó con una caña	She jumped on top of me with a club
Y encima me la cascó!	And gave me a thorough drubbing!

Again, the term *encima* has emotional resonance. Literally "above," or "on top of," it is used to express social hierarchy and domination, as in the commonly heard expression *los ricos nos están encima,* "the rich are on top of us." To be "encima" also has obvious sexual connotations.

While these men clearly felt abused by the outcome of Eulogio's premarital squabble, I am unfortunately unable to provide his antagonists' view. For reasons of discretion, I was unable to interview Carmen or her mother alone. Despite recent arguments to the contrary, it is still inadvisable for a male fieldworker to approach unchaperoned women in places like Andalusia, because men take umbrage at such things.

Yet I did get some casual female input. The few women I was able to query regarded Carmen's victory as "only natural" because, as they said, technical matters involving marriage are a "woman's business" (*cosa de mujeres*). For a man to interfere in such matters was to them as unseemly as his attempting to dictate a silverware pattern or an upholstery color. So here is an area where male "right" seems to contrast with female "prerogative" or sexual "seemliness," and the former may indeed be contested, since the prerogatives of sex role seem ambiguous.

CONJUGAL DECISIONS

Once a couple marries, the newlyweds are faced with three immediate problems, the solutions of which will have permanent impact upon their future: first, where to set up residence; second, how to administer domestic finances and how to allocate previous savings in order to set up an immediately comfortable home; and, finally, when to have children and how many to have. Naturally there are other questions that arise, depending upon idiosyncrasies, but these three represent the major, initial, seminal or "organic" decisions that all newlyweds must make at the outset of establishing an independent household.

Postmarital residence in Fuenmayor shows a very strong neolocal, but "matrivicinal" tendency; that is, newlyweds tend to choose a new home that is near that of the wife's family. By "near" is normally meant within five minutes' walking distance. Minuscule degrees of distance are a major issue among engaged couples. I have heard both men and women state seriously that a house two blocks away was *lejos,* or "distant." People describe a house on the other side of town (about ten minutes' walking time) as *muy lejos,* or very far away. In addition, when the newlyweds must remain in one of the parental homes because of financial constraints (neolocality is preferred), there is a marked uxorilocal [residence with the parents of the bride] tendency. In Fuenmayor, 71 percent of households show a matrilateral extension. This same matrilateral tendency is equally well marked in El Castillo, where 79 percent of the extended multigenerational families were living with the wife's parents in the 1970s.

As a result, many Andalusian towns display a female-oriented residence pattern and sororal neighborhoods [neighborhoods in which sisters live close together], as is true of some Greek, Portuguese, and southern Italian peasants. These data challenge conventional wisdom about patriarchal, patrilocal peasantries. As Davis reports for the town of Pisticci in southern Italy, this residential preference tends to create a permanent female infrastructure, or matri-core; that is, neighborhoods are dominated by women's ties because women remain co-residential more often and longer than men and because they reside in close association with childhood neighbors, kinswoman, and parents after marriage. According to village perceptions of spatial-social distance, it is the husband who is most often the "stranger" in his home or neighborhood, residing "very far" from his parents, who may be located more than two blocks away, and from his agnates.[5] In a statement that may serve for Andalusia, Davis writes: "The neighborhood is a community of women: women bring their husbands to live there; women have their close kin there; daughters will continue to live there when parents are dead." As Davis astutely notes, this matri-core is a woman's "chief source of power," since it provides her access to allies and to sources of information and gossip, and establishes a continual basis of kinship support.

Equally true in western Andalusia, this quasi-matrilocality raises two epistemological questions in considering domestic power: first, to what degree is this matrilocal-matrivicinal pattern consonant with the assumed male domestic prerogatives; and second, what is the effect of such a residence pattern on conjugal decision making? Although there is the usual amount of individual variation, certain patterns emerge.

When I first became aware of the matrilocal tendency, I queried men about it, since it seemed at variance with the androcentric emphasis. Most men said that they quietly acquiesced to the wife's request to "live near mamma," for a number of reasons, any one of which may have been paramount in any particular case. As in Seville City, some men said they wanted to evade the continuing supervision of their fathers, although this seems less pressing in these rural towns. The most common response was that residence was an issue that meant a great deal to women and less to men, as men are by nature more "independent" of parental ties. The wife, men allow, especially a new bride, needs the support of her mother in establishing a new home; so why break up this proven domestic team?

Basically the men felt that any attempt on their part to "come between" wife and mother-in-law by insisting on virilocal residence [residence with the parents of the groom] would backfire, leading to a passive-aggressive campaign by both to undermine his comfort and his peace of mind for the rest of his life, and that therefore the battle for dominance was just not worth the penalty.

To be sure, part of the answer reflects selfishness rather than mere passivity, since men want their homes to be run well and efficiently. Andalusians believe that since women are in charge of domestic operations they must be allowed full control; otherwise the man's life will suffer from disorganization. As one man put it: wife and mother are a "clique" that works well only when there is physical proximity. In a sense, therefore, the mother-in-law is regarded as a necessary nuisance, a kind of existential penance. The most common response to questions about the uxorial dominance in residence choice was therefore a resigned acceptance of proven practice with the frequently heard conversational suffix: *no hay remedio* (there is no remedy for it). This is a rhetorical device that one encounters in many male pronouncements concerning wives, mothers-in-law, and women's capacity to get their own way in general. Although this may reflect, in part, the usual male indifference to "feminine" preoccupations, it also seems to indicate a degree of moral surrender, as the issues concerned were indeed of great importance to men and were often, as they knew, the sources of dissatisfaction later. In this sense, we may characterize male abstention from such domestic matters as de facto, although ambivalent, recognition of uncontested female authority in domestic decision making.

The most important consequence of the husband's ambiguous acquiescence is that the *suegra* maintains a high profile in the man's life, often intruding into domestic arrangements and sometimes asserting the balance of power in marital quarrels or disagreements. The powerful image of this invasive female scourge is found also among urbanites in western Andalusia, testifying to a regional stereotype deeply rooted in male consciousness. On the surface, the Andalusian's fearful attitude about his mother-in-law seems ubiquitous rather than area-specific, aside from the possibly anomalous intensification of affinal ties as a result of matrivicinal residence. Most bilateral societies, including our own, have their own folklore about the horrors of this stock villain in the domestic comedy. Yet, because of the associated structural preponderance of the domestic matri-core, the Andalusian husband often finds himself outmatched by the weight this fierce harridan throws in supporting her daughter, and his laments often evoke a revealing sense of masculine alienation before a female dyad elevated to domestic sovereignty.

Naturally the *suegra*'s power is enhanced by simple residential propinquity, but even more psychologically salient is the fact that she and her daughter enjoy a moral symbiosis that the husband cannot match. Although he may have many friends, his male friendships are founded as much on competition as cooperation, and he cannot plead for help in domestic skirmishes without endangering his reputation as a "strong man." His own mother of course may intercede, but no man wants to have his mother fight his battles. So for various reasons, he acquiesces, maintaining a respectable facade of indifference before his peers. In addition the husband knows all too well that "trouble" (*jaleo*) with the *suegra* leads to marital discord, unless the wife is "strong" and prefers to mollify her husband while alienating her own mother. However, this is said to be rare.

With their vibrant oral traditions, Andalusians are consummate artists of the human condition. Because of the powerful proscription on fighting and violence in their culture, they prefer to express their sorrows and troubles in song and art rather than in outbursts. Accordingly, the alliance of wife and *suegra*, with the latter assuming mythopoetic status as a masculine nemesis, has achieved a kind of apotheosis in verse and poetry.

In both Fuenmayor and El Castillo, the men sing *coplas* during Carnival to great acclaim and applause, reflecting common male concerns. What is most interesting about these verses is the formidable physical power ascribed to the *suegra* in metaphors and tropes of specifically virile animal and military imagery, a tradition rendering "marital" as "martial," in which the male appears victimized and indecisive. This may reflect, as Driessen perceptively suggests, deep-seated insecurity or cognitive dissonance about the power of women, which the "cover" of male indifference or self-abstention is meant to assuage. During the Fuenmayor Carnival of 1970, one famous poet sang the following *copla,* receiving accolades from the cheering men:

> All mothers-in-law in the world
> Are pretty much the same.
> I fight with mine, too,
> So listen how it goes.
> She kicks me out of her house
> Forty times a day.
> Good, bad, indifferent,
> They all belong in the cavalry.[6]

Another poet describes his *suegra* as a *bicho fiero* ("fierce beast") which he hopes someday to *desbravacer* ("tame" or, more colorfully, "geld") as though she were a wild animal.[7] One man told me that his *suegra* was a "dragon" who expelled him from "her house" (which was his house, as well) whenever he disagreed with her. Other men described their *suegra* as a "brave bull," a "tomcat," an "armor-plated lizard," and other such scaly or vicious animals.

With all their hyperbole, these pseudo-jocular laments are revealing because of the intimations of sex-role reversal and power inversion with their unconscious implications of sublimated male gender-identity insecurities. Also revealing is the sense of powerlessness expressed as an evanescent integration into the domestic setting as a result of the man's tenuous connection to the home, which is, after all, haunted—sometimes owned outright—by his *suegra*. Even if the man lives neolocally, the *suegra*'s intrusion into his home is so all-encompassing that the man feels menaced in his own house. As we have seen, this domestic weakness is partly attributable to a masculine abdication of domestic responsibilities in exchange for a full larder and efficient housekeeping, but belying the ready acceptance of this domestic "service" is the continual eulogizing over lost powers.

Faced with this powerful matri-core, the working-class husband often finds some of the most basic decisions in his life taken over unilaterally by affines. For example, many men complain plaintively that although they hate to emigrate to work outside of Andalusia, they are literally forced to go when faced with the *fait accompli* of a decision made by wife and *suegra*. One man in El Castillo, a peasant farmer, echoed a commonly heard complaint when he confided that he went to work in Madrid after his wife decided they needed a new refrigerator—a prestige item that many women buy for competitive "show" rather than real need (since women shop daily, the refrigerator often stands empty in the kitchen). Most men are committed to providing as well as possible for their families, but often decisions about consumption needs and therefore about employment, are made by the joint demands of kinswoman, with the *suegra* again figuring demonically in this process. Another popular carnival *copla* puts it this way:

> Working, working,
> Working night and day,
> Because when I'm unemployed
> And not earning any money,
> No one can control my
> Wife and mother-in-law.[8]

Later in this song the *suegra* and wife are scolded for their voracious appetite for consumer goods, which forces the poor man to emigrate to Germany as "the only way to pay back what I owe in Spain." Again, the point to be made is that a worker or poor peasant, who has very little input into purchasing decisions, senses a helplessness before the power of the matri-core. The wife, in alliance with her mother, may make the most important life decision, and the man may feel a passive victim.

Occasionally, a man may express the opinion that his wife cares more about her mother than her husband, a complaint that may convey a hidden sense of both injustice and affective exclusion. For example, there was one man in Fuenmayor, Adolfo, whose wife kept forgetting his lunch (the main meal of the day). Her excuse was that her mother was old and needed her constant attention. One day I went home with Adolfo directly from the bar where we had been enjoying a pre-prandial beer. He had invited me home for the midday meal, after which I was to interview him. But when we arrived, Adolfo was chagrinned to find that no lunch had been prepared and there was nothing in the family larder but a small sausage. A note taped on the wall announced that his wife had gone to visit her ill mother. Although embarrassed and disappointed, Adolfo took it all in stride, confiding to me that "that's how women are." A man is a fifth wheel in his own house, he noted, adding peevishly that at least he had the consolation of knowing that the "old dragon" would not be bossing him around that day, since she was sick. It is clear that many lower-class men feel marginalized in their own homes.

In addition to her dominance in economic planning (with her mother's active support), the non-elite Andalusian wife usually acts as the unofficial administrator of domestic finances. This is especially true among the rural proletarians in both Fuenmayor and El Castillo, where the husband may surrender his entire day-wage to his wife each night. In return he expects the house to be run properly, and will himself be given a small "allowance" for his expenses at the bar and for his nightly card game. Many laborers refer to their wives in a semi-ironic vein as the *ama* ("boss") or *jefa* ("chief") of the house—words reserved in the wider public context for such authority figures as employers and political leaders. One man in Fuenmayor spoke of his wife seriously as the "generalissima" of household finances (using the feminized form of Generalissimo Franco's[9] title), adding that he did not care what she did with the money he earned so long as he was returned enough to buy refreshments at the neighborhood tavern.

I remember one worker getting up from an exciting card game to run home to wheedle his wife for more money. His fellows remarked that his wife was a "peseta pincher," but they agreed that her supervision of his gambling was probably a good thing, as he tended to bet poorly at cards. Most men present admitted that their own wives held the family purse strings and that this was unavoidable, since they (the men) were rarely at home. They said that a man works (or "sacrifices") to give money to his wife and his family and that a man who withheld his wages from his wife was "mean" and a reprobate: he was depriving his children. Again, male acquiescence here may be seen as morally ambivalent. Men evade onerous responsibilities by giving the wife final authority, but there is a lingering self-doubt about it; as usual, this tension finds expression in self-deprecating humor.

DOMESTIC POWER AND CLASS

This tendency to let the wife and her mother run the family's finances correlates with class status. Among the wealthier peasants, most husbands retain rights over the domestic economy and play a more active part in allocating resources for the family. Among the gentry in Fuenmayor, most husbands take a more active role in finances and may even control the family purse strings through bank accounts and investments that the wife rarely knows about. Or, in some landowning families, a husband may simply provide his wife with a monthly allowance, while she does little more than distribute this to various domestic employees with instructions on purchases.

In the working classes, however, where surplus cash is a rarity and where the domestic economy is often managed on a credit or deficit basis because of the vagaries of agrarian employment, the wife "rules" the household economy and the husband accepts this. Although he may realize that it further diminishes his "power" in the domestic sphere, he is often willing to trade this power for the peace of mind that comes from being shielded from petty fiscal annoyances. Again, working-class male remoteness here is a trade-off in which the man sacrifices control for a modicum of comfort. Conversely, in the propertied classes, comfort is assured through the practice of hiring servants; in addition, or perhaps because of this, the rich tend to live either patrilocally or patrivicinally after marriage: the *suegra* is not "needed."

Although we could not advise them on this issue, the conversation soon turned to more concrete subjects, such as the importance of having a first child exactly nine months after the wedding. Husband and wife agreed that this is necessary to quell gossip about the man's potency. If a first child is delayed, they added, people assume that the husband has sexual problems and they gossip about his manhood. They also implied that since this is so, some brides are able to "lead the groom about by the nose" by threatening to withhold sex. The man has to placate her so that she quickly becomes pregnant. This is another example of female "power" wielded without respect to "right."

POWER AND SEXUALITY

Finally, there is the "power" exercised by wives through their ability to withhold sex, which is the same in all classes. Generally it is assumed among men in Andalusia that women are highly sexed, although it is the man who awakens and directs this amorphous source of female sexual energy. Yet there is also a general understanding that in marital relations, it is the woman who "uses" the strategy of withholding sex as a means of controlling or persuading.

Some men naturally are "flojo" sexually (weak or impotent), and their wives may be frustrated by this lamentable failing. But according to informants—both male and female—a husband never withholds sex purposefully in order to manipulate his wife. "He could not do that if he were a man," one man asserted firmly, adding that this is an exclusively feminine weapon that would be humiliating for a man.

Withholding sex is also a weapon that carries more than just psychological weight. I was once talking to a couple of newlyweds, who quite spontaneously asked me and my wife (a medical doctor, as they knew) about the best way to conceive a child. They had heard rumors that the impregnation of the wife could be assured and the sex of the child could be determined by "positions."

CONCLUSIONS

If power is defined as personal autonomy and the ability to impose one's will regardless of the source of this ability, then one must conclude, along with Rogers that men have less of this ability than their wives—at least in the lower classes of these Andalusian communities. Although the lower-class men claim that this imbalance is by design and that it "frees" them to concentrate on more important matters, I am inclined to regard this as Rogers seems to do, as farcical face-saving, rather than an inverse "power" to evade work.

Beyond the domestic realm, real power is a scarce commodity denied to most men. Most Andalusian workers have little or no political power; nor do they exercise power in relations with their peers, all of whom start from the same point of equivalency in basically egalitarian relationships. They may have influence with their cronies, but few men can be said to have power, whatever its provenance—except perhaps over their sons, but even this is equivocal (Murphy 1983). Since working-class men have virtually no alternative sources of power over their peers in communities like Fuenmayor and El Castillo, one may conclude that they are relatively powerless compared to women, whose domestic power is real and unqualified.

One very important point should be made about relations of dominance and subordination in the context of class-stratified marginal communities like those in rural Andalusia. This is that any approach to the dimension of power that uses only gender as a criterion is probably epistemologically invalid. Where power is concerned, there are men and men, and there are women and women. As Davis has pointed out, what matters is not only sex, but also relative access to resources. One may not speak of a category "men" opposed to another category "women," because this is an oversimplification that, in Herzfeld's phrase, "sacrifices *complementarity* to *opposition*" and conflates theoretically subtle symbols. Europeanist ethnography shows us the pervasiveness of social class and its power to determine, not sex of course, but the principles of group formation. Gender is one additional or parallel dimension of the social organization of production, not an arbitrary symbolic schema imposed independent of structural and historical context. Almost everywhere we look, "Alpha males"[10] dominate women *because* they dominate men and so one must speak more generally of multidimensional *human* rather than unidimensional gender hierarchies.

NOTES

1. Research for this study was made possible by grants from the National Institute of Mental Health, the National Science Foundation, the Wenner-Gren Foundation, the National Endowment for the Humanities, the Council for the International Exchange of Scholars, and the H. F. Guggenheim Foundation.
2. See, for example, Giovannini (1985); Uhl (1985); Dubisch (1986). I also follow Dubisch (1986:16); and Salamone and Stanton (1986:97) in use of the term "domestic power."
3. Names of both towns are pseudonyms.
4. A latifundium is a landed estate on which workers in a state of partial servitude practice labor-intensive agriculture.
5. Agnates are kin related through the male line.
6. From a poem by Marcelin Lora.
7. From a poem by Juanillo "El Gato."
8. From a poem by Juanillo "El Gato."
9. Generalissimo Franco ran Spain with an iron hand from 1936 until his death in 1975.
10. "Alpha male" is a term developed in studies of nonhuman primates. It refers to the dominant male of a local primate group.

REFERENCES

Bem, Sandra. 1983. "Gender Schema Theory and Its Implications for Child Development." *Signs,* 8: 598–616.

Brandes, Stanley H. 1980. *Metaphors of Masculinity.* Philadelphia: University of Philadelphia Press.

Brøgger, Jan. 1990. *Pre-Bureaucratic Europeans.* Oslo: Norwegian University Press.

Carrasco, Pedro. 1963. "The Locality Referent in Residence Terms." *American Anthropologist,* 65: 133–134.

Casselberry, Samuel F. and Nancy Valavanes. 1976. "Matrilocal Greek Peasants and Reconsideration of Residence Terminology." *American Ethnologist,* 3:215–226.

Davis, John. 1973. *Land and Family in Pisticci.* London: Athlone Press.

Driessen, Henk. 1983. "Male Sociability and Rituals of Masculinity in Rural Andalusia." *Anthropological Quarterly,* 56:125–133.

Dubisch, Jill, ed. 1986. *Gender and Power in Rural Greece.* Princeton: Princeton University Press.

Giovannini, Maureen J. 1985. "The Dialectics of Women's Factory Work in a Sicilian Town." *Anthropology,* 9:45–64.

Gregory, James R. 1984. "The Myth of the Male Ethnographer and the Woman's World." *American Anthropologist,* 86:316–327.

Herzfeld, Michael. 1986. "Within and Without: The Category of 'Female' in the Ethnography of Modern Greece," in Jill Dubisch, ed., *Gender and Power in Rural Greece.* Princeton: Princeton University Press.

Murphy, Michael. 1983. "Emotional Confrontations between Sevillano Fathers and Sons: Cultural Foundations and Social Consequences." *American Ethnologist,* 10:650–664.

Pina-Cabral, João de. 1986. *Sons of Adam, Daughters of Eve: The Peasant Worldview of the Alto Minho.* Oxford: Clarendon Press.

Press, Irwin. 1979. *The City as Context: Urbanism and Behavioral Constraints in Seville.* Urbana: University of Illinois Press.

Rogers, Susan C. 1975. "Female Forms of Power and the Myth of Male Dominance: A Model of Female/Male Interaction in Peasant Society." *American Ethnologist,* 2:727–756.

Salamone, S. D., and J. B. Stanton. 1986. "Introducing the Nikokyra: Ideality and Reality in Social Process," in Jill Dubisch, ed., *Gender and Power in Rural Greece.* Princeton: Princeton University Press.

Uhl, Sarah C. 1985. "Special Friends; The Organization of Intersex Friendship in Escalona (Andalusia) Spain." *Anthropology,* 9:129–152.

35

Delicate Transactions

Gender, Home, and Employment among Hispanic Women

M. PATRICIA FERNÁNDEZ KELLY

The days have vanished when scholars could comfortably speak about the roles of men and women as if they were immutable biological or temperamental traits. More than a decade of feminist thought and research in the social sciences has brought about a complex understanding of gender as a process reflecting political, economic, and ideological transactions, a fluid phenomenon changing in uneasy harmony with productive arrangements. The theoretical focus of this essay is on the way class, ethnicity, and gender interact.

I compare two groups of Hispanic women involved in apparel manufacturing: One includes native- and foreign-born Mexicans in Southern California; another, Cuban exiles in Southern Florida.[1] All the women have worked in factories at different stages in their lives, and they have also been involved in industrial work in the home. In a broad sense, women's incorporation into the work force is part and parcel of economic strategies that have allowed manufacturing firms to compete in domestic and international markets. From a more restricted perspective, it is also the result of personal negotiations between men and women in households and workplaces. Combining these perspectives, it is possible to compare the two groups of women to see the influence of economic resources and immigration histories on conceptions and institutions of gender. Despite sharing important characteristics, the two groups represent distinct economic classes and social situations. I use the cases to examine how economic and social factors can reinforce or undermine patriarchal values and affect women's attitudes toward and relationships with men.

A complex conceptualization of gender has emerged over the past two decades from the dialogue between Marxist and feminist scholars. In this dialogue, theorists have focused on the relationship between productive and reproductive spheres to uncover the varied content of gender relations under differing conditions of production and in different periods.[2] Here "gender" refers to meshed economic, political, and ideological relations. Under capitalism gender designates fundamental economic processes that determine the allocation of labor into remunerated and non-remunerated spheres of production. Gender also circumscribes the alternatives of individuals of different sexes in the area of paid employment. Women's specific socioeconomic experience is grounded in the contradiction that results from the wage labor/unpaid domestic labor split.

In addition, gender is political as it contributes to differential distributions of power and access to vital resources on the basis of sexual difference. The political asymmetry between men and women is played out both within and outside of the domestic realm. In both cases it involves conflict, negotiation, and ambivalent resolutions which are, in turn, affected by economic and ideological factors.

Finally, gender implicates the shaping of consciousness and the elaboration of collective discourses which alternatively explain, legitimate, or question the position of men and women as members of families and as workers. While all societies assign roles to individuals on the basis of perceived sexual characteristics, these roles vary significantly and change over time. Gender is part of a broader ideological process in constant flux. Moreover, adherence to patriarchal mores may have varying outcomes depending on their economic and political context.

This interplay of economic, political, and ideological aspects of gender is particularly evident in studying the relationship between women's paid employment and household responsibilities. Women's work—whether factory work, industrial homework, or unpaid domestic work—always involves negotiations of gendered boundaries, such as the line between wage labor and domestic responsibilities, and the arrangements that tie household organization and family ideals. Industrial homework, for example, both contradicts and complies with the ideological split between "work" and "family" as this sets standards for male-female differentiation; women who do homework work for wages but do not leave their homes and families.

Employers rely on homework to lower the wage bill, evade government regulations, and maintain competitiveness in the market;[3] none of these goals seem consistent with women's attempts to raise their economic status. Yet homework has been used by women to reconcile the responsibilities of domestic care with the need to earn a wage. Furthermore, women use and interpret homework as a strategy for bridging employment and family goals in a variety of ways. Women move between factory work, homework, and unpaid domestic labor on different trajectories, depending on both household organization and class-based resources.

Some conceptual clarification is needed for this analysis. It is necessary to distinguish "family" and "household." "Family" is an ideological notion that includes marriage and fidelity, men's roles as providers and women's roles as caretakers of children, and the expectation that nuclear families will reside in the same home. Rayna Rapp

notes the prevalence of a family ideal shared by working- and middle-class people in the United States.[4] While "family" designates the way things should be, "household" refers to the manner in which men, women, and children actually join each other as part of domestic units. Households represent mechanisms for the pooling of time, labor, and other resources in a shared space. As households adjust to the pressures of the surrounding environment, they frequently stand in sharp, even painful, contrast to ideals regarding the family.

Class accounts largely for the extent to which notions about the family can be upheld or not. The conditions necessary for the maintenance of long-term stable unions where men act as providers and women as caretakers of children have been available among the middle and upper classes but absent among the poor. Nuclear households are destabilized by high levels of unemployment and underemployment or by public policy making it more advantageous for women with children to accept welfare payments than to remain dependent upon an irregularly employed man. The poor often live in highly flexible households where adherence to the norms of the patriarchial family are unattainable.

Class differences in the relation between household patterns and family ideals are apparent in women's changing strategies of factory work, homework, and unpaid labor. Homework, for example, can maintain family objectives or help compensate for their unattainability. In describing two contrasting ways women link household organization, paid employment, and gender and family ideals, my study creates a model for class and ethnic specific analyses of gender negotiations.

THE HISPANIC COMMUNITIES IN MIAMI AND LOS ANGELES

Although there are many studies comparing minorities and whites in the U.S., there have been few attempts to look at variations of experience within ethnic groups. This is true for Hispanics in general and for Hispanic women in particular; yet contrasts abound. For example, Mexicans comprise more than half of all Hispanics between eighteen and sixty-four years of age living in the U.S. Of these, approximately 70% were born in this country. Average levels of educational attainment are quite low with less than 50% having graduated from high school. In contrast, Cubans represent about 7% of the Hispanic population. They are mostly foreign-born; 58% of Cubans have 12 or more years of formal schooling.[5]

Both in Southern California and in Southern Florida most direct production workers in the garment industry are Hispanic. In Los Angeles most apparel firm operatives are Mexican women, in Miami, Cuban women.[6] The labor force participation rates of Mexican and Cuban women dispel the widespread notion that work outside the home is a rare experience for Hispanic women.[7] Yet the Los Angeles and Miami communities differ in a number of important respects. One can begin with contrasts in the garment industry in each area.

The two sites differ in the timing of the industry, its evolution, maturity, and restructuring. In Los Angeles, garment production emerged in the latter part of the nineteenth century and expanded in the 1920s, stimulated in part by the arrival of runaway shops evading unionization drives in New York. The Great Depression sent the Los Angeles garment industry into a period of turmoil, but soon fresh opportunities for the production of inexpensive women's sportswear developed, as the rise of cinema established new guidelines for fashion. During the 1970s and 1980s the industry reorganized in response to foreign imports; small manufacturing shops have proliferated, as has home production. In contrast, the apparel industry in Miami has had a shorter and more uniform history. Most of the industry grew up since the 1960s, when retired manufacturers from New York saw the advantage of opening new businesses and hiring exiles from the Cuban Revolution.

The expansion of the Los Angeles clothing industry resulted from capitalists' ability to rely on continuing waves of Mexican immigrants, many of whom were undocumented. Mexican migration over the last century ensured a steady supply of workers for the apparel industry; from the very beginning, Mexican women were employed in nearly all positions in the industry.[8] By contrast, the expansion of garment production in Miami was due to an unprecedented influx of exiles ejected by a unique political event. Cubans working in the Florida apparel industry arrived in the United States as refugees under a protected and relatively privileged status. Exile was filled with uncertainty and the possibility of dislocation but not, as in the case of undocumented Mexican aliens, with the probability of harassment, detention, and deportation.

Mexican and Cuban workers differ strikingly in social class. For more than a century, the majority of Mexican immigrants have had a markedly proletarian background. Until the 1970s, the majority had rural roots, although in more recent times there has been a growing number of urban immigrants.[9] In sharp contrast, Cuban waves of migration have included a larger proportion of professionals, mid-level service providers, and various types of entrepreneurs ranging from those with previous experience in large companies to those qualified to start small family enterprises. Entrepreneurial experience among Cubans and reliance on their own ethnic networks accounts, to a large extent, for Cuban success in business formation and appropriation in Miami.[10] Thus, while Mexican migration has been characterized by relative homogeneity regarding class background, Cuban exile resulted in the transposition of an almost intact class structure containing investors and professionals as well as unskilled, semi-skilled, and skilled workers.

In addition to disparate class compositions, the two groups differ in the degree of their homogeneity by place of birth. Besides the sizable undocumented contingent mentioned earlier, the Los Angeles garment industry also employs U.S.-born citizens of Mexican heritage. First-hand reports and anecdotal evidence indicate that the fragmentation between "Chicana" and "Mexicana" workers causes an unresolved tension and animosity within the labor force. Cubans, on the other hand, were a highly cohesive population until the early 1980s, when the arrival of the so-called "Marielitos" resulted in a potentially disruptive polarization of the community.

Perhaps the most important difference between Mexicans in Los Angeles and Cubans in Florida is related to their distinctive labor market insertion patterns. Historically, Mexicans have arrived in the U.S. labor market in a highly individuated and dispersed manner. As a result, they have been extremely dependent on labor market supply and demand forces entirely beyond their control. Their working-class background and stigma attached to their frequent undocumented status has accentuated even further their vulnerability vis-à-vis employers. By contrast, Cubans have been able to consolidate an economic enclave formed by immigrant businesses, which hire workers of a common cultural and national background. The economic enclave partly operates as a buffer zone separating and often shielding members of the same ethnic group from the market forces at work in the larger society. The existence of an economic enclave does not preclude exploitation on the basis of class; indeed, it is predicated upon the existence of a highly diversified immigrant class structure. However, commonalities of culture, national background, and language between immigrant employers and workers can become a mechanism for collective improvement of income levels and standards of living. As a result, differences in labor market insertion patterns among Mexicans and Cubans have led to varying social profiles and a dissimilar potential for socioeconomic attainment.

THE WOMEN GARMENT WORKERS

These differences between the two Hispanic communities have led to important differences between the two groups of women who work in the garment industry. For Mexican women in Southern California, employment in garment production is the consequence of long-term economic need. Wives and daughters choose to work outside the home in order to meet the survival requirements of their families in the absence of satisfactory earnings by men. Some female heads of household join the labor force after losing male support through illness, death, and, more often, desertion. In many of these instances, women opt for industrial homework in order to reconcile child care and the need for wage employment. They are particularly vulnerable members of an economically marginal ethnic group.

By contrast, Cuban women who arrived in Southern Florida during the 1960s saw jobs in garment assembly as an opportunity to recover or attain middle-class status. The consolidation of an economic enclave in Miami, which accounts for much of the prosperity of Cubans, was largely dependent upon the incorporation of women into the labor force. While they toiled in factories, men entered business or were self-employed. Their vulnerability was tempered by shared goals of upward mobility in a foreign country.

Despite their different nationalities, migratory histories, and class backgrounds, Mexicans and Cubans share many perceptions and expectations. In both cases, patriarchal norms of reciprocity are favored; marriage, motherhood, and devotion to family are high priorities among women, while men are expected to hold authority, to be good providers, and to be loyal to their wives and children. However, the divergent economic and political conditions surrounding Mexicans in Southern California and Cubans in Southern Florida have had a differing impact upon each group's ability to uphold these values. Mexican women are often thrust into financial "autonomy" as a result of men's inability to fulfill their socially assigned role. Among Cubans, by contrast, men have been economically more successful. Indeed, ideological notions of patriarchal responsibility have served to maintain group cohesion; that offers women an advantage in getting and keeping jobs within the ethnic enclave.

Cuban and Mexican women both face barriers stemming from their subordination in the family and their status as low-skilled workers in highly competitive industries. Nevertheless, their varying class backgrounds and modes of incorporation into local labor markets entail distinctive political and socioeconomic effects. How women view their identities as women is especially affected. Among Mexican garment workers disillusion about the economic viability of men becomes a desire for individual emancipation, mobility, and financial independence as women. However, these ideals and ambitions for advancement are most often frustrated by poverty and the stigmas attached to ethnic and gender status.

Cuban women, on the other hand, tend to see no contradiction between personal fulfillment and a strong commitment to patriarchal standards. Their incorporation and subsequent withdrawal from the labor force are both influenced by their acceptance of hierarchical patterns of authority and the sexual division of labor. As in the case of Mexicans in Southern California, Cuban women's involvement in industrial homework is an option bridging domestic and income-generating needs. However, it differs in that homework among them was brought about by relative prosperity and expanding rather than diminishing options. Women's garment work at home does not contradict patriarchal ideals of women's place at the same time as it allows women to contribute to the economic success that confirms gender stratification.

The stories of particular women show the contrasts in how women in each of these two groups negotiate the links among household, gender, and employment arrangements. Some of the conditions surrounding Mexican home workers in Southern California are illustrated by the experience of Amelia Ruíz.[11] She was born into a family of six children in El Cerrito, Los Angeles County. Her mother, a descendant of Native American Indians, married at a young age the son of Mexican immigrants. Among Amelia's memories are the fragmentary stories of her paternal grandparents working in the fields and, occasionally, in canneries. Her father, however was not a stoop laborer but a trained upholsterer. Her mother was always a homemaker. Amelia grew up with a distinct sense

of the contradictions that plague the relationships between men and women:

All the while I was a child, I had this feeling that my parents weren't happy. My mother was smart but she could never make much of herself. Her parents taught her that the fate of woman is to be a wife and mother; they advised her to find a good man and marry him. And that she did. My father was reliable and I think he was faithful but he was also distant; he lived in his own world. He would come home and expect to be served hand and foot. My mother would wait on him but she was always angry about it. I never took marriage for granted.

After getting her high school diploma, Amelia found odd jobs in all the predictable places: as a counter clerk in a dress shop, as a cashier in a fast-food establishment, and as a waitress in two restaurants. When she was 20, she met Miguel— Mike as he was known outside the barrio. He was a consummate survivor, having worked in the construction field, as a truck driver, and even as an English as a Second Language instructor. Despite her misgivings about marriage, Amelia was struck by Mike's penchant for adventure:

He was different from the men in my family. He loved fun and was said to have had many women. He was a challenge. We were married when I was 21 and he 25. For a while I kept my job but when I became pregnant, Miguel didn't want me to work any more. Two more children followed and then, little by little, Miguel became abusive. He wanted to have total authority over me and the children. He said a man should know how to take care of a family and get respect, but it was hard to take him seriously when he kept changing jobs and when the money he brought home was barely enough to keep ends together.

After the birth of her second child, Amelia started work at Shirley's, a women's wear factory in the area. Miguel was opposed to the idea. For Amelia, work outside the home was an evident need prompted by financial stress. At first, it was also a means to escape growing disenchantment:

I saw myself turning into my mother and I started thinking that to be free of men was best for women. Maybe if Miguel had had a better job, maybe if he had kept the one he had, things would have been different, but he didn't.... We started drifting apart.

Tension at home mounted over the following months. Amelia had worked at Shirley's for almost a year when, one late afternoon after collecting the three children from her parents' house, she returned to an empty home. She knew, as soon as she stepped inside, that something was amiss. In muted shock, she confirmed the obvious: Miguel had left, taking with him all personal possessions; even the wedding picture in the living room had been removed. No explanations had been left behind. Amelia was then 28 years of age, alone, and the mother of three small children.

As a result of these changes, employment became even more desirable, but the difficulty of reconciling home responsibilities with wage work persisted. Amelia was well regarded at Shirley's, and her condition struck a sympathetic chord among the other factory women. In a casual conversation, her supervisor described how other women were leasing industrial sewing machines from the local Singer distributor and were doing piecework at home. By combining factory work and home assembly, she could earn more money without further neglecting the children. Mr. Driscoll, Shirley's owner and general manager, made regular use of home workers, most of whom were former employees. That had allowed him to retain a stable core of about 20 factory seamstresses and to depend on approximately 10 home workers during peak seasons.

Between 1979, the year of her desertion, and 1985, when I met her, Amelia had struggled hard, working most of the time and making some progress. Her combined earnings before taxes fluctuated between $950 and $1,150 a month. Almost half of her income went to rent for the two-bedroom apartment which she shared with the children. She was in debt and used to working at least 12 hours a day. On the other hand, she had bought a double-needle sewing machine and was

thinking of leasing another one to share additional sewing with a neighbor. She had high hopes:

Maybe some day I'll have my own business; I'll be a liberated woman...I won't have to take orders from a man. Maybe Miguel did me a favor when he left after all....

With understandable variations, Amelia's life history is shared by many garment workers in Southern California. Three aspects are salient in this experience. First, marriage and a stable family life are perceived as desirable goals which are, nonetheless, fraught with ambivalent feelings and burdensome responsibilities.

Second, tensions between men and women result from contradictions between the intent to fulfill gender definitions and the absence of the economic base necessary for their implementation. The very definition of manhood includes the right to hold authority and power over wives and children, as well as the responsibility of providing adequately for them. The difficulties in implementing those goals in the Mexican communities I studied are felt equally by men and women but expressed differently by each. Bent on restoring their power, men attempt to control women in abusive ways. Women often resist their husbands' arbitrary or unrealistic impositions. Both reactions are eminently political phenomena.

Third, personal conflict regarding the proper behavior of men and women may be tempered by negotiation. It can also result in the breach of established agreements, as in the case of separation or divorce. Both paths are related to the construction of alternative discourses and the redefinition of gender roles. Women may seek personal emancipation, driven partly by economic need and partly by dissatisfaction with men's performance as providers. In general, individuals talk about economic and political conflict as a personal matter occurring in their own homes. Broader contextual factors are less commonly discussed.

The absence of economic underpinnings for the implementation of patriarchal standards may bring about more equitable exchanges between men and women, and may stimulate women's search for individual well-being and personal autonomy as women. However, in the case at hand, such ideals remain elusive. Mexican garment workers, especially those who are heads of households, face great disadvantages in the labor market. They are targeted for jobs that offer the lowest wages paid to industrial workers in the United States; they also have among the lowest unionization rates in the country. Ironically, the breakdown of patriarchal norms in the household draws from labor market segmentation that reproduces patriarchal (and ethnic) stratification.

Experiences like the ones related are also found among Cuban and Central American women in Miami. However, a larger proportion have had a different trajectory. Elvira Gómez's life in the U.S. is a case in point. She was 34 when she arrived in Miami with her four children, ages three to twelve. The year was 1961.

> Leaving Havana was the most painful thing that ever happened to us. We loved our country. We would have never left willingly. Cuba was not like Mexico: we didn't have immigrants in large numbers. But Castro betrayed us and we had to join the exodus. We became exiles. My husband left Cuba three months before I did and there were moments when I doubted I would ever see him again. Then, after we got together, we realized we would have to forge ahead without looking back.
>
> We lost everything. Even my mother's china had to be left behind. We arrived in this country as they say, "covering our nakedness with our bare hands" (una mano delante y otra detrás). My husband had had a good position in a bank. To think that he would have to take any old job in Miami was more than I could take; a man of his stature having to beg for a job in a hotel or in a factory? It wasn't right!

Elvira had worked briefly before her marriage as a secretary. As a middle-class wife and mother, she was used to hiring at least one maid. Coming to the United States changed all that:

> Something had to be done to keep the family together. So I looked around and finally found a job

in a shirt factory in Hialeah. Manolo (her husband) joined a childhood friend and got a loan to start an export-import business. All the time they were building the firm, I was sewing. There were times when we wouldn't have been able to pay the bills without the money I brought in.

Elvira's experience was shared by thousands of women in Miami. Among the first waves of Cuban refugees there were many who worked tirelessly to raise the standards of living of their families to the same levels or higher than those they had been familiar with in their country of origin. The consolidation of an ethnic enclave allowed many Cuban men to become entrepreneurs. While their wives found unskilled and semi-skilled jobs, they became businessmen. Eventually, they purchased homes, put their children through school, and achieved comfort. At that point, many Cuban men pressed their wives to stop working outside of the home; they had only allowed them to have a job, in the first place, out of economic necessity. In the words of a prominent manufacturer in the area:

> You have to understand that Cuban workers were willing to do anything to survive. When they became prosperous, the women saw the advantage of staying at home and still earn additional income. Because they had the skill, owners couldn't take them for granted. Eventually, owners couldn't get operators anymore. The most skilled would tell a manager "my husband doesn't let me work out of the home." This was a worker's initiative based on the values of the culture. I would put ads in the paper and forty people would call and everyone would say "I only do homework." That's how we got this problem of the labor shortages. The industry was dying; we wouldn't have survived without the arrival of the Haitians and the Central Americans.

This discussion partly shows that decisions made at the level of the household can remove workers, actively sought and preferred by employers, from the marketplace. This, in turn, can threaten certain types of production. In those cases, loyalty to familial values can mitigate against the interests of capitalist firms. Interviews with Cuban women involved in homework confirm the general accuracy of this interpretation. After leaving factory employment, many put their experience to good use by becoming subcontractors and employing neighbors or friends. They also transformed so-called "Florida rooms" (the covered porches in their houses) into sewing shops. It was in one of them that Elvira Gómez was first interviewed. In her case, working outside the home was justified only as a way to maintain the integrity of her family and as a means to support her husband's early incursions into the business world:

> For many long years I worked in the factory but when things got better financially, Manolo asked me to quit the job. He felt bad that I couldn't be at home all the time with the children. But it had to be done. There's no reason for women not to earn a living when it's necessary; they should have as many opportunities and responsibilities as men. But I also tell my daughters that the strength of a family rests on the intelligence and work of women. It is foolish to give up your place as a mother and a wife only to go take orders from men who aren't even part of your family. What's so liberated about that? It is better to see your husband succeed and to know you have supported one another.

Perhaps the most important point here is the unambiguous acceptance of patriarchal mores as a legitimate guideline for the behavior of men and women. Exile did not eliminate these values; rather, it extended them in telling ways. The high labor force participation rates of Cuban women in the United States have been mentioned before. Yet, it should be remembered that, prior to their migration, only a small number of Cuban women had worked outside the home for any length of time. It was the need to maintain the integrity of their families and to achieve class-related ambitions that precipitated their entrance into the labor force of a foreign country.

In descriptions of their experience in exile, Cuban women often make clear that part of the motivation in their search for jobs was the preservation of known definitions of manhood and womanhood. Whereas Mexican women worked as a response to what they saw as a failure of patriarchal arrangements, Cuban women worked in the name of dedication to their husbands and children, and in order to preserve the status and authority of the former. Husbands gave them "permission" to work outside the home, and only as a result of necessity and temporary economic strife. In the same vein, it was a ritual yielding to masculine privilege that led women to abandon factory employment. Conversely, men "felt bad" that their wives had to work for a wage and welcomed the opportunity to remove them from the marketplace when economic conditions improved.

As with Mexicans in Southern California, Cuban women in Miami earned low wages in low- and semi-skilled jobs. They too worked in environments devoid of the benefits derived from unionization. Nevertheless, the outcome of their experience as well as the perceptions are markedly different. Many Cuban women interpret their subordination at home as part of a viable option ensuring economic and emotional benefits. They are bewildered by feminist goals of equality and fulfillment in the job market. Yet, the same women have had among the highest rates of participation in the U.S. labor force.

CONCLUSIONS

For Mexican women in Southern California, proletarianization is related to a high number of female-headed households, as well as households where the earnings provided by women are indispensable for maintaining standards of modest subsistence. In contrast, Cuban women's employment in Southern Florida was a strategy for raising standards of living in a new environment. These contrasts in the relationship between households and the labor market occurred despite shared values regarding the family among Mexicans and Cubans. Both groups partake of similar mores regarding the roles of men and women; nevertheless, their actual experience has differed significantly. Contrasting features of class, educational background, and immigration history have created divergent gender and family dilemmas for each group.

This analysis underscores the impact of class on gender. Definitions of manhood and womanhood are implicated in the very process of class formation. At the same time, the norms of reciprocity sanctioned by patriarchal ideologies can operate as a form of social adhesive consolidating class membership. For poor men and women, the issue is not only the presence of the sexual division of labor and the persistence of patriarchal ideologies but the difficulties of upholding either.

Thus, too, the meaning of women's participation in the labor force remains plagued by paradox. For Mexican women in Southern California, paid employment responds to and increases women's desires for greater personal autonomy and financial independence. Ideally, this should have a favorable impact upon women's capacity to negotiate an equitable position within their homes and in the labor market. Yet these women's search for paid employment is most often the consequence of severe economic need; it expresses vulnerability, not strength within homes and in the marketplace. Indeed, in some cases, women's entry into the labor force signals the collapse of reciprocal exchanges between men and women. Women deserted by their husbands are generally too economically marginal to translate their goals of gender equality and autonomy into socially powerful arrangements. Conversely, Cuban women in Southern Florida have more economic power, but this only strengthens their allegiance to patriarchal standards. The conjugal "partnership for survival" Elvira Gómez describes is not predicated on the existence of a just social world, but rather an ideological universe entailing differentiated and stratified benefits and obligations for men and women.

NOTES

A different version of this essay appears in Women, Work, and Politics, *Louise Tilly and Patricia Guerin, eds. (New York: Russell Sage Foundation, 1990).*

1. This essay is based on findings from the "Collaborative Study of Hispanic Women in Garment and Electronics Industries" supported by the Ford Foundation under grant number 870 1149. Initial funding for the same project was also provided by the Tinker Foundation. The author gratefully acknowledges the continued encouragement of Dr. William Díaz from the Ford Foundation.

2. Joan W. Scott, "Gender: A Useful Category of Historical Analysis," *The American Historical Review,* 91, 5 (1986): 1053–75; Felicity Edholm, "Conceptualizing Women," *Critique of Anthropology,* 3, 9/10: 101–30. For a relevant analysis of class, see Michael Buroway, *The Politics of Production* (London: New Left Books, 1985).

3. M. Patricia Fernández Kelly and Anna M. García, "Informalization at the Core: Hispanic Women, Homework and the Advanced Capitalist State," in *The Informal Economy: Comparative Studies in Advanced and Third World Societies,* eds. Alejandro Portes, Manuel Castels, and Lauren Benton (Baltimore: Johns Hopkins University Press, 1989).

4. Rayna Rapp, "Family and Class in Contemporary America: Notes Toward an Understanding of Ideology," in *Rethinking the Family,* eds. Barrie Thorne and Marilyn Yalom (New York: Longman, 1982). See also Eli Zaretsky, *Capitalism, The Family and Personal Life* (New York: Harper and Row, 1976).

5. Frank D. Bean and Marta Tienda, *The Hispanic Population of the United States* (New York: Russell Sage Foundation, 1987). There are almost twenty million Hispanics in the United States, that is, 14.6% of the total population.

6. Approximately 75% and 67% of operatives in Los Angeles and Miami apparel firms are Mexican and Cuban women, respectively.

7. Note 54.2% of native-born and 47.5% of foreign-born Mexican women were employed outside the home in 1980. The equivalent figure for the mostly foreign-born Cuban women was almost 65%. Non-Hispanic white women's labor force participation in 1980 was assessed at 57.9% (U.S. Census of Population, 1980).

8. Peter S. Taylor, "Mexican Women in Los Angeles Industry in 1928," *Aztlán: International Journal of Chicano Studies Research,* 11, 1 (Spring, 1980): 99–129.

9. Alejandro Portes and Robert L. Bach, *Latin journey: Cuban and Mexican Immigrants in the United States* (Berkeley: University of California Press, 1985), 67.

10. Alejandro Portes, "The Social Origins of the Cuban Enclave Economy of Miami," *Pacific Sociological*

Review, Special Issue on the Ethnic Economy. 30, 4 (October, 1987): 340–372. See also Lisandro Perez, "Immigrant Economic Adjustment and Family Organization: The Cuban Success Story Reexamined," *International Migration Review,* 20 (1986): 4–20.

11. The following descriptions are chosen from a sample of 25 Mexican and 10 Cuban women garment workers interviewed in Los Angeles and Miami Counties. The names of people interviewed, and some identifying characteristics, have been changed.

36

Culture, Social Class, and Income Control in the Lives of Women Garment Workers in Bangladesh

NAZLI KIBRIA

My father and mother can't feed me, my brothers can't feed me, my uncles can't feed me. So that is why I am working in garments, to stand on my own feet. Since I am taking care of my own expenses, I have no obligation to give money to my family. (Unmarried garment worker, late teens)

It's natural that I give my wages to my husband. It is the custom (niyom) *of our society to cater to the wishes of the husband. For a woman, heaven is at her husband's feet. In this world, a woman without a husband is no better off than a beggar on the street. (Married garment worker, late thirties)*

The recent emergence of export-oriented garment production factories in Bangladesh, the first modern industry in the country to employ primarily women, has been accompanied by vigorous debate among scholars and policymakers about its effects on women (Bangladesh Unnayan Parishad 1990; Chaudhuri and Majumdar 1991; United Nations Industrial Development Organization 1991). In this article I explore this issue through an indepth analysis of how Bangladeshi women garment workers view and experience their income. Of particular interest is the ability of the women workers to exercise authority over their wages, because income control has been identified as a

critical variable in the relationship of women's wagework to family power (Blumberg 1984, 1991).

Analyses of gender and wage control in developing societies emphasize the role of traditional social and cultural patterns in determining the ability of women to control their income (Fapohunda 1988; Hoodfar 1988; Papanek and Schwede 1988; Wolf 1992). The experience of Bangladeshi women workers, however, suggests the need to move away from an analysis of income control that relies heavily on *tradition* as an explanation.

Despite the fact that cultural traditions in Bangladesh are not favorable to the economic autonomy of women, the relationship of women workers to their wages is varied, ranging from complete control over its expenditure to virtually none. Underlying this diversity are differences in the socioeconomic background of the women workers, which shape the relevance and meaning of cultural traditions, particularly those surrounding family life, for women.

SOCIAL CLASS AND THE RELATIONSHIP OF CULTURAL TRADITION TO INCOME CONTROL

Women's access to wage income has the potential to generate egalitarian shifts in gender relations at the household level by providing women the bargaining chips with which to assert power in

AUTHOR'S NOTE: I would like to thank M. Anisul Islam and Ashrafe Khandekar for their research assistance, and Susan Eckstein, Hanna Papanek, and Diane Wolf for their helpful comments on earlier drafts.

household decision-making processes; however, this potential for positive change is not always realized (Sen 1990). One of the crucial intervening factors is the ability of women to exercise control over their income. As Blumberg (1984, 1991) notes in her work on gender stratification, it is women's *control* over key economic resources rather than mere economic ownership or participation that is critical to women's family power. When women exercise control over the expenditure of their income, they can more effectively use it as a bargaining chip with the implicit threat of withdrawing their wages from the household economy.

Studies on the ability of Third World women to control their wages emphasize the importance of traditional social patterns (Fapohunda 1988; Hoodfar 1988; Papanek and Schwede 1988; Wolf 1992). That is, established cultural beliefs and expectations about women furnish a normative template, one that guides the relationship of employed women to their income. Across societies, the ability of women to control their wages varies by the degree of social and economic autonomy that they have traditionally enjoyed.

Clearly, societies in which women have traditionally engaged in valued productive activities and maintained control over the fruits of their labor are social settings in which the potential ability of women to control their wages is high. For example, sub-Saharan African societies, in which women and men have traditionally maintained separate economic activities and resources, are a context in which women are likely to govern their own wages (Fapohunda 1988; Kandiyoti 1988). Women are also more likely to control their income within kinship systems that have traditionally accorded power and authority to women in their relations with men. The Javanese kinship system, favorable to women because of bilateral inheritance, descent, and flexible rules of residence, is one in which women are able to resist the authority of men over their wages (Wolf 1991). In stark contrast, the Chinese kinship system, with its patriarchal rules of descent, inheritance, and residence, is one that expects women to defer to male authority, an expectation that women factory workers fulfill by turning over their wages to the male household head (Gallin 1990; Greenhalgh 1988; Kung 1983; Salaff 1981).

The emphasis on cultural tradition that marks the analysis of gender and wage control in developing societies has fostered a perspective that is inattentive to differentiation among women and its consequences for income control processes. Cultural traditions regarding the autonomy of women vary in meaning and relevance for women, depending on such factors as age and stage in the family life cycle. A major source of differentiation among women, one that is important to consider when evaluating the impact of tradition on income control, is social class.

By determining access to social and economic resources, social class can shape the ability of women and their families to fulfill the dictates of cultural tradition. Economic necessity, for example, often triggers the movement of women into the labor force, despite traditional cultural prohibitions against women's employment (Geschwender 1992). When families are unable to meet traditional gender expectations, women may deal with their income in ways that are a departure from traditional patterns. In the context of a patriarchal family system that assumes the social and economic protection of women by men, the inability of male kin to offer such protection may shift the dynamics of power within the family (Fernández Kelly 1990). Under such circumstances, women may refuse to relinquish control of their wages to men. In short, social class can affect income control patterns by either affirming or challenging the traditional dynamics of relations between women and men.

Social class will also influence income control patterns by shaping the symbolic meanings that are attached to women's income earning. Scholars concerned with the familial consequences of women's wagework have argued that how income is viewed by the woman and her family may be far more important to understanding family power dynamics than the material value of the money per se (Hochschild and Machung 1989; Hood 1983; Pyke 1994). As suggested by the following discussion, the impact of a woman's income on her family power depends on the symbolic meanings and interpretations that are attached to the income by the woman and her family members:

> A woman married to a man who views her employment as a threat rather than as a gift for which he should reciprocate will derive less power from her employment. Similarly, a nonemployed woman married to a man who values his wife's domestic work as a gift will derive more power from her role. Conversely, the extent to which a woman views her own paid and unpaid labor as a gift or burden will also affect her marital power. (Pyke 1994, 75)

Studies suggest that understandings of women's employment are shaped by the socioeconomic status of those involved. For example, in her research on marital power, Pyke (1994) found that among working-class men, the absence of a sense of control in the workplace resulted in a need to assert one's authority at home. The woman's wagework was then viewed unfavorably, as something for which she was expected to compensate to her husband. Such situations, in which the employment of the woman is burdensome due to status insecurities, may detract from the ability of women to control their wages. This is suggested by Safilios-Rothschild (1988), who observes that in patriarchal societies, men may be less inclined to directly assert their authority and demand control of the income of women when their economic superiority and headship over women is firmly established and not under question. In short, social class, through its impact on perceptions of male dominance and authority, affects the symbolic meaning of women's income, and thus potentially the patterns of control that surround women's wages.

In the analyses that follow, I explore the impact of variations in socioeconomic status on women's income-related experiences. Contrary to the widespread image of Bangladeshi women as a monolithic mass, one whose behavior is guided in uniform ways by cultural tradition, women garment workers relate to the traditional family system in diverse ways. The diversity of women's experiences reflects recent economic and social shifts in Bangladesh, which have increased socioeconomic differentiation among women.

CHALLENGES TO TRADITION AND THE RISE OF THE GARMENT INDUSTRY

The basic features of the traditional normative family system in Bangladesh concur with those noted by Kandiyoti (1988) in her description of "classic patriarchy." The system's rules of residence, inheritance, and lineage work to limit the social and economic autonomy of women. Although the status and power of women improve with age, women remain dependent on men throughout the life cycle. At a young age, girls are married and go to live in their husband's home. The custom of village exogamy, or marrying outside the home village, only heightens the isolation of the new bride, who finds herself in a position of subordination to not only the men but also the older women (mother-in-law and sisters-in-law) in the joint family household.[1] Marriage is traditionally accompanied by gifts from the groom's family to the bride, and sometimes to the bride's family. There is also an agreement of a bride price (*mahre*) that is typically deferred with the understanding that it can be claimed by the wife in the event of divorce. Besides this, women enter into marriage with no independent economic assets of their own. As specified by Islamic law, daughters have the right to inherit the equivalent of half the son's share of the father's property; however, the customary practice is for women to waive their land rights to their brothers in exchange for the promise of future economic protection in the event of divorce, abandonment, or other calamity.

The subordination of women in the traditional Bangladeshi family system as I have described is powerfully supported by the institution of *purdah,* or female seclusion. *Purdah* functions as a system of social control that emphasizes the separation of women from men and the seclusion of women from the world outside the home. Whereas the outward symbol of *purdah* is the veil, in Bangladesh, *purdah* operates through a more generalized system in which women are confined to the household compound (*ghare*), away from the outside (*baire*) world of men. The seclusion of women is supported by a powerful ideological apparatus whereby women are socialized into modesty and submission, and family honor (*izzat*) rests on the ability of the family to seclude its women. As Feldman and McCarthy (1983) have observed, it is a system that simultaneously ensures women's participation in agricultural production as well as the inability of women to control the fruits of production. Within the confines of the household compound, women are involved in the processing of crops (e.g., winnowing, husking) as well as the maintenance of household gardens and livestock (Chen 1983). Men, on the other hand, specialize in those economic activities carried out in public spaces, such as the marketplace, thus facilitating their control over economic resources.

As this brief description suggests, the traditional context in Bangladesh is clearly not favorable to women's control over their income, but in Bangladesh, as elsewhere, cultural traditions are not experienced and interpreted by people in uniform ways. Contemporary social and economic shifts in Bangladesh have in fact heightened the diversity of women's understanding of and relationship to the traditional normative family system. The expansion of the state sector following national independence in 1971 has resulted in the expansion of an urban, salaried middle class whose family life is shaped by nonagrarian economic concerns and exposure to Western ideas (Siddiqui et al. 1990). The more widespread challenge to the traditional organization of family life, however, has come from the growing landlessness and impoverishment of rural Bangladesh, trends that have been sharply evident since the 1970s.[2] Under the pressures of extreme poverty, the tradi-

tional family system is becoming increasingly distant from the immediate realities of life for many in rural Bangladesh. For women, it is a system that is increasingly unreliable, one on which they cannot depend for survival.

One of the effects of landlessness has been the disintegration of the joint family household, an economic unit previously held together by shared land interests. Observers of rural Bangladesh have also noted how, under the pressures of extreme poverty, traditional familial and village-based mutual-aid networks have declined in value, and subsistence has become a largely individual matter (Cain, Khanan, and Nahar 1979; Feldman 1992). For women, the erosion of traditional sources of mutual aid, including the ability to rely on the natal family in the event of calamity, has been especially devastating because of a rise in the number of women who find themselves without men's economic support. Conditions of widespread impoverishment and the concurrent inability of men to economically support their families are reflected in the growing incidence of divorce and abandonment by men of their wives and children. As a result, there has been a steady rise in the number of female-headed households in the country.[3]

A central assumption of the traditional family system—the economic and social protection of women by men in exchange for deference to male authority—has been challenged by the widespread poverty of rural Bangladesh. In light of these conditions, growing numbers of women in contemporary Bangladesh have been compelled to go outside the bounds of the traditional family system to ensure their livelihood. The 1970s witnessed the movement of growing numbers of rural women into wagework (e.g., road construction), despite both the traditional prohibitions against women's presence in public spaces and extremely limited employment opportunities for women (Hossain, Jahan, and Sobhan 1990, 34).

Since the mid-1980s, the garment industry has been an important source of urban employment for women. The Bangladesh Garment Manufacturers and Exporters Association (BGMEA 1992) reports more than 1,000 garment manufacturing units in the country in 1992, compared to just 47 in 1983. In fact, by 1992, Bangladesh had become the eighth largest exporter of garments to the United States and the tenth largest to the EEC (European Economic Community). Two factors favored the entry of Bangladesh into the global clothing market at this time. First, the rising costs of production and the imposition of export quotas on major garment-supplying countries, such as Taiwan and South Korea, spurred the movement of garment production to quota-free countries such as Bangladesh that had cheap labor. Second, government policy in Bangladesh, as reflected in the New Industrial Policy (NIP) of 1982, sought to create a favorable investment climate for export-oriented industries by such measures as the creation of export processing zones and the extension of tax benefits and tariff protection to investors (Hossain, Jahan, and Sobhan 1990, 37).

The BGMEA (1992) reports that of the 500,000 workers employed by the industry, more than 78 percent were women who had no previous work experience in the organized industrial sector. The high numbers of women in the industry reflect both the preference of employers for women workers and the growing need for income generation among women. How much control do these women workers retain over their wages? It is clear that the traditional Bangladeshi family system, centered on the deference and dependence of women on men, is a setting in which women are likely to defer to men in the control of their wages. How does this normative system operate to affect income control, particularly in light of structural challenges to traditional family life in Bangladesh?

STUDY METHODS

The analyses that follow draw on materials from a study of the Bangladesh garment industry conducted in 1992. As part of this study, I interviewed garment factory workers, as well as managers and owners. On two occasions, I also observed recruitment interviews for workers at a small-sized factory. I conducted my research in five different export garment production facilities. In two of the factories, managers allowed me to approach workers randomly and ask for interviews; in others, the management selected interviewees. Whereas the majority of the interviews were conducted at the production site, a few were done at the homes of interviewees.

I conducted 46 interviews with workers in their native language, Bengali. The analysis here focuses on the 34 female sewing machine operators in the sample who had similar salary levels and who faced potential demands for control of their income from male kin.[4] The semistructured interviews, which lasted an average of an hour to an hour and a half, were tape-recorded and later transcribed. Whereas the interviews covered a range of issues surrounding socioeconomic status, work, and family, a series of questions focused on what women did with their income and how they felt about it.

The majority of the women workers had not been employed prior to their work in the garment industry, a finding that concurs with that noted by other studies of the industry (Bangladesh Unnayan Parishad 1990; Chaudhuri and Majumdar 1991). In other ways, the sample was a diverse group. The median age of workers ranged from early to late 20s. Of the 41 women, 26 lived in households that were conventionally structured, headed by husbands or male family elders. Eight of the interviewees were young, unmarried women who were living in the city without family elders, either in a dormitory (*mess*) or in an apartment shared with other young women workers.

Reflecting the general paucity of employment opportunities for women in Bangladesh, the female sewing machine operators came from socioeconomically diverse backgrounds. This is suggested by the range of education levels among the women. A total of 12 women had been to school for one to five years, 13 for six to ten years, and 1 had attended a year of college. Based on the women's years of schooling as well as other factors that have been identified as important in determining social class in contemporary Bangladesh (e.g., family income, occupation, involvement in formal versus informal sector, land ownership), I analyzed the socioeconomic background of the women (Siddiqui et al. 1990). Sixteen of the women were from urban working-class backgrounds, as suggested by the relatively low levels of income, schooling (six years or less), and involvement in manual jobs in the informal sector (e.g., rickshaw puller) of family members. Ten of the women were distinguished from others in the sample by their relative economic prosperity, as indicated by their levels of education and household income. On average, these women had completed 7 to 10 years of schooling, and they had at least one family member in a low-level salaried government job—all indicators of lower-middle-class status. Eight of the interviewees were from poor rural backgrounds. These were women who had arrived in the city from the villages with the specific intent of working in the garment factories. Their families were from the impoverished, landless sectors of rural Bangladesh. In what follows, I explore the relationship of these variations in socioeconomic background to the income control experiences of the women.

Urban Working-Class Women: Handing over Wages

The women from urban working-class backgrounds lived with what may be described as *male-dominant budgets*—financial arrangements in which a male family member exercised substantial or complete control over the woman's income. Many of these women initially indicated that they placed their money into a common household fund. Further questioning revealed, however, that most had little say over the uses of the common fund, revealed by the fact that they were unable to provide any specific accounting of the areas of income expenditure. The dominant pattern was to hand over their entire pay to the

male household heads who maintained complete control over household expenditures. In many cases the household head, after receiving the woman's pay, would then give her a small allowance from it for supplemental housekeeping and/or personal expenses. I encountered only three cases among male-dominant budgets in which women were in charge of basic housekeeping expenses. The absence of women's control over even housekeeping budgets may be explained by the responsibility traditionally held by men in Bangladesh for purchasing food for the household, because of cultural prohibitions against women appearing in public places such as the market. Reinforcing this tradition of male responsibility for grocery shopping was the women's long working hours at the factory; many women said that they simply did not have the time or energy to undertake the time-consuming task of shopping for food.

Not surprisingly, the imprint of traditional Bangladeshi familial principles emerged in the sharpest and most predictable fashion in the interviews with women in male-dominant budgets. These women, both married and unmarried, legitimated their surrender of pay to the male household heads with reference to ideological elements of the traditional Bangladeshi family system. The first of these was a view of the family as a unit with common interests and a single, unified identity. Women spoke of how the distinction between their own wages and that of other household members was an artificial one, because all of these were collective rather than individual resources. The reality of conflicting intrahousehold interests was also minimized as women spoke of the male household head as the *benevolent dictator,* whose authority over financial matters was justified by the fact that he acted in ways that protected the interests of all household members. These views emerged in the words of Rokeya, an unmarried 18-year-old woman who had been working as a sewing machine operator for almost two years. She lived in her brother's household and dutifully handed over her wages to him every month:

I give all my pay to my brother. I can't imagine acting in another way. After all, my brother is not spending the money on his own pleasure, on luxuries for himself. When he spends the money it's for my own good, for the good of our family.

Further bolstering the legitimacy of the financial authority of the male household head were traditional beliefs regarding the *natural* place of men and women. Because financial matters were in the realm of the *baire* rather than the *ghare,* they fell under the purview of men's responsibility and expertise. A number of the women garment workers remarked that men were naturally more clever at outside worldly matters, in contrast to women who were smart in household matters.

The traditional family system entered into the construction of the male-dominant budgets not only by furnishing ideological justifications for women's relinquishment of income control but also by providing the basis for the expectation that conformity to traditional norms, specifically, acts of deference to male authority, would ensure the fulfillment of male familial economic responsibilities. In other words, women's surrender of their income solidified the gender contract that was a central dynamic of the traditional family system, that of women's submission to male authority in exchange for the economic and social protection of men.

Of central importance to understanding the significance and value that the women placed on the traditional gender contract is their socioeconomic status. As members of the urban working class, these women had entered into garment work in a context of financial scarcity and insecurity. Despite the added household income generated by their garment factory work, their families had trouble making ends meet and had little or no surplus income. In fact, the urban working-class women, both married and unmarried, had entered into garment factory work because of the inability of men in the family to adequately meet basic household costs, a situation that also provided the justification for women breaking the norms of *purdah* to enter the workplace. They thus saw

themselves as living on the edge of poverty, a situation that strengthened their resolve to solidify the contract that ensured men's participation in the household economy.

Further highlighting women's fears about men's economic participation were the financial struggles of fellow women workers who had become heads of household in the absence of men. The impoverished women heads of households, struggling to support themselves and their children, were symbolic warnings of the dire consequences of men's withdrawal from familial economic responsibilities. This view was shared by the women heads of households themselves, who saw their poverty to be a result of the failure of the family system to deliver on its promise of protection to women.

The significance of these economic fears to the income control behavior of the women in male-dominant budgets was vividly illustrated by the situation of Ameena, a married woman in her mid-20s with two children. Ameena said that a year ago, she had fought with her husband when he discovered that to generate savings she had been withholding about 20 percent of her pay from him. Ameena eventually acceded to her husband's demands that she turn over all her pay to him. She saw this as an act that preserved the implicit gender contract of the marriage:

After that time I stopped keeping money for myself; every time I get paid I come home and give all the money to my husband. I see some of the marriages of women in the garment factory ruined over money; they don't give all the money when he asks for it, the husband leaves her, and then she and her children will be struggling to find rice to eat. After all, women have only one dream in life, to remain with their husband forever.

If the fear of men's withdrawal from their familial economic responsibilities caused women to hand over their wages, it also, somewhat ironically, encouraged women to covertly withhold a portion of their pay from the male household heads. Women were extremely aware of the potential for breakdown of the traditional gender contract. Six of the 16 women in the male-dominant budgets said that they secretly withheld a portion of their pay, despite the possibility of physical violence and other retribution from family members. One of the most common means of withholding money was not to inform family members of special holiday and overtime bonus pay received at work. The withheld money was typically accumulated and then used by women to purchase gold jewelry—a common method of saving in Bangladesh. The women saw such savings as protective insurance that could enable them to survive if faced with such calamity as the departure of the male family breadwinner, an increasingly common occurrence. The income control behavior of women in male-dominant budgets, while driven by the promises of the traditional gender contract, was also being affected by the contract's growing unreliability.

To summarize, women garment workers from urban working-class backgrounds did not exercise much control over their income; however, women's acceptance of male financial authority was not a simple reflection of patriarchal cultural tradition. Rather, the male-dominant budgets were the outcome of the complex interaction of cultural tradition and economic circumstance. Economic conditions affected the symbolic meanings that were attached to the women's income earning. Used to meet basic household subsistence costs, the women's pay symbolized the inadequacy of men's breadwinning capacities. Women worked, however, to mute the potential challenge of this situation to men's authority in the family. The handing over of wages to men was a gesture that diverted attention from men's economic inadequacies. Women also affirmed the economic primacy and, thus, the authority of men by the ways in which they spoke of their pay. For example, they spoke of their pay as a supplement rather than a replacement for male wages.

Such efforts to affirm male authority were not simply a reflection of women's socialization into patriarchal cultural tradition. They reflected a concern for maintaining male participation in the household economy. Whereas the men's income was not enough to support the household completely, it was essential to keep the household from sinking into extreme poverty. Given these circumstances, it is not surprising that entry into wagework had not apparently increased the women's family power in significant ways. Whereas many of the women felt that employment had enhanced their sense of self-worth, they did not associate wagework with a strengthened ability to exercise authority in family decision making.

Lower-Middle-Class Women: Keeping Wages with Permission

In stark contrast to the budgetary arrangements described above, the women workers from lower-middle-class backgrounds said that they did not pool their money with other household members; they maintained control of 90 percent or more of their own income. Although the women paid heed to the financial advice of knowledgeable elders, they alone made decisions about how to spend their pay, and they also spent the money themselves, *with their own hands (nijer hate)*.

The financial autonomy of the women reflects, I suggest, the symbolic meanings attached to their wagework, meanings that were deeply colored by the meaning of lower-middle-class status in Bangladesh. Unlike the previous case, the entry of these women into the outside world of the garment industry could not be justified by basic economic scarcity. Instead, the women spoke of how their wagework was legitimated by the fact that they were working to achieve economic mobility into the secure upper sectors of the middle class for their families. The unmarried women in this group, for example, spoke of how garment factory work enabled them to save money for marriage expenses. Not only would these savings spare their families from incurring wedding and dowry costs on their behalf, but they could also facilitate marriage into a prosperous family, a situation that held potential economic and social benefits both for themselves and for their families. They could also use their earnings to purchase luxury goods such as televisions and VCRs for the household, items that promoted a middle-class identity.

Among married women, the notion that their wagework was of benefit to the family was even more strongly invoked; they argued that they were being good wives and mothers by working. One woman told me that she was saving her wages to pay the bribe that was necessary for her husband to get a salaried government job, an important marker of middle-class status in Bangladesh. Simmi, a 22-year-old married woman with two children, felt that she was fulfilling the dictates of good motherhood by working. Whereas the household was financially able to get by on the income of her husband, who was a shopkeeper, she felt compelled to work for some extra money. Her husband had initially opposed her employment arguing that the factories were filled with uncouth lower-class persons who generated an unsuitable environment for women. Simmi persisted in her request, however, arguing that her income would give them the extra means necessary to ensure a middle-class future for their children. In keeping with this goal, Simmi indicated that she placed a large share of her monthly income into a savings account that was earmarked for the private schools and tutoring that were necessary to ensure the educational success of her children. She spent the remainder of her income on milk (an expensive item in Bangladesh) for the children, household goods, and personal expenses. These items had become indispensable to her, and she could not imagine not working.

Despite the fact that these women spoke of their wagework as an activity aimed toward the collective welfare of their households, they maintained virtually complete control of their wages. The lower-middle-class women spoke of their wage control as an expression of the ability of men to fulfill their provider obligations. Some told of how, according to Islamic principles, men were expected to provide for the upkeep of their families, regardless of the women's resources. It was a matter of honor and pride for men to not take money from women in the family. Nasreen, a single woman who lived in the household of her older brother, said that no one touched her pay because, after all, it was the family's responsibility to look after her, a young woman, rather than the other way around; her brother would feel shameful to take her money.

The status-related meanings surrounding men's insistence that women keep their wages are revealed by the comments of a married woman. Her words also show how the belief that the woman's wages went only toward incidental expenses, publicly affirmed by all involved, was not always entirely accurate:

> My husband likes that my income is for luxuries, for the little things that catch my fancy. Although sometimes I pay for household things, during difficult months. He tells me, it is his job to provide for food, clothing, rent and other necessities. Why should he take my money like the lower-class men?

Whereas the income control of these women was a sharp contrast to the patterns noted among working-class women, in both cases, budgetary arrangements were legitimated by traditional family ideology, albeit different elements of it. These differing interpretations of tradition highlight the malleability of family ideologies and the critical role of social class in structuring interpretations of tradition. For the working-class women, male authority was affirmed by women's relinquishment of wages to men, but for the lower-middle-class women, male authority was affirmed by men's refusal to touch their wages. Indeed, allowing one's wife or daughter to retain her wages for incidental luxury expenses was perhaps especially important for the lower-middle-class men, given their insecurity about their place in the middle class. That is, the ability of the men to adequately provide for their families was an important marker of middle-class status, a way of affirming distance from the lower socioeconomic strata.

Given the ways in which women's income control symbolically affirmed rather than challenged male authority, it is not surprising that the wage earning of the lower-middle-class women had only modest effects on their family power. The women did not associate their entry into wagework with a notably enhanced ability to assert their power in family decision-making processes. At the same time, almost all of the women felt that greater respect was accorded them because of their status as income earners.

Rural Poor Women: Controlling Wages

Women garment workers who controlled their income included eight young unmarried women who were living in the city without family elders. Like that of the lower-middle-class women, the income control of these women is counterintuitive when viewed against the backdrop of cultural tradition. In the traditional Bangladeshi family system, before marriage, women are under the authority of fathers, brothers, and other male kin who control all aspects, including economic aspects, of their lives; however, contrary to the dictates of tradition, none of these young women remitted all or even a portion of their wages to family members. Underlying this pattern of financial independence were conditions of poverty, which had challenged the set of expectations traditionally guiding relations between daughters and kin.

The women in this group were from impoverished and typically landless rural families. It was the inability of the families to economically provide for daughters that allowed the young women to enter into garment work in the city unaccompanied by family members. In Bangladeshi tradition, the honor of the family is tied to its ability to protect the sexual purity of its women. Young unmarried women who do not conform to *purdah* norms and whose activities are not subject to familial supervision are automatically sexually suspect and a threat to family honor. It is not surprising, then, that for these women, entering into garment factory work and relocating to the city were both events that were typically accompanied by a period of opposition to these moves from parents and other family elders because of the implications for family honor. The ability of families to persist in their opposition was weakened by their poverty and subsequent inability to adequately provide for basic subsistence needs as well as the ever-rising costs of providing a dowry to daughters.[5] This was suggested by the words of two young women who had initially encountered family opposition to their plans to work in the garment industry:

> *Rehana: At first, my mother and uncle [chacha] said no, if you work in garments and live alone in Dhaka city you will lose your innocence; you will mix with men and all kinds of low people, and you will learn undesirable things from them. But then I said, how long can I eat your rice? Now there's not enough for two meals a day, and I'm just another mouth to feed. They had no reply to what I said.*

> *Sayeeda: In my home in the village there were five of us [brothers and sisters] and my father couldn't support us. When I heard about garments work from some people in the village I asked my father about it and he said that if it was necessary I would eat just one meal a day but still I couldn't work in garments. That was how much he opposed it. But later I persuaded him to change his mind. I asked him to think about my future because if I worked in garments I would be self-sufficient and I could save some money for my married life.*

Within the traditional family system, girls could expect natal families to ensure their upkeep and eventual marriage. But poverty had eroded the ability of these families to fulfill obligations to daughters. This familial failure enabled the young women to take the unconventional step of working and living in the city alone and also maintain virtually no financial ties with their families. As I have mentioned, young single women did not remit money to parents or other family members in the home village. Their wages instead went toward personal living expenditures and, occasionally, consumer items (e.g., clothes, cosmetics, and small pieces of gold jewelry). The only regular flow of resources from daughters to their families occurred on such occasions as Eid (a Muslim religious holiday), when the young women traveled back to their home villages, armed with gifts of clothes, food, and other items.

The failure to remit wages, a sharp contrast to the behavior of working daughters in many societies (Fernandez Kelly 1982; Greenhalgh 1988; Harevan 1982; Ong 1987; Tilly and Scott 1978), reflected the inability of families to provide for their daughters and the subsequent breakdown of obligation in daughter-parent relations. One young woman, when questioned about how her parents felt about the fact that she did not send money home, replied that they did not expect her to do so. On the contrary, they felt shameful about the fact that they could not provide for her, and so they did not want to accept her money. Another woman refused to cave in to her elder brother's demands for her wages. She resented that he and other family members had been unable to take care of her. It was clear that the circumstances under which the young women had entered into garment work had shaped the symbolic meanings of the work. Rather than daughterly obligation, the work was associated with familial inefficacy and perhaps even shame.

The financial autonomy of these young women was the outcome of a process in which economic circumstances, specifically, conditions of poverty, had worked to challenge the traditional dynamics of family life. To put it simply, the traditional family system had little meaning for these young women, certainly far less than it did for the other groups of women that I have described. Unlike the other women in the study, these young women expressed ideals and conceptions of family life that were far removed from traditional ones. They spoke with great satisfaction about their greater freedom of movement (in contrast to their village sisters) and their ability to exercise control over such important life events as marriage. Whereas it was clear that garment factory work, combined with an independent living situation, damaged the sexual reputation and thus marriage opportunities of young women, the benefits

of such work, including the ability to make one's own marriage choices, far outweighed the disadvantages. Perhaps most significantly, these women spoke of how, after marriage, they expected to continue to move around freely and to make their own decisions about such issues as employment and the expenditure of their income:

If you work in garments you can better yourself. What's the use of sitting at home? If I lived in the village I would be married by now, but I'm glad that my life is different. Because I'm self-sufficient I can go where I want and marry whom I want. Even after I'm married, I will continue to live my life in my own way.

Both the working-class and lower-middle-class women related to their income within a social context in which the traditional family system was meaningful and attractive, at least in certain aspects. But this was not the case for the young women from poor rural families. These young women felt that they were economically better off at present than they were when they lived with their families in the home village. Unencumbered by economic dependents, they experienced their financial situation as adequate, one that enabled them to meet basic living as well as occasional discretionary expenses. They did not place much meaning or significance on what is perhaps the fundamental attraction of the patriarchal family system for the women—the promise of men's economic support. Also relevant were the combined effects of the young age (mid- to late teens) and the living situation of the women. Unlike the other women in the sample, they had moved out of the parental home during early to mid-adolescence, thus avoiding the critical gender socialization processes of this phase of the life cycle. This, combined with the absence of family guardians who could monitor their activities in the city, was potent ground for change. It was the combined effect of these conditions, rather than income control per se, that made wage employment an extremely powerful force of change for these women.

CONCLUSION

Research on Third World women is often marked by an inattention to the sources of differentiation in their lives. This is particularly the case with studies of Bangladeshi women, who are often portrayed as a monolithic group whose behavior is uniformly guided by cultural traditions such as that of *purdah*.[6] My analyses reveal Bangladeshi women garment workers to be a diverse group, one that experiences employment in varied ways.

The diversity of the women's experiences highlights the difficulty of assuming a simple relationship between cultural tradition and women's income control, particularly in societies that are in the throes of rapid economic and social transformation. In Bangladesh, one of the effects of such transformation has been to heighten socioeconomic differentiation among women. It is not surprising that women workers deal with the issue of male control over their income differently, in ways that reflect the particular socioeconomic realities of their lives. These socioeconomic realities place them in varied relationships to the traditional family system. For example, the financial autonomy of the young, unmarried women garment workers living without family in the city reflects the failure of the traditional family system to deliver on its promise of economic and social protection; however, as illustrated by the situation of the women in male-headed, working-class and lower-middle-class households, the traditional family system remains economically attractive to some women, despite increasing uncertainty about it (cf. Kandiyoti 1988). The varied ways in which women relate to the traditional family system highlight the fact that family life is in a process of rapid change in Bangladesh.

There were, however, important differences in income control patterns even among those women who valued the maintenance of the traditional family system. Lower-middle-class women retained control over their wages, whereas working-class women relinquished control to men.

These divergent patterns stemmed from differences in socioeconomic status, which colored the ways in which men viewed the implications of women's income earning for their own authority in the family. Working-class men associated women's wagework with their own economic impotence; seizing control of women's income was a gesture that affirmed their economic headship. In contrast, lower-middle-class men affirmed their economic authority by allowing women to control their wages. By not touching the women's pay, they affirmed an understanding of women's income as peripheral and inessential to the household economy. Ironically, whereas quite different in substance, both sets of behaviors served to affirm rather than challenge male authority in the family. Efforts to maintain male dominance in the family can result, then, in quite different patterns of income control. The relationship of social class to women's income control may be explored in more detail by studies that look at the effects of household economic mobility, or how the ability of women to control income shifts along with changes in socioeconomic status.

Income control is not a guarantee of greater family power for women, as highlighted by the experiences of the lower-middle-class women. More significant than income control per se is the extent to which the broader social context that surrounds women's income earning offers opportunities and options for women. The importance of the broader context is also suggested by Blumberg (1991) when she asserts that the relationship between women's income control and family power is one that is mediated by a variety of complex factors such as the extent of gender inequality at the macrosocietal level and the gender role ideology of family members. For the young unmarried *unaccompanied* women workers, the larger social context surrounding their work accounts for the seemingly dramatic changes in their lives. It is not simply their income earning but a combination of circumstances, including the independent living situation of the young women and the economic inefficacy of their families, that creates the conditions for both their financial and social autonomy. Unlike the other women in the sample, these women responded to the growing uncertainty of the traditional family system with a new and more egalitarian vision of family life. Further research may illuminate the specific conditions that generate changes in attitudes and ideals for these women. It is possible, for example, that the workplace subcultures in which the young women are involved play an important role in the construction of egalitarian family ideals.

Given the controversy that has surrounded the participation of women in the garment industry of Bangladesh, it is worth noting that the overwhelming majority of the women garment workers spoke of their employment in positive terms, as an activity that had enhanced their sense of self-esteem and worth in the household. Because of the paucity of other job opportunities, they valued the presence of the garment factories in the country. At the same time, for those who are concerned with the improvement of women's status in Bangladesh, the women's experiences do not legitimate an overly optimistic view of the consequences of the industry for women. With respect to family power, the benefits of garment factory work for women in Bangladesh seem to be uneven at best. The most significant and powerful challenge to patriarchal family relations stems not from women's involvement in the industrial sector but from the ongoing macrostructural shifts that have questioned the core dynamics of traditional family relations.

NOTES

1. The term *joint family household* refers to a household in which the sons of the family continue to live under one roof, with their parents, after marriage.

2. Feldman (1992, 220) reports that in 1978, 80 percent of the rural population was found to be landless or functionally landless, owning less than one acre of land. For other statistics on this issue, see Hossain, Jahan, and Sobhan (1990, 32).

3. In 1982, 16.5 percent of all households were estimated to be female headed, based on a sample survey by Bangladesh Bureau of Statistics (Islam 1991).

4. Besides the operators, the sample included two quality inspectors, women who inspected garments for errors after they had been produced. It also included three "helpers" or assistants to sewing machine operators. To control for levels of income, the analysis here is confined to operators because of their similar salary levels. Because control over wages was not a problematic issue for these women, I have also not included the seven women who were heads of their households. The female heads of households tended to have only distant relations with fathers, brothers, and other male kin who could potentially challenge their authority.

5. Whereas marriage was traditionally accompanied by a flow of gifts from the groom's family to the bride, the past three decades have witnessed a steady inflation in the economic demands made by the groom of the bride's family, a situation that both signifies and reinforces the low economic value of women (Lindenbaum 1981).

6. For a review and critique of the monolithic depiction of Bangladeshi women in academic literature, see Kabeer (1991) and White (1992).

REFERENCES

Bangladesh Garment Manufacturers and Exporters Association (BGMEA). 1992. The garment industry: A look ahead at Europe of 1992. Bangladesh Garment Manufacturers and Exporters Association, Dhaka, Bangladesh. Mimeographed.

Bangladesh Unnayan Parishad (BUP). 1990. A study on female garment workers in Bangladesh: A draft report. Bangladesh Unnayan Parishad, Dhaka, Bangladesh.

Blumberg, R. L. 1984. A general theory of gender stratification. In *Sociological theory*, edited by R. Collins. San Francisco: Jossey-Bass.

———. 1991. Income under female versus male control: Hypotheses from a theory of gender stratification and data from the Third World. In *Gender, family and economy: The triple overlap,* edited by R. L. Blumberg. Newbury Park, CA: Sage.

Cain, M., S. R. Khanan and S. Nahar. 1979. Class, patriarchy, and women's work in Bangladesh. *Population and Development Review* 5:408–16.

Chaudhuri, S., and P. P. Majumdar. 1991. The conditions of garment workers in Bangladesh: An appraisal. Bangladesh Institute of Development Studies, Dhaka, Bangladesh.

Chen, Martha. 1983. *A quiet revolution: Women in transition in rural Bangladesh.* Cambridge, MA: Schenkman.

Fapohunda, E. R. 1988. The nonpooling household: A challenge to theory. In *A home divided: Women and income in the Third World,* edited by D. Dwyer and J. Bruce. Stanford, CA: Stanford University Press.

Feldman, S. 1992. Crisis, Islam and gender in Bangladesh: The social construction of a female labor force. In *Unequal burden: Economic crises, persistent poverty and women's work,* edited by L. Beneria and S. Feldman. Boulder, CO: Westview.

Feldman, S., and F. E. McCarthy. 1983. Purdah and changing patterns of social control among rural women in Bangladesh. *Journal of Marriage and the Family* 4:949–59.

Fernández Kelly, Maria Patricia. 1982. *For we are sold, I and my people: Women and industry in Mexico's frontier.* Albany, NY: SUNY Press.

———. 1990. Delicate transactions: Gender, home, and employment among Hispanic women. In *Uncertain terms: Negotiating gender in American culture,* edited by P. Ginsburg and A. L. Tsing. Boston: Beacon.

Gallin, R. 1990. Women and the export industry in Taiwan: The muting of class consciousness. In *Women, work and global restructuring,* edited by K. Ward. Ithaca, NY: ILR.

Geschwender, James A. 1992. Ethgender, women's waged labor, and economic mobility. *Social Problems* 39:1–16.

Greenhalgh, S. 1988. Intergenerational contacts: Familial roots of sexual stratification in Taiwan. In *A home divided: Women and income in the Third World,* edited by D. Dwyer and J. Bruce. Stanford, CA: Stanford University Press.

Harevan, Tamara. 1982. *Family time and industrial time.* New York: Cambridge University Press.

Hochschild, A., and A. Machung. 1989. *The second shift.* New York: Viking.

Hood, Jane. 1983. *Becoming a two-job family.* New York: Praeger.

Hoodfar, H. 1988. Household budgeting and financial management in a lower-income Cairo neighborhood. In *A home divided: Women and income in the Third World,* edited by D. Dwyer and J. Bruce. Stanford, CA: Stanford University Press.

Hossain, H., R. Jahan, and S. Sobhan. 1990. *No better option? Industrial women workers in Bangladesh.* Dhaka, Bangladesh: University Press Limited.

Islam, Mahmuda. 1991. *Women heads of household in Bangladesh: Strategies for survival.* Dhaka, Bangladesh: Flair Print.

Kabeer, Naila. 1991. Cultural dopes or rational fools? Women and labour supply in the Bangladesh garment industry. *European Journal of Development Research* 3:133–60.

Kandiyoti, Deniz. 1988. Bargaining with patriarchy. *Gender & Society* 2:274–90.

Kung, Lydia. 1983. *Factory women in Taiwan.* Ann Arbor: University of Michigan Press.

Lindenbaum, Shirley. 1981. Implications for women of changing marriage transactions in Bangladesh. *Studies in Family Planning* 1:394–401.

Ong, Aihwa. 1987. *Spirits of resistance and capitalist discipline: Factory women in Malaysia.* Albany, NY: SUNY Press.

Papanek, H., and L. Schwede. 1988. Women are good with money: Earning and managing in an Indonesian city. In *A home divided: Women and income in the Third World,* edited by D. Dwyer and J. Bruce. Stanford, CA: Stanford University Press.

Pyke, Karen D. 1994. Women's employment as gift or burden? Marital power across marriage, divorce and remarriage. *Gender & Society* 8:73–91.

Safilios-Rothschild, C. 1988. The impact of agrarian reform on men's and women's incomes in rural Honduras. In *A home divided: Women and income in the Third World,* edited by D. Dwyer and J. Bruce. Stanford, CA: Stanford University Press.

Salaff, Janet. 1981. *Working daughters of Hong Kong.* New York: Cambridge University Press.

Sen, A. K. 1990. Gender and cooperative conflicts. In *Persistent inequalities: Women and world development,* edited by I. Tinker. New York: Oxford University Press.

Siddiqui, K., S. Qadir, S. Alamgir, and S. Huq. 1990. *Social formation in Dhaka city.* Dhaka, Bangladesh: University Press Limited.

Tilly, L. and J. Scott. 1978. *Women, work and family.* New York: Holt, Rinehart and Winston.

United Nations Industrial Development Organization (UNIDO). 1991. Bangladesh's textile and clothing industry: A working paper. United Nations Industrial Development Organization, Dhaka, Bangladesh.

White, Sarah. 1992. *Arguing with the crocodile: Gender and class in Bangladesh.* London: Zed Books.

Wolf, D. L. 1991. Female autonomy, the family and industrialization in Java. In *Gender, family and economy: The triple overlap,* edited by R. L. Blumberg. Newbury Park, CA: Sage.

———. 1992. *Factory daughters: Gender, household dynamics and rural industrialization in Java.* Berkeley: University of California Press.

37

Moving Up with Kin and Community

Upward Social Mobility for
Black and White Women

ELIZABETH HIGGINBOTHAM
LYNN WEBER

... When women and people of color experience upward mobility in America, they scale steep structural as well as psychological barriers. The long process of moving from a working-class family of origin to the professional-managerial class is full of twists and turns: choices made with varying degrees of information and varying options; critical junctures faced with support and encouragement or disinterest, rejection, or active discouragement; and interpersonal relationships in which basic understandings are continuously negotiated and renegotiated. It is a fascinating process that profoundly shapes the lives of those who experience it, as well as the lives of those around them. Social mobility is also a process engulfed in myth. One need only pick up any newspaper or turn on the television to see that the myth of upward mobility remains firmly entrenched in American culture: With hard work, talent, determination, and some luck, just about anyone can "make it."...

The image of the isolated and detached experience of mobility that we have inherited from past scholarship is problematic for anyone seeking to understand the process for women or people of color. Twenty years of scholarship in the study of both race and gender has taught us the importance of interpersonal attachments to the lives of women

and a commitment to racial uplift among people of color....

...Lacking wealth, the greatest gift a Black family has been able to give to its children has been the motivation and skills to succeed in school. Aspirations for college attendance and professional positions are stressed as *family* goals, and the entire family may make sacrifices and provide support.... Black women have long seen the activist potential of education and have sought it as a cornerstone of community development—a means of uplifting the race. When women of color or White women are put at the center of the analysis of upward mobility, it is clear that different questions will be raised about social mobility and different descriptions of the process will ensue....

Research Design

These data are from a study of full-time employed middle-class women in the Memphis metropolitan area. This research is designed to explore the processes of upward social mobility for Black and White women by examining differences between women professionals, managers, and administrators who are from working- and middle-class backgrounds—that is, upwardly mobile and middle-class stable women. In this way, we isolate subjective processes shared among women who have been upwardly mobile from those common to women who have reproduced their family's

AUTHORS' NOTE: The research reported here was supported by National Institute for Mental Health Grant MH38769.

professional-managerial class standing. Likewise, we identify common experiences in the attainment process that are shared by women of the same race, be they upwardly mobile or stable middle class. Finally, we specify some ways in which the attainment process is unique for each race-class group....

...We rely on a model of social class basically derived from the work of Poulantzas (1974), Braverman (1974), Ehrenreich and Ehrenreich (1979), and elaborated in Vanneman and Cannon (1987). These works explicate a basic distinction between social class and social status. Classes represent bounded categories of the population, groups set in a relation of opposition to one another by their roles in the capitalist system. The middle class, or professional-managerial class, is set off from the working class by the power and control it exerts over workers in three realms: economic (power through ownership), political (power through direct supervisory authority), and ideological (power to plan and organize work; Poulantzas 1974; Vanneman and Cannon 1987).

In contrast, education, prestige, and income represent social statuses—hierarchically structured relative rankings along a ladder of economic success and social prestige. Positions along these dimensions are not established by social relations of dominance and subordination but, rather, as rankings on scales representing resources and desirability. In some respects, they represent both the justification for power differentials vested in classes and the rewards for the role that the middle class plays in controlling labor.

Our interest is in the process of upward social class mobility, moving from a working-class family of origin to a middle-class destination—from a position of working-class subordination to a position of control over the working class. Lacking inherited wealth or other resources, those working-class people who attain middle-class standing do so primarily by obtaining a college education and entering a professional, managerial, or administrative occupation. Thus we examine carefully the process of educational at-

tainment not as evidence of middle-class standing but as a necessary part of the mobility process for most working-class people.

Likewise, occupation alone does not define the middle class, but professional, managerial, and administrative occupations capture many of the supervisory and ideologically based positions whose function is to control workers' lives. Consequently, we defined subjects as *middle class* by virtue of their employment in either a professional, managerial, or administrative occupation.... Classification of subjects as either professional or managerial-administrative was made on the basis of the designation of occupations in the U.S. Bureau of the Census's (1983) "Detailed Population Characteristics: Tennessee." Managerial occupations were defined as those in the census categories of managers and administrators; professionals were defined as those occupations in the professional category, excluding technicians, whom Braverman (1974) contends are working class.

Upwardly mobile women were defined as those women raised in families where neither parent was employed as a professional, manager, or administrator. Typical occupations for working-class fathers were postal clerk, craftsman, semiskilled manufacturing worker, janitor, and laborer. Some working-class mothers had clerical and sales positions, but many of the Black mothers also worked as private household workers. *Middle-class stable* women were defined as those women raised in families where *either* parent was employed as a professional, manager, or administrator. Typical occupations of middle class parents were social worker, teacher, and school administrator as well as high-status professionals such as attorneys, physicians, and dentists....

Family Expectations for Educational Attainment

Four questions assess the expectations and support among family members for the educational attainment of the subjects. First, "Do you recall your father or mother stressing that you attain an education?" Yes was the response of 190 of the 200 women. Each of the women in this study had obtained a college degree, and many have graduate degrees. It is clear that for Black and White women, education was an important concern in their families....

The comments of Laura Lee,[1] a 39-year-old Black woman who was raised middle class, were typical:

> Going to school, that was never a discussable issue. Just like you were born to live and die, you were going to go to school. You were going to prepare yourself to do something.

It should be noted, however, that only 86 percent of the White working-class women answered yes, compared to 98 percent of all other groups. Although this difference is small, it foreshadows a pattern where White women raised in working-class families received the least support and encouragement for educational and career attainment.

"When you were growing up, how far did your father expect you to go in school?" While most fathers expected college attendance from their daughters, differences also exist by class of origin. Only 70 percent of the working-class fathers, both Black and White, expected their daughters to attend college. In contrast, 94 percent of the Black middle-class and 88 percent of the White middle-class women's fathers had college expectations for their daughters.

When asked the same question about mother's expectations, 88 percent to 92 percent of each group's mothers expected their daughters to get a college education, except the White working-class women, for whom only 66 percent of mothers held such expectations. In short, only among the White working-class women did a fairly substantial proportion (about one-third) of both mothers and fathers expect less than a college education from their daughters. About 30 percent of Black working-class fathers held lower expectations for their daughters, but not the mothers; virtually all middle-class parents expected a college education for their daughters.

Sara Marx is a White, 33-year-old director of counseling raised in a rural working-class family. She is among those whose parents did not expect a college education for her. She was vague about the roots of attending college:

> It seems like we had a guest speaker who talked to us. Maybe before our exams somebody talked to us. I really can't put my finger on anything. I don't know where the information came from exactly.

"Who provided emotional support for you to make the transition from high school to college?" While 86 percent of the Black middle-class women indicated that family provided that support, 70 percent of the White middle class, 64 percent of the Black working class, and only 56 percent of the White working class received emotional support from family.

"Who paid your college tuition and fees?" Beyond emotional support, financial support is critical to college attendance. There are clear class differences in financial support for college. Roughly 90 percent of the middle-class respondents and only 56 percent and 62 percent of the Black and White working-class women, respectively, were financially supported by their families. These data also suggest that working-class parents were less able to give emotional or financial support for college than they were to hold out the expectation that their daughters should attend.

Family Expectations for Occupation or Career

When asked, "Do you recall your father or mother stressing that you should have an occupation to succeed in life?" racial differences appear. Ninety-four percent of all Black respondents said yes. In the words of Julie Bird, a Black woman raised-middle-class junior high school teacher:

> My father would always say, "You see how good I'm doing? Each generation should do more than the generation before." He expects me to accomplish more than he has.

Ann Right, a 36-year-old Black attorney whose father was a janitor, said:

> They wanted me to have a better life than they had. For all of us. And that's why they emphasized education and emphasized working relationships and how you get along with people and that kind of thing.

Ruby James, a Black teacher from a working-class family, said:

> They expected me to have a good-paying job and to have a family and be married. Go to work every day. Buy a home. That's about it. Be happy.

In contrast, only 70 percent of the White middle-class and 56 percent of the White working-class women indicated that their parents stressed that an occupation was needed for success. Nina Pentel, a 26-year-old white medical social worker, expressed a common response: "They said 'You're going to get married but get a degree, you never know what's going to happen to you.' They were pretty laid back about goals."

When the question focuses on a career rather than an occupation, the family encouragement is lower and differences were not significant, but similar patterns emerged. We asked respondents, "Who, if anyone, encouraged you to think about a career?" Among Black respondents, 60 percent of the middle-class and 56 percent of the working-class women answered that family encouraged them. Only 40 percent of the White working-class women indicated that their family encouraged them in their thinking about a career, while 52 percent of the White middle-class women did so. . . .

When working-class White women seek to be mobile through their own attainments, they face conflicts. Their parents encourage educational attainment, but when young women develop professional career goals, these same parents sometimes become ambivalent. This was the case with Elizabeth Marlow, who is currently a public interest attorney—a position her parents never intended her to hold. She described her parents' traditional expectations and their reluctance to support her career goals fully.

> My parents assumed that I would go college and meet some nice man and finish, but not necessarily work after. I would be a good mother for my children. I don't think that they ever thought I would go to law school. Their attitude about my interest in law school was, "You can do it if you want to, but we don't think it is a particularly practical thing for a woman to do."

Elizabeth is married and has three children, but she is not the traditional housewife of her parents' dreams. She received more support outside the family for her chosen lifestyle.

Although Black families are indeed more likely than white families to encourage their daughters to prepare for careers, like White families, they frequently steer them toward highly visible traditionally female occupations, such as teacher, nurse, and social worker. Thus many mobile Black women are directed toward the same gender-segregated occupations as White women. . . .

Marriage

Although working-class families may encourage daughters to marry, they recognize the need for working-class women to contribute to family income or to support themselves economically. To achieve these aims, many working-class girls are encouraged to pursue an education as preparation for work in gender-segregated occupations. Work in these fields presumably allows women to keep marriage, family, and child rearing as life goals while contributing to the family income and to have "something to fall back on" if the marriage does not work out. This interplay among marriage, education, financial need, and class mobility is complex (Joslin 1979).

We asked, "Do you recall your mother or father emphasizing that marriage should be your primary life goal?" While the majority of all respondents did not get the message that marriage was the *primary* life goal, Black and White women's parents clearly saw this differently. Virtually no Black parents stressed marriage as the primary life goal (6 percent of the working class and 4 percent of the middle class), but significantly more White parents did (22 percent of the working class and 18 percent of the middle class).

Some White women said their families expressed active opposition to marriage, such as Clare Baron, a raised-working-class nursing supervisor, who said, "My mother always said, 'Don't get married and don't have children!'"

More common responses recognized the fragility of marriage and the need to support oneself. For example, Alice Page, a 31-year-old White raised-middle-class librarian, put it this way:

> I feel like I am really part of a generation that for the first time is thinking, "I don't want to have to depend on somebody to take care of me because what if they say they are going to take care of me and then they are not there? They die, or they leave me or whatever." I feel very much that I've got to be able to support myself and I don't know that single women in other eras have had to deal with that to the same degree.

While White working-class women are often raised to prepare for work roles so that they can contribute to family income and, if necessary, support themselves, Black women face a different reality. Unlike White women, Black women are typically socialized to view marriage separately from economic security, because it is not expected that marriage will ever remove them from the labor market. As a result, Black families socialize all their children—girls and boys—for self-sufficiency (Clark 1986; Higginbotham and Cannon 1988)....

...Fairly substantial numbers of each group had never married by the time of the interview, ranging from 20 percent of the White working-class to 34 percent of the Black working-class and White middle-class respondents. Some of the women were pleased with their singlehood, like Alice Page, who said:

> I am single by choice. That is how I see myself. I have purposely avoided getting into any kind of romantic situation with men. I have enjoyed going out but never wanted to get serious. If anyone wants to get serious, I quit going out with him.

Other women expressed disappointment and some shock that they were not yet married. When asked about her feeling about being single, Sally Ford, a 32-year-old White manager, said:

> That's what I always wanted to do: to be married and have children. To me, that is the ideal. I want a happy, good marriage with children. I do not like being single at all. It is very, very lonesome. I don't see any advantages to being single. None!

Subjective Sense of Debt to Kin and Friends

McAdoo (1978) reports that upwardly mobile Black Americans receive more requests to share resources from their working-class kin than do middle-class Black Americans. Many mobile Black Americans feel a "social debt" because their families aided them in the mobility process and provided emotional support. When we asked the White women in the study the following question: "Generally, do you feel you owe a lot for the help given to you by your family and relatives?" many were perplexed and asked what the question meant. In contrast, both the working- and middle-class Black women tended to respond immediately that they felt a sense of obligation to family and friends in return for the support they had received. Black women, from both the working class and the middle class, expressed the strongest sense of debt to family, with 86 percent and 74 percent, respectively, so indicating. White working-class women were least likely to feel that they owed family (46 percent), while 68 percent of white middle-class women so indicated. In short, upwardly mobile Black women were almost twice as likely as upwardly mobile White women to express a sense of debt to family.

Linda Brown, an upwardly mobile Black woman, gave a typical response, "Yes, they are there when you need them." Similar were the words of Jean Marsh, "Yes, because they have been supportive. They're dependable. If I need them I can depend upon them."

One of the most significant ways in which Black working-class families aided their daughters and left them with a sense of debt related to care for their children. Dawn March expressed it thus:

> They have been there more so during my adult years than a lot of other families that I know about. My mother kept all of my children until they were old enough to go to day care. And she not only kept them, she'd give them a bath for me during the daytime and feed them before I got home from work. Very, very supportive people. So, I really would say I owe them for that.

Carole Washington, an upwardly mobile Black woman occupational therapist, also felt she owed her family. She reported:

> I know the struggle that my parents have had to get me where I am. I know the energy they no longer have to put into the rest of the family even though they want to put it there and they're willing. I feel it is my responsibility to give back some of that energy they have given to me. It's self-directed, not required.

White working-class women, in contrast, were unlikely to feel a sense of debt and expressed their feelings in similar ways. Irma Cox, part owner of a computer business, said, "I am appreciative of the values my parents instilled in me. But I for the most part feel like I have done it on my own." Carey Mink, a 35-year-old psychiatric social worker, said, "No, they pointed me in a direction and they were supportive, but I've done a lot of the work myself." Debra Beck, a judge, responded, "No, I feel that I've gotten most places on my own.". . .

Commitment to Community

The mainstream "model of community stresses the rights of individuals to make decisions in their own self interest, regardless of the impact on the larger society" (Collins 1990, 52). This model may explain relations to community of origin for mobile White males but cannot be generalized to other racial and gender groups. In the context of well-recognized structures of racial oppression, America's racial-ethnic communities develop collective survival strategies that contrast with the individualism of the dominant culture but ensure the community's survival (Collins 1990; McAdoo 1978; Stack 1974; Valentine 1978). McAdoo (1978) argues that Black people have *only* been able to advance in education and attain higher status and higher paying jobs with the support of the wider Black community, teachers in segregated schools, extended family networks, and Black mentors already in those positions. This widespread community involvement enables mobile people of color to confront and challenge racist obstacles in credentialing institutions, and it distinguishes the mobility process in racial-ethnic communities from mobility in the dominant culture. For example, Lou Nelson, now a librarian, described the support she felt in her southern segregated inner-city school. She said:

> There was a closeness between people and that had a lot to do with neighborhood schools. I went to Tubman High School with people that lived in the Tubman area. I think that there was a bond, a bond between parents, the PTA . . . I think that it was just that everybody felt that everybody knew everybody. And that was special.

Family and community involvement and support in the mobility process means that many Black professionals and managers continue to feel linked to their communities of origin. Lillian King, a high-ranking city official who was raised working class, discussed her current commitment to the Black community. She said:

> Because I have more opportunities, I've got an obligation to give more back and to set a positive example for Black people and especially for Black women. I think we've got to do a tremendous job in building self-esteem and giving people the desire to achieve.

Judith Moore is a 34-year-old single parent employed as a health investigator. She has been able to maintain her connection with her community, and that is a source of pride.

> I'm proud that I still have a sense of who I am in terms of Black people. That's very important to

me. No matter how much education or professional status I get, I do not want to lose touch with where I've come from. I think that you need to look back and that kind of pushes you forward. I think the degree and other things can make you lose sight of that, especially us Black folks, but I'm glad that I haven't and I try to teach that [commitment] to my son.

For some Black women, their mobility has enabled them to give to an even broader community. This is the case with Sammi Lewis, a raised-working-class woman who is a director of a social service agency. She said, "I owe a responsibility to the entire community, and not to any particular group."...

Crossing the Color Line

Mobility for people of color is complex because in addition to crossing class lines, mobility often means crossing racial and cultural ones as well. Since the 1960s, people of color have increasingly attended either integrated or predominantly White schools. Only mobile White ethnics have a comparable experience of simultaneously crossing class and cultural barriers, yet even this experience is qualitatively different from that of Black and other people of color. White ethnicity can be practically invisible to White middle-class school peers and co-workers, but people of color are more visible and are subjected to harsher treatment. Our research indicates that no matter when people of color first encounter integrated or predominantly White settings, it is always a shock. The experience of racial exclusion cannot prepare people of color to deal with the racism in daily face-to-face encounters with White people.

For example, Lynn Johnson was in the first cohort of Black students at Regional College, a small private college in Memphis. The self-confidence and stamina Lynn developed in her supportive segregated high school helped her withstand the racism she faced as the first female and the first Black to graduate in economics at Regional College. Lynn described her treatment:

I would come into class and Dr. Simpson (the Economics professor) would alphabetically call the roll. When he came to my name, he would just jump over it. He would not ask me any questions, he would not do anything. I stayed in that class. I struggled through. When it was my turn, I'd start talking. He would say, "Johnson, I wasn't talking to you" [because he never said Miss Johnson]. I'd say, "That's all right, Dr. Simpson, it was my turn. I figured you just overlooked me. I'm just the littlest person in here. Wasn't that the right answer?" He would say, "Yes, that was the right answer." I drove him mad, I really did. He finally got used to me and started to help me.

In southern cities, where previous interaction between Black and White people followed a rigid code, adjustments were necessary on both sides. It was clear to Lynn Johnson and others that college faculty and students had to adapt to her small Black cohort at Regional College.

Wendy Jones attended a formerly predominantly White state university that had just merged with a formerly predominantly Black college. This new institution meant many adjustments for faculty and students. As a working-class person majoring in engineering, she had a rough transition. She recalled:

I had never gone to school with White kids. I'd always gone to all Black schools all my life and the Black kids there [at the university] were snooty. Only one friend from high school went there and she flunked out. The courses were harder and all my teachers were men and White. Most of the kids were White. I was in classes where I'd be the only Black and woman. There were no similarities to grasp for. I had to adjust to being in that situation. In about a year I was comfortable where I could walk up to people in my class and have conversations.

For some Black people, their first significant interaction with White people did not come until graduate school. Janice Freeman described her experiences:

I went to a Black high school, a Black college and then worked for a Black man who was a former teacher. Everything was comfortable until I had to go to State University for graduate school. I felt very insecure. I was thrown into an environment that was very different—during the 1960s and 1970s there was so much unrest anyway—so it was extremely difficult for me.

It was not in graduate school but on her first job as a social worker that Janice had to learn to work *with* White people. She said, "After I realized that I could hang in school, working at the social work agency allowed me to learn how to work *with* White people. I had never done that before and now I do it better than anybody."

Learning to live in a White world was an additional hurdle for all Black women in this age cohort. Previous generations of Black people were more likely to be educated in segregated colleges and to work within the confines of the established Black community. They taught in segregated schools, provided dental and medical care to the Black communities, and provided social services and other comforts to members of their own communities. They also lived in the Black community and worshiped on Sunday with many of the people they saw in different settings. As the comments of our respondents reveal, both Black and White people had to adjust to integrated settings, but it was more stressful for the newcomers.

SUMMARY AND CONCLUSIONS

Our major aim in this research was to reopen the study of the subjective experience of upward social mobility and to begin to incorporate race and gender into our vision of the process. In this exploratory work, we hope to raise issues and questions that will cast a new light on taken-for-granted assumptions about the process and the people who engage in it. The experiences of these women have certainly painted a different picture from the one we were left some twenty years ago. First and foremost, these women are not detached, isolated, or driven solely by career goals. Relationships with family of origin, partners, children, friends, and the wider community loom

large in the way they envision and accomplish mobility and the way they sustain themselves as professional and managerial women.

Several of out findings suggest ways that race and gender shape the mobility process for baby boom Black and White women. Education was stressed as important in virtually all of the families of these women; however, they differed in how it was viewed and how much was desired. The upwardly mobile women, both Black and White, shared some obstacles to attainment. More mobile women had parents who never expected them to achieve a college education. They also received less emotional and financial support for college attendance from their families than the women in middle-class families received. Black women also faced the unique problem of crossing racial barriers simultaneously with class barriers.

There were fairly dramatic race differences in the messages that the Black and White women received from family about what their lives should be like as adults. Black women clearly received the message that they needed an occupation to succeed in life and that marriage was a secondary concern. Many Black women also expressed a sense that their mobility was connected to an entire racial uplift process, not merely an individual journey.

White upwardly mobile women received less clear messages. Only one-half of these women said that their parents stressed the need for an occupation to succeed, and 20 percent said that marriage was stressed as the primary life goal. The most common message seemed to suggest that an occupation was necessary, because marriage could not be counted on to provide economic survival. Having a career, on the other hand, could even be seen as detrimental to adult happiness.

Upward mobility is a process that requires sustained effort and emotional and cognitive, as well as financial, support. The legacy of the image of mobility that was built on the White male experience focuses on credentialing institutions, especially the schools, as the primary place where talent is recognized and support is given to ensure that the talented among the working class are mobile. Family and friends are virtually invisible in this portrayal of the mobility process.

Although there is a good deal of variation in the roles that family and friends play for these women, they are certainly not invisible in the process. Especially among many of the Black women, there is a sense that they owe a great debt to their families for the help they have received. Black upwardly mobile women were also much more likely to feel that they give more than they receive from kin. Once they have achieved professional managerial employment, the sense of debt combines with their greater access to resources to put them in the position of being asked to give and of giving more to both family and friends. Carrington (1980) identifies some potential mental health hazards of such a sense of debt in upwardly mobile Black women's lives.

White upwardly mobile women are less likely to feel indebted to kin and to feel that they have accomplished alone. Yet even among this group, connections to spouses and children played significant roles in defining how women were mobile, their goals, and their sense of satisfaction with their life in the middle class.

These data are suggestive of a mobility process that is motivated by a desire for personal, but also collective, gain and that is shaped by interpersonal commitments to family, partners and children, community, and the race. Social mobility involves competition, but also cooperation, community support, and personal obligations. Further research is needed to explore fully this new image of mobility and to examine the relevance of these issues for White male mobility as well.

NOTE

1. This and all the names used in this article are pseudonyms.

REFERENCES

Braverman, Harry. 1974. *Labor and monopoly capital.* New York: Monthly Review Press.

Carrington, Christine. 1980. Depression in Black women: A theoretical appraisal. In *The Black woman*, edited by La Frances Rodgers Rose. Beverly Hills, CA: Sage.

Clark, Reginald. 1986. *Family life and school achievement.* Chicago: University of Chicago Press.

Collins, Patricia Hill. 1990. *Black feminist thought: Knowledge, consciousness, and the politics of empowerment.* Boston: Routledge.

Ehrenreich, Barbara, and John Ehrenreich. 1979. The professional-managerial class. In *Between labor and capital*, edited by Pat Walker. Boston: South End Press.

Higginbotham, Elizabeth, and Lynn Weber Cannon. 1988. *Rethinking mobility: Towards a race and gender inclusive theory.* Research Paper no. 8.

Center for Research on Women, Memphis State University.

Joslin, Daphne. 1979. Working-class daughters, middle-class wives: Social identity and self-esteem among women upwardly mobile through marriage. Ph.D. diss., New York University, New York.

McAdoo, Harriette Pipes. 1978. Factors related to stability in upwardly mobile Black families. *Journal of Marriage and the Family* 40:761–76.

Poulantzas, Nicos. 1974. *Classes in contemporary capitalism.* London: New Left Books.

U.S. Bureau of the Census. 1983. Detailed population characteristics: Tennessee. Census of the Population, 1980. Washington, DC: GPO.

Vanneman, Reeve, and Lynn Weber Cannon. 1987. *The American perception of class.* Philadelphia: Temple University Press.

PART SIX

Constructing Gender
in the Workplace

How much does gender influence one's status at work? Does the feminization of paid labor around the world place women on a more equal footing with men? Or is paid labor another arena intensifying women's disadvantage? Is it an arena that intensifies some women's disadvantage more than others, and how do race, class, and nationality shape women's workplace disadvantage and resistance? The readings in this part rely on various empirical studies to address these questions.

Paid workers and workplaces are increasingly diverse. Today's average worker in the global economy may be either a man or a woman, of any age, race, class, sexual orientation, or nationality. The average worker in the global economy may labor virtually unseen inside the home, or may work in a public workplace, as a mechanic, teacher, secretary, or assembler. Yet whatever the average worker does for a living, he or she is very likely to work at a job assigned on the basis of gender.

Everywhere, gender differentiation organizes workplaces. Even five-year-olds can readily identify what is a "man's job" and what is a "woman's job." Women's jobs and men's jobs are structured with different characteristics and different rewards. In every society, we find a familiar pattern: Women earn less than men, even when they work in similar occupations and have the same level of education. But exactly *how* does work become gendered? How does occupational segregation take hold? How do people normalize gendered jobs? Can these gender boundaries be dismantled? These questions are addressed in the first reading of this section. By probing the work environment of men who work in secretarial jobs—which is today widely recognized as a "woman's job"—Rosemary Pringle reveals how men's secretarial jobs are redefined as higher status "administrative" or "managerial" jobs.

Workplaces are racialized as well as gendered. Racism and sexism interact so that women and men of different races, national origins, and immigrant groups become clustered in certain kinds of work. Job opportunities are shaped by *who* people are—by their being women or men, educated or uneducated, of a certain race, sexual orientation, and residents of specific geopolitical settings—rather than by their skills and talents. These hierarchies also define what constitutes acceptable behavior on the job. In their study of restaurant workers, Patti A. Giuffre and Christine L. Williams discover that even the definition of sexual harassment depends on *who* the perpetrator is and *who* the victim is. Double standards of race, class, and sexual orientation mask a good deal of sexual discrimination in workplaces.

As the global economy presses forward, relying on established patterns of race and gender subordination to structure local workplaces, women and men throughout the world are affected differently. The same changes making women the main facilitators of these economic transformations have eroded many men's ability to be breadwinners. This would appear to benefit women by expanding their opportunities, but women around the world continue to earn low wage levels and face limited opportunities for advancement.

The next two readings in this section consider some of the complex matters related to race, gender, and economic transformations in the United States. Karen Hossfeld's study, based on research conducted among assembly workers in the widely acclaimed Silicon Valley, illustrates how divisions of race and gender can also be used by workers themselves to resist coercive measures of control in the workplace. Teresa Amott explains how economic restructuring has reconfigured work for women and men in different races and classes.

The final reading introduces the concept of "gender harassment," which is different from the more popularly recognized, yet ill-defined, "sexual harassment." Sociologist Laura L. Miller's study of women and men in the U.S. army reveals that although men remain structurally and numerically dominant, they often use a bag of subtle techniques to resist women's advancement in the military. The techniques that military men use, such as sabotage or spreading rumors, are difficult to regulate with official rules, but they have very real consequences for women's stalled advancement in the military.

38

Male Secretaries

ROSEMARY PRINGLE

Two years ago I was appointed to a promotions committee at a provincial university. Complicated travel arrangements had to be made each time for the 12 or so out-of-town members, and there were difficulties finding dates that were mutually compatible. Extensive documentation had to be collected and circulated, interviews arranged, referees contacted. At each meeting Pat, the secretary, not only took minutes but frequently left the room to make telephone calls and send faxes. Pat's role was clearly to do the bidding of the chair. Pat did all this cheerfully and was warmly thanked by members of the committee at the end for taking care of them. The work was secretarial in the broadest sense, including organizing lunches and daily travel arrangements, and helping to clear the cups away after morning tea. But Pat was a man. And nobody thought it at all odd that he should be doing this work. It was, after all, a high-level, confidential committee chaired by the Vice-Chancellor. Pat was a besuited, slightly swarthy man in his late forties, not in any way effeminate. He was doing work that was clearly defined as appropriate to a man, and he was formally classified, not as a secretary but as an administrative officer.

Pat is not unique. Every large organization has dozens of men like him, performing a similar range of tasks to those done by female secretaries, often under the direction of a "boss" and often, as in Pat's case, including a range of semipersonal services. Rather than being called secretaries, they are generally classified as clerical, administrative, or even managerial workers. At the same time, male secretaries are thought to be few and far between. The media have found novelty value in

such role reversals, and have posed the question of whether, in response to feminist demands for equality in the workplace, men will return to secretarial work, perhaps serving women bosses. It is important, therefore, to consider the relationship between the minority who are labeled "male secretaries" and the much larger group who are doing broadly secretarial work.

This chapter derives from a larger study, *Secretaries Talk* (Pringle, 1988), based on historical and statistical data, census returns, representations of secretaries in the media and in student text books, and interviews with both secretarial and nonsecretarial workers in a range of workplaces, large and small, government and nongovernment. While the material on which I draw is mostly Australian, similar processes have taken place throughout the Western industrialized world (Benet, 1972; Crompton & Jones, 1984; Davies, 1982; Kanter, 1977). Some variation can be expected at the level of the region, the firm, and the individual. It will be argued that while there are key discourses that structure secretaries' working lives, these discourses are not imposed in a deterministic way. Rather, they exist as frameworks of meaning within which individuals negotiate their relationships: There is room for different outcomes and for shifts in emphasis. Though male secretaries were sought, there are only 7 in the sample of 149 secretaries interviewed for *Secretaries Talk,* and most of these were found only after I eventually stopped asking for "male secretaries" and substituted job profiles (Pringle, 1988, p. 271). Once I began to realize how the categorization was limiting the data, it became relatively easy to locate men doing broadly similar work. Had I started doing this earlier, I might well have included a higher proportion of men. This is indicative of the extent to which occupational groupings, which at first seem self-evident, are shaped by the categories that are used to organize them. The emphasis on gender polarity can mask a great deal of common ground between men's and women's work. It was thus not only the changing labor process of secretarial work that needed to be studied but also shifts in its definition and meaning.

FEMINIST APPROACHES

Feminist scholars have provided a clear outline of the processes whereby secretarial work, which until the third quarter of the nineteenth century was done almost entirely by men, came in the twentieth century to be perceived as quintessentially women's work. Once an apprenticeship for management, or a way of learning the business before taking it over, secretarial work changed dramatically as the result of both new office technology and the growth of a more complex corporate economy. Middle management expanded, opening up new opportunities to men who might once have been clerks and simultaneously creating new low-status keyboard and stenographic positions that were filled by women. Secretarial work became mechanized and deskilled, and no longer served as a gateway to power. The sexual division of labor was redefined to include a sharp differentiation between secretarial jobs on the one hand and administrative and managerial jobs on the other. Work has continued to be organized around gender polarities, with clear-cut distinctions between men's and women's work. As argued in *Gender at Work,* gender is not only about difference but also about power: the domination of men and the subordination of women. This power relation is maintained by the creation of distinctions between male and female spheres (Game & Pringle, 1983, p. 16). Not only are jobs defined according to a clear gender dichotomy, but the gendering of jobs has been important to the construction of gender identity. Gen-

der is not constructed in the family and then taken out to work but is continually reconstituted in a number of arenas, including work. Men need to experience their work as empowering. Performing secretarial work, as it conveyed ancillary service functions carried out by women, was increasingly seen as a threat to masculine power and identity.

One of the limitations of such an analysis is that it assumes that both occupational and gender categories are empirically given. It will be argued here that neither occupational titles nor gender labels merely describe a pregiven reality, but exist in discourses that actively constitute that reality. Discourse is precisely this—the ways of understanding, interpreting, and responding to a "reality," which it is impossible to know in any other way. This is not to imply that reality does not exist—in this case, substantial differences in the tasks performed by men and women. But occupations do not emerge straightforwardly from an observation of the labor process. These occupational divisions could equally well have been described in a number of other ways and need not have assumed a gender polarity. In any case, secretaries are not sitting at their desks waiting to be counted. Their numbers vary enormously, depending on which meaning is being produced: In Australia it could range between 25,000 and a half million, depending on whether one wanted to differentiate between executive assistants and routine filing clerks. It is notable, too, that secretarial work is still routinely described in terms of individual boss/secretary relationships, even though such relationships are now largely restricted to senior management (Pringle, 1988, pp. 174–194).

If we cannot take occupations as given in reality, neither can we take gender as given. Kessler and McKenna (1978, pp. 102–103) point out that by assuming in advance the centrality of gender categories, we inevitably reproduce such categories. The possibility of describing social relations in any other way is then systematically excluded, and gender is presented as fixed and given. Most questions posed about gender assume a sharp dichotomy, that is, that everyone fits one and only one category, and that one's gender is invariant. On the contrary, they suggest, it is "our seeing two genders" that leads to the "discovery" of biological, psychological, and social differences. They argue for a more open approach, suggesting that if gender is a social construction, it might be treated as more fluid. Judith Butler has made the case against essentialism even more strongly, arguing that gender coherence is a regulatory fiction (1990, pp. 329–339). She rejects the assumption that individuals have a deep psychic investment in gender identity, socially constructed or otherwise, and insists that this is imposed purely through discourse.

While Butler's anti-essentialist position is extreme, it does open up new ways of thinking about gender and occupations. It calls into question the deep connections between gender and occupational identities and suggests that it may be possible to resituate the issues. The subject of male secretaries is a particularly promising area to investigate this approach, for it poses the contradiction between men's horror of being labeled "male secretaries," while they are willing to do the same or very similar work as long as they are not so labeled. Why does a simple change of label make it acceptable? On the one hand gender seems so rigid that secretarial work presents a threat to a man's core gender identity. On the other, it may be relatively straightforward to resituate the subject in a different occupational discourse, recasting the "reality" in a different frame. The question that needs to be raised is not, why there are so few male secretaries; but rather, why the title "secretary" is reserved almost exclusively for women, and how it affects the negotiation of workplace identities and power relations.

WHAT IS A SECRETARY?

It is impossible to answer the question "what is a secretary?" by describing what a secretary *does*. If it were so, the many thousands of Pats in existence would surely be included. There are actually a range of discourses, statistical and cultural, in which meanings are produced about what a secretary *is* (Pringle, 1988). We come to know secretaries and to identify them as a group through the ways in which they are represented. This is true of all groups, but in most cases the emphasis is on the actual work and the social relations surrounding it. A plumber, or for that matter a stenographer or typist, does not have a particularly strong cultural presence. By contrast, the secretary is constructed in popular culture in a way that plays down the importance of what she does, in favor of discussion of what she is. Secretary is one of the few employment categories for which there has never been a clear job description. Secretaries do a wide variety of things, and there is not even one task, such as typing, that we can confidently say they all perform. This ambiguity about what constitutes a secretary's work makes it easily available for cultural redefinition. Secretaries are part of folklore and popular culture and are represented in stereotypical ways in advertising and the media, even in pornography.

In the twentieth century secretaries have come to be defined first as exclusively women, and second in familial and sexual terms. If, as the psychoanalysts suggest, woman is perceived as lacking what it takes to be a man, so secretaries were assumed to lack the qualities that make a successful boss. The equating of secretary with woman or wife, and boss with man, has been important in establishing the normative versions of what a secretary is. So powerful are these norms that female bosses and male secretaries are perceived as out of step, and the relationship may be difficult to read in traditional boss/secretary terms—it may simply be perceived as two people working together (Pringle, 1988, pp. 82–83).

The question "what is a secretary" may be answered with reference to three discourses, which have coexisted at times peacefully and at others in open competition with one another. The first of these, the "office wife," emerged early this century and had its origins in the debate about whether (middle-class) women should work outside the home. It may be found in serious journals, teaching manuals, and the practices of a good many secretarial studies teachers, as well as the more traditional bosses and secretaries. It signified that women's primary place was in the home, that her other tasks would be redefined in relation to this and restricted to support roles. The two main requirements of the office wife were that she be deferential and that she be ladylike. The office wife is portrayed as the extension of her boss: loyal, trustworthy, and devoted. Though the discourse has been modernized, debate about changes in secretarial work is frequently cast in terms of how far office marriages are changing. Are they being transformed into more compassionate and egalitarian relations, where the wife might have other interests or refuse to do certain aspects of the housework?

By the 1950s the prim, spinsterish figure with the bun had been challenged by alternative images, appearing regularly in tabloid cartoons, of the blonde "dolly bird" figure, with large breasts, long legs, and short skirts. Where the office wife had been a workhorse, putting order into the office, the dolly was presented as a source of chaos and diversion. The office wife is subservient, passive, and reserved; but the dolly is cheeky and loud and is represented as having an active sexuality and a degree of sexual power over the boss. What the two had in common was their definition in gendered and familial terms. Secretaries could be wives, mothers, mistresses, dragons, or spinster aunts.

A third set of meanings has struggled to emerge, which resists the familial and sexual definitions, treats secretaries as having serious careers, emphasizes skill and experience, and plays down the special relationship between boss and secretary in favor of viewing both as part of a management team. Although this "equal opportunity" discourse gathered strength by the 1970s, and proclaimed that gender should not be important in the construction of occupational categories, the earlier meanings live on and need to be addressed seriously in the discussion of work.

The inclusion of a sexual dynamic in the boss/secretary relationship has largely excluded men

from being defined as secretaries. It would be tantamount to declaring both boss and secretary to be gay. Male secretaries are often assumed to be gay. This is both a conventional way of interpreting a male sexuality that is perceived as lacking power and a statement about the place of sexuality in people's perceptions of the boss/secretary relation. Alternately, male secretaries may be incorporated in familial terms as sons and brothers. (Sons who are currently performing filial duties but will, in the course of time, move on to establish their autonomous place in the world.) In the fantasies of women managers, male secretaries may at times appear as boy toys and playthings—but significantly *never* in the powerful subject positions of husbands or fathers. I shall return to these questions, drawing on interview data, in the final section.

SHIFTING DEFINITIONS OF SECRETARIES

The history of men and women in secretarial work must take account of not only technological and organizational change, but also shifting frameworks of meaning. Far from being a fixed, identifiable group, secretaries are a fluid and shifting category; and sociologists, economists, journalists, managers, clerks, keyboard operators, personal assistants, and so on, may have quite different notions of who should be included. The changing definitions of secretaries are amplified by the decisions of the statisticians as to how to count and classify them. Official statistics are no more neutral a discourse than any other; they too produce specific meanings for *secretary*. This section looks at the ongoing presence of men in secretarial work since the late nineteenth century, and the ways in which that presence has been discursively disguised, particularly by statisticians who have interpreted the occupational structure in ways that emphasized sexual polarities.

Even though in the nineteenth century secretaries were men, it is now assumed that secretaries have been women since time immemorial. Secretarial work is now seen as so traditionally women's work that it is hard to remember how recently this work has become feminized. Although in the United States women began to move into secretarial work during the Civil War period, it was not until about 1930 that a clear majority of secretaries were women, and not until the 1950s that male secretaries began to seem strange or unusual (Benet, 1972; Davies, 1982). In the space of a very few decades, the secretarial workforce underwent a sex change. This feminization occurred in conjunction with a major shift in the meaning and status of *secretary*.

The shift is signified by the three definitions offered by the *Oxford English Dictionary* (1979), which will be discussed in turn. The first of these definitions invokes the older meaning, which lives on in titles like Secretary of State or Press Secretary.

> One who is entrusted with private or secret matters; one whose office is to write for another, especially one who is employed to conduct correspondence, to keep records and (usually) to transact other business for another person or for a society, corporation or public body.

It usually appears in capitals and still signifies largely male preserves. While the British Foreign Secretary and the American Defense Secretary are there to serve a monarch and a president, respectively, they exercise enormous power. Men who are Secretaries in this earlier sense are often impatient or uncomfortable about comparing themselves with "small s" secretaries. Had anyone used the word *secretary* to refer to Pat, they would have implicitly added, "in the old sense," more akin to a company or union secretary than to somebody who served a boss.

The second Oxford definition indicates a transition of meaning:

> Private secretary—a secretary employed by a minister of state or other high official for the personal correspondence connected with his official positions. Also applied to a secretary in the employ of a particular person (as distinguished from the secretary to a society, etc).

As assistants to senior managers, private secretaries still act as officers of the company or organization, but their continuity with secretaries in the earlier sense goes largely unacknowledged and they are, for counting purposes, usually included with typists and stenographers.

The third definition more accurately conveys what most contemporary secretaries do and is indicative of the shift to "women's work":

> A person employed to help deal with correspondence, typing, filing and similar routine work.

HISTORICAL TRANSITIONS

The changes signified by the dictionary definitions did not take place overnight but happened gradually over half a century. They are linked to major changes in the occupational structure and the development of new tiers of clerical work, made possible by new technologies. This section attempts a broad periodization from the 1890s, when the first two definitions still held sway, to the developments since World War II, when the third definition became the most widely used one.

1890–1920

Of all the components of what is now called secretarial work, telephoning was the first to be designated as feminine (Kingston, 1975, p. 93). Typing was initially considered to require not only manual dexterity but also some practical knowledge of the material being processed (Fitzsimmons, 1980, p. 24). It was therefore perceived as appropriate work for men. As typewriters came into general use, in the first decade of the twentieth century, and the demand for operators increased, typing became accepted as a woman's subject. Shorthand retained a masculine image, but had, before World War I, become paired with typing by employers to create the feminine job classification of "shorthand-typiste." The first two national censuses in Australia replaced "secretary" with "officer in a public company," a small group which remained predominantly male. Typists and stenographers were included in the general categories of "office caretaker, keeper, attendant" and "clerk, cashier, accountant undefined." The proportion of women in the latter category rose to 35% by 1921 and, when this is checked against the job advertisements for the period, it is reasonable to assume that many of them were typists, stenographers, and private secretaries.

1920–1945

Though men continued to engage in secretarial work in the inter-war period, their proportion steadily declined. The feminine "typiste" came to be used in the job advertisements of the 1920s to distinguish "women's work." The statisticians caught up with this terminology and, in the 1933 census created the gendered category "typiste, office machinist," from which men were absent by definition. Until World War II advertisements for typists (without the "e") still routinely appeared in the classifieds, which indicates that a number of men were employed as typist/clerks. The majority of secretaries, as distinct from stenographers, were also still men. But for the male secretaries, unlike most of the women, stenographic work was the start rather than the end of a career. The key way that young men without a tertiary education could get promotion in the public service, for example, was by going to night school and studying either shorthand or accountancy. Shorthand was taken as a kind of alternative evidence of intellectual ability. Even in the 1980s there were senior male public servants and company managers who had started their careers as stenographic and secretarial workers (Byrne, 1982, p. 10).

Late 1940s–Present

In the late 1940s the term *secretary* began to be used more loosely in the classifieds to describe what had previously been understood in more precise terms as stenographers and typists. The statisticians were obviously concerned that company secretaries might get confused with humbler typing varieties. "Secretary" disappeared entirely as a census category. Rather than making any effort to distinguish private secretaries as a professional group, they collapsed them into the category of "typists and shorthand writers." From a masculinist viewpoint it was convenient to do this because they then did not have to identify or acknowledge levels of skill. "Women's work" could be seen as an undifferentiated category of unskilled labor.

In the 1947 census men were again counted among typists and stenographers, but their numbers were small: 245 out of 71,000. Although officially gender-neutral, the "typist, stenographer" category was treated, by the statisticians, as a feminine one. The coders were actually allowed to take gender into account in deciding how to categorize people. Men who did shorthand or typing (and there were still a large number of them in the public service) were thus recoded as clerks. If "shorthand typist" was a category reserved for women, so too was "receptionist." So that there could be no mistake about this, the 1976 and 1981 censuses actually labeled the group "receptionist, female." A man, by definition, could not be a receptionist and would have to be placed in some other category.

As a result of these processes, men in secretarial work became literally invisible as "secretaries" and were treated as part of a clerical and administrative workforce with a separate career path. Male secretaries gained novelty value. Newspapers have loved to "discover" the occasional "brave" man who is attending secretarial college. In Australia, they have been discovering him every few months since at least 1968! (*Sun-Herald,* November 10, 1968). In 1973, when employers faced the prospect of equal pay, we were told that Caulfield Institute had just enrolled their first male in a secretarial postgraduate course (*Australian,* March 4, 1973); that Stella Cornelius (furrier and arbiter of women's fashion) had a male personal assistant (*Sydney Morning Herald,* March 14, 1973); and that such men were earning nearly twice as much as the women and saw their jobs as stepping-stones to more important careers (*Sydney Morning Herald,* February 7, 1973). After equal pay for work of equal value became official policy in 1975, the popular press threatened that "the first male secretaries are sharpening their pencils to lead the men's lib march down the corridors of power" and that they were "edging out boardroom blondes." One of their number allegedly commented: "Female secretaries are two a penny. Men beat them for efficiency and stability.... We don't fall pregnant and don't come and go" (*Sun-Herald,* January 9, 1977). A year later it was "Take a letter MR Jones" (*Sun-Herald,* March 5, 1977). In 1982 a policeman was chosen as Queensland's Secretary of the Year: As the *Herald* put it, "Sergeant Greg takes on the girls and cops it sweet." He had started 20 years earlier as a foot patrolman and gone on to become assistant to the police commissioner. With admirable secretarial tact, he commented: "The police in Queensland have received a lot of unwarranted criticism lately and I hope my award can do a little bit to help our cause" (*Sydney Morning Herald,* April 22, 1982).

The strong associations of "secretary" with femininity and sexuality have a number of implications for men doing broadly secretarial work. Currently, men are rarely called secretaries. They are generally described as assistants of some kind, or as computer operators, clerks, or trainees. As late as 1970 a textbook for secretarial students noted that:

> *In industries where secretaries are required to represent their employers, in factories or on construction sites, and in strictly masculine provinces, male secretaries are in great demand... they are frequently employed in the legal field, in purchasing, mining, the oil and rubber industries, public utilities and in the newspaper field. (Solly et al., 1970, pp. 6–7)*

Men continued to use stenographic skills in the armed forces, the police, and journalism. The State Rail Authority insisted that its junior recruits learn to type, and in the 1960s still required shorthand as a qualification for its clerks. Court reporting also remained a male preserve, although women had taken over the typing side. In what seems a strange division of labor, the reporters took down the proceedings in shorthand and dictated them directly to typists. Men only dropped out in the 1980s, when the work apparently became less attractive to them after equal pay was implemented (Pringle, 1988, p. 170). While the number of men doing secretarial work has undoubtedly dropped, a number remain who are simply not perceived as secretaries because of their gender. As a result, the extent to which secretarial work has been feminized has been overemphasised.

"MALE SECRETARIES"

While the majority of men in secretarial work are not called secretaries, a few are quite self-consciously given that label, and it is necessary to ask why they have been singled out in this way, rather than incorporated into an "assistant" category. According to my research, men labeled as secretaries are often thought, by those with whom they work, to have some "problem" with their masculinity. Said one manager:

> *I had a male secretary once. He was a clerk who came from the Air Force and I discovered one day, quite by accident, that he wrote shorthand and he typed.... I didn't have a secretary at the time and he was one of those guys who was quite happy to fill a secretarial role.... He was an effeminate sort of person and he appeared to enjoy the subservient role. He was one of those people who always wanted to help you.*

The boss's assumption appeared to be: What "real" man would want to be subservient, let alone helpful! Male secretaries may also be sensitive to assumptions made about their sexuality, as another interviewee insists:

> *An old retired bloke comes in regularly to relive the old days.... The other morning he came in. He stopped and he looked at me and I was typing. And I was aware that he was looking at me...and he said, what's your name, Miss? And I looked at him*

and said, it's Jacqueline, actually! He didn't get it. He just sort of grunted and walked off.

I don't object to having overtones of femininity. I mean, everyone's got their yin and their yang. But the implication in a male-dominated society, and particularly in the last bastion of male domination... is that femininity is associated with homosexuality, which is taboo... which conjures up all sorts of nasty images. So that's what I cope with every day.

Any "feminized" occupation is presumed to draw homosexual men: Fashion, hairdressing, entertainment, and more recently nursing are cases in point. A firm connection is made between gender and sexual preference, and the stronger the sex-typing of the job, the stronger the resulting stereotype. The popular press reinforces such connections, for example, by seeking out gay secretaries. The Sydney *Sun-Herald,* for example, in an article titled "Sex Changes in the Typing Pool" (July 1982), described the unhappy experience of Ashley, before he joined the safety of the public service: "'It was disastrous,' he said. 'The boss tried to chase me around the desk. I left after only three-and-a-half weeks.'" The passage probably says more about the fear expressed by the interviewer, of what happens to men in an occupation that is not only subordinate and feminized, but perceived in such strongly sexual terms. The sexuality of the boss is not problematical here—he is represented as sexually dominant and willing to take sexual liberties with the secretary, regardless of either gender or sexual preference.

Ashley *was* actually gay (I interviewed him 4 years later) but he is in the minority. In my research it was easier to find gay nurses than gay secretaries; and even in nursing, gays are a minority. Gay secretaries were largely a newspaper fiction of the 1970s and 1980s. There is no reason to believe that gay men are congregated in secretarial work. A gay lawyer, with a high proportion of gay clients, told me he had advertised widely for a male secretary and had not been able to find anyone suitably qualified. He thought the legal profession was probably too staid for such people. A

spokesman for the Gay Business Association in Sydney suggested that gay men may perceive secretaries as "dowdy," and the work as involving long hours of drudgery. He suggested that they were more likely to be working as receptionists or switchboard operators than as secretaries. Secretarial work does not necessarily represent femininity for gay men. In some cases it may represent the opposite. The only other gay secretary I interviewed grew up in a country town and wanted to be a court or Hansard reporter, he explained, to reconcile his sexuality with "something masculine." When he did not get the necessary speeds, he joined the State Rail Authority, which had also retained a masculine image, and it was only when he became dissatisfied with the promotional prospects there that he became willing to consider more stereotypically secretarial positions in the private sector.

The media discourse about gay male secretaries now seems a little dated, particularly since the emergence of "gay machismo." Since the mid-1980s more women have moved into senior executive positions (particularly in the public service) and often find themselves dealing with male subordinates. These women often joked to me about the "male secretary" as a subject of titillation, a possible object of desire or a status symbol (a boy toy or a handbag). Given the notorious difficulties that women bosses often report with female secretaries (Pringle, 1998, pp. 57–83), a male personal assistant has both practical and erotic appeal. To reverse the master/slave relationship is to represent the woman as both powerful and stylish. It is to imply that she is cared for by a man, who both finds her sexually attractive and admires and respects her, offering the same kind of loyalty that men have in the past extracted from their female secretaries. It is also to exploit the traditionally higher status of the manservant or butler over the female domestic (the status of male secretaries might be lower than that of men in many other occupations, but they are likely to earn more than their female counterparts). The numbers of female boss/male secretary pairs are not vast, but their appearance in the discourse of women managers is indicative of a shift in the way male secretaries are being regarded. It is notable that they continue to be sexually defined, though in new ways. Perhaps because of this sexualization, most men doing secretarial work still express discomfort at the prospect of being labeled "male secretaries."

MALE BOSSES

Some male managers said they "could not imagine" having a man as a secretary, and it is quite possible that male applicants face discrimination. One of my subjects recalled that when he was living in London two other men he knew were "temping" for solicitors and found it very difficult to get work "until they had tried them once. And it took 3 or 4 months for these guys to get established. It is a very staid industry." To many male bosses the relationship with a "secretary" is of an intimate nature and is more appropriately with a woman. Yet managers are constantly in the position of supervising those below them in the chain of command. Why should it be so different in principle when the person concerned is a "secretary"? As soon as the person concerned is renamed an "assistant" of some kind, the problem appears to go away. A professor spoke warmly of his "technical officer," who, "to my delight writes letters almost in the words I would have used." He relies on him for "higher level secretarial tasks" and sees a future for a lot more men in these positions.

Bosses may deal with the sexualization issue by denying that their male secretaries are secretaries or by treating them differently. One senior manager commented:

> A male secretary... would not be called my secretary but my assistant.... I think I would get a male secretary to do additional work because he was male.... Simply because other males here that are helping me, the marketing manager, the accountant, the product manager... are doing work of a particular level.... I would imagine this guy taking on more and more responsibility and then one day I would say, "Why don't we get a typist?"

Once appointed, male secretaries appear to receive very favorable treatment and the "discrimination" works to their advantage. In a rather similar way male doctors, embarrassed by the sexual connotations of the doctor/nurse relationship, often treat male nurses as junior doctors, explain more processes to them, and facilitate their speedier progress through the system (Game & Pringle, 1983, pp. 110–111). Since it is "unimaginable" that men might be secretaries, they tend to be paid more and to move quickly up the career ladder.

Male secretaries earn about 20% more than their female counterparts, a figure that directly parallels the differential for full-time workers overall (Pringle, 1988, p. 171). The self-confidence and assertiveness of the two male secretaries discussed below thus has a solid financial basis. The higher rate cannot be explained in terms of the different occupation distributions of men and women, and can only signify that the men are receiving more favorable treatment and moving into personal assistant positions.

FAMILY GAMES

Where male secretaries are not defined sexually, they may be integrated, in family terms, as brothers or sons. Tim, for example, works in the family law firm. He tells close friends that he is a secretary but otherwise describes himself as a legal clerk. He picked up typing while working in a bank and works from Dictaphone. He does not take shorthand. His brother and sister, both solicitors, say he is the best secretary they have had because he wants to know exactly what each piece of work is about. He behaves as though he were one of the legal staff and, like many other male secretaries, is treating it as a stepping-stone. He is currently taking an accountancy course.

Phillip Warton works for a family-based pharmaceutical company, where he is treated by both husband and wife as the son. While this has its frustrations, particularly with the wife, it also gives him a stronger power base than that usually available to sisters or daughters. Phillip agreed to talk to me after a woman friend of his saw my advertisement for "male secretaries" and volunteered him. He had not identified himself as a secretary until that time because his description says he is a "marketing assistant." Now in his early 20s he had started work in a bank and had taken it upon himself to learn to type when he found he kept making mistakes on bank cheques and international drafts.

> *I went to tech for 6 months and learned to type. . . . There was two other guys there but it was very sexist actually in that the woman who was teaching me to type came to me and said that I didn't have to bother too much about spacing and those aspects of typing because I wouldn't be using that in my role. And I said, but if I was going to be a secretary I would. She said, "But you're not—what are you doing it for?" She automatically presumed I was not going to be a secretary. . . . I didn't have to do typing tests on spacing and setting out letters and what have you. I just went strictly on speed typing.*

He earns 30% to 40% more than he was getting in the bank. Despite his lack of a science or pharmacy degree, he is being groomed for a long-term position in the company. But he does not see a future in it, and it is unlikely that he will stay. Phillip has taken the job to get marketing experience and plans to do a marketing diploma. How does he describe his current job?

> *Basically it is to look after the managing director. I run after him, and organize him, keep his desk tidy, make sure he goes to appointments. . . . Get things done that he should do and doesn't get time for.*

But he is always introduced as "my assistant," my offsider, Phillip who runs around after me . . . never as secretary. Phillip claims a degree of power in relation to his boss:

> *I think he feels, not threatened by me, but I feel I have the ability to tell him what to do. I tell him what to do and he does it. I'll go in there and I'll say, "Your desk is utterly disgusting. How can you find anything?" And I'll come back into his office and there will be piles on the floor for me to take*

away to file. His wife thinks it's wonderful that he's got me to run around after him. . . . But in regard to a power play he's still M.D., and he knows he still is . . . and knows that it's just a game. . . . Sometimes I feel like that and other times I feel he's a bit wimpy, because someone who's only been in the company for 3 months has the ability to say something to him.

It was unusual to hear female secretaries talk like this in an interview situation, regardless of what they might have felt privately.

Though he replaced a woman who did a lot of typing, Phillip rarely uses his typing skills at work. He says:

> *. . . The only time I'll type is if I need it and there's no one to do it. I've heard it said that the girl that is doing the typing now has had to do more because I'm there. . . . Mind you, typing was a stipulation of the job . . . but he [the boss] didn't even ask me if I could type . . . he just assumed I didn't.*
>
> *And I said to him, "You didn't ask me about typing." He said, "Do you type?" I said, "Of course I do, I did a tech course." "Oh, really? That's an added advantage, isn't it?" I thought, oh, well, he must have taken me on on the basis of my other attributes.*

This "girl" appears a few minutes later as the boss's wife and a director of the company. Her relationship with Phillip is complex. He asserts his ascendancy over her, too, as the typist who lacks many of his skills, but at the same time he regards her as the power behind the throne.

> *So you give typing to her?*
> *Yes but it doesn't work that way because she . . . is not the typist. She is a director and she will take time out.*

As the interview continues, her authority increases rapidly. She controls the office, keeps everything under surveillance, and basically manages things. If there is conflict between her and her husband, she gets her way. She intervenes on every level. She insists on a high standard of dress and routinely comments on Phillip's ties, clothes, hairstyle, and so on. At first this is presented in terms of mother-son intimacy. The two of them talk about PLU—people like us. You are either PLU or you are not. But before long, he switches again and says that if he were going to resign, it would be because of her. He finds it "frustrating" that she constantly goes behind his back to the boss:

> If I do something that she disagrees with...she won't tell me, she'll go to Douglas. And then he will ask me, "Why did you do that?"... Everything that goes on, she is always overseeing. If I resign from the job, it will be basically because of her. I find her a very frustrating woman to deal with. Because I cannot find my footing with her. She is not direct. She is behind my back.

Perhaps it is not accidental that Phillip's own mother had been a secretary and in all likelihood intervened in similar ways in her relationship with his father.

Phillip's role is considerably more high profile than that of the "girl" he replaced. He does no routine typing, and as a result the boss's wife, herself a director and actively engaged in managing the company, takes on additional typing work. A conflict ensues in which she is constantly putting him in his place, showing that ultimately it is she rather than he who will have her way with Douglas, the patriarch. He can be the favored son only by conforming to her whims, and he has made the judgment that his future will be better served by moving on.

GENDER AND POWER

Clearly, gender does alter the boss-secretary relationship. Raoul, unlike Phillip, is actually defined as a secretary and is thus placed at a cultural disadvantage, subject to ridicule. Yet he is able to develop strategies of asserting masculine power. His boss, Geraldine Milner, is a senior manager with a large merchant bank, for which she has worked for the past 15 years. Her main responsibilities are with advisory services and public relations. She is

41 and single. Beyond that she revealed virtually nothing about her private life.

Though very aware of the problems of being a woman in a male-dominated industry, she does not attach any significance to having a male secretary. I asked her what she thought about the common view that it would be hard for men to be in those sorts of support positions:

> Rubbish! What a load! Have they ever tried it? I mean, this is it! It's crazy! I've always had men working for me and I haven't noticed any difference.... I've never really expected my secretaries to get my cups of coffee or cups of tea or anything like that...if that's what they term support.... I suppose some men expect their secretaries to go out and buy their wives' birthday presents and all that sort of nonsense.... I would never consider asking them to do anything other than what was required in a professional capacity.

Her secretary, Raoul Wicks, is 26 and single. He was dressed in a crumpled suit, which barely fulfilled the formal dress requirements, and he appeared to thumb his nose at the style associated with merchant banks. Having dropped out of a Bachelor of Business degree halfway through, he has had a rather checkered career as an actor and odd-jobs person. He is in this position rather accidentally, having originally contacted the bank about another clerical job.

Geraldine stressed there was no difference between what Raoul did and what previous female secretaries had done:

> I want someone who can do the basic school lectures for us. Someone who can handle the phones and preferably who knows the industry, at least enough to answer a lot of the basic queries. I don't really have sufficient typing and normal things like that to warrant a full-time secretary.
>
> Raoul's here because he studied and wants to work in the industry, so it's a very good training position for someone in the long term. Another former secretary has now gone into a broker's office and is doing extremely well.

Raoul, on the other hand, is not happy about being called a secretary, and goes out of his way to explain why the term is inappropriate. He says that when the job was first discussed, the term *secretary* was never mentioned. They just said:

> I would need to do a little bit of typing.... It looked like an attractive job. There's a certain amount of prestige in working for this organization.... At that point in time I couldn't type but I rapidly learned.... I went and did one of those bloody student receptionist center courses...

He stressed the ways in which his job is different from that of a secretary—and went on to give what is a very typical job description:

> My job involves doing all the administration in the department.... I answer all the mail...and discern where it should go and who should answer it. If I can answer it, I answer it. I handle all the bookings for schools for our educational talks...for community organizations...and for companies.... I also take lectures for school and community groups. I handle all the merchandising for the department. I sell all the sweatshirts. I am in charge of the accounts.... I do the banking.... I also take phone inquiries.

"Lecturing" to school and community groups is beyond the duties of most secretaries, but it is the only task that stands out. There had been some concern to find him an alternative title, befitting his status as a male, but Geraldine would have none of this. Where his strategy of power was to emphasize his difference from secretaries, hers was to assert his similarity with his female predecessors. The connections between discourse and power are very obvious here, in the two quite different interpretations of "secretary" that are put forward as the terms of the relationship are negotiated.

On this occasion Geraldine won. As Raoul describes it:

> The personnel officer rang me.... She was updating the telephone directory...and she said to me. "Oh, Raoul, what are we going to call you? You're not really a "secretary," are you...you do more than that...how about we call you "Information Officer"? I said that's fine, that sounds good. And

she said, "I'll talk to Geraldine and get back to you.".... No more was said...and when the telephone list came out, there I was, a secretary and that was that.... I didn't say anything to Geraldine about it. I didn't feel I could.

He goes to some lengths to enlist sympathy for his "predicament":

> If one wants to belong to a club, particularly a men's club, there are certain do's and don'ts. There are certain mores, and it therefore doesn't augur well to be a secretary. Maybe 30 years ago...if you had been a private secretary...that may have been different.... Now if you're doing a woman's job, the implication is that you are somehow feminine. And femininity has no place in a men's club.

He claims to get teased by young girls in the office who imply he is not a proper man. And yet what comes across is the power that this man is able to exercise. Typically, when I interviewed both members of a boss/secretary pair, the male boss was loquacious and open, while the female secretary was more guarded. On this occasion, the female boss restricts her range of comments, while the male secretary talks freely, explicitly, and quite personally about her. I did not meet a single female secretary who talked in quite this way about a boss, male or female. On this occasion gender clearly overrides formal position in determining what can be said. Thus he comments:

> I think she's perceived as a hard arse. But I think she's had to be a hard arse to get where she's got to. I also think she's perceived as pretty neurotic and I do know that she has a nickname around here.
>
> She gets bad-mouthed a lot behind her back. I have to be careful, as there may be times when I agree with what people are saying. I have found myself slip on a couple of occasions and say, yes, you're right...or enforce their prejudices rather than just taking a neutral stance.
>
> Yes, she's perceived as being hard and tough, particularly with women. She's tougher on women than she is on men.... So I think...you know, jobs for the boys doesn't necessarily operate with jobs for the girls.

He talks at length about the way in which Geraldine exercises power over him. As he talks it becomes clear that the flow of power between them fluctuates very much more than is the case with female secretaries and either male or female bosses. He thinks she has "very definite limits and very definite boundaries that cannot be overstepped," but seems to delight in playing games with them. On one occasion Geraldine asserts her authority because Raoul has forgotten to leave her a message. His comeback is, first, that only a woman would be concerned with such "trivia," dismissing the possibility that it may have been important to make every effort to return the call. Second, he implies it is because he is a man that she has to bother asserting herself in this way at all:

> I think she expects that she doesn't have to exert any authority with women. I mean, someone who has authority doesn't feel the need to display it.... With women I don't think she feels the need to display it. But with men she does have a need to display it.

Raoul continues in this vein, ostensibly describing her power and his subordination, but actually imposing his own power in the situation and reducing hers through stereotyping her—first as a dragon and then as a typical neurotic woman.

> The male bosses I have had are more even. They're less prone to ups and downs. With my boss at the moment...I leave her alone for at least a good hour. I've learned that now. Leave her alone till half past 10 and probably it'll be okay. But as soon as she walks in the door, the first thing I have to do is sum her up...and see what kind of mood she's in.

It is hardly unusual for secretaries to discern their bosses' moods, and adjust their behavior accordingly. But he turns this into a kind of reverse power base. He concedes that men's moods fluctuate too:

> ...but I don't think it's as visible.... That's kind of more dangerous because they're actually prone to exploding on you without any warning,

> whereas with Geraldine, I've got a pretty fair idea in advance.

He claims the power to read her accurately, literally placing her via a detailed description of her clothes. None of the women interviewed said anything like this of her boss:

> I can tell a lot from the way she's dressed.... There was one dress that has a very high collar...it's quite rigid...and it's pleated all the way down.... I know that she's in a very no-nonsense mood when I see that dress.... Like today we've got work to do.... She has a little crimson suit and that's another no-nonsense outfit. But it says...I'm more available today. I'm more open. I will probably be meeting executives or important VIPs.... There is another dress that has a split up the center, and that has its own connotations. And that's usually when she's far more relaxed. The perfume she wears tells me how she feels that day, too. So I try to sum those things up.

While Geraldine denies that the gender of her secretary makes any difference, Raoul thinks she is very aware of his maleness. Unlike female secretaries, he is quite happy to talk about sexual fantasies and interactions, assuming that he has control.

> I can imagine having an affair with Geraldine. But I can't imagine having an affair with Geraldine and working here, because I just think it would just alter the relationship entirely, and it would become untenable for her and for me.

He thinks in the first few weeks in the job there was a kind of sexual attraction going on. Whether the attraction was mutual or his fantasy we do not know, but he curtailed it. As if to have the last word he says:

> I've never told her when I'm pissed off, never. I think that would be to take advantage of the relationship between the sexes, so I don't. Because I couldn't do it with a man. I couldn't go to a man and say, "Look, what you have just done really annoys me," or "The way you've spoken to me really annoys me."

In other words, he believes he could take advantage of male power but claims he does not. The implication is that she depends on his gallantry and cooperation. Remembering his unease at being called secretary, he has had to turn the situation around in fantasy, and to some extent in practice, to make it acceptable to his masculine ego. Geraldine's counter-strategy is to deny that his masculinity has any relevance to the situation and to try to ensure that it brings him no extra privileges. It is clear that, on this occasion at least, gender does matter.

SUMMARY

The normative boss/secretary relationship involves a male boss and a female secretary. When the gender of either is changed, the relationship is quite considerably transformed. Despite stereotyping of male secretaries as "inadequate" men, they are often able to draw on images of masculine power and competence to negotiate significant power in relation to managers. While one must be cautious about generalizing on the basis of a small number of interviews, the discursive strategies that are available to men in secretarial work are fairly clear.

Men have always maintained a presence, albeit a minority one, in secretarial work; the reason this cannot be seen is because of the sexual and gendered nature of the cultural construction of "secretary." Men can and do type, though they often decline to do so at work, for fear of losing their status or their masculinity. Increasingly, managers have computer terminals on their desks, and the old distinction between clerical and secretarial work is breaking down.

The question is not how to get more men into secretarial work but the terms on which they come in. As with other areas of "traditional" women's work, the danger for women is that men will take over the best-paid, most prestigious jobs; that the division between gendered categories of work will be replaced by a horizontal division in which women are restricted to the bottom rungs. This has already happened to some extent in nursing, where men become charge nurses more quickly and move up the administrative hierarchy. But in nursing the movement of some men into positions of power has been counter-balanced by powerful unions, by strong moves toward professionalization and the upgrading of nursing qualifications. It can be argued that the presence of men has assisted in the upgrading of status and working conditions for everyone. In secretarial work the position is quite different. Outside the public sector, the unions are weak and the movement of men into the area does not signify that secretarial work is being acknowledged as professional or managerial in any genuine sense. The fact that "male secretaries" as well as female ones are so often perceived in sexual terms probably does currently limit their capacity to challenge women for many of the most prestigious jobs. While in the short term it may be to the benefit of the women that the sexual definitions are extended in this way, in the long term it will be necessary to challenge the sexualized meanings of "secretary" to ensure that it does not continue to be used to limit the areas available to women. This involves not only a change of label but also struggles around the discursive frameworks within which meanings are constituted.

REFERENCES

Australian. (1973, March 3).

Benet, M. K. (1972). Secretary: An inquiry into the female ghetto. London: Sidgwick & Jackson.

Butler, J. (1990). Gender trouble, feminist theory and psychoanalytic discourse. In L. J. Nicholson (Ed.), Feminism/postmodernism (pp. 324–340). New York: Routledge.

Byrne, R. (1982). Occupation—secretary: An historical perspective. A paper presented at the seminar, Secretarial Education: A New Direction. Melbourne: Chisholm Institute of Technology.

Crompton, R., & Jones, G. (1984). White collar proletariat: Deskilling and gender in clerical work. London: Macmillan.

Davies. M. (1982). *Woman's place is at the typewriter.* Philadelphia: Temple University Press.

Fitzsimmons, K. (1980). The involvement of women in the commercial sector 1850–1891. *Second women and labor conference papers.* Melbourne: Melbourne University.

Game, A., & Pringle, R. (1983). *Gender at work.* Sydney: Allen & Unwin.

Kanter, R. M. (1977). *Men and women of the corporation.* New York: Basic Books.

Kessler, S., & McKenna, W. (1978). *Gender: An ethnomethodological approach.* London: Verso.

Kingston. B. (1975). *My wife, my daughter and poor Mary Ann.* Melbourne: Nelson.

Oxford English dictionary. (1979). Oxford: Oxford University Press.

Pringle. R. (1988). *Secretaries talk.* London: Verso.

Solly, E., et al. (1970). *The secretary at work* (3rd ed.) Melbourne: McGraw-Hill.

Sun-Herald. (1968, November 10).

Sun-Herald. (1977, January 9).

Sun-Herald. (1977, March 5).

Sydney Morning Herald. (1973, February 7).

Sydney Morning Herald. (1973, March 14).

Sydney Morning Herald. (1982, April 22).

Sydney Sun-Herald. (1982, July).

39

Boundary Lines

Labeling Sexual Harassment in Restaurants

PATTI A. GIUFFRE
CHRISTINE L. WILLIAMS

Sexual harassment occurs when submission to or rejection of sexual advances is a term of employment, is used as a basis for making employment decisions, or if the advances create a hostile or offensive work environment (Konrad and Gutek 1986). Sexual harassment can cover a range of behaviors, from leering to rape (Ellis, Barak, and Pinto 1991; Pryor 1987; Reilly et al. 1992; Schneider 1982). Researchers estimate that as many as 70 percent of employed women have experienced behaviors that may legally constitute sexual harassment (MacKinnon 1979; Powell 1986); however, a far lower percentage of women claim to have experienced sexual harassment. Paludi and Barickman write that "the great majority of women who are abused by behavior that fits legal definitions of sexual harassment—and who are traumatized by the experience—do not label what has happened to them 'sexual harassment'" (1991, 68).

Why do most women fail to label their experiences as sexual harassment? Part of the problem is that many still do not recognize that sexual harassment is an actionable offense. Sexual harassment was first described in 1976 (MacKinnon 1979), but it was not until 1986 that the U.S. Su-

AUTHORS' NOTE: We would like to thank Margaret Andersen, Dana Britton, Kirsten Dellinger, Ricardo Gonzalez, Elizabeth Grauerholz, Suzanne Harper, Beth Schneider, Tracey Steele, Teresa Sullivan, and an anonymous reviewer for their helpful comments and criticisms.

preme Court included sexual harassment in the category of gender discrimination, thereby making it illegal (Paludi and Barickman 1991); consequently, women may not yet identify their experiences as sexual harassment because a substantial degree of awareness about its illegality has yet to be developed.

Many victims of sexual harassment may also be reluctant to come forward with complaints, fearing that they will not be believed, or that their charges will not be taken seriously (Jensen and Gutek 1982). As the Anita Hill-Clarence Thomas hearings demonstrated, women who are victims of sexual harassment often become the accused when they bring charges against their assailant.

There is another issue at stake in explaining the gap between experiencing and labeling behaviors "sexual harassment": many men and women experience some sexual behaviors in the workplace as pleasurable. Research on sexual harassment suggests that men are more likely than women to enjoy sexual interactions at work (Gutek 1985; Konrad and Gutek 1986; Reilly et al. 1992), but even some women experience sexual overtures at work as pleasurable (Pringle 1988). This attitude may be especially strong in organizations that use and exploit the bodies and sexuality of the workers (Cockburn 1991). Workers in many jobs are hired on the basis of their attractiveness and solicitousness—including not only sex industry workers, but also service sector workers such as receptionists, airline attendants, and servers in trendy restaurants. According to Cockburn (1991), this sexual exploitation is not completely forced: many people find this dimension of their jobs appealing and reinforcing to their own sense of identity and pleasure; consequently, some men and women resist efforts to expunge all sexuality from their places of work.

This is not to claim that all sexual behavior in the workplace is acceptable, even to some people. The point is that it is difficult to label behavior as sexual harassment because it forces people to draw a line between illicit and "legitimate" forms of sexuality at work—a process fraught with ambiguity. Whether a particular interaction is identified as harassment will depend on the intention of the harasser and the interpretation of the interchange by the victim, and both of these perspectives will be highly influenced by workplace culture and the social context of the specific event.

This article examines how one group of employees—restaurant workers—distinguishes between sexual harassment and other forms of sexual interaction in the workplace. We conducted an in-depth interview study of waitpeople and found that complex double standards are often used in labeling behavior as sexual harassment: identical behaviors are labeled sexual harassment in some contexts and not others. Many respondents claimed that they enjoyed sexual interactions involving coworkers of the same race/ethnicity, sexual orientation, and class/status backgrounds. Those who were offended by such interactions nevertheless dismissed them as natural or inevitable parts of restaurant culture.[1] When the same behavior occurred in contexts that upset these hegemonic heterosexual norms—in particular, when the episode involved interactions between gay and heterosexual men, or men and women of different racial/ethnic backgrounds—people seemed willing to apply the label sexual harassment

We argue that identifying behaviors that occur only in counterhegemonic contexts as sexual harassment can potentially obscure and legitimate more insidious forms of domination and exploita-

tion. As Pringle points out, "Men control women through direct use of power, but also through definitions of pleasure—which is less likely to provoke resistance" (1988, 95). Most women, she writes, actively seek out what Rich (1980) termed "compulsory heterosexuality" and find pleasure in it. The fact that men and women may enjoy certain sexual interactions in the workplace does not mean they take place outside of oppressive social relationships, nor does it imply that these routine interactions have no negative consequences for women. We argue that the practice of labeling as "sexual harassment" only those behaviors that challenge the dominant definition of acceptable sexual activity maintains and supports men's institutionalized right of sexual access and power over women.

METHODS

The occupation of waiting tables was selected to study the social definition of sexual harassment because many restaurants have a blatantly sexualized workplace culture (Cobble 1991; Paules 1991). According to a report published in a magazine that caters to restaurant owners, "Restaurants...are about as informal a workplace as there is, so much so as to actually encourage—or at the very least tolerate—sexual banter" (Anders 1993, 48). Unremitting sexual banter and innuendo, as well as physical jostling, create an environment of "compulsory jocularity" in many restaurants (Pringle 1988, 93). Sexual attractiveness and flirtation are often institutionalized parts of a waitperson's job description; consequently, individual employees are often forced to draw the line for themselves to distinguish legitimate and illegitimate expressions of sexuality, making this occupation an excellent context for examining how people determine what constitutes sexual harassment. In contrast, many more sexual behaviors may be labeled sexual harassment in less highly sexualized work environments.[2]

Eighteen in-depth interviews were conducted with male and female waitstaff who work in restaurants in Austin, Texas. Respondents were selected from restaurants that employ equal proportions of men and women on their wait staffs. Overall, restaurant work is highly sex segregated: women make up about 82 percent of all waitpeople (U.S. Department of Labor 1989), and it is common for restaurants to be staffed only by either waitresses or waiters, with men predominating in the higher-priced restaurants (Cobble 1991; Hall 1993; Paules 1991). We decided to focus only on waitpeople who work in mixed-sex groups for two reasons. First, focusing on waitpeople working on integrated staffs enables us to examine sexual harassment between co-workers who occupy the same position in an organizational hierarchy. Co-worker sexual harassment is perhaps the most common form of sexual harassment (Pryor 1987; Schneider 1982); yet most case studies of sexual harassment have examined either unequal hierarchical relationships (e.g., boss-secretary harassment) or harassment in highly skewed gender groupings (e.g., women who work in nontraditional occupations) (Benson and Thomson 1982; Carothers and Crull 1984; Gruber and Bjorn 1982). This study is designed to investigate sexual harassment in unequal hierarchical relationships, as well as harassment between organizationally equal co-workers.

Second, equal proportions of men and women in an occupation implies a high degree of male-female interaction (Gutek 1985). Waitpeople are in constant contact with each other, help each other when the restaurant is busy, and informally socialize during slack periods. In contrast, men and women have much more limited interactions in highly sex-segregated restaurants and indeed, in most work environments. The high degree of interaction among the wait staff provides ample opportunity for sexual harassment between men and women to occur and, concomitantly, less opportunity for same-sex sexual harassment to occur.

The sample was generated using "snowball" techniques and by going to area restaurants and asking waitpeople to volunteer for the study. The sample includes eight men and ten women. Four respondents are Latina/o, two African American,

and twelve White. Four respondents are gay or lesbian; one is bisexual; thirteen are heterosexual. (The gay men and lesbians in the sample are all "out" at their respective restaurants.) Fourteen respondents are single; three are married; one is divorced. Respondents' ages range from 22 to 37.

Interviews lasted approximately one hour, and they were tape-recorded and transcribed for this analysis. All interviews were conducted by the first author, who has over eight years' experience waiting tables. Respondents were asked about their experiences working in restaurants; relationships with managers, customers, and other co-workers; and their personal experiences of sexual harassment. Because interviews were conducted in the fall of 1991, when the issue was prominent in the media because of the Hill-Thomas hearings, most respondents had thought a lot about this topic.

FINDINGS

Respondents agreed that sexual banter is very common in the restaurant: staff members talk and joke about sex constantly. With only one exception, respondents described their restaurants as highly sexualized. This means that 17 of the 18 respondents said that sexual joking, touching, and fondling were common, everyday occurrences in their restaurants. For example, when asked if he and other waitpeople ever joke about sex, one waiter replied, "about 90 percent of [the jokes] are about sex." According to a waitress, "at work...[we're] used to patting and touching and hugging." Another waiter said, "I do not go through a shift without someone...pinching my nipples or poking me in the butt or grabbing my crotch.... It's just what we do at work."

These informal behaviors are tantamount to "doing heterosexuality," a process analogous to "doing gender" (West and Zimmerman 1987).[3] By engaging in these public flirtations and open discussions of sex, men and women reproduce the dominant cultural norms of heterosexuality and lend an air of legitimacy—if not inevitability—to heterosexual relationships. In other words, heterosexuality is normalized and naturalized through its ritualistic public display. Indeed, although most respondents described their workplaces as highly sexualized, several dismissed the constant sexual innuendo and behaviors as "just joking," and nothing to get upset about. Several respondents claimed that this is simply "the way it is in the restaurant business," or "just the way men are."

With only one exception, the men and women interviewed maintained that they enjoyed this aspect of their work. Heterosexuality may be normative, and in these contexts, even compulsory, yet many men and women find pleasure in its expression. Many women—as well as men—actively reproduce hegemonic sexuality and apparently enjoy its ritual expression; however, in a few instances, sexual conduct was labeled as sexual harassment. Seven women and three men said they had experienced sexual harassment in restaurant work. Of these, two women and one man described two different experiences of sexual harassment, and two women described three experiences. Table 1 describes the characteristics of each of the respondents and their experiences of sexual harassment.

We analyzed these 17 accounts of sexual harassment to find out what, if anything, these experiences shared in common. With the exception of two episodes (discussed later), the experiences that were labeled "sexual harassment" were not distinguished by any specific words or behaviors, nor were they distinguished by their degree of severity. Identical behaviors were considered acceptable if they were perpetrated by some people, but considered offensive if perpetrated by others. In other words, sexual behavior in the workplace was interpreted differently depending on the context of the interaction. In general, respondents labeled their experiences sexual harassment only if the offending behavior occurred in one of three social contexts: (1) if perpetrated by someone in a more powerful position, such as a manager; (2) if by someone of a different race/ethnicity; or (3) if perpetrated by someone of a different sexual orientation.

Our findings do not imply that sexual harassment did not occur outside of these three contexts.

Instead, they simply indicate that our respondents *labeled* behavior as "sexual harassment" when it occurred in these particular social contexts. We will discuss each of these contexts and speculate on the reasons why they were singled out by our respondents.

Powerful Position

In the restaurant, managers and owners are the highest in the hierarchy of workers. Generally, they are the only ones who can hire or fire waitpeople. Three of the women and one of the men interviewed said they had been sexually harassed by their restaurants' managers or owners. In addition, several others who did not personally experience harassment said they had witnessed managers or owners sexually harassing other waitpeople. This finding is consistent with other research indicating people are more likely to think that sexual harassment has occurred when the perpetrator is in a more powerful position (e.g., Ellis et al. 1991).

Carla describes being sexually harassed by her manager:

> One evening, [my manager] grabbed my body, not in a private place, just grabbed my body, period. He gave me like a bear hug from behind a total of four times in one night. By the end of the night I was livid. I was trying to avoid him. Then when he'd do it, I'd just ignore the conversation or the joke or whatever and walk away.

She claimed that her co-workers often give each other massages and joke about sex, but she did not label any of their behaviors sexual harassment. In fact, all four individuals who experienced sexual harassment from their managers described very similar types of behavior from their co-workers, which they did not define as sexual harassment. For example, Cathy said that she and the other waitpeople talk and joke about sex constantly: "Everybody stands around and talks about sex a lot. . . . Isn't that weird? You know, it's something about working in restaurants and, yeah, so we'll all sit around and talk about sex." She said that talking with her co-workers about sex does not constitute sexual harassment because it is "only

TABLE 1   Description of Respondents and Their Reported Experiences of Sexual Harassment at Work

PSEUDONYM	AGE	RACE[a]	SO[b]	MS[c]	YEARS IN RESTAURANT[d]	SEXUALIZED ENVIRONMENT[e]	SEXUALLY HARASSED[f]
Kate	23	W	H	S	1	yes	yes (1)
Beth	26	W	H	S	5	yes	yes (1)
Ann	29	W	H	S	1*	yes	yes (2)
Cathy	29	W	H	S	8 mos.*	yes	yes (3)
Carla	22	W	H	M	5 mos.*	yes	yes (3)
Diana	32	L	H	M	6	no	no
Maxine	30	L	H	M	4	yes	no
Laura	27	W	B	S	2*	yes	yes (1)
Brenda	23	W	L	S	3	yes	yes (2)
Lynn	37	B	L	D	5*	yes	no
Jake	22	W	H	S	1	yes	yes (1)
Al	23	W	H	S	3	yes	no
Frank	29	W	H	S	8	yes	yes (1)
John	31	W	H	S	2	yes	no
Trent	23	W	G	S	1*	yes	no
Rick	24	B	H	S	1.5	yes	yes (2)
David	25	L	H	S	5	yes	no
Don	24	L	G	S	1*	yes	no

a. Race: B = Black, L = Latina/o, W = White.

b. SO = sexual orientation: B = bisexual, G = gay, H = heterosexual, L = lesbian.

c. MS = marital status: D = divorced, M = married, S = single.

d. Years in restaurant refers to length of time employed in current restaurant. An asterisk indicates that respondent has worked in other restaurants.

e. Whether or not the respondent claimed sexual banter and touching were common occurrences in their restaurant.

f. Responded yes or no to the question: "Have you ever been sexually harassed in the restaurant?" Number in parentheses refers to number of incidents described in the interview.

joking." She does, however, view her male manager as a sexual harasser:

> *My employer is very sexist. I would call that sexual harassment. Very much of a male chauvinist pig. He kind of started [saying] stuff like, "You can't really wear those shorts because they're not flattering to your figure.... But I like the way you wear those jeans. They look real good. They're tight." It's like, you know [I want to say to him], "You're the owner, you're in power. That's evident. You know, you need to find a better way to tell me these things." We've gotten to a point now where we'll joke around now, but it's never ever sexual ever. I won't allow that with him.*

Cathy acknowledges that her manager may legitimately dictate her appearance at work, but only if he does so in professional—and not personal—terms. She wants him "to find a better way to tell me these things," implying that he is not completely out-of-line in suggesting that she wear tight pants. He "crosses the line" when he personalizes his directive, by saying to Cathy "*I like* the way you wear those jeans." This is offensive to Cathy because it is framed as the manager's personal prerogative, not the institutional requirements of the job.

Ann described a similar experience of sexual harassment from a restaurant owner:

Yeah, there's been a couple of times when a manager has made me feel real uncomfortable and I just removed myself from the situation.... Like if there's something I really want him to hear or something I think is really important there's no touching. Like, "Don't touch me while I'm talking to you." You know, because I take that as very patronizing. I actually blew up at one of the owners once because I was having a rough day and he came up behind me and he was rubbing my back, like up and down my back and saying, you know, "Oh, is Ann having a bad day?" or something like that and I shook him off of me and I said, "You do not need to touch me to talk to me."

Ann distinguishes between legitimate and illegitimate touching: if the issue being discussed is "really important"—that is, involving her job status—she insists there be no touching. In these specific situations, a back rub is interpreted as patronizing and offensive because the manager is using his powerful position for his *personal* sexual enjoyment.

One of the men in the sample, Frank, also experienced sexual harassment from a manager:

I was in the bathroom and [the manager] came up next to me and my tennis shoes were spray-painted silver so he knew it was me in there and he said something about, "Oh, what do you have in your hand there?" I was on the other side of a wall and he said, "Mind if I hold it for a while?" or something like that, you know. I just pretended like I didn't hear it.

Frank also described various sexual behaviors among the waitstaff, including fondling, "joking about bodily functions," and "making bikinis out of tortillas." He said, "I mean, it's like, what we do at work.... There's no holds barred. I don't find it offensive. I'm used to it by now. I'm guilty of it myself." Evidently, he defines sexual behaviors as "sexual harassment" only when perpetrated by someone in a position of power over him.[4]

Two of the women in the sample also described sexual harassment from customers. We place these experiences in the category of "powerful position" because customers do have limited economic power over the waitperson insofar as they control the tip (Crull 1987). Cathy said that male customers often ask her to "sit on my lap" and provide them with other sexual favors. Brenda, a lesbian, described a similar experience of sexual harassment from women customers:

One time I had this table of lesbians and they were being real vulgar towards me. Real sexual. This woman kind of tripped me as I was walking by and said, "Hurry back." I mean, gay people can tell when other people are gay. I felt harassed.

In these examples of harassment by customers, the line is drawn using a similar logic as in the examples of harassment by managers. These customers acted as though the waitresses were providing table service to satisfy the customers' private desires, instead of working to fulfill their job descriptions. In other words, the customers' demands were couched in personal—and not professional—terms, making the waitresses feel sexually harassed.

It is not difficult to understand why waitpeople singled out sexual behaviors from managers, owners, and customers as sexual harassment. Subjection to sexual advances by someone with economic power comes closest to the quid pro quo form of sexual harassment, wherein employees are given the option to either "put out or get out." Studies have found that this type of sexual harassment is viewed as the most threatening and unambiguous sort (Ellis et al. 1991; Fitzgerald 1990; Gruber and Bjorn 1982).

But even in this context, lines are drawn between legitimate and illegitimate sexual behavior in the workplace. As Cathy's comments make clear, some people accept the employers' prerogative to exploit the workers' sexuality, by dictating appropriate "sexy" dress, for example. Like airline attendants, waitresses are expected to be friendly, helpful, and sexually available to the male customers (Cobble 1991). Because this expectation is embedded in restaurant culture, it becomes difficult for workers to separate sexual harassment from the more or less accepted forms of sexual exploitation that are routine features of their jobs. Consequently, some women are reluctant to label blatantly offensive behaviors as sexual harassment. For example, Maxine, who claims that she has never experienced sexual harassment, said that customers often "talk dirty" to her:

> I remember one day, about four or five years ago when I was working as a cocktail waitress, this guy asked me for a "Slow Comfortable Screw" [the name of a drink]. I didn't know what it was. I didn't know if he was making a move or something. I just looked at him. He said, "You know what it is, right?" I said, "I bet the bartender knows!" (laughs).... There's another one, "Sex on the Beach." And there's another one called a "Screaming Orgasm." Do you believe that?

Maxine is subject to a sexualized work environment that she finds offensive; hence her experience could fit the legal definition of sexual harassment. But because sexy drink names are an institutionalized part of restaurant culture, Maxine neither complains about it nor labels it sexual harassment: Once it becomes clear that a "Slow Comfortable Screw" is a legitimate and recognized restaurant demand, she accepts it (albeit reluctantly) as part of her job description. In other words, the fact that the offensive behavior is institutionalized seems to make it beyond reproach in her eyes. This finding is consistent with others' findings that those who work in highly sexualized environments may be less likely to label offensive behavior "sexual harassment" (Gutek 1985; Konrad and Gutek 1986).

Only in specific contexts do workers appear to define offensive words and acts of a sexual nature as sexual harassment—even when initiated by someone in a more powerful position. The interviews suggest that workers use this label to describe their experiences only when their bosses or their customers couch their requests for sexual attentions in explicitly personal terms. This way of defining sexual harassment may obscure and legitimize more institutionalized—and hence more insidious—forms of sexual exploitation at work.

Race/Ethnicity

The restaurants in our sample, like most restaurants in the United States, have racially segregated staffs (Howe 1977). In the restaurants where our respondents are employed, men of color are concentrated in two positions: the kitchen cooks and bus personnel (formerly called busboys). Five of the White women in the sample reported experiencing sexual harassment from Latino men who worked in these positions. For example, when asked if she had ever experienced sexual harassment, Beth said:

> Yes, but it was not with the people . . . it was not, you know, the people that I work with in the front of the house. It was with the kitchen. There are boundaries or lines that I draw with the people I work with. In the kitchen, the lines are quite different. Plus, it's a Mexican staff. It's a very different attitude. They tend to want to touch you more and, at times, I can put up with a little bit of it but . . . because I will give them a hard time too but I won't touch them. I won't touch their butt or anything like that.

> [Interviewer: So sometimes they cross the line?]

> It's only happened to me a couple of times. One guy, like, patted me on the butt and I went off. I lost my shit. I went off on him. I said, "No. Bad. Wrong. I can't speak Spanish to you but, you know, this is it." I told the kitchen manager who is a guy and he's not . . . the head kitchen manager is not Hispanic. . . . I've had to do that over the years only a couple of times with those guys.

Beth reported that the waitpeople joke about sex and touch each other constantly, but she does not consider their behavior sexual harassment. Like many of the other men and women in the sample, Beth said she feels comfortable engaging in this sexual banter and play with the other waitpeople (who were predominantly White), but not with the Mexican men in the kitchen.

Part of the reason for singling out the behaviors of the cooks as sexual harassment may involve status differences between waitpeople and cooks. Studies have suggested that people may label behaviors as sexual harassment when they are perpetrated by people in lower status organizational positions (Grauerholz 1989; McKinney 1990); however, it is difficult to generalize about the relative status of cooks and waitpeople because of the varied and often complex organizational hierarchies of restaurants (Paules 1991, 107–10). If the cook is a chef, as in higher-priced restaurants, he or she may actually have more status than waitpeople, and indeed may have the formal power to hire and fire the waitstaff. In the restaurants where our respondents worked, the kitchen cooks did not wield this sort of formal control, but they could exert some informal power over the waitstaff by slowing down food orders or making the orders look and/or taste bad. Because bad food can decrease the waitperson's tip, the cooks can thereby control the waitperson's income; hence servers are forced to negotiate and to some extent placate the wishes and desires of cooks to perform their jobs. The willingness of several respondents to label the cooks' behavior as sexual harassment may reflect their perception that the cooks' informal demands had become unreasonable. In such cases, subjection to the offensive behaviors is a term of employment, which is quid pro quo sexual harassment. As mentioned previously, this type of sexual harassment is the most likely to be so labeled and identified.

Because each recounted case of sexual harassment occurring between individuals of different occupational statuses involved a minority man sexually harassing a White woman, the racial context seems equally important. For example, Ann also said that she and the other waiters and waitresses joke about sex and touch each other "on the butt" all the time, and when asked if she had ever experienced sexual harassment, she said,

> I had some problems at [a previous restaurant] but it was a communication problem. A lot of the guys in the kitchen did not speak English. They would see the waiters hugging on us, kissing us and pinching our rears and stuff. They would try to do it and I couldn't tell them, "No. You don't understand this. It's like we do it because we have a mu-

tual understanding but I'm not comfortable with you doing it." So that was really hard and a lot of times what I'd have to do is just sucker punch them in the chest and just use a lot of cuss words and they knew that I was serious. And there again, I felt real weird about that because they're just doing what they see go on everyday.

Kate, Carla, and Brenda described very similar racial double standards. Kate complained about a Mexican busser who constantly touched her:

> This is not somebody that I talk to on a friendly basis. We don't sit there and laugh and joke and stuff. So, when he touches me, all I know is he is just touching me and there is no context about it. With other people, if they said something or they touched me, it would be funny or... we have a relationship. This person and I and all the other people do not. So that is sexual harassment.

And according to Brenda:

> The kitchen can be kind of sexist. They really make me angry. They're not as bad as they used to be because they got warned. They're mostly Mexican, not even Mexican-American. Most of them, they're just starting to learn English.
>
> [Interviewer: What do they do to you?]
>
> Well, I speak Spanish, so I know. They're not as sexual to me because I think they know I don't like it. Some of the other girls will come through and they will touch them like here [points to the lower part of her waist].... I've had some pretty bad arguments with the kitchen.
>
> [Interviewer: Would you call that sexual harassment?]
>
> Yes. I think some of the girls just don't know better to say something. I think it happens a lot with the kitchen guys. Like sometimes, they will take a relleno in their hands like it's a penis. Sick!

Each of these women identified the sexual advances of the minority men in their restaurants as sexual harassment, but not the identical behaviors of their white male co-workers; moreover, they all recognize that they draw boundary lines differently for Anglo men and Mexican men: each of them willingly participates in "doing heterosexuality" only in racially homogamous contexts. These women called the behavior of the Mexican cooks "sexual harassment" in part because they did not "have a relationship" with these men, nor was it conceivable to them that they *could* have a relationship with them, given cultural and language barriers—and, probably, racist attitudes as well. The white men, on the other hand, can "hug, kiss, and pinch rears" of the white women because they have a "mutual understanding"—implying reciprocity and the possibility of intimacy.

The importance of this perception of relationship potential in the assessment of sexual harassment is especially clear in the cases of the two married women in the sample, Diana and Maxine. Both of these women said that they had never experienced sexual harassment. Diana, who works in a family-owned and -operated restaurant, claimed that her restaurant is not a sexualized work environment. Although people occasionally make double entendre jokes relating to sex, according to Diana, "there's no contact whatsoever like someone pinching your butt or something." She said that she has never experienced sexual harassment:

> Everybody here knows I'm married so they're not going to get fresh with me because they know that it's not going to go anywhere, you know so . . . and vice versa. You know, we know the guys' wives. They come in here to eat. It's respect all the way. I don't think they could handle it if they saw us going around hugging them. You know what I mean? It's not right.

Similarly, Maxine, who is Colombian, said she avoids the problem of sexual harassment in her workplace because she is married:

> The cooks don't offend me because they know I speak Spanish and they know how to talk with me because I set my boundaries and they know that. . . . I just don't joke with them more than I should. They all know that I'm married, first of all, so that's a no-no for all of them. My brother

> used to be a manager in that restaurant so he probably took care of everything. I never had any problems anyway in any other jobs because, like I said, I set my boundaries. I don't let them get too close to me.

> *[Interviewer. You mean physically?]*

> Not physically only. Just talking. If they want to talk about, "Do you go dancing? Where do you go dancing?" Like I just change the subject because it's none of their business and I don't really care to talk about that with them . . . not because I consider them to be on the lower levels than me or something but just because if you start talking with them that way then you are just giving them hope or something. I think that's true for most of the guys here, not just talking about the cooks. . . . I do get offended and they know that so sometimes they apologize.

Both Maxine and Diana said that they are protected from sexual harassment because they are married. In effect, they use their marital status to negotiate their interactions with their co-workers and to ward off unwanted sexual advances. Furthermore, because they do not view their co-workers as potential relationship "interests," they conscientiously refuse to participate in any sexual banter in the restaurant.

The fact that both women speak Spanish fluently may mean that they can communicate their boundaries unambiguously to those who only speak Spanish (unlike the female respondents in the sample who only speak English). For these two women, sexual harassment from co-workers is not an issue. Diana, who is Latina, talks about "respect all around" in her restaurant; Maxine claims the cooks (who are Mexican) aren't the ones who offend her. Their comments seem to reflect more mutual respect and humanity toward their Latino co-workers than the comments of the white waitresses. On the other hand, at least from Maxine's vantage point, racial harassment is a bigger problem in her workplace than is sexual harassment. When asked if she ever felt excluded from any groups at work, she said:

Yeah, sometimes. How can I explain this? Some-times, I mean, I don't know if they do it on purpose or they don't but they joke around you about being Spanish.... Sometimes it hurts. Like they say, "What are you doing here? Why don't you go back home?"

Racial harassment—like sexual harassment—is a means used by a dominant group to maintain its dominance over a subordinated group. Maxine feels that, because she is married, she is protected from sexual harassment (although, as we have seen, she is subject to a sexualized workplace that is offensive to her); however, she does experience racial harassment where she works, and she feels vulnerable to this because she is one of very few nonWhites working at her restaurant.

One of the waiters in the sample claimed that he had experienced sexual harassment from female co-workers, and race may have also been a factor in this situation. When Rick (who is African American) was asked if he had ever been sexually harassed, he recounted his experiences with some White waitresses:

Yes. There are a couple of girls there, waitpeople, who will pinch my rear.

[Interviewer: Do you find it offensive?]

No (laughs) because I'm male.... But it is a form of sexual harassment.

[Interviewer: Do you ever tell them to stop?]

If I'm really busy, if I'm in the weeds, and they want to touch me, I'll get mad. I'll tell them to stop. There's a certain time and place for every-thing.

Rick is reluctant about labeling this interaction "sexual harassment" because "it doesn't bother me unless I'm, like, busy or something like that." In those cases where he is busy, he feels that his female co-workers are subverting his work by pinching him. Because of the race difference, he may experience their behaviors as an expression of racial dominance, which probably influences his willingness to label the behavior as sexual harassment.

In sum, the interviews suggest that the per-ception and labeling of interactions as "sexual ha-rassment" may be influenced by the racial context of the interaction. If the victim perceives the ha-rasser as expressing a potentially reciprocal re-lationship interest they may be less likely to label their experience sexual harassment. In cases where the harasser and victim have a different race/ethnicity and class background, the possibil-ity of a relationship may be precluded because of racism, making these cases more likely to be la-beled "sexual harassment."

This finding suggests that the practices associ-ated with "doing heterosexuality" are profoundly racist. The White women in the sample showed a great reluctance to label unwanted sexual behavior sexual harassment when it was perpetrated by a po-tential (or real) relationship interest—that is, a White male co-worker. In contrast, minority men are socially constructed as potential harassers of White women: any expression of sexual interest may be more readily perceived as nonreciprocal and unwanted. The assumption of racial homog-amy in heterosexual relationships thus may protect White men from charges of sexual harassment of White women. This would help to explain why so many White women in the sample labeled behav-iors perpetrated by Mexican men as sexual harass-ment, but not the identical behaviors perpetrated by White men.

Sexual Orientation

There has been very little research on sexual ha-rassment that addresses the sexual orientation of the harasser and victim (exceptions include Reilly et al. 1992; Schneider 1982, 1984). Surveys of sexual harassment typically include questions about marital status but not about sexual orienta-tion (e.g., Fain and Anderton 1987; Gruber and Bjorn 1982; Powell 1986). In this study, sexual orientation was an important part of heterosexual men's perceptions of sexual harassment. Of the four episodes of sexual harassment reported by the men in the study, three involved openly gay men sexually harassing straight men. One case involved a male manager harassing a male waiter (Frank's experience, described earlier). The other two cases involved co-workers. Jake said that he had been sexually harassed by a waiter:

> Someone has come on to me that I didn't want to come on to me.... He was another waiter [male]. It was laughs and jokes the whole way until things got a little too much and it was like, "Hey, this is how it is. Back off. Keep your hands off my ass."... Once it reached the point where I felt kind of threatened and bothered by it.

Rick described being sexually harassed by a gay baker in his restaurant:

> There was a baker that we had who was really, really gay.... He was very straightforward and blunt. He would tell you, in detail, his sexual experiences and tell you that he wanted to do them with you.... I knew he was kidding but he was serious. I mean, if he had a chance he would do these things.

In each of these cases, the men expressed some confusion about the intentions of their harassers—"I knew he was kidding but he was serious." Their inability to read the intentions of the gay men provoked them to label these episodes sexual harassment. Each man did not perceive the sexual interchange as reciprocal, nor did he view the harasser as a potential relationship interest. Interestingly, however, all three of the men who described harassment from gay men claimed that sexual banter and play with other *straight* men did not trouble them. Jake, for example, said that "when men get together, they talk sex," regardless of whether there are women around. He acceded, "people find me offensive, as a matter of fact," because he gets "pretty raunchy" talking and joking about sex. Only when this talk was initiated by a gay man did Jake label it as sexual harassment.

Johnson (1988) argues that talking and joking about sex is a common means of establishing intimacy among heterosexual men and maintaining a masculine identity. Homosexuality is perceived as a direct challenge and threat to the achievement of masculinity and consequently, "the male homo-

sexual is derided by other males because he is not a real man, and in male logic if one is not a real man, one is a woman" (p. 124). In Johnson's view, this dynamic not only sustains masculine identity, it also shores up male dominance over women; thus, for some straight men, talking about sex with other straight men is a form of reasserting masculinity and male dominance, whereas talking about sex with gay men threatens the very basis for their masculine privilege. For this reason they may interpret the sex talk and conduct of gay men as a form of sexual harassment.

In certain restaurants, gay men may in fact intentionally hassle straight men as an explicit strategy to undermine their privileged position in society. For example, Trent (who is openly gay) realizes that heterosexual men are uncomfortable with his sexuality, and he intentionally draws attention to his sexuality in order to bother them:

> [Interviewer: Homosexuality gets on whose nerves?]
>
> The straight people's nerves.... I know also that we consciously push it just because, we know, "Okay. We know this is hard for you to get used to but tough luck. I've had my whole life trying to live in this straight world and if you don't like this, tough shit." I don't mean like we're shitty to them on purpose but it's like, "I've had to worry about being accepted by straight people all my life. The shoe's on the other foot now. If you don't like it, sorry."
>
> [Interviewer: Do you get along well with most of the waitpeople?]
>
> I think I get along with straight women. I get along with gay men. I get along with gay women usually. If there's ever going to be a problem between me and somebody it will be between me and a straight man.

Trent's efforts to "push" his sexuality could easily be experienced as sexual harassment by straight men who have limited experience negotiating unwanted sexual advances. The three men who reported being sexually harassed by gay men seemed genuinely confused about the intentions of their harassers, and threatened by the possibility that they would actually be subjected to and harmed by unwanted sexual advances. But it is important to point out that Trent works in a restaurant owned by lesbians, which empowers him to confront his straight male co-workers. Not all restaurants provide the sort of atmosphere that makes this type of engagement possible; indeed, some restaurants have policies explicitly banning the hiring of gays and lesbians. Clearly, not all gay men would be able to push their sexuality without suffering severe retaliation (e.g., loss of job, physical attacks).

In contrast to the reports of the straight men in this study, none of the women interviewed reported sexual harassment from their gay or lesbian co-workers. Although Maxine was worried when she found out that one of her co-workers was lesbian, she claims that this fact no longer troubles her:

> Six months ago I found out that there was a lesbian girl working there. It kind of freaked me out for a while. I was kind of aware of everything that she did towards me. I was conscious if she walked by me and accidently brushed up against me. She's cool. She doesn't bother me. She never touches my butt or anything like that. The gay guys do that to the [straight] guys but they know they're just kidding around. The [straight] guys do that to the [straight] girls, but they don't care. They know that they're not supposed to do that with me. If they do it, I stop and look at them and they apologize and they don't do it anymore. So they stay out of my way because I'm a meanie (laughs).

Some heterosexual women claimed they feel *more* comfortable working with gay men and lesbians. For example, Kate prefers working with gay men rather than heterosexual men or women. She claims that she often jokes about sex with her gay co-workers, yet she does not view them as potential harassers. Instead, she feels that her working conditions are more comfortable and more fun because she works with gay men. Similarly, Cathy prefers working with gay men over straight men because "gay men are a lot like women in that

they're very sensitive to other people's space." Cathy also works with lesbians, and she claims that she has never felt sexually harassed by them.

The gays and lesbians in the study did not report any sexual harassment from their gay and lesbian co-workers. Laura, who is bisexual, said she preferred to work with gays and lesbians instead of heterosexuals because they are "more relaxed" about sex. Brenda said she feels comfortable working around all of her male and female colleagues—regardless of their sexual orientation:

> The guys I work with [don't threaten me]. We always run by each other and pat each other on the butt. It's no big deal. Like with my girlfriend [who works at the same restaurant], all the cocktailers and hostesses love us. They don't care that we're gay. We're not a threat. We all kind of flirt but it's not sexual. A lesbian is not going to sexually harass another woman unless they're pretty gross anyway. It has nothing to do with their sexuality; it has to do with the person. You can't generalize and say that gays and lesbians are the best to work with or anything because it depends on the person.

Brenda enjoys flirtatious interactions with both men and women at her restaurant, but distinguishes these behaviors from sexual harassment. Likewise, Lynn, who is a lesbian, enjoys the relaxed sexual atmosphere at her workplace. When asked if she ever joked about sex in her workplace, she said:

> Yes! (laughs) All the time! All the time—everybody has something that they want to talk about on sex and it's got to be funny. We have guys. We have lesbians. We have straights. We have people who are real Christian-oriented. But we all jump in there and we all talk about it. It gets real funny at times…. I've patted a few butts…and I've been patted back by men, and by the women, too! (laughs)

Don and Trent, who are both gay, also said that they had never been sexually harassed in their restaurants, even though both described their restaurants as highly sexualized.

In sum, our interviews suggest that sexual orientation is an important factor in understanding each individual's experience of sexual harassment and his or her willingness to label interactions as sexual harassment. In particular, straight men may perceive gay men as potential harassers. Three of our straight male respondents claimed to enjoy the sexual banter that commonly occurs among straight men, and between heterosexual men and women, but singled out the sexual advances of gay men as sexual harassment. Their contacts with gay men may be the only context where they feel vulnerable to unwanted sexual encounters. Their sense of not being in control of the situation may make them more willing to label these episodes sexual harassment.

Our findings about sexual orientation are less suggestive regarding women. None of the women (straight, lesbian, or bisexual) reported sexual harassment from other female co-workers or from gay men. In fact, all but one of the women's reported cases of sexual harassment involved a heterosexual man. One of the two lesbians in the sample (Brenda) did experience sexual harassment from a group of lesbian customers (described earlier), but she claimed that sexual orientation is not key to her defining the situation as harassment. Other studies have shown that lesbian and bisexual women are routinely subjected to sexual harassment in the workplace (Schneider 1982, 1984); however, more research is needed to elaborate the social contexts and the specific definitions of harassment among lesbians.

The Exceptions

Two cases of sexual harassment were related by respondents that do not fit in the categories we have thus far described. These were the only incidents of sexual harassment reported between co-workers of the same race: in both cases, the sexual harasser is a white man, and the victim, a white woman. Laura—who is bisexual—was sexually harassed at a previous restaurant by a cook:

This guy was just constantly badgering me about going out with him. He like grabbed me and took me in the walk-in one time. It was a real big deal. He got fired over it too.... I was in the back doing something and he said, "I need to talk to you," and I said, "We have nothing to talk about." He like took me and threw me against the wall in the back.... I ran out and told the manager, "Oh my God. He just hit me," and he saw the expression on my face. The manager went back there...and then he got fired.

This episode of sexual harassment involved violence, unlike the other reported cases. The threat of violence was also present in the other exception, a case described by Carla. When asked if she had ever been sexually harassed, she said,

I experienced two men, in wait jobs, that were vulgar or offensive and one was a cook and I think he was a rapist. He had the kind of attitude where he would rape a woman. I mean, that's the kind of attitude he had. He would say totally, totally inappropriate [sexual] things.

These were the only two recounted episodes of sexual harassment between "equal" co-workers that involved white men and women, and both involved violence or the threat of violence.[5]

Schneider (1982, 1991) found the greatest degree of consensus about labeling behavior sexual harassment when that behavior involves violence. A victim of sexual harassment may be more likely to be believed when there is evidence of assault (a situation that is analogous to acquaintance rape). The assumption of reciprocity among homogamous couples may protect assailants with similar characteristics to their victims (e.g., class background, sexual orientation, race/ethnicity, age)—*unless* there is clear evidence of physical abuse. Defining only those incidents that involve violence as sexual harassment obscures—and perhaps even legitimizes—the more common occurrences that do not involve violence, making it all the more difficult to eradicate sexual harassment from the workplace.

DISCUSSION AND CONCLUSION

We have argued that sexual harassment is hard to identify, and thus difficult to eradicate from the workplace, in part because our hegemonic definition of sexuality defines certain contexts of sexual interaction as legitimate. The interviews with wait-people in Austin, Texas, indicate that how people currently identify sexual harassment singles out only a narrow range of interactions, thus disguising and ignoring a good deal of sexual domination and exploitation that take place at work.

Most of the respondents in this study work in highly sexualized atmospheres where sexual banter and touching frequently occur. There are institutionalized policies and practices in the workplace that encourage—or at the very least tolerate—a continual display and performance of heterosexuality. Many people apparently accept this ritual display as being a normal or natural feature of their work; some even enjoy this behavior. In the in-depth interviews, respondents labeled such experiences as sexual harassment in only three contexts: when perpetrated by someone who took advantage of their powerful position for personal sexual gain; when the perpetrator was of a different race/ethnicity than the victim—typically a minority man harassing a white woman; and when the perpetrator was of a different sexual orientation than the victim—typically a gay man harassing a straight man. In only two cases did respondents label experiences involving co-workers of the same race and sexual orientation as sexual harassment—and both episodes involved violence or the threat of violence.

These findings are based on a very small sample in a unique working environment, and hence it is not clear whether they are generalizable to other work settings. In less sexualized working environments, individuals may be more likely to label all offensive sexual advances as sexual harassment, whereas in more highly sexualized environments (such as topless clubs or striptease bars), fewer sexual advances may be labeled sexual harassment.

Our findings do suggest that researchers should pay closer attention to the interaction context of sexual harassment taking into account not only gender but also the race, occupational status, and sexual orientation of the assailant and the victim.

Of course, it should not matter who is perpetrating the sexually harassing behavior: sexual harassment should not be tolerated under any circumstances. But if members of oppressed groups (racial/ethnic minority men and gay men) are selectively charged with sexual harassment, whereas members of the most privileged groups are exonerated and excused (except in cases where institutionalized power or violence are used), then the patriarchal order is left intact. This is very similar to the problem of rape prosecution: minority men are the most likely assailants to be arrested and prosecuted, particularly when they attack white women (LaFree 1989). Straight white men who sexually assault women (in the context of marriage, dating, or even work) may escape prosecution because of hegemonic definitions of "acceptable" or "legitimate" sexual expression. Likewise, as we have witnessed in the current debate on gays in the military, straight men's fears of sexual harassment justify the exclusion of gay men and lesbians, whereas sexual harassment perpetrated by straight men against both straight and lesbian women is tolerated and even endorsed by the military establishment, as in the Tailhook investigation (Britton and Williams, forthcoming). By singling out these contexts for the label "sexual harassment," only marginalized men will be prosecuted, and the existing power structure that guarantees privileged men's sexual access to women will remain intact.

Sexual interactions involving men and women of the same race and sexual orientation have a hegemonic status in our society, making sexual harassment difficult to identify and eradicate. Our interviews suggest that many men and women are active participants in the sexualized culture of the workplace, even though ample evidence indicates that women who work in these environments suffer negative repercussions to their careers because of it (Jaschik and Fretz 1991; Paludi and Barickman 1991; Reilly et al. 1992; Schneider 1982). This is how cultural hegemony works—by getting under our skins and defining what is and is not pleasurable to us, despite our material or emotional interests.

Our findings raise difficult issues about women's complicity with oppressive sexual relationships. Some women obviously experience pleasure and enjoyment from public forms of sexual engagement with men; clearly, many would resist any attempt to eradicate all sexuality from work— an impossible goal at any rate. Yet it is also clear that the sexual "pleasure" many women seek out and enjoy at work is structured by patriarchal, racist, and heterosexist norms. Heterosexual, racially homogamous relationships are privileged in our society: they are institutionalized in organizational policies and job descriptions, embedded in ritualistic workplace practices, and accepted as legitimate, normal, or inevitable elements of workplace culture. This study suggests that only those sexual interactions that violate these policies, practices, and beliefs are resisted and condemned with the label "sexual harassment."

We have argued that this dominant social construction of pleasure protects the most privileged groups in society from charges of sexual harassment and may be used to oppress and exclude the least powerful groups. Currently, people seem to consider the gender, race, status, and sexual orientation of the assailant when deciding to label behaviors as sexual harassment. Unless we acknowledge the complex double standards people use in "drawing the line," then sexual domination and exploitation will undoubtedly remain the normative experience of women in the workforce.

NOTES

1. It could be the case that those who find this behavior extremely offensive are likely to leave restaurant work. In other words, the sample is clearly biased in that it includes only those who are currently employed in a restaurant and presumably feel more comfortable with the level of sexualized behavior than those who have left restaurant work.

2. It is difficult, if not impossible, to specify which occupations are less highly sexualized than waiting tables. Most occupations probably are sexualized in one way or another; however, specific workplaces may be more or less sexualized in terms of institutionalized job descriptions and employee tolerance of sexual banter. For example, Pringle (1988) describes some offices as coolly professional—with minimal sexual joking and play—whereas others are characterized by "compulsory jocularity." Likewise, some restaurants may de-

emphasize sexual flirtation between waitpeople and customers, and restrain informal interactions among the staff (one respondent in our sample worked at such a restaurant).

3. We thank Margaret Andersen for drawing our attention to this fruitful analogy.

4. It is also probably significant that this episode of harassment involved a gay man and a heterosexual man. This context of sexual harassment is discussed later in this article.

5. It is true that both cases involved cooks sexually harassing waitresses. We could have placed these cases in the "powerful position" category, but did not because in these particular instances, the cooks did not possess institutionalized power over the waitpeople. In other words, in these particular cases, the cook and waitress had equal organizational status in the restaurant.

REFERENCES

Anders, K. T. 1993. Bad sex: Who's harassing whom in restaurants? *Restaurant Business,* 20 January, pp. 46–54.

Benson, Donna J., and Gregg E. Thomson. 1982. Sexual harassment on a university campus: The confluence of authority relations, sexual interest and gender stratification. *Social Problems* 29:236–51.

Britton, Dana M., and Christine L. Williams. Forthcoming. Don't ask, don't tell, don't pursue: Military policy and the construction of heterosexual masculinity. *Journal of Homosexuality.*

Carothers, Suzanne C., and Peggy Crull. 1984. Contrasting sexual harassment in female- and male-dominated occupations. In *My troubles are going to have trouble with me: Everyday trials and triumphs of women workers,* edited by K. B. Sacks and D. Remy. New Brunswick, NJ: Rutgers University Press.

Cobble, Dorothy Sue. 1991. *Dishing it out: Waitresses and their unions in the twentieth century.* Urbana: University of Illinois Press.

Cockburn. Cynthia. 1991. *In the way of women.* Ithaca, NY: I.L.R. Press.

Crull, Peggy. 1987. Searching for the causes of sexual harassment: An examination of two prototypes. In *Hidden aspects of women's work,* edited by Christine Bose, Roslyn Feldberg, and Natalie Sokoloff. New York: Praeger.

Ellis, Shmuel, Azy Barak, and Adaya Pinto. 1991. Moderating effects of personal cognitions on experienced and perceived sexual harassment of women at the workplace. *Journal of Applied Social Psychology* 21:1320–37,

Fain, Terri C., and Douglas L. Anderton. 1987. Sexual harassment: Organizational context and diffuse status. *Sex Roles* 17:291–311.

Fitzgerald, Louise F. 1990. Sexual harassment: The definition and measurement of a construct. In *Ivory power: Sexual harassment on campus,* edited by Michele M. Paludi. Albany: State University of New York Press.

Grauerholz, Elizabeth. 1989. Sexual harassment of women professors by students: Exploring the dynamics of power, authority, and gender in a university setting. *Sex Roles* 21:789–801.

Gruber, James E., and Lars Bjorn. 1982. Blue-collar blues: The sexual harassment of women auto workers. *Work and Occupations* 9:271–98.

Gutek, B. A. 1985. *Sex and the workplace.* San Francisco: Jossey-Bass.

Hall, Elaine J. 1993. Waitering/waitressing: Engendering the work of table servers. *Gender & Society* 7:329–46.

Howe, Louise Kapp. 1977. *Pink collar workers: Inside the world of women's work.* New York: Avon.

Jaschik, Mollie L., and Bruce R. Fretz. 1991. Women's perceptions and labeling of sexual harassment. *Sex Roles* 25:19–23.

Jensen, Inger W., and Barbara A. Gutek. 1982. Attributions and assignment of responsibility in sexual harassment. *Journal of Social Issues* 38: 122–36.

Johnson, Miriam. 1988. *Strong mothers, weak wives.* Berkeley: University of California Press.

Konrad, Alison M., and Barbara A. Gutek. 1996. Impact of work experiences on attitudes toward sexual harassment. *Administrative Science Quarterly* 31:422–38.

LaFree, Gary D. 1989. *Rape and criminal justice: The social construction of sexual assault.* Belmont, CA: Wadsworth.

MacKinnon, Catherine A. 1979. *Sexual harassment of working women: A case of sex discrimination.* New Haven, CT: Yale University Press.

McKinney, Kathleen. 1990. Sexual harassment of university faculty by colleagues and students. *Sex Roles* 23:421–38.

Paludi, Michele, and Richard B. Barickman. 1991. *Academic and workplace sexual harassment.* Albany: State University of New York Press.

Paules, Greta Foff. 1991. *Dishing it out: Power and resistance among waitresses in a New Jersey restaurant.* Philadelphia. Temple University Press.

Powell, Gary N. 1986. Effects of sex role identity and sex on definitions of sexual harassment. *Sex Roles* 14:9–19.

Pringle, Rosemary. 1988. *Secretaries talk: Sexuality, power and work.* London: Verso.

Pryor, John B. 1987. Sexual harassment proclivities in men. *Sex Roles* 17:269–90.

Reilly, Mary Ellen, Bernice Lott, Donna Caldwell, and Luisa DeLuca. 1992. Tolerance for sexual harassment related to self-reported sexual victimization. *Gender & Society* 6:122–38.

Rich, Adrienne, 1980. Compulsory heterosexuality and lesbian existence. *Signs* 5:631–60.

Schneider, Beth E. 1982. Consciousness about sexual harassment among heterosexual and lesbian women workers. *Journal of Social Issues* 38:75–98,

———. 1984. The office affair. Myth and reality for heterosexual and lesbian women workers. *Sociological Perspectives* 27:443–64.

———. 1991. Put up and shut up: Workplace sexual assaults. *Gender & Society* 5:533–48.

U.S. Department of Labor, Bureau of Labor Statistics. 1989, January. *Employment and earnings.* Washington, DC: Government Printing Office.

West, Candace, and Don H. Zimmerman. 1987. Doing gender. *Gender & Society* 1:125–51.

40

"Their Logic against Them"

Contradictions in Sex, Race, and Class in Silicon Valley

KAREN J. HOSSFELD

The bosses here have this type of reasoning like a seesaw. One day it's "you're paid less because women are different than men," or "immigrants need less to get by." The next day it's "you're all just workers here—no special treatment just because you're female or foreigners."

Well, they think they're pretty clever with their doubletalk, and that we're just a bunch of dumb aliens. But it takes two to use a seesaw. What we're gradually figuring out here is how to use their own logic against them.

—*Filipina circuit board assembler in Silicon Valley (emphasis added)*

This chapter examines how contradictory ideologies about sex, race, class, and nationality are used as forms of both labor control and labor resistance in the capitalist workplace today. Specifically, I look at the workplace relationships between Third World immigrant women production workers and their predominantly White male managers in high-tech manufacturing industry in Silicon Valley, California. My findings indicate that in workplaces where managers and workers are divided by sex and race, class struggle can and does take gender- and race-specific forms. Managers encourage women immigrant workers to identify with their gender, racial, and national identities when the managers want to "distract" the workers from their class concerns about working conditions. Similarly, when workers have workplace needs that actually are defined by gender, nationality, or race, managers tend to deny these identities and to stress the workers' generic class position. Immigrant women workers have learned to redeploy their managers' gender and racial tactics to their own advantage, however, in order to gain more control

over their jobs. As the Filipina worker quoted at the beginning of the chapter so aptly said, they have learned to use managers' "own logic against them.". . .

This chapter draws from a larger study of the articulation of sex, race, class, and nationality in the lives of immigrant women high-tech workers (Hossfeld 1988b). Empirical data draw on more than two hundred interviews conducted between 1982 and 1986 with Silicon Valley workers; their family members, employers, and managers; and labor and community organizers. Extensive in-depth interviews were conducted with eighty-four immigrant women, representing twenty-one Third World nationalities, and with forty-one employers and managers, who represented twenty-three firms. All but five of these management representatives were U.S.-born White males. All of the workers and managers were employed in Santa Clara County, California, firms that engaged in some aspect of semiconductor "chip" manufacturing. I observed production at nineteen of these firms. . . .

SILICON VALLEY

"Silicon Valley" refers to the microelectronics-based high-tech industrial region located just south of San Francisco in Santa Clara County, California.[1]...

Class Structure and the Division of Labor

Close to 200,000 people—one out of every four employees in the San Jose Metropolitan Statistical Area labor force—work in Silicon Valley's microelectronics industry. There are more than 800 manufacturing firms that hire ten or more people each, including 120 "large" firms that each count over 250 employees. An even larger number of small firms hire fewer than ten employees apiece. Approximately half of this high-tech labor force—100,000 employees—works in production-related work: at least half of these workers—an estimated 50,000 to 70,000—are in low-paying, semiskilled operative jobs (Siegel and Borock 1982; *Annual Planning Information* 1983).[2]

The division of labor within the industry is dramatically skewed according to gender and race. Although women account for close to half of the total paid labor force in Santa Clara County both inside and outside the industry, only 18 percent of the managers, 17 percent of the professional employees, and 25 percent of the technicians are female. Conversely, women hold at least 68 percent and by some reports as many as 85 to 90 percent of the valley's high-tech operative jobs. In the companies examined in my study, women made up an average of 90 percent of the assembly and operative workers. Only rarely do they work as production managers or supervisors, the management area that works most closely with the operatives.

Similar disparities exist vis-à-vis minority employment.... Within the microelectronics industry, 12 percent of the managers, 16 percent of the professionals, and 18 percent of the technicians are minorities—although they are concentrated at the lower-paying and less powerful ends of these categories. An estimated 50 to 75 percent of the operative jobs are thought to be held by minorities.[3] My study suggests that the figure may be closer to 80 percent.

Both employers and workers interviewed in this study agreed that the lower the skill and pay level of the job, the higher the percentage of Third World immigrant women who were employed. Thus assembly work, which is the least skilled and lowest-paying production job, tends to be done predominantly by Third World women....

This occupational structure is typical of the industry's division of labor nationwide. The percentage of women of color in operative jobs is fairly standardized throughout various high-tech centers; what varies is *which* minority groups are employed, not the job categories in which they are employed.[4]

Obviously, there is tremendous cultural and historical variation both between and within the diverse national groups that my informants represent. Here I emphasize their commonalities. Their collective experience is based on their jobs, present class status, recent uprooting, and immigration. Many are racial and ethnic minorities for the first time. Finally, they have in common their gender and their membership in family households.

LABOR CONTROL ON THE SHOP FLOOR

Gender and Racial Logic

In Silicon Valley production shops, the ideological battleground is an important arena of class struggle for labor control. Management frequently calls upon ideologies and arrangements concerning sex and race, as well as class, to manipulate worker consciousness and to legitimate the hierarchical division of labor. Management taps both traditional popular stereotypes about the presumed lack of status and limited abilities of women, minorities, and immigrants and the workers' own fears, concerns, and sense of priorities as immigrant women.

But despite management's success in disempowering and devaluing labor, immigrant women workers have co-opted some of these ideologies and have developed others of their own, playing on management's prejudices to the workers' own advantage. In so doing, the workers turn the "logic" of capital against managers, as they do the intertwining logics of patriarchy and racism. The following section examines this sex- and race-based logic and how it affects class structure and struggle. I then focus on women's resistance to this manipulation and their use of gender and racial logics for their own advantage.

From interviews with Silicon Valley managers and employers, it is evident that high-tech firms find immigrant women particularly appealing workers not only because they are "cheap" and considered easily "expendable" but also because management can draw on and further exploit pre-existing patriarchal and racist ideologies and arrangements that have affected these women's consciousness and realities. In their dealings with the women, managers fragment the women's multifaceted identities into falsely separated categories of "worker," "ethnic," and "woman." The effect is to increase and play off the workers' vulnerabilities and splinter their consciousness. But I also found limited examples of the women drawing strength from their multifaceted experiences and developing a unified consciousness with which to confront their oppressions. These instances of how the workers have manipulated management's ideology are important not only in their own right but as models. To date, though, management holds the balance of power in this ideological struggle.

I label management's tactics "gender-specific" and "racial-specific" forms of labor control and struggle, or gender and racial "logic." I use the term *capital logic* to refer to strategies by capitalists to increase profit maximization. Enforcement by employers of a highly stratified class division of labor as a form of labor control is one such strategy. Similarly, I use the terms *gender logic* and *racial logic* to refer to strategies to promote gender and racial hierarchies. Here I am concerned primarily with the ways in which employers and managers devise and incorporate gender and racial logic in the interests of capital logic.

Attempts to legitimate inequality form my main examples.

I focus primarily on managers' "gender-specific" tactics because management uses race-specific (il)logic much less directly in dealing with workers. Management clearly draws on racist assumptions in hiring and dealing with its workforce, but usually it makes an effort to conceal its racism from workers. Management recognizes, to varying degrees, that the appearance of blatant racism against workers is not acceptable, mainly because immigrants have not sufficiently internalized racism to respond to it positively. Off the shop floor, however, the managers' brutal and open racism toward workers was apparent during "private" interviews. Managers' comments demonstrate that racism is a leading factor in capital logic but that management typically disguises racist logic by using the more socially acceptable "immigrant logic." Both American and immigrant workers tend to accept capital's relegation of immigrants to secondary status in the labor market.

Conversely, "gender logic" is much less disguised: management uses it freely and directly to control workers. Patriarchal and sexist ideology is *not* considered inappropriate. Because women workers themselves have already internalized patriarchal ideology, they are more likely to "agree" with or at least accept it than they are racist assumptions. This chapter documents a wide range of sexist assumptions that management employs in order to control and divide workers.

Gender Ideology

A growing number of historical and contemporary studies illustrate the interconnections between patriarchy and capitalism in defining both the daily lives of working women and the nature of work arrangements in general. Sallie Westwood, for example, suggests that on-the-job exploitation of women workers is rooted in part in patriarchal ideology. Westwood states that ideologies "play a vital part in calling forth a sense of self linked to class and gender as well as race. Thus, a patriarchal ideology intervenes on the shop floor culture to make anew the conditions of work under capitalism" (1985:6).

One way in which patriarchal ideology affects workplace culture is through the "gendering" of workers—what Westwood refers to as "the social construction of masculinity and femininity on the shop floor" (page 6). The forms of work culture that managers encourage, and that women workers choose to develop, are those that reaffirm traditional forms of femininity. This occurs in spite of the fact that, or more likely because, the women are engaged in roles that are traditionally defined as nonfeminine: factory work and wage earning. My data suggest that although factory work and wage earning are indeed traditions long held by working-class women, the dominant *ideology* that such tasks are "unfeminine" is equally traditional. For example, I asked one Silicon Valley assembler who worked a double shift to support a large family how she found time and finances to obtain elaborate manicures, makeup, and hair stylings. She said that they were priorities because they "restored [her] sense of femininity." Another production worker said that factory work "makes me feel like I'm not a lady, so I have to try to compensate."

This ideology about what constitutes proper identity and behavior for women is multileveled. First, women workers have a clear sense that wage earning and factory work in general are not considered "feminine." This definition of "feminine" derives from an upper-class reality in which women traditionally did not need (and men often did not allow them) to earn incomes. The reality for a production worker who comes from a long line of factory women does not negate the dominant ideology that influences her to say, "At work I feel stripped of my womanhood. I feel like I'm not a lady anymore. It makes me feel . . . unattractive and unfeminine."

Second, women may feel "unwomanly" at work because they are away from home and family, which conflicts with ideologies, albeit changing ones, that they should be home. And third, earning wages at all is considered "unwifely" by some women, by their husbands, or both because it strips men of their identity as "breadwinner."

On the shop floor, managers encourage workers to associate "femininity" with something contradictory to factory work. They also encourage women workers to "compensate" for their perceived loss of femininity. This strategy on the part of management serves to devalue women's productive worth.

Under contemporary U.S. capitalism, ideological legitimation of women's societal roles and of their related secondary position in the division of labor is already strong outside the workplace. Management thus does not need to devote extreme efforts to developing new sexist ideologies within the workplace in order to legitimate the gender division of labor. Instead, managers can call on and reinforce preexisting ideology. Nonetheless, new forms of gender ideology are frequently introduced. These old and new ideologies are disseminated both on an individual basis, from a manager to a worker or workers, and on a collective basis, through company programs, policies, and practices. Specific examples of informal ways in which individual managers encourage gender identification, such as flirting, dating, sexual harassment, and promoting "feminine" behavior, are given below. The most widespread company practice that encourages engenderment, of course, is hiring discrimination and job segregation based on sex.

An example of a company policy that divides workers by gender is found in a regulation one large firm has regarding color-coding of smocks that all employees in the manufacturing division are required to wear. While the men's smocks are color-coded according to occupation, the women's are color-coded by sex, regardless of occupation. This is a classic demonstration of management's encouragement of male workers to identify according to job and class and its discouragement of women from doing the same. Regardless of what women do as workers, the underlying message reads, they are nevertheless primarily women. The same company has other practices and programs that convey the same message. Their company newsletter, for example, includes a column entitled "Ladies' Corner," which runs features on cooking and fashion tips for "the working gal." A manager at this plant says that such "gender tactics," as I call them, are designed to "boost morale by reminding the gals that even though they do unfeminine work, they really are still feminine." But although some women workers may value femininity, in the work world, management identifies feminine traits as legitimation for devaluation.

In some places, management offers "refeminization" perks to help women feel "compensated" for their perceived "defeminization" on the job. A prime example is the now well-documented makeup sessions and beauty pageants for young women workers sponsored by multinational electronics corporations at their Southeast Asian plants (Grossman 1979; Ong 1985). While such events are unusual in Silicon Valley, male managers frequently use flirting and dating as "refeminization" strategies. Flirting and dating in and of themselves certainly cannot be construed as capitalist plots to control workers; however, when they are used as false compensation for and to divert women from poor working conditions and workplace alienation, they in effect serve as a form of labor control. In a society where women are taught that their femininity is more important than other aspects of their lives—such as how they relate to their work—flirting can be divisive. And when undesired, flirting can also develop into a form of sexual harassment, which causes further workplace alienation.

One young Chinese production worker told me that she and a co-worker avoided filing complaints about illegal and unsafe working conditions because they did not want to annoy their White male supervisor, whom they enjoyed having flirt with them. These two women would never join a union, they told me, because the same supervisor told them that all women who join unions "are a bunch of tough, big-mouthed dykes." Certainly these women have the option of ignoring

this man's opinions. But that is not easy, given the one-sided power he has over them not only because he is their supervisor, but because of his age, race, and class.

When women workers stress their "feminine" and female characteristics as being counter to their waged work, a contradictory set of results can occur. On one hand, the women may legitimate their own devaluation as workers, and, in seeking identity and solace in their "femininity," discard any interest in improving their working conditions. On the other hand, if turning to their identities as female, mother, mate, and such allows them to feel self-esteem in one arena of their lives, that self-esteem may transfer to other arenas. The outcome is contingent on the ways in which the women define and experience themselves as female or "feminine." Femininity in White American capitalist culture is traditionally defined as passive and ineffectual, as Susan Brownmiller explores (1984). But there is also a female tradition of resistance.

The women I interviewed rarely pose their womanhood or their self-perceived femininity as attributes meriting higher pay or better treatment. They expect *differential* treatment because they are women, but "differential" inevitably means lower paid in the work world. The women present their self-defined female attributes as creating additional needs that detract from their financial value. Femininity, although its definition varies among individuals and ethnic groups, is generally viewed as something that subtracts from a woman's market value, even though a majority of women consider it personally desirable.

In general, both the women and men I interviewed believe that women have many needs and skills discernible from those of male workers, but they accept the ideology that such specialness renders them less deserving than men of special treatment, wages, promotions, and status. Conversely, both the men and women viewed men's special needs and skills as rendering men more deserving. Two of the classic perceived sex differentials cited by employers in electronics illustrate this point.

First, although Silicon Valley employers consistently repeat the old refrain that women are better able than men to perform work requiring manual skills, strong hand-eye coordination, and extreme patience, they nonetheless find it appropriate to pay workers who have these skills (women) less than workers who supposedly do not have them (men). Second, employers say that higher entry-level jobs, wages, and promotions rightly belong to heads of households, but in practice they give such jobs only to men, regardless of their household situation, and exclude women, regardless of theirs.

When a man expresses special needs that result from his structural position in the family—such as head of household—he is often "compensated," yet when a woman expresses a special need resulting from her traditional structural position in the family-child care or her position as head of household—she is told that such issues are not of concern to the employer or, in the case of child care, that it detracts from her focus on her work and thus devalues her productive contribution. This is a clear illustration of Heidi Hartmann's definition of patriarchy: social relationships between men, which, although hierarchical, such as those between employer and worker, have a material base that benefits men and oppresses women (1976).

Definitions of femininity and masculinity not only affect the workplace but are in turn affected by it. Gender is produced and reproduced in and through the workplace, as well as outside it. Gender identities and relationships are formed on the work floor both by the labor process organized under capitalism and by workers' resistance to that labor process. "Femininity" in its various permutations is not something all-bad and all-disempowering: women find strength, pride, and creativity in some of its forms. . . . I turn now to one of the other tenets of women workers' multi-tiered consciousness that employers find advantageous: gender logic that poses women's work as "secondary."

THE LOGIC OF "SECONDARY" WORK

Central to gender-specific capital logic is the assumption that women's paid work is both secondary and temporary. More than 70 percent of the employers and 80 percent of the women workers I interviewed stated that a woman's primary jobs are those of wife, mother, and homemaker, even when she works full time in the paid labor force. Because employers view women's primary job as in the home, and they assume that, prototypically, every woman is connected to a man who is bringing in a larger paycheck, they claim that women do not need to earn a full living wage. Employers repeatedly asserted that they believed the low-level jobs were filled only by women because men could not afford to or would not work for such low wages.

Indeed, many of the women would not survive on what they earned unless they pooled resources. For some, especially the nonimmigrants, low wages did mean dependency on men—or at least on family networks and household units. None of the women I interviewed—immigrant or nonimmigrant—lived alone. Yet most of them would be financially better off without their menfolk. For most of the immigrant women, their low wages were the most substantial and steady source of their family's income. *Eighty percent of the immigrant women workers in my study were the largest per annum earners in their households.*

Even when their wages were primary—the main or only family income—the women still considered men to be the major breadwinners. The women considered their waged work as secondary, both in economic value and as a source of identity. Although most agreed that women and men who do exactly the same jobs should be paid the same, they had little expectation that as women they would be eligible for higher-paying "male" jobs. While some of these women—particularly the Asians—believed they could overcome racial and class barriers in the capitalist division of labor, few viewed gender as a division that could be changed. While they may believe that hard work can overcome many obstacles and raise their *families'* socioeconomic class standing, they do not feel that their position in the gender division of labor will change. Many, of course, expect or hope for better jobs for themselves—and others expect or hope to leave the paid labor force altogether— but few wish to enter traditional male jobs or to have jobs that are higher in status or earnings than the men in their families.

The majority of women who are earning more than their male family members view their situation negatively and hope it will change soon. They do not want to earn less than they currently do; rather, they want their menfolk to earn more. This was true of women in all the ethnic groups....

As in the rest of America, in most cases, the men earned more in those households where both the women and men worked regularly. In many of the families, however, the men tended to work less regularly than the women and to have higher unemployment rates. While most of the families vocally blamed very real socioeconomic conditions for the unemployment, such as declines in "male" industrial sector jobs, many women also felt that their husbands took out their resentment on their families. A young Mexicana, who went to a shelter for battered women after her husband repeatedly beat her, described her extreme situation:

> He knows it's not his fault or my fault that he lost his job: they laid off almost his whole shift. But he acts like I keep my job just to spite him, and it's gotten so I'm so scared of him. Sometimes I think he'd rather kill me or have us starve than watch me go to work and bring home pay. He doesn't want to hurt me, but he is so hurt inside because he feels he has failed as a man.

Certainly not all laid-off married men go to the extreme of beating their wives, but the majority of married women workers whose husbands had gone through periods of unemployment said that the men treated other family members significantly worse when they were out of work. When capitalism rejects male workers, they often use patriarchal channels to vent their anxieties. In a world where men are defined by their control over their environment, losing control in one arena, such as that of the work world, may lead them to tighten control in another arena in which they still have power—the family. This classic cycle is not unique to Third World immigrant communities, but as male unemployment increases in these communities, so may the cycle of male violence.

Even some of the women who recognize the importance of their economic role feel that their status and identity as wage earners are less important than those of men. Many of the women feel that men work not only for income but for respect and dignity. They see their own work as less noble. Although some said they derive satisfaction from their ability to hold a job, none of the women considered her job to be a primary part of her identity or a source of self-esteem. These women see themselves as responsible primarily for the welfare of their families: their main identity is as mother, wife, sister, and daughter, not as worker. Their waged work is seen as an extension of caring for their families. It is not a question of *choosing* to work—they do so out of economic necessity.

When I asked whether their husbands' and fathers' waged work could also be viewed as an extension of familial duties, the women indicated that they definitely perceived a difference. Men's paid labor outside the home was seen as integral both to the men's self-definition and to their responsibility vis-à-vis the family; conversely, women's labor force participation was seen as contradictory both to the women's self-image and to their definitions of female responsibility.

Many immigrant women see their wage contribution to the family's economic survival not only as secondary but as *temporary*, even when they have held their jobs for several years. They expect to quit their production jobs after they have saved enough money to go to school, stay home full time, or open a family business. In actuality, however, most of them barely earn enough to live on, let alone to save, and women who think they are signing on for a brief stint may end up staying in the industry for years.

That these workers view their jobs as temporary has important ramifications for both employers and unions, as well as for the workers themselves. When workers believe they are on board a company for a short time, they are more likely to put up with poor working conditions, because they see them as short term.. . .

Employers are thus at an advantage in hiring these women at low wages and with little job security. They can play on the women's *own* consciousness as wives and mothers whose primary identities are defined by home and familial roles. While the division of labor prompts the workers to believe that women's waged work is less valuable than men's, the women workers themselves arrive in Silicon Valley with this ideology already internalized.

A young Filipina woman, who was hired at a walk-in interview at an electronics production facility, experienced a striking example of the contradictions confronting immigrant women workers in the valley. Neither she nor her husband, who was hired the same day, had any previous related work experience or degrees. Yet her husband was offered an entry-level job as a technician, while she was offered an assembly job paying three dollars per hour less. The personnel manager told her husband that he would "find [the technician job] more interesting than assembly work." The woman had said in the interview that she wanted to be considered for a higher-paying job because she had two children to support. The manager refused to consider her for a different job, she said, and told her that "it will work out fine for you, though, because with your husband's job, and you *helping out* [emphasis added] you'll have a nice little family income."

The same manager told me on a separate occasion that the company preferred to hire members of the same families because it meant that workers' relatives would be more supportive about their working and the combined incomes would put less financial strain on individual workers. This concern over workers and their families dissipated, however, when the Filipino couple split up, leaving the wife with only the "helping-out" pay

instead of the "nice little family income." When the woman requested a higher-paying job so she could support her family, the same manager told her that "family concerns were out of place at work" and did not promote her.. . .

RESISTANCE ON THE SHOP FLOOR

There is little incidence in Silicon Valley production shops of *formal* labor militancy among the immigrant women, as evidenced by either union participation or collectively planned mass actions such as strikes. Filing formal grievances is not common in these workers' shop culture. Union activity is very limited, and both workers and managers claim that the incidence of complaints and disturbances on the shop floor is lower than in other industries. Pacing of production to restrict output does occur, and there are occasionally "informal" incidents, such as spontaneous slowdowns and sabotage. But these actions are rare and usually small in scale. Definitions of workplace militancy and resistance vary, of course, according to the observer's cultural background, but by their *own* definitions, the women do not frequently engage in traditional forms of labor militancy.

There is, however, an important, although often subtle, arena in which the women do engage in struggle with management: the ideological battleground. Just as employers and managers harness racist, sexist, and class-based logic to manipulate and control workers, so too workers use this logic against management. In the ideological arena, the women do not merely accept or react to the biased assumptions of managers: they also develop gender-, class-, and race-based logic of their own when it is to their advantage. The goal of these struggles is not simply ideological victory but concrete changes in working conditions. Further, in Silicon Valley, immigrant women workers have found that managers respond more to workers' needs when they are couched in ethnic or gender terms, rather than in class and labor terms. Thus, class struggle on the shop floor is often disguised as arguments about the proper place and appropriate behavior of women, racial minorities, and immigrants.

When asked directly, immigrant women workers typically deny that they engage in any form of workplace resistance or efforts to control their working conditions. This denial reflects not only workers' needs to protect clandestine activities, but also their consciousness about what constitutes resistance and control. In their conversations with friends and co-workers, the women joke about how they outfoxed their managers with female or ethnic "wisdom." Yet most of the women do not view their often elaborate efforts to manipulate their managers' behavior as forms of struggle. Rather, they think of their tactics "just as ways to get by," as several workers phrased it. It is from casual references to these tactics that a portrait of worker logic and resistance emerges. . . .

The vast majority of these women clearly wish to avoid antagonizing management. Thus, rather than engaging in confrontational resistance strategies, they develop less obvious forms than, say, work stoppages, filing grievances, and straightforwardly refusing to perform certain tasks, all of which have frequently been observed in other industrial manufacturing sectors. Because the more "quiet" forms of resistance and struggle for workplace control engaged in by the women in Silicon Valley are often so discrete and the workers are uncomfortable discussing them, it is probable that there are more such acts and they are broader in scope than my examples imply. As a Chinese woman in her forties who has worked as an operative in the valley for six years explained:

> Everybody who does this job does things to get through the day, to make it bearable. There are some women who will tell you they never do anything unproper or sneaky, but you are not to believe them. The ones that look the most demure are always up to something. . . . There's not anybody here who has never purposefully broken something, slowed down work, told fibs to the supervisor, or some such thing. And there's probably no

one but me with my big mouth who would admit it! . . .

The most frequently mentioned acts of resistance against management and work arrangements were ones that played on the White male managers' consciousness—both false and real—about gender and ethnic culture. Frequently mentioned examples involved workers who turned management's ideologies against them by exploiting their male supervisors' misconceptions about "female problems." A White chip tester testified:

> It's pretty ironic because management seems to have this idea that male supervisors handle female workers better than female supervisors. You know, we're supposed to turn to mush whenever he's around and respect his authority or something. But this one guy we got now lets us walk all over him. He thinks females are flighty and irresponsible because of our hormones—so we make sure to have as many hormone problems as we can. I'd say we each take hormone breaks several times a day. My next plan is to convince him that menstrual blood will turn the solvents bad, so on those days we have to stay in the lunchroom!

A Filipina woman production worker recounted another example:

> The boss told us girls that we're not strong enough to do the heavy work in the men's jobs—and those jobs pay more, too. So, I suddenly realized that gosh, us little weak little things shouldn't be lifting all those heavy boxes of circuit board parts we're supposed to carry back and forth all the time—and I stopped doing it.
>
> The boss no longer uses that "it's too heavy for you girls" line anymore . . . but I can tell he's working on a new one. That's okay; I got plenty of responses.

A Mexican wafer fabricator, whose unit supervisor was notorious for the "refeminization" perks discussed above, told of how she manipulated the male supervisor's gender logic to disguise what was really an issue of class struggle:

I was getting really sick from all the chemicals we have to work with, and I was getting a rash from them on my arms. [The manager] kept saying I was exaggerating and gave the usual line about you can't prove what caused the rash. One day we had to use an especially harsh solvent, and I made up this story about being in my sister's wedding. I told him that the solvents would ruin my manicure, and I'd be a mess for the wedding. Can you believe it? He let me off the work! This guy wouldn't pay attention to my rash, but when my manicure was at stake, he let me go!

Of course, letting this worker avoid chemicals for one day because of a special circumstance is more advantageous to management than allowing her and others to avoid the work permanently because of health risks. Nonetheless, the worker was able to carve out a small piece of bargaining power by playing off her manager's gender logic. The contradiction of these tactics that play up feminine frailty is that they achieve short-term, individual goals at the risk of reinforcing damaging stereotypes about women, including the stereotype that women workers are not as productive as men. From the workers' point of view, however, the women are simply using the prejudices of the powerful to the advantages of the weak.

Another "manicure" story resulted in a more major workplace change at one of the large plants. Two women fabricator operatives, one Portuguese and one Chicana, applied for higher-paying technician jobs whereupon their unit supervisor told them that the jobs were too "rough" for women and that the work would "ruin their nails." The women's response was to pull off their rubber gloves and show him what the solvents and dopants had done to their nails, despite the gloves. (One of the most common chemicals used in chip manufacturing is acetone, the key ingredient in nail polish removal. It also eats right through "protective" rubber gloves.) After additional goading and bargaining, the supervisor provisionally let them transfer to technician work.

Although the above are isolated examples, they represent tactics that workers can use either to challenge or play off sexist ideology that employers use to legitimate women's low position in the segregated division of labor. Certainly there are not enough instances of such behavior to challenge the inequality between worker and boss, but they do demonstrate to managers that gender logic cannot always be counted on to legitimate inequality between male and female workers. And dissolving divisions between workers is a threat to management hegemony.

RACIAL AND ETHNIC LOGIC

Typically, high-tech firms in Silicon Valley hire production workers from a wide spectrum of national groups. If their lack of a common language (both linguistically and culturally) serves to fragment the labor force, capital benefits. Conversely, management may find it more difficult to control workers with whom it cannot communicate precisely. Several workers said they have feigned a language barrier in order to avoid taking instructions; they have also called forth cultural taboos—both real and feigned—to avoid undesirable situations. One Haitian woman, who took a lot of kidding from her employer about voodoo and black magic, insisted that she could not work the night shift because evil spirits were out then. Because she was a good worker, the employer let her switch to days. When I tried to establish whether she believed the evil spirits were real or imagined, she laughed and said, "Does it matter? The result is the same: I can be home at night with my kids."

Management in several plants believed that racial and national diversity minimized solidarity. According to one supervisor, workers were forbidden from sitting next to people of their own nationality (i.e., language group) in order to "cut down on the chatting." Workers quickly found two ways to reverse this decision, using management's own class, racial, and gender logic. Chinese women workers told the supervisor that if they were not "chaperoned" by other Chinese women, their families would not let them continue to work there. Vietnamese women told him that the younger Vietnamese women would not work hard unless they were under the eyes of the older workers and that a group of newly hired Vietnamese workers would not learn to do the job right unless they had someone who spoke their language to explain it to them. Both of these arguments could also be interpreted as examples of older workers wanting to control younger ones in a generational hierarchy, but this was not the case. Afterwards both the Chinese and the Vietnamese women laughed among themselves at their cleverness. Nor did they forget the support needs of workers from other ethnic groups: they argued with the supervisor that the same customs and needs held true for many of the language groups represented, and the restriction was rescinded.

Another example of a large-scale demonstration of interethnic solidarity on the shop floor involved workers playing off supervisors' stereotypes regarding the superior work of Asians over Mexicans. The incident was precipitated when a young Mexicana, newly assigned to an assembly unit in which a new circuit board was being assembled, fell behind in her quota. The supervisor berated her with racial slurs about Mexicans' "laziness" and "stupidity" and told her to sit next to and "watch the Orientals." As a group, the Asian women she was stationed next to slowed down their production, thereby setting the average quota on the new boards at a slower than usual pace. The women were in fits of laughter after work because the supervisor had assumed that the speed set by the Asians was the fastest possible, since they were the "best" workers.

Hispanic workers also turn management's anti-Mexican prejudices against them, as a Salvadorean woman explained:

First of all, the bosses think everyone from Latin American is Mexican, and they think all Mexicans

are dumb. So, whenever they try to speed up production, or give us something we don't want to do, we just act dumb. It's not as if you act smart and you get a promotion or a bonus anyway.

A Mexicana operative confided, "They [management] assume we don't understand much English, but we understand when we want to."

A Chinese woman, who was under five feet tall and who identified her age by saying she was a "grandmother," laughingly told how she had her White male supervisor "wrapped around [her] finger." She consciously played into his stereotype that Asian women are small, timid, and obedient by frequently smiling at and bowing to him and doing her job carefully. But when she had a special need, to take a day or a few hours off, for example, she would put on her best guileless, ingratiating look and, full of apologies, usually obtained it. She also served as a voice for co-workers whom the supervisor considered more abrasive. On one occasion, when three White women in her unit complained about poor lighting and headaches, the supervisor became irritated and did not respond to their complaint. Later that week the Chinese "grandmother" approached him, saying that she was concerned that poor lighting was limiting the workers' productivity. The lighting was quickly improved. This incident illustrates that managers can and do respond to workers' demands when they result in increased productivity.

Some workers see strategies to improve and control their work processes and environments as contradictory and as "Uncle Tomming." Two friends, both Filipinas, debated this issue. One argued that "acting like a China doll" only reinforced white employers' stereotypes, while the other said that countering the stereotype would not change their situation, so they might as well use the stereotype to their advantage. The same analysis applies to women workers who consciously encourage male managers to view women as different from men in their abilities and characteristics. For women and minority workers, the need for short-term gains and benefits and for long-term equal treatment is a constant contradiction. And for the majority of workers, short-term tactics are unlikely to result in long-term equality.

POTENTIAL FOR ORGANIZING

Obviously, the lesson here for organizing is contradictory. Testimonies such as the ones given in these pages clearly document that immigrant women are not docile, servile people who always follow orders, as many employers interviewed for this study claimed. Orchestrating major actions such as family migration so that they could take control of and better their lives has helped these women develop leadership and survival skills. Because of these qualities, many of the women I interviewed struck me as potentially effective labor and community organizers and rank-and-file leaders. Yet almost none of them were interested in collective organizing, because of time limitations and family constraints and because of their lack of confidence in labor unions, the feminist movement, and community organizations. Many were simply too worn out from trying to make ends meet and caring for their families. And for some, the level of inequality and exploitation on the shop floor did not seem that bad, compared to their past experiences....

Nonetheless, their past torment does not reduce the job insecurity, poor working conditions, pay inequality, and discrimination so many immigrant workers in Silicon Valley experience in their jobs. In fact, as informants' testimonies suggest, in many cases, past hardships have rendered them less likely to organize collectively. At the same time, individual acts of resistance do not succeed on their own in changing the structured inequality of the division of labor. Most of these actions remain at the agitation level and lack the coordination needed to give workers real bargaining power. And, as mentioned, individual strategies that workers have devised can be contradictory. Simultaneous to winning short-run victories, they can also reinforce both gender and racial stereotypes in the long run. Further, because many of these victories are isolated and individual, they can often be divisive. For workers to gain both greater workplace control *and* combat sexism and racism, organized *collective* strategies hold greater possibilities....

My findings indicate that Silicon Valley's immigrant women workers have a great deal to gain from organizing, but also a great deal to contribute. They have their numeric strength, but also a wealth of creativity, insight, and experience that could be a shot in the arm to the stagnating national labor movement. They also have a great deal to teach—and learn from—feminist and ethnic community movements. But until these or new alternative movements learn to speak and listen to these women, the women will continue to struggle on their own, individually and in small groups. In their struggle for better jobs and better lives, one of the most effective tactics they have is their own resourcefulness in manipulating management's "own logic against them."

NOTES

1. For a comprehensive analytical description of the development of Silicon Valley as a region and an industry, see Saxenian 1981.
2. These production jobs include the following U.S. Department of Labor occupational titles: semiconductor processor; semiconductor assembler; electronics assembler; and electronics tester. Entry-level wages for these jobs in Silicon Valley in 1984 were $4.00 to $5.50; wages for workers with one to two years or more experience were $5.50 to $8.00 an hour, with testers sometimes earning up to $9.50.
3. "Minority" is the term used by the California Employment Development Department and the U.S. Department of Labor publications in reference to people of color. The statistics do not distinguish between immigrants and non-immigrants within racial and ethnic groupings.
4. In North Carolina's Research Triangle, for example, Blacks account for most minority employment, whereas

in Albuquerque and Texas, Hispanics provide the bulk of the production labor force. Silicon Valley has perhaps the most racially diverse production force, although Hispanics—both immigrant and nonimmigrant—still account for the majority.

REFERENCES

Annual Planning Information: San Jose Standard Metropolitan Statistical Area, 1983–1984. 1983. Sacramento: California Department of Employment Development.

Brownmiller, Susan. 1984. *Femininity.* New York: Simon and Schuster.

Grossman, Rachel. 1979. "Women's Place in the Integrated Circuit." *Southeast Asia Chronicle* 66—*Pacific Research* 9:2–17.

———. 1980. "Bitter Wages: Women in East Asia's Semiconductor Plants." *Multinational Monitor* 1 (March):8–11.

Hartmann, Heidi. 1976. "Capitalism, Patriarchy, and Job Segregation by Sex." In *Women in the Workplace,* ed. Martha Blaxall and Barbara Reagan, 137–70. Chicago: University of Chicago Press.

Hossfeld, Karen. 1988a. "Divisions of Labor, Divisions of Lives: Immigrant Women Workers in Silicon Valley." Ph.D. diss., University of California, Santa Cruz.

———. 1988b. "The Triple Shift: Immigrant Women Workers and the Household Division of Labor in Silicon Valley." Paper presented at the annual meetings of the American Sociological Association, Atlanta.

Ong, Aihwa. 1985. "Industrialization and Prostitution in Southeast Asia." *Southeast Asia Chronicle* 96: 2–6.

Saxenian, Annalee. 1981. *Silicon Chips and Spatial Structure: The Industrial Basis of Urbanization in Santa Clara County, California.* Working Paper no. 345. Berkeley: Institute of Urban and Regional Planning, University of California.

Siegel, Lenny, and Herb Borock. 1982. *Background Report on Silicon Valley.* Prepared for the U.S. Commission on Civil Rights. Mountain View, Calif.: Pacific Studies Center.

Westwood, Sallie. 1985. *All Day, Every Day: Factory and Family in the Making of Women's Lives.* Champaign: University of Illinois Press.

41

Shortchanged
Restructuring Women's Work

TERESA AMOTT

...The [economic] crisis has had different effects on men and women. In some ways, and for some women, the economic crisis has not been as severe as it has been for men. In other ways, and for other women, the crisis has been far more severe.

Throughout the crisis women continued to join the labor force, both to support themselves and their families and to find satisfaction in working outside the home. Companies, seeking to bolster their profits, hired women in order to cut labor costs. In fact, hiring women was a central part of the corporate strategy to restore profitability because women were not only cheaper than men, but were also less likely to be organized into unions and more willing to accept temporary work and no benefits. Women were hired rather than men in a variety of industries and occupations, in the United States and abroad. This led to what has been called the "feminization" of the labor force, as women moved into jobs that had previously been held only by men and as jobs that were already predominantly female became even more so.... This "feminization" of the workforce, in which women substitute for men, explains why women's unemployment rates, on average, were lower than men's during the 1980s.

Each of the corporate and government responses to the crisis...had its most damaging effects on a particular group (or groups) of workers. Union-busting, for instance, took its toll *primarily* on the manufacturing jobs that have been dominated by White men (although a weakened labor movement damages the bargaining power of all workers, as we see below). Capital flight also *pri-marily* affected men's manufacturing jobs, although it also affected women in the service sector and women who work in primarily female manufacturing jobs, such as the garment industry.

SEGREGATION AND SEGMENTATION

The way women experience the economic crisis depends on where they are located in the occupational hierarchy. One concept that will help us understand this hierarchy is *occupational segregation,* which can be by gender—most jobs are held by either men *or* women and few are truly integrated. To take one extreme example, in 1990, 82 percent of architects were male; 95 percent of typists were female. Occupational segregation can also be by race-ethnicity, although this is sometimes more difficult to detect—since racial-ethnic workers are a minority, they rarely dominate a job category numerically, although they may be in the majority at a particular workplace or in a geographical region. At the national level, we have to look for evidence of occupational segregation by race-ethnicity by examining whether a particular group is over- or underrepresented relative to its percent of the total workforce. For instance, if African American women make up 5.1 percent of the total workforce, they are underrepresented in an occupation if they hold less than 5.1 percent of the jobs.[1] Law would be such an occupation: African American women made up only 1.8 percent of all lawyers in 1990. In contrast, they are overrepresented in licensed practical nursing, where they hold 16.9 percent of the jobs.

A second concept that will be helpful in our examination of women's situation during the economic crisis is *labor market segmentation,* a term that refers to the division of jobs into categories with distinct working conditions. Economists generally distinguish two such categories, which they call the *primary* and *secondary* sectors. The first includes high-wage jobs that provide good benefits, job security, and opportunities for advancement. The upper level of this sector includes elite jobs that require long years of training and certification and offer autonomy on the job and a chance to advance up the corporate ladder. Access to upper level jobs is by way of family connections, wealth, talent, education, and governmental programs (like the GI bill, which guaranteed higher education to veterans returning from World War II). The lower level includes those manufacturing jobs that offer relatively high wages and job security (as a result of unionization), but do not require advanced training or degrees. The fact that unionized workers are part of this lower level is the result of the capital-labor accord...through which employers offered some unionized workers better pay and working conditions in exchange for labor peace. In both levels of the primary sector, job turnover is relatively low because it is more difficult for employers to replace these workers. Both the upper and lower levels of the primary sector were for many years the preserve of White men, with women (mostly White women) confined to small niches, such as schoolteaching and nursing.

The secondary sector includes low-wage jobs with few fringe benefits and little opportunity for advancement. Here too, there is a predominantly white-collar upper level (which includes sales and clerical workers), where working conditions, pay, and benefits are better than in the blue-collar lower level (private household, laborer, and most service jobs). Turnover is high in both levels of this sector because these workers have relatively few marketable skills and are easily replaced. For decades, the majority of women of all racial-ethnic groups, along with most men of color, were found in the secondary sector. Mobility between the primary and secondary sectors is limited: no career ladder connects jobs in the secondary sector to jobs in the primary sector.

While most jobs fall into these two sectors...during the economic crisis a third sector began to grow rapidly. This is known as the *informal sector,* or the underground economy. This name is not entirely accurate, however, since these activities do not make up a separate, distinct *economy* but are linked in many ways to the formal, above-ground sectors. Journalist and economist Philip Mattera believes that economic activity can be lined up along a continuum of formality and regulation.[2] At one end there is formal, regulated, and measured activity, where laws are observed, taxes are paid, inspections are frequent, and the participants report their activities to the relevant government entities. At the other end is work "off the books," where regulations are not enforced, participants do not report their activities, and taxes are evaded. Many economic activities exist somewhere in the middle. As the economic crisis deepens, many large corporations, whose own jobs are in the primary sector, have subcontracted some of their work out to underground firms that hire undocumented workers and escape health and safety, minimum wage, and environmental regulations. For example, in El Paso, Texas, only half of all garment industry workers earn adequate wages in union shops.[3] The other half work in sweatshops that contract work from big-name brands, such as Calvin Klein and Jordache, pay the minimum wage, and sometimes fail to pay anything at all. In 1990, the Labor Department fined one contractor for owing $30,000 in back wages and forced him to pay up. Fortunately for the employees, there is some justice in this world: the International Ladies' Garment Workers Union (ILGWU) then won a contract at his shops. According to Mattera,

operating a business off the books—i.e., without any state regulation or union involvement—is the logical conclusion of the restructuring process. It represents the ultimate goal of the profit-maximizing entrepreneur: proverbial free enterprise.... The type of restructuring that has taken place makes it possible for firms that cannot or do not want to go underground to take advantage of un-protected labor nonetheless.[4]

Another reason for the growth in the informal sector is that worsening wages and conditions in the two formal sectors lead people to seek additional work "off the books" to supplement their shrinking incomes and inadequate welfare or social security benefits. Thus the numbers of people suffering what Mattera calls "the nightmarish working conditions of unregulated capitalism" grow rapidly. Women and men of color, particularly immigrants, are those most likely to be found in the informal sector....

CAPITAL FLIGHT: A FLIGHT TO WOMEN?

...Over the past twenty years, many U.S. corporations shifted manufacturing jobs overseas. The creation of this "global assembly line" became a crucial component of the corporate strategy to cut costs. In their new locations, these companies hired women workers at minimal wages, both in the third world and in such countries as Ireland. Poorly paid as these jobs were, they were attractive to the thousands of women who were moving from impoverished rural villages into the cities in search of a better life for their families.

But in the United States, millions of workers lost their jobs as the result of capital flight or corporate downsizing. When workers lose their jobs because their plants or businesses close down or move, or their positions or shifts are abolished, it is called worker *displacement*. Over 5 million workers were displaced between 1979 and 1983, and another 4 million between 1985 and 1989.[5] In both periods, women were slightly *less* likely to lose their jobs than men of the same racial-ethnic group. Women in secondary sector factory jobs were hit hardest, primarily because they lacked union protection and the education and skills to find better jobs. (In 1989, over 35 percent of the women in manufacturing operative jobs had less than a high school education.)[6]

The overall result was that even though women lost jobs to capital flight and corporate downsizing, they did so at a slower rate than men. In fact, the share of manufacturing jobs going to women *rose* between 1970 and 1990. Women, in other words, claimed a growing share of a shrinking pie. Sociologist Joan Smith studied this growing tendency to replace male workers with women (as well as a parallel tendency to replace White workers with African Americans and Latinos). In her research on heavy manufacturing industries such as steel and automobiles, Smith found that employers hired men and/or White workers only in those areas of manufacturing where profits were high, jobs were being created, and there was substantial investment in new plant and equipment. In contrast,

in sectors where profits were slipping, the obvious search for less expensive workers led to the use of Black and women workers as a substitute for White workers and for men.... Close to 70 percent of women in these sectors and well over two-fifths of Blacks held their jobs as either substitutes or re-placements for Whites or men.[7]

While manufacturing jobs were feminizing, the rapidly expanding service sector was also hiring women in larger and larger numbers—both women entering the labor market for the first time and women displaced from manufacturing. In fact, all the jobs created during the 1980s were in the service sector....[8]

A large part of this service sector growth took place in what were already predominantly female jobs, such as nurses' aides, child care workers, or hotel chambermaids (jobs that men would not take), as employers took advantage of the availability of a growing pool of women workers who were excluded from male-dominated jobs.[9] Chris Tilly argues that these sectors were able to grow so rapidly during the 1980s precisely *because* they were able to use low-wage, part-time labor.[10] In other words, if no women workers had been available, the jobs would not have been filled by men;

instead, service employment would not have grown as rapidly.

The availability of service sector jobs helped hold the average official unemployment rates for women below those for men. However, the overall figure for women masks important differences by race-ethnicity....[11] In addition, the official unemployment rate doesn't tell the whole story. If we construct a measure of underemployment, we get a different sense of the relative hardships faced by women and men. The underemployed are those who are working part-time but would prefer full-time work, those who are so discouraged that they have given up looking for work, and those who want a job but can't work because home responsibilities—such as caring for children or aged parents—or other reasons keep them out of the labor force. If we look at underemployment rather than unemployment, the rankings change: in contrast to the official unemployment rates, the underemployment rates are higher for women than for men....

Even though the entire service sector grew during this period, service workers still risked losing their jobs. According to the Census Bureau's study of displaced workers, nearly half of those who lost their jobs between 1981 and 1983, and nearly two-thirds of those between 1985 and 1989, were in the service sector. As the crisis dragged on, in other words, corporate downsizing hit services as well as manufacturing. The financial sector, where women make up 60 percent of the workforce, was particularly hard hit, as jobs in banking, insurance, and real estate were lost as a result of the savings and loan scandal and other financial troubles.

UNION-BUSTING

...A second corporate strategy to bolster profitability was to attack labor unions. As the assault took its toll, union membership and union representation declined until by 1990 only 14 percent of women and 22 percent of men were represented by a union—compared to 18 percent of women and 28 percent of men only six years earlier. Even though women are less likely to be represented by unions than men, the *drop* in unionization was not as severe for women, largely because they are concentrated in the service sector where there were some organizing victories. In addition, most women do not hold jobs in factories, the area most vulnerable to union-busting. The drop in unionization was highest among Latinas, who are over-represented in manufacturing, followed closely by African American women. Still, African American women have the highest rate of union representation among women (22 percent) because so many work in the public sector.[12]

The drop in unionized jobs is dangerous for women for several reasons. The most obvious is that unionized women earn an average weekly wage that is 1.3 times that of nonunionized women. The gap is especially large in the service sector, where unionized workers earn 1.8 times as much as nonunionized workers....[13]

The loss of unionized jobs also hurts women in nonunion jobs because of what economists call a "spillover" effect from union to nonunion firms in the area of wages and benefits. While it is difficult to estimate the extent of this spillover, Harvard economists Richard Freeman and James Medoff suggest that it raises wages in blue-collar jobs in large nonunion firms (those with lower level primary sector jobs) by anywhere from 10 to 20 percent, and also improves benefits and working conditions.[14] This happens for two reasons: (1) nonunion firms must compete for labor with the union firms and therefore have to meet unionized rates, and (2) some firms will keep wages higher than necessary in order to keep unions out. Thus when union workers lose wages and benefits, these spillover effects diminish, lowering wages and benefits in nonunion jobs as well.

Higher wages are only part of what women achieve when there is a strong labor movement. Unionization has an important spillover effect in the political as well as economic arena. For instance, support from the labor movement is responsible for the passage of most of the major safety net legislation in the United States, including the minimum wage and the Social Security Act. When the labor movement is weakened, important items on labor's agenda—including national health care, national child care, improved enforcement of job safety and health regulations, and broadened unemployment insurance coverage—all become more difficult to achieve, even though they address the needs of *all* workers. Further evidence of the critical role played by the labor movement comes from Europe, where family policies (parental leave, child allowances, and national day care) were all enacted with the backing, and sometimes at the initiative, of the labor movement.

WOMEN AND THE RESTRUCTURING OF WORK

...Another component of restructuring, and one that particularly affects women, is the use of homework. While homework can provide incomes for women who are unable to locate affordable child care or who live in rural areas, far from other employment, it also exposes women to intense exploitation. Both men and women homeworkers typically earn much less than those who do the same work outside the home: according to the federal Office of Technology Assessment, the poverty risk for homeworkers is nearly double that for other workers. In addition, working conditions in the home can be dangerous. In semiconductor manufacturing homework, for instance, workers are exposed to hazardous substances that can also contaminate residential sewage systems.[15]

Many homeworkers are undocumented immigrants who work out of their homes in order to escape detection by the Immigration and Naturalization Service (INS). During the early 1970s, the majority of undocumented immigrants were male, but since then women have begun to arrive in ever larger numbers:

> Women's migration has traditionally been ignored by researchers.... The INS reported a "dramatic rise" in the number of women apprehended at the U.S.-Mexico border between 1984 and 1986.... Many authors describe a new spirit of "indepen-

> dence" among women choosing to cross the border alone to reunite with family already in the U.S., or to seek employment on their own to support family left behind.[16]

In the spring of 1990, the Coalition for Immigration and Refugee Rights and Services in San Francisco surveyed over 400 undocumented women in the Bay Area. Nearly half of them reported employment discrimination by employers who abused them sexually, physically, or emotionally, paid them less than their co-workers, or failed to pay them at all. Most of those surveyed worked as domestic servants, in stores, restaurants, and factories.

WOMEN'S RESPONSES TO RESTRUCTURING

As wages fell and employers pushed more and more work into the secondary and informal sectors, women responded with a variety of individual strategies. Some started small businesses. Others sought "nontraditional" jobs in areas formerly dominated by men, hoping to earn a man's wage. And a growing number took on multiple jobs, "moonlighting" in a desperate effort to make a living wage out of two, or even three, different jobs. Each of these individual strategies...held some promise, but all failed to deliver substantial gains except to the lucky few....

...Self-employment did not solve women's economic problems. The vast majority of these businesses remained small in scale: although they made up nearly 33 percent of all the businesses in the United States, they earned only 14 percent of the receipts. Nearly 40 percent had total receipts of less than $5,000 a year; only 10 percent had any employees.[17] Even the most successful women entrepreneurs faced difficulties finding affordable health insurance and pension coverage, which they had to buy for themselves out of their profits. Despite conservative rhetoric about the glories of entrepreneurship, self-employment has not proved to be a cure-all for women's economic troubles....

As the number of poverty-level jobs has increased, more and more women have been forced to turn to moonlighting to boost their incomes. By 1989, 3.5 times as many women were working two or more jobs as in 1973. In contrast, the number of men moonlighting only rose by a factor of 1.2.[18] And many more women were moonlighting because of economic hardship—to meet regular household expenses or pay off debts—not to save for something special, get experience, or help out a family member or friend. African American women and Latinas were the most likely to report that they were moonlighting to meet *regular* household expenses, while White women were more likely to report saving for the future or other reasons—a difference caused by the lower average income of women of color and the greater likelihood that they were raising children on their own.

But moonlighting is ultimately limited by the number of hours in the day.... As the crisis wears on and more and more women become fully employed, more families turn to children to help out. According to recent estimates, at least 4 million children under the age of 19 are employed legally, while at least 2 million more work "off the books," and the number is growing.[19]

NEW JOBS FOR WOMEN

During the 1980s, the female labor force grew by over 10 million. Most of the new entrants found traditionally female jobs in secondary, sector service and administrative support occupations, since that is where the majority of job growth took place.... However, some women made inroads into traditionally male jobs in the highly paid primary sector, and these gains are likely to be maintained. In addition, graduate degrees show how women are increasingly willing to prepare themselves for male-dominated occupations.... There has been an occupational "trickle down" effect, as White women improved their occupational status by moving into male-dominated professions such as law and medicine, while African American

women moved into the *female-dominated* jobs, such as social work and teaching, vacated by White women. There is some evidence that the improvement for White women was related to federal civil rights legislation, particularly the requirement that firms receiving federal contracts comply with affirmative action guidelines.[20]

The movement of women into highly skilled blue-collar work, such as construction and automaking, was sharply limited by the very slow growth in those jobs. Not coincidentally, male resistance to letting women enter these trades stiffened during the 1980s, when layoffs were common and union jobs were under attack. Moreover, all women lost ground in secondary sector manufacturing jobs, such as machine operators and laborers. Latinas were particularly hard hit, losing ground in most manufacturing jobs....

UP THE DOWN ESCALATOR

If the postwar economic boom had continued into the 1970s and 1980s, women's economic status today would be substantially improved. The crisis produced some gains for women, but many of these evaporate on close inspection. The wage gap narrowed, but partly because men's wages fell. The gap between men's and women's rates of unionization and access to fringe benefits fell, but again partly because men's rates fell. More women entered the workforce, but they also worked longer hours than ever before, held multiple jobs, and sought work in the informal economy in order to maintain their standard of living. Finally, women's gains were not evenly distributed: highly educated women moved even further ahead of their less-educated counterparts.

All this took place against a backdrop of rising family responsibilities.... The most serious stress faced by married women ... was associated with the reduced standard of living their families faced as a result of the cutbacks: "Their continued need to reduce what their wages can buy for their families means that the conflicts they feel between work and family life intensify. Earning less makes it feel harder and harder for them to continue to work and take care of their families."[21]

For these women, who depended on manufacturing jobs, it is not surprising that the economic crisis took a heavy toll. What is surprising is that they experienced it most acutely in the home rather than on the job. Work for them was not a career, a satisfying route to self actualization, but a fate they accepted in order to provide for their families.

When their earnings fell, it was their work at home—the work of marketing, cooking, cleaning, caring—that became more difficult. An increasing number were the sole support of their households. Others found that their household's standard of living could only be maintained if they took on one— or more—paid jobs in addition to their homemaking. They were caught between shrinking incomes and growing responsibilities....

NOTES

1. Unpublished data, Bureau of Labor Statistics.
2. Philip Mattera, *Off the Books: The Rise of the Underground Economy* (New York: St. Martin's Press, 1985), p. 38.
3. Colatosti, Camille, "A Job Without a Future," *Dollars and Sense* (May 1992), p. 10.
4. Philip Mattera, *Prosperity Lost* (Reading, MA: Addison-Wesley, 1992), pp. 34–35.
5. For instance, between 1985 and 1989 the displacement rate—the number of workers displaced for every 1,000 workers employed—was 6.3 for white women compared to 6.7 for white men; 6.1 for African American women compared to 7.3 for African American men; and 8.3 for Latinas compared to 9.0 for Latinos. See U.S. Department of Labor, Bureau of Labor Statistics, *Displaced Workers, 1985–89*, June 1991, Bulletin 2382, Table 4.
6. U.S. Bureau of the Census, *Statistical Abstract of the United States 1991*, Table 656, p. 400. African American women factory operatives are better educated than Whites: only 29 percent lack a high school degree, compared to 36 percent of whites.
7. Joan Smith, "Impact of the Reagan Years: Race, Gender, and the Economic Restructuring," *First Annual Women's Policy Research Conference Proceedings* (Washington, DC: Institute for Women's Policy Research, 1989), p. 20.
8. U.S. Bureau of the Census, *Statistical Abstract of the United States 1991*, Table 658, p. 401. The number of jobs in durable manufacturing fell by 0.8 percent a year between 1980 and 1988 and in nondurable manufacturing (i.e., light manufacturing, such as food processing) fell by 0.2 percent; service jobs grew an average of 2.7 percent. Manufacturing jobs did see some growth in the last half of the 1970s, however, so that over the two decades there was a small amount of overall growth in manufacturing.

9. Because the number of jobs held by women increased more than the number held by men, the percent of service sector jobs held by women increased from 43 percent to 52 percent between 1970 and 1990.
10. Polly Callaghan and Heidi Hartmann, *Contingent Work* (Washington, DC: Economic Policy Institute, 1991), p. 24.
11. For Latinas, on the other hand, women's unemployment was higher than that of men's. While it is difficult to pinpoint the reason for this, it may be because of the relatively rapid growth of Latina participation in the labor force. Although Latinas have lowest labor force participation rate of the three groups of women, their participation rates are growing the most rapidly. It may be that this growth in the Latina workforce outstripped job creation in the secondary sector, which had traditionally hired Latinas while discrimination still barred their way into the primary sector—resulting in high unemployment. See National Council of La Raza, *State of Hispanic America 1991*, p. 26.
12. Paula Ries and Anne J. Stone, eds., *The American Woman 1992–93: A Status Report* (New York, W. W. Norton and Co., 1991), p. 369.
13. U.S. Bureau of Labor Statistics, *Employment and Earnings,* January 1992, Tables 59–60.
14. Richard Freeman and James Medoff, *What Do Unions Do?* (New York: Basic Books, 1981), p. 153.
15. Virginia DuRivage and David Jacobs, "Home-Based Work: Labor's Choices," in *Homework: Historical and Contemporary Perspectives on Paid Labor at Home*, ed. Eileen Boris and Cynthia R. Daniels (Urbana: University of Illinois Press, 1989), p. 259.
16. Chris Hogeland and Karen Rose, *Dreams Lost, Dreams Found: Undocumented Women in the Land of Opportunity* (San Francisco, CA: Refugee Rights and Services, 1990), p. 4.

17. Ries and Stone, *The American Woman,* pp. 347–48.

18. Lawrence Mishel and David M. Frankel, *The State of Working America* (Armonk, NY: M. E. Sharpe, 1991), p. 142.

19. Gina Kolata, "More Children Are Employed, Often Perilously," *New York Times,* 21 June 1992, p. 1.

20. Barbara Bergman, *The Economic Emergence of Women* (New York: Basic Books, 1986), p. 147.

21. Ellen Israel Rosen, *Bitter Choices: Blue Collar Women in and out of Work* (Chicago: University of Chicago Press, 1987), p. 164.

42

Not Just Weapons of the Weak

Gender Harassment as a Form of Protest for Army Men

LAURA L. MILLER

Structural and cultural analyses would describe men as the dominant and more powerful gender in the military. The military has been virtually all male for most of its history, and the role of soldier reinforces the traditionally masculine role. Men make up the majority of personnel, overwhelmingly hold the highest positions, and, unlike women, are not barred from participating in any branch of the service.

Why, then, are some Army men using what the resistance literature calls "weapons of the weak" against women soldiers? These weapons are reportedly the masked strategies that subordinates use to resist oppression from above. Army women do not appear to rely on these strategies at all, even though they are a minority and their rights to full participation in the military are still the subject of debate. Rather, it is the men in the dominant structural position who employ the resistance modes typically used by the powerless.

An effort to solve this seeming paradox reveals two critical flaws in most analyses of resistance. First, most of these studies rely exclusively on structural measures of power to draw conclusions about individuals' interactional strategies. Individuals' perceptions of power, however, do not always echo our academic assessments of it. These perceptions of power, whether or not we find them accurate, influence behavior. Thus, to explain power and resistance at the interactional

level, the analysis must include the social psychology of power and its emphasis on perceptions.

The second problem with studies of resistance is that they begin by dividing the population into the powerful and the powerless. Such a framework is limited because it assumes that people hold only one relevant social status in society, rather than many. Individuals can simultaneously enjoy privilege and suffer disadvantages according to their gender, race, class, age, occupation, or position within an organization. Thus people can be powerful and powerless at the same time because their lives are situated in several coexisting hierarchies.

In the case of gender relations in the Army, perceptions matter because some Army men believe that women, not men, are the privileged and powerful group in the military. These men then act as "an oppressed group" on the basis of those perceptions. Most of these men object to women's increased participation in the military, but fear negative organizational consequences for expressing their objections openly. Therefore they resort to interactional, indirect forms of protest. I call Army men's resistance strategies "gender harassment." This behavior includes sabotage, foot-dragging, feigning ignorance, constant scrutiny, gossip and rumors, and indirect threats. This harassment targets women but is not sexual; often it cannot be traced to its source.

Because multiple hierarchies are also at work, the structure of gender interactions is more complex than that presented in the literatures on resistance or on women in the military. Within the broad organization of the military, some men are less powerful than others and find it safer to vent their frustrations on hierarchical equals or inferiors. Even men in more powerful positions may feel powerless in the face of civilian actors seeking to change military policy. That many men feel prohibited from overtly expressing their discontent demonstrates that women indeed have made headway in deterring overt sexist comments. Unfortunately the consequence may be that some men resort to more covert and less easily controllable forms of harassment.

METHODS

The data presented here are taken from multiple stages of field research on active-duty Army soldiers from early 1992 to late 1994. I used a multimethod strategy to capture both large-scale attitudinal patterns and individual viewpoints. To collect the data, I traveled to eight stateside Army posts and two national training centers, where soldiers conduct war games on a simulated battlefield. I also lived with Army personnel for 10 days in Somalia during Operation Restore Hope, for seven days in Macedonia during Operation Able Sentry, and for six days in Haiti during Operation Uphold Democracy.

In designing the study, I drew on the "grounded theory" tradition. That is, my approach to studying gender relations was inductive because I wished to learn how people constructed the issues for themselves. Therefore I collected qualitative data through discussion groups, one-on-one unstructured interviews, participant and nonparticipant observation, and informal conversations with soldiers. Given the military context and the sensitive nature of some of the issues, I relied on written notes rather than tape-recording. I had no formal interview schedule: instead I carried a short list of topics that interested me and to which

I could steer the discussion. These topics included the nature of gender relations, conflict and cooperation among women, the management of work and family obligations, women's experiences in deployment environments, and the assignment and promotion of Army women across different occupational fields.

I also collected large-scale survey data in order to analyze the relationships between soldiers' demographics and their attitudes on a wide array of issues. The ethnographic data were cross-validated by multiple stages of questionnaires totaling more than 4,100. Soldiers were encouraged to write their own responses if they did not find their opinion represented among the choices, or if they wanted to introduce or expand on an important topic. Many soldiers wrote extensive comments, providing qualitative material that could be tied to demographic data and attitudes on other topics.

…Because of my focus on gender, I oversampled women: Only about 12 percent of the Army population at the time of the research was female, but women account for 40 percent of my sample. Enlisted personnel are slightly oversampled: noncommissioned officers (NCOs) are slightly undersampled. Most of the officers in the sample hold the rank of lieutenant, captain, or major. Higher-ranking officers (colonels and generals) typically were not asked to fill out written surveys, but instead were interviewed in depth. Whites were slightly undersampled; Blacks were slightly oversampled. This difference is due in part to the oversampling of women, who are more likely than men in the military to be Black. Hispanics and other minorities were included in representative numbers.

THE RESISTANCE LITERATURE: A GOOD FIT, UPSIDE DOWN

In *Domination and the Arts of Resistance,* James C. Scott (1990) provides an extensive historical analysis explaining how powerless groups resist and subvert the efforts of those with power over them. His work demonstrates that people's fear of negative sanctions often drives them to resist in ways that cannot be traced to the initiator, or are lost in the anonymity of crowds. The greater the power exerted from above, the more fully masked the resistance from below.

Scott's examples closely parallel behavior that I found in gender relations in the Army, except for one very significant anomaly: It is the structurally dominant group, Army men, who employ the strategies of resistance that are generally seen as the weapons of the weak. My research shows that some men devote a great deal of energy to resisting their women coworkers and commanders through methods such as sabotage, name-calling, foot-dragging, and spreading rumors. Women, paradoxically, do not appear to be using any of these strategies of the weak to gain power from men, according to either their accounts or men's.

What explains the use of weapons of the weak by the structurally dominant group but not by the subordinate minority? My investigation led me to social psychological studies of power (Cartwright 1959; Lips 1981; Ng 1980). In this literature it is argued that people act according to perceptions of power based on their own experiences and knowledge, not according to some objective analysis of resources. A social psychological analysis of my own data revealed how frequently military men described themselves as unjustly constrained or controlled by military women. Furthermore, these men tend to believe that women's power is usually gained illegitimately and that women take advantage of their gender to promote their own careers.

…The military contains many levels of dominance and subordination including those based on rank, job specialty, education, race, gender, age, marital and family status, and mission experience. For example, enlisted men may not enjoy the privileges of their sex as much as men at the higher command levels, particularly in relation to women officers; also, in this era of organizational downsizing, male career officers sometimes blame their limited opportunities on increased participation by women. Thus not all military men experience male privilege, and even some of the more privileged members are constrained within the organization.

GENDER HARASSMENT

Distinguishing Gender Harassment from Sexual Harassment

Sexual harassment implies that you can only be harassed through sexual means. Women can also be harassed through the job in other ways. If your commander doesn't like you, you will encounter harassment, i.e., the shit details, made to work later than everyone else, constant field problems, low efficiency ratings, etc. "It's more prejudice than harassment towards females in the Army" (Black NCO in administrative support).

Gender harassment refers to harassment that is not sexual, and is used to enforce traditional gender roles, or in response to the violation of those roles. This form of harassment also may aim to undermine women's attempts at gaining power or to describe that power as illegitimately obtained or exercised. Examples include men proclaiming "Women can't drive trucks" in the presence of female drivers or refusing to follow a superior's directives simply because that superior is a woman. Many Army women report that gender harassment on the job is more prevalent than sexual harassment.

Gender harassment also can be used against men who violate gender norms. For example, men who fail to live up to the "masculine ideal" by showing insecurity or hesitation during maneuvers may be called "fags" or "girls" by their comrades. (For a classic description of this type of harassment in socializing new male soldiers, see Eisenhart 1975.) Because behavior that conflicts with one's gender role is stereotypically associated with homosexuality, both heterosexuality and traditional gender roles are enforced through gender harassment.

Because of the prevalence of gender harassment, workshops and policies that address only sexual harassment miss much of the picture.

Women report that gender harassment can be just as disruptive in their lives as sexual harassment: It can interfere with their ability to do their work, with their private lives, and with their opportunities to receive recognition and promotions. Gender harassment is often difficult to attribute to individuals, may not be recognized by command as a problem, and is often invisible in debates about harassment of women in the military.

What I call gender harassment does not fall under the official Department of Defense definitions of discrimination or sexual harassment. Some of these behaviors violate codes for working conditions or rules of good order and discipline, but because women tend to view these actions as harassment and as gender-specific, they categorize them alongside sexual harassment. Yet because much gender harassment is untraceable, women tend to think that filing a complaint is futile and may even backfire by bringing negative attention to themselves.

Some Forms of Gender Harassment

Below are some illustrative examples of gender harassment. By no means are these an exhaustive categorization of the possible types of harassment.

Resistance to Authority.   Women who are officers or NCOs commonly complained of male subordinates, especially older enlisted men, who "just don't like answering to a woman." When give orders, they feign ignorance about what is expected of them, or encase in foot-dragging. This method is effective because the men do not risk the official reprimand warranted by an outright refusal to obey orders; yet they challenge women's authority by not complying completely. As one White NCO hypothesized, "Men are intimidated by women superiors and most try to undermine their work." Several women leaders reported having to "pull rank" more often than their male counterparts to get things done.

Women commanders' age alone cannot account for the men's resistance. These men do not

appear to be so aggrieved when taking orders from younger male officers. Indeed, in Army parlance, senior NCOs in their thirties and forties commonly refer to company commanders, who are in their late twenties, as "the old man." The term old lady is not used in this sense, however.[1]

Resentment of women in powerful positions can also come from above, as reported by a White woman captain in the medical field:

> There should be some recourse for female commanders…when they are falsely taken out of command because their superiors don't want them there. I went to the [equal opportunity] office, [the inspector general], and [the commanding general] on [this post], and no one would even look at the proof I had that they were wrong and lying. Because of that, I now have to get out of the Army that I was going to make a career of. Thank you for the injustice to the women of the U.S. Army because the offices set up to supposedly protect us from bias and harassment aren't working.

Women sometimes hesitate to report uncooperative behavior because it could be interpreted as lack of leadership skills or as inability to get along with other officers. Such an appraisal in turn could affect work evaluations and promotion opportunities.

Constant Scrutiny.   Hostile men use constant scrutiny to catch individual women making mistakes, and then use the mistakes to criticize the abilities of women in general.[2] Because of this scrutiny women often feel obligated to work harder than those under less supervision. Women report that they experience such scrutiny as relentless harassment, and that it can make them feel self-conscious and extremely stressed.

Both enlisted and officer women report that as women they are subject to closer scrutiny than men. When women are singled out for observation by suspicious peers and superiors, they often feel they have to work harder than their coworkers just to be accepted as equal members of the unit. In the words of a Black enlisted woman in craftswork, "Women are still having to prove themselves. Women work a lot harder at things because they have to prove they can maintain." This complaint has long been registered in the literature on women in the military (Holm [1982] 1992; Schneider and Schneider 1988; Stiehm 1989; Williams 1989).

The behavior of a few women is often projected onto the entire gender, but the same is not true for men. To illustrate, some women soldiers serving in the early phases of operations in Haiti pointed out that if the three soldiers who committed suicide there had been women, a discussion would have ensued: People would have asked whether women could handle the stress of deployments or separation from their families. Yet because they were "just men," they were reported as *soldiers,* and the suicides were not interpreted as saying anything about men in general.

Because some Army men question women's abilities or commitment to perform their jobs effectively, they not only scrutinize women's activities but sometimes also set up unofficial hurdles to see if the women will "hold up." The women's performance during these tests is then scrutinized. One White NCO even referred to this behavior as harassment:

> *I think probably [there is] more harassment along the lines [of] "Well, you're trying to be a man— let's see how tough you really are." I have never been sexually harassed. However, I did at one time have problems with a supervisor who didn't like women. Especially women in the Army. There is still a lot of that going on.*

Women leaders are rendered less flexible than men because of the constant scrutiny. Sometimes they believe that the people watching them are waiting for them to make mistakes or deviate from regulations; this is a disconcerting environment in which to make decisions. As a result, some men as well as some women classify female superiors as unfair or "too hard." They prefer to serve under men, who have more freedom to bend the rules in favor of their troops: "Women seem to feel they have something to prove. They do, but should not abuse their soldiers [in the process]" (White enlisted man in electronics).

Scrutiny as a harassment strategy is particularly safe in the military because it fits into the functioning of the organization. One cannot be punished for seeking out and correcting errors, and it would be quite difficult to prove that women are being watched more closely than men.

Gossip and Rumors.   Research on power and social interaction has found that "rumors are especially likely to flourish among people who see [that] their fates are in other people's hands" (Cartwright 1959:9). Rumors abound in the military.

Army women are often the subject of untrue gossip about their sex lives. Repeatedly I heard that if a woman dates more than one man in the Army, she is labeled a "slut." If she doesn't date, she is labeled a "dyke." Unlike men, women who are promoted quickly or who receive coveted assignments are often rumored to have "slept their way to the top." At every post I visited, soldiers had heard the rumor (which has never been verified) that a few women soldiers in the Persian Gulf War made a fortune by setting up a tent and serving as prostitutes for their male counterparts.

Young Army women in particular feel that their personal lives are under intense scrutiny at all times, and that ridiculous lies can emerge from the rumor mill for no apparent reason. One enlisted woman was shocked when her commander took her aside one day and said, "Look, I know you're sleeping with all the guys in your unit." She could not imagine why he said that to her; who would have started such a rumor, or why; or why fellow soldiers—her friends—would have contributed to spreading the stories.

Stories of sexual harassment or sexual activity between men and women soldiers were often framed in terms of the natural consequences of women "being there":

> *I'm in the infantry. The reason why I'm anti-women in combat MOS is because of the sexual harassment that the women will receive. When we go to the field on maneuvers, it can take up a month or more at times. Guys would sexually harass the*

*women for the heck of it. Also, if we get into an-
other conflict, and women end up as POWs, they're
most likely to get harassed worse than men. (White
enlisted man)*

Although sexual activity with local women
and prostitutes by male soldiers stationed overseas
has always been accepted and even sanctioned as a
part of military life, female soldiers' sexual activity was often a subject of conversation. In the case
of women soldiers, sexual behavior was described
as unacceptable and disruptive to the mission:

*Women have a place in life, just as men do, and
both are equally important, but I do not recommend women to serve in combat units because of
the amount of sexual activities that take place in
stateside units. The finger can be pointed at both
sides, because I have seen male and female soldiers encourage sexual advances. It's a shame that
adults can't control their emotions and sexual feelings, but it's true, and putting both genders together in that type of situation would just make the
situation ten times worse. (White enlisted woman
in equipment repair)*

Men voiced concerns only about men's sexual attraction to *American* women, as though no other
women exist during an overseas deployment:

*Although women should be allowed to serve in
combat units, some problems may arise when/if
young women and men are in isolated situations
for long/short periods of time. Hormones cause
natural attraction. Morale could be rapidly undermined if a few men and women engaged in sexual
activities. Others (majority being male) may become angry, even jealous. Readiness could very
well be impaired. Some constraints should be
placed on utilizing women soldiers and men soldiers in combat roles to help reduce potential morale problems, pregnancies, discipline problems,
etc. (White male captain)*

Rumors and gossip about sexuality thus communicated the inappropriateness of women serving among men, or implied that women's power
was often gained illegitimately through sexual fa-

vors. Because rumors are usually untraceable,
they cannot be addressed through a formal complaint system....

Sabotage.   I found evidence of sabotage, as a
form of gender harassment, only in work fields
that are nontraditional for women. Because these
nontraditional occupations can be strenuous and
dangerous, the sabotage of equipment can be quite
threatening. Literature on women in the trades has
documented injuries and near misses because of
sabotage by workers, assignment of women to
faulty equipment, or failure to give women the
proper tools or training (M. Martin 1988;
Schroedel 1985; Walshok 1981). Thus sabotage
not only can challenge women's abilities in nontraditional work; it can jeopardize their lives.

In one instance of sabotage from my research,
two women new to an all-male vehicle maintenance and repair unit arrived at work every morning to find that the heavy, difficult-to-change track
had been removed from their assigned vehicle. After a few weeks, during which they patiently replaced the track each day, the harassment ended.
They had earned the men's respect by proving
their skills and their willingness to work hard. The
men's doubts were dispelled when they decided
that the women's abilities had earned them a position in the unit, and that they would not use their
gender to exempt themselves from dirty and difficult work. (I heard this story from two of the men
in the unit, who were describing how they evolved
from challenging to respecting women in their
workplace.)

Sabotage of equipment and tools was reported by women in mechanical fields, but I never
heard of sabotage in the form of disappearing
files, erased computer data, jammed typewriters,
hidden medical supplies, or misplaced cooking
utensils.

Indirect Threats.   Some soldiers reported that
some of their fellow men would rape women who
dared to enter infantry or armor units. The com-

ments written on surveys include these remarks by a Black enlisted man in the combat arms:

> *The majority of men in the Army are sexist. I know, because I'm a man. Women in combat units would be harassed, if not raped. I say this because I've seen it and have nothing to hide. If you want the truth about issues, don't ask NCOs or officers. They'll tell you everything is all peaches and cream!! If you want the truth ask an E4 that's been in about 5 years. Women only have a fair shake as cooks or nurses. They'll be extremely harassed, if not molested, if they enter combat arms. I know, trust me.*

Another infantryman echoed that assessment, although he proposed that male violence toward women is due to the conditions of deployments, not to sexism:

> *In a situation where times are hard—less food, no showers, road marching, with 70–100 lbs ruck on your back, and [you] don't know when the next supply shipment will be in, the male soldiers will start thinking of sex and the female soldiers may be raped or something.*

Only once did a group of men in the combat arms tell me that they personally would "rape the women if you send them out to the tanks and foxholes with us." The men almost always wrote or spoke in terms of what other men would do: "Now I don't have a problem with women, but some of these guys, I know them and they're animals. They won't hesitate to take what they want or let a woman get killed to get her out of the way."

These comments were not made only to me during interviews, but are typically raised in soldiers' debates among themselves about women's roles in the military. Often these "warnings" are given by men in the combat arms, who see themselves as experts on the nature of combat and the requirements of combat units. The threats are usually communicated in a tone of concern for women's safety, for morale, or for combat effectiveness. This concern, whether genuine or not, gives the teller some sense of safety from repri-

mand for his statements. An underlying function of these stories, however, is to intimidate women and to invoke their fear of entering predominantly male domains.

I contend that these forms of gender harassment are employed as a resistance strategy against women's current status in the military as well as against any potential expansion of that status. To establish this connection, I will give a brief overview of women's military participation, and explain why. Then I will discuss why disgruntled men resort to gender harassment to register their discontent.

ADVANCEMENT OF WOMEN IN THE MILITARY

Women's participation in the military has been restricted since gender integration began. About 33,000 women served in World War I—20,000 of them in the Army and Navy Nurse Corps, which was separate from the regular Army and Navy. In World War II, manpower shortages and reports of valuable performance by women in other countries' armed forces led the United States to utilize approximately 350,000 women for its own military effort. The attack on Pearl Harbor resulted in the creation of the Women's Army Auxiliary Corps (WAAC) and Women Accepted for Volunteer Emergency Service (WAVES). Women typically filled nursing and administrative jobs, which were consistent with civilian women's work, although they also served in all other noncombat jobs. These 350,000 women who served in World War II were regarded as temporary support that would free more men for combat.

After the war, women's future role with the military was called into question. In 1948, the year when racial integration was mandated by President Truman, Congress passed the Women's Armed Services Integration Act, which placed highly specific limits on the women who would now be allowed to join the Army. Women could make up no more than 2 percent of the total enlisted ranks; the proportion of female officers could equal no more than 10 percent of enlisted women. No woman could serve in a command position, attain the rank of general, or hold permanent rank above lieutenant colonel. Later the Army adopted the regulation prohibiting women from serving in combat. (For a detailed history of women in the military, see Holm [1982] 1992.)

The doors for women have been pried open slowly over the past four decades. In 1967 the 2 percent cap on enlisted women and some restrictions on promotions were lifted; in 1972 ROTC was opened to women; in 1976 the first women entered West Point; in 1978 the separate Women's Army Corps was dissolved; in 1989 two women led their units into combat in Panama; and in 1991, in the Persian Gulf War, large numbers of women moved forward with their units into combat zones, which they were officially forbidden to enter. The policy prohibiting women from such zones was a new limit placed on women's participation as late as 1988. A Department of Defense Task Force on Women in the Military created a "risk rule" to bar women from areas on the battlefield where the "risk of exposure to direct combat, hostile fire, or capture is equal to or greater than that experienced by associated combat units in the same theater of operations" (Wekesser and Polesetsky 1991:87).

In 1996 women made up 13 percent of active-duty military personnel: 16 percent of the Air Force, 14 percent of the Army, 12 percent of the Navy, 9 percent of the Coast Guard, and 5 percent of the Marines (DEOMI 1996). Many concerns raised about women's roles have persisted over time. During my research interviews, both men and women confirmed that the typical reasons for wanting to limit women's roles in the military, as present in the literature, still flourish in the 1990s: Women's psychology, limited upper-body strength, and reproductive system, as well as the mere presence of women among men, would reduce combat efficiency and result in a greater loss of life during war. The literature on women in the military covers both sides of these issues exhaustively (Binkin

1993; Devilbiss 1990; Donnelly 1991; Enloe 1983; Holm [1982] 1992; Mitchell 1989; Presidential Commission 1992; Segal 1982; Stiehm 1981, 1983, 1989; Tuten 1982; Wekesser and Polesetsky 1991).

In the 1990s women have served with men in peacekeeping and humanitarian missions, such as those in Somalia, Rwanda, Haiti, and Bosnia, with little public attention to their gender. Although women now attend the service academies and work in all branches of the armed forces, they are still prohibited from serving in most ground combat positions. The "risk rule" has been abandoned, however. Women recently have been integrated into some combat aviation positions and seagoing vessels, though not without controversy. Debates about policies excluding women from most combat specialties are currently muted, but certainly will continue as long as the present policies remain in force. While feminist activists continue to challenge restrictions on women's roles in the military, some people charge that the military has already gone too far and has compromised military effectiveness in order to meet affirmative action goals.

WHICH MEN ARE MOST LIKELY TO OBJECT TO WOMEN'S CURRENT OR EXPANDED PARTICIPATION IN THE MILITARY?

In my survey I found that the Army men who are most likely to resist expanded or even current roles of women in the military are White officers. Yet even these men are not a monolithic group; some are very supportive of their female coworkers. For the purposes of this analysis, however, I focus primarily on men who object to expanding women's roles to include the combat arms, as well as those who object to women's current degree of participation in the service.

Table 1 presents soldiers' satisfaction or dissatisfaction with the present number of women in the military by the most significant variables: gender and rank.[3] Women made up 12 percent of military personnel at the time when this survey was

TABLE 1   Soldiers' Opinions of Whether There Are Too Many or Too Few Women in the Armed Forces, by Rank*** and Gender***

	ENLISTED		NCOs		OFFICER	
	Men	Women	Men	Women	Men	Women
Too many women in the armed forces	11%	2%	16%	1%	24%	—
About the right amount	36	31	38	48	59	44
Too few women in the armed forces	33	50	22	38	7	49
Not sure	20	17	24	13	10	7
Totals	100%	100%	100%	100%	100%	100%
(N)	(277)	(299)	(146)	(92)	(41)	(72)

***$p < .001$.

administered. The polar extremes appear to exist between men and women officers: Male officers were most likely to think there are too many women in the armed forces; female officers were most likely to think there are too few women.

Table 2 shows soldiers' opinions, again by gender and rank, about the roles that women should hold in the military. This item sets aside the question of whether women should be assigned to combat roles or should be allowed to volunteer. When the question was presented in this way, men did not vary by race, rank or MOS. Sixty-six percent of men thought that more roles should be opened to women, but some men (14 percent) would roll back opportunities already available to military women. Thus, in an average group of 25 men, three or four think that women's roles are already beyond acceptable levels. Even this minority of men could have a significant impact on the lives of their women coworkers if they resort to harassment strategies in protest. Women were not a monolithic group either, and varied significantly

TABLE 2   Soldiers' Opinions on the Roles Army Women Should Fill, by Rank *** and Gender***

	MEN	WOMEN		
	All Ranks[a]	Enlisted	NCOs	Officers
All roles, including combat, should be open to women.	44%	64%	48%	68%
We should open more assignments to women, but stop short of infantry and armor.	22	19	30	26
The assignment of women in the Army is pretty much all right the way it is now.	20	15	19	6
Women should be restricted to assignments in office and technical work.	10	2	3	—
Women have no place in the Army.	4	—	—	—
Totals	100%	100%	100%	100%
(N)	(469)	(301)	(95)	(72)

[a]Rank was significant only for women.
***$p < .001$.

on this item by rank, but not by race or MOS. Among women, 94 percent of officers would expand women's roles, followed by 83 percent of junior enlisted women and 78 percent of NCO women. The tiny proportion (2–3 percent) of women who would reduce women's options from their present level belong to the junior enlisted or NCO ranks.

Table 3 shows men's opinions on combat policy for women, analyzed by race and rank (MOS was not significant). Statistical analyses of variance found significant variation between White and minority men (there was no variation among Black, Hispanic, and "other race" men). White men varied among themselves by rank: White officers were by far the most satisfied with the status quo and the least likely to support either a voluntary or a same-as-men combat option for women. Minority men did not vary by rank, were least likely to support the current policy, and were most likely to prefer to allow women to volunteer for the combat arms if they so desired. Men of color, regardless of rank, may be more likely than White men to identify with women, who are fellow members of a minority; or they

may be less likely to feel threatened by equal opportunity issues.

Being an officer can influence men's opinions in several ways. While one might expect more liberal values to emerge from this more highly educated group, other factors are also at work. As women advance up the career ladder in a downsizing Army, male career officers may attribute their own limited opportunities to competition from women, who they fear may have an unfair advantage because of their minority status. If officers believe that the presence of women may compromise the performance of their unit, they have a personal stake in limiting women's entrance because as leaders they are accountable for that performance. When women are added to a unit, commanders must learn to deal with issues such as sexual harassment, assignments for pregnant soldiers, and fraternization between men and women soldiers. Some officers object to integrating women into their units because they must manage not only their own feelings but also the opinions and reactions of their male subordinates and any disciplinary problems that may arise as a result. Especially problematic is the reaction of officers

TABLE 3   Army Men's Opinions on the Combat Exclusion Policy, by Race*** and Rank***

	WHITES			BLACKS, HISPANICS, AND OTHER RACES
	Enlisted	NCOs	Officers	All Ranks[a]
I am satisfied with the present Army regulations that exclude women from direct combat roles.	42%	50%	68%	34%
I think that women who want to volunteer for the combat arms should be allowed to do so.	39	32	18	48
I think that women should be treated exactly like men and serve in the combat arms just like men.	19	18	14	18
Totals	100%	100%	100%	100%
(N)	(402)	(214)	(146)	(550)

[a]Rank was significant only for White men; race differences were significant only between Whites and nonwhites. Among men of color, race and rank were not significant.
***$p < .001$.

who have never worked with women: They often base their projections about integration on rumors they have heard from units containing women.

WHY GENDER HARASSMENT?
PERCEPTIONS OF POWER
AND LIMITED FORMS OF PROTEST

Some men resort to gender harassment to protect changing gender norms, either because they personally prefer traditional norms or because they think that men and women are not capable of successfully working outside traditional roles. Many of these men believe that women's attempts to claim equality have resulted in favorable treatment for women who have been largely unwilling or unable to fully meet the demands of being a soldier. Gender harassment is an attempt to push women back into their more "natural" roles, restore the meritocratic order of the organization, and ensure that all soldiers on the battlefield can do their jobs and assist the wounded in times of war. Certainly these views are considered sexist by many, and potentially could cause problems for any soldier who expresses them openly in mixed company. Thus gender harassment is preferred as an often unattributable way to protest the expansion of women's roles and to attempt to balance scales that are perceived to be tilted in women's favor.

Hostile Proponents and Another Version of Equality

"Women should be given totally equal treatment and standards. But I don't see it happening." This assertion by a male Army captain expresses the views of many Army men. Rather than championing women's rights, however, this officer is among the men who feel that women, not men, are the privileged and powerful group in the military. These men oppose expanding women's opportunities because they believe that women already enjoy too many advantages in the organization and have not yet met the requirements of the roles they already fill.

Some men believe that women use the term *equality* to advance their personal interests, and that they would object if true equality were offered:

My opinion is that if women want the right to be in combat roles, they should have to register with selective service. Also, if women want to be treated and have the same rights as men, they should be treated equally all of the time and not just when it is convenient for them. (White enlisted man)

Table 4 displays Army women's opinions on combat policy. Without the ethnographic data, one might compare this table with Table 3 and incorrectly deduce that men support equality more strongly than do women: Nearly four times as

TABLE 4 Army Women's Opinions on the Combat Exclusion Policy, by Rank***

	ENLISTED	NCOs	OFFICERS
I am satisfied with the present Army regulations that exclude women from direct combat roles.	16%	24%	16%
I think that women who want to volunteer for the combat arms should be allowed to do so.	78	72	70
I think that women should be treated exactly like men and serve in the combat arms just like men.	6	4	14
Totals	100%	100%	100%
(*N*)	(799)	(404)	(235)

***$p < .001$.

many men endorse treating women the same as men with regard to assignment to the combat arms. Indeed, some respondents, such as one White enlisted man in the combat arms, said that if women prove to be capable, they should be given the same assignments as men: "Women should be given a one time chance to see if they could be in the combat arms. Like a test platoon!"

Interview data, however, reveal that most of the men who favor opening combat roles to women on the same terms as men do so only because they are confident that women will fail in those roles. I term this group "hostile proponents" of women in combat. Such hostile proponents reason that the issue of women in the combat arms will not be put to rest until women have been given the opportunity to prove their incompetence. For example, a male driver agreed that women should be allowed to volunteer for combat roles— until he dropped off the female officer who was traveling with us. As soon as she left our group, he added that he thought women should be allowed into combat because they would see how hard the combat arms really are, and no one would have to listen any longer to their complaints about wanting to be included. This "treat women the same to watch them fail" attitude was expressed in writing by a White NCO in the combat arms:

> My feelings are that women just want a door open that is closed. If they want to be totally equal with us, shave their head in basic training [and] give them the same [physical training] test as men. Women in the infantry would ruin male bonding and get soldiers killed or hurt trying to cover for them in combat. Try an all female infantry basic training and [advanced individual training] with the exact same standards as males.

The idea of testing women's abilities to assess their limitations for military service has a precedent. In the 1970s the Army experimentally integrated women into various exercises to determine what percentage of women would be required to decrease military effectiveness (Army Research Institute 1977, 1978). The Army suggested that these surveys (known as the MAX WAC and REF WAC studies) be conducted in response to instructions from the Department of Defense to the Army to double its proportion of women. Yet even when the studies showed that women performed well and without a negative impact on unit performance, the true skeptics did not change their opinions. When the subject of these tests came up during my interviews, men who oppose women's serving in combat roles charged that field exercises do not accurately represent combat conditions. According to this logic, we cannot risk sending women into war as combat soldiers because we do not have systematic evidence showing how they would perform; yet we will never have this kind of evidence because experimental environments cannot replicate the actual conditions of war.

These hostile proponents have found that they can voice their objections by appropriating the language of the feminist activists. Arguments that women should stay home and raise children can be denounced as sexist: agreeing with activists that women and men are "equal" and should be expected to be treated equally cannot. When women are kept out of certain occupations, feminists can continue to argue that women, given the chance, could perform as well as men. Hostile proponents believe that admitting women is a better strategy for reducing the credibility of such arguments because, they insist, the reality will prove the arguments false.

I examined a cluster of survey items to identify hostile proponents of expanding women's roles. Some soldiers indicated that women should be assigned to combat roles on the same terms as men, but also believed that doing so would reduce military effectiveness and that most or all women are incapable of filling such roles successfully. I assumed these soldiers to be hostile proponents because this combination of beliefs reflected those found in interviews. In each wave of the surveys, virtually the entire 20 percent of the men who selected the "same-as-men" combat option for women fell into this category.

One resistant male soldier provided the formula "(Equal pay = equal job = equal responsibility = equal risk) = equal opportunity" to stress that equality should be sought across the board, not only in pay or opportunity. He was one of many men who believed that the differential policies actually work in women's favor, disrupt the meritocratic order, and are likely to imperil soldiers in times of war.

A few combat soldiers in my survey were motivated by self-interest to support admitting women to their MOSs. One such man, a Black NCO, wrote:

> If women are allowed in combat they should be made to shave their heads like men, or let men grow their hair like women. And if women are allowed, field duly would become better for men, because of [women's] needs. So therefore, I'm for them in combat. Yes, let them in.

Men's Perceptions of Women's Privileges

Why do some Army men perceive themselves, and not women, to be the disadvantaged gender in the military? Although other respondents offer counterarguments to these men's opinions, I focus here on the viewpoint of men who record themselves as underdogs. In this section I demonstrate how a structurally dominant group can perceive itself to be a disadvantaged group, and therefore resort to the types of resistance strategies that Scott attributes to the weak. The unifying theme of these examples is the belief that most military women do not take the same risks or work as hard as do military men, and yet are promoted more quickly than men because of their gender.

Easier Physical Training Standards.   Both men and women reported that women's physical training requirements are not only different from men's, but easier for most women to meet than men's are for most men. Although this training is supposed to maintain physical fitness, most soldiers interpret it as a measure of strength. That the women's requirements are easier than the men's is seen by many as proof that women are less well qualified for physically strenuous work:

> I can't be adamant enough. There is no place for women in the infantry. Women do not belong in combat units. If you haven't been there, then you wouldn't understand. As far as equal rights, some women say they are as physically strong as a man. Then why are the [physical training] standards different? (White NCO in the combat arms)

Thus some soldiers argue that only one standard should exist for men and for women, and that such a standard should reflect the requirements of the job. A White lieutenant in intelligence and communications explained his view:

> The standards are never the same for men and women. The [Army Physical Fitness Test] is a perfect example. [W]hat most junior leaders feel (that I have discussed the topic with)…there should be no difference for either sex. [The Department of the Army] has established minimum standards and they should apply across the board, regardless of sex. Which means the female standards would have to go out the window. A man who can only do 18 pushups is unfit for service, so it should be [the same] for females. If a female can meet the same standards as me, I will gladly serve with, for, or over her. But if she can't I will also gladly chapter her out of the Army as unfit for service. I've seen action in Grenada and Iraq and know there are females who could've done my job. Few, but some. However my wife, who went to Saudi, is 104 lbs, 5'4" and couldn't carry my 201 lbs across the living room, much less the desert if I was wounded. Whose standards should apply?

In deployments and field exercises, the differences are most apparent. Some commanders find them difficult to know how to handle:

> The topic about women in combat MOS's has finally cleared up with me. I have completed [platoon leadership training], and found that the women on my patrol team could not perform their squad duties. For example, being a 60-gunner, or radio operator, I was patrol leader. I assigned the females on my team the 60 and the radio. After about 2 miles of patrolling, the females could not

do their jobs. I was accused of being sexist, but when it came down to it, men had to take those assigned jobs in my squad from these women. I'm sure that there are some females that could "keep up" or "hang" with the men, but the fact is that women are not physically strong enough. (White enlisted man in the combat arms)

Pregnancy as an Advantage.   Some men find it unfair that women have an honorable option out of the service, deployments, or single barracks that men do not have: pregnancy. A White enlisted man in intelligence and communications wrote:

There seems to be a trend that females in the Army take advantage of free medical and have kids while serving. The 9 months of pregnancy limits them to no physical labor and is bad on morale. They are still a soldier, but they are only working at about 30% of their potential, forcing men or non-pregnant women to compensate.

A White lieutenant in the medical field noted, "I am currently in a unit with female soldiers, about 60–75% are pregnant or on some type of profile." "Profile" is a standing in which soldiers' physical abilities are limited; therefore they are exempt from physically strenuous tasks, including daily physical training. Pregnant women are among the most common sources of resentment and thus are targets of harassment. Pregnancy then, is another way in which some men feel that women are receiving equal pay and promotion, but are not doing equal work and not taking equal risks and responsibilities.

Better Educational Opportunities.   Many men feel that restrictions on women's roles are unfair not because they limit women, but because they appear to give women opportunities to receive more schooling than men, thus improving their chances for promotion. A White enlisted man wrote, "Most women are in rear units and have the chance to go to school and complete correspondence courses." A Black NCO viewed these opportunities as tipping the balance in women's favor in competitions for promotion: "Of most of the units that I've served, the female soldier is

more apt to attend schools, i.e. military and civilian. This constant trend allows them better opportunities for career progression."

Some men feel that with this extra training, women will be more qualified than men, with the result that "Most women are promoted above their peers" (White NCO). One White enlisted man expressed the view that it is wasteful to allow women to take coveted slots in combat-related training to help their careers when they are currently restricted from performing those tasks in the event of a real war:

Each person male or female will perform according to his or her gifts. We cannot make that determination. Congress needs to get off its lazy butt and make a decision one way or the other. Until that time, it remains a waste of time and taxpayer's money to send women to combat related schools (jump schools and air assault, etc.) just for the sake of being "stylish" and to appease those women who whine about discrimination when they're not allowed to do something a male soldier does.

Exemption from Combat Arms as a Way to Faster Promotion, Better Assignments, and "Cushy" Jobs.   In some units there is a hierarchy of assignments, which is sometimes disrupted by the way women are integrated. The lowest jobs are often the "grunt work"—hard, mindless labor. Some men protested to me that when women are assigned to such a unit, they are spared the grunt work and placed (often by male superiors) ahead of men for more desirable assignments. Not only are they excused from doing what men have to do, they also delay men's progress into better positions and sometimes have authority over the men they have bumped. A White lieutenant cited an example of the problems created because a man in a signal MOS can be assigned to a combat unit and required to do grunt work, but a woman is always assigned elsewhere:

Currently, females in combat support roles (e.g., signal, chemical, [military police], medical services) cannot hold a designated position in Combat Units. For example, females are allowed to serve in the signal corps, but they are not allowed to serve as a signal [platoon leader] in a combat arms unit. There is too much animosity towards females in a specific branch if they can't hold the same positions that their male counterparts [do]. The females are seen as getting the "cushy" jobs and interesting jobs as the males have to fulfill the combat roles. If a female cannot hold a position in their designated specialty, they should not be allowed in that specific specialty.

These men view women not only as obtaining easier work, but as jumping up the hierarchy without earning it. As a White lieutenant explains, this can breed resentment:

Chemical corps: females should not be allowed in this branch if they cannot serve in all positions. For example, they get sent to this division, but cannot serve in the infantry, armor, or forward artillery units. This leaves very few slots for them to fill. [The Army] does not manage this very [well] at all. As a new lieutenant, we must put in our time at the battalion staff level, first, then we are awarded a platoon at the chem company. (One company per division). [The Department of the Army) sends us more females than we have slots for, so they wind up being platoon leaders at the company ahead of the males who have put in their time at the battalions. A lot of hard feelings about this. They (females) should not be branched chemical or some of the other combat support branches.

In a related situation reported by both men and women, in units that perform blue-collar-type work, women are assigned office or paperwork tasks because of stereotypic beliefs that they are naturally more skilled in that area: "They are more likely to be pulled to work as clerks" (White lieutenant). Men resent that women receive what they see as the "cushy" jobs.

Men complained that women are not required to do the heaviest or dirtiest part of any job, and that they can get away with it without reprimand because of their sex. Although men may find it humorous when Beetle Bailey shirks his assignments, they may become resentful when women have an unfair advantage based on their sex. One Black enlisted man wrote: "Today all you hear in the Army is that we are equal, but men do all the

hard and heavy work whether it's combat or not." A White enlisted man with experience in mixed units complained: "I've served with females in the Army. It sucks, they're weak and all they want to do is get over, which in most cases they do because they're female."

According to some men, women's current behavior is proof that most are unable or unwilling to do the work required of soldiers in the combat arms. Thus they resist putting their lives on the line with such soldiers: "I feel women are useless to the Army, most do not do their part when it comes to real work! Most won't change a tire, or pick up a box if it weighs more than 5 lbs. I would not go to war with women in or out of a combat role." Some of these conclusions are based on experience in the States:

When given the same opportunity, most [women] look for excuses not to do the work. You in your position cannot see it, However, I am exposed to it daily. The majority of females I know are not soldiers. They are employed. Anything strenuous is avoided with a passion. I would hate to serve with them during combat! I would end up doing my job and 2/3 of theirs just to stay alive. (Black NCO in administrative work)

I feel as if women in the military are ordered to do less work, get out of doing things such as field problems, and when it comes to doing heavy work, they just stand around and watch the work until it is completed. This is part of the reason I feel they could not handle a combat role because of a weaker physical and mental capability under such a stressful situation. I say this because it is proved in an everyday day of work. (Black enlisted man in a technical field)

Perhaps even stronger are the protests from those who had unpleasant experiences with women during overseas operations:

I feel that there is a majority of women who use their gender as a way of getting out of some heavy and difficult [assignments]. Working with women in [Southeast Asia] has led me to stand firm that women are not physically able to handle combat

MOSs. (White enlisted man in the intelligence and communications branch)

Women's gender identity traditionally has been tied to "delicacy," while men's identity has been tied to the ability to be tough and strong. So men may try to avoid work in general, but avoiding heavy labor in particular would make them look weak, cast doubt on their masculinity, and draw ridicule from other men about their "femininity." Thus many men resent that women can avoid a great deal of dirty, heavy work and still succeed in the military, while men's lives are considerably tougher. Although men tend to lay most of the blame for "getting by" on women, this behavior could not persist unless the leaders allowed it.

Paternalism Allowing Women to Get Away With More. Several men commented that favoritism, not limited opportunity, is holding Army women back: "As long as women continue to get special breaks, they will not be able to realize their full potential" (White NCO in equipment repair). A White enlisted man in the medical field was frustrated because, he believes, "Women are given easier treatment than men on a daily basis!" Indeed, differential assignment of tasks is often based on leaders' stereotypes of what women can and should do.

Both men and women may try to bend the rules, but when women succeed because of their gender, male coworkers may hold it against them. Several times women told me how they could avoid certain duties by complaining of cramps to particular male commanders. At the first mention of anything "menstrual" their commander would grimace and wave them away. (This did not work with women superiors, who sent them to sick call if they thought the cramps were serious.) Two women told me that they could hide off-limits items such as candy by placing tampons or underwear on top of the contents of their lockers or drawers. During inspections, their male commander took one look at their belongings, saw the personal items, and moved on, apparently too embarrassed to examine the rest of the contents.

As another example, one man wrote on his survey,

I don't think women can withstand not being able to take showers for as long as men. When I was in the Gulf, we were ordered to use the water that we had only for drinking. But after one week the women were using our drinking water to take bird baths. This made me very upset.

This problem is framed as a matter of women's behavior, not the command's enforcement of rules.

Male commanders enforce rules differently for women, for several reasons. In the case of the water, the leader may have made this exception for women because he perceived them as more fragile than men, or felt that some sort of chivalry was appropriate. Padavic and Reskin (1990) call such behavior "paternalism," which they measured in their study of blue-collar workers according to whether women "had been relieved of some hard assignments, whether male coworkers had given them special treatment because of their sex, and whether their supervisors had favored them because of their sex" (p. 618).

Men in command positions sometimes fear disciplining women or pushing them to excel. These men worry that they will be accused of harassing women soldiers because of their gender, or of being insensitive to women's needs or limitations. Also, some are too embarrassed about women's underwear or hygiene to perform the ritual invasion of privacy men must undergo. As a result, even when sensitivity to women is intended, women receive privileges that men do not; this situation breeds disdain for women soldiers among some of the men.

In the military, some believe that male leaders' unwillingness to push women to excel creates a weakness among the troops that could have grave consequences during a war:

The more fundamental question is whether women should be in the military at all. They have served well, but are victims of a male dominated system which has always demanded less of them than they would (hopefully) of themselves. If every soldier in the U.S. Army today had been trained at the same low level of expectation that female soldiers routinely are, the U.S. Army today would be either dead or in Prisoner of War camps. (an "other race" major)

Quotas, Sex, and Other Paths to the Top. As noted earlier, some men believe that women can "sleep their way" to the top, and that quotas allow women to receive undeserved promotions and assignments because of their minority status. Some men also believe that women can and do challenge poor performance reviews by claiming discrimination, and that they can use false harassment claims to punish or remove men they do not like. The perception is that women usually are believed over men in harassment cases; as a result, men's careers are ruined by the whims of ambitious or vengeful women.

Most of these perceptions reinforce the view that women want the prestige and promotions that come with serving in the combat arms, but do not intend to make the same efforts as men: "They want equal rights, but don't want to do what it takes to become equal" (White enlisted man in administration).

Limited Forms of Protest

When I asked men who opposed women in combat roles what they thought would happen in the future, they all asserted that integration was inevitable. They concluded that women eventually would "have their way" despite any reasonable objections. Perhaps because women's gains have been made gradually over the years, men perceive this progression not as a series of slow, incremental changes toward one goal but as a string of victories for women over men.

One white major said, "As minorities, women have advantages." White men were likely to have a similar attitude about race; for example, they tended to think that nonwhite soldiers unfairly charge racial discrimination to challenge negative performance reviews. One White NCO spoke for

many of his comrades in defining himself as a member of the oppressed minority: "I feel that the White enlisted male has more prejudice against him than any other sector in the military." He specified not only his gender but also his race and rank as contributing to his position.

Scott analyzes both the micro interactional forms of resistance by subjugated people and the outward rebellion of the powerless that occurs when "an entire category of people suddenly finds it's public voice no longer stifled" (1990:210). I found the reverse among military men: a category of people who have assumed and enjoyed gender privilege, and who rebel because their public voice has been deemed sexist and has been silenced.

Because of the nature of the military organization, many forms of protest are not realistic options for men who contend that they are disadvantaged. Army men cannot strike, circulate petitions, organize rallies or demonstrations, walk out during the workday, or quit collectively in response to a policy change. (Before quitting they would have to meet their enlistment obligations or complete time-consuming formal exit procedures and paperwork.) Boycotts and "client preference" arguments are generally irrelevant here. Thus men who are silent in mixed-sex environments may be channeling their frustrations into underground grumbling.

I experienced firsthand evidence of men's perception that they must hide their opinions. Often the men who eventually voiced their objections to working with women were not initially forthright. When asked about gender issues, they first told me what they imagined I wanted to hear, or recited the "party line" that would keep them out of trouble should any statements be attributed to them. After calculating my opinion on the basis of my status as a young civilian woman conducting research on military women, they hesitated at my opening questions and then said reluctantly that they thought women should and could serve in any military roles. Then, when I raised an opposing argument (such as "So you don't see any problem with close contact between men and women serving in tanks together?"), their true feelings burst forth.[4]

In mixed-sex groups (particularly groups of officers), some of the men squirmed, rolled their eyes, or shook their heads, but did not speak up during discussions about gender. After I dismissed the group, I privately asked those men to stay behind, and asked them why they were silent but seemingly dissatisfied. They revealed that they refrained from participating because they believed that organizational constraints prohibited them from stating their true opinions, particularly in the presence of officer women. In this way I learned which arguments were considered legitimate in the organization (at least when women were present) and which would be censured. The opportunity to write anonymous comments on the formal questionnaires may have been particularly appreciated by soldiers who felt their views were controversial. Men were concerned that they would be held accountable for any statements that could be considered sexist; they feared an official reprimand and negative consequences for their career.

These soldiers' perceptions are evidence that the Army has made some headway in controlling men's willingness to make openly sexist statements. (Soldiers' self-censorship about gender contrasted sharply with their comments about allowing open gays and lesbians to serve in the military; men did not hesitate to make loud, violent threats against any gays they might discover.) Many of these men resent the inability to speak their minds. They believe that even if they could speak candidly, their concerns would not be addressed formally because they think women have the advantage in gender-based disputes. Therefore they express their resentment in ways that the institution cannot control.

Male soldiers interpret the "suppression" of some arguments against women as proof that those arguments are valid and that women have no legitimate counterargument. Thus some men are angry because they perceive women as having gained their power in the military illegitimately or as having taken advantage of that power. Others simply object to changing gender norms and increasing participation of women in non-traditional roles. This tension is exacerbated by the perceived prohibition against expressing their dissatisfaction. Therefore many men hold their tongues in public, but complain among themselves and retaliate with gender harassment. Although grumbling is certainly a part of military culture, the resistance strategies I found directed against women are rarely employed for similar complaints against male leaders or fellow soldiers in general.

IMPLICATIONS OF GENDER HARASSMENT

Publicized cases of sexual harassment in the 1990s have taught many men the definitions and the possible consequences of this behavior.

Yet improvements in controlling sexual harassment do not necessarily mean that women are now working in a supportive or even a tolerant environment. Although women can be hurt by public sexist comments that express doubts about their abilities, it is also debilitating when such comments are forced underground, where they cannot be challenged. In addition, because many men perceive themselves as unable to safely voice their concerns about women as coworkers, some men feel that gender harassment is a justified means of registering their complaints.

Although sexual harassment policies and education were overhauled in the Army in 1994, gender harassment is likely to persist, if not to increase. Gender harassment is more subtle than sexual harassment and often impossible to trace. Even if policy makers were to address it, attempts at regulation would be ineffective when no initiator could be identified.

As previously disadvantaged groups gain some power in legislating discriminatory behavior, their opponents may come to rely on forms of resistance that are difficult to regulate. These implications go beyond gender and affect areas such as race, ethnicity, and sexual orientation. Even as minorities enjoy increased success in controlling overt harassment, they must recognize that people will seek other ways to express hostility. When minority groups call for equality, they should be prepared to be informed about inequities that favor them, and to learn how the language of equality might be used against them.

NOTES

1. I am grateful to Charles Moskos for bringing this custom to my attention.

2. I use the term *constant scrutiny* rather than Rosabeth Moss Kanter's (1977) *visibility* because the latter connotes an unintentional result due to the small numerical size of the minority.

3. All analyses of variance in this study included a search for possible interaction among variables: the appropriate controls were employed when necessary.

4. Men who I believe truly support women in combat roles responded to this probing technique with assertions such as "No. I don't think it would be a problem. Men and women can work together without having sex all the time: I've seen it."

REFERENCES

Army Research Institute. 1977. *Women Content in Units Force Deployment Test* (MAX WAC). Alexandria, VA: Army Research Institute.

———. 1978. *Women Content in the Army—Reforger 77* (REF WAC). Alexandria, VA: Army Research Institute.

Binkin, Martin. 1993. *Who Will Fight the Next War? The Changing Face of the American Military.* Washington, DC: Brookings Institute.

Cartwright, Dorwin, ed. 1959. *Studies in Social Power.* Ann Arbor: University of Michigan Press.

Collins, Patricia Hill. 1991. *Black Feminist Thought.* New York: Routledge.

Davis, Angela Y. 1981. *Women, Race & Class.* New York: Random House.

Defense Equal Opportunity Management Institute (DEOMI). 1996. *Semi-Annual Race/Ethnic/Gender Profile.* Patrick Air Force Base. FL: DEOMI.

Devilbiss, M. C. 1990. *Women and Military Service: A History, Analysis, and Overview of Key Issues.* Maxwell Air Force Base, AL: Air University Press.

Donnelly, Elaine. 1991. "Politics and the Pentagon: The Role of Women in the Military." Unpublished manuscript.

Eisenhart, R. Wayne. 1975. "You Can't Hack It, Little Girl: A Discussion of the Covert Psychological Agenda of Modern Combat Training." *Journal of Social Issues* 31(4):13–23.

Enloe, Cynthia. 1983. *Does Khaki Become You? The Militarization of Women's Lives.* Boston: South End Press.

Ferguson, Trudi C. with Madeline Sharples. 1994. *Blue Collar Women: Trailblazing Women Take On Men-Only Jobs.* Liberty Corner, NJ: New Horizon Press.

Halle, David. 1984. *America's Working Man.* Chicago: University of Chicago Press.

Holm, Jeanne. [1982] 1992. *Women in the Military: An Unfinished Revolution.* Novato, CA: Presidio Press.

Hooks, Bell. 1984. *Feminist Theory: From Margin to Center.* Boston: South End Press.

Kanter, Rosabeth Moss. 1977. *Men and Women of the Corporation.* New York: Basic Books.

Lips, Hilary M. 1981. *Women, Men, and the Psychology of Power.* Englewood Cliffs, NJ: Prentice-Hall.

Mansfield, Phyllis Kernoff, Patricia Barthalow Koch, Julie Henderson, Judith R. Vicary, Margaret Cohn, and Elaine W. Young. 1991. "The Job Climate for Women in Traditionally Male Blue-Collar Occupations." *Sex Roles* 25(½):63–79.

Martin, Molly, ed. 1988. *Hard Hatted Women: Stories of Struggle and Success in the Trades.* Seattle: Seal Press.

Martin, Susan Ehrlich. 1980. *Breaking and Entering: Police Women on Patrol.* Berkeley: University of California Press.

Miles, Matthew B. and A. Michael Huberman. 1994. *Qualitative Data Analysis.* Thousand Oaks, CA: Sage.

Mitchell, Brian. 1989. *Weak Link: The Feminization of the American Military.* Washington, DC: Regnery Gateway.

Ng, Sik Hung. 1980. *The Social Psychology of Power.* NY: Academic Press.

O'Farrell, Brigid and Sharon L. Harlan. 1982. "Craftworkers and Clerks: The Effect of Male Co-Worker Hostility on Women's Satisfaction with Non-Traditional Jobs." *Social Problems* 29: 252–65.

Padavic, Irene and Barbara F. Reskin. 1990. "Men's Behavior and Women's Interest in Blue-Collar Jobs." *Social Problems* 37:613–28.

Presidential Commission on the Assignment of Women in the Armed Forces. 1992. *Report to the President, November 15, 1992.* Washington, DC: U.S. Government Printing Office.

Reskin, Barbara F. and Irene Padavic. 1988. "Supervisors as Gatekeepers: Male Supervisors' Response to Women's Integration in Plant Jobs." *Social Problems* 35:536–50.

Schneider, Dorothy and Carl J. Schneider. 1988. *Sound Off! American Military Women Speak Out.* New York: Dutton.

Schroedel, Jean R. 1985. *Alone in a Crowd: Women in the Trades Tell Their Stories.* Philadelphia: Temple University Press.

Scott, James C. 1985. *Weapons of the Weak: Everyday Forms of Peasant Resistance.* New Haven: Yale University Press.

———. 1990. *Domination and the Arts of Resistance: Hidden Transcripts.* New Haven: Yale University Press.

Segal, Mady Wechsler. 1982. "The Argument for Female Combatants." Pp. 267–87 in *Female Soldiers: Combatants or Noncombatants?* edited by Nancy Loring Goldman. Westport, CT: Greenwood.

Stiehm, Judith Hicks. 1981. *Bring Me Men and Women.* Berkeley: University of California Press.

———. ed. 1983. *Women and Men's Wars.* New York: Pergamon.

———. 1989. *Arms and the Enlisted Woman.* Philadelphia: Temple University Press.

Tuten, Jeff M. 1982. "The Argument Against Female Combatants." Pp. 137–65 in *Female Soldiers: Combatants or Noncombatants?* edited by Nancy Loring Goldman, Westport, CT: Greenwood.

Waite, Linda J. and Sue E. Berryman. 1985. *Women in Nontraditional Occupations: Choice and Turnover.* Santa Monica: RAND.

Walshok, Mary L. 1981. *Blue-Collar Women.* Garden City, NY: Anchor.

Wekesser, Carol and Matthew Polesetsky. eds. 1991. *Women in the Military.* San Diego: Greenhaven.

Williams, Christine L. 1989. *Gender Differences at Work: Women and Men in Nontraditional Occupations.* Berkeley: University of California Press.

Willis, Paul. 1977. *Learning to Labor.* New York: Columbia University Press.

Zimmer, Lynn E. 1986. *Women Guarding Men.* Chicago: University of Chicago Press.

PART SEVEN

Popular Culture

Most of the articles in this book have examined gender and other relations of inequality primarily in terms of peoples' lived experiences within social institutions such as families and workplaces. This reflects, in our minds, the importance of examining gender, race, class, and sexual orientation within a social structural perspective. However, an examination of peoples' lived experiences within institutions does not tell the whole story about gender relations. The arena of ideas, beliefs, and values is also of crucial importance. And one of the most dynamic places in which people learn, contest, and forge values and beliefs is in the vast and varied arena of popular culture. In this part, the articles reflect on how the magazines we read, the sports we watch, and the music we listen to are cultural creations through which dominant values are often imposed on people, but may also become arenas in which these values are contested and new values forged.

In the first article, Catherine A. Lutz and Jane L. Collins argue that, for White U.S. readers, *National Geographic Magazine* has provided an opportunity to gaze upon the bodies and lives of non-Western women in a particular way that articulates White middle-class women's ambivalences about motherhood, sexuality, and wage labor. Although millions of readers may think of *National Geographic* as their window on the world, Lutz and Collins's analysis of the magazine's contents suggests that the way it presents non-Western women may tell us more about ourselves than about the "other." Next, Shari Lee Dworkin and Faye Linda Wachs's systematic analysis of newspaper coverage of the HIV-positive announcements by professional athletes Magic Johnson, Greg Louganis, and Tommy Morrison illustrates how the mass media responds to what might be a moment of "crisis" for dominant conceptions of masculinity. By linking the virus to gay, Black, and working-class bodies, the mass media frames the meanings of the "athlete with AIDS" news story in a way that shores up the image of White, middle-class, heterosexual masculinity as the healthy and safe norm.

These first two articles, on *National Geographic* and media coverage of HIV-positive professional athletes, share one thing in common: They are "textual analyses" that reveal the ways that dominant gender, race, sexual, and national meanings are encoded in popular icons. But they do not delve into the various ways that consumers might themselves use or "read" these popular texts—and these readings might sometimes express skeptical, critical, or even resistant reactions to the dominant encoded meanings. Popular music—and the youth cultures that surround it—sometimes play this sort of resistant role. In the final article in this section, Melissa Klein discusses how she and other young women have come to define themselves as "Third Wave Feminists" within the context of punk and "Riot Grrrrl" cultures. Alternative music, Klein argues, provided girls and young women like her an empowering context in which to forge feminist identities that are continuous with, but different from, the "second wave" feminism of their mothers. In short, alternative music may be a popular cultural expression that points to one avenue through which the goal of this book might be achieved—the building of a movement toward a more just society in which race, class, gender, and other inequalities are simultaneously confronted.

43

The Color of Sex

Postwar Photographic Histories of Race and Gender in *National Geographic Magazine*

CATHERINE A. LUTZ
JANE L. COLLINS

THE WOMEN OF THE WORLD

National Geographic photographs of the women of the world tell a story about the women of the United States over the post–World War II period. It is to issues of gender in White American readers' lives, such as debates over women's sexuality or whether women doing paid labor can mother their children adequately, that the pictures refer as much as to the lives of third world women. Seen in this way, the *National Geographic*'s women can be placed alongside the other women of American popular culture: the First lady, the woman draped over an advertisement's red sports car, the Barbie doll, the woman to whom the Hallmark Mother's Day card is addressed. Rather than treating the photos as simply images of women, we can set them in the context of a more complex cultural history of the period, with the sometimes radical changes it brought to the lives of the women who are the readers (or known to the male readers) of the magazine.

The photographs of *National Geographic* are indispensable to understanding issues of gender because the magazine is one of the very few popular venues trafficking in large numbers of images of Black women. While the photographs tell a story about cultural ideals of femininity, the narrative threads of gender and race are tightly bound up with each other. In the world at large, race and gender are clearly not separate systems, as Trinh (1989), Moore (1988), Sacks (1989), and others have reminded us.

For the overwhelmingly White readers of the *Geographic,* the dark-skinned women of distant regions serve as touchstones, giving lessons both positive and negative about what women are and should be (compare Botting 1988). Here, as elsewhere, the magazine plays with possibilities of the other as a flexible reflection—even a sort of funhouse mirror—for the self. The women of the world are portrayed in sometimes striking parallel to popular images of American womanhood of the various periods of the magazine's production—for instance, as mothers and beautiful objects. At certain times, with certain races of women, however, the *Geographic*'s other women provide a contrast to stereotypes of White American women—they are presented as hard-working breadwinners in their communities.

As with American women in popular culture, Third World women are portrayed less frequently than men: one-quarter of the pictures we looked at focus primarily on women.[1] The situation has traditionally not been that different in the anthropological literature covering the non-Western world, and it may be amplified in both genres where the focus is on cultural difference or exoticism. Given the association between women and the natural world, men and things cultural (Ortner 1974), a magazine that aspires to describe the distinctive achievements of civilizations might be expected to highlight the world of men. But like the "people of nature" in the Fourth World, women have been treated as all the more precious for their nonutilitarian, nonrationalistic qualities. Photographs of women become one of the primary devices by which the magazine depicts "universal human values," and these include the values of family love and the appreciation of female beauty itself.[2] We turn to these two issues now, noting that each of them has had a consistent cultural content through the postwar period, during historical changes that give the images different emphases and form through the decades.

The motherhood of man. There is no more romantic set of photographs in the *Geographic* than those depicting the mothers of the world with their children. There is the exuberant picture showing the delight of a Kurd mother holding her infant. Filling much space, as an unusually high percentage of the magazine's mother-child pictures do, the photograph covers two pages despite the relative lack of information in it. Its classical composition and crisp, uncluttered message are similar to those in many such photos. They often suggest the Western tradition of madonna painting, and evoke the Mother's Day message: this relationship between mother and child, they say, is a timeless and sacred one, essentially and intensely loving regardless of social and historical context—the foundation of human social life rather than cultural difference. The family of man, these pictures might suggest, is first of all a mother-child unit, rather than a brotherhood of solidarity between adults.[3]

For the magazine staff and readers of the 1950s, there must have been even more power in these images than we see in them today. The impact of the photos would have come from the intense cultural and social pressures of middle-class women to see their most valued role as that of mother (Margolis 1984). The unusually strong pressure of this period is often explained as motivated by desires to place returning World War II veterans (and men in general) in those jobs available and by anxieties about the recent war horror and the future potential for a nuclear conflagration, which made the family seem a safe haven (May 1988). As a new cult of domesticity emerged, women were told—through both science and popular culture—that biology, morality, and the psychological health of the next generation required their commitment to full-time mothering. This ideological pressure persisted through the 1950s despite the rapid rise in female employment through the decade.

The idealization of the mother-child bond is seen in everything from the warm TV relationships of June Clever with Wally and the Beaver to the cover of a *Life* magazine issue of 1956 devoted to "The American Woman" showing a glowing portrait of a mother and daughter lovingly absorbed in each other; all of this is ultimately and dramatically reflected in the period's rapidly expanding birth rate. This idealization had its counterpoint in fear of the power women were given in the domestic domain. In both science and popular culture, the mother was criticized for being smothering, controlling, oversexualized, and, a bit later, overly permissive (Ehrenreich and English 1978, 1988).

The *National Geographic*'s treatment of children can be seen as an extension of these ideologies of motherhood and the family. As the "woman question" came to be asked more angrily in the late 1950s, there was a gradual erosion of faith in the innocence of the mother-infant bond and even in the intrinsic value of children (Ehrenreich and English 1978), centered on fears of juvenile delinquency and the later 1960's identification of a "generation gap." The *National Geographic,* however, continued to print significant numbers of photographs of children, perhaps responding to their increasingly sophisticated marketing information which indicated that photographs of children and cute animals were among their most popular pictures.

In the *National Geographic*'s pictures of mother and child, it often appears that the non-

White mother is backgrounded, with her gaze and the gaze of the reader focused on the infant. The infant may in fact be an even more important site for dealing with White racial anxieties, by virtue of constituting an acceptable Black love object. A good number of pictures in the postwar period have the form of these two: one a Micronesian and the other an Iraqi infant, from 1974 and 1976 respectively, each peacefully asleep in a cradle with the mother visible behind. The peacefulness constitutes the antithesis of the potentially threatening differences of interest, dress, or ritual between the photographed adult and the reader.

Women and their breasts. The "nude" woman sits, stands or lounges at the salient center of *National Geographic* photography of the non-Western world. Until the phenomenal growth of mass circulation pornography in the 1960s, the magazine was known as the only mass culture venue where Americans could see women's breasts. Part of the folklore of Euramerican men, stories about secret perusals of the magazine emerged time after time in our conversations with *National Geographic* readers. People vary in how they portray the personal or cultural meaning of this nakedness, some noting it was an aid to masturbation, others claiming it failed to have the erotic quality they expected. When White men tell these stories about covertly viewing Black women's bodies, they are clearly not recounting a story about a simple encounter with the facts of human anatomy or customs; they are (perhaps unsuspectingly) confessing a highly charged—but socially approved—experience in this dangerous territory of projected, forbidden desire and guilt. Such stories also exist (in a more charged, ironic mode) in the popular culture of the African Americans—for example, in Richard Pryor's characterization of *National Geographic* as the Black man's *Playboy.*

The racial distribution of female nudity in the magazine conforms, in pernicious ways, to Euramerican myths about Black women's sexuality. Lack of modesty in dress places Black women closer to nature. Given the pervasive tendency to interpret skin color as a marker of evolutionary progress, it is assumed that White women have acquired modesty along with other characteristics of civilization. Black women remain backward on this scale, not conscious of the embarrassment they should feel at their nakedness (Gilman 1985: 114–15, 193). Their very ease unclothed stigmatizes them.

In addition, Black women have been portrayed in Western art and science as both exuberant and excessive in their sexuality. While their excess intrigues, it is also read as pathological and dangerous. In the texts produced within White culture, Haraway writes, "Colored women densely code sex, animal, dark, dangerous, fecund, pathological" (1989: 154). Thus for the French surrealists of the 1930s, the exotic, unencumbered sexuality of non-Western peoples—and African women in particular—represented an implicit criticism of the repression and constraint of European sexuality. The Africanism of the 1930s, like an earlier Orientalism, evidenced both a longing for—and fear of—the characteristics attributed to non-Western peoples (Clifford 1988: 61). The sexuality of Black women that so entertained French artists and musicians in cafes and cabarets, however, had fueled earlier popular and scientific preoccupation with the Hottentot Venus and other pathologized renditions of Black women's bodies and desires (Gilman 1985).

Cultural ambivalence toward women working outside the home has been profound during the postwar period, when women's waged employment grew from 25 percent in 1940 to 40 percent in 1960. More of this is accounted for by African American women, half of whom were employed in 1950, with their waged work continuing at high rates in the following decades. The ideological formulation of the meaning of women's work has changed. Working women in the fifties were defined as helpmates to their husbands. Only much later did women's work come to be seen by some as a means to goals of independence and self-realization (Chafe 1983), although even here, as Traube (1989) points out, messages were widely available that women's success in work was threatening to men. This ambivalence occasionally shows up in the *Geographic* when the laboring woman is presented as a drudge or when her femininity, *despite her working,* is emphasized. An example of the latter is found in a photograph of a Burmese woman shown planting small green shoots in a garden row (June 1974: 286). Retouching has been done both to her line of plants and to the flowers which encircle her hair. The sharpening and coloring of these two items lets the picture much more clearly tell a narrative about her femininity and her productivity and about how those two things are not mutually exclusive.

More often, however, the labor of women as well as other aspects of their lives are presented by the *Geographic* as central to the march of progress in their respective countries. Women are constructed as the vanguard of progress in part through the feminizing of the developing nation state itself (Kabbani 1986; cf. Shaffer 1988). How does this work? In the first instance, those foreign states are contrasted, in some Western imaginations, with a deeply masculine American national identity (Krasniewitz 1990; Jeffords 1989), a gendering achieved through the equation of the West (*in* the West, of course) with strength, civilization, rationality, and freedom, its other with vulnerability, primitivity, superstition, and the binds of tradition. Once this equation has been made, articles can be titled as in the following instance where progress is masculinized and the traditional nation feminized: "Beneath the surge of progress, old Mexico's charm and beauty live undisturbed" (October 1961).

Fanon (1965: 39) pointed out in his analysis of French colonial attitudes and strategies concerning the veil in Algeria that the colonialists' goal, here as elsewhere in the world, was "converting the woman, winning her over to the foreign values, wrenching her free from her status" as a means of "shaking up the [native] man" and gaining control of him. With this and other motives, those outsiders who would "develop" the Third World have often seen the advancement of non-

Western women as the first goal to be achieved, with their men's progress thought to follow rather than precede it. In the nineteenth century, evolutionary theory claimed that the move upward from savagery to barbarism to civilization was indexed by the treatment of women, in particular by their liberation "from the burdens of overwork, sexual abuse, and male violence" (Tiffany and Adams 1985: 8). It "saw women in non-Western societies as oppressed and servile creatures, beasts of burden, chattels who could be bought and sold, eventually to be liberated by 'civilization' or 'progress,' thus attaining the enviable position of women in Western society" (Etienne and Leacock 1980: 1), who were then expected to be happy with their place.[4] The *Geographic* has told a much more upbeat version of this story, mainly by presenting other women's labors positively.

The continuation of these ways of thinking into the present can be seen in how states defined as "progressive" have been rendered by both Western media like the *National Geographic* and the non-Western state bureaucrats concerned. Graham-Brown (1988) and Schick (1990) describe how photographic and other proof of the progress of modernity of states like Turkey and pre-revolutionary Iran has often been found primarily in the lives of their women, and particularly in their unveiling.[5] Indeed, as Schick points out, "a photograph of an unveiled woman was not much different from one of a tractor, an industrial complex, or a new railroad; it merely symbolized yet another one of men's achievements" (1990: 369).

Take the example from the *Geographic*'s January 1985 article on Baghdad. Several photographs show veiled women walking through the city's streets. One shot shows women in a narrow alley. The dark tones of the photograph are a function of the lack of sunlight reaching down into the alley, but they also reproduce the message of the caption. Playing with the associations between veil and past that are evoked for most readers, it says, "In the shadows of antiquity, women in long black abayas walk in one of the older sections of the city." A few pages earlier, we learn about the

high-rise building boom in the city and the changing roles of women in a two-page layout that shows a female electrical engineer in a hard hat and jeans organizing a building project with a male colleague. The caption introduces her by name and goes on: "Iraqi women, among the most progressive in the Arab world, constitute 25 percent of the country's work force and are guaranteed equality under Baath Party doctrine." On the opposite page, the modern buildings they have erected are captioned, "New York on the Tigris." The equation of the end point (Manhattan) with the unveiled woman is neatly laid out.

The celebration of simultaneous women's liberation and national progress is not the whole story, of course. The magazine also communicates—in a more muted way through the fifties and into the sixties—a sense of the value of the "natural," Gemeinshaft-based life of the people without progress. Progress can be construed as a socially corrosive process as it was in the late nineteenth century, when non-Western women were seen as superior to their Western counterparts because too much education had weakened the latter (Ehrenreich and English 1978: 114), sapping vitality from their reproductive organs. The illiterate woman of the non-Western world still lives with this cultural inheritance, standing for the woman "unruined" by progress.

An example of the contradictory place of progress is found in two photographs that draw attention to housewives. In the first, an Inuit woman wearing a fur trimmed parka stands in front of a washing machine: "Unfamiliar luxury" the caption says, "a washing machine draws a housewife to the new 'Tuk' laundromat, which also offers hot showers" (July 1968). This picture is explicitly structured around the contrast between the premodern and the modern, with the evaluative balance falling to the luxurious present. It might have still resonated for readers with the image from 1959 of Nixon and Khrushchev arguing over the benefits of capitalism next to a freshly minted washing machine and dryer at the American National Exhibition in Moscow. In those debates,

Nixon could argue that the progress of American society under capitalism is found in its ability to provide labor-saving devices to women. "I think that this attitude toward women is universal. What we want is to make easier the life of our housewives," he said. In the gender stories told during the cold war, family life and commodities provided what security was to be found in the post-Hiroshima, post-Holocaust world (May 1988). The non-Western woman, too, could be deployed as proof of capitalism's value, of the universal desire for these goods, and of the role of women in the evolution of society.

From January 1971, however, an article titled "Housewife at the End of the World" documents the adventures of an Ohio woman settling in Tierra del Fuego, and congratulates her on adapting to local norms of self-sufficiency and simplicity. The last photo's caption articulates the theme of the whole article: "Life in this remote land spurs inventiveness.... My special interests keep me so busy I have little time to miss the conveniences I once knew." The North American woman chooses to forgo the benefits of progress in search of an authentically simple place, as her "younger sister" climbs the ladder in the other direction.

In stories of progress and/or decline, Western and non-Western women have often been played off of one another in this way, each used to critique the other in line with different purposes and in the end leaving each feeling inadequate. The masculine writer/image maker/consumer thereby asserts his own strength, both through his right to evaluate and through his completeness in contrast to women. Although non-Western men cannot be said to fare well in these cultural schemes, they are used less frequently and in other ways (Honour 1989) to either critique or shore up White men's masculinity.

In sum, the women of the non-Western world represent a population aspiring to the full femininity achieved in Western cultures, and, in a more secondary way, they are a repository for the lost femininity of "liberated" Western women. Both an ideal and thus a critique of modern femininity, they are also a measure to tell the Western family how for it has advanced. They are shown working hard and as key to their countries' progress toward some version of the Western consumer family norm. The sometimes contradictory message these pictures can send to middle class women is consistent with cultural ideologies in the United States that both condemn and affirm the woman who would be both mother and wage laborer. We can see the women of the *National Geographic* playing a role within a social field where the Cold War was being waged and where social changes in kinship structures and gender politics were precipitated by the entrance of White women into the paid labor force in larger and larger numbers.

NOTES

1. This proportion is based on those photos in which adults of identifiable gender are shown (N = 510). Another 11 percent show women and men together in roughly equal numbers, leaving 65 percent of the photos depicting mainly men.

2. The popularity of this notion in American culture, which *National Geographic* relies on as much as feeds, is also one wellspring for American feminism's focus on universal sisterhood, that is, its insistence, particularly in the 1970s, that Western and non-Western women will easily see each other as similar or sharing similar experiences.

3. Edward Steichen's *Family of Man* exhibition, first displayed in the United States in 1955, also included a substantial section devoted to mothers and infants, nicknamed "Tits and Tots" by the staff of photographers who organized it (Meltzer 1978). This exhibit was immensely popular when it toured, and the catalogue became a bestselling book.

4. Western feminism in the 1970s may have simply transformed rather than fundamentally challenged the terms of this argument as well when it argued that the women of the world were oppressed by men and to be liberated by feminism as defined in the West (see Amos and Parmar 1984).

5. Although feminist anthropology has analyzed and critiqued these kinds of assumptions, it has nonetheless often continued a basic evolutionary discourse in the assumption that Ong has identified: "Although a common past may be claimed by feminists, Third World women are often represented as mired in it, ever arriving at modernity when Western feminists are already adrift in postmodernism" (1988: 87).

REFERENCES

Amos, V., and Prathiba Parmar. 1984. Challenging Imperial Feminism. *Feminist Review* 17: 3–20.

Betterton, Rosemary, ed. 1987. *Looking On: Images of Femininity in the Visual Arts and Media.* London: Pandora.

Botting, Wendy. 1988. *Posing for Power/Posing for Pleasure: Photographies and the Social Construction of Femininity.* Binghamton, NY: University Art Gallery.

Canaan, Joyce. 1984. *Building Muscles and Getting Curves: Gender Differences in Representations of the Body and Sexuality among American Teenagers.* Paper presented at the Annual Meeting of the American Anthropological Association, Denver.

Carby, Hazel. 1985. "On the Threshold of Woman's Era": Lynching, Empire and Sexuality in Black Feminist Theory. In *Race, Writing and Difference,* ed. H. Gates, pp. 301–16. Chicago: University of Chicago Press.

Carson, Claybourne. 1981. *In Struggle: SNCC and the Black Awakening of the 1960s.* Cambridge: Harvard University Press.

Chafe, William. 1983. Social Change and the American Woman, 1940–70. In *A History of Our Time: Readings on Postwar America,* ed. William Chafe and Harvard Sitkoff, pp. 147–65. New York: Oxford University Press.

Clifford, James. 1988. *The Predicament of Culture: Twentieth-Century Ethnography, Literature and Art.* Cambridge, MA: Harvard University Press.

Collins, Patricia Hill. 1991. *Black Feminist Thought.* Boston: Unwin Hyman.

Ehrenreich, Barbara and Dierdre English. 1978. *For Her Own Good: 150 Years of the Experts' Advice to Women.* Garden City, NY: Anchor Press/Doubleday.

Fanon, Frantz. 1965. *A Dying Colonialism.* New York: Grove Press.

Gaines, Jane. 1988. White Privilege and Looking Relations: Race and Gender in Feminist Film Theory. *Screen* 29 (4): 12–27.

Gilman, Sander. 1985. *Difference and Pathology: Stereotypes of Sexuality, Race, and Madness.* Ithaca: Cornell University Press.

Graham-Brown, Sarah. 1988. *Images of Women: The Portrayal of Women in Photography of the Middle East, 1860–1950.* London: Quartet Books.

Haraway, Donna. 1989. *Primate Visions: Gender, Race, and Nature in the World of Modern Science.* New York: Routledge.

Honour, Hugh. 1989. *The Image of the Black in Western Art.* Vol. 4, From the American Revolution to World War I. New York: Morrow.

Jeffords, Susan. 1989. *The Remasculinization of America: Gender and the Vietnam War.* Bloomington: Indiana University Press.

Kabbani, Rana. 1986. *Europe's Myths of the Orient.* Bloomington: Indiana University Press.

Krasniewicz, Louise. 1990. *Desecrating the Patriotic Body: Flag Burning, Art Censorship, and the Powers of "Prototypical Americans."* Paper presented at the Annual Meeting of the American Anthropological Association, New Orleans.

Margolis, Maxine. 1984. *Mothers and Such.* Berkeley and Los Angeles: University of California Press.

May, Elaine Tyler. 1988. *Homeward Bound: American Families in the Cold War Era.* New York: Basic Books.

Meltzer, Milton. 1978. *Dorothea Lange: A Photographer's Life.* New York: Farrar Straus Giroux.

Moore, Henrietta. 1988. *Feminism and Anthropology.* Cambridge: Cambridge University Press.

Ong, Aihwa. 1988. Colonialization and Modernity: Feminist Re-presentation of Women in Non-Western Societies. *Inscriptions* 3/4: 79–93.

Ortner, Sherry. 1974. Is Female to Male as Nature Is to Culture? In *Woman, Culture and Society,* ed. M. Rosaldo and L. Lamphere, Pp. 67–88. Stanford: Stanford University Press.

Sacks, Karen. 1989. Toward a Unified Theory of Class, Race and Gender. *American Ethnologist* 16: 534–50.

Schaffer, Kay. 1988. *Women and the Bush: Forces of Desire in the Australian Cultural Tradition.* Cambridge: Cambridge University Press.

Tiffany, Sharon, and Kathleen Adams. 1985. *The Wild Woman: An Inquiry into the Anthropology of an Idea.* Cambridge, MA: Schenkman.

Traube, Elizabeth G. 1989. Secrets of Success in Postmodern Society. *Cultural Anthropology* 4: 273–300.

Trinh Minh-Ha. 1989. *Woman, Native, Other: Writing Postcoloniality and Feminism.* Bloomington: Indiana University Press.

44

"Disciplining the Body"

HIV-Positive Male Athletes, Media Surveillance, and the Policing of Sexuality

SHARI LEE DWORKIN
FAYE LINDA WACHS

In the U.S., sport and success at sports signify masculinity, and particular sports are linked to the "right" kind of masculinity. Connell applies the term hegemonic masculinity to this form of masculinity. He argues that hegemonic masculinity is the most valued form of masculinity, which is defined hierarchically in relation to what is feminine and to subordinated masculinities (1987). At the turn of the 20th century, changes in men's and women's roles challenged social ideologies of male physical superiority. Competitive team sports were popularized in the United States as a means for symbolically reaffirming male physical superiority over women and socially subordinated men (Crosset, 1990; Kimmel, 1990; Messner, 1988). From these early influences, modern sport has evolved as a bastion of masculinity in which one particular form of masculinity (white, middle class, heterosexual, and physically dominating) is constructed as the most highly valued (Connell, 1987, 1990, Davis, 1997; Messner, 1988).

Participation in particular types of sport, especially collision sports and often team sports, is understood as "masculine appropriate." For example, sports like basketball, football, and boxing are coded as masculine appropriate sports (Metheny, 1965; Kane, 1988; Kane & Snyder, 1989). These sports are not merely "masculine appropriate" in the sense that they are considered inappropriate for women, but these sports reinforce the ideologies of hegemonic masculinity. As a general rule, the sports in which men dominate or display the elements linked to ideologies of masculine physical superiority are those most valued by our culture (Messner, 1988). These sports are the ones which garner the bulk of television and print media attention (Duncan, Messner, & Jensen, 1994). By extension, the men who participate in these sports are seen as heroes.

Sport may be highly adored and valued in U.S. culture, but it has not gone without its critics. While some applaud the role of sport in reproducing masculinity, others are distinctly apprehensive about what type of masculinity is valued and reproduced. Often, male sports stars are excused from wrongdoing by the term *boys will be boys* and are valorized for their sexual conquests of women (McKay, 1993). Ironically, the media often frame these events so as to privilege and protect "excessive" male heterosexual activity through the classification of women as the aggressors, the "problem," or the temptation upon which any "normal" man would act (McKay, 1993; Wachs & Dworkin, 1997, in press). The media can be said to carry out ideological repair work which protects sports heroes in a gender regime which privileges heterosexual manhood and pathologizes gay male and female (hetero)sexuality (McKay, 1993; Wachs & Dworkin, 1997).

...In Western thought the athletic male body has historically been a mark of power and moral superiority for those who bear it (Dutton, 1995).

Thus, an interesting question remains: How might the mainstream American print media construct sports heroes' bodies once they announce they have a socially stigmatized disease, such as HIV/AIDS? Will the print media protect the widely celebrated virility of male sport heroes, or will it mark the athletes' bodies with symbols of "immorality" and "inappropriate" sexuality? Through an analysis of the different ways in which professional athletes with HIV/AIDS have been framed by print media, we will unpack the racialized, sexualized, and classed iconography of the body. In particular, we will explore how power relations, as expressed in public discourse, normalize certain sexual acts and identities while stigmatizing others.

THE HISTORICAL CONFLATION OF SEXUAL ACT AND IDENTITY

In 1981 the first case of what is now known as Acquired Immune Deficiency Syndrome (AIDS) was reported (Patton, 1990; Seidman, 1992; Weeks, 1985). The disease was first termed GRID or Gay-Relayed Immune Disorder (Patton, 1990; Seidman, 1992). Although the virus was known to be transmitted primarily through blood and "bodily fluids" in sexual acts, AIDS was automatically attached to a specific sexual identity—the gay identity. Ironically, the medical community did not immediately ask *which* sex *acts* were correlated to high risks, but rather, which sexual identities were high risk. Today, numerous mainstream media accounts jump to the same conclusion, so much so that being gay and having AIDS are nearly synonymous (Connell, 1987; LePoire, 1994; Patton, 1990; Watney, 1989; Weeks, 1985)....

Although millions of gay men have died from AIDS and currently constitute the largest category of deaths in the United States, there is no reason to assume that being gay "causes" AIDS any more than being straight "caused" the international reemergence of syphilis prior to the discovery of penicillin. In other words, it is inaccurate to conflate specific sexual identities with the performance of particular sexual acts. This point is exemplified by Alfred Kinsey's work (1948, 1953), wherein he revealed the wide range of sexual behaviors which are practiced by individuals across multiple sexual identity categories.

A current example of the complex relationship between sex acts and sexual identity clarifies this point. For years rumors have circulated about Magic Johnson's alleged bisexual activities. In 1996, several newspapers published articles claiming that Magic Johnson had numerous boyfriends as part of "life in the fast lane." Magic Johnson self-identifies as a heterosexual man and publicly denies any accusations of same-sex activity. Whether he does so in fear of public stigmatization or because the "heterosexual" descriptor is accurate, sexual identity categories by themselves clearly provide little help in unfolding the complexities of HIV/AIDS transmission, behavior, and risk. In fact, there are potentially dangerous consequences of conflating act and identity, especially if the goal is to provide the public with accurate information about HIV transmission.

Equally dangerous is the conflation of sexual identity and risk. For example, gay men are assumed always to engage in high-risk activity. This error is repeated frequently by the medical community and the mass media (Watney, 1989). Despite the dangers of such assumptions, the medical establishment for some time formed sexual "risk groups" largely on the basis of sexual identity. Several researchers (Duggan & Hunter, 1995; Watney, 1989; Weeks, 1985) have highlighted how sexual act, sexual identity, and risk are not necessarily linked. These same researchers note how medicine, law, and the mass media have continued to make and enforce discourses on this basis. As we will demonstrate, mainstream news media perpetuate myths about HIV/AIDS through the absence of any discussion of acts while implicitly fixing sexual identity in relation to specific acts. By assuming a "natural" and "fixed" identity which is assumed to include some acts and partners while excluding others, mainstream news media reinforce ignorance about both sexual practices and risk.

The mass media have historically problematized gay sexuality by marking it as inherently dangerous. While no longer assumed to be a problem solely for the gay community, HIV/AIDS is still solidly and consistently blamed on the gay community (Connell, 1987; Grosz, 1994; LePoire, 1994; Patton, 1990; Seidman, 1992; Sontag, 1989; Watney, 1989; Weeks, 1985). At the same time, members of the heterosexual community, especially heterosexual men in the athletic community who engage in high risk behaviors, are largely absolved of the stigma of HIV/AIDS.[1]

METHODOLOGICAL CONSIDERATIONS

We performed a textual analysis on all articles from the *Los Angeles Times (LAT), New York Times (NYT),* and *The Washington Post (WP)* which followed the HIV-positive announcements of Olympic diver Greg Louganis, professional basketball player Earvin "Magic" Johnson, and professional boxer Tommy Morrison. For Magic Johnson, we also collected all available articles for 3 months following his announcement and 10% of the articles which appeared the following year. These three mainstream newspapers were chosen from three major cities in the United States in order to represent the dominant or mainstream print media's treatment of HIV/AIDS. Indeed, other papers, such as *USA Today,* may have large circulations, and the gay and alternative presses may offer different framings of these events. However, the selected newspapers garner prestige and respect as reliable sources of accurate information.[2]

Numerous scholars discuss the importance of the mass media in social, political, and cultural life (DeFleur & Ball-Rokeach, 1989; Fiske, 1994; McLuhan, 1964; McQuail, 1987). While media texts can be read by agents who construct meaning from the text in various ways, power limits which texts are presented to a mass audience (Fiske, 1994). As Herman and Chomsky (1988) discuss, relatively few corporations own, produce, and distribute most of our "news." Using textual analysis,

we focus primarily on the cultural assumptions built into the text rather than the text itself. Cultural assumptions demonstrate how power constitutes certain practices as normal, while marking others as deviant (Foucault, 1978). At the same time, these cultural assumptions also reveal what is completely left out of our mass cultural discourse, that is, what is unrepresentable.

Given the social importance of male team sports, it is hardly surprising that there were over 100 articles about Magic Johnson, 12 articles about Greg Louganis, and 6 articles about Tommy Morrison. Perhaps the difference in the sheer number of articles highlights not only Magic Johnson's celebrity status within the basketball community, but also the popularity of basketball in our culture and its link to the symbolic production of masculinity. By contrast, the fewer number of articles about Morrison and Louganis may reflect their lower popularity as individuals or the status of the sports in which they participate.

The relative lack of coverage of Louganis likely reflects that diving, which involves no direct physical confrontation, is not linked to the construction of hegemonic masculinity. Where Morrison participates in a sport with heavy doses of physical contact, boxing's historic links to working class blood sports (Gorn & Goldstein, 1993) undermine it as an icon of middle class masculinity. However, it is interesting to note that Morrison received almost as much coverage as Louganis, despite his mediocre success as compared to Louganis, who dominated the sport of diving for most of his career. Greg Louganis' sexual identity may have been a key issue in keeping the media from covering him in greater depth.

…After our initial reading of the articles, four themes emerged. Articles were then coded around these themes. First, we explored whether or not the media conflates sexual identity with risk group. Second, we investigated whether the mainstream print media commits the historical error of conflating act with identity. Third, in order to uncover cultural assumptions in the texts, we analyzed frames which emphasized notions of family and/or relationships, personal responsibility, and "failure." Finally, we explicated how social location (consisting of multiple axes of power) led to a differential interpretation of an individual athlete's behavior depending upon which axis media coverage highlighted. The list of relevant articles is included in an appendix.

SHOCK AND SILENCE: "IT'S NOT JUST A GAY DISEASE!"

Consistent with the conflation of risk groups and HIV/AIDS status, the articles on Magic Johnson express overwhelming surprise that he contracted HIV/AIDS. Questions arise immediately as to how Magic Johnson could have contracted HIV/AIDS. Once we learn that he contracted HIV/AIDS through "heterosexual sex," articles report "shock" and "surprise" and repeatedly use exclamations such as: "startling," "totally mind blowing," "seems ridiculous," and "stunning." Forty-two of 100 articles express the sentiment that the public is caught totally off guard by Johnson's announcement, such as: "Even Hearing News Was Not Believing It," (Bonk, *LAT*, 11/8/91), "Hero's Shocker Leaves Teens Grasping For Answers," (Shen, *WP*, 11/9/91), "A Jarring Reveille For Sports," (Lipsyte, *NYT*, 11/10/91), and "A Day Later, It Remains a Shock Felt Around the World," (Thomas, Jr., *NYT*, 11/9/91).

The "shock" registered in these articles arises from the historic conflation of gay identity with risk of and blame for the disease. Essentially, Magic Johnson is lauded for showing the public that AIDS is not restricted to gays and that it in fact can be transmitted to "heterosexuals" through "heterosexual sex." What heterosexual sex consists of is never explained, since it is assumed that identity explains act. One phrase which appeared repeatedly is "it's not just a gay disease," generally followed by a discussion of how heterosexuals can also "get AIDS." Media coverage does not highlight behaviors and the risks associated with those behaviors. The coverage focuses, instead, on sexual identity while assuming that sex is inher-

ently risky. For example, one article is entitled, "Johnson's HIV Caused by Sex: Heterosexual Transmission Cited, Wife is Pregnant" (Cannon & Cotton, *WP*, 11/9/91).

Ultimately, the shock directed at a heterosexually-identified individual announcing that he has HIV/AIDS implies that if a man is gay, he is necessarily at risk regardless of his lifestyle. The articles ignore the reality that high (and low) risk acts, including intravenous drug use, are practiced across the spectrum of sexualities. The media's expression of shock and linkage of risk and identity (as opposed to act and risk), reinforce the conflation of identity and risk group. Specifically, the conflation of gay and HIV/AIDS is both reinforced, through an expression of shock, and destabilized, through the existence of a heterosexual with HIV/AIDS.

None of the articles mentioned the sexual acts which put Magic Johnson at risk. Rather, they stated that he contracted the disease through "heterosexual sex" and ended the inquiry there (e.g., Cannon & Cotton, *WP*, 11/9/91; McNeil, *NYT*, 11/10/91; see Note 13). The mainstream media overwhelmingly took as their focus a confirmation of Magic Johnson's heterosexuality and "surprise" that he contracted the virus. This is consistent with the findings of Gamson and Modigliana (1989) and Messner and Solomon (1993), who argue that mass media use "ready made" packages to construct meanings around stories. In this case, part of the ready made package is the affirmation of a hero's heterosexuality. The media centers on Johnson's contraction of the "heterosexual disease," with Johnson claiming that he is "far from homosexual." He immediately reassures the public that he contracted the virus through "heterosexual sex." Though "straights can get it too," media coverage continues to imply that gay men are primarily at risk. In other words, the conflation between risk (or the act which puts one at risk) and identity remains unchallenged.

Rather than leading to a questioning of Magic Johnson's heterosexuality, his HIV-positive condition is framed by the media as a reaffirmation of his desirability to women. Magic Johnson's unprotected sexual activity is not problematized as his "responsibility" or his "risk," but rather, is blamed on female groupies. As McKay (1993) argues, the media privileges and protects virile male heterosexuality in sport while making consistent references to aggressive women who wait for the athletes. The implication is that any normal man would have done the same thing (e.g., "boys will be boys").

Magic Johnson's "promiscuity" is not only blamed on women, but he is painted as a kind man who says he tries "accommodating" as many women as possible. In one article Magic Johnson says, "There were just some bachelors that almost every woman in Los Angeles wanted to be with: Eddie Murphy, Arsenio Hall and Magic Johnson. I confess that after I arrived in L.A. in 1979 I did my best to accommodate as many women as I could" (editors, *NYT,* 11/14/91). A second article agrees: "The groupies, the 'Annies.' They are the ancient entitlements of the locker room, the customary fringe benefits of muscles" (Callahan, *WP,* 11/10/91). Such views are reminiscent of the Victorian Era whereby men's sexual appetites were assumed to be naturally more powerful and aggressive than women's. At the same time, women are expected to be the moral guardians of civilization by not eliciting or provoking male desire (Gilder, 1973). Similar arguments are by no means confined to past history. Gilder's (1986) modern version substantially influenced Ronald Reagan during his presidency. . . .

Even though over 4 years separate Magic Johnson's and Tommy Morrison's HIV announcements, the articles still expressed shock that a self-identified heterosexual man contracted the disease. Morrison says he thought he "had a better chance of winning the lottery than contracting this disease" (Romano, *NYT,* 2/16/96) and that he thought it was a disease which only could be transmitted to homosexuals and drug users. The remaining articles on Morrison deal in some way with the risk of acquiring HIV/AIDS in the box-

ing ring. Over half the articles focus on the risk of transmission in the ring, even though all of the authors agree that the probability of acquiring HIV in the boxing ring is "infinitesimally small." While some articles simply use Morrison as a way to advocate new boxing policies, the articles which focus on Morrison note his "promiscuous lifestyle" and the fact that he was surprised, as no doubt were others, that a heterosexual man could contract the disease.

Rather than elevating Morrison to hero status for overcoming the stigma of the illness, the media more often treated him as a tragic figure who, through his ignorance about HIV transmission, cut short a promising career. Similar to the Johnson version, though, women are framed as pursuers, and Morrison is framed as one who is unable to resist temptation. For example, Romano framed as the problem the women who "wait outside the door fighting over who was going to get Tommy that night," (*NYT,* 2/16/96) not Morrison's pursuit of these women or his failure to practice safe sex. Though Morrison accepts some personal responsibility for contacting the "young ladies" and is blamed for making "irrational, immature decisions" in his "fast lane" life, he is not framed as the threatening pursuer but as the "world's biggest bimbo magnet."

While the articles hold Morrison accountable for his ignorance of HIV/AIDS transmission, he is not held responsible for the risk to which he may have subjected others. Romano highlights the way Morrison's "inner circle" sums up the situation: "It wasn't uncommon for me to go to his hotel room and find three or four women outside the door fighting over who was going to get Tommy that night. We had groupies all the way up to career women" (*WP,* 2/16/96). Similar to their treatment of Johnson, the media's confirmation of Morrison's heterosexuality serves to affirm his sexual desirability to women, his presumed "normal" sexuality, and his participation in only "normal" sexual acts.

Most importantly, the articles convey very little information about the transmission of HIV/

AIDS. While most of the articles mention the small chance of contracting HIV in the ring, there is no mention of the types of specific activities that put one at risk outside the ring. "Promiscuity" and a "fast and reckless lifestyle" are implied risks, but promiscuity alone does not have to be risky (Watney, 1989), and in fact no acts pose an HIV risk if none of the participants are HIV-positive. There is no focus in the Morrison articles on "safe sex" or the specific types of acts which are high-risk. This type of omission likely contributes to the moral panic over AIDS and sex (Weeks, 1985). Further, the assumed risk of promiscuity implies that heterosexual monogamy is the only imaginable moral and responsible alternative. Later, we will return to this point.

SILENCE SURROUNDING GAYS AND HIV/AIDS

In contrast to the coverage of Johnson and Morrison's announcements, the print media makes no mention of shock or surprise when Greg Louganis makes his announcement that he is HIV-positive. There is no discussion of promiscuity, no mention of a relationship, no indictment of a "fast lane" lifestyle, and no indication of surprise by Louganis or the public. Additionally, there are no questions as to how he could have contracted the disease. Apparently, when "Louganis says he has AIDS," his homosexuality is a catch-all which signifies participation in high-risk activities, promiscuity, and inevitable contraction.

We argue that the lack of inquiry into how Louganis could have contracted the disease works to reinforce the undiscussed (assumed) inevitability of HIV/AIDS for homosexual men. This works to perpetuate the assumption that Greg Louganis' body is necessarily diseased, thereby exemplifying the conflation of gay identity with HIV/AIDS. This stands in stark contrast to the way the mainstream print media informed the public that Magic Johnson and Tommy Morrison acquired HIV/AIDS through heterosexual activity, thus maintaining the illusion that identity explains act. In

both cases, however, the specific high-risk sex acts are never discussed.

SEXUAL HIERARCHIES, LEGITIMATE RELATIONSHIPS, AND THE THREAT OF TRANSMISSION

Cultural norms affect how one conceptualizes and hierarchicalizes relationships. We argue that these norms are reproduced in the discourse found in mainstream print media. This is revealed in how "straight" and "gay" men are framed differently with regard to the mention of long-term partners and/or spouses. Magic Johnson and Tommy Morrison are discussed vis-à-vis a wife and fiancé, respectively, while our previous discussion highlights the fact that no mention is made of Greg Louganis' long-term partner. Thus, by inquiring into Johnson and Morrison's risk of infecting loved ones while never mentioning Louganis' partner, the media perpetuates the hegemony of heterosexual relationships, sex, and nuclear families. Consistent with Rubin's (1993) sexual hierarchy, we find that heterosexual relationships are more valued than homosexual relationships.

While the "blame" or responsibility for the pollution of the bodies of Magic Johnson and Tommy Morrison is placed on the aggressive women who pursued successful male sports stars, the print media offer no corollary absolution for Greg Louganis. There is no discussion about the aggressive men who may have pursued Louganis. Ironically, Greg Louganis stated in his television interview with Barbara Walters that he was in a monogamous relationship with a man who both cheated on him and abused him (*20/20*, February 24,1995). However, none of the newspaper articles ask Louganis' partner who is responsible for transmission.

The athletes also are framed differently vis-à-vis the risk of transmission they present to others. Here, Magic Johnson and Tommy Morrison's threat to women is discussed nearly always in relation to their "legitimate" sex partners, while they are not presented often as a threat to their numerous other sex partners. Only 3 of the 100 articles on Magic Johnson mention the risks he posed to the many women with whom he slept. Morrison, by contrast, was said to be remorseful for putting other women at risk and urged any woman with whom he had sexual contact to "get tested." Yet, he is not criticized specifically for putting these women at risk, because blame for the risk of transmission is placed on the women.

Morrison and Johnson are framed with a lifestyle which is consistent sexually with hegemonic masculinity. Their behavior may be judged as a bit "reckless," but indeed it is seen as non-problematized heterosexuality—the "female groupies" who have enticed and tainted them are the problem, and the men did what any "normal" man would do. However, the print media see no need even to ask about the men Greg Louganis may have infected, nor even to inquire about his long-term relationship, nor the risk each partner poses to the other. In this way, gay men and "promiscuous" women are problematized, while hegemonic masculinity is reaffirmed.

CLASS, RACE, SPORTS, AND AIDS: "BOYS WILL BE BOYS"

Historically, African-American and working class peoples' bodies have been seen as hypersexualized, primitive, and "closer to nature" (Collins, 1990).... By contrast, White, middle class men are defined by the mind or rationality (Synnott, 1993). This ideogical belief has been reinforced and reproduced in the sports world through the disproportionate representation of men of color and working class men (Edwards, 1973; Messner, 1990). The limited structure of opportunity disproportionately funnels men of color and working class men into particular sports (Messner, 1990). Articles which mention Morrison and Johnson's class background simultaneously praise these men for their current career success, yet their HIV announcements dangerously reifies historical links between sexual excess and minority and working class peoples.

Sports media tend to focus on those sports which reproduce hegemonic masculinity (Messner, 1988). Since disproportionate numbers of Black and working class bodies are featured in professional sports, and since HIV/AIDS cases are well publicized when sporting bodies are involved, it is implied that individual minority and working class bodies are "excessively" sexual and "morally depraved." Rather than problematizing male sexuality in sport through an examination of its social norms, including the validation of masculinity through sexual conquest, the media focus on individual moral failings. In this way, the media preserve male (hetero)sexual privilege, including the conquest of women, while displacing the blame for the spread of HIV/AIDS onto Black and working class bodies.

The previous analysis revealed that Johnson and Morrison's social locations are simultaneously marginalized and privileged. While both men occupy marginalized race and/or class statuses, they occupy a privileged position through their contribution to the maintenance of hegemonic masculinity. However, they are also subordinated through the symbolic reaffirmation of the link between sexual immorality and socially marginalized race and class positions. Thus, while the sports-promoted norms of hegemonic masculinity are protected, the media potentially reinvigorates cultural ideas about the threatening and excessive sexualities of minority and working class peoples.

Through such coverage, "bad" (gay, Black, or working class) sexuality is juxtaposed against the unstated norms of (heterosexual, White, middle class) reproductive, monogamous, familial sex. White, middle class, heterosexual men are left out of the picture and are absolved altogether from any involvement with HIV/AIDS or promiscuity. They are left out of the print media picture of sports, not because of individual differences in morality but because of a greater structure of opportunity whereby men are likely to pursue numerous career options ahead of a sports career (Edwards, 1973; Messner, 1990). These men are the invisible, mythical "good" or normal icons against which "bad" men and women are highlighted. In short, hegemonic masculinity is constructed as good and pure, while the bodies of women, gay men, and other subordinated masculinities are framed as corrupt.

Conservative rhetoric surrounding HIV/AIDS has emphasized abundantly the view that the sexual liberationist era of the 1960s and 1970s produced the individual moral failures of today. Gay men have been criticized for "fast lane" lifestyles and made to seem deserved of AIDS, no matter their sexual practices. Consistent with Eisenstein (1994), our analysis highlights how modern public discussions of HIV/AIDS have extended the signifier of AIDS beyond the gay community to include heterosexual minorities and the working class. Ultimately, the idea of heterosexuality is reinforced as "good," while these particular individuals are seen to have practiced "bad" heterosexuality by failing to meet dominant cultural norms of reproductive, monogamous, familial sex.

CHALLENGING "NATURAL" SEXUAL ACTS AND IDENTITIES

…There are a wide range of sexual practices enacted across a multitude of sexualities. Indeed, there are numerous sex acts in common between gays, lesbians, bisexuals, and heterosexuals. Rather than emphasizing the commonalities between identities, our culture and mass media tend to construct boundaries between these identities which in effect create and emphasize difference. Media discourse assumes that particular practices are limited by definition to certain identities; however, actual practices transcend identity. In our analysis, we highlight how the media has made no mention of high-risk sexual acts the three men may have had in common. Instead, the media has focused on affirming, declaring, and reifying a fixed inner essence which our culture refers to as *sexual identity.*

The maintenance of discrete categories is one means through which power is exercised. In this way, some identities are privileged legally and so-

cially, while others are excluded and/or condemned regardless of actual practices. Through the maintenance of these boundaries, good and bad sexualities are defined, and sexual identity is linked definitely to particular individuals and practices. By assuming that risk correlates to identity, not practice, the myth of dangerous and bad sexualities is maintained. In our analysis, the assumption that being gay "causes" HIV/AIDS, combined with the overwhelming inquiry into how a heterosexual could possibly have acquired HIV/AIDS, both reinforces and problematizes the conflation between act and identity. That is, the very fact that "straights can get it too" is destabilizing the assumption that only gays are at risk or that only acts associated with "being" gay create risk. However, by ignoring the common sexual practices of the three men and by focusing on fixed identities rather than acts, the media works to maintain discrete sexual identity categories that are thought automatically to correspond to specific acts and, hence, risk.

As a more accurate alternative, we propose analyzing these categories without the set boundaries imposed on them through the use of Haraway's (1991) metaphor of the cyborg. The cyborg metaphor demonstrates that individuals often transgress the "rules" or boundaries which mark their identities. Hence, we might expect a fusion and implosion of categories. While this appears to be occurring in lived experiences, the mainstream print media's framing of these experiences maintains the distinction between these identities, acts, and risk groups.

Clearly, American discomfort with public discussion of specific sexual matters and acts contributes to the confirmation, policing, and hierarchicalization of sexual identity categories. More accurate information about AIDS/HIV transmission and human sexuality could be conveyed through the mass media if AIDS/HIV were associated with particular acts rather than particular fixed identities. Instead of destabilizing the conflation between risk and identity, our analysis has highlighted how the media merely broadened the definition of bad sexuality, from gay identity to non-monogamous, non-familial, straight identity, while fully excluding discussions about actual behaviors and risks.

WHO CAN BE "SAVED" FROM THE FATE OF HIV/AIDS: THE DISCOURSE OF INDIVIDUAL RESPONSIBILITY AND NEW RIGHT IDEOLOGY

...The assumptions embedded in the texts—specifically, the conflation of gay with promiscuity and the inevitability of HIV/AIDS—demonstrate how power is exercised. In terms of the way their sexual identities are framed, Magic Johnson and Tommy Morrison may be redeemed from the stigma of HIV/AIDS. Johnson and Morrison, as heterosexual "family men"—Johnson is married and has a child, Morrison is engaged—are framed as having made "mistakes." Johnson says, "Sometimes you're a little naïve.... You think it can never happen to you" (Downey, *LAT*, 11/8/91). Morrison says he "blew it with irresponsible, irrational, immature decisions" (Romano, *WP*, 2/16/96). Johnson's current familial role is praised and held out as an example to young Black men. In particular, he touts marriage and abstinence. Johnson asks "teenagers to be less promiscuous" and recommended they "remain virgins until marriage" (French, *WP*, 1/14/92). The heterosexual, monogamous body is normalized, while non-monogamous heterosexuals are labeled as deviant but redeemable through abstinence and/or by returning to the confines of heterosexual monogamy. In other words, self-identified heterosexual men are presented as temporarily lapsing from an otherwise "good" sexuality, and these lapses are presented as individual moral "failings." For these men, HIV/AIDS may be a "punishment" for transgressions but not an irremovable stigma or "inevitable."

By contrast, the homosexual body is framed as necessarily immoral, deviant, and stigmatized. Louganis is not framed as having the option of abstinence or monogamy which could have "saved" him from HIV/AIDS. Being gay conflates him

with the "evils of promiscuity," a dangerous gay sexuality, and an inevitable HIV/AIDS outcome. This is accomplished through the absence of any comment about Louganis' sexual practices or any inquiry into the cause of his HIV-positive condition. Because gay sexuality is already marked as deviant and immoral, the gay body is assumed to be doomed necessarily. While Magic Johnson is given a presidential appointment as national spokesman and is lauded for being a public educator, a local senator attempts to ban Greg Louganis from speaking at a Florida university because of his "moral decadence" and for being "an embarrassment to the university community" (Associated Press, *LAT*, 1/26/97).

Mainstream mass media often ignore how political and social ideologies and policies enforce a particular lifestyle and the public perception of a lifestyle. For instance, we see in our analysis how heterosexual relationships are legitimated when the mass media highlight Johnson and Morrison's partners while ignoring Louganis' long-term partner. This is consistent with the hierarchy of sexual value which privileges heterosexual over homosexual sex (Rubin, 1993). In addition, there was a definitive shift in the years between Johnson and Morrison's HIV-positive announcements. Earlier media frames labeled certain behavior (safe sex, monogamy, and abstinence) acceptable and responsible, while later frames only included abstinence and monogamy. Numerous articles stress safe sex and Johnson's role in current and future safe sex campaigns. By contrast, media attention surrounding Tommy Morrison's announcement 4 years later included no discussion of safe sex. Instead, the focus was on Morrison's promiscuity, which is roundly condemned.

Such a shift is explained largely by the recent resurgence of the New Right, which offers "clear cut and familiar" moral strategies which are seen as best regulating "personal and social life" (Weeks, 1985, p. 53). Historically, there have been three different approaches to regulating sexuality: liberal, libertarian, and absolutionist (Weeks, 1985). Rooted in Christianity, absolutionist strategies are becoming increasingly popular in the U.S. in this post-sexual liberation era. Under these strategies, participants value limited notions of relationships and family forms, along with abstinence and monogamy. Here, our analysis has shown how the mass media act to promote as "moral," and hence safe, monogamous nuclear family forms. The media frame excludes a discussion of numerous viable forms of relationships and safe erotic pluralism across sexual identity categories. Given the current rise of a New Right ideology which stresses "family values" and which is obvious in its backlash against gay and lesbian political progress, it is not surprising that sexual liberation is not a part of the cultural discourse presented by the mainstream print media.

CONCLUSION

In sum, the media polices sexuality by presenting the causes of and solutions to the HIV/AIDS epidemic by framing marriage, heterosexuality, and monogamy as "safe" and by condemning homosexuality, promiscuity, and casual sex as "dangerous." Here, we see male sporting bodies of "promiscuous" minority and working class heterosexuals grouped with "immoral" gay men. Despite challenging the automatic conflation of gays and HIV/AIDS by adding heterosexuals to the list of those at-risk, the mass media maintain the assumption that gays will get AIDS and that a gay lifestyle is synonymous with promiscuity. Because the lifestyles of only some heterosexuals are stigmatized, the "moral panic" surrounding sex is reinvigorated (Rubin, 1993), and the stigmatization and fear about homosexuality being anti-family is reinforced subtly.

Invoking a moral panic through an emphasis on the "evils of promiscuity" falsely reinforces the idea that sex is inherently dangerous (Rubin, 1993; Watney, 1989; Weeks, 1985). This occurs through the perpetuation of the myth that promiscuity is necessarily dangerous and risky. Watney (1989) predicted such tendencies when he posited that, as we see more people with HIV/AIDS

across social groups, we will see a more frantic push for monogamy and a denunciation of the promiscuous. It should be noted that AIDS is neither caused by promiscuity nor prevented by monogamy, as "one can contract AIDS if one has one sexual partner in one's life—with AIDS" (Watney, 1989, p. 32). What needs to be emphasized if we are going to highlight individual solutions is not the lessening of sexual activities or "the demonology of sex" (Rubin, 1993), but a discussion of the *kinds* of activities which put one at risk. The challenges posed by Segal (1994), Weeks (1989), Watney (1989), and Patton (1990) include creative ideas on how a safe and active erotic plurality could easily be formed and, in fact, already exists.

The print media coverage of HIV-positive athletes reveals how sports media are active in the reproduction of ideologies which privilege heterosexual male behavior. How athletes are framed by the mass media with regards to their social locations reveals and reproduces cultural assumptions about normal and deviant behavior. Even when exemplars of hegemonic masculinity contract a highly stigmatized illness, print media coverage does not problematize norms of male sexual conquest in sport, norms which are consistent with hegemonic masculinity. Rather, print media coverage focuses blame on failed individual bodies and subordinate sexualities, specifically those of women, minorities, and working-class and gay men.

Social fears surrounding HIV/AIDS, a "moral panic" over sex, the spread of HIV/AIDS in sport, and concerns for a "dissipating" nuclear family structure make such an analysis especially timely. As Rubin notes, "It is precisely at times such as these" that "disputes over sexual behavior…become the vehicles for displacing social anxieties, and discharging their attendant emotional intensity" (1993, p. 4). We must be critical, however, of the media's role in forming erroneous links in the culture at large between HIV/AIDS, sexual identity, and risk. As noted by Weeks (1985), we tend to invent "new victims" in times of social apprehension. This may be true, but we are also finding new villains. Clearly, the media is playing an important role in the policing of bodies and acts and in the fixing of identities through a hierarchical

sexual morality which is embedded in the "cultural anxiousness" of our time.

REFERENCES

Bordo, S. (1993). *Unbearable weight: Feminism, Western culture, and the body.* Berkeley: University of California Press.

Cole, C. L., & Andrews, D. L. (1996). Look, it's NBA Showtime!: A research annual. *Cultural Studies, 1,* 141–181.

Cole, C. L., & Denny, H. (1994). Visualizing deviance in post-Reagan America: Magic Johnson, AIDS and the promiscuous world of professional sport. *Critical Sociology, 20,* 123–147.

Collins. P. H. (1990). *Black feminist thought: Knowledge, consciousness, and the politics of empowerment.* London: Harper Collins.

Connell, R. W. (1987). *Gender and power: Society, the person and sexual politics.* Stanford: Stanford University Press.

Connell, R. W. (1990). An iron man: The body and some contradictions of hegemonic masculinity. In M. Messner & D. Sabo (Eds.), *Sport, men and the gender order* (pp. 83–96). Champaign, IL: Human Kinetics.

Crosset, T. (1990). Masculinity, sexuality, and the development of early modern sport. In M. Messner & D. Sabo (Eds.), *Sport, men and the gender order* (pp. 45–54). Champaign, IL: Human Kinetics.

Davis, L. (1997). *The swimsuit issue and sport: Hegemonic masculinity in* Sports Illustrated. New York: SUNY Press.

DeFleur, M., & Ball-Rokeach, S. (1989). *Theories of mass communication.* New York: Longman.

Duggan, L., & Hunter, N. D. (1995). *Sex wars: Sexual dissent and political culture.* New York: Routledge.

Duncan, M. C., Messner, M. A., & Jensen, K. (1994). *Gender stereotyping in televised sports: A follow-up to the 1989 study.* Los Angeles: The Amateur Athletic Foundation.

Dutton, K. (1995). *The perfectible body: The Western ideal of male physical development.* New York: Continuum.

Edwards, H. (1973). *Sociology of sport.* Homewood, IL: Dorsey Press.

Eisenstein, Z. (1994). *The color of gender: Reimaging democracy.* Berkeley: University of California Press.

Firestone, S. (1970). *The dialectic of sex: The case for feminist revolution.* New York: Quill.

Fiske, J. (1994). *Media matters: Everyday culture and political change.* Minneapolis: University of Minnesota Press.

Foucault, M. (1978). *The history of sexuality.* New York: Vintage Books.

Foucault, M. (1979). *Discipline and punish: The birth of the prison.* New York: Vintage Books.

Gamson, W., & Modigliana, A. (1989). Media discourse and public opinion on nuclear power: A constructionist approach. *American Journal of Sociology, 95,* 1–37.

Gilder, G. (1973). *Sexual suicide.* New York: Quadrangle.

Gilder, G. (1986). *Men and marriage.* Gretna, LA: Pelican.

Gorn, E., & Goldstein, W. (1993). *A brief history of American sports.* New York: Hill & Wang.

Grosz, E. (1994). *Volatile bodies: Towards a corporeal feminism.* Bloomington, IN: Indiana University Press.

Haraway, D. (1991). *Simians, cyborgs, and women: The reinvention of nature.* London: Free Association.

Herman, E. S., & Chomsky, N. (1988). *Manufacturing consent: The political economy of the mass media.* New York: Pantheon.

Kane, M. J. (1988). Media coverage of the female athlete before, during, and after Title IX: *Sports Illustrated* revisited. *Journal of Sport Management, 2,* 87–99.

Kane, M. J., & Snyder, E. (1989). Sport typing: The social "containment" of women in sport. *Arena Review, 13,* 77–96.

Katz, J. N. (1995). *The invention of heterosexuality.* New York: Penguin.

Kimmel, M. (1990). Baseball and the reconstitution of American masculinity, 1880–1920. In M. Messner & D. Sabo (Eds.), *Sport, men and the gender order* (pp. 55–66). Champaign, IL: Human Kinetics.

Kinsey, A. (1948). *Sexual behavior in the human male.* Philadelphia: W. B. Saunders.

Kinsey, A. (1953). *Sexual behavior in the human female.* Philadelphia: W. B. Saunders.

Klein, R. (1993). *The bisexual option*. New York: Haworth Press.

LePoire, B. (1994). Attraction toward and nonverbal stigmatization of gay males and persons with AIDS: Evidence of symbolic over instrumental attitudinal structures. *Human Communication Research, 21*(2), 241–279.

Lule, J. (1995). The rape of Mike Tyson: Race, the press and symbolic stereotypes. *Critical Studies in Mass Communication, 12,* 176–195.

McKay, J. (1993). "Marked men" and "wanton women": The politics of naming sexual "deviance" in sport. *The Journal of Men's Studies, 2,* 69–87.

McLuhan, M. (1964). *Understanding media: The extensions of man.* Cambridge: The MIT Press.

McQuail, D. (1987). *Mass communication theory.* London: Sage.

Messner, M. A. (1990). Masculinities and athletic careers: Bonding and status differences. In M. Messner & D. Sabo (Eds.), *Sport, men and the gender order* (pp. 97–108). Champaign, IL: Human Kinetics.

Messner, M. A. (1988). Sports and male domination: The female athlete as contested ideological terrain. *Sociology of Sport Journal, 12,* 197–211.

Messner, M. A., & Solomon, W. S. (1993). Outside the frame: Newspaper coverage of the Sugar Ray Leonard wife abuse story. *Sociology of Sport Journal, 10,* 119–134.

Metheny, E. (1965). *Connotations of movement in sport and dance.* Dubuque, IA: Wm. C. Brown.

Patton, C. (1990). *Inventing AIDS.* New York: Routledge.

Phelan, S. (1994). *Getting specific: Postmodern lesbian politics.* Minneapolis: University of Minnesota Press.

Rubin, G. (1993). Thinking sex: Notes for a radical theory of the politics of sexuality. In H. Abelove, M. A. Barale, & D. M. Halperin (Eds.), *The lesbian and gay studies reader* (pp. 3–62). New York: Routledge.

Rust, P. (1995). *Bisexuality and the challenge to lesbian politics: Sex, loyalty, and revolution.* New York: New York Press.

Sedgwick, E. K. (1990). *Epistemology of the closet.* Berkeley: University of California Press.

Segal, L. (1994). *Straight sex: Rethinking the politics of pleasure.* Berkeley: University of California Press.

Seidman, S. (1992). *Embattled eros: Sexual politics and ethics in contemporary America.* New York: Routledge.

Sontag, S. (1989). *AIDS and its metaphors.* New York: Farrar, Straus, and Giroux.

Synnott, A. (1993). *The body social: Symbolism, self and society.* London: Routledge.

Wachs, F. L., & Dworkin, S. L. (1997). There's no such thing as a gay hero: Magic = hero, Louganis = carrier: Sexual identity and media framing of HIV positive athletes. *Journal of Sport and Social Issues, 21,* 335–355.

Wachs, F. L., & Dworkin, S. L. (in press). The morality/manhood paradox: Masculinity, sport, and the media. In M. Messner, J. McKay, & D. Sabo (Eds.), *Masculinities and sport.* London: Sage.

Watney, S. (1989). *Policing desire: Pornography, AIDS, and the media.* Minneapolis: University of Minnesota Press.

Weeks, J. (1985). *Sexuality and its discontents: Meanings, myths, and modern sexualities.* New York: Routledge.

Weinberg, M. S., Williams, C., & Pryor, D. (1994). *Dual attraction: Understanding bisexuality.* New York: Oxford University Press.

APPENDIX

Magic Johnson

11/8/91 Harris, S. "Announcement hailed as a way to teach public," *Los Angeles Times,* A32.

11/8/91 Heisler, M. "Magic Johnson's career ended by HIV-positive test," *Los Angeles Times,* A1.

11/8/91 Murphy, D. E., & Griego, T. "An icon falls and his public suffers the pain," *Los Angeles Times,* Al.

11/8/91 Kindred, D. "Magic's gift for inspiring us tests reality," *Los Angeles Times,* B7.

11/8/91 Bonk, T. "Even hearing news was not believing it," *Los Angeles Times,* C1.

11/8/91 Downey, M. "Earvin leaves NBA, but his smile remains," *Los Angeles Times,* C1.

11/8/91 Springer, S. "Through the years, he stayed the same," *Los Angeles Times,* C1.

11/8/91 Stevenson, R. W. "Basketball star retires on advice of his doctors," *New York Times,* Al.

11/8/91 Berkow, I. "Magic Johnson's legacy," *New York Times,* B11.

11/8/91 Thomas, R. M., Jr. "News reverberates through basketball and well beyond it," *New York Times,* B13.

11/8/91 Brown, C. "A career of impact, a player with heart," *New York Times,* B11.

11/8/91 Araton, H. "Riley leads the prayers," *New York Times,* B11.

11/8/91 Specter, M. "Magic's loud message for young black men," *New York Times,* B12.

11/8/91 Aldridge, D. "Lakers star put imprint on finals, records, money," *The Washington Post,* C1.

11/8/91 Gladwell, M., & Muscatine, A. "Legend's latest challenge," *The Washington Post,* front page.

11/8/91 Cannon, L. "Basketball star Magic Johnson retires with AIDS virus," *The Washington Post,* front page.

11/8/91 Castaneda, R., & Sanchez, R. "Johnson's AIDS virus revelation moves teenagers, fans," *The Washington Post,* D1.

11/9/91 Bonk, T., & Scott, J. "'Don't feel sorry for me,' Magic says," *Los Angeles Times,* Al.

11/9/91 Lacey, M. & Martin, H. "Student's cry a bit, learn life lessons," *Los Angeles Times,* A26.

11/9/91 Gerstenzang, J., & Cimons, M. "Bush calls Johnson a hero, defends administration's policy on AIDS," *Los Angeles Times,* A26.

11/9/91 Horovitz, B. "Sponsors may use magic in ads to encourage safe sex," *Los Angeles Times,* D1.

11/9/91 Editors, "A magical cure for lethargy," *Los Angeles Times,* B5.

11/9/91 Thomas, R. M., Jr. "A day later, it remains a shock felt around the world," *New York Times,* 33.

11/9/91 Specter, M. "When AIDS taps hero, his 'children' feel pain," *New York Times,* front page.

11/9/91 McMillen, T. "Magic, now and forever," *New York Times,* 23.

11/9/91 Stevenson, R. W. "Johnson's frankness continues," *New York Times,* 33.

11/9/91 Mathews, J. "Los Angeles stunned as hero begins future with HIV," *The Washington Post,* A12.

11/9/91 Cannon, L., & Cotton, A. "Johnson's HIV caused by sex: 'Heterosexual transmission' cited; wife is pregnant," *The Washington Post,* front page.

11/9/91 Lewis, N. "Apprehensive callers swamp hotline," *The Washington Post,* A12.

11/9/91 Shen, F. "Hero's shocker leaves teens grasping for answers," *The Washington Post,* front page.

11/10/91 Callahan, T. "What it boils down to is playing with fire," *The Washington Post,* D2.

11/10/91 Jones, R. A. "A shock that shifted the world," *Los Angeles Times,* A3.

11/10/91 Lipsyte, R. "A jarring reveille for sports," *New York Times,* S1.

11/10/91 McNeil, D. "On the court or off, still Magic," *New York Times,* E9.

11/10/91 Muscatine, A. "Magic's revelation transcends sports," *The Washington Post,* D1.

11/10/91 Aldridge, D. "For moments like these," *The Washington Post,* D4.

11/11/91 Horovitz, B. "Advertisers try to handle this Magic moment carefully," *Los Angeles Times,* D1.

11/14/91 Editors, "Sorry but Magic isn't a hero," *New York Times,* B19.

11/14/91 Editors, "Converse's AIDS efforts features Magic Johnson," *New York Times,* D10.

11/18/91 Almond, E., & Ford, A. "Wild ovation greets Magic at Lakers game," *Los Angeles Times,* A1.

11/30/91 Editors, "Keep Magic in the mainstream," *New York Times,* B7.

1/1/92 Araton, H. "Advertisers shying from Magic's touch," *New York Times,* 44.

1/14/92 French, M. A. "Magic, rewriting the rules of romance," *The Washington Post,* B1.

11/11/91 Chase, M. "Johnson disclosure underscores facts of AIDS in heterosexual population," *Wall Street Journal,* B1.

4/5/97 Editors, "Johnson's HIV level drops, AIDS virus in Earvin "Magic" Johnson is significantly reduced," *New York Times,* 36.

Greg Louganis

2/23/95 Weyler, J. "Olympic diver Louganis reveals that he has AIDS," *Los Angeles Times,* Al.

2/23/95 Sandomir, R. "Louganis, Olympic champion, says he has AIDS," *New York Times,* B11.

2/23/95 Longman, J. "Doctor at games supports Louganis," *New York Times,* B15.

2/24/95 Boxall, B., & Williams, F. "Louganis disclosure greeted with sadness," *Los Angeles Times,* B1.

2/24/95 Editors, "Louganis: Breaks his silence, another world-famous athlete disclosed he has AIDS," *Los Angeles Times*, B6.

2/24/95 Vecsey, G. "Tolerance, not blame, for Louganis," *New York Times,* B7.

2/24/95 Longman. J. "Olympians won't have to take H.I.V. test," *New York Times,* B7.

2/26/95 Longman, J. "Olympian blood: Debate about HIV tests sparked by diver with AIDS," *New York Times*, 2.

2/28/95 Quintanilla, M. "The truth shall set you free," *Los Angeles Times*, E11.

3/5/95 Alfano, P. "The Louganis disclosure: AIDS in the age of hype," *New York Times Magazine*, E1.

5/5/95 Ammon, R. "Gay athletes," *Los Angeles Times*, M5.

1/26/97 "Senator seeks to ban Louganis," *Los Angeles Times*, C11.

Tommy Morrison

2/12/96 Eskenazi, G. "Morrison suspension: An HIV concern," *New York Times*, B6.

2/13/96 Springer, S. "Magic Johnson plans to call boxer," *Los Angeles Times*, A9.

2/13/96 Springer, S., & Gustkey, E. "Boxer's HIV test heats up debate over risk to others," *Los Angeles Times*, A1.

2/13/96 Eskenazi, G. "Morrison confirms positive HIV test," *New York Times*, B13.

2/14/96 "HIV test for Morrison ref," *New York Times*, B11.

2/16/96 Vecsey, G. "Morrison didn't pay enough attention," *New York Times*, B20.

2/16/96 Eskenazi, G. "Remorseful Morrison has words of caution," *New York Times*, B7.

2/16/96 Romano, L. "Heavyweight deals with serious blow," *The Washington Post*, A1.

9/20/96 Kawakami, T. "HIV-positive Morrison says he'll fight again," *Los Angeles Times*, C9.

NOTES

1. Other analyses of media coverage reveal frames of Magic Johnson as a "hero" for living with a stigmatized illness with little to no mention of how his unprotected "promiscuity" posed a threat of transmission to women. Gay men, on the other hand, are not only held responsible for their illness but also are villainized as a threat to the heterosexual community (Wachs & Dworkin, 1997). For example, Greg Louganis was framed by mass media as a "carrier" of the virus, which emphasizes his HIV-positive status as a threat to the heterosexual community.

2. We recognize the use of Associated Presses by all three of these newspapers. However, most major newspapers use the Associated Press. In many ways, this strengthens our arguments, as it demonstrates the homogenization of information dissemination among the mainstream print media.

45

Duality and Redefinition

Young Feminism and the Alternative Music Community

MELISSA KLEIN

I am twenty-five years old. On my left upper arm I have a six-inch long tattoo of a voluptuous cowgirl. One of her hands rests jauntily on her jutting hip. The other is firing a gun. An earlier feminist might frown upon my cowgirl's fringed hot pants and halter top as promoting sexual exploitation, and might see her pistol as perpetuating male patterns of violence. Yet I see this image as distinctly feminist. Having a tattoo signifies a subculture that subverts traditional notions of feminine beauty. That this tattoo is a pinup girl with a gun represents the appropriation and redefinition of sexuality, power, and violence—ideas characteristic of third wave punk feminism.

I was born in 1971 and am part of a generation of young women who grew up during or after the feminist "second wave" and who, as a result, have mixed feelings about traditional feminism. Many young women hesitate to take on the mantle of feminism, either because they fear being branded as fanatical "feminazis" or because they see feminism not as a growing and changing movement but as a dialogue of the past that conjures up images of militantly bell-bottomed "women's libbers." The issues pertinent to older women do not necessarily resonate in our lives. We do not, for instance, experience the double burden of the proverbial "superwoman"—attempting to be both model mother and ambitious professional—because we often have neither "real" jobs nor children.

A new social context means that within the alternative music community and elsewhere, girls have created a new form of feminism. Much in the same way that race relations in this country have moved from the ideal of the "color-blind society" toward the promotion of diversity and multiculturalism, feminism has moved away from a struggle for equality toward an engagement with difference, an assertion that girls can have the best of both worlds (that they, for example, can be both violently angry and vampily glamorous). This feminism owes much to the struggles of the second wave, yet it differs in many ways, especially in the way it is defined by contradiction.

Third wave feminism is certainly not confined to punk culture. For many women in my age range, because *sexism* is a word in our vocabulary, we have the means to recognize it in our lives, even if this recognition does not occur immediately and even if we have had to find new ways to analyze sexism and to take action. Though we grew up in the so-called aftermath of feminism and have taken some of its gains for granted, we experienced the backlash in areas such as reproductive rights as a rude jolt into action. Activism in the arena of AIDS drew renewed attention to gay and lesbian rights. The resurgence of interest in these and other issues began to shape a new feminism, a new kind of activism emphasizing our generation's cynical and disenfranchised temperament, born of distaste for the reactionary politics and rat-race economics of the 1980s. Our politics reflects a postmodern focus on contradiction and duality, on the reclamation of terms. S-M, pornography, the words *cunt* and *queer* and *pussy* and *girl*—are all things to be re-examined or re-claimed. In terms of gender, our rebellion is to make it camp. The underground music community has served as a particularly fertile breeding ground for redefining a feminism to fit our lives.

For many of us, our paradoxical identity with traditional feminism began in childhood. Thanks to the gains of second wave feminists, we grew up in a comparatively less gender-segregated environment and with expanded expectations of ourselves. My parents made sure the idea that girls are equal to boys was strongly ingrained in me. My mother marched at pro-choice rallies and tried to teach the neighborhood boys how to sew. She subscribed to *Ms.,* and each month I would look over the "No Comment" section (which I liked because it had pictures) and read the stories for kids. My father taught me to read when I was four, ordered science projects by mail for me and my two younger sisters, and played softball and soccer with us in our overgrown backyard. I even had an early introduction to the subject of gay pride when, at my day camp, I kissed another girl on the cheek and a boy said, "Eeeewww! You're a lesbian!" That afternoon when my mom picked me up in our old Ford Falcon, I asked her to explain the word *lesbian,* and she told me it meant a woman who loved other women. Reasoning that I loved my mother and sisters, and not quite comprehending the difference between loving and being in love, I went back to camp the next day and fiercely told the boy, "So what if I'm a lesbian? I'm proud I'm a lesbian."

The remarks of my less-than-enlightened fellow camper demonstrate that despite substantial gains made by the second wave and the influence of these gains in my life, the world around me was not a totally radical place. Within my family I was encouraged to do whatever I wanted, yet in the outside world I was encouraged toward "female" pursuits. I could throw a ball, and I could do more chin-ups than anyone else in my class, yet I spent more time on gymnastics, ballet, and diving—"female" activities that emphasized aesthetics, individual achievement, and grace, rather than aggression, strength, and teamwork. Like many girls, my self-confidence dwindled in adolescence. As I approached an age when peer support became more important than family support, my alienation grew, because I did not fit into the ideal of the popular girl. Whereas before, my self-confidence had come from my status as an academic achiever, I now suspected that my worth depended on my attractiveness to boys.

In the year I turned thirteen, I would smile whenever a female classmate came to school wearing a T-shirt that said, "A woman's place is in the House…and in the Senate." Yet that was the year I tried on high heels for the first time and started taking off my glasses at lunch when the boy I liked was nearby, even though it reduced my vision to such a blur that I could barely make him out. As I reached a crisis of confidence, my grades suffered. An often-praised A student in seventh-grade science class, by ninth grade I was getting D's in biology. Instead of doing my homework, I watched soaps, lounged in bed, or experimented in the mirror with makeup. In tenth grade at my new high school, I decided not to try out for the diving team and weaseled my way out of a semester of swimming, because I didn't want anyone looking at me in a bathing suit.

Around fourteen, I became interested in the punk scene. Here mainstream tastes in music and other things were scorned, and thriftstore clothes and outcast status worn with pride. Though my original style was more "traditionally" punk—I favored raccoon-style black eyeliner, combat boots, and the Sex Pistols—I soon gravitated toward the more politicized style prevalent at the time in Washington, D.C., where the close-knit punk community centered on Dischord, a record label started by Ian MacKaye and Jeff Nelson in 1981. The underground music scene provided an alternative to mainstream culture and politics in many ways. There were women within the punk scene who challenged gender ideals and who served as examples of strength and independence: they rode and fixed their own motorcycles, worked at clubs or booked shows, or documented their scene by taking photographs. Yet the punk scene was predominantly male. At this time in punk music (the mid-1980s), there were very few women in bands.

Rock, in this regard, has been a kind of last frontier for women. The rock image—being confrontational, lewd, angst-ridden, wild, and loud—has been a male domain met with a head-shaking but tolerant "boys will be boys" attitude. The "bad boy" has always had a sanctioned niche in the mainstream that the "bad girl" has not. The rebel, the James Dean character, wins the heart of the wholesome pretty girl next door. The rock star (even if supremely ugly) marries the supermodel, a scenario that has no parallel with the gender roles reversed. Though many girls in the alternative community held as fierce and well thought-out opinions as boys did, when it came to the all-important subject of music, they felt relegated to sideline roles such as fan or girlfriend.

The boys we associated with led "bohemian" lifestyles, questioned mainstream values, and held politically leftist viewpoints. They were unfailingly pro-choice, played benefit shows, believed in gay rights, and so on. And because they had been raised in a society that had assimilated feminist values, they, like us, held less fixed or negative assumptions about gender than any generation before them. Yet the music around which the scene revolved was generally played by boys. Boys occupied the public sphere. They were the ones onstage, the ones literally making the noise; girls occupied a supplementary place.

I see punk, like the antiwar and civil rights movements before it, as a place where young women learned or solidified radical means of analyzing the world and then applied these powers of analysis to their own lives, only to realize that, as girls, they felt disenfranchised within their own supposedly "alternative" community.

In 1970, women's rights leader Robin Morgan wrote of the experience of women in the student movement, "Thinking we were involved in the struggle to build a new society, it was a slowly dawning and depressing realization that we were doing the same work and playing the same roles in the Movement as out of it: typing speeches that men delivered, making coffee but not policy..."[1] Despite the similarities in coming to consciousness, the means and methods through which women in the alternative music community chose to express themselves differed from those of earlier feminists, because they stemmed from our experiences as girls in a subculture whose roots lay in disaffection, destruction, and nihilism rather than in peace and love; that is, we were punk rather than hippie. The 1960s counterculture represented a challenge to conformity and an optimism that society could change. Punk was also a reaction against conformity, but one tempered by a disillusionment with the 1960s. Punk feminism grew not out of girls wanting sensitive boys so much as girls wanting to be tough girls; instead of boys wearing their hair long and getting called pansies, girls cut their hair and were called dykes.

Yet the seeds of our feminism did grow out of our participation in structures established by the second wave: taking women's studies classes in college, volunteering at a battered women's shelter or at the rape crisis hotline, attending pro-choice events. For me, the foreshadowing of my punk feminism was the frustration I felt when I would go out with my boyfriend, who was in a band, and other boys would come over, sit down without saying hello to me, and start talking to him about music and "the revolution," which was mainly one of aesthetics rather than politics. I began to wonder what was so damned revolutionary about staying up all night and combing your hair a certain way, when I had gotten up at four o'clock on a freezing January morning to hold hands with other women defending a clinic, and had listened to a boy whose girlfriend was inside having an abortion as he confided that he had sold his stereo to pay for the procedure and asked me how he could help her when it was over. I began to wonder, as many other girls did before and after, why we did not get or give each other credit for the contributions we made, and why toughness, anger, and acts of rebellion were considered a male province.

As we began thinking individually about how we had experienced oppression on the basis of gender, we also started making connections with each other. We critiqued both popular culture and the underground culture in which we participated. We thought about school and the books we had read, about the way that despite the second wave, we had learned history with no idea how or whether women could be great or brave. We realized that early on in life we had learned a self-conscious sense of the male gaze, a constant awareness of the physical impression we make. Boys cannot appreciate this, unless perhaps they imagine as constant the feeling of walking alone at night through an unfamiliar neighborhood under hostile scrutiny. Upon examination, we saw that we shared with other girls experiences of being made uncomfortable, unsure of ourselves, or even abused because we were female. Girls began to draw parallels between different experiences: shame at being fat and bitterness at caring so much about our looks; secret competitiveness with other girls, coupled with self-dislike for being jealous; the unsettling feeling that we could not communicate with a boy without flirting; the sudden, engulfing shock of remembering being molested by a father or stepfather when we were too small to form words for such a thing. Straight and bi girls talked about having to give anatomy lessons every time we had sex with a boy. Queer and questioning girls talked about isolation and about mothers bursting into tears when they learned their daughters were gay. Girls who wanted to play music talked about not knowing how to play a guitar because they had never gotten one for Christmas like the boys did. Girls who played music complained that they were treated like idiots by condescending male employees when they went to buy guitar strings or drum parts.

We began to see the world around us with a new vision, a revelation that was both painful and filled with possibility.

Young women's anger and questioning fomented and smoldered until it became an all-out gathering of momentum toward action. In the summer of 1991, the bands Bratmobile and Bikini Kill, self-proclaimed "angry grrrl" bands, came to D.C. for an extended stay, on loan from Olympia, Washington. Bikini Kill promoted its ideas under the slogans "Revolution Girl Style Now" and "Stop the J-Word Jealousy from Killing Girl Love." While subletting a room in the house where I lived, Allison Wolfe worked with Bratmobile bandmate Molly Neuman to produce Riot Grrrl's earliest manifestation, a pocket-sized fanzine by the same name. An initial experimental all-girl meeting evolved into a weekly forum for girls to discuss political, emotional, and sexual issues. That August also saw the International Pop Underground Convention (IPU), a brainchild of stalwart Olympia indie K ("No lackeys to the corporate ogre allowed"). IPU opened with Girl Day. As the idea of Riot Grrrl spread via band tours, fanzines, high school and college networks, and word of mouth, chapters sprang up around the country....

Riot Grrrl meetings owed much to the "personal as political" precedent set by second wave feminists.... Like earlier movements, Riot Grrrl also relied on the strength of numbers to question male territory, but for purposes specific to punk. In "Revolution Girl Style Now," a 1992 *L.A. Weekly* article later reprinted in *Rock She Wrote*, Emily White writes:

> One of the most engaging metaphors of the Riot Girls [sic] is their dramatic invasion of the mosh pit. In Olympia, bands often don't perform on risers, so only the people up front can really see, and, given the violent crush of the pit, those people are almost always boys. The girls got tired of this. But most of them didn't want to dance in the pit—it hurts your boobs. And getting touched by a bunch of sweaty male strangers has all-too-familiar, nightmarish connotations for many girls. Perhaps

moshing is just another one of what Barbara Kruger calls those "elaborate rituals" men have invented "in order to touch the skin of another man." But the girls wanted a space to dance in, so they formed groups and made their way to the front, protecting each other the whole way. Any boy who shoved them had a whole angry pack to deal with.[2]

Early Riot Grrrl ideology was much like the "safe-space," women-only feminism that characterized the second wave. Riot Grrrl often used second wave activist techniques but applied them to third wave forms. The "safe space" Riot Grrrl created was more often the mosh pit than the consciousness-raising group, but lyrically the music often functions as a form of CR. And whereas some second wave feminists fought for equal access to the workplace, some third wave feminists fought for equal access to the punk stage.

One of the most obvious ways that girls strove collectively to end the disparities within punk music was to put women onstage. The phenomenon of girls playing music grew explosively and exponentially. Girls taught their friends how to play instruments and encouraged through words or examples. Some chose to play with other girls to demonstrate unity, whereas others avoided the "girl band" stereotype and proved that they could "rock with the guys" by doing exactly that. There was encouragement to overcome intimidation, to just get up and play. Sometimes this resulted in debate about whether just playing, or "going for it," was the most important thing, or whether it undermined the status of women in rock to perform ill-played sets.... While reworking feminism, these girls were simultaneously reworking punk, getting back to its roots, to a time when raw honesty of expression counted for more than perfect playing....

It is important to remember that not all music created by young women was the same, despite press coverage that made it sound that way. Nor did all feminists in the alternative scene identify themselves as Riot Grrrls, though journalistic overgeneralization sometimes made it seem so.... Rather than constituting a homogeneous mass,

the different bands girls played in were characterized by the contradictions that distinguished other aspects of their lives. They reflected the full spectrum of personas among which young women felt pulled. The music and lyrics combined toughness and tenderness, vengefulness and vulnerability. A political message was often conveyed through graphic personal stories. The songs ranged from fierce exaltation in female anger, to anguish about the pain of relationships, to celebration of non-competitive love between girls. Stage presence often reflected duality as well, for example, contrasting a physical emphasis on overt sexuality with lyrics about sexual abuse. Vocals swung back and forth between harsh, wrenching screams, sweet, soulful siren intonations, and childish singsong.

As women began to form and perform in more bands, they not only changed the face of punk but changed its fabric. They reclaimed punk as the legacy of the outsider, and previously marginalized issues became more prominent....

Feeling in multiple ways like outsiders as feminism became more prevalent among younger women, these musicians demonstrated the punk ethic of bypassing the co-option of the mainstream through self-sufficiency, by photocopying fanzines and distributing them by hand or by mail. These 'zines became a means of feverish expression and collaboration. They employed a format traditionally used to review records and conduct band interviews, not only to spotlight female musicians but also to share insights, ideas, and information (such as how to induce a late period through herbal teas), to rant and reflect, and to tell personal stories—some humorous, some horrifying, some uplifting. Like other means of expression, fanzines embodied an attempt to process a wide variety of past and present images of femininity. Illustrations ran the gamut from photographs hyping girls currently involved in music, to cartoon sex kittens, to torrid lesbian pulp-fiction covers, to hilariously wholesome advertisements from old *Life* magazines. Fanzines helped girls form a network with each other, not only between towns such as Olympia, D.C., and San Francisco, but also among other places, smaller places, suburbs. Hard-core enabled young suburban boys to vent their anger at the world; Riot Grrrl allowed young suburban girls to vent their anger at the world of suburban boys.

Like the women's bands, not all angry-girl fanzines will go down in history as brilliant masterpieces. Often they were crudely constructed and consisted entirely of free-form rants, fragmented diatribes, and uncensored accusation. I have picked up fanzines that I have found literally impossible to read. Yet because young women are so often made to feel invisible, it is vital for them to elevate their everyday lives outside the everyday. I liken this to Frida Kahlo painting herself over and over. It is the pounding of the fist on the table, claiming, "I exist, I exist." Maybe creating a fanzine is cathartic to one young girl alone in her bedroom. Maybe it helps another young girl, reading it alone in her bedroom, come out or speak out or just feel less alone. And if these things are true, then that fanzine has fulfilled its fundamental task of fostering creativity and communication.

Fanzines and punk shows created forums for young women to speak out as survivors of sexual abuse and to share success stories and painful secrets.... As with some aspects of second wave feminism, issues of violence against women form a basis for biracial, cross-cultural coalition. But, perhaps because our scene has punk rather than hippie roots, because we grew up in a more violent society, and because we feel frustrated at the seeming lack of progress in preventing rape, we are more likely than some second wavers to see violence as a legitimate form of equalizing gender dynamics, of reclaiming power....

Although reflections about rape, relationships, and reclaiming our sexuality constituted the burgeoning of our feminism, they also revealed important differences between our definition of it and that of the second wave. Though old stereotypes reverberate in modern gender dynamics, they do not exist in the same clear-cut form. In a society that takes premarital sex for granted, the "virgin/whore" dichotomy that underpins much earlier feminist theory has mutated. Instead of experiencing strict sexual repression, we are taught through advertising that sexuality determines how we are rated; it is a potent form of power we must struggle to possess. Yet it is not a power we ask for or control. In the aftermath of 1970s feminism, we experience both the loss of chivalrous standards that require "respect for ladies," and the post-"free-love" backlash against women's prominent sexuality, which uses our sexuality to thwart us.

Conflicting ideas about the meaning of sex and sexiness are often reflected in the way punk feminists look. Punk fashion has always reflected irony. Because clothes come from thrift stores, they reflect whatever era of clothing people are discarding at any given time. Wardrobes consist of the past, bought for pennies and reworked, reinvented. In this way, the idea of identity is turned on its head. This might mean wearing a gas station attendant's jacket with someone else's name on it. It might mean wearing army gear although you are antimilitary. It might mean mocking capitalism by wearing a T-shirt advertising a ridiculous product you would never buy. For women, punk fashion irony has often been reflected through gender parody.

During the heyday of hard-core and the early politicization of punk in D.C., girls felt compelled to dress and act like guys—black jeans and no makeup were de rigueur. But ultimately, as girls came into their own, the solution became not to demand equity but to celebrate difference, whether this meant strutting their butchness or being a vampy femme or combining both. Punk female fashion trends have paired 1950s dresses with combat boots, shaved hair with lipstick, studded belts with platform heels. We dye our hair crazy colors or proudly expose chubby tummies in a mockery of the masculine ideal of beauty. At the same time, we fiercely guard our right to be sexy and feminine. We might get harassed less if we dressed and acted exactly like boys, but we would see this as giving up. We are interested in creating not models of androgyny so much as models of contradiction. We want not to get rid of the trappings of traditional femininity or sexuality so much as to pair them with demonstrations of strength or power. We are much less likely to burn our bras communally than to run down the street together clad in nothing but our bras, yelling, "Fuck you!"...

Early Riot Grrrl publications pointed out that the name was not copyrighted and encouraged other women to start their own groups. It was never a movement with membership rolls and dues; thus, the media pronouncements of its rise and fall are mostly hype. I am less interested in the EKG status of Riot Grrrl than in the idea that women's work is definitely thriving, though, for what it is worth, Riot Grrrl does currently exist online and as a fanzine-distribution press.

For me, looking at the past, present, and future of women in the alternative music community, I see a continuum of struggle, spiraling upward. This struggle does not depend on the name it takes. Punk has assimilated the demands of girl revolutionaries—there are women tour managers, engineers, and label owners, as well as a plethora of women musicians. But perhaps more important to me is not only that women make up a much more equal balance of those playing music, but also that as women occupy a more respected space, support grows for their work outside the traditional punk music arena. Initially we had to fight just to breathe, to keep ourselves alive. Now that we can stop and take a breath, we can go more in-depth, we are freer to branch off into our specific interests, to leave our own lasting landmarks combining creativity and social change.

NOTES

This essay is dedicated to Sharon Cheslow for her great encouragement, Jen Smith for her genius and friendship, and to my mother, Kim Florence Klein, for constant inspiration.

1. Robin Morgan, ed., *Sisterhood Is Powerful: An Anthology of Writings from the Women's Liberation Movement* (New York: Vintage, 1970), xxiii.

2. Emily White, "Revolution Girl Style Now," *L.A. Weekly,* July 10–16, 1992; reprinted in *Rock She Wrote,* ed. Evelyn McDonnell and Ann Powers (New York: Dell, 1995), 398–99.

PART EIGHT

Change and Politics

Section 1   Resistance and Social Movements

Section 2   Visions of the Future

A husband convicted of spousal rape contends that Catholocism and the U.S. Constitution protect him, while his wife argues that her wedding vows do not include vows of abuse. A group of mothers takes to the streets on behalf of their children, demanding that politicians invest in job creation and safe streets. Activities such as these challenge orthodox definitions of motherhood and marriage. The articles in this section examine how social change is emerging in the daily practices of families and communities, through social movements, and in the forward-looking visions of the future.

The first sequence of articles challenges traditional assumptions about the participation of poor women of color in social and political movements. Mary Pardo's article reveals how Mexican American women's identities as mothers helped to fuel grassroots political mobilization, which in turn sparked political transformations and expanded meanings of motherhood. Helen Safa explores how poor women in Latin America challenge public–private dichotomies by organizing around collective consumption issues. Even outside of organized social movements, we see women disadvantaged by racism, poverty and global inequalities actively strategizing for social change, as Tracy Bachrach Ehlers suggests with her exploration of women's economic dependence on men in Guatemala. And Mindy Stombler and Irene Padavic find in their study of college fraternity "little sisters" that Black women were more likely than their White counterparts to directly confront their sexist fraternity peers, in part because the Black women "drew on an ideological script rooted in the historical legacy of oppositional culture." Poor women of color living in developed, industrial societies or in developing nations are not generally recognized as feminist activists, but the articles in this segment begin to suggest how the diversity of these women's experiences and concerns fuels a more expansive range of feminist political activities.

The concluding section brings together reflections on difference and social change. In the first article, Audre Lorde urges us to work for justice by confronting and reshaping the meanings attached to difference. It is not difference, Lorde observes, but the refusal to recognize differences and "the distortions which result from our misnaming them" that leads to institutionalized inequalities. Continuing with this theme of embracing difference, Walter L. Williams examines several non-Western cultures and points to some of the ways that respect for sexual diversity and gender nonconformity might prove beneficial for our society. Finally, the dialogue between bell hooks and Cornel West suggests that social change needs to encompass spirituality, love, respect, and a rejection of all exclusionary impulses toward difference. Together, these authors show us that embracing the prism of difference is a vital step toward building a more democratic future.

46

Mexican American Women, Grassroots Community Activists

"Mothers of East Los Angeles"

MARY PARDO

The following case study of Mexican American women activists in "Mothers of East Los Angeles" (MELA) contributes another dimension to the conception of grassroots politics. It illustrates how these Mexican American women transform "traditional" networks and resources based on family and culture into political assets to defend the quality of urban life. Far from unique, these patterns of activism are repeated in Latin America and elsewhere. Here as in other times and places, the women's activism arises out of seemingly "traditional" roles, addresses wider social and political issues, and capitalizes on informal associations sanctioned by the community. Religion, commonly viewed as a conservative force, is intertwined with politics. Often, women speak of their communities and their activism as extensions of their family and household responsibility. The central role of women in grassroots struggles around quality of life, in the Third World and in the United States, challenges conventional assumptions about the powerlessness of women and static definitions of culture and tradition.

In general, the women in MELA are long-time residents of East Los Angeles; some are bilingual and native born, others Mexican born and Spanish dominant. All the core activists are bilingual and have lived in the community over thirty years. All have been active in parish-sponsored groups and activities; some have had experience working in community-based groups arising from schools, neighborhood watch associations, and labor support groups. To gain an appreciation of the group and the core activists, I used ethnographic field methods.... The following discussion briefly chronicles an intense and significant five-year segment of community history from which emerged MELA and the women's transformation of "traditional" resources and experiences into political assets for community mobilization.[1]

THE COMMUNITY CONTEXT: EAST LOS ANGELES RESISTING SIEGE

...MELA initially coalesced to oppose the state prison construction but has since organized opposition to several other projects detrimental to the quality of life in the central city.[2] Its second large target is a toxic waste incinerator proposed for Vernon, a small city adjacent to East Los Angeles. This incinerator would worsen the already debilitating air quality of the entire county and set a precedent dangerous for other communities throughout California.[3] When MELA took up the fight against the toxic waste incinerator, it became more than a single-issue group and began working with environmental groups around the state.[4] As a result of the community struggle, AB58 (Roybal-Allard), which provides all Californians with the minimum protection of an environmental impact report before the construction of hazardous waste incinerators, was signed into law. But the law's effectiveness relies on a watchful community network. Since its emergence, "Mothers of East Los Angeles" has become centrally important to just such a network of grassroots activists including a select number of Catholic priests and two Mexican American political representatives. Furthermore, the group's very formation, and its continued spirit and activism, fly in the face of the conventional political science beliefs regarding political participation....

...All the women live in a low-income community. Furthermore, they identify themselves as active and committed participants in the Catholic Church; they claim an ethnic identity—Mexican American; their ages range from forty to sixty; and they have attained at most high school educations. However, these women fail to conform to the predicted political apathy. Instead, they have transformed social identity—ethnic identity, class identity, and gender identity—into an impetus as well a basis for activism. And, in transforming their existing social networks into grassroots political networks, they have also transformed themselves.

TRANSFORMATION AS A DOMINANT THEME

...First, women have transformed organizing experiences and social networks arising from gender-related responsibilities into political resources.[5] When I asked the women about the first community, not necessarily "political," involvement they could recall, they discussed experiences that predated the formation of MELA. Juana Gutiérrez explained:

Well, it didn't start with the prison, you know. It started when my kids went to school. I started by joining the Parents Club and we worked on different problems here in the area. Like the people who come to the parks to sell drugs to the kids. I got the neighbors to have meetings. I would go knock at the doors, house to house. And I told them that we should stick together with the Neighborhood Watch for the community and for the kids.[6]...

Part of a mother's "traditional" responsibility includes overseeing her child's progress in school, interacting with school staff, and supporting school activities. In these processes, women meet other mothers and begin developing a network of acquaintanceships and friendships based on mutual concern for the welfare of their children.

Although the women in MELA carried the greatest burden of participating in school activities, Erlinda Robles also spoke of strategies they used to draw men into the enterprise and into the networks:

At the beginning, the priests used to say who the president of the mothers guild would be; they used to pick 'um. But, we wanted elections, so we got elections. Then we wanted the fathers to be involved, and the nuns suggested that a father should be president and a mother would be secretary or be involved there [at the school site].

Of course, this comment piqued my curiosity, so I asked how the mothers agreed on the nuns' suggestion. The answer was simple and instructive:

At the time we thought it was a "natural" way to get the fathers involved because they weren't involved; it was just the mothers. Everybody [the women] agreed on them [the fathers] being president because they worked all day and they couldn't be involved in a lot of daily activities like food sales and whatever. During the week, a steering committee of mothers planned the group's activities. But now that I think about it, a woman could have done the job just as well!

So women got men into the group by giving them a position they could manage. The men may have held the title of "president," but they were not making day-to-day decisions about work, nor were they dictating the direction of the group. Erlinda Robles laughed as she recalled an occasion when the president insisted, against the wishes of the women, on scheduling a parents' group fundraiser—a breakfast—on Mother's Day. On that morning, only the president and his wife were present to prepare breakfast. This should alert researchers against measuring power and influence by looking solely at who holds titles.

Each of the cofounders had a history of working with groups arising out of the responsibilities usually assumed by "mothers"—the education of children and the safety of the surrounding community. From these groups, they gained valuable experiences and networks that facilitated the formation of "Mothers of East Los Angeles."...

Second, the process of activism also transformed previously "invisible" women, making them not only visible but the center of public attention. From a conventional perspective, political activism assumes a kind of gender neutrality. This means that anyone can participate, but men are the expected key actors. In accordance with this pattern, in winter 1986 an informal group of concerned businessmen in the community began lobbying and testifying against the prison at hearings in Sacramento. Working in conjunction with Assemblywoman Molina, they made many trips to Sacramento at their own expense. Residents who did not have the income to travel were unable to join them. Finally, Molina, commonly recognized as a forceful advocate for Latinas and the community, asked Frank Villalobos, an urban planner in the group, why there were no women coming up to speak in Sacramento against the prison. As he phrased it, "I was getting some heat from her because no women were going up there."

In response to this comment, Veronica Gutiérrez, a law student who lived in the community, agreed to accompany him on the next trip to Sacramento.[7] He also mentioned the comment to Father John Moretta at Resurrection Catholic Parish. Meanwhile, representatives of the business sector of the community and of the 56th assembly district office were continuing to compile arguments and supportive data against the East Los Angeles prison site. Frank Villalobos stated one of the pressing problems:

We felt that the Senators whom we prepared all this for didn't even acknowledge that we existed. They kept calling it the "downtown" site, and they argued that there was no opposition in the community. So, I told Father Moretta, what we have to do

is demonstrate that there is a link (proximity) between the Boyle Heights community and the prison.[8]

The next juncture illustrates how perceptions of gender-specific behavior set in motion a sequence of events that brought women into the political limelight. Father Moretta decided to ask all the women to meet after mass. He told them about the prison site and called for their support. When I asked him about his rationale for selecting the women, he replied:

I felt so strongly about the issue, and I knew in my heart what a terrible offense this was to the people. So, I was afraid that once we got into a demonstration situation we had to be very careful. I thought the women would be cooler and calmer than the men. The bottom line is that the men came anyway. The first times out the majority were women. Then they began to invite their husbands and their children, but originally it was just women.[9]

Father Moretta also named the group. Quite moved by a film, *The Official Story,* about the courageous Argentine women who demonstrated for the return of their children who disappeared during a repressive right-wing military dictatorship, he transformed the name "Las Madres de la Plaza de Mayo" into "Mothers of East Los Angeles."[10]

However, Aurora Castillo, one of the cofounders of the group, modified my emphasis on the predominance of women:

Of course the fathers work. We also have many, many grandmothers. And all this IS with the support of the fathers. They make the placards and the posters; they do the security and carry the signs; and they come to the marches when they can.

Although women played a key role in the mobilization, they emphasized the group's broad base of active supporters as well as the other organizations in the "Coalition Against the Prison." Their intent was to counter any notion that MELA was composed exclusively of women or mothers and to stress the "inclusiveness" of the group. All the women who assumed lead roles in the group had long histories of volunteer work in the Boyle

Heights community; but formation of the group brought them out of the "private" margins and into "public" light.

Third, the women in "Mothers of East L.A." have transformed the definition of "mother" to include militant political opposition to state-proposed projects they see as adverse to the quality of life in the community. Explaining how she discovered the issue, Aurora Castillo said,

> You know if one of your children's safety is jeopardized, the mother turns into a lioness. That's why Father John got the mothers. We have to have a well-organized, strong group of mothers to protect the community and oppose things that are detrimental to us. You know the governor is in the wrong and the mothers are in the right. After all, the mothers have to be right. Mothers are for the children's interest, not for self-interest; the governor is for his own political interest.

The women also have expanded the boundaries of "motherhood" to include social and political community activism and redefined the word to include women who are not biological "mothers." At one meeting a young Latina expressed her solidarity with the group and, almost apologetically, qualified herself as a "resident," not a "mother," of East Los Angeles. Erlinda Robles replied:

> When you are fighting for a better life for children and "doing" for them, isn't that what mothers do? So we're all mothers. You don't have to have children to be a "mother."

At critical points, grassroots community activism requires attending many meetings, phone calling, and door-to-door communications—all very labor-intensive work. In order to keep harmony in the "domestic" sphere, the core activists must creatively integrate family members into their community activities. I asked Erlinda Robles how her husband felt about her activism, and she replied quite openly:

> My husband doesn't like getting involved, but he takes me because he knows I like it. Sometimes we would have two or three meetings a week. And my husband would say, "Why are you doing so much? It is really getting out of hand." But he is very supportive. Once he gets there, he enjoys it and he starts in arguing too! See, it's just that he is not used to it. He couldn't believe things happened the way that they do. He was in the Navy twenty years and they brainwashed him that none of the politicians could do wrong. So he has come a long way. Now he comes home and parks the car out front and asks me, "Well, where are we going tonight?"...

Working-class women activists seldom opt to separate themselves from men and their families. In this particular struggle for community quality of life, they are fighting for the family unit and thus are not competitive with men.[11] Of course, this fact does not preclude different alignments in other contexts and situations.[12]

Fourth, the story of MELA also shows the transformation of class and ethnic identity. Aurora Castillo told of an incident that illustrated her growing knowledge of the relationship of East Los Angeles to other communities and the basis necessary for coalition building:

> And do you know we have been approached by other groups? [She lowers her voice in emphasis.] You know that Pacific Palisades group asked for our backing. But what they did, they sent their powerful lobbyist that they pay thousands of dollars to get our support against the drilling in Pacific Palisades. So what we did was tell them to send their grassroots people, not their lobbyist. We're suspicious. We don't want to talk to a high-salaried lobbyist; we are humble people. We did our own lobbying. In one week we went to Sacramento twice.

The contrast between the often tedious and labor-intensive work of mobilizing people at the "grassroots" level and the paid work of a "high-salaried lobbyist" represents a point of pride and integrity, not a deficiency or a source of shame. If the two groups were to construct a coalition, they must communicate on equal terms.

The women of MELA combine a willingness to assert opposition with a critical assessment of their own weaknesses. At one community meeting, for example, representatives of several oil companies attempted to gain support for placement of an oil pipeline through the center of East Los Angeles. The exchange between the women in the audience and the oil representative was heated, as women alternated asking questions about the chosen route for the pipeline:

> *"Is it going through Cielito Lindo [Reagan's ranch]?" The oil representative answered, "No." Another woman stood up and asked, "Why not place it along the coastline?" Without thinking of the implications, the representative responded, "Oh, no! If it burst, it would endanger the marine life." The woman retorted, "You value the marine life more than human beings?" His face reddened with anger and the hearing disintegrated into angry chanting.*[13]...

People living in Third World countries as well as in minority communities in the United States face an increasingly degraded environment.[14] Recognizing the threat to the well-being of their families, residents have mobilized at the neighborhood level to fight for "quality of life" issues. The common notion that environmental well-being is of concern solely to white middle-class and upper-class residents ignores the specific way working-class neighborhoods suffer from the fallout of the city "growth machine" geared for profit.[15]...

Mexican American women living east of downtown Los Angeles exemplify the tendency of women to enter into environmental struggles in defense of their community. Women have a rich historical legacy of community activism....

But something new is also happening. The issues "traditionally" addressed by women—health, housing, sanitation, and the urban environment—have moved to center stage as capitalist urbanization progresses. Environmental issues now fuel the fires of many political campaigns and drive citizens beyond the rather restricted, perfunctory political act of voting. Instances of political mobilization at the grassroots level, where women often play a central role, allow us to "see" abstract concepts like participatory democracy and social change as dynamic processes.

The existence and activities of "Mothers of East Los Angeles" attest to the dynamic nature of participatory democracy, as well as to the dynamic nature of our gender, class, and ethnic identity. The story of MELA reveals, on the one hand, how individuals and groups can transform a seemingly "traditional" role such as "mother." On the other hand, it illustrates how such a role may also be a social agent drawing members of the community into the "political" arena. Studying women's contributions as well as men's will shed greater light on the networks dynamic of grassroots movements....

NOTES

1. During the last five years, over 300 newspaper articles have appeared on the issue. Frank Villalobos generously shared his extensive newspaper archives with me. See Leo C. Wolinsky, "L.A. Prison Bill 'Locked Up' in New Clash," *Los Angeles Times,* 16 July 1987, sec. 1, p. 3; Rudy Acuña, "The Fate of East L.A.: One Big Jail," *Los Angeles Herald Examiner,* 28 April 1989, A15; Carolina Serna, "Eastside Residents Oppose Prison," *La Gente UCLA Student Newspaper* 17, no. 1 (October 1986): 5; Daniel M. Weintraub, "10,000 Fee Paid to Lawmaker Who Left Sickbed to Cast Vote," *Los Angeles Times,* 13 March 1988, sec. 1, p. 3.

2. MELA has also opposed the expansion of a county prison literally across the street from William Mead Housing Projects, home to 2,000 Latinos, Asians, and Afro-Americans, and a chemical treatment plant for toxic wastes.

3. The first of its kind in a metropolitan area, it would burn 125,000 pounds per day of hazardous wastes. For an excellent article that links recent struggles against hazardous waste dumps and incinerators in minority communities and features women in MELA, see Dick Russell, "Environmental Racism: Minority Communities and Their Battle against Toxics," *The Amicus Journal* 11, no. 2 (Spring 1989): 22–32.

4. Miguel G. Mendívil, field representative for Assemblywoman Lucille Roybal-Allard, 56th assembly district, Personal Interview, Los Angeles, 25 April 1989.

5. Karen Sacks, *Caring by the Hour.*

6. Juana Gutiérrez, Personal Interview, Boyle Heights, East Los Angeles, 15 January 1988.

7. The law student, Veronica Gutiérrez, is the daughter of Juana Gutiérrez, one of the cofounders of MELA. Martín Gutiérrez, one of her sons, was a field representative for Assemblywoman Lucille Roybal-Allard and also central to community mobilization. Ricardo Gutiérrez, Juana's husband, and almost all the other family members are community activists. They are a microcosm of the family networks that strengthened community mobilization and the Coalition Against the Prison. See Raymundo Reynoso, "Juana Beatrice Gutiérrez: La incansable lucha de una activista comunitaria," *La Opinion,* 6 Agosto de 1989, Acceso, p. 1, and Louis Sahagun, "The Mothers of East L.A. Transform Themselves and Their Community," *Los Angeles Times,* 13 August 1989, sec. 2, p. 1.

8. Frank Villalobos, Personal Interview.

9. Father John Moretta, Resurrection Parish, Personal Interview, Boyle Heights, Los Angeles, 24 May 1989.

10. The Plaza de Mayo mothers organized spontaneously to demand the return of their missing children, in open defiance of the Argentine military dictatorship. For a brief overview of the group and its relationship to other women's organizations in Argentina, and a synopsis of the criticism of the mothers that reveals ideological camps, see Gloria Bonder, "Women's Organizations in Argentina's Transition to Democracy," in *Women and Counter Power,* edited by Yolanda Cohen (New York: Black Rose Books, 1989): 65–85. There is no direct relationship between this group and MELA.

11. For historical examples, see Chris Marín, "La Asociación Hispano-Americana de Madres Y Esposas: Tucson's Mexican American Women in World War II," *Renato Rosaldo Lecture Series 1: 1983–1984* (Tucson, Ariz.: Mexican American Studies Center, University of Arizona, Tucson, 1985) and Judy Aulette and Trudy Mills, "Something Old, Something New: Auxiliary Work in the 1983–1986 Copper Strike," *Feminist Studies* 14, no. 2 (Summer 1988): 251–69.

12. Mina Davis Caulfield, "Imperialism, the Family and Cultures of Resistance."

13. As reconstructed by Juana Gutiérrez, Ricardo Gutiérrez, and Aurora Castillo.

14. For an overview of contemporary Third World struggles against environmental degradation, see Alan B. Durning, "Saving the Planet," *The Progressive* 53, no. 4 (April 1989): 35–59.

15. John Logan and Harvey Molotch, *Urban Fortunes* (Berkeley: University of California Press, 1988). Logan and Molotch use the term in reference to a coalition of business people, local politicians, and the media.

47

Women's Social Movements in Latin America

HELEN ICKEN SAFA

The past decade has witnessed a marked increase in participation by women in social movements in Latin America. Latin American women are participating in organizations led by and for women, struggling for their rights as workers in trade unions, as housewives in squatter settlements, and as mothers defending human rights against state repression. While undoubtedly influenced by the feminist movements that developed earlier and were largely middle class in origin, these social movements are distinguished by the widespread participation by poor women, who focus their demands on the state in their struggle for basic survival and against repression.

While many studies trace the origin of these movements to the current economic and political crisis in the region, I believe they are indicative of a broader historical trend toward the breakdown of the traditional division between the private and public spheres in Latin America.[1] The private sphere of the family has always been considered the domain of women, but it is increasingly threatened by economic and political forces. Industrialization and urbanization have reduced the role of the family and strengthened the role of the state. There have been marked occupational changes, including an increasing incorporation of women into the labor force. The importance of women as wage earners has been made even more acute by the economic crisis now gripping Latin America, while state services upon which women have come to depend have been reduced or curtailed. Authoritarian military regimes have invaded the very heart of the family by taking the lives of children and other loved ones and subjecting them to terror and state repression.

However, women in Latin America are not just defending the private domain of the family against increasing state and market intervention. They are also demanding incorporation into the state, so that their rights as citizens will be fully recognized. In this sense, these movements not only are symptomatic of the breakdown between the public and private spheres in Latin America but are themselves furthering this process. Women are demanding to be recognized as full participants in the public world and no longer wish to have their interests represented solely by men, whether as heads of household, *barrio* leaders, politicians, or union officials.

At the same time, as Jelin notes (1987), Latin American women are insisting upon distinct forms of incorporation that reaffirm their identity as women, and particularly as wives and mothers. This form of incorporation differs from the contemporary U.S. and Western European expedience, in which women seek a gender-neutral participation in the public sphere. Latin American women, in contrast, think that their roles as wives and mothers legitimize their sense of injustice and outrage, since they are protesting their inability to effectively carry out these roles, as military governments take away their children or the rising cost of living prevents them from feeding their families adequately. In short, they are redefining and transforming their domestic role from one of private nurturance to one of collective, public protest, and in this way challenging the traditional seclusion of women into the private sphere of the family.

The prominence of women in these new social movements challenges Marxist theory in at

467

least two fundamental ways. In the first place, participation in these women's movements is based primarily on gender rather than on class, which Marxists have emphasized as the principal avenue for collective action. Most of the poor women who participate in these movements are conscious of both class and gender exploitation, but they tend to legitimize their concerns over issues such as human rights or the cost of living primarily in terms of their roles as wives and mothers rather than as members of a subordinated class. This tendency points out the weakness of Marxist theory in addressing the importance of gender, racial, or religious differences within the working class. Second, and as a consequence of their gender emphasis, the primary arena of confrontation for women's social movements in Latin America has not been with capital but with the state, largely in terms of their reproductive role as wives, mothers, and consumers of both state services and private consumer goods. The state has assumed a major role in social reproduction in Latin America, particularly in terms of the provision of basic services, such as health, education, and transportation. At the same time, the need for these services has grown with the rapid increase in urbanization and industrialization in the post-World War II period.

Women are not the only subordinated group to challenge the state, and social movements have arisen as well among youth, peasants, the urban poor, and broader-based human rights groups. Latin American women have also demanded greater participation in labor unions, political parties, and peasant movements that have attempted to make the state more responsive to their needs. They have worked with feminists in establishing day-care centers or in developing ways to cope with sexual violence and other problems. However, this article focuses on Latin American women's movements for human rights and those centering around consumer issues. It explores the factors that contributed to the increased participation of women in social movements in Latin America and why women have chosen the state as

the principal arena of confrontation rather than capital, as in workplace-related issues of collective action. It also discusses how successful these social movements have been in bringing about fundamental changes in gender roles in Latin America.

THE BASES OF WOMEN'S SOCIAL MOVEMENTS IN LATIN AMERICA

Women's social movements in Latin America are commonly seen as a response to military authoritarian rule and the current economic crisis, both of which create particular hardships for the working class. In an attempt to address the growing debt crisis, many Latin American governments have set up structural adjustment programs designed by the International Monetary Fund. These programs have had a devastating impact on women and children, since they have resulted in increased unemployment and underemployment, a decline in real wages coupled with accelerated inflation, the elimination of state subsidies for basic foods, as well as cuts in government expenditures for social services, such as health and education (Cornia 1987). The economic crisis has reinforced the need for collective action, particularly among poor urban women who organize primarily on a neighborhood basis.

The urban poor in Latin America have a long history of collective action, as demonstrated by the squatter settlements and other neighborhood actions to improve urban services (e.g., Safa 1974). Women have always played a prominent role in these neighborhood forms of collective action, though their importance has seldom been explicitly acknowledged (Caldeira 1987, 77). At the same time, women commonly resort to informal networks of mutual aid, including extended family and neighbors, to help stretch the family income and resolve community problems. Women also add to the family income through participation in the informal economy as domestic servants, street vendors, industrial homeworkers, and other forms of self-employment. With the economic crisis, these survival strategies have been intensified and institutionalized into formal organizations, such as the *comedores populares* or *ollas comunes* (communal kitchens) for food distribution or *talleres productivos* (workshops) for making garments or doing other types of piecework. In Santiago, Chile, in 1986, there were 768 organizations dedicated to collective consumption, including consumer cooperatives (Arteaga 1988, 577).

The participation of women in social movements in Latin America is also a product of the changes in women's roles in Latin America in the past two decades. Fertility has been declining steadily in most countries of the region, so that by 1980–85, only three Latin American countries registered average fertility rates in excess of six children per woman, while eight countries had rates of fewer than four children per woman (ECLAC 1988a, 2). Fertility decline was associated with women's higher educational levels and increased labor-force participation, as well as with greater access to contraceptives and the promotion of family-planning programs in several Latin American countries. Women's educational levels rose at a faster rate than men's as part of the enormous expansion in primary and, in particular, secondary education between 1950 and 1970. The number of women in higher education rose from 35 percent to 45 percent from 1970 to 1985 (ECLAC 1988a, 3–4). As a result, the female labor force increased threefold in Latin America between 1950 and 1980, with overall participation rates rising from almost 18 percent to over 26 percent in the same period (ECLAC 1988b, 15). Work-force participation rates for women grew faster than those for men, and while all age groups experienced growth, single women between the ages of 20 and 29 continued to have the highest level of paid employment among women.

Women industrial workers in the Caribbean are now making a major contribution to their household economies, which has resulted in a shift toward more egalitarian conjugal relationships (Safa 1990). In contrast to the assumptions of some feminist theorists (e.g., Barrett 1980), women in Latin America and the Caribbean seem to have been more successful in negotiating change within the home than at the level of the workplace or the state, where their needs are still not given legitimacy.

The increased educational and occupational levels of Latin American women also contributed to the growth of a feminist movement among middle-class women, who felt their exclusion from the public sphere even more sharply than poor women did. These feminists have devoted much attention to the poor through research and involvement in action projects, such as day care, health services, and centers for raped and battered women. These programs helped to transmit feminist concerns for greater gender equality and have stimulated poor women to challenge their traditional role. The visibility these gender issues received during the U.N. Decade for the Equality of Women through numerous conferences, publications, and projects reinforced their appeal.

Poor women in Latin America also received considerable support from the church (Alvarez 1989, 20–26). Women played a major role in the Catholic church's organization of ecclesiastic base communities (CEBs) in Brazil and other Latin American countries. The CEBs were part of the church's efforts to give more support to social justice for the poor in Latin America, emanating from liberation theology, which is now under increasing attack from the Vatican. The CEBs were also an attempt by the church to reinforce grassroots support, which was weakening with the growth of Protestantism and the church's elitist stance. Women were organized into mothers' clubs for the provision of food, sewing classes, and other traditional domestic tasks. Many of women's collective consumption strategies, such as communal kitchens, have received church support. While based on traditional women's roles, these clubs provided an additional organizational base from which women could challenge the existing order.

Under military rule, the church often provided the only legitimate umbrella under which women and other groups could organize, since all other forms of mobilization were prohibited. In some Latin American countries, such as Chile and Brazil, women from all class levels, with church support, organized into human rights groups to protest the disappearance or killing of their loved ones, or to seek amnesty for political prisoners or exiles. Catholic doctrine played an important role in these women's self-definition and quest for legitimacy, and they rarely questioned traditional gender roles. On the contrary, these women often appealed to Catholic symbols of motherhood and the family in legitimizing their protest—values that these authoritarian states also proclaimed but destroyed in the name of national security. Women themselves were often victims of this repression: They were systematically sought out for violent sexual torture designed to destroy their femininity and human dignity (Bunster-Burotto 1986).

In sum, many factors have contributed to the recent increased participation of women in social movements in Latin America. Women had long been active at the neighborhood level, both through informal networks and more organized forms of collective action, such as squatter settlements and *barrio* committees. With economic crisis and military rule, these activities took on added importance and also received the support of important groups, such as the Catholic church and nongovernmental agencies. Increased educational and occupational opportunities made women more aware of previous restrictions and more vocal in protesting them. Poor women became more receptive to the largely middle-class feminist movement in Latin America and began to redefine their traditional role, including their relationship to the state.

WOMEN'S SOCIAL MOVEMENTS AND THE STATE

Women's social movements have been described as a new form of doing politics (*nueva forma de hacer política*) in Latin America, but the impetus for most of these movements has not come from traditional political parties and labor unions in the region. Most women's movements have consciously avoided partisan political connections, in part because of the weakness of these traditional avenues of political action during the period of authoritarian military rule when most of these movements arose. The attempt of these regimes to limit legitimate political action contributed to the politicization of women and other groups who had not been participating actively in the public arena (Jelin 1987).

The other reason women's social movements took place largely outside the realm of traditional political parties is that politics is seen as men's sphere, particularly by poor women. Latin American political parties traditionally have been dominated by men and have been seen as engaged in struggles for power in which the poor are essentially clients. Poor people's loyalty to the party is exchanged for favors, such as paving a road, providing state services, guaranteeing title to land, or getting jobs. The Centros de Madres in Chile, which had begun to acquire some autonomy under the governments of Frei and Allende, were, under the military dictatorship of Pinochet, completely subverted to the needs of the state for the control and co-optation of poor women (Valdes et al. 1989). Although the Centros de Madres were privatized, they were run by a staff of volunteers appointed by the government and headed by Pinochet's wife, who offered to both rural and urban women such services as training courses that focused largely on improving their domestic role. Political participation was discouraged as "unfeminine," although members were often called upon to display their loyalty to the regime by participating in rallies and other activities. As a result, membership in the Centros de Madres declined drastically from the premilitary period, and new nonofficial women's groups arose, in the areas of both human rights and collective survival strategies, in response to Chile's severe economic crisis and rising rates of unemployment (Arteaga 1988, 573). These nonofficial groups provided the base for the women's movement against Pinochet starting in 1983.

Latin American women appear to have chosen the state as the principal arena of their collective action rather than the workplace as men traditionally have, partly because industrial capitalism transformed the organization and social relations of production and the gendered division of labor. While industrial capitalism initially drew women into the paid labor force in many areas, they were never as fully incorporated as men, who became the chief breadwinners. Women were relegated to a role as supplementary wage earners, while their reproductive role as housewives and consumers assumed new importance. Despite recent significant increases in women's labor-force participation in Latin America, this image of women as supplementary workers persists and helps explain women's comparatively low level of consciousness as workers. Most poor women are relatively recent and less-stable entrants to the formal labor force in Latin America and work primarily to support themselves and their families, obtaining little gratification or self-fulfillment from their jobs. Their primary identification, even when they are working, is as wives and mothers.

The gendered division of labor in the workplace may reinforce gender hierarchies rather than weaken them, by relegating women to inferior jobs. Even in São Paulo, Brazil, where the spectacular industrial boom of the 1970s led to a 181 percent increase in women's employment in manufacturing between 1970 and 1980, women workers were largely concentrated in exclusively women's jobs at the bottom of the job hierarchy (Humphrey 1987). These gender asymmetries in the workplace were reflected in the conflict between male-dominated unions and working women. Souza-Lobo's study (forthcoming) of the metallurgy industry found that although women formed union committees, and some individually active women were integrated into the union structure, women continued to see the union as a men's sphere that remained largely unresponsive to their demands.

As a result of their frustration in working through political parties and labor unions, the recognized channels for collective action, Latin American women presented their demands to the state directly. One of the principal demands was for the provision of public services, such as running water, electricity, and transportation, all of which are sorely lacking in the squatter settlements in which most of these poor women live. Women's reproductive role as housewives and mothers has tended to push them into the foreground as champions of these collective consumption issues, and they have been in the forefront of protests against the cost of living and for demands for programs to provide day care, health services, and even food.

One of the most successful and unique collective consumption strategies to combat the growing economic crisis is the *comedores populares* or communal kitchens organized by women in Lima, Santiago, and other Latin American cities. Groups of 15 to 50 households buy and prepare food collectively for the neighborhood, with each family paying according to the number of meals requested. Many of these *comedores* sprang up spontaneously, while others have been started or at least supported by the church, the state, and other local and international agencies. UNICEF-Peru in 1985 estimated that there were 300 in Lima (Cornia 1987, 99), while Blondet (1989) recently estimated their number at 1,000–1,200. Their growing number is evidence of women's collective response to the increasing severity of the economic crisis in Peru and other Latin American countries in the past decade.

In Lima, popular organizations may be the only alternative to acquire basic services, such as health, education, and food, yet the *asistencialismo* (welfare dependency) that this policy encourages may be exploited by the government, political parties, and other agencies (Blondet 1989). Traditional district and neighborhood organizations are controlled by male leaders, who attempt to usurp the popular support enjoyed by women's groups for their own partisan ends. Blondet (1989) recounts, for example, how the popular women's federation in Villa El Salvador, a large shanty town in Lima, split and was partially absorbed through pressure brought by the traditional men's organization. The political fragmentation then occurring among leftist political parties in Peru was reproduced within the women's organizations, further weakening their base of support.

Some feminists have been critical of these women's self-help organizations because they focus almost exclusively on traditional women's tasks and do not challenge the traditional division of labor. I would argue that the collectivization of private tasks, such as food preparation and child care, is transforming women's roles, even though they are not undertaken as conscious challenges to gender subordination. These women never reject their domestic role but use it as a base to give them strength and legitimacy in their demands on the state (Alvarez 1989, 20; Caldeira 1987, 97). In moving their domestic concerns into the public arena, they are redefining the meaning associated with domesticity to include participation and struggle rather than obedience and passivity.

Nowhere is their militancy more apparent than in the demands Latin American women have placed on the state for the recognition of human rights. One of the best-known cases in contemporary Latin America is Las Madres del Plaza de Mayo, who played a decisive role in the defeat of the military dictatorship that ruled Argentina from 1976 to 1983. Composed mostly of older women with no political experience, Las Madres take their name from the Plaza de Mayo, the principal seat of government power in Buenos Aires, in which they march every Thursday, wearing a white kerchief and carrying photographs of their missing children as a symbol of protest. Although the military government attempted to discredit them as mad women or mothers of subversives, they continued to march, publish petitions in the newspaper, organize trips abroad, and seek cooperation with other human rights groups and youth movements, with whom they organized larger demonstrations in 1981 and 1982. The publicity they received from the foreign media and the support given them by some European countries and the United States during the Carter administration contributed to

their popular support (Reimers 1989). In order to maintain their legitimacy during the military regime, they refused any identification with political parties or feminism. They maintained, "*Nosotros no defendemos ideologías, defendemos la vida*" ("We don't defend ideologies, we defend life"; Feijoo and Gogna 1987, 155). Their demands were not political power for themselves, but that the state guarantee the return of their loved ones and punish the military who had violated the sanctity of the home and family. These demands remain largely unfulfilled. Though the top military were prosecuted, most officers were granted amnesty, and even some of those imprisoned were later released.

After the end of military rule, Las Madres were weakened by internal struggles that reflected a split between those who wished to remain aloof from partisan politics and those who sought alliances with political parties, chiefly the Peronists, to achieve their goals. Although women's human rights groups similar to Las Madres del Plaza de Mayo have arisen in Uruguay, Chile, Brazil, Honduras, El Salvador, Guatemala, and other Latin American countries subject to military rule, the decline in popular support for Las Madres reflects the difficulty women's social movements have in converting political mobilization into institutional representation (cf. Jaquette 1989, 194).

THE TRANSFORMATIVE POTENTIAL OF WOMEN'S SOCIAL MOVEMENTS IN LATIN AMERICA

Most participation by women in social movements arises out of women's immediate perceived needs and experiences, or out of what Molyneux (1986) terms women's "practical gender interests." Molyneux claims these practical gender interests do not challenge gender subordination directly, whereas strategic gender interests question or transform the division of labor. As we have seen, women's social movements are often based on their roles as wives and mothers and may reinforce or defend women's domestic role. However, as these practical gender interests are collectivized and politicized, they may also lead to a greater consciousness of gender subordination and the transformation of practical into strategic gender interests.

Although neither women's movements for human rights not collective consumption were designed as challenges to gender subordination, participation in those movements has apparently led to greater self-esteem and recognition by women of their rights, as the following statement by a Brazilian woman, leader of a neighborhood organization, underlines:

> *Within the Women's Movement, as a woman, I discovered myself, as a person, as a human being. I had not discovered that the woman … always was oppressed. But it never came to my mind that the woman was oppressed, although she had rights. The woman had to obey because she was a woman. … It was in the Women's Movement that I came to identify myself as a woman, and to understand the rights I have as a woman, from which I have knowledge to pass on as well to other companions. (Caldeira 1987, 95–96, my translation)*

As this statement exemplifies, women's participation in social movements has produced changes in Latin American women's self-definition. Such changes are the best guarantee that these women will resist any attempt to reestablish the old order and will continue to press for their rights. They imply a redefinition of women's roles from a purely domestic image as guardians of the private sphere into equal participants as citizens in a democratic state. However, this redefinition must occur not only in the minds of women themselves but in the society at large, so that women are no longer treated as supplementary wage earners and pawns in the political process. To achieve such goals, there must be unity within the women's movement, across class, ethnic, and ideological lines; and women must also gain support from other groups in the society, such as political parties and labor unions, whom we have seen often try to utilize women's movements for their own ends.

A glaring example of co-optation comes from an earlier period in Bolivia, when women's committees within the party then in power and the housewives' committee of the miners' union were used for partisan politics, and neither the party nor the union ever addressed demands specific to women (Ardaya 1986). Neither of these women's committees had sought autonomy, since they saw themselves serving class rather than gender interests.

Tension between the primacy of class and gender interests in women's organizations throughout Latin America produces differences between women who are feminists and those who are *políticas* (party militants of the left) (Kirkwood 1986, 196). While feminists view politics as a way of furthering their own interests, *políticas* subordinate women's needs to a political program in the hope of their future incorporation. Those who profess to uphold both feminist and partisan political goals are said to be practicing *doble militancia* or double militancy.

This tension between feminists and *políticas* has become more apparent with the end of military rule in Latin America and the reemergence of political parties, which reactivate divisions within the women's movement formerly united in the opposition. The women's movement in Chile suffered less partisan fragmentation than other social sectors opposing the military dictatorship and was an important force in the plebiscite to oust General Pinochet. A group of 12 women's organizations were able to draft the Demands of Women for Democracy, which were presented to the opposition shortly before the plebiscite, and which included the constitutional guarantee of equality between men and women; the reform of civil, penal, and labor legislation that discriminates against women; and an affirmative action policy to reserve 30 percent of government posts for women. However, although the military and the opposition political parties have recognized the importance of women's electoral support, few have given women access to power (Valenzuela 1989). Since the newly elected democratic government in Chile has only recently taken power, it is too early at this writing to see whether women's demands will be implemented, but the small number of women elected or appointed to government office does not augur well for the future.

The Brazilian liberal, democratic state that supplanted military rule has been more successful in addressing women's needs and electing women to public office, including 26 women in the 1986 congressional elections (Alvarez 1989, 58). The initial impetus given by the church through the development of base communities (CEBs) and by feminist groups for the women's movement was critical in building a wider base of support, even though these groups remain divided on some issues, such as family planning. Women also gained greater representation within the state through the government-appointed Council on the Status of Women in São Paulo, which was subsequently established in 23 other states and municipalities, and through the National Council on Women's Rights, which played a critical role in developing women's proposals for the new Brazilian constitution. Pressure put on the council, particularly in São Paulo, by an active grass-roots constituency operating outside the state has kept it responsive to women's needs (Alvarez 1989, 53). However, in Brazil as in Chile, the increased importance of elections rekindled old political divisions between rival political parties formerly united in the opposition. The recent election of a conservative president and the continuing economic crisis weakens the possibility of implementing women's demands, because of budgetary constraints and because of the election and appointment of women with less identification with women's interests.

Women's organizations under socialism have been accused of being imposed from above and of being instruments of state policy. Molyneux (1986) claims that although women's emancipation is officially recognized and supported by the socialist state, it is contained within defined limits. Both Cuba and Nicaragua have been eminently successful in the incorporation of women into the labor force, which is considered a key to women's emancipation, and have supported working women with education and training programs, day-care centers, ample maternity leaves, and other measures. Women's employment has helped the state to meet its labor needs but has also been costly because of the support services women require, which make women considerably more expensive to employ than men (Safa 1989). Therefore, it is hard to argue, as some critics have, that socialist states have simply taken advantage of women's labor power.

Perhaps the most controversial issue for socialist feminists is continued state support of the family, embodied in legal reforms such as the Family Code in Cuba and the Provision Law in Nicaragua. While both reforms aim at greater sharing of responsibility in the household and financial support for women and children, they are also attempts by the state to make the family responsible for needs the state at present cannot meet, given its limited resources (Molyneux 1989). Thus, the goal of these socialist states is to modify the family, to make it more egalitarian rather than to do away with it. This does not differ radically from the goal of most women's social movements in capitalist Latin American countries.

The tenacity of the family in Latin American socialist or capitalist societies derives not only from the needs of the state, or Catholic doctrine, but from the strong identification and emotional gratification women feel in their roles as wives and especially mothers (Safa 1990). The family fulfills their emotional needs for giving and receiving affection, needs that men tend to deny or undervalue. Women continue to value the family because their role within it is never questioned, while they continue to seek legitimacy in the public sphere. As Jaquette (1989, 193) notes, "The feminist perception of the family as an arena of conflict between men and women directly contradicts how women in urban poor neighborhoods understand and justify their politicization—*for* the family." The strong attachment to the family may be one reason why the distinction between the public and private spheres is still more prevalent in Latin America than in more advanced industrial countries like the United States.

CONCLUSION

What is the future of women's social movements in Latin America? Are we to conclude with Jelin (1987) that Latin American women participate more frequently in short-term, sporadic protest movements than in long-term, formalized institutional settings? Or does women's political mobilization represent part of a progressive longer-term trend that may suffer setbacks but not total eclipse?

I would argue for the latter perspective. Latin American women have been too incorporated into the public sphere to retreat back into the private domestic sphere. They have become increasingly important members of the labor force and contributors to the household economy; they have organized social movements for human rights and social welfare; and they are trying to voice their demands in labor unions and political parties. Even if these activities are not undertaken as conscious challenges to gender subordination, they show that women have broken out of the domestic sphere and that gender roles are changing. Latin American women's emergence into the public sphere is both cause and effect of profound cultural changes in the private sphere, in which women are demanding more "democracy in the home" as well as in the state. These changes in Latin American women's self-definition are most likely to endure and to give women the confidence to continue bringing pressure on public authorities for greater recognition of women's rights.

Despite the political and economic problems Latin American countries are facing in the transition to democracy, important gains in women's rights have been made as a result of these social movements. The new Brazilian constitution adopted in 1988 guarantees women equality before the law, including right to property ownership, equal rights in marriage, maternity leave, and the prohibition of salary differences based on sex, age, or civil status (*Debate Sindical* 1989, 24). Argentina has legalized divorce and modified *patria potestad* to give women joint custody of children and equality in other family matters (Jaquette 1989, 199–200). Despite concerted efforts by the Pinochet dictatorship to court women's support in the 1988 plebiscite, 52 percent of Chilean women rejected the continuation in power of the military government, reflecting in part the effectiveness of opposition women's groups.[2] Whether current governments in power in these countries will continue to support women's needs depends on the importance of their electoral support and on the strength and unity of the women's movement in each country.

When women's demands are confined to domestic issues like child care, communal kitchens, or even human rights, they pose less of a threat than when women attempt to gain leverage in men's power structures, such as political parties or labor unions. In short, as women move away from practical to strategic gender interests, they are likely to encounter more opposition on both gender and class lines from established interest groups who are unwilling to grant them the same legitimacy as men in the public arena.

Latin American women are attempting to establish a new relationship to the state, one based not on subordination, control, and dependency but on rights, autonomy, and equality (Valdes and Weinstein 1989). They have passed beyond the stage in which women's needs were largely invisible and ignored, to where women are now heard, even if some may be co-opted for partisan political ends. By politicizing the private sphere, women have redefined rather than rejected their domestic role and extended the struggle against the state beyond the workplace into the home and community. This shift does not invalidate the Marxist theory of class struggle but calls for its reinterpretation to accommodate these new political voices. As Kirkwood (1986, 65) reminds us, the issue is not simply one of women's incorporation into a male-defined world but of transforming this world to do away with the hierarchies of class, gender, race, and ethnicity that have so long subordinated much of the Latin American population, men as well as women.

NOTES

1. While the concept of public-private spheres have been criticized by many feminists and has been largely replaced by the notion of production and reproduction, it has validity for Latin America, the Caribbean, and Mediterranean Europe, where it has been widely used in the study of gender roles. While the reasons for its usefulness for this region lie beyond the scope of this article, it should be noted that I am using the concept of public-private spheres as poles of a continuum rather than as a dichotomy between mutually exclusive categories (cf. Tiano 1988, 40). It is this fluidity that makes possible the domination of the private by the public sphere.

2. The importance of women's labor-force participation in arousing political consciousness can be seen in a study conducted two months prior to the plebiscite, according to which a greater percentage of housewives supported Pinochet than working women (Valenzuela 1989).

REFERENCES

Alvarez, Sonia. 1989. Women's movements and gender politics in the Brazilian transition. In *The women's movement in Latin America: Feminism and the transition to democracy,* edited by Jane Jaquette. Winchester, MA: Unwin Hyman.

Ardaya, Gloria. 1986. The Barzolas and the housewives committee. In *Women and change in Latin America,* edited by J. Nash and H. Safa. Westport, CT: Bergin & Garvey/Greenwood.

Arteaga, Ana María. 1988. Politización de lo privado y subversión de lo cotidiano (Politicization of the private and subversion of everyday life). In *Mundo de Mujer: Continuida y Cambio* (Woman's world: Continuity and change). Santiago: Centro de Estudios de la Mujer.

Barrett, Michèle. 1980. *Women's oppression today.* London: Verso.

Blondet, Cecilia. 1989. Women's organizations and politics in a time of crisis. Paper presented at the Helen Kellogg Institute for International Studies, University of Notre Dame, Notre Dame, IN.

Bunster-Burotto, Ximena. 1986. Surviving beyond fear: Women and torture in Latin America. In *Women and changes in Latin America,* edited by J. Nash and H. Safa. Westport, CT: Bergin & Garvey/Greenwood.

Caldeira, Teresa. 1987. Mujeres, cotidianidad y política (Women, everyday life & politics). In *Ciudadanía e Identidad: Las Mujeres en los Movimientos Sociales Latino-Americanos* (Citizenship and identity: Women and Latin American social movements), edited by E. Jelin. Geneva: UNRISD

(United Nations Research Institute for Social Development).

Cornia, Giovanni. 1987. Adjustment at the household level: Potentials and limitations of survival strategies. In *Adjustment with a human face,* edited by G. Cornia, R. Jolly, and F. Stewart. New York: UNICEF/Oxford: Clarendon Press.

Debate Sindical. 1989. *A mujer trabalhadora* (The woman worker). São Paulo: Depanamento de Estudos Socio-Económicos, Central Unicas dos Trabalhadores (Department of Socioeconomic Studies, Central Workers Federation).

ECLAC (Economic Commission for Latin America and the Caribbean). 1988a. *Women, work and crisis.* LC/L. 458 (CRM. 4/6). Santiago, Chile.

———. 1988b. *Latin American and Caribbean women: Between change and crisis.* LC/L. 464 (CRM. 4/2). Santiago, Chile.

Feijoo, María del Carmen and Monica Gogna. 1987. Las mujeres en la transición a la democrácia (Women in the transition to democracy). In *Ciudadanía e Identidad. Las Mujeres en los Movimientos Sociales Latino-Americanos* (Citizenship and identity: Women and Latin American social movements), edited by E. Jelin. Geneva: UNRISD (United Nations Research Institute for Social Development).

Humphrey, John. 1987. *Gender and work in the Third World.* London: Tavistock.

Jaquette, Jane. 1989. Conclusion: Women and the new democratic politics. In *The women's movement in*

Latin America: Feminism and the transition to de-mocracy, edited by J. Jaquette. Winchester, MA: Unwin Hyman.

Jelin, Elizabeth. 1987. Introduction. In *Ciudadanía e Identidad: Las Mujeres en los Movimientos Sociales Latino-Americanos* (Citizenship and identity: Women and Latin American social movements), edited by E. Jelin. Geneva: UNRISD (United Nations Research Institute for Social Development).

Kirkwood, Julieta. 1986. *Ser política en Chile: Las feministas y los partidos* (*To be political in Chile: Feminists and parties*). Santiago: FLACSO (Latin American Faculty of Social Science).

Molyneux, Maxine. 1986. Mobilization without emancipation? Women's interests, state, and revolution. In *Transition and development: Problems of Third World socialism,* edited by R. Fagen, C. D. Deere, and J. L. Corragio. New York: Monthly Review Press.

———. 1989. Women's role in the Nicaraguan revolutionary process: The early years. In *Promissory notes: Women in the transition to socialism,* edited by S. Kruks, R. Rapp, and M. Young. New York: Monthly Review Press.

Reimers, Isolde. 1989. *The decline of a social movement: The Mothers of the Plaza de Mayo.* Master's thesis, Center for Latin American Studies, University of Florida, Gainesville.

Safa, Helen I. 1974. *The urban poor of Puerto Rico: A study in development and inequality.* New York: Holt, Rinehart & Winston.

———. 1989. Women, industrialization and state policy in Cuba. Working Paper no. 133. Helen Kellogg Institute for International Studies, University of Notre Dame, Notre Dame, IN.

———. 1990. Women and industrialization in the Caribbean. In *Women, employment and the family in the international division of labor,* edited by S. Stichter and J. Parpart. London: Macmillan.

Souza-Lobo, Elizabeth. Forthcoming. Brazilian social movements, feminism and women worker's struggle in the São Paulo trade unions. In *Strength in diversity: Anthropological perspectives on women's collective action,* edited by Constance Sutton.

Tiano, Susan. 1988. Women's work in the public and private spheres: A critique and reformulation. In *Women, development and change: The Third World experience,* edited by M. F. Abraham and P. S. Abraham. Bristol, IN: Wyndham Hall Press.

Valdés, Teresa, and Marisa Weinstein. 1989. *Organizaciones de pobladoras y construción en Chile* (Organizations of squatter settlements and democratic reconstruction in Chile). Documento de Trabajo 434 (Working Paper 434), Santiago: FLACSO-CHILE.

Valdés, Teresa, Marisa Weinstein, M. Isabel Toledo, and Lilian Letelier. 1989. *Centros de Madres 1973–1989: Sólo disciplinamiento?* (*Mothers' Centers 1973–1989: Only imposed discipline?*). Documento de Trabajo 416 (Working Paper 416). Santiago: FLACSO-CHILE.

Valenzuela, María Elena. 1989. Los nuevos roles de las mujeres y la transición democrática en Chile (The new roles of women and the democratic transition in Chile). Paper presented at Conference on Transformation and Transition in Chile, 1982–89, University of California, San Diego.

48

Debunking Marianismo

Economic Vulnerability and Survival Strategies among Guatemalan Wives

TRACY BACHRACH EHLERS

In highland Guatemala, an old riddle asks, "How is a husband like an avocado?" The answer, "A good one is hard to find," is well known to every woman. My fieldnotes are filled with stories testifying to the truth of this adage. Marcela's common-law husband gambles every night and refuses to marry her because he has another wife—and five children—in the next town. Dona Violeta is called a widow, but everyone knows she was abandoned by her husband after the birth of her third child. Carmen had to send her children to live with her mother since their father left her and her new husband refuses to raise another man's offspring. Dona Magdalena's husband drank up her wages, beat her when she complained about it, then spent the next two weeks with his lover, leaving Magdalena penniless. Rich or poor, in towns and villages across the highlands, rarely a day passes without another woeful tale of offenses, abuses, and bad habits of men.

The research on gender relations in Latin America is replete with descriptions of women tormented by unhappy marriages and with explanations of male behavior in this context.[1] As early as the seventeenth century, Fray Alonso called it *"la mala vida,"* or "the bad life" (Boyer 1989). Where analysis fails us is when we ask why women put up with persistent male abuse and irresponsibility. In trying to explain this pattern, authors have often turned to the *machismo/marianismo* model of gender relations, which

suggests that women welcome abusive male behavior as the spiritual verification of their true womanhood. Men's wickedness, this argument claims, is the necessary precondition for women's superior status as semidivine figures, without whose intercession men would have little chance of obtaining forgiveness for their transgressions (Stevens 1973a).

There are several problems with this model. First, *marianismo* is often considered as a complement to machismo, where the passive, long-suffering woman acts in response to male irresponsibility; without *marianismo, machismo* could not exist. Second, it alleges that this pattern offers women a positive and private realm and that, relegated to a separate domestic sphere, they are content with their feminine power in the home, and do not wish to change the sexual balance of power. On both counts, *marianismo* blames the victim, suggesting wives accept callousness from men because they benefit from the status of wife/mother. In addition, *marianismo* has evolved into a nearly universal model of the behavior of Latin American women.[2]

Some see *marianismo* as a powerful positive stance,[3] but I maintain that in Guatemala's patriarchal society, the sexual division of labor excludes women from valuable income-producing activities, thus giving them no choice but to accept irresponsible male behavior. Among Mayas and ladinos, the prevailing ideology of male domination in the economy minimizes the contribution women make to family survival and their ability to manage without a resident man. In this system, men are valuable scarce resources who can misbehave with impunity, assured that their wives and mistresses need them for economic reasons. In this paper, I argue that:

1. While female subordination is present, it comes in many different forms and in varying degrees.
2. Women's behavior vis-à-vis men is not merely a response to *machismo*, but is a survival strategy emerging from female economic, social, and sexual dependence in a society where men hold economic, political, and legal power.
3. Gender relations are not a static construction of ideal roles, but evolve and change with the material conditions of women's lives, and over the life span of each woman.

This article focuses on two highland communities where women have distinctly different relations to production. San Pedro Sacatepequez, San Marcos, is a changing indigenous town (pop. 15,000) in highland Guatemala. San Pedro's rapidly developing economy has created a myriad of income-producing activities for both sexes, reflected in a diversity of male/female relations. In contrast to San Pedro's urbanity, I also examine material from San Antonio Palopó, a traditional Cakchiquel-speaking village on Lake Atitlán. San Antonio (pop. 2600) has a subsistence-based economy, largely dependent upon corn and onion production. In the last dozen years the rapid growth of commercial weaving has resulted in a dramatic change in the sexual division of labor. These contrasting communities have in common a shift in relations of production, i.e., development, albeit on vastly different scales. My discussion focuses on how each town's increasing market integration has changed the sexual division of labor, emphasizing and exacerbating patriarchal relations to the detriment of women.[4]

THE MARIANISMO MODEL

Latin American women are aware of the realities of marriage. Safa's (1976) interviews in Puerto Rico revealed that two-thirds of the women regarded marriage as an unhappy situation doomed from the start because of male vices. Similarly, female Mexican textile workers considered marriage to be problem-ridden and thought themselves better off alone (Piho 1975). Still, 92 percent of Latin American women marry (Youseff 1973), and continue to speak fatalistically about the state of marriage. Peasant women in the Dominican Republic also believe marriage to be a matter of luck, that one must suffer whatever comes and make the best of it (Brown 1975).

This fatalistic acceptance of women suffering at the hands of men has been traced to the colonial period, when women were taught to emulate the virtues of the Virgin Mary. The Spanish fostered a nontemporal, spiritual, and therefore secondary, role for women with laws and social codes limiting women's rights and defining women as subservient (Leahy 1986). This tradition relegates the unquestioning, obedient woman to the home, the church and the family.

Stevens (1973a) coined the term *marianismo* to suggest the sacred significance of women's subordinate posture in Latin America, and described the idealized belief that women are semidivine, morally superior, spiritually strong beings who manifest these attributes in personal abnegation, humility and sacrifice. These attributes she believes appropriate, given the tensions surrounding the exaggerated masculinity (*machismo*) of their spouses. Thus women must be patient with frivolous and intemperate husbands. When men are truly sinful, women, who are closer to God, will intervene and, by their prayers, guide men along the difficult road to salvation. Above all, women are submissive and resigned to their status as pure, long-suffering martyrs to the irresponsible but domineering men in their lives.

Women use their subordinate status to their own advantage in "having their *marianismo* cake and eating it too," (Stevens 1973b:98). The myth of Marian martyrdom is perpetuated in order to assure the "security blanket" which covers all women, giving them a strong sense of identity and historical continuity (Stevens 1973b:98). By this way of reasoning, female power emerges from the private, domestic domain where women rule and are as liberated as they wish to be, free from the pressures of the male-oriented business world. Women are satisfied with their domestic domain and will likely work hard to hold onto a system that supports it. However, the price for controlling this powerful resource can be a lifetime of suffering, both in childbearing and in the trials and humiliations of the marriage itself. Nonetheless, as Neuhouser (1989:690) notes, "the positive impact of marianismo as a resource for women increases over the life course," as a woman's accumulated pain is transformed into sainthood.

Critics of the *marianismo* concept take issue with the notion that women consciously place themselves within the domestic safety net of *la mala vida*. Bourque and Warren (1981) reject the idea that women enjoy parity with men through their control of the domestic sphere. They argue, that where female status is undercut by a hierarchy of men in the larger world, women cannot have power in the home no matter how much they are venerated. Nash (1989) adds that combining public isolation with the spiritual emulation of the Virgin acts to rationalize female powerlessness as it condones male superiority. Moreover, the ideal of the good woman reigning at home rarely corresponds to daily reality (Kinzer 1973; Browner and Lewin 1982). I suggest that as men move away from agricultural dependence, fatherhood becomes an expression of male virility or proof of masculine control over females, and the home becomes the realm of a tyrannical husband, not the idealized domain of women.

Where the *marianismo* model breaks down entirely is among the millions of poor women for whom work is a necessity. They are often underreported and underestimated, especially in subsistence or domestic production. Urban and rural women are rarely idle; their children might not eat if they do not work. Employed as maids, factory workers, in subsistence or export agriculture, as artisans, petty commodity producers, etc., Latin American women work and, when compared to men, occupy the more onerous, insecure, and unrewarding jobs. Female laborers have fewer productive opportunities than men (Deere and Leon de Leal 1981), are severely restricted in what choices they do have (Schminck 1977), and are often forced to accept oppressive conditions and physically taxing work (Piho 1975).

While the sexual division of labor in productive activities is mixed, reproductive responsibilities for Latin American women are relatively uniform. Women perform the bulk of household duties, which proscribes their potential productivity outside the home. Men can find wage labor while many women take up subsistence activities "almost as an extension of domestic work" (Deere and Leon de Leal 1981:360). Even cottage industry, which allows women to direct child labor and is compatible with housework, is usually an extension of labor-intensive domestic skills (Beuchler 1985) and can be a highly exploitative, low-profit endeavor (Ehlers 1982). Moreover, whether a woman works in the informal sector or in the home, she still works two shifts, juggling children, cooking, washing, and cleaning with income-production. Managing these two full-time jobs impinges upon female income potential and diminishes the seriousness with which women are treated in jobs and careers. In short, the *marianismo* model does not fully take into account Latin American male domination.

Male dominance over economic and political institutions limits female access to economic resources. Because it marginalizes women as economic actors, patriarchy does not have to dominate women physically, but can use indirect market control to limit female independence. This may vary by class, ethnicity, or geography, but any examination of gender relations in Latin America shows male dominance in economic control, access to critical roles in society, and in maintaining cultural stereotypes which reinforce male power. Women are therefore economically and socially vulnerable. Modernization and the accompanying elaboration of market relations usually make this situation worse.

Wolf (1966) and Adams (1960) argue that egalitarian relations among indigenous Mayan men and women emerge from a traditional culture that supports a strong, positive husband-father role. Bossen (1984) correctly observes that this argument underestimates the importance of economic roles in determining gender values. In peasant economies where the family productive system functions, as a cooperative unit, women's productive and reproductive labor is as valuable as men's work. Loucky's (1988:119) research in two Lake Atitlan towns convinced him that, "so indispensable is this partnership that individual accumulation and highly unequal distribution of goods is rare." Women are confident of their roles and have little reason to be submissive. Both sexes acknowledge the mutuality of their labor contributions within a flexible, supportive social system. This domestic balance would encourage a woman to leave an abusive husband and return to her natal home (Wagley 1949).

All this changes when individualized cash income enters the system, creating a redivision of labor that negatively affects women. The interdependency, cooperation, and equal distribution of labor characteristic of couples in small traditional communities breaks down when men work autonomously outside the home. Male accessibility to private income production establishes female dependency characteristic of nuclear families in a situation of industrialization (Bossen 1984).

The increasing value given to male income from outside employment is problematic for women in the two communities I examine. In each, women's economic status diminishes with the increasing occupational fortunes of their spouses. In one community, new male-dominated industry has begun to make complementary peasant production irrelevant. In the other, modernization has undermined women's independent businesses while it greatly enhanced male external trade opportunities. The evidence suggests that with increased autonomous income, men devalue their wives, who are no longer essential to them. The economic vulnerability of women from these two very different towns compels them to accept male callousness or irresponsibility because they have no alternative sources of economic security. Those middle-class women who are able to manage without a man do so through resources not available to the ordinary Guatemalan wife.

SAN ANTONIO PALOPÓ

San Antonio Palopó is a traditional, Cakchiquel-speaking community on the eastern shore of Lake Atitlán, whose people have depended upon *milpa* agriculture (small-scale corn agriculture) supplemented by small-scale cash crops (namely onions and previously, anise), and seasonal plantation labor. Families live in tiny, one-room houses, few of which have access to running water, and nearly half the households are landless. Harvested maize (corn) lasts about six months, after which cash must be generated to buy food. The precarious quality of life is perhaps best reflected in the poor diet and the high frequency of chronic illness.

Men and women share this impoverished life, but women carry a larger share of the burden. Half marry by age sixteen and 60 percent have their first child by eighteen. Families with six or seven children under twelve years old are common, although 43 percent have lost one or more children to illness associated with malnutrition. Beyond nursing and child care, women bear an arduous and repetitive domestic routine that takes up to nine hours each day, and which diminishes the time for income production.

Although both men and women are poor and socially marginalized, men have more familiarity with and access to the dominant ladino culture. Women are rarely educated (77 percent have no schooling), with only a 15 percent literacy rate, compared with 32 percent for men. Eighty-four percent of men are fluent in Spanish, while women speak Cakchiquel almost exclusively. All indigenous women wear the local costume, compared to three-quarters of men, a figure that will no doubt decrease since men are beginning to insist their sons wear Western dress.

Cultural, economic, and physical isolation handicap Tunecas[5] in many ways. Only a few women regularly travel beyond San Antonio to sell handweavings in the nearby tourist town of Panajachel, and their sales are sporadic at best. In fact, most Tunecas avoid Panajachel, preferring to do their shopping from itinerant traders who charge high prices when they pass through town. Women who choose the forty-minute bus ride to Panajachel to shop are uncomfortable and shy beyond the market, where Cakchiquel is spoken. They usually accomplish their errands quickly and go home on the next bus.

Female social vulnerability is clearest when women interact with outsiders—doctors, teachers, ladino traders—and must defer to men. In part this is because they do not speak Spanish, but also because of cultural prescriptions that deny respectability to those women who openly converse with strangers. Without men present, women can be outspoken about themselves. Tunecas visiting me needed little encouragement to talk about sex and contraception. They agreed that where children were concerned, women suffered on many counts: they did not like intercourse, they hated pregnancy, feared childbirth, and resented having to care for several small children because it made income production so difficult. Like the women of San Pedro la Laguna interviewed more than fifty years before (Paul 1974), my Tuneca informants characterized men as "curs" who wanted sex all the time, but had little consideration for their wives' needs.

While skewed gender relations have long existed in San Antonio, a clear pattern of male dominance is more evident now than in the past. Until recently, men and women worked together to survive. Men were responsible for agricultural production, women for processing grains, preparing onions for market, and maintaining the home.

Both sexes traveled to the coast to pick cotton on large plantations. There was little money to be made beyond this, and the cash generated from migratory labor was quickly absorbed in consumption or fertilizer for corn. In 1978, however, a handful of entrepreneurial men and women worked with the Peace Corps and the Catholic Church to establish a commercial weaving industry in the town. This innovation totally realigned the relations of production, creating a severe discrepancy in the contributions men and women make to the family income.

Today, 60 percent of Tuneco homes have looms. These families generate an average of nearly $50 a month, more than replacing plantation labor as a source of cash income. The average plantation income is approximately $25 a month, and few work for more than one month. Coastal weather is hot and extremely humid, the work is arduous and food and housing are abysmal. Weaving is home-based, often year-round, and clean. One man said he likes to weave because while he works he can listen to his new radio and look at his new watch. Moreover, instead of eating *frijoles* (beans) three times a day, his wife cooks various dishes for him, keeps his clothes clean, and generally provides domestic support services for his productive efforts.

In San Antonio in 1978, no men wove, but nearly all their wives did. Women used their backstrap looms to produce the blouses, shirts, and handcloths for the family and for a small tourist trade. It seemed obvious that women should lead in the introduction of four-harness footlooms since they understood the basic weaving system and could easily adapt to the new technology. In fact, women far outnumbered men at the early co-operative meetings, but later, when it was clear that the new production system was to be ongoing, men signed up in increasing numbers. As an indication of their incipient dominance of commercial weaving, a handful of entrepreneurial male leaders took over as officers of the co-operative, pushing women into peripheral organizational positions.

In a very short time, the sexual division of labor evolved to afford female weavers a small part in the town's new economic profile. Only five percent of commercial weavers are women, despite their prominent role in the establishment of the textile co-operative. Quite simply, with all the other (non-paying) labor they have to do, women do not have the time to weave. Men replace themselves in the fields with day laborers paid from their weaving earnings. The demand for local fieldhands to tend the corn fields has risen with the popularity of weaving and become a secondary occupation replacing plantation labor. In fact, so many men weave there is a scarcity of fieldhands. Women cannot do the same in their domestic work, and this compromises their effectiveness as weavers. While men can start weaving upon rising and work all day, female domestic responsibilities seriously diminish the number of hours available for commercial textile production. Weaving contractors admit they would rather not give work to women because of their longer delivery time compared to men. Despite their traditional skill as weavers, women's labor is now less valuable than their husbands'.

Men have readily taken advantage of the opportunity to weave, as evidenced by the cash purchases of new tape decks, watches, roofs, and cement block houses. Several men have invested their earnings in motorboats, bars, *tiendas* (stores), and other businesses. As soon as they learned how to market belts and table linens, a dozen or so enterprising men began their own weaving organizations as *contratistas* (middlemen), a system paralleling the co-operative, but with one distinction. Rather than putting the standard 20 percent of each order back into the co-operative, the *contratistas* keep it for themselves. Every few months, someone else decides to try being a middleman by drumming up new business. Since looms can produce only so much, new weavers regularly enter the labor pool. Thus, privatization of the weaving business enlarged the small existing bourgeoisie by infusing it with male entrepreneurs. The men of San Antonio Palopá

have embraced a new productive activity affording them a better living.

It is too soon to state unequivocally how development has disrupted male-female interactions in San Antonio. However, given the new relations of production accompanying weaving, we might gain some insight by looking to those who have profited most from the individualization of income, the entrepreneurial class. The incidence of *casitas* (parallel marriages) is highest among the town's wealthier men. While few men have the opportunity for more than casual affairs, men with money can take second wives, and they tend to flaunt their behavior. In a flagrant case of polygyny, one of the new *contratistas* built a house for his second wife and their children next to his first wife's house. The families involved have complained to the local authorities about these arrangements, making the affair a public scandal. In another case, one of the town's well-to-do middlemen brought his parallel family to San Antonio's saint's day fiesta, an action so outrageous that his first wife tried to kill him. Both these wives took action to stop their husbands' infidelities, but neither has been successful.

San Antonio women are at a considerable disadvantage in maintaining themselves as partners in the family productive system. Like other rural Maya, they shared their impoverishment with the men in their lives. Currently, a discrepancy in income and control of earnings deprives them of that comfort, however small, and the security of knowing that their husbands need them as much as they need their husbands. It is clear that development has been beneficial to men, creating a large new job category (weaving), and expanding another (day laborer). Although men still require female domestic service, the traditional complementarity of peasant agricultural production has been replaced by individualization of income and concentration of business in the hands of men. At the same time, women's productive contribution has been devalued and marginalized, exacerbating female economic vulnerability and creating worrisome implications for gender relations in the future.

SAN PEDRO SACATEPEQUEZ

San Pedro Sacatepequez is a busy Indian commercial center in San Marcos, located between the high altiplano and the coastal towns and hotland plantations. The town has a heterogeneous, stratified population made even more diverse by the large hinterland comprising seventeen hamlets (*aldeas*), a favorable location for trade. Since World War II, expansion of commerce, cottage industry, transportation and education has placed San Pedro and several other large, enterprising Indian towns in stark contrast to the poverty of most highland communities.

The pace of business is such that townsfolk are fully employed, with few families relying entirely upon *milpa* production for food. Evidence of decades of entrepreneurial vigor are found in the town's educated children, handsome new houses, and imported automobiles. Although consumerism is rampant among the growing middle-class, poor townspeople and rural *aldeanos* also have disposable income. Few rural Sampedranos need to work on coastal plantations to feed their families. Those in the four or five nearest *aldeas* are well-integrated into the commercial activity of the town whose middle-class values they now emulate.

The creation of a middle-class (15 percent of the urban population) in a mere forty years is an indication of the potential for material gain in San Pedro. Since the late 1940s, business opportunities have multiplied with better transportation and the demand for more consumer goods, and many commercial families have dramatically expanded their earning power. Nowadays, grandchildren of itinerant textile peddlers have comfortable lives and successful careers as doctors, lawyers, architects, teachers, and engineers. Education has become a valuable and accessible commodity as the desire for learning and diploma-related employment has grown. Oddly enough, the local passion for business often supersedes entering the positions that come with post-graduate training. There are several cases where new professionals postponed establishing a practice to return to their first love, the family store.

The good fortune of the middle-class is built upon the same strategy used by poorer Sampedranos, the family productive system. But middle-class families have been able to educate enough children to generate reliable salaries, thus providing capital for the commercial development of household-based businesses. Poorer families must continue to invest in labor-intensive enterprises and jobs. While the poor, too, are beginning to send their children to school, class differences handicap *aldeanos* as wage earners, making their material progress slower.

Women, more than men, exploit the available labor supply, depending upon the free labor of children working side-by-side with supervising mothers in what I have called the female family business (Ehlers 1982). Female members of the family cooperate in the home, store, or small workshop for the efficient running of both business and household. Domestic functions are undisturbed since daughters care for babies, cook meals, and run errands to free their older siblings and mothers for income production. The family productive system maximizes the potential for under-capitalized, labor-intensive work while socializing girls for the same occupations when they are mature.

Women must engage in several productive activities to survive, and it is the rare woman who has only one strategy for earning money. A teacher is an after-school knitter or shopkeeper or both. A weaver comes to the huge Thursday market to sell the week's *huipil* (a woven blouse or dress), but also stocks up on candies and breads for her little *aldea* store. When their live chicken market closes, three teenage girls help their mother make *piñatas* and paper floral decorations for graves. The woman who sells vegetables returns home at 7:00 P.M. to her knitting machine, and will bake several dozen breads for sale if she has time. The dedication to work is near-constant and Sunday mass provides the only respite most women have from productive activities.

To justify their workaholism, Sampedranas claim they live to work, but the opposite is equally true: they must work in order to live. The pace of commercial development in San Pedro is brisk enough and the new middle-class large enough, that it is an easy mistake to assume that the locals are doing well. They are better off than other highland communities, but in most cases their earnings are grossly insufficient. A growing population, competition, and unstable markets have kept profit margins for female cottage industry or trade only slightly above cost. Labor is never figured into the price of a handmade product since a woman's saleable work is considered part of her normal domestic responsibility. Accordingly, in ten day's time, a woman and her two daughters might produce a *huipil* in which they have invested $50 in thread, but for which they will garner only $60. Their profit of just over one dollar a day is standard.

Weaving and other female family businesses provide women with their own productive enterprises where they control family labor, manage money, and make creative decisions, but profits from female enterprises are so low that few can completely depend upon them to sustain the family. For the family to survive and flourish, men must do their part as well. The standard highland budgetary division of labor assumes men will contribute the household staples of corn and firewood, while their wives provide everything else through domestic manufacture or cash production. Until recently, women were able to fulfil their obligations by producing goods domestically. Today, women are buying more items because the demands of earning a living do not allow for the home manufacture of necessities like bread, soap, candies, or clothes. Budgets from nearby *aldeas* show that families require a cash minimum of $80 each month, far more than a woman can earn by herself.

An alliance with a male pays off for women in another way. Men father children and, most important, daughters. While boys are valuable for potential remittances from salaried jobs, girls are a necessary requirement for their mother's immediate security. In the poorest households, girls help with domestic chores or low-level cottage industry, and mothers benefit from the small income their teenage daughters provide as domestics. Artisan women use their daughters' labor through the female family business and keep up handicraft output. In both situations, women are keenly aware of the crucial productive and reproductive contributions of men.

Middle-class women are in a somewhat different situation, one complicated by the diversity of productive options among the socially mobile. Some middle-class women have jobs as teachers, but most who work are *comerciantes* (business operators). Rarely do they have their own businesses, however. Instead they function as the retail end of a commercial enterprise which their husbands own and manage. Few of these women control the money their stores take in, being little more than front office overseers. Other wives of this class do not work at all, in many cases because their husbands insist they remain at home as a visible sign of male affluence. In either situation, these women control little of their families' resources and are entirely reliant upon their husbands for money. Children in this case legitimate a woman's role as a mother, but require expensive outlays to outfit and educate, rather than being productive assistants. Nonetheless, children of the professional middle-class do contribute to household expenses and are often regarded as fiscal safety nets in the event that their mother is widowed or abandoned.

FEMALE VULNERABILITY AND DEVELOPMENT

Since World War II, men in San Pedro have been able to take advantage of their town's burgeoning commercial enterprises by establishing relatively lucrative commercial networks and artisanal occupations (Smith 1977). Men now control transportation, storefront retail businesses, and professions. Men have more tools for investment than women (among them better education, easier credit and, most important, exclusive control of the external market), and have done remarkably well in taking advantage of the bullish economy. Quite the opposite is true for their wives.

One by-product of modernization has been the undermining of women's traditional occupations in cottage industry and trade. For generations, woman-centered artisan shops satisfied indigenous consumer habits. Now, however, they are unable to compete with the cheaper, commercially manufactured modern products merchandized by local men, and their handiworks are no longer even minimally profitable. Identification with the national culture has also meant that handwoven textiles and handmade household goods are now considered old-fashioned. Without their customary markets, independent female family businesses are dying out. They have been replaced by employment or piece-work jobs which transfer control of production from the woman to a male patron or supervisor. Overall, while most women in San Pedro have work if they want it, the relations of production are changing. Analysis of production data I collected in town and three *aldeas* shows the following:

1. Women's work is segregated into a handful of occupations, while male jobs are spread across a much wider spectrum.
2. Women's occupations were overwhelmingly labor-intensive and based on family production. Men do take advantage of their sons' labor to some extent, but they generally work in more solitary jobs.
3. Nearly half the women surveyed currently worked only in nonpaying household duties, compared to a small fraction of men primarily occupied with *milpa* production.
4. Female family business made an average of one dollar a day while solitary male workers made nearly three times as much for about the same hours worked per week.

In sum, women's work is narrowly confined to traditional production systems which are steadily declining as a viable part of the economy. Lacking the skills or capital to begin new businesses, many traditional producers have returned to being housewives, being able to do this because their husbands are making more money. As women's traditional enterprises fade, men's productive opportunities have expanded, particularly in solitary occupations

and businesses. Education has afforded them more jobs and access to credit for start-up companies. The result of this transition in the sexual division of labor has been an increase in female economic vulnerability and, correspondingly, a greater dependence upon male wage earners for family survival.

The repercussions of decades of modernization are sizeable, and one clear problem for women is that diminishing economic responsibility translates directly into a loss in female status. Women who no longer manage a household productive system forfeit fiscal independence, supervision of child labor, business decision-making, and personal mobility. Instead they move toward a peripheral productive role in the family, where they are minor contributors to the household budget, dependent upon husbands' earnings, and thus more vulnerable to male domination.

MATING PATTERNS

Adult Sampedranas regard marriage and the bearing of children as the only way to fully legitimize their status as women. Emphasis on the domestic role is so pervasive that middle-aged *senoritas* are extremely rare. Women are invariably newly married, married with children, single but with children, abandoned with children, or widowed. Women understand that at some stage in their relationships with men they will become hapless victims of their *mal caracter* (bad character). Even the early stages of married life are seldom enjoyable for women. Sampedranas tend to marry or, more commonly, move in with a man before they know much about sexuality or the reproductive system. In most cases, girls marry when their parents discover they have been seduced and/or impregnated, and few of these *unido* marriages are legally binding. Thus women are mothers before they are out of their teens, often forced into marriages with boys they hardly know or care for. Patrilocal residence extracts them from their natal families and the female family business into which they were socialized. They come under the direction of an often hostile mother-in-law, who may oblige the new wife to work for her for no wages. Young wives begin their marriages lacking power, and remain that way until their daughters are old enough to provide a modicum of economic security.

These mating patterns and the alternatives to *la mala vida* have been disparately affected by developments in San Pedro. Lacking the resources for personal survival, poor unskilled women have little choice but to stay with abusive husbands. Artisans have traditional skills, but their declining market share is quickly rendering them obsolete as independent producers. They are becoming instead a cottage proletariat, dependent upon work orders from their husbands and other men, or they are unemployed. As the productive mobility and individualized incomes of their spouses rises, these women experience more seriously problematic relationships. What they have that unskilled women lack is a family productive system into which they were socialized as children. For the time being, abused artisans can still return to their natal homes and find a certain amount of economic security, however fragile.

Middle-class male infidelity is likely to increase with the advent of an affluent lifestyle and the status that accompanies it. Middle-class women are often powerless to rein in a wayward spouse since their welfare is entirely based upon a male breadwinner. However, middle-class women have more latitude than poor women when they are unmarried. Educated girls have begun to spurn irresponsible suitors, even if the young woman has become pregnant. With schooling, a job, and a family business for support, these young women are not obligated to marry. They can support themselves and their children without men, and can thus afford to be more selective in choosing a husband.

From late childhood, Sampedranas worry about being abandoned, mostly because of the money difficulties involved. They are taught to prepare themselves so that when and if their husbands leave them, they will be able to feed their children. Some women are able to do this better than others, but modernization has made single

motherhood more troublesome for many Sampedranas who are forfeiting their traditional businesses and the personal status it provides. Moreover, in today's economy women are making less money and men more, further skewing the relations of production. Sampedranas are more economically vulnerable than ever, with less leverage to control male behavior, and fewer resources to retreat to if abandoned. Survival demands that women passively accept male irresponsibility or suffer the consequences.

CONCLUSIONS

Although *marianismo* has been widely accepted as an ideological explanation for why Latin American women endure abuse, this concept does not address the economic basis for gender relations. Instead, *marianismo* provides a rationale for female subordination and idealizes the harsh reality of women's lives. Women tolerate abusive husbands and continue in bad marriages because they have no alternatives. Most highland Guatemalan women rely upon male economic support and to a lesser extent their children, which men provide. The arrangement between men and women is simple. When men abandon the home, women rarely miss them as much as the money or the corn they supply. Deserted women repeatedly enter into temporary or fragile alliances with married men for the same reasons they originally wed: the money and the children that will result.

The basis for this dependence on men lies in the unprofitable and tangential connection women have to production. In two very different highland Guatemalan communities there exists a trend toward female economic degradation associated with accelerated male integration into entrepreneurial activities, cash income, and the external labor market. While this tendency has just begun in San Antonio, if men continue to monopolize income production, female subordination will eventually come to resemble that of San Pedro, where parallel marriages and abandonment are common.

NOTES

1. See, for example, Basham (1976); Lewis (1959, 1961); Peñalosa (1968); Hewes (1954).
2. Some writers exclude traditional indigenous families who maintain their "cultural purity" (Stevens 1973b).
3. See, for example, Paul (1974); Neuhouser (1989); Stevens (1973c); Jacquette (1976).
4. Research in San Antonio began in 1988. In the summer of 1989, I administered a comprehensive sociode-mographic survey of 80 Tuneco families from which the current analysis emerges. The study of San Pedro Sacatepequez began with a year's dissertation research (1976–1977) and research visits continued in the 1980s.
5. Female residents of San Antonio are called Tunecas; males are called Tunecos.

REFERENCES

Adams, R. N. 1960. "An Inquiry in the Nature of the Family," in G. Dole and R. Carneiro, eds., *Essays in the Science of Culture: In Honor of Leslie A. White*. New York: Thomas Y. Crowell.

Basham, R. 1976. "Machismo." *Frontiers,* 1:126–143.

Beuchler, J. M. 1985. "Women in Petty Commodity Production in La Paz, Bolivia," in J. Nash and H. Safa, eds., *Women and Change in Latin America*. South Hadley, MA: Bergin and Garvey.

Bossen, Laurel. 1984. *The Redivision of Labor: Women and Economic Change in Four Guatemalan Communities*. SUNY Series in the Anthropology of Work, June Nash, ed. Albany: State University of New York Press.

Bourque, S. C. and K. B. Warren. 1981. *Women of the Andes: Patriarchy and Social Change in Two Peruvian Towns*. Ann Arbor: University of Michigan Press.

Boyer, R. 1989. "Women, 'La Mala Vida' and the Politics of Marriage," in A. Lavrin, ed., *Sexuality and Marriage in Colonial Latin America*. Lincoln: University of Nebraska Press.

Browner, C. and E. Lewin. 1982. "Female Altruism Reconsidered: The Virgin Mary as Economic Woman." *American Enthologist,* 9:61–75.

Deere, C. D., and M. Leon de Leal. 1981. "Peasant Production, Proletarianization, and the Sexual Division of Labor in the Andes." *Signs,* 7:338–360.

Ehlers, T. B. 1982. "The Decline of Female Family Business: A Guatemalan Case Study." *Women and Politics,* 7:7–21.

Hewes, G. W. 1954. "Mexicans in Search of the 'Mexican': Notes on Mexican National Character." *American Journal of Economics and Sociology,* 13:209–305.

———. 1976. "Female Political Participation in Latin America," in L. B. Iglitzin and R. Ross, eds., *Women in the World, A Comparative Study*. Santa Barbara:ABC-Clio.

Kinzer, N. S. 1973. "Women Professionals in Buenos Aires," in A. Pescatello, ed., *Female and Male in Latin America*. Pittsburgh: University of Pittsburgh Press.

Leahy, M. E. 1986. *Development Strategies and the Status of Women. A Comparative Study of the United States, Mexico, the Soviet Union, and Cuba*. Boulder: Westview.

Lewis, O. 1959. *Five Families*. New York: Basic Books.

———. 1961. *Children of Sánchez*. New York: Random House.

Loucky, J. 1988. *Children's Work and Family Survival in Highland Guatemala*. Ph.D. dissertation, University of California, Los Angeles.

Nash, June. 1989. "Gender Studies in Latin American," in Sandra Morgen, ed. *Gender and Anthropology: Critical Reviews for Research and Teaching*. Washington, DC: American Anthropological Association.

Neuhouser, K. 1989. "Sources of Women's Power and Status among the Urban Poor in Contemporary Brazil." *Signs,* 14:685–702.

Paul, L. 1974. "The Mastery of Work and the Mystery of Sex in a Guatemalan Village," in Michelle Zimbalist Rosaldo and Louise Lamphere, eds., *Women, Culture and Society*. Stanford: Stanford University Press.

Peñalosa, F. 1968. "Mexican Family Roles." *Journal of Marriage and the Family,* 30:681–689.

Piho, V. 1975. "Life and Labor of the Women Textile Worker in Mexico City," in Ruby Rohrlicht-Leavitt, ed., *Women Cross-Culturally: Change and Challenge*. The Hague: Mouton.

Safa, H. I. 1976. "Class Consciousness among Working Class Women in Latin America: A Case Study in Puerto Rico," in J. Nash and H. Safa, eds. *Sex and Class in Latin America.* New York: Praeger.

Wagley, Charles. 1949. *The Social and Religious Life of a Guatemalan Village.* Menosha, WI: American Anthropological Association.

Wolf, E. 1966. *Peasants.* Englewood Cliffs, NJ: Prentice-Hall.

Youseff, N. H. 1973. "Cultural Ideals, Feminine Behavior and Family Control." *Comparative Studies in Society and History,* 15: 326–347.

49

Sister Acts

Resisting Men's Domination in Black and White Fraternity Little Sister Programs

MINDY STOMBLER
IRENE PADAVIC

College offers most late adolescents their first extended contact with extra-familial life and the opportunity to develop alternative conceptions of gender and sexuality (Sanday 1990).

The Greek system often quashes these alternatives and reasserts male privilege, though its success is not uniform. This paper examines how female members of one kind of peer group—little sisters—both uphold and challenge, accommodate and resist men's domination on college campuses. Little sister programs are organizations of women who serve fraternity men in the supportive capacity of hostesses or boosters. These groups exist on both predominantly Black (where they sometimes are called "sweethearts") and predominantly White college campuses, although programs differ in important ways. In all cases, little sisters are affiliates of the fraternity, but receive few privileges and rights associated with full membership (Martin and Stombler 1993).[1]

Researchers (Stombler and Martin 1994) and the press (Lifetime Television 1993; *New York Times* 1989a, 1989b) paint a bleak picture of male dominance and female subordination in little sister programs. Institutional oversight of these programs is minimal: university officials, national fraternities, local alumni and advisors, and women students have little supervisory authority.[2] Fraternity men can thus exploit little sisters for their physical labor (e.g., cleaning up after parties or fulfilling brothers' community service obligations), for their emotional labor (e.g., using little sisters as confidantes or intramural sports cheerleaders), and for their sexuality (e.g., having little sisters model in bikinis for full-color fraternity-rush advertisements).

This research shows that Black little sisters have been more successful than their White counterparts in resisting men's exploitation through collective resistance. Some White little sisters resisted, mostly as individuals, but they were more likely to be accommodating than the Black little sisters. In order to understand why we found White little sisters more likely to engage in "foot dragging" methods while Black little sisters engaged in more confrontational ones, we examine quotidian interactional events—the "micropractices of everyday life"[3] (Davis and Fisher 1993)—that can be "raced" as well as gendered (Morrison 1992). There are several reasons for these differences: Black and White women had different goals, selection processes and expectations differed between the groups, and Black women drew on an ideological script rooted in the historical legacy of an oppositional culture....

METHODS AND DATA

In-depth interviews over a five-year period in the early 1990s on public university campuses in the

Southeast provide most of the data for this study. The first author conducted interviews with 40 women (21 Black, 19 White) of traditional college age who currently or recently participated in little sister organizations in eight different fraternity chapters. Most respondents were recommended by Interfraternity councils, individual fraternities, or fellow little sisters, although in some cases we asked for referrals to women whose experiences were different from those of the recommender. Interviews averaged an hour an a half and took place in settings chosen by the respondents, including restaurants, student apartments, empty classrooms, fraternity houses, and university offices. Seven interviewees participated in a focus group.

The interviewer was close in age to the women she interviewed. Because she is White, her race potentially could have made Black women reluctant to speak openly, but we do not believe this was the case for two reasons. First, both groups of women frankly discussed both positive and negative (sometimes painful) experiences; we had not expected such candor in light of fraternity members' typical defensiveness about a system they perceive to be (and often is) under attack. Second, we had very few refusals: Black women eagerly agreed to be interviewed, perhaps because we emphasized the need for documenting experiences that had long been ignored in popular press and scholarly accounts.

Interviews with several others gave us a broader view: an Interfraternity Council president who had led a campus drive to disband little sister organizations; two little sister program coordinators (fraternity men appointed by the fraternity to work closely with little sister programs); a fraternity president; the head of a Greek Affairs Task Force that had recommended disbanding little sister organizations; eight university officials; and a live-in adult supervisor at a fraternity. We changed the names of respondents, fraternities, and fraternity symbols.

The first author also conducted participant observation in one predominantly White fraternity: she attended little sister rush, several parties and social events, and an orientation meeting of newly chosen little sisters. Although the interview and participant observation data are from the Southeast, national data, including national fraternity and sorority newsletters, televised news reports, and talk show transcripts, support our findings. While geographically limited ethnographic research cannot offer definitive answers about fraternity little sister programs, it suggests how gender inequality is reproduced and resisted on campus.

RESULTS

Black little sister programs offered more liberating structural and cultural elements than white organizations; this predisposed Black women toward a more activist stance than their White counterparts. We discuss these differences and then turn to the types of resistance strategies the two groups tended to use.

Structural and Cultural Factors Enabling Resistance

…At the structural level, several features distinguished Black from White programs: Black programs gave veteran little sisters a say in little sister selection; used a little sister pledge period to enhance women's bonding; created separate, semi-autonomous organizational forms for little sister programs; and, in most cases, sponsored question-and-answer interest meetings instead of more sexualized rush events. White little sister organizations, in contrast, had none of these structural features. They provided no official role for veteran little sisters. Their organizations had no autonomy. Their recruitment process involved rush-style events where women visited a fraternity party *en masse,* trying to impress as many men as possible to enhance their chances of being chosen as little sisters. Nor did White little sisters have a structured "bonding" mechanism—such as a serious pledge period—because it was considered more important for White women to become acquainted with brothers than with other little sisters.

Cultural differences also help explain different resistance strategies. Little sisters of both races described an organizational culture where fraternity men viewed little sisters as partial and inferior members of the fraternity. (National and local fraternity officials described little sisters as "half-members" and "quasi-members.") Rarely did little sisters question their position. Little sisters outwardly accepted the fraternity as the men's property and domain; their purpose was to provide support for the brothers. However, ideological distinctions between the White and Black groups fostered different propensities to critique the brothers' behavior. Below we discuss the differences in the ideologies that undergirded both women's motivations for joining and their orientations to sisterhood. We then show how, within the structure of female subordination, Black women were able to draw on the empowering ideology of "getting ahead" to mobilize for opposition more effectively than White women, who relied on an ideology of "getting a man," leading to a more accommodationist stance. We now turn to specific discussions of the structural and ideological features that informed the selection process, women's motivations for joining little sister programs, and women's notions of sisterhood.

Differences in Little Sister Selection: Pretty Girls and Strong Women.   White and Black little sister organizations had very different notions of the characteristics desirable in little sisters. The recruiting and selection practices that they instituted to realize these preferences yielded little sisters with differing propensities to resist exploitation; this partially explains the different types of resistance that the Black and White women tended to adopt. At White fraternities, the main qualities that men sought in potential little sisters were beauty and sociability. In contrast, according to our respondents, men at Black fraternities—along with veteran little sisters, who actively participated in recruitment in most fraternities—sought women who had strong characters and were willing to work for the fraternity.

Describing the qualities men looked for in recruits, a White little sister reported, "First of all

they look at your face, then they look at your body, and then they say, 'Hi!'" Another said that requirements included:

> *Personality, maybe, [but] it's minuscule…[What matters are] your body and your whole outlook on the guys.… We didn't have to do anything but look good.*

Another gave more credit to personality, which she believed gave her the edge over another would-be little sister:

> *I'm usually really upbeat and outgoing and really easygoing. I like to go up to a brother and just talk to him. [Women the brothers reject are] shy people when you first meet them.*

Black little sisters rarely mentioned beauty or sociability as elements in selection. Instead, recruiters emphasized their desire for "strong" women, an attribute ferreted out with questions such as:

> *"I'm going to give you three categories: woman, XYZ sweetheart, and Black woman. What order would you put them in and why?"*

Or this one:

> *[They asked me,] "Who do you think is the epitome of the Black woman and why?" I said that I felt like it was a close race between my mother and Oprah Winfrey.… You want to give the impression that you're sure of yourself.*

According to our respondents, brother and veteran little sisters looked for a woman who "remained collected" during her response; but poise and self-confidence were not the only selection criteria, as this veteran little sister pointed out:

> *We are looking for someone who is headstrong— who knows that there is a time to play and a time to work. We want people who are not selfish, because in order to do community service you can't be selfish.… We are really looking for strong Black women, to tell you the truth, because a chain is only as strong as its weakest link and we don't want any weak links.*

White little sisters, in contrast, were more likely to be punished than rewarded for being headstrong, as when a fraternity forced a group to close their little sister bank account because their president had been "too bossy."

The selection event was much more emotionally charged for White women than for Black women, highlighting the importance of women's relationships with men. Black fraternities—who accepted the vast majority of rushees—simply notified the women by mailing letters of acceptance. The proportion of women accepted for membership in the White organizations was much smaller, fostering the women's sense of being among the chosen few. Moreover, White fraternity men publicly acknowledged a woman's selection by taking her for a limousine ride, serenading her in public, or regaling her with flowers. One woman described the process:

> They come in and they sing and put you on their lap and lean on one knee. They sit you down, give you a rose and sing a [fraternity] love song.

Another:

> It was seen as a big honor. It feels good that so many guys have picked you. When they came and got me, I was so light-headed that I almost fell over.

Thus, the symbolic importance of being chosen by men to be affiliated with a men's group, structures differently in Black and White organizations, was far more integral to White women's experience than to Black women's, perhaps helping them to identify more closely with the fraternity men's interests than with the interests of their little sister fraternity subgroup. More importantly, white organizations selected women for their beauty and sociability, hardly traits associated with opposition, while Black organizations' choice of "headstrong" women promoted the opposite effect.

Motivations for Joining: Getting a Man versus Getting Ahead.

Black and White little sisters shared some motivations for joining: a desire to meet people, to have a social outlet, to be con-

nected to Greek and campus life, and to be part of a "family" away from home. Interviews clarified, however, that White little sisters primarily joined to meet, befriend, and date men. The White women desired the privileged access to fraternity men that membership brought and saw this access as the main benefit of little sisterhood. For example, when asked why she joined, one little sister replied:

> You get to meet the brothers.... They are always calling the little sisters and telling them to go places with them.

Another credited the program with finding her a boyfriend:

> I date a boy...that I probably wouldn't be dating if I wasn't a little sister. You get to meet men.

Black little sisters' focus was quite different. They acknowledged men as potential dates and good friends or "real brothers" who could protect them or come to their aid if necessary, but many downplayed the importance of meeting men. A large majority claimed that their chief motivation for joining was to have an outlet for community service work, and their substantial time investments in this work corroborated the claim. One said:

> When I first went to hear about sweethearts I wasn't interested at all until the brothers really stressed community service. Then I said I would do it.

Beyond the genuine desire to help the Black community, many women used participation in community service activities instrumentally, to enhance their attractiveness to sororities:

> Sororities want to know...what you have done in the community. So I thought that by being a sweetheart I could get my community service.

In a roundabout way, Black women used little sisterhood as an opportunity to get ahead in their careers. The first step, according to many, was acceptance into a *sorority* (see also Berkowitz and

Padavic 1997; Giddings 1988; Glover 1993). Beyond the high status that women achieve on campus through association with sororities, Black women turned to sororities as networks for future professional achievement and community involvement. Black sororities facilitate career advancement, train Black women leaders, and mobilize political and social practices that improve the Black community (Giddings 1988; Glover 1993). In fact, members of Black sororities tend to be more active after college graduation than before, quite unlike members of White sororities. Our black respondents clearly viewed sororities, not little sister programs, as organizations that would "help you get along in whatever you do." One explained:

> I see sororities as a way to get ahead. Many women in national and state politics are XYZ [sorority]. It is a way to get ahead. That name can help you get connections in the job world. It could help you get hired.

Black little sisters said that little sisterhood could enhance their likelihood of sorority acceptance in three ways: it allowed them to accumulate the hours of community service that sororities consider crucial for admittance; it proved that they could forge bonds with other women; and it provided access to sorority members, who attended fraternity functions. Thus, for most, little sister status opened doors to their desired end—sorority membership—and was not an end in itself.

> I kind of see it as them [the brothers] introducing us to the sororities.... I do remember a lot of sorority girls being there [at a fraternity ball] and they [the brothers] kind of showed us off.... The sororities look among the sweethearts for potential pledges.

Another described her little sisterhood as: "something I needed to learn to go on to better things, like a sorority."

Black little sisters' tendency to regard their affiliation with a men's group as a means to achieve a more important affiliation with a woman's group underscores their collective realization of the importance of connections with other women, in contrast to White little sisters' unadulterated focus on men. Black little sisters, situated in a context where men dominate women, worked the existing system on their own behalf. While it is ironic that Black men had any connection at all to women's participation in sorority life, in a further twist of irony, the little sisters were essentially "using" fraternity men.

Sisterhood.   The most marked difference between White and Black little sister organizations involves their conceptions of sisterhood. White women reported few, if any, experiences of closeness to other women in the program: "You always knew the guys; the guys stood out.... I didn't like the lack of communication between all the girls." Many White women reported competing with one another to get men's attention, or, in one instance, to avoid it. In a striking display of unsisterly behavior, during a fraternity event that called for little sisters to dance provocatively, one woman corralled another sister:

> This is so bad!...I got a girl I know could dance [excitingly]...and got her to go up there with me so they wouldn't be watching me, they would be watching her!

In contrast, the Black little sisters stressed the importance of the bonds between women in the little sister program. Many aspects of the pledging process structured such bonding. In sharp contrast to White women's experiences, at initial interest meetings at one Black fraternity, veteran little sisters and brothers explained to rushees that they were pledging the little sister organization, not the fraternity, and instructed rushees to meet other little sisters so they could "begin to bond." One veteran little sister explained:

> You would want to know the sweethearts on a personal level a little bit more than you would the brothers, because you're not trying to become a brother.... This is our organization and the girls want to come into our organization.

...Not surprisingly, given such training, feelings of sisterhood sometimes superseded loyalty to the brothers. One woman pointed out:

> We had enough people [little sisters] to say [to the fraternity brothers], "You're not going to run over us." The women stuck up for one another.

In short, sisterhood was the *modus vivendi* for Black little sisters but not for their white counterparts and it became a resource for them to draw on in altercations with fraternity men. Black women—and men—drew heavily on an ideology of "strong, black womanhood" to formulate their notions of sisterhood and the qualities desirable in a sister.

Why would men select women for these traits when they heighten women's ability to resist? We speculate that powerful women—and many little sisters were campus leaders—added to the fraternities' campus prestige, which the men appreciated, just as they would appreciate the prestige attending to a male campus leader. It is also possible that Black men are familiar with and accept strength in women because of the larger history and valorization of Black women's labor force participation, family headship, and participation in the civil rights struggle—a movement in which many fraternity chapters were active. Or Black fraternity men's encouragement of sisterhood ties may have resulted from earlier institutional battles between brothers and little sisters that were resolved in the women's favor and whose results are now a normalized part of the institution.

To return to the issue of Black women's sisterhood, Lerner (1979) described turn-of-the-century women's clubs whose goal was to "uplift the race" and to dispel negative stereotypes about Black women. Updating this mission, some little sister organizations defined their organizations as part of the movement to improve Black women's social status. For example, one little sister president organized a seminar on Black women:

> I figured that while I'm in office I'm going to make sure that I'm going to do things that go down in history. We organized a seminar called "The Up-

> lifting of the Black Woman" and we got a professor, a female Black psychologist at the university, to speak. The whole fraternity [brother and sisters] was there.

This type of activity—unheard of in White little sister programs—sends the message that strong women are desired in Black little sister programs because they foster the ideology—begun 100 years ago—that Black women are not merely victims of oppression but generator's of their own successes.[4]

The structures and ideologies of Black little sister programs that emphasized the bonds of sisterhood and mitigated invalidation by men sharply contrasted with the lack of these structures and empowering ideologies in White little sister programs. Structural elements, like having a voice in recruitment, a pledge period that facilitates bonding with women, and some degree of organizational autonomy, lay the necessary foundation for empowerment. Ideologies gave Black little sisters a language of collective resistance with which to fight oppressive situations; these women drew on resources within little sister programs to make the organization less oppressive. As we show below, without these structures and ideologies to legitimate collective resistance, White women responded by accommodating or resisting as individuals.

Strategies of Resistance

Most conflicts between fraternity brothers and little sisters emerged over women's attempts at self-governance and men's resistance to it. Fraternity structure and culture rarely legitimated the *rights* of little sisters to speak up, object, express an opinion, or share in deciding how things were done, although in some cases fraternity men granted them permission. Most women found ways to accommodate their second-class citizenship. This White little sister, irate at the fraternity's practice of using little sisters as "bait"—expecting them to hostess at men's rush parties where they serve drinks, make name tags and show their "smiling faces"—spoke for many interviewees who felt disgruntled, but were unwilling to rock the boat:

> Something that made me so mad was when they would tell us to go up to the would-be [male fraternity] pledge and make sure that he is having a good time. "Dance with him or give him a drink or something or walk outside with him." I wouldn't complain about this in front of everybody. I wouldn't stand up at a little sister meeting and say, "They're using us!" I didn't feel like I had the power to do that.

Most women complied with men's expectations and viewed whatever was asked of them as legitimate; they served the fraternity men in exchange for the men's approval and companionship. One White little sister echoed this acceptance of male dominance, claiming that little sisters "didn't deserve any rights whatsoever." Others resented the fraternities' demands and their lack of rights but felt powerless to oppose them. By participating in activities requiring subservience, little sister programs generally helped to structure and reproduce gender inequality on campus. Although some women did resist, White women tended to resist as individuals, while Black women tended to resist collectively—with more successful results.

Individual Actions. Disaffected White women chose listless compliance and quitting as ways to act on their frustration. For example, at some White fraternities little sisters participated in an annual fundraiser called the "Slave Auction." Some women felt it was degrading because it called for dancing seductively on stage for the brothers and then being auctioned off to the highest bidder to perform a week of "slave" services (such as baking brownies, cleaning, and chauffeuring). Brothers at one fraternity bid more money and cheered louder for women who simulated sex on a pole erected in the middle of the stage.

Despite feeling intensely embarrassed or humiliated by this ritual, the little sisters never considered refusing to participate as a group. Instead, they adopted individual strategies of resistance. Several chose not to attend:

> I didn't do it. That's one thing I don't approve of. I skipped town.

Another:

> Some guys said you had to do it. I was like, 'I don't have to do anything!'

Another was willing to dance but only in a decidedly non-provocative way. By participating half-heartedly, she was still a good sport but had not soiled her reputation by responding to the brothers' chant, "Hump the pole!" After much agonizing and discussion with her biological brother, another adopted a similar strategy of "safe" rebellion:

> I just got up there and stood there. I didn't move.... I wouldn't try to stop the whole thing...and [wouldn't want to] make everybody mad. But, yeah, I personally wouldn't do it.

Quitting was the other option that individual resisters in predominantly-White fraternities employed. One White woman quit upon discovering the brothers' practice of "selecting" women: choosing a woman that several men decide to have sex with by a certain date. She confronted the fraternity president and asked him if what she had heard about a particular woman's "selection" was true. He replied, "Let's just put it this way: one, two and three are done [three brothers had had sex with the woman so far]." She admonished two more brothers for "taking advantage of drunk girls." They said, "What do you want us to do about it?" She replied, "Stop it!" They replied that what they chose to do sexually was their own business and it wasn't her place to lecture them about it. After warning the woman who had been selected, she quit. "After that situation, I came to a realization …that I didn't want to be involved with this…. I [even] started doing research on date rape."

Another little sister quit in anger when her fraternity "revamped" the program by discharging all the little sisters and inviting only the "pretty girls" to come back:

I'm disgusted with it. I think they are slime.

She was incensed that her close friend had not been asked back and described how:

> *The more my roommate and I talked about it, the madder we got.... We ended up talking to the little sister coordinator...and I was just bitching him out, totally.... He expected me to come back?! That's ridiculous!*

Thus, in White fraternities, resistance involved individual acts of half-hearted participation or quitting, akin to Scott's (1985) subterfuge strategies. We found only one instance of a White little sister group that attempted a collective strategy to control the brothers' behavior, and their plan backfired. These little sisters devised "Snake, Slug, Goose" awards corresponding to individual brothers' exhibition of nice behavior (e.g., helping a little sister with a tax return), rude behavior (e.g., vomiting in a little sister's purse), or unbecoming behavior (e.g., standing up a little sister on a date). The brothers ridiculed those men who received the awards of niceness and celebrated those who received the dishonorable awards, undermining the White little sisters' attempts at solidarity.

Collective Actions. Black sisters were much more likely to use collective, above ground strategies to resist fraternity men's exploitation. The most bitter collective protests centered on men's tight control of the organization. In one such protest:

> *The little sisters had a car wash and the brothers tried to control [the proceeds]. The little sisters got angry and broke away and had a big cookout with some of the money and split the rest of it. They got kicked out...but the brothers really learned their lesson after that and treated [the next group] well.*

New little sisters were aware of their predecessors' mobilization and said that this realization tightened their sisterly bonds, making them feel like respected members of the fraternity. Thus, this act of resistance led to at least semi-permanent change: it emboldened incoming little sisters and improved

the men's treatment of future little sisters. However, the brothers' final authority was another "lesson," whether or not the women attended to it: the militant sisters were, in fact, ousted.

Fraternities often discourage women from acting collectively on their own behalf. When several Black little sisters wanted to party on their own at a different hotel during a regional fraternity conference, the brothers attempted to escort the women back to the brothers' hotel. When the women protested, claiming they had the right to act as they chose, the men threatened them:

> *So we were upstairs at my friend's hotel and all of a sudden there was this knock at the door. Our chapter's brothers were outside and they asked me to come into the hall. They said, "Tell the rest of the sweethearts that they have to come back with us." I said, "Those are grown females in there; why don't you tell them to come." We stayed. The brothers started calling us trouble-makers. They told us that if we did anything else like it, that they would refund our activity fee and tell all the other chapters of our fraternity in the country that we couldn't be sweethearts. We were like, "We're not your children [but] that is how you talk to us! We're just as able to do what you can do."*

She "understood" the terms of little sisterhood: "if it wasn't for the frat, sweethearts wouldn't exist," but felt that disobeying was necessary to prove the point that, "we are not beneath them...and we're not going to be subservient to anyone—you can forget that—it's not gonna happen."

If enough clashes occurred—if the women could no longer accommodate the terms of the little sister bargain—it was not unusual for Black little sister organizations, unlike White organizations, to create semi-autonomous little sister organizations. (Another reason for creating semi-autonomous organizations was some national fraternity organizations' unwillingness to allow officially affiliated women's groups.) These groups still operated within the fraternity but coined separate names, assumed more self-governance and autonomy, planned their own social events, and chose their own community service projects.

Redefining their relationship to the men's group made the women feel empowered and enhanced their focus on women:

> I felt closest to the women [rather than to the men]. We had our own meetings and our own projects and things that we were working on. So the women were the people that I had more constant contact with.

In no instance did reorganizing resolve the fundamental disagreement between the women and men over the fraternity authority structure, and clashes continually surfaced, particularly about choosing new little sisters.

> [We] pledged our own girls. That was a problem because the guys were also allowed to participate …and were doing things like groping the pledges. They would blindfold them and grab on them and then say, "Oh, that was a mistake! I didn't mean to do that."

As this example illustrates, many brothers met little sisters' resistance with continued social control. In several fraternities where men tried to remove little sisters' say in selection and pledging, the women argued with them at chapter meetings. According to hooks (1989: 8), "talking back" is an "act of resistance, a political gesture that challenges the politics of domination…a courageous act—as such, it represents a threat." Often the men did not accommodate such threats. For example:

> We had chosen who we wanted on the line and then the brothers wanted to go back and re-choose the line. We had done all the work!… And yet the brothers wanted to come behind us and rechoose! That caused friction.… We got mad because they should have listened to us! We all protested to the brothers.

Black little sisters realized that the men were uncomfortable with even the relatively modest amount of power the women held:

> All of the sweethearts stuck together.… The brothers stopped us from having meetings by ourselves because we were starting to get too much power [laughs proudly]. I know [another university] can-

celed their sweethearts right in the middle of the semester because their sweethearts started getting too much power.

She continued to reflect on little sisters' power:

> We thought we were getting a lot of power, but in reality we weren't, because we could not do anything without going through them. They stopped us from having regular meetings. We still had meetings like once a week or once every two weeks [for a while] but they didn't seem worth the problems.

These little sisters' lack of true membership rights meant that brothers won most altercations. Even when Black little sisters formed separate organizations, their impact was more cosmetic than fundamental. Fraternity men still controlled the little sisters' actions; the men retained the power to abolish these organizations when they saw fit. Clearly, little sisters did not undo the fraternity's overarching system of patriarchy, but in their own backyards, we found little sister resistance that challenged the organizations and actions of their fraternity brothers.

Despite the considerable constraints on their autonomy, little sisters of both races fought back, as either individuals or groups. White women were much more likely to use individual strategies, but on at least one occasion, they, too, tried collective action. We find it interesting that they felt the need to cast their critique in jocular terms (the "Snake, Slug, Goose" awards), probably because overt rebellion ran a higher risk of annihilation. Black little sisters were far more likely to use collective strategies to protest injustices and seemed less concerned with making the message palatable to the men. Not all of their protests were collective, of course; Black women, too, objected as individuals. One, for example, stood up to a fraternity man who claimed he had slept with her: "I confronted him at a large gathering and I set the record straight loud enough so that those in the fraternity heard." So while individual strategies were not exclusively the province of White women nor collective ones the province of Black women, clearly, the tendencies toward particular forms of resistance lay in those directions. Neither form sought to overthrow or even question the fraternity system, only to create more room for autonomous action or dignity.

DISCUSSION

Fraternity little sister organizations are features of campus culture that help reproduce men's dominance. Yet both Black and White women continued to participate in them to further their goals. These goals differed, however, as did the strategies women used to obtain them. Our results show that White women's primary goal was to find a man, perhaps to make him a life partner. This goal and the structure and ideology of their little sister organizations—which provided no niche for veteran little sisters and no support for the concepts of sisterhood or womanly strength—inhibited their ability to mobilize for their rights. Nevertheless, they engaged in resistance, characterized by "noncompliance, subtle sabotage, evasion, and deception" (Scott 1985:31) instead of overt rebellion.

While meeting men was a benefit for Black little sisters, performing community service and negotiating access to sororal life were more important. Because Black little sister organizations offered them more room to maneuver than White little sisters—by giving them a say in recruitment and endorsing sisterhood—they created a space for actions on their own behalf. Their emphasis on sisterhood bonds and the desirability of strength in women allowed them to collectively protest injustices with some success.

We draw two larger conclusions from these themes. First, our data show that existing gender relations are not immutable; even in retrograde organizations, they are subject to the "countervailing processes of resistance, challenge, conflict, and change" (Thorne 1995:497). Because they could draw on liberating elements in the interstices of their organizations, Black little sisters' acts of resistance had greater success than White women's, but even White women tried to change some aspects of their organizations to better serve their purposes.

Second, while Black and White women both experienced a campus peer culture replete with gender inequities and exploitation, their reactions were remarkably different. We argue that both endogenous and exogenous factors account for their different resistance strategies. Regarding the former, we have shown that different resistance strategies are partly due to the more liberating ideologies of the Black little sister organizations that endorsed sisterhood and the relative importance of relations with women over men. They are also undoubtedly partly due to the different levels of tenacity with which Black and White brothers maintained their claims on little sisters. According to Scott (1958:299):

> The parameters of resistance are also set, in part, by the institutions of repression. To the extent that such institutions do their work effectively, they may all but preclude any forms of resistance other than the individual, the informal, and the clandestine.

Yet this analysis begs the question of why Black fraternity little sister programs were structured to allow greater female empowerment and why the goals and strategies of the two groups differed. To understand these factors, we must turn to exogenous explanations.

One such explanation draws on differences in the cultural prescriptions for women's survival. The economic oppression of Black men forced a measure of economic independence on Black women from the time of emancipation (Jones 1985; King 1988). Due in part to the scarcity of good jobs at good wages for men, Black culture relied on women's labor force participation and on an extended family system in which women provided material help to one another (Cherlin 1992; Stack 1974). These emphases diminished the economic basis of the husband-wife bond that characterizes white culture (Cherlin 1992). As Collins (1991:42) discovered when asking young Black women about lessons they learned from their mothers, most answers stressed self-reliance, e.g., "want more for yourself than just a man." Higginbotham and Weber (1992:429) drew a similar conclusion from their quantitative analysis of parents' instructions: "Unlike White women, Black women are typically socialized to view marriage separately from economic security, because it is not expected that marriage will ever remove them from the labor market." Culturally, then, these women's notions of "strong, Black womanhood" and life success do not include future economic dependence on men. White little sisters can more straightforwardly follow the cultural prescription of "getting a man" as a route to success. This prescription is based on the nineteenth-century social construction of women's economic dependency on men (Cancian 1989:19), and encourages women to shape their lives on the basis of intimate relationships (Blumstein and Schwartz 1989:125). From their cultural "legacy," they extract "the culture of romance" on which to pin their hopes (Holland and Eisenhart 1990). Drawing from their culture, Black women extricate notions of strength and sisterhood. Neither group is simply victimized by fraternity men; women draw on their cultural resources to further their goals as they see them in a fraternity structure designed to subordinate them.

A different exogenous explanation might be that Black and White women enter these organizations with different bases of knowledge about individual and collective resistance. The Civil Rights Movement, for example, galvanized many Black women into political action against injustice. Black women of all backgrounds, while rarely recognized as leaders, not only initiated and strategized protests, but also mobilized the resources to successfully complete these actions. This participation taught Black women about the strategies for and effectiveness of collective action (Barnett 1993). Black little sisters' collective resistance is also reminiscent of church women in the Civil Rights Movement who vigorously fought the conservatism of the men who controlled the church hierarchies. Thus, while our evidence clearly shows that endogenous forces were at work, they may have combined with repertoires of resistance and orientations to men and women that were imported from other social venues, organizations, and past experiences.

More broadly, we argue, along with postmodern feminists, that knowledge about White women does not automatically translate into knowledge about Black women: their experiences are often just too different. Nevertheless, we agree with standpoint feminists' claim that a political focus on local interest groups can sidetrack a "collective feminist struggle against women's persistent location at the margins of power" (Davis and Fisher 1993:10). While the postmodern and standpoint perspectives might seem irreconcilable, through empirical exploration of the tensions between structured forms of constraint and women's agency, we may make some headway in understanding and perhaps improving women's lives. This paper has tried to bridge the gap between these orientations by pointing out both the constraints that fraternities place on women and the different factors that underlie women's resistance.

NOTES

1. Some little sisters are also sorority members, although the relationship between sororities and little sister programs differs across campuses. Interviews with little sisters show that some join both organizations in order to increase the variety of connections they have with Greek men. Some join as a less expensive and less structured alternative to sororities that nevertheless facilitates participation in the Greek system.

2. Since the early 1990s, many national and local fraternity organizations and university administrators have disbanded little sister programs. National fraternity organizations cite increased insurance rates, possible loss of legal sex-segregated organizational status, diversion of resources away from chapter operations, disharmony among brothers, and the distraction of chapter members from the "performance of essential duties" as reasons to disband little sister programs. University officials cite sexism and rape prevention as reasons for abolishing the programs. While no national level data on the number of little sister programs exist, national fraternity and sorority organizations and college administrators recognize that, each semester, thousands

of college women in all regions of the country continue to "rush" these organizations. Some fraternities ignore national resolutions and continue to sponsor little sister programs, while others "work the system" by calling their little sisters by a new name. Still other fraternities have pushed their organizations underground (sources listed in Stombler 1994, Appendix).

3. Researchers in the critical education tradition document such micropractices as they appear in students' repertoires of resistance. For example, McRobbie (1978:104) found that British schoolgirls would often, "jettison the official ideology...and replace it with a *more* feminine, even sexual one" and Thomas (1980) found sexually defiant behaviors among Australian schoolgirls.

4. Black women assumed central leadership roles in the community and in liberation politics. As King (1988) noted, "We founded schools, operated social welfare services, sustained churches, organized collective work groups and unions, and even established bands and commercial enterprises. That is, we were the backbone of racial uplift...." The same message of racial uplift, geared to masculine accomplishments, is a part of black fraternities' mission statements, and partly may account for the brothers' acceptance of little sisters' independent sisterhood.

REFERENCES

Barnett, Bernice McNair. 1993. "Invisible southern black women leaders in the civil rights movement: The triple constraints of gender, race, and class." *Gender & Society* 7(2):162–182.

Berkowitz, Alexandra, and Irene Padavic. 1997. "Getting a man or getting ahead: A comparison of White and Black sororities." Unpublished manuscript, Department of Sociology, Florida State University.

Blumstein, Phillip, and Pepper Schwartz. 1989. "Intimate relationships and the creation of sexuality." In *Gender and Intimate Relations: A Microstructural Approach,* Barbara J. Risman and Pepper Schwartz (eds.), 120–129. Belmont, Calif.: Wadsworth.

Cancian, Francesca M. 1989. "Love and the rise of capitalism." In *Gender and Intimate Relations: A Microstructural Approach,* Barbara J. Risman and Pepper Schwartz (eds.), 12–25. Belmont, Calif.: Wadsworth.

Cherlin, Andrew. 1992. *Marriage, Divorce, and Remarriage.* Cambridge, Mass.: Harvard University Press.

Collins, Patricia Hill. 1991. "The meaning of motherhood in Black culture and Black mother-daughter relationships." In *Double Stitch: Black Women Write About Mothers and Daughters,* Patricia Bell-Scott, Beverly Guy-Sheftall, Jacqeline Jones Royster, Janet Sims-Wood, Miriam DeCosta-Willis, and Lucille P. Fultz (eds.), 42–60. New York: Harper Perennial.

Davis, Kathy, and Sue Fisher. 1993. "Power and the female subject." In *Negotiating at the Margins: The Gendered Discourses of Power and Resistance,* Sue Fisher and Kathy Davis (eds.), 3–22. New Brunswick, N.J.: Rutgers University Press.

Giddings, Paula. 1988. *In Search of Sisterhood: The History of Delta Sigma Theta Sorority, Inc.* New York: Morrow.

Glover, Cynthia. 1993. "Sister Greeks: African-American sororities and the dynamics of institutionalized sisterhood at an Ivy league university." Paper presented at the annual meetings of the Eastern Sociological Society, Boston, Mass.

Higginbotham, Elizabeth, and Lynn Weber. 1992. "Moving up with kin and community: Upward social mobility for black and white women." *Gender & Society* 6:416–440.

Holland, Dorothy C., and Margaret Eisenhart. 1990. *Educated in Romance: Women, Achievement, and College Culture.* Chicago: University of Chicago Press.

hooks, bell. 1989. *Talking Back: Thinking Feminist, Thinking Black.* Boston: South End Press.

Jones, Jacqueline. 1985. *Labor of Love, Labor of Sorrow: Black Women, Work, and the Family from Slavery to Present.* New York: Basic Books.

King, Deborah H. 1988. "Multiple jeopardy, multiple conciousness: The context of a Black feminist ideology." *Signs* 19:42–72.

Lerner, Gerda. 1979. *The Majority Finds Its Past: Placing Women in History.* New York: Oxford.

Lifetime Television. 1993. "Scary frat boys." Aired on *The Jane Pratt Show,* April 17.

Martin, Patricia Yancey, and Mindy Stombler. 1993. "Gender politics in fraternity little sister groups: How men take power away from women."

Unpublished manuscript, Department of Sociology, Florida State University.

McRobbie, Angela. 1978. "Working class girls take issue." In *Women Take Issue: Aspects of Women's Subordination,* Centre for Contemporary Cultural Studies Working Papers in Cultural Studies (ed.), 96–108. London: Hutchinson.

Morrison, Toni. 1992. *Race-ing Justice, En-gendering Power: Essays on Anita Hill, Clarence Thomas, and the Construction of Social Reality.* N.Y.: Pantheon Books.

New York Times. 1989a. Fraternities phase out "little sister groups." September 17:59.

———. 1989b. "'Little sisters' program stopped after assaults." October 22:43.

Riley, Kathryn. 1985. "Black girls speak for themselves." In *Just a Bunch of Girls: Feminist Approaches to Schooling,* Gary Weiner (ed.), 63–76. London: Open University Press.

Sanday, Peggy Reeves. 1990. *Fraternity Gang Rape: Sex, Brotherhood, and Privilege on Campus.* New York: New York University Press.

Scott, James C. 1985. *Weapons of the Weak: Everyday Forms of Peasant Resistance.* New Haven: Yale University Press.

———. 1990. *Domination and the Art of Resistance.* New Haven: Yale University Press.

Stack, Carol B. 1974. *All Our Kin: Strategies for Survival in a Black Community.* New York: Harper and Row.

Stombler, Mindy. 1994. "'Buddies' or 'slutties': The collective sexual reputation of fraternity little sisters." *Gender & Society* 8(3):297–323.

Stombler, Mindy, and Patricia Yancey Martin. 1994. "Bringing women in, keeping women down: Fraternity 'little sister' organizations." *Journal of Contemporary Ethnography* 23(2):150–184.

Thorne, Barrie. 1995. "Symposium on West and Fenstermaker's 'Doing difference." *Gender & Society* 9:497–499.

50

Age, Race, Class, and Sex
Women Redefining Difference

AUDRE LORDE

Much of western European history conditions us to see human differences in simplistic opposition to each other: dominant/subordinate, good/bad, up/down, superior/inferior. In a society where the good is defined in terms of profit rather than in terms of human need, there must always be some group of people who, through systematized oppression, can be made to feel surplus, to occupy the place of the dehumanized inferior. Within this society, that group is made up of Black and Third World people, working-class people, older people, and women.

As a forty-nine-year-old Black lesbian feminist socialist mother of two, including one boy, and a member of an interracial couple, I usually find myself a part of some group defined as other, deviant, inferior, or just plain wrong. Traditionally, in american society, it is the members of oppressed, objectified groups who are expected to stretch out and bridge the gap between the actualities of our lives and the consciousness of our oppressor. For in order to survive, those of us for whom oppression is as american as apple pie have always had to be watchers, to become familiar with the language and manners of the oppressor, even sometimes adopting them for some illusion of protection. Whenever the need for some pretense of communication arises, those who profit from our oppression call upon us to share our knowledge with them. In other words, it is the responsibility of the oppressed to teach the oppressors their mistakes. I am responsible for educating teachers who dismiss my children's culture in

school. Black and Third World people are expected to educate White people as to our humanity. Women are expected to educate men. Lesbians and gay men are expected to educate the heterosexual world. The oppressors maintain their position and evade responsibility for their own actions. There is a constant drain of energy which might be better used in redefining ourselves and devising realistic scenarios for altering the present and constructing the future.

Institutionalized rejection of difference is an absolute necessity in a profit economy which needs outsiders as surplus people. As members of such an economy, we have all been programmed to respond to the human differences between us with fear and loathing and to handle that difference in one of three ways: ignore it, and if that is not possible, copy it if we think it is dominant, or destroy it if we think it is subordinate. But we have no patterns for relating across our human differences as equals. As a result, those differences have been misnamed and misused in the service of separation and confusion.

Certainly there are very real differences between us of race, age, and sex. But it is not those differences between us that are separating us. It is rather our refusal to recognize those differences, and to examine the distortions which result from our misnaming them and their effects upon human behavior and expectation.

Racism, the belief in the inherent superiority of one race over all others and thereby the right to dominance. Sexism, the belief in the inherent superiority of one sex over the other and thereby the right to dominance. Ageism. Heterosexism. Elitism. Classism.

It is a lifetime pursuit for each one of us to extract these distortions from our living at the same time as we recognize, reclaim, and define those differences upon which they are imposed. For we have all been raised in a society where those distortions were endemic within our living. Too often, we pour the energy needed for recognizing and exploring difference into pretending those differences are insurmountable barriers, or that they do not exist at all. This results in a voluntary isolation, or false and treacherous connections. Either way, we do not develop tools for using human difference as a springboard for creative change within our lives. We speak not of human difference, but of human deviance.

Somewhere, on the edge of consciousness, there is what I call a *mythical norm*, which each one of us within our hearts knows "that is not me." In America, this norm is usually defined as White, thin, male, young, heterosexual, Christian, and financially secure. It is with this mythical norm that the trappings of power reside within this society. Those of us who stand outside that power often identify one way in which we are different, and we assume that to be the primary cause of all oppression, forgetting other distortions around difference, some of which we ourselves may be practicing. By and large within the women's movement today, White women focus upon their oppression as women and ignore differences of race, sexual preference, class, and age. There is a pretense to a homogeneity of experience covered by the word *sisterhood* that does not in fact exist.

Unacknowledged class differences rob women of each others' energy and creative insight. Recently a women's magazine collective made the decision for one issue to print only prose, saying poetry was a less "rigorous" or "serious" art form. Yet even the form our creativity takes is often a class issue. Of all the art forms, poetry is the most economical. It is the one which is the most

secret, which requires the least physical labor, the least material, and the one which can be done between shifts, in the hospital pantry, on the subway, and on scraps of surplus paper. Over the last few years, writing a novel on tight finances, I came to appreciate the enormous differences in the material demands between poetry and prose. As we reclaim our literature, poetry has been the major voice of poor, working class, and Colored women. A room of one's own may be a necessity for writing prose, but so are reams of paper, a typewriter, and plenty of time. The actual requirements to produce the visual arts also help determine, along class lines, whose art is whose. In this day of inflated prices for material, who are our sculptors, our painters, our photographers? When we speak of a broadly based women's culture, we need to be aware of the effect of class and economic differences on the supplies available for producing art.

As we move toward creating a society within which we can each flourish, ageism is another distortion of relationship which interferes without vision. By ignoring the past, we are encouraged to repeat its mistakes. The "generation gap" is an important social tool for any repressive society. If the younger members of a community view the older members as contemptible or suspect or excess, they will never be able to join hands and examine the living memories of the community, nor ask the all important question, "Why?" This gives rise to a historical amnesia that keeps us working to invent the wheel every time we have to go to the store for bread.

We find ourselves having to repeat and relearn the same old lessons over and over that our mothers did because we do not pass on what we have learned, or because we are unable to listen. For instance, how many times has this all been said before? For another, who would have believed that once again our daughters are allowing their bodies to be hampered and purgatoried by girdles and high heels and hobble skirts?

Ignoring the differences of race between women and the implications of those differences presents the most serious threat to the mobilization of women's joint power.

As White women ignore their built-in privilege of Whiteness and define *woman* in terms of their own experience alone, then women of Color become "other," the outsider whose experience and tradition is too "alien" to comprehend. An example of this is the signal absence of the experience of women of Color as a resource for women's studies courses. The literature of women of Color is seldom included in women's literature courses and almost never in other literature courses, nor in women's studies as a whole. All too often, the excuse given is that the literatures of women of Color can only be taught by Colored women, or that they are too difficult to understand, or that classes cannot "get into" them because they come out of experiences that are "too different." I have heard this argument presented by White women of otherwise quite clear intelligence, women who seem to have no trouble at all teaching and reviewing work that comes out of the vastly different experiences of Shakespeare, Molière, Dostoyefsky, and Aristophanes. Surely there must be some other explanation.

This is a very complex question, but I believe one of the reasons White women have such difficulty reading Black women's work is because of their reluctance to see Black women as women and different from themselves. To examine Black women's literature effectively requires that we be seen as whole people in our actual complexities— as individuals, as women, as human—rather than as one of those problematic but familiar stereotypes provided in this society in place of genuine images of Black women. And I believe this holds true for the literatures of other women of Color who are not Black.

The literatures of all women of Color recreate the textures of our lives, and many White women are heavily invested in ignoring the real differences. For as long as any difference between us means one of us must be inferior, then the recognition of any difference must be fraught with guilt. To allow women of Color to step out of stereo-

types is too guilt provoking, for it threatens the complacency of those women who view oppression only in terms of sex.

Refusing to recognize difference makes it impossible to see the different problems and pitfalls facing us as women.

Thus, in a patriarchal power system where Whiteskin privilege is a major prop, the entrapments used to neutralize Black women and White women are not the same. For example, it is easy for Black women to be used by the power structure against Black men, not because they are men, but because they are Black. Therefore, for Black women, it is necessary at all times to separate the needs of the oppressor from our own legitimate conflicts within our communities. This same problem does not exist for White women. Black women and men have shared racist oppression and still share it, although in different ways. Out of that shared oppression we have developed joint defenses and joint vulnerabilities to each other that are not duplicated in the white community, with the exception of the relationship between Jewish women and Jewish men.

On the other hand, White women face the pitfall of being seduced into joining the oppressor under the pretense of sharing power. This possibility does not exist in the same way for women of Color. The tokenism that is sometimes extended to us is not an invitation to join power; our racial "otherness" is a visible reality that makes that quite clear. For White women there is a wider range of pretended choices and rewards for identifying with patriarchal power and its tools.

Today, with the defeat of ERA, the tightening economy, and increased conservatism, it is easier once again for White women to believe the dangerous fantasy that if you are good enough, pretty enough, sweet enough, quiet enough, teach the children to behave, hate the right people, and marry the right men, then you will be allowed to co-exist with patriarchy in relative peace, at least until a man needs your job or the neighborhood rapist happens along. And true, unless one lives and loves in the trenches it is difficult to remember that the war against de-humanization is ceaseless.

But Black women and our children know the fabric of our lives is stitched with violence and with hatred, that there is no rest. We do not deal with it only on the picket lines, or in dark midnight alleys, or in the places where we dare to verbalize our resistance. For us, increasingly, violence weaves through the daily tissues of our living—in the supermarket, in the classroom, in the elevator, in the clinic and the schoolyard, from the plumber, the baker, the saleswoman, the bus driver, the bank teller, the waitress who does not serve us.

Some problems we share as women, some we do not. You fear your children will grow up to join the patriarchy and testify against you, we fear our children will be dragged from a car and shot down in the street, and you will turn your backs upon the reasons they are dying.

The threat of difference has been no less blinding to people of Color. Those of us who are Black must see that the reality of our lives and our struggle does not make us immune to the errors of ignoring and misnaming difference. Within Black communities where racism is a living reality, differences among us often seem dangerous and suspect. The need for unity is often misnamed as a need for homogeneity, and a Black feminist vision mistaken for betrayal of our common interests as a people. Because of the continuous battle against racial erasure that Black women and Black men share, some Black women still refuse to recognize that we are also oppressed as women, and that sexual hostility against Black women is practiced not only by the White racist society, but implemented within our Black communities as well. It is a disease striking the heart of Black nationhood, and silence will not make it disappear. Exacerbated by racism and the pressures of powerlessness, violence against Black women and children often becomes a standard within our communities, one by which manliness can be measured. But these woman-hating acts are rarely discussed as crimes against Black women.

As a group, women of Color are the lowest paid wage earners in America. We are the primary targets of abortion and sterilization abuse, here and abroad. In certain parts of Africa, small girls are still being sewed shut between their legs to keep them docile and for men's pleasure. This is known as female circumcision, and it is not a cultural affair as the late Jomo Kenyatta insisted, it is a crime against Black women.

Black women's literature is full of the pain of frequent assault, not only by a racist patriarchy, but also by Black men. Yet the necessity for and history of shared battle have made us, Black women, particularly vulnerable to the false accusation that anti-sexist is anti-Black. Meanwhile, womanhating as a recourse of the powerless is sapping strength from Black communities, and our very lives. Rape is on the increase, reported and unreported, and rape is not aggressive sexuality, it is sexualized aggression. As Kalamu ya Salaam, a Black male writer points out, "As long as male domination exists, rape will exist. Only women revolting and men made conscious of their responsibility to fight sexism can collectively stop rape."*

Differences between ourselves as Black women are also being misnamed and used to separate us from one another. As a Black lesbian feminist comfortable with the many different ingredients of my identity, and a woman committed to racial and sexual freedom from oppression, I find I am constantly being encouraged to pluck out some one aspect of myself and present this as the meaningful whole, eclipsing or denying the other parts of self. But this is a destructive and fragmenting way to live. My fullest concentration of energy is available to me only when I integrate all the parts of who I am, openly, allowing power from particular sources of my living to flow back

---

*From "Rape: A Radical Analysis, An African-American Perspective" by Kalamu ya Salaam in *Black Books Bulletin*, vol. 6, no. 4 (1980).

and forth freely through all my different selves, without the restrictions of externally imposed definition. Only then can I bring myself and my energies as a whole to the service of those struggles which I embrace as part of my living.

A fear of lesbians, or of being accused of being a lesbian, has led many Black women into testifying against themselves. It has led some of us into destructive alliances, and others into despair and isolation. In the White women's communities, heterosexism is sometimes a result of identifying with the White patriarchy, a rejection of that interdependence between women-identified women which allows the self to be, rather than to be used in the service of men. Sometimes it reflects a diehard belief in the protective coloration of heterosexual relationships, sometimes a self-hate which all women have to fight against, taught us from birth.

Although elements of these attitudes exist for all women, there are particular resonances of heterosexism and homophobia among Black women. Despite the fact that woman-bonding has a long and honorable history in the African and African-American communities, and despite the knowledge and accomplishments of many strong and creative women-identified Black women in the political, social and cultural fields, heterosexual Black women often tend to ignore or discount the existence and work of Black lesbians. Part of this attitude has come from an understandable terror of Black male attack within the close confines of Black society, where the punishment for any female self-assertion is still to be accused of being a lesbian and therefore unworthy of the attention or support of the scarce Black male. But part of this need to misname and ignore Black lesbians comes from a very real fear that openly women-identified Black women who are no longer dependent upon men for their self-definition may well reorder our whole concept of social relationships.

Black women who once insisted that lesbianism was a White woman's problem now insist that Black lesbians are a threat to Black nationhood, are consorting with the enemy, are basically un-Black. These accusations, coming from the very women to whom we look for deep and real understanding, have served to keep many Black lesbians in hiding, caught between the racism of White women and the homophobia of their sisters. Often, their work has been ignored, trivialized, or misnamed, as with the work of Angelina Grimke, Alice Dunbar-Nelson, Lorraine Hansberry. Yet women-bonded women have always been some part of the power of Black communities, from our unmarried aunts to the amazons of Dahomey.

And it is certainly not Black lesbians who are assaulting women and raping children and grandmothers on the streets of our communities.

Across this country, as in Boston during the spring of 1979 following the unsolved murders of twelve Black women, Black lesbians are spearheading movements against violence against Black women.

What are the particular details within each of our lives that can be scrutinized and altered to help bring about change? How do we redefine difference for all women? It is not our differences which separate women, but our reluctance to recognize those differences and to deal effectively with the distortions which have resulted from the ignoring and misnaming of those differences.

As a tool of social control, women have been encouraged to recognize only one area of human difference as legitimate, those differences which exist between women and men. And we have learned to deal across those differences with the urgency of all oppressed subordinates. All of us have had to learn to live or work or coexist with men, from our fathers on. We have recognized and negotiated these differences, even when this recognition only continued the old dominant/subordinate mode of human relationship, where the oppressed must recognize the masters' difference in order to survive.

But our future survival is predicated upon our ability to relate within equality. As women, we must root out internalized patterns of oppression within ourselves if we are to move beyond the most superficial aspects of social change. Now we must recognize differences among women who are our equals, neither inferior nor superior, and devise ways to use each others' difference to enrich our visions and our joint struggles.

The future of our earth may depend upon the ability of all women to identify and develop new definitions of power and new patterns of relating across difference. The old definitions have not served us, nor the earth that supports us. The old patterns, no matter how cleverly rearranged to imitate progress, still condemn us to cosmetically altered repetitions of the same old exchanges, the same old guilt, hatred, recrimination, lamentation, and suspicion.

For we have, built into all of us, old blueprints of expectation and response, old structures of oppression, and these must be altered at the same time as we alter the living conditions which are a result of those structures. For the master's tools will never dismantle the master's house.

As Paulo Freire shows so well in *The Pedagogy of the Oppressed,** the true focus of revolutionary change is never merely the oppressive situations which we seek to escape, but that piece of the oppressor which is planted deep within each of us, and which knows only the oppressors' tactics, the oppressors' relationships.

Change means growth, and growth can be painful. But we sharpen self-definition by exposing the self in work and struggle together with those whom we define as different from ourselves, although sharing the same goals. For Black and White, old and young, lesbian and heterosexual women alike, this can mean new paths to our survival.

> We have chosen each other
> and the edge of each others battles
> the war is the same
> if we lose
> someday women's blood will congeal
> upon a dead planet
> if we win
> there is no telling
> we seek beyond history
> for a new and more possible meeting.**

*Seabury Press, New York, 1970.

**From "Outlines," unpublished poem.

51

Benefits for Nonhomophobic Societies

An Anthropological Perspective

WALTER L. WILLIAMS

In a recent publication of the Coalition for Traditional Values, the Reverend Lou Sheldon commits himself to "open warfare with the gay and lesbian community.... [This is] a battle with one of the most pernicious evils in our society: homosexuality."[1] What does the Christian Right think is so bad about homosexuality? We are all familiar with the litany: homosexuals are seen as evil because they are said to be a threat to children, the family, religion, and society in general.

In sharp contrast to the heterosexist views of some people in Western society, the majority of other cultures that have been studied by anthropologists condone at least some forms of same-sex eroticism as socially acceptable behavior.[2] Beyond that, quite a number of societies provide honored and respected places for people who are roughly comparable to what we in Western culture would call gay men and lesbians. One example is the Navajo people of Arizona and New Mexico, the largest American Indian group in North America. *Nadle*, a Navajo word meaning "one who is transformed," is applied to androgynous male or female individuals who combine elements of both masculinity and feminity in their personalities. The rare case of a person who is born hermaphroditic, with ambiguous genitalia or with the sexual organs of both the male and the female, is also considered to be a *nadle,* but most *nadle* are individuals whom Western society would characterize as effeminate men or masculine women. While each society of course constructs its own categories of sexuality in different ways, Navajo people traditionally accepted the fact that such androgynous people almost always have inclinations to be sexually active with people of the same biological sex.

Today's Navajos, like other Native Americans, have been significantly affected by Christian attitudes condemning homosexuality, but among those who value their traditions, there still continues a strong respect for *nadle*. We can see traditional Navajo attitudes more clearly by reading the testimony of an anthropologist who lived among the Navajos in the 1930s, before they had been so affected by Western values. This anthropologist documented the extremely reverential attitudes toward *nadle*. He wrote that traditional Navajo families who had a child who behaved androgynously were "considered by themselves and everyone else as very fortunate. The success and wealth of such a family was believed to be assured. Special care was taken in the raising of such children and they were afforded favoritism not shown to other children of the family. As they grew older and assumed the character of *nadle,* this solicitude and respect increased.... This respect verges almost on reverence in many cases."[3]

To illustrate these attitudes, this anthropologist quoted what the Navajo people told him about *nadle:*

> *They know everything. They can do both the work of a man and a woman. I think when all the nadle are gone, that will be the end of the Navajo.*
>
> *If there were no nadle, the country would change. They are responsible for all the wealth in*

the country. If there were no more left, the horses, the sheep, and Navajo would all go. They are leaders, just like President Roosevelt. A nadle around the hogan will bring good luck and riches. They have charge of all the riches. It does a great deal for the country if you have a nadle around.

You must respect a nadle. They are, somehow, sacred and holy.[4]

On reading such quotations, the insight that immediately springs to mind is how attitudes toward similar phenomenon may differ widely from one culture to another. Presented above are opposing views of homosexually oriented people, condemned by Christian fundamentalist as "one of the most pernicious evils in society," but seen by the Navajo as something "sacred and holy." Why the difference?

My research in societies that do not discriminate against homosexuals suggests that the main reason for nonprejudicial attitudes is that those societies have figured out specific ways that homosexuality can contribute positively to the good of society as a whole. In other words, acceptance of sexual diversity is due not so much to "toleration" on the part of the heterosexual majority as it is to distinct advantages perceived by the general populace in having a certain proportion of the population homosexually inclined.

In Western culture, where only heterosexuality is valued, it occurs to few people that homosexuality might enrich society. From over a decade of research on this topic, I have come to have a different perspective than most Americans. The knowledge that I have gained has come primarily from fieldwork with native people of North American, Pacific, and Southeast Asian cultures. After three years of documentary research in many libraries, I lived among the American Indians of the Great Plains and the Southwest (1982), the Mayas of Yucatan (1983), and Native Alaskans (1989). I also did field research among the peoples of Hawaii (1984, 1985, 1990), Thailand (1987), and Indonesia (1987–88).[5] This essay will refer to the results of my fieldwork among these indigenous peoples. Much more ethnographic fieldwork certainly needs to be conducted in these

and other societies before we can draw firm conclusions, but I have formulated some tentative points that I outline below.

BENEFITS TO RELIGION

In Western writings about homosexuality, the emphasis has usually been on its "cause," with the implication that homosexuality is an "abnormality" that must be prevented. In contrast, among American Indians the reaction is usually acceptance, based on the notion that all things are "caused" by the spirits and therefore have some, spiritual purpose. It is left to them only to discover each individual's spiritual purpose.

Traditional American Indians seem more interested in finding a useful social role for those who are different than in trying to force people to change character. One's basic character is a reflection of one's spirit, and to interfere with that is dangerously to disrupt the instructions from the spirit world. Many native North American religions are of a type called "animistic"; they emphasize not one creator god but a multiplicity of spirits in the universe. Everything that exists has a spirit; all things that exist are due equal respect because they are part of the spiritual order of the universe. The world cannot be complete without them.

In this religious view, there is no hierarchy among the beings—the humans, animals, and plants—that populate the earth. Humans are not considered to be any more spiritual or any more important than the other beings. Neither is the spirit of man more important than the spirit of woman. Each spirit may be different, but all are of equal value. However, American Indian religions see an androgynous individual as evidence that that person has been blessed by being bestowed with *two* spirits. Because both women and men are respected for their equal but distinct qualities, a person who combines attributes of both is considered as higher, as above the regular person— who only has one spirit.

In contrast to Western sexist views, where a male who acts like a woman is considered to be "lowering himself" to the subordinate female status, in the egalitarian American Indian religions feminine roles are accorded equal respect with men's roles. Therefore, a male who acts like a woman is not "lowering himself"; rather, he is indicating that he has been favored with an extra gift of spirituality. He is respected as a "double person." Such an individual is considered to be not entirely man and not entirely woman but a mixture of both masculine and feminine elements with additional unique characteristics. Such a distinctive personality is respected as a different gender, distinct from either man or woman.

This concept of respect for gender nonconformity is quite foreign to mainstream American society today. Despite the gains made in recent decades by the women's movement, our culture still does not respect the social contributions of anyone other than masculine men. Perhaps the best way to see this is to look at attitudes toward androgynous males. On American schoolyards today, the worst insult that can be thrown at a boy is to call him a *sissy*. What does it say about a society's gender values when the worst insult that can be directed toward a man is to say that he is like a woman?

While androgyny among males is seldom defended in mainstream American culture, it can be argued that many men need social permission to express those aspects of their personalities that in our society are more commonly associated with women. American men in particular are under constant pressure to conform, to maximize their masculine side —to "be tough," not to show emotion. Seldom verbalized are the dangers to society of excessive masculinity, even though the evidence appears daily in newspaper headlines. Violence is preponderantly a characteristic of masculine personalities: physical and sexual violence by men against women, children, and other men is a major social problem. Not only are men's tempers not conducive to cooperation in the workplace, but they also lead to stress-related health problems for hot-headed men themselves.

In contrast, American Indian cultures that are not prejudiced against androgynous persons allow more flexibility among personality types. A major

reason for this flexibility is the basic respect that their religions accord human diversity. According to these religions, since everything that exists comes from the spirit world, people who are different have been made that way by the spirits and therefore maintain an especially close connection to the spirit world. Accordingly, androgynous people are often seen as sacred, as spiritually gifted individuals who can minister to the spiritual needs of others. In many tribes, such androgynous men—called *berdache* by the early explorers and by modern anthropologists—were often shamans or sacred people who work closely with shamans. Females who were inclined to take the traditional masculine role of hunter and warrior were called *amazons* by the early explorers, after the ancient Greek legend of warrior women.

Nonprejudiced Native American societies recognized that the berdache and the amazon were almost always homosexual, but an androgynous personality, not sexual behavior, was the defining characteristic. Many tribes had special career roles for berdache and amazons. Many Indian tribes, believing that sickness can be cured by the intervention of the spirits, will turn to the spiritually powerful as healers. While conducting my fieldwork on a Lakota reservation in South Dakota, I often observed people who were ill calling on *winkte* (the word in the Lakota language meaning "half man/half woman") to perform healing ceremonies for them. *Winktes* spend much of their time helping others, visiting the ill and infirm, comforting those in distress, and drawing on their spiritual connections to help people get well.

With a spiritual justification provided by the culture, berdache and amazons are not seen as a threat to religion. Instead, they are often considered sacred. Sexuality—indeed bodily pleasure—is seen not as sinful but as a gift from the spirit world. Both the spirit and the flesh are sacred. The homosexual inclinations of such berdache and amazons are accepted as a reflection of their spiritual nature. The American Indian example shows that it is not enough for a religion to "tolerate" sexual diversity; it must also provide a specific religious explanation for such diversity.

Some worldviews see reality as pairs of opposites: everything is viewed as good versus evil, black versus white, the spiritual versus the physical. The latter derides the needs and desires of the physical body as "temptations of the flesh," in contrast to the devotions of the spirit. The American Indian religions take a different view, seeing both the body and the spirit as good, as reflections of each other. As a consequence, sexual behavior—the epitome of the physical body—may be seen as something positively good, as something spiritual in and of itself, at the same time as it is physical.

The conceptualization by Native American societies of the berdache and the amazons as sacred has its practical applications. Those male berdache whom I have met and read about are uniformly gentle, peaceful people who would simply not fill the traditional Indian man's role of hunter and warrior effectively. By recognizing that they are special and encouraging them to become religious leaders and healers, Indian cultures give such people a means by which to contribute constructively to society. Rather than wasting time and energy trying to suppress their true nature or assuming an unsuitable role, they are encouraged to see their uniqueness as a special spiritual gift and to maximize their capabilities to help others. A Crow elder told me, "We don't waste people, the way White society does. Every person has their gift, every person has their contributions to make."[6]

BENEFITS TO THE FAMILY

This emphasis on the social usefulness of the person who is different can be seen especially clearly in the contributions of such people to their families. Because most pre-Columbian Native Americans lived in extended families, with wide networks of kin who depended on one other, it was not necessary for everyone to have children. In contrast to a society with only nuclear families (father-mother-children), where all must reproduce to have someone take care of them in old age, an extended family offers some adults the opportunity not to reproduce. Childless people have nephews

and nieces care for them. It is actually economically advantageous to the extended family for one or two adults *not* to reproduce because then there is a higher ratio of food-producing adults to food-consuming children. Also, by assuming gender roles that mix both the masculine and the feminine, the berdache and the amazon can do both women's and men's work. Not being burdened with their own childcare responsibilities, they can care for others' children or for their aged parents and grandparents.

The same pattern occurs in Polynesian culture, where an androgynous role similar to that of the berdache exists. Called *mahu* in Hawaii and Tahiti and *fa'afafine* among Samoans, such alternatively gendered people were traditionally those who took care of elderly relatives while their heterosexual siblings were busy raising their own children. With this kind of gender flexibility, and with their families holding high expectations for them (since they are spiritual people), berdache and amazons are often renowned for being hard workers, productive, and intelligent.

Since they are not stigmatized or alienated, berdache and amazons are free to make positive contributions to family life. Today, they often allow adolescent nieces and nephews to move in with them when the parents' home gets overcrowded and also help them finance schooling. A Navajo woman whose cousin is a respected *nadle* healer told me,

> *They are seen as very compassionate people, who care for their family a lot and help people. That's why they are healers.* Nadles *are also seen as being great with children, real Pied Pipers. Children love* nadles, *so parents are pleased if a* nadle *takes an interest in their child. One that I know is now a principal of a school on the reservation.... Nadles are not seen as an abstract group, like "gay people," but as a specific person, like "my relative so-and-so." People who help their family a lot are considered valuable members of the community.*[7]

It is thus in the context of individual family relations that much of the high status of the berdache and amazon must be evaluated. When such people play a positive and valued role in their societies, and when no outside interference disrupts the normal workings of those societies, unprejudiced family love can exert itself.

In most Western cultures, such people are often considered misfits, an embarrassment to the family. They often leave the family in shame or are thrown out by homophobic relatives, the family thereby losing the benefit of their productive labor. In contrast, traditional Native American families will often make such people central to the family. Since other relatives do not feel threatened by them, family disunity and conflict are avoided. The male berdache is not pressured to suppress his feminine behavior, nor is the female amazon pressured to suppress her masculine inclinations. Neither are they expected to deny their same-sex erotic feelings. Berdache and amazons thereby avoid the tendency of those considered deviant in Western culture to harbor a low self-esteem and to engage in self-destructive behavior. Because they are valued by their families, few become alcoholic or suicidal, even in tribes where such problems are common.

Male berdache are often highly productive at women's work. Unlike biological females, who must take time away from farming or foraging when they are menstruating, pregnant, or nursing children, the berdache is always available to gather or prepare food. Anthropologists have often commented on the way in which berdache willingly take on the hardest work. Many berdache are also renowned for the high quality of their craftswork, whether pottery, beadwork, weaving, or tanning. In many tribes, berdache are known as the best cooks in the community and are often called on to prepare feasts for ceremonies and funerals. Women in particular seem to appreciate the help provided by berdache. An elderly Papago woman for example, spoke fondly of a berdache she had known in her youth (referring to him as *she*): "The man-woman was very pleasant, always laughing and talking, and a good worker. She was so strong! She did not get tired

grinding corn.... I found the man-woman very convenient."[8]

The female amazon is often appreciated for her prowess at hunting and fighting. In the Crow tribe of the Great Plains, one of the most famous warriors of the nineteenth century was an amazon called "Woman Chief." Edward Denig, a White frontier trader who lived with the Crows for over twelve years, wrote that Woman Chief "was equal if not superior to any of the men in hunting, both on horseback and foot." After single-handedly warding off an attack by an enemy tribe, she developed a reputation as a brave fighter. She easily attracted male warriors to follow her in battle, where she always distinguished herself by her bravery. According to Denig, the Crows believed that she had "a charmed life which, with her daring feats, elevated her to a point of honor and respect not often reached by male warriors." Crow singers composed special songs to commemorate her gallantry, and she eventually became the third highest ranked chief in the entire tribe. Her status was so high, in fact, that she easily attracted women to marry her. By 1850, she had four wives, which also gave her additional status in the tribe. Denig concluded his biography of Woman Chief by saying in amazement, "Strange country this, where [berdache] males assume the dress and perform the duties of females, while women turn [like] men and mate with their own sex!"[9]

Whether attaining status as a warrior, a hunter, a healer, or an artist or simply by being hard working and generous, most amazons and berdache share an urge for success and prestige. They might not be good at doing the kinds of things that are typically expected of their sex, but instead of feeling deviant, they merely redirect their efforts into other kinds of prestigious activities. Moreover, berdache and amazons can gain notable material prosperity by selling their craftwork. Since they are considered sacred, their work is highly valued for its magical power as well as for its beauty.

The economic opportunities open to berdache and amazons are especially evident among the

Navajo. Whereas average men and women are restricted to certain economic activities, *nadle* know no such constraints. Goods produced by them are much in demand. Also, because they are believed to be lucky, they usually act as the head of the family and make decisions about family property. They supervise the family's farming, sheepherding, and selling or trading. With such opportunities, talented *nadle* are valued and respected for their contributions to the family's prosperity.

More than economic success is involved in such people's striving for excellence, however. Atypical children soon recognize their difference from other people. Psychological theory suggests that, if a family does not love and support such children, they will quickly internalize a negative self-image. Severe damage can result from feelings of deviance or inferiority. The way out of such self-hatred is either to deny any meaningful difference or to appreciate uniqueness. Difference is transformed—from *deviant* to *exceptional*—becoming a basis for respect rather than stigma. American Indian cultures deal with such atypical children by offering them prestige and rewards beyond what is available to the average person.

Masculine females and effeminate males in Western culture are often equally productive and successful, but they are so in the face of overwhelming odds. They may eventually come to appreciate their difference, but such self-acceptance comes more easily when one is considered "special" rather than "deviant." Few Western families show such youths more than grudging tolerance. If American families would adopt an appreciative attitude when faced with difference, much conflict and strife could be avoided when a family member turns out to be gay, lesbian, or bisexual. Such children could be nurtured and supported, and such nonprejudiced treatment would ultimately rebound to the family's great benefit.

BENEFITS FOR CHILDREN

From the Native American and Polynesian viewpoints, then, homosexuality and gender noncon-
formity do not threaten the family. An unusual phenomenon is instead incorporated into the kinship system in a productive and nondisruptive manner. Similarly, berdache and amazons are not seen as a threat to children. In fact, because they often have the reputation for intelligence, they are encouraged in some tribes to become teachers. In my fieldwork on Indian reservations and in the Yucatan, Alaska, Hawaii, and Thailand, I met a number of gender nonconformists who are highly respected teachers. Many of the venerated teachers of the sacred traditional hula ceremony among native Hawaiians are *mahus*.

Native American amazons also have the opportunity to become fathers. Among the Mohave, for example, the last person to have sex with the mother before she gives birth is considered to be the true father of the child. This allows an amazon to choose a male to impregnate her wife yet still claim paternity. The child is thus socially recognized as having an amazon father, who is thus able to fulfill all social roles that any other father would do.

Berdache have the opportunity to become parents through adoption. In fact, since they have a reputation for intelligence and generosity, they are often the first choice to become adoptive parents when there is a homeless child. For example, a Lakota berdache with whom I lived while conducting my 1982 fieldwork had adopted and raised four boys and three girls in his lifetime. The youngest boy was still living with him at the time, a typical teenager who was doing well in school. The household consisted of the berdache, his adopted son, the berdache's widowed mother, a number of nephews and nieces, and an elderly aunt.

Such an extended family contrasts sharply with contemporary American society, where gays, lesbians, and bisexuals are often alienated from their families, have trouble becoming adoptive or foster parents, and are often denied custody of their own children. Whereas American Indian communities can remedy the tragedy of a homeless child quickly and easily, foster and adoptive families are not so easy to come by in mainstream American society. As a result, the costs that Americans pay are high—in terms of both tax dollars and crimes committed by homeless youths.

Of course, the main reason for preventing gays and lesbians from becoming adoptive or foster parents—or even Big Brothers or Big Sisters—is the often expressed fear that the youths will be sexually molested. Since recent statistics show that well over 90 percent of child molesters are heterosexual men and their victims young girls, sexual orientation by itself is not a valid criterion on which to base adoption decisions. If it were, heterosexual men would not be allowed to adopt. The fact that homophobic leaders continue to oppose gay and lesbian adoptions when they know the statistics suggests that this issue is merely a rhetorical ploy. The real issue emerges most clearly in custody cases. Children are taken away from lesbian mothers or gay fathers, not because of molestation, but because they will provide "bad role models."

To consider an adult lesbian, gay man, or bisexual a bad role model is simple heterosexism. Children growing up in America today, no matter who their parents are, will see plenty of heterosexual role models—on television, at school, among neighbors and the parents of friends. Why not have a few gay and lesbian role models as an alternative? The answer is simple: American culture still regards it as a tragedy if a youth turns out to be lesbian, gay, or bisexual.

Nonheterosexist cultures, by contrast, emphasize an individual's freedom to decide his or her own fate. Paradoxically, those cultures often see sexual variance or gender nonconformity not as matters of choice but as inborn or as determined by the spirit world. Ironically, while the professed American ideal is "freedom of choice," in reality every child is subjected to extreme social pressures to conform. Despite the omnipresent American rhetoric of freedom, mainstream American culture continues to deny lesbian, gay, and bisexual youths the freedom to choose their own lifestyles. Ever since Freud, however, research has

made it abundantly clear that many psychological problems arise when childhood sexual desires are repressed. In fact, a greater incidence and severity of mental illness has been documented among more repressive cultures.[10]

BENEFITS FOR FRIENDSHIP

In America today, many men are prevented from expressing their feelings or developing close friendships with other men by the fear that others will think them homosexual. Men can be coworkers, sports buddies, even social companions, but nothing more personal. Consequently, many American men are left with only one legitimate, socially sanctioned intimate relationship in their lives—that with their wives. Is it therefore surprising that most men equate intimacy with sex or that, starved for intimacy, many elect to keep a mistress? To expect marriage to meet all a person's needs—to expect a spouse or significant other to be sexual playmate, economic partner, and best friend—places too heavy a burden on what today is an infirm institution.

During my fieldwork in Indonesia, by contrast, I was struck by the intensity of friendships between men (friendships that reminded me of the intense "blood brother" relationships between Native American men). In Indonesia, the highly structured mixed-sex marriage and kinship system is balanced and strengthened by unstructured same-sex friendship networks. The one complements the other, and both provide men with the support that they need to get through their lives.

Once gay men, lesbians, and bisexuals have transcended the fear of being thought homosexual, they open themselves to whole new possibilities for more satisfying same-sex friendships. In nonhomophobic societies, heterosexual men are free to develop same-sex friendships and nurture their same-sex friends. Because no stigma is attached to same-sex friendship, no pressure exists to choose between an exclusively homosexual or heterosexual orientation. In contemporary America, by contrast, where men are socialized to equate intimacy with a sexual relationship, some may feel forced to abandon an exclusively heterosexual identity for an exclusively homosexual one. Homophobia creates two distinct classes of men, self-identified "heterosexuals" and self-identified "homosexuals." More flexible notions of same-sex friendship in nonhomophobic societies mean less of a need to compartmentalize people on the basis of sexual behavior and less social consternation should the relationship between same-sex friends become erotic.

BENEFITS FOR SOCIETY AT LARGE

A culture that does not try to suppress the same-sex desires of its people can focus instead on the contributions that can be made by those who are different. We have already seen that American Indian berdache and amazons are honored for their spirituality, their artistic skills, and their hard work, all of which benefit the entire community. They are also often called on to mediate disputes between men and women. Married couples in particular turn to them since, as "half men/half women," they can see things from the perspective of both sexes. Their roles as go-betweens is integral to the smooth functioning of Native American communities.

Although there is not as much information on the social roles of amazons, the historical documents suggest that berdache performed their go-between function in traditional Indian cultures for males and females on joyous occasions as well. A number of tribes were noted to have employed berdache to facilitate budding romances between young women and men, a role that reached its highest development among the Cheyenne tribe of the Great Plains. One Cheyenne informant reported that berdache "were very popular and special favorites of young people, whether married or not, for they were noted matchmakers. They were fine love talkers.... When a young man wanted to send gifts for a young woman, one of these half-men-halfwomen was sent to the girl's relatives to do the talking in making the marriage."[11] Because

of their spiritual connection, berdache were believed to possess the most potent love medicines. A Cheyenne bachelor who gained the assistance of a berdache was believed to be fortunate indeed since the berdache could often persuade the young woman and her family to accept the gift-laden horses that a man offered when he made a marriage proposal.

Whereas American Indian societies recognize and incorporate sexual diversity, others simply ignore it. When I was in Southeast Asia in 1987 and 1988, I learned that it was commonly known in both Thailand and Indonesia that some major government figures were homosexual. Although those men did not publicly broadcast their homosexuality, neither did they make any attempt to hide their same-sex lovers from public view. Such tolerance benefits both the individuals, who are allowed to live their lives as they choose, and the nation, which utilized their leadership skills.

In my research, I have found that those societies with accepted homosexual roles ironically do not emphasize the sexual activities of homosexuals. Everyone knows their sexual preferences, but those preferences are considered matters for private, not public, concern. Homosexuality is therefore not politicized. In America, however, the homophobic Right has made such an issue of what it considers to be deviant sexuality that it has stimulated the development of a politically active gay community.

The suppression of sexual diversity *inevitably* results in social turmoil. Families and communities are divided by the issue. Suicides are occasioned by the discovery, or the fear of discovery, of secret sex lives. When the individuals whose secrets are uncovered are public figures, the ensuing media scandal can bring a community to the point of hysteria—witness Boise, Idaho, in the 1950s and schoolteacher firings in countless communities.

The persecution of gays, lesbians, and bisexuals also endangers the freedom of other groups—indeed, any group. For persecution rarely confines itself to one group. For example, Adolf Hitler tried to rid Germany of Jews, but also extended his campaign to include homosexuals. The Ayatollah Khomeini similarly exterminated infidels and beheaded homosexuals. The point here is that no one group is safe until all groups are safe.

By continuing to discriminate against lesbians, gay men, and bisexuals, the United States is losing the respect of many in the world community—the Dutch and other progressive governments have already made formal diplomatic protests against discriminatory U.S. policies. Sodomy laws remain on the books and are enforced in many states, homosexuals are excluded from the military, sexual minorities are denied equal protection under the law—all this in a nation devoted to "life, liberty, and the pursuit of happiness." The situation today is similar to that in the early 1960s, when progressive governments in Europe, Asia, and especially the newly independent African nations voiced their support for African-American civil rights protestors. Such diplomatic action helped pressure the Kennedy administration to take action against racial segregation. For how could America champion its ideals of freedom and expect to maintain its position as the leader of the "free" world when people of color were treated so unequally?

Acceptance of people's right to be different is the certain hallmark of democracy and freedom. This is why the New Right's attempt to suppress homosexuality is so dangerous for the larger society. The dominant message propounded by the New Right in the 1980s has been that everyone should be the same. That desire for sameness has a strong attraction for people living in a diverse and changing society. Instead, we should be thankful that we are *not* all the same. If we were, society would lose the creativity and vitality that comes from difference. Faced with the new global competitiveness of the 1990s, we as Americans are hardly in a position *not* to promote independent thinking and creativity. Mindless conformity is an economic and emotional and intellectual dead end.

An appreciation of diversity, not just a tolerance of minorities, is what will promote future American progress. As the American Indian example illustrates so well, far from being a threat to religion, to the family, to children, and to society in general, homosexuality can benefit both men and women as well as bring freedom to all.

NOTES

1. Quoted in *Project 10 Newsletter* (March 1989), 1.
2. Clellan Ford and Frank Beach, *Patterns of Sexual Behavior* (New York: Harper, 1951).
3. W. W. Hill, "The Status of the Hermaphrodite and Transvestite in Navaho Culture," *American Anthropologist* 37 (1935): 274.
4. Ibid.
5. The results of my 1979–84 fieldwork are reported in Walter L. Williams, *The Spirit and the Flesh: Sexual Diversity in American Indian Culture* (Boston: Beacon, 1986). Part of my Indonesian research is contained in Walter L. Williams, *Javanese Lives: Women and Men in Modern Indonesian Society* (New Brunswick, N.J.: Rutgers University Press, 1991). My research among Polynesians and Native Alaskans has not yet been written up. I express my gratitude to the Council for the International Exchange of Scholars, for a Fulbright research grant to Indonesia (with a side trip to Thailand and Malaysia), to the University of Southern California faculty research fund for trips to conduct research in Hawaii, and to the Institute for the Study of Women and Men for a travel grant to go to Alaska. My main work there was among Aleuts and Yupik Eskimos.
6. Quoted in Williams, *Spirit and Flesh*, 57.
7. Ibid., 54.
8. Ibid., 58–59.
9. Ibid., 245–46,
10. George Devereux, Mohave Ethnopsychiatry (Washington, D.C.: Smithsonian Institution, 1969), viii–ix, xii–xiii, and "Institutionalized Homosexuality of the Mohave Indians," *Human Biology* 9 (1937): 498–499, 518. For examples of other sexually free societies, see Williams, *Spirit and Flesh*, chap. 12.
11. Quoted in Williams, *Spirit and Flesh*, 70–71.

52

Breaking Bread

BELL HOOKS
CORNEL WEST

bh: In the past you have talked about "combative spirituality" that seeks to, as you put it, "develop a mode of community that sustains people in their humanity." What do you feel is eroding that kind of dynamic spirituality in Black life?

CW: Well, there's no doubt about it, what is eroding it is market forces. What is eroding it is consumerism, hedonism, narcissism, privatism, and careerism of Americans in general, and Black Americans in particular. You cannot have a tradition of resistance and critique along with pervasive hedonism. It means then that we must have spokesmen for genuine love, care, sacrifice, and risk in the face of market forces that highlight buying, selling, and profit making. And poor communities of course have been so thoroughly inundated and saturated with the more pernicious forms of buying and selling, especially drugs and women's bodies and so forth, that these traditions of care and respect have almost completely broken down.

When our grandmothers are not respected, so that mothers are not respected, fathers have no respect, preachers have no respect—no one has respect. Respect is externalized, given to those who exercise the most brutal forms of power. Respect goes to the gun; that's what market forces lead to....

CW: ...I want to suggest that there are only three ways out. All of them are forms of conversion. There is either personal conversion by means of love of another, love of a mother, father, a mate, a spouse, that's strong enough to convince one to shift from a nihilistic mode to a meaningful mode. The second is political conversion, in which an ideology or a cause becomes strong enough to shift from a nihilistic mode to a meaningful mode.

And the third form of conversion is that of religious conversion, be it Christianity or Islam, or any faith that convinces you that there are, in fact, reasons to live and serve, so that one sidesteps the nihilistic traps, be it drugs, alcoholism, or any of the various forms of addiction that are so deeply ingrained in our society. Without some form of conversion, we will simply lose thousands of people, especially Black people. This will have serious repercussions for the next generation.

bh: When people talk about the growing popularity of Black women writers, or when they try to contrast that and say somehow Black male writers are receiving less attention, I always find that problematic, because people often don't go on to talk about what it is in these works that are giving them the quality of appeal that we may not see in many works by Black male writers.

And I would say that one of the things that's in all these works is a concern with spiritual well-being. Toni Cade Bambara begins her novel *The Salt Eaters* with the question, "are you sure that you want to be well?" And she is not just talking about physical well-being, she is talking about a well-being of the spirit.

CW: That's right. Of the spirit and the soul.

bh: Certainly a novel like Paule Marshall's *Praise Song for the Widow* has to do with a politicized spiritual reawakening.

CW: I think something else is going on, too. And I think, for example, of Toni Morrison's *Beloved*, in which the love ethic sits at the center. You don't see that kind of self-love affirmed in many works by Black male writers.

bh: When I think about *Beloved* I remember that the person who brings the prophetic message of redemptive love, it is the grandmother, in her role of preacher—she goes into the field —and preaches that sermon about the necessity of love.

CW: That sermon is one of the great moments in American literature. One of the great moments in modern literature. And you don't find that kind of sermon in a Richard Wright or a James Baldwin or even Ralph Ellison. You just don't find it. There is a depth of love for Black humanity which is both affirmed and enacted that, I think, speaks very deeply to these spiritual issues. And I think this relates precisely to the controversy in the relations between Black men and women.

bh: That is exactly what I was going to ask you. What does it mean for a progressive Black male on the Left to ally himself with the critique of patriarchy and sexism, to be supportive of feminist movement?

CW: We have to recognize that there cannot be relationships unless there is commitment, unless there is loyalty, unless there is love, patience, persistence. Now, the degree to which these values are eroding is the degree to which there cannot be healthy relationships. And if there are no relationships then there is only the joining of people for the purposes of bodily stimulation.

And if we live in a society in which these very values are eroding, then it's no accident that we are going to see less and less qualitative relations between Black men and women.

At the same time, and this is one reason why I think many Black men and women are at each other's throats, is because there is tremendous rage in Black men.

bh: Talk about it.

CW: Just as there is a tremendous sense of inadequacy and rage in Black women. That feeling of inadequacy and rage is also in Black men.

bh: But this rage takes a different form.

CW: That's right. The rage takes a different form, the sense of inadequacy takes a different form.

bh: You are one of the few men who's talked about the fact that often suppressed rage takes the form of Black male violence against Black women.

CW: That's right, it is one of the most insidious manifestations imaginable. This rage and this inadequacy, when they come up in their raw form in a violent culture means combat. We have always had the rage—don't get me wrong. We have always felt the inadequacy, but we've also had traditions that were able to channel it in such a way that we could remain in that boat with the tension, with the hostility, because there was also love, care, loyalty, and solidarity.

bh: Well, one of the things that you talked about earlier and I think you can link that rage to is the whole question of fear and failure.

CW: That's right. That's the fundamental problem. This is what Marcus Garvey understood. In many ways he was the first one to understand it. He understood the fact that Black people could only be fully human when they were free enough from the fear and failure which is imposed upon them by a larger racist society, but it would not be a matter of blaming that society, it would be a matter of understanding that society and asserting themselves boldly and defiantly as human beings. Very few Black folk ever reach that level, and more must.

bh: I think we also have to break away from the bourgeois tradition of romantic love which isn't necessarily about creating the conditions for what you call critical affirmation. And I think this produces a lot of the tensions between heterosexual Black men and Black women, and between gays. We must think of not just romantic love, but of love in general as being about people mutually meeting each other's needs and giving and receiving critical feedback.

CW: That's so, so very true. We actually see some of the best of this in the traditions of contemporary Africa that has a more deromanticized, or less romanticized, conception of relationship, talking more about partnership. I know this from my loving Ethiopian wife.

bh: That's where, as Black people, we have much to learn from looking at global revolutionary struggles, looking at, for example, the work of Nicaraguans. There has to be a re-conceptualization of what it means to be engaged in a primary liberation struggle as we also try to alter issues of gender.

That's what we haven't done enough of yet, theoretically, as African Americans, to begin to conceptualize how we re-envision Black liberation struggle in ways that allow us to look at gender and the pain that we feel negotiating gender politics.

CW: Sexuality in general must be discussed. There is a reluctance in the Black community to talk seriously about sexuality. We've got significant numbers of gays and lesbians who often-times are rendered invisible, as if their humanity somehow ought to be hidden and concealed.

bh: It's interesting when you think about the kind of compassion, love, and openness that many of us remember in the traditional Black church, because in fact we don't remember those Black gay folk as going off to set up a separate sub-culture that alienates and estranges them from Black community. But in fact we remember them vitally engaged in the maintenance and sustaining of Black culture.

CW: There's no doubt, good God almighty, if you look at Black music in the Black church and the crucial role that Black gays and lesbi-

ans have played there, this is the grand example. And it's the failure of the Black religious leadership to come to terms with these issues of sexuality, but it's also a fear on behalf of the congregation that talking about this may undermine some of the consensus in other areas and thereby render the community less able to confront other issues.

bh: So the people won't think I'm stereotyping, when we talk about the roles people play musically, I think that we have to remember that there has always been in the realm of Black cultural production an acceptance of certain forms of radical behavior, behavior that, within the status quo of everyday life, people might object to, but certainly when we look at the tradition of blues singers, the Black women who were cross-dressing, if we look at the career of someone like Josephine Baker, I mean, we see an openness, a tolerance within the sphere of cultural production that may not have made itself known in other spheres of Black life.

CW: That is so very true.

bh: Well, Cornel, as we bring this discussion to a close, are there any last words that you want to give us? Will we have a renewed Black liberation struggle? Will the struggle take another form? Will it be a more inclusive struggle? Or will we have simultaneous movements?

CW: It's hard to say, but, I think the important thing is that we must never give up hope. Black people have always been in a very difficult predicament, we must always preserve our subversive memory, which is to say our attempt to stay in tune with the best of our history. And at the same time we must always be explicitly moral in an all-inclusive manner so that we resist all forms of xenophobia.

bh: How do you define xenophobia?

CW: Xenophobia is a hatred of the other, be it a hatred of individuals different from one's self, be it a Black, White, Jewish, or Korean person.

All forms of racism must be rejected directly and openly.

I have hope for the next generation. I think that they're up against a lot. Market forces are stronger now than they've been in American history. But I also believe in the ingenuity, in the intelligence, the beauty, the laughter and the love that Black people can give both themselves and to others. And that is the raw stuff out of which any major movement for justice is made.

bh: When you talked about the need for a politics that deals with death, dread, despair, disappointment, you talked about the fact that even as we identify strategic conflicts and problems, we also have to identify the location of our joys.

CW: That's right.

bh: You certainly identified that one way cultural production functions in Black communities is to awaken our joy. And I was thinking, as we close, of the impact of Anita Baker's song, "You Bring Me Joy."

CW: Yes.

bh: Which returns us to that notion of redemptive care, reciprocal, mutual sharing, that brings about a sense of joy. It's the kind of joy and fellowship I feel always in talking with you. Thank you.

CW: Thank you.

CREDITS

Amott, Teresa. "Shortchanged: Restructuring Women's Work" is copyright © 1993 by Teresa Amott. Reprinted by permission of Monthly Review Foundation.

Anderson, Margaret L. "Studying across Difference: Race, Class, and Gender in Qualitative Research" is from *Race and Ethnicity and Research Methods* by John H. Stanfield, pp. 39–52, copyright © 1993 by Sage Publications. Reprinted by permission of Sage Publications, Inc.

Anzaldúa, Gloria. Poetry quote is from *Borderlands/La Frontera: The New Mestiza,* © 1987 by Gloria Anzaldúa.

Baca Zinn, Maxine, and Bonnie Thornton Dill. "Theorizing Difference from Multiracial Feminism" is from *Feminist Studies 22,* no. 2 (Summer 1996). Copyright © 1994 by Temple University Press. Reprinted by permission of Temple University Press.

Bordo, Susan. "Pills and Power Tools" is from *Men and Masculinities, 1,* pp. 87–90, copyright © 1999 by Sage Publications. Reprinted by permission of Sage Publications, Inc.

Collins, Patricia Hill. "The Meaning of Motherhood in Black Culture and Black Mother–Daughter Relationships" is from *Double Stitch: Black Women Write about Mothers and Daughters,* pp. 42–60, edited by Patricia Bell-Scott. Copyright © 1991 Beacon Press. Reprinted by permission of the author.

Connell, R. W. "Masculinities and Globalization" is from *Men and Masculinities, 1,* pp. 3–23, copyright © 1999 by Sage Publications. Reprinted by permission of Sage Publications, Inc.

Drakulic, Slavenka. "A Letter from the United States: The Critical Theory Approach" is from *How We Survived Communism and Even Laughed* by Slavenka Drakulic. Copyright © 1991 by Slavenka Drakulic. Reprinted by permission of W. W. Norton & Company, Inc.

Dworkin, Shari Lee, and Faye Linda Wachs. "'Disciplining the Body': HIV-Positive Male Athletes, Media Surveillance, and the Policing of Sexuality" is adapted by permission. From *Sociology of Sport Journal,* 15(1):1–20, © 1998.

Ehlers, Tracy Bachrach. "Debunking Marianismo: Economic Vulnerability and Survival Strategies among Guatemalan Wives" is reprinted by permission of *Ethnology.*

Enloe, Cynthia. "It Takes More Than Two: The Prostitute, the Soldier, the State, and the Entrepreneur" is from *The Morning After: Sexual Politics at the End of the Cold War,* pp. 152–160, copyright © 1993 The Regents of the University of California.

Espiritu, Yen Le. "'Americans Have a Different Attitude': Family, Sexuality, and Gender in Filipina American Lives" is reprinted by permission of the author.

Fernández Kelly, M. Patricia. "Delicate Transactions: Gender, Home, and Employment among Hispanic Women" is from *Uncertain Terms* by Faye Ginsburg and Anna Lowenhaupt Tsing. © 1992 by Faye Ginsburg and Anna Lowenhaupt Tsing. Reprinted by permission of Beacon Press, Boston.

Frye, Marilyn. "Lesbian 'Sex'" is from *Willful Virgin: Essays in Feminism,* pp. 109–119, copyright © 1992 The Crossing Press. Reprinted by permission of the author.

Gerschick, Thomas J., and Adam Stephen Miller. "Coming to Terms: Masculinity and Physical Disability" is from *Men's Health and Illness: Gender, Power, and the Body,* edited by Donald Sabo and David F. Gordon, copyright © 1995 by Sage Publications. Reprinted by permission of Sage Publications, Inc.

Gilmore, David D. "Men and Women in Southern Spain: 'Domestic Power' Revisited" is reproduced by permission of the American Anthropological Association from *American Anthropologist* 91:4, December 1990. Not for further reproduction.

Giuffre, Patti A., and Christine L. Williams. "Boundary Lines: Labeling Sexual Harassment in Restaurants" is from *Gender & Society, 8,* pp. 378–401, copyright © 1994 by Sage Publications. Reprinted by permission of Sage Publications, Inc.

Gutmann, Matthew C. "Male Discretion and Sexual Indiscretion in Working Class Mexico City" is from *The Meanings of Macho: Being a Man in Mexico City,* copyright © 1996 The Regents of the University of California.

Higginbotham, Anastasia. "Chicks Goin' at It" reprinted from *Listen Up: Voices from the Next Feminist Generation,* edited by Barbara Findlen (Seattle: Seal Press, 1995), pp. 3–11. Copyright © 1995 by Barbara Findlen. Reprinted by permission of Seal Press.

Higginbotham, Elizabeth, and Lynn Weber. "Moving Up with Kin and Community: Upward Social Mobility for Black and White Women" is from *Gender & Society, 6,* pp. 416–440, copyright © 1992 by Sage Publications. Reprinted by permission of Sage Publications, Inc.

Hondagneu-Sotelo, Pierrette, and Ernestine Avila. "'I'm Here, but I'm There': The Meanings of Latina Transnational Motherhood" is from *Gender & Society, 11,* pp. 548–571, copyright © 1997 by Sage Publications. Reprinted by permission of Sage Publications, Inc.

Hondagneu-Sotelo, Pierrette, and Michael A. Messner. "Gender Displays and Men's Power: The 'New Man' and the Mexican Immigrant Man" is from *Theorizing Masculinities* edited by Harry Brod, pp. 200–218, copyright © 1994 by Sage Publications. Reprinted by permission of Sage Publications, Inc.

hooks, bell, and Cornel West. "Breaking Bread" is reprinted by permission of South End Press.

Hossfeld, Karen J. "'Their Logic against Them': Contradictions in Sex, Race, and Class in Silicon Valley" is from *Women Workers and Global Restructuring,* edited by Kathryn Ward. Copyright © 1990. Used by permission of Cornell University Press.

Kibria, Nazli. "Culture, Social Class, and Income Control in the Lives of Women Garment Workers in Bangladesh" is from *Gender & Society, 9,* pp. 289–309, copyright © 1995 by Sage Publications. Reprinted by permission of Sage Publications, Inc.

Kimmel, Michael S. "Judaism, Masculinity, and Feminism" is reprinted by permission of the author.

Klein, Melissa. "Duality and Redefinition: Young Feminism and the Alternative Music Community" is reprinted by permission of the author.

Lamm, Nomy. "It's a Big Fat Revolution" reprinted from *Listen Up: Voices from the Next Feminist Generation,* edited by Barbara Findlen (Seattle: Seal Press, 1995), pp. 85–94. Copyright © 1995 by Barbara Findlen. Reprinted by permission of Seal Press.

LaRossa, Ralph. "Fatherhood and Social Change" is copyrighted 1988 by the National Council on Family Relations, 3989 Central Ave. NE, Suite 550, Minneapolis, MN 55421. Reprinted by permission.

Lorber, Judith. "Believing Is Seeing: Biology as Ideology" is from *Gender & Society, 7,* pp. 568–581, copyright © 1993 by Sage Publications. Reprinted by permission of Sage Publications, Inc.

Lorde, Audre. "Age, Race, Class, and Sex: Women Redefining Difference" is from *Sister Outsider* © 1984 by Audre Lorde, The Crossing Press.

Lutz, Catherine A., and Jane L. Collins. "The Color of Sex: Postwar Photographic Histories of Race and Gender in *National Geographic Magazine*" is from *Reading National Geographic,* edited by Catherine A. Lutz and Jane L. Collins, copyright © 1993. Reprinted by permission of The University of Chicago Press.

Marable, Manning. "The Black Male: Searching beyond Stereotypes" is from *The American Black Male,* edited by Richard G. Majors and Jacob U. Gordon. Reprinted by permission of Nelson Hall.

Matthews, Nancy A. "Surmounting a Legacy: The Expansion of Racial Diversity in a Local Anti-Rape Movement" is from *Gender & Society, 3,* pp. 518–532, copyright © 1989 by Sage Publications. Reprinted by permission of Sage Publications, Inc.

McIntosh, Peggy. "White Privilege: Unpacking the Invisible Knapsack," © 1988 Peggy McIntosh. Reprinted by permission of the author.

Messner, Michael A. "Becoming 100% Straight" © Michael A. Messner, 1999, is from *Inside Sports,* pp. 104–110, edited by Jay Coakley and Peter Donnelly. Reprinted by permission of Routledge.

Messner, Michael A. "When Bodies Are Weapons" reprinted by permission of *Changing Men* magazine.

Miller, Laura L. "Not Just Weapons of the Weak: Gender Harassment as a Form of Protest for Army Men" is reprinted by permission of the American Sociological Association.

Nathan, Debbie. "Abortion Stories on the Border," copyright © Debbie Nathan, 1991. Originally published in *Women and Other Aliens: Essays from the U.S.–Mexico Border.* Reprinted by permission of Cinco Puntos Press.

Pardo, Mary. "Mexican American Women, Grassroots Community Activists: 'Mothers of East Los Angeles'" is excerpted from *Frontiers 11,* pp. 1–7. Copyright © 1990 Frontiers Editorial Collective.

Pringle, Rosemary. "Male Secretaries" is from *Doing 'Women's Work': Men in Nontraditional Occupations,* pp. 128–151, edited by Christine L. Williams, copyright © 1993 by Sage Publications. Reprinted by permission of Sage Publications, Inc.

Richie, Beth E., and Valli Kanuha. "Battered Women of Color in Public Health Care Systems: Racism, Sexism, and Violence" reprinted from *Wings of Gauze: Women of*

Color and the Experience of Health and Illness, edited by Barbara Bair and Susan E. Cayleff, by permission of the Wayne State University Press. Copyright © 1993.

Safa, Helen Icken. "Women's Social Movements in Latin America" is from *Gender & Society, 4,* pp. 354–369, copyright © 1990 by Sage Publications. Reprinted by permission of Sage Publications, Inc.

Scheper-Hughes, Nancy. "(M)Other Love: Culture, Scarcity, and Maternal Thinking" is excerpted from Chapter 8 in *Death Without Weeping: Mother Love and Child Death in Northeast Brazil,* pp. 340–365. Copyright © 1992 The Regents of the University of California.

Stack, Carol B. "Different Voices, Different Visions: Gender, Culture, and Moral Reasoning" reprinted by permission of the author.

Stein, Arlene. "Seventies Questions for Nineties Women" is from *Sex and Sensibility: Stories of a Lesbian Generation,* pp. 184–201. Copyright © 1997 The Regents of the University of California.

Stombler, Mindy, and Irene Padavac. "Sister Acts: Resisting Men's Domination in Black and White Fraternity Little Sister Programs" is reprinted from *Social Problems* 44(2), May, 1997, pp. 257–275. Copyright © 1997 by The Society for the Study of Social Problems. Reprinted by permission.

Straton, Jack C. "The Myth of the 'Battered Husband Syndrome,'" © 1995 by *Masculinities.* All rights reserved.

Thorne, Barrie. "Children and Gender: Constructions of Difference" is from *Theoretical Perspectives on Sexual Difference,* edited by Deborah L. Rhode, pp. 100–113, copyright © 1990. Reprinted by permission from Yale University Press.

Tolman, Deborah L. "Doing Desire: Adolescent Girls' Struggles for/with Sexuality" is from *Gender & Society, 8,* pp. 324–342, copyright © 1994 by Sage Publications. Reprinted by permission of Sage Publications, Inc.

Williams, Walter L. "Benefits for Nonhomophobic Societies: An Anthropological Perspective" is from *Homophobia: How We All Pay the Price* by Warren J. Blumenfeld. Copyright © 1992 by Warren J. Blumenfeld. Reprinted by permission of Beacon Press, Boston.

Witherow, Judith K. "Native American Mother" is reprinted by permission of the author.

Zones, Jane Sprague. "Beauty Myths and Realities and Their Impact on Women's Health" is from *Women's Health: Complexities and Differences,* edited by Sheryl B. Ruzek, Virginia L. Olesen, and Adele E. Clarke, copyright © 1997 by Ohio State University Press. Reprinted by permission of Ohio State University Press and the author.